Intercultural Counseling

Bridging the Us and Them Divide

Intercultural Counseling

Bridging the Us and Them Divide

Gerald Monk, John Winslade,
Stacey Sinclair, and marcela polanco

cognella®
SAN DIEGO

Bassim Hamadeh, CEO and Publisher
Amy Smith, Project Editor
Berenice Quirino, Associate Production Editor
Emely Villavicencio, Senior Graphic Designer
Stephanie Kohl, Licensing Associate
Natalie Piccotti, Director of Marketing
Kassie Graves, Vice President of Editorial
Jamie Giganti, Director of Academic Publishing

Printed in the United States of America.

3970 Sorrento Valley Blvd., Ste. 500, San Diego, CA 92121

Brief Contents

Detailed Contents

Foreword

KENNETH J. GERGEN

L ife in the helping professions has always been fraught with ambiguity. How can we come to understand the problems we confront, what are the origins of untoward and irrational actions, what are the best forms of counseling or therapeutic practice we can offer, how can we assess the effects of our work, and what are the ethical and political implications of our engagement? For over a century, such issues have stimulated lively and sometimes rancorous debate. Schools of thought have come and gone, and we seem no closer to the answers today than we were a century ago.

In recent decades, this search for clear answers has taken a different turn, at once liberating and perilous. In earlier years, the search largely took place within the professional classes, and the grounds for debate were typically furnished by the then-dominant conception of empirical science. Reason and evidence were the key criteria for knowing. However, as the technologies of communication became increasingly available to society, grassroots organization was facilitated. Multiple pockets of consciousness developed; groups of the like-minded sprang to political life. There were sharp differences among such groups in the way they understood the world and the values they placed on various outcomes. Further, for many of these groups, the debates within the helping professions not only seemed irrelevant, but posed a threat to the very ways of life they so valued. Thus, the "helping" professions came under sharp critique for biases of race, class, gender, and sexual preference. And, too, their assumptions and practices seemed wholly insensitive to the vast ethnic and cultural differences within a society.

This multi-hued eruption has been enormously liberating. It has placed in critical question long-standing traditions, given voice to myriad minorities, and set new agendas for how to think about and foster human well-being. The space of freedom and creativity has been substantially expanded. At the same time, these movements have fostered both fragmentation and alienation. There are strong tendencies for various enclaves, just as in the case of "old-stream" empiricism, to seek to claim the high ground in both knowledge and values. Each strives to set its own course for the future. Those outside an enclave are often viewed with suspicion or derision. There is a pervasive view that no group has the right to conceptualize those outside, to study them, or offer entrapping practices of help. To extend such logic, we are all invited to live in isolation from each other.

In the present volume, Gerald Monk, John Winslade, Stacey Sinclair, and marcela polanco invite us into a new world of thought and practice. They write from long experience in the roiling waters of multicultural counseling; they are not afraid to expose their passions or their shortcomings; they search beyond the early tradition of counseling for useful insights. And their conclusion is of enormous importance: *it is not the clear and compelling answer for which we should be striving, but a continuing and ever-extended participation in dialogue.* In effect, they render honor to the full array of traditions, values, and visions that now circulate globally, and they invite an open and honest sharing. They soften the boundaries of separation and see within the process of dialogue the possibilities for new, more fully informed, more thoroughly sensitive, and more broadly responsible ways of going on. In offering such visions to those entering the field of counseling today, they make a major contribution to a more viable tomorrow.

This spirit of participatory inquiry is secreted into every corner of this work, from the emphasis on the intercultural as opposed to the multicultural, the personal openness of the initial prologue, the inclusion of "outsider" reflections at the end of each chapter, to a final chapter in which the reader is invited to join in thinking about the next steps. Traditional understandings are thrust into question at every turn; where clarity on matters of culture, race, ethnicity, identity, community, and competence once reigned, there is now careful and caring reflection. Nor are the authors satisfied by developing highly sophisticated and far-reaching accounts of the subject matter. They also invite readers into experiences that will enable them to add to the deliberation in their own terms. The chapters also bring a wealth of wide-ranging scholarship to bear on the topics they treat, thus adding depth and breadth to the discussions.

To be sure, it is most gratifying to me that the authors have made such excellent use of social constructionist ideas. Deliberations on social construction have absorbed my interests and enthusiasm for over 25 years. At the same time, the present work speaks importantly to a critical issue in contemporary constructionism. Early constructionist writings were important in removing foundational claims to truth, rationality, or value. All traditions have a place at the table. Yet, while constructionist ideas are often used by various groups to deconstruct the dominant discourse, they are infrequently turned upon the users themselves. One's own tradition remains unquestioned. Under these conditions we approach a war of all against all, only in this case it is war among traditions as opposed to individuals. Given the potential for any social movement to expand globally, and the simultaneous democratization of weaponry, the conditions turn perilous.

For me, the pragmatic dimension of constructionist writings provides direction: let us cease in this battle for ultimate good, relying on attack and defense as our means of survival. Rather, we may ask, "Is this the kind of world *we* wish to create together?" And, if the answer is "No," the invitation is given for a collaborative search into more viable futures. It is precisely here that one discerns the profound significance of this volume. In the case of counseling, the authors answer "No" to an embattled future. Thus, we find within these pages not simply a groundbreaking entry into the domain of intercultural counseling; rather, this volume gives rise to the kinds of practices on which global well-being will ultimately depend.

Kenneth J. Gergen, PhD, is a senior research professor at Swarthmore College and the president of the Taos Institute. He is widely known for his inquiries in social construction and professional practice, relational theory, and contemporary cultural life. His work has merited numerous awards, including honorary degrees in both Europe and the United States. Among his major writings are *Realities and Relationships, The Saturated Self, An Invitation to Social Construction*, and *Relational Being: Beyond Self and Community*.

February 4, 2019

Preface

The Us and Them Divide

More than ever before, there is a demand for counseling practice that adequately addresses the multicultural worlds in which people live. We are witnessing a growing Us and Them divide in our diverse society, as groups of people with common cultural identity markers (for example, identifying as Democrat or Republican) find solace in being with people who think like them and sound like them. Many of these human groupings retreat into echo chambers that reinforce ideas of the Self versus the Other, through regular immersion in particular versions of social media and community life that resonate with their sense of common purpose and vision for the future. Within a 24-hour period, we can observe diverse news outlets and be quickly reminded of how polarized our communities are, and how there are so many versions of what reality "truly" is.

At the same time, there are stark historical and current inequities experienced by many people across multiple social locations, especially pertaining to ethnicity, class, sexual orientation, body abilities, nationality, language, immigration status, gender, and mental health. For example, there are long histories of inequities against people of color, and strong identity politics form around ethnic/racial groupings. The voices speaking from specific ethnic identity and political identity landscapes have intensified and become a chorus. These performances of identity politics pertaining to the people of color stay alive due to the sustained neglect, disrespect, and exhaustion experienced by those who are demeaned by a significant segment of society.

Simultaneously, there is an emergent, virulent display of White identity politics, fueled by negative reactions to the economic despair of the White working class. This public demonstration of White identity politics has gathered momentum, due in part to rural and small-town communities' sense of disenfranchisement and exclusion from the economic recovery of the upper-middle- and upper-class communities in large urban areas. The very public display of strident White identity politics in the media seems also to be invigorated by this group's sense of entitlement and coinciding rejection of the rights of people of color to give voice to their ongoing inequities. These powerful, historical, and current-day political and social forces, amplified by a segregated social media, are exacerbating the Us and Them divide.

As culturally diverse clients and mental health professionals meet to address mental health issues in various contexts, these organizing forces that separate and partition groups of people, based upon the histories of specific identity markers, are rumbling in the background, contributing to the mental health challenges unleashed in our communities. It is therefore our view that nowhere is it more important to bridge the Us and Them divide, and to engage one another interculturally, than in therapeutic settings, where important and personal problems are addressed.

There are many people of goodwill in the helping professions committed to bridging a cultural divide and endeavoring to work in multicultural ways. However, we argue that there are some serious unresolved problems in the counseling field that cannot be resolved by goodwill and commitment alone. They are problems of how we think about or conceptualize even such basic concepts as culture and cultural groupings. While most multicultural practitioners now abandon the belief in the cultural melting pot ideal, the ideas that have replaced this conceptualization continue to contain many shaky assumptions and lead to counter-productive strategies in professional practice. These problems need to be addressed in order to bridge these cultural divides and realize the ambitions of the multicultural counseling movement. What is needed is some fresh thinking in this domain; and this is what this book seeks to offer, first by laying out what we see as currently problematic in this domain, and then by suggesting some ways forward that we think hold promise.

Interculturality—A New Force in the Multicultural Movement

Interculturality, as we have adopted it here, is a project proposed from decolonial activism in the Andean region. It is grounded on the work of the Peruvian sociologist Anibal Quijano (2000), who articulated that the structure of colonial patterns of power are deeply implanted in the actions and the choices we make in all sectors of modern life. This project emerged as an Indigenous and African bottom-up reaction to colonial patterns of power embedded in Eurocentric, universal, monocultural, and modern conceptions of thinking, sensing, being, believing, and doing (Walsh, 2012).

The fundamental characteristic of colonial power is the organization of social life on the basis of race. Race, however, is not defined in terms of a person's color or absence of color. It is a Eurocentric practice of hierarchical categorization of people in terms of naturalized identities by gender, class, ethnicity, sexual orientation, and so on. In other words, Quijano conceptualizes race as a practice or experience of intersecting identities rather than as a single identity. At the heart of the intercultural project is challenging the pervasive effects that racializing systems of power have in shaping both the organization of human life and the ways in which these systems influence how human problems are understood and addressed. The vision of interculturality is a world in which humanity is not categorized by racial superiority and inferiority. We argue it is time to shift away from racialized practices in the counseling field and begin to challenge the categorizations of humanity used to frame how mental health systems are understood and how counseling services should be delivered. Humanity has choices. We can live in our corners and only interact with others across differences if we have to. Alternatively, we can move toward interculturality, by being suspicious of the lines that categorization draws among us to separate us. We can approach one another in the spirit of curiosity, open-heartedness and empathy, seeking to understand one another and make a connection—to build bridges that, among other things, can change the very same practices that have separated us. Our hope is that the material laid out in this book will help prepare you to practice as intercultural counselors who build across the intersections to bridge the Us and Them divide.

Moving Beyond Cultural Competence

For a few decades now, students training to be counselors, psychologists, and therapists have been assessed and evaluated on the extent to which they are competent to work with culturally diverse clients. This movement seeks to teach current and future practitioners respectful and socially just ways of working with people representing culturally diverse backgrounds. There are still efforts being made to develop more accurate and objective methods to assess, teach, and evaluate cultural competence that center upon the development of appropriate knowledge, skills, and attitudes.

While the contributions of many researchers, writers, and practitioners have been enormously impactful on the promotion of respectful and socially just practice, the multicultural field is still largely captured by a formulaic and rigid approach to engaging with cultural diversity, based on the assumption of coherency of thought, action, and identity within particular, identifiable cultural groupings. In part, this growing trend is caused by one-dimensional characterizations of cultural difference and by the ongoing impact of humanist and critical theories on the nature of the self and identity. One-dimensional portrayals of ethnicity and the uncritical acceptance of the stability of a core, "true" self, implicit in contemporary humanist theories, create divisions and place significant constraints on expanding a new range of possibilities to produce socially just practices.

This book provides a wide range of new resources for respectful and socially just practice in intercultural counseling. These new resources are, to a significant but not exclusive extent, based upon the theoretical potency of constructionist epistemologies that have emerged within a postmodern paradigm, and more recently from Andean decolonial activists from South America. We explore relevant theoretical and practice-based models aiming to advance the original aspirations of the multicultural counseling movement. In addition, we engage literature outside multiculturality and across various disciplines, in search of alternative understandings that support our intercultural efforts and also have the potential to advance the counseling profession's aspirations toward social transformation. For example, we include the new literature on topics such as decoloniality, intersectionality, interculturality, and minority stress.

We pay special attention to the multiplicity, contextuality, and active construction of the self and identity. This emphasis represents a different approach to the relationship between self and culture. It suggests that the self is socially constructed and multiply dimensioned in response to the demands of particular variations of social, historical, and cultural settings. This view contrasts with more established and conventional conceptions of the self as a naturally occurring, independent object, devoid of cultural significance. The world of culture, in the conventional view, is arrayed around the outside of the boundaries of the self. By contrast, from a postmodern perspective, the self is deeply penetrated by the (often complex and shifting) cultural milieu in which it is surrounded. The self of the therapist, moreover, is also dependent upon the social world, including the culture of therapy. In fact, this is a notion of the self that is far from being stable and singular but is, instead, a multiple of selves. These ideas shape and organize this book.

There are dozens of books currently available on themes of culture and counseling. We think this is a positive development, given that the issue of responding to difference across a range of domains is critical to modern life. But it does raise the question, why yet another book? To answer this question, we need to be up-front about our purposes in writing this text. We have a number of specific goals that we are trying to achieve in this book. We shall outline these here so that they are transparent, and so that you can measure your reading of the book against these goals rather than against some other idea of what a book like this should be.

Constructionist Foundations and Decolonial Threads

In this proposed core text for multicultural counseling, we explore in detail the current major episte-mological developments in the multicultural counseling movement, and then present two additional epistemological approaches. First, we present a Eurocentric social constructionist approach, in order to highlight the potency of this metaphor for working with diversity; and second, in parallel, we present a decolonial approach, a non-Eurocentric framework that provides a historical analysis of the way in which colonial systems of power have prevented the realization of the modern promise of freedom, liberty, autonomy, and equality. In an effort to make complex decolonial, social constructionist, and postmodern concepts and vocabulary more accessible to the reader, we include significant case material and short vignettes to assist the reader in grappling with the comprehensive intercultural material presented throughout the text.

Efforts to Connect with Classroom Requirements

We have aimed to write a book that will be of use to students and faculty instructors, not only in a multicultural counseling class, but across various counseling classes. We believe that thinking about how to navigate intercultural considerations and apply intercultural skills should not just be empha-sized as a subject of one class; it should cut across the entirety of the counselor training curriculum. We consider, too, that others in the field of general helping relations—for example, students of psy-chology, family therapy, and social work—might find this work of value, and hope that this book will stimulate interest among practitioners of counseling.

We have kept an eye on the requirements of the American Counseling Association's multicultural counseling competencies and the Council of Accreditation of Counseling and Related Educational Programs (CACREP) standards in the writing of this text. As we discuss these standards and compe-tencies, our aim has been to introduce some new material into the discourse of culture and counseling, or at least to gather a number of ideas together from various sources for increased consideration in relation to culture and counseling practice.

One book can't do everything. We have sought here to address what we see as some of the most important domains of cultural influence, while intentionally avoiding normalizing descriptions within those domains. Because our focus has been on the complexity of identity issues and the epistemological underpinnings of an intercultural perspective, we have not been able to adequately address all of the multicultural domains that you might be looking for. For example, you will find very little discussion on the specific counseling needs of ethnic groups, or counseling needs related to disability, religion, and spirituality, or of the cultural experience of the elderly. Fortunately, there are numerous publica-tions that address the discrete needs of identity groups, including the following:

Brammer, R. (2012). *Diversity in counseling* (2nd ed.). Belmont, CA: Brooks/Cole.
Diller. J. V. (2015). *Cultural diversity: A primer for the human services* (5th ed.). Stamford. CT: Cengage.
Duan, C., & Brown, C. (2015). *Becoming a multiculturally competent counselor*. Thousand Oaks, CA: Sage.
Hays, D., & Erford, B. (Eds.). (2018). *Developing multicultural counseling competence: A systems approach* (3rd ed.). New York, NY: Pearson.
Lewis, J. A., Lewis, M. D., Daniels, J. A., & D'Andrea, M. J. (2010). *Community counseling: A multicultural-social justice perspective* (4th ed.). Stamford. CT: Cengage.

McAuliffe, G. (2019). *Culturally alert counseling. A comprehensive introduction* (3rd ed.). Thousand Oaks, CA: Sage.

McGoldrick, M., & Hardy, K. V. (2008). *Re-visioning family therapy, second edition: Race, culture, and gender in clinical practice.* New York, NY: Guilford Press.

Murphy, B. C., & Dillon, C. (2015). Interviewing in action in a multicultural world (5th ed.). Stamford. CT: Cengage.

Pedersen, P. B., Lonner, W. J., Draguns, J. G., Trimble, J. E., & Scharrón-del Río, M. R. (2015). *Counseling across cultures* (7th ed.). Thousand Oaks, CA: Sage.

Ponterotto, J. (2010). *Handbook of multicultural counseling* (3rd ed.). Thousand Oaks, CA: Sage.

Robinson-Wood, T. (2017). *The convergence of race, ethnicity, and gender: Multiple identities in counseling.* Thousand Oaks, CA: Sage.

Sue D. W., & Sue, D. S. (2019). *Counseling the culturally diverse: Theory and practice* (8th ed.). Hoboken, NJ: John Wiley & Sons.

Our Efforts to Add to the Dialogue on Culture and Counseling

We have taken a different approach in our book than that taken in the textbooks listed above, in part because we take the multicultural movement seriously enough to believe that it should provoke substantial rethinking of many of the commonly accepted assumptions in the counseling field. We consider one of the primary functions of a textbook to be the provocation and stimulation of thought. You may not always agree with our arguments in this book. That is okay. We expect that. But we would invite you to at least consider the ideas we present in a culturally respectful way; to adopt a questioning stance in relation to accepted knowledge; and to test that knowledge against criteria that place cultural difference at the forefront.

Some may argue (we have heard these arguments expressed to us) that we should not focus so much on the "intellectual" issues of culture but should promote the more humanistic concept of "awareness" in this text. We are not persuaded by these arguments. It is not that we are opposed to the idea of awareness; it is just that awareness can only exist within a framework of assumptions about people and about life. There is no such thing as pure awareness, only awareness that is located in culture and discourse and history. We think that students should engage in understanding, and sometimes questioning, these background assumptions in the process of developing awareness of cultural relations. We prefer not to patronize students by suggesting that they are not capable of such thought.

Our intention, therefore, has been to contribute a problematizing element to the conversation on these issues. To problematize means to take a step back from something that seems familiar and taken for granted, rendering it an object worthy of thinking more about (Marshall, 2007). Rather than just asking students or practitioners to, say, be more aware of their own race or culture, we want to ask them to step back and think carefully about some of the problems associated with the conventional concepts of race and culture, and to understand these concepts as contestable ideas rather than hard realities, as ideas produced through a history riven with power relations.

In this process, we anticipate that the subject matter might initially become less certain and less familiar. Many texts start with defining the terms of race and culture and so on. We want to encourage a discussion about how these terms get to be so defined, on the grounds that the control of definitions is a basis for power in itself. We trust that the opening up of these terms for searching discussion will also open up new forms of practice and the development of some conceptual tools that may assist counselors and students as they make sense of their own experience and that of the clients who seek their help.

For these reasons, we endeavor to incorporate scholarship on the assumptions and experience of culture and cultural difference from several other fields into our consideration of multicultural counseling.

For example, we have sought to draw from the recent developments in the field of cultural studies. We have also consciously drawn upon the literature of Andean decoloniality, postcolonial studies, and critical race theory. We've used material based in the philosophy of culture and in postmodern social theory. Others in the field of multicultural counseling have dipped into these sources, of course, but not all texts in this field have used them as fully as we have sought to do here.

All texts are written from a philosophical perspective; ours is no different. Sometimes this isn't mentioned because it's assumed that everyone will share the same perspective. Sometimes, too, confusion results when people talk across different assumptions without being transparent about where they're coming from. We want to avoid that. So let's declare our preference for thinking about counseling and multicultural practice from a social constructionist perspective, as discussed above. To be more specific, following are some guiding principles that have informed our approach.

Our Issue with Essentialism

We have not written this book from a humanistic perspective, or from a structuralist perspective. We certainly have respect for the vast majority of counselors who hold to one or the other of these frameworks. But, like them, we have our own biases. We would prefer that you know this from the start. One of our premises as social constructionists is that essentialist ideas about culture should be eschewed. Because essentialist thinking about meanings, personhood, groups of people, and culture itself is so familiar in our patterns of thought and in our ways of speaking, essentialism is hard to step out of. Nevertheless, we believe that new possibilities open up when we do so. We have therefore aimed to write about cultural issues using language and concepts that are as nonessentialist as possible.

Some may find this very effort to be Eurocentric. They are, in a sense, right. Essentialist thinking has dominated the modern world from its origins in European culture. Even the word "culture" itself is a European concept, as is the word "race." Indigenous cultures around the world have nurtured very different ways of thinking. Our intention in questioning essentialist assumptions in multicultural counseling is partly to create space for other ways of making sense of life to be considered and granted legitimacy. Even when we're not speaking about different cultural frameworks of thought, we would like you to remember that this is our intention.

Another premise we hold is that cultural relations in the modern world are not just constructed out of contemporary thinking. They have a history and they developed in a social context. We have therefore placed considerable emphasis in this text on locating concepts of culture in context, rather than implying that they exist in the present in some kind of temporal suspension. People do not hold to cultural stereotypes because, for example, they have independently developed faulty thinking in their heads. They do so because they are the products of a history that has produced these stereotypes and passed them down through the generations. We think it's important to make that history explicit without turning this book into a history text. We work with the assumption that locating concepts in history helps deconstruct some of their taken-for-granted authority.

We also seek to avoid essentialist language in our consideration of racism, sexism, heteronormative bias, and other ideological issues. We don't believe that these ideologies are essential to any person's existence. Therefore, we have sought to avoid the common practice of assigning their origins to the hearts of persons. We do not believe that people are racist, for example, in the core of their being.

Rather, we assume that racism is a social construct that existed long before any individual who now utters its lines. It has been passed on through social discourse and may have achieved a degree of influence over a person's heart and mind. But we shall avoid talking about any individual as a racist person, a sexist person, and so on. Such discipline is based on our philosophical standpoint, and we ask that you consider it. In this discipline, we draw from Michael White's (1989) aphorism: "The person is not the problem; the problem is the problem" (p. 7).

Our Implications for Practice

A by-product of this assumption is that we are doubtful about classroom practices that seek to make students more aware of, for example, their own racism or sexism. We would invite students to step out of the racist or sexist ideas that may have affected them, rather than to step further into them. We are more interested, therefore, in exercises that help students deconstruct the work done by powerful ideologies, including in their own thinking, to produce life experiences of privilege and disadvantage.

Chapter 1 examines the Us and Them divide and sets the scene for how this text seeks to build bridges and make connections with people subjected to all manner of separating forces occurring in North America and elsewhere. The chapter explores the social justice implications too that occur in these emergent, often conflict-bound identity politics.

Chapter 2 raises questions about the concept of culture. Many texts on multiculturalism simply define culture and move on. We think it's important for a book on culture to consider the concept of culture in more complexity. We begin, therefore, with a problematizing discussion in which we briefly trace the genealogy of the concept of culture and of the ways this concept has been used in the therapeutic literature. We introduce many aspects of added complexity that we believe need to be taken into account in relation to culture. In particular, we argue for a focus on the multiplicity of cultural influences rather than an essentializing notion of singular cultural belonging. Here we explain the usefulness of considering cultural narratives that run through our lives rather than focusing on simple identities.

In Chapter 3 we move to a focus on the major social divisions that were created by the processes of Western colonization of most of the earth's land surface, and the ongoing psychological effects of this process. We take a historical perspective here in order to signify that the cultural relations that exist today do so because of a particular history rather than just because of current policies and practices.

The historical and genealogical focus continues in Chapter 4, where we pay particular attention to the concept of race. Our focus on these topics before all others signifies the centrality in the modern world of the forms of social organization that have been built on concepts of race through colonizing practices.

In Chapter 5 we lay out some theoretical and epistemological emphases that we want to make use of through the rest of the book; specifically, we explore the relevance of the concepts of discourse, deconstruction, and positioning. Drawn from poststructuralism and used extensively in cultural studies, these concepts are, we believe, useful for counselors to master in order to speak in fresh ways about cultural identity influences.

Chapter 6 addresses power relations, highlighting and teasing out three different ways of thinking about power. We explain the liberal humanist approach that emphasizes personal power, a structuralist approach to power that reviews the workings of power through societal structural organization, and the poststructuralist (largely Foucauldian) analytic of power. We advocate for understanding the role of therapy in terms of the latter approach.

In Chapter 7, we return to the question of racism. It is such a central and such a damaging ideological formation that we felt this book deserved another chapter devoted to how counselors might think about and respond to expressions of racism.

Chapter 8 addresses the processes of cultural identity formation. We believe this to be a crucial consideration for counselors because it is the material that counselors and clients are dealing with on a daily basis. Our aim in this chapter is essential to do justice to the complexities of identity formation in the face of the array of swirling forces at work in the modern world.

In Chapter 9, we pick up the subject of gender and sexuality as critically important domains of cultural experience. This chapter traces some of the different approaches to thinking about the construction of gender and sexuality, with something of a historical emphasis, and includes a consideration of both women's and men's enculturation into gendered narratives.

Chapter 10, written by Penelope (Nel) Mercer, explores the major shifts occurring in the expressions of gender, sexuality, and relationship styles over the last few decades. This chapter builds on Chapter 9 by discussing the important new knowledges required of therapists working with clients embodying diverse gender, sexual, and relational identities and practices. Nel makes a case for providing affirmative therapy, including the deconstruction of problematic dominant discourses relating to gender, sexuality, and relationship structures.

Chapter 11 surveys both nationalist forces shaping the cultural landscape of the United States, and the major social forces at work in the process of globalization, pertaining to migration, mass social media, and the growth of technology. In Chapter 12, we explore social class issues and the positioning of people in places of economic privilege or disadvantage. We investigate how personal stories develop in relation to socioeconomic cultural formations, and the degree of access these formations give people to the "American dream" or its equivalent in other countries.

In Chapter 13, we consider the community contexts in which individuals are developing their personal identity. Here we pose the following question: Just what kind of community can we imagine that intercultural counseling approaches might contribute to? We use Charles Taylor's concept of social imaginaries and explore the shifts away from the melting pot idea to a range of possible alternatives.

In Chapter 14, we take a critical look at the competency-oriented framework of training, multiculturality, and the centeredness of European practices that inform counseling. We review the literature on cultural humility and psycho-politics, adding to a project of interculturality in counseling. We also link the decolonial analysis of colonial power with interculturality.

Acknowledgments

This book is a major reworking of our book published in 2008 and titled *New Horizons in Multicultural Counseling*. We are grateful to many people who have contributed to it along the way. We most want to give thanks to Wendy Drewery, who provided wonderful mentorship to Gerald and John in their early scholarship and research that proved to be a great source of inspiration for this first text, and the material presented in this book. We have deliberately sought to include a range of voices by taking special care to give space to a richly diverse group of writers. These writers include experts and teachers in the field of culture and counseling, as well as students of these subjects. We have invited them all to contribute their ideas on culture and counseling, primarily in the United States (and in other homelands), and to include their reflections on the nature of culture, identity, ethnicity, race, gender and sexual orientation, class, geographic location, disability, religion, relationship style, and numerous other salient cultural markers. Our goal has been to create a polyphonic range of responses that represents the complexity and multiplicity of perspectives we have been at pains to explain. We trust that the result of this process is that the book has something of the dialogic quality of a conversation rather than being a monologue.

Each chapter ends with a reflection on the content of the chapter by an author who we believe has an important perspective to offer on its content. You may recognize some of these authors as established and well-known writers in the multicultural field. Others represent the new generation of teachers of culture and counseling. When we approached these people to ask them to write their reflections, we specified two things. One was that they need not agree with our perspective but might take issue with it wherever they saw fit, as we hope that the differences expressed here will provide readers with stimulation to their own thinking. We also asked the writers to include a story illustrating the impact of the issues in the chapter on their own or others' lives. We are grateful to those who so willingly contributed their reflections to this book, and we acknowledge their thoughtfulness and integrity in doing so.

Our students and graduates have also contributed many stories to this book. We acknowledge the richness and poignancy of these stories and the freshness and complexity of lived experience that they exemplify. They serve as valuable illustrations of the ideas we have sought to represent. We acknowledge the contributions of the following people, whose stories were written for our first *New Horizons* book, and then transferred with copyright permission from Sage Publications to this new book. They are Sara Ackelson, Lorena Arias, Abbie Castel, Danielle Castillo, Heather Conley-Higgins, Natasha Crawford, Mark Darby, Esmelda Gonzalez, Maiko Ikeda, Sarah Johnson, Mikela Jones, Andy Kim, Mayra Lorenzo, Monica Loyce, Sarah Mamaril, Jesus Miranda, Fredy Moreno, Mandana Najimi, Rieko Onuma, Elynn Oropilla, Lorena Ortega, Florence Park, Michael Perales, An Pham, Hien Pham, Stephanie Picon, Belen Robles, Deborah Ann Samson, Randy Tone, Deanna Toombs, Jaime Tran, Grace Tsai, Mary Suzette Tuason, Tristan Turk, Lucille Vail, Michelle Wiese, and Daphne Zacky. A special thanks is due to new authors of personal stories in this text, including Sarah Hancock and Farah Hussein.

We would like to give particular thanks to Nel Mercer for the hundreds of hours she spent writing a new, comprehensive Chapter 10 on current trends, research, and the lived experience of a diverse community embodying gender, sexual, and relational diversity. We also acknowledge Nel's significant editorial contributions to other chapters of the book. We would further like to acknowledge Nel's extensive community of colleagues, family, and friends, who contributed rich personal statements and/or critical editorial feedback to Chapter 10. Specifically, we thank Katie Mercer, Amanda Mercer, Lilliana, Meera Dhebar, Mia Little, Monica Cham, Isaac Gomez, Paola, Sofia, Greg, Jane, Charlie, David Findlay, Cassia Holstein, George Mercer, Amanda Mercer, Chris Mercer, Montse Gómez Núñez, Jennifer Rehor, Diana Lozoya, Bonnie Clayton, Michael Giancola, Navid Zamani, and Val Delane.

A number of people read and commented on drafts of many chapters in the book, helping us to re-evaluate many small and not-so-small issues as we wrote. Some were particularly helpful in asking us to adopt a less strident tone in certain places; we shall leave it to you to judge how well we took their advice. We are grateful to the following people for their comments and suggestions on this current book: Wonyoung Cho, Justine Darling, Rose Hartzell-Cushanick, Rian Hancock, Sarah Kahn, Tri Nguyen, Meg Rogers, Maggie Slaska, and Navid Zamani. We would like to reserve special appreciation for Kimberly Ayres, who provided important editing work integrating chapters for this new text; Ayesha Schuster, who contributed some helpful exercises for readers; and to Da Hee Christina Kim, who completed the laborious task of checking all references and finding some missing ones, too! We also thank Krystal Colwell, Edward Delgado-Romero, Changming Duan, Mia Hardy, Brenda Ingram, Michael Jabbra, Larissa Jefferson-Allen, Richard Lee, Paul Pedersen, Tracy Shelton, Sue Strong, and Allen Wilcoxon for their contributions to the original text on which this present book is based.

Those at Cognella who supported us in rewriting the original book deserve our acknowledgment and gratitude. We are particularly grateful to Kassie Graves for seeing value in our proposal for this new book and for helping us initiate the project. We thank Amy Smith, project editor, for her hard work in getting the book into production and Emely Villavicencio, senior graphic designer for Cognella, who worked with her team to produce a great cover for the book. We thank Berenice Quirino, Associate Production Editor for her rapid feedback on getting our book to its final stages.

Our universities have provided both general and specific assistance for the completion of this project. In particular, San Diego State University's College of Education and Department of Counseling and School Psychology have provided research support to Gerald Monk over the last two years. California State University, San Bernardino, also supported John Winslade while he contributed to completing in the book through the 2018 to 2019 period.

Chapter 1

The Challenges of Bridging the Us and Them Divide

How the Categories of Us and Them Are Made

Introduction

The evidence that many genetic scientists are examining suggests that our human origins can be tracked back to a common mother who lived in Africa 200,000 years ago (Cavalli-Sforza & Feldman, 2003; Henn, Cavalli-Sforza, & Feldman, 2012). Mukherjee (2017), pooling multiple research studies on human genetics, argued that we originated from a small geographical location in sub-Saharan Africa and migrated north to Europe and east to the Middle East, Asia, and on to the Americas. Current evidence suggests that our human genomic variation is extremely low: we share 99.688% of the same genetic makeup, even though we might outwardly have different phenotypical characteristics. There is a case to be made that in every way, genetically, "We" and "Us" is a single species. In the course of this chapter, the "We" and the "Us" that is referenced here is based upon a considerable body of genetic data indicating that we belong to one identifiable category—a homo sapiens human species.

There is a long-standing history in the West, spanning over 500 years, that suggests there are distinct classes of human phenotype that clearly distinguish us as belonging in identifiable categories. However, the genetic reality is that our differences are more wide ranging within identifiable broad groups, like Asian or African, than between groups that are normally thought of as biologically distinct. For example, Mukherjee (2017), in his landmark book *The Gene: An Intimate History*, writes that, from a genetic perspective, the construct of race is a thoroughly inadequate identifier to use to group human beings. For example, one might think that Africans would have more genetic similarities with people who live on the African continent, rather than people from other continents. However, according to Mukherjee's sources, the genetic makeup of an African man from Nigeria is more different from a man from Namibia than an African man is from an Asian man. Geneticists therefore argue that it makes no sense to lump people together in a racial category.

Despite our extraordinary similar genetic makeup, our day-to-day interactions with others seem to tell us to congregate with well-defined, conspicuously discrete groups, such as a "We" or an "Us." Based upon everyday human interactions, it would be easy to conclude that human beings belong to uniquely different, highly separate and distinct categorizations. In fact, many of us notice that we seem to belong within different categories even within our extended families. Many of us have had experiences as a "Them"—being the other—in school, on social media, playing sports, in a religion, or in some community activity. Just as we are aware of our differences, we seem to long for belonging in a group that we can call an "Us." Berscheid and Reis (1998) suggest that human beings need a community, in a psychological sense, to thrive. They claim we have an evolutionary need to belong and a strong aversion to social exclusion. They cite evidence to suggest that social exclusion leads to loneliness and alienation, and our well-being suffers. Our modern-day social media, in all its forms, pays close attention to where we seem to belong. Then, our online activity gets reflected back to us, often intensifying separate, sharp, and distinct divisions of human kinds with whom we create connection or disconnection. As a human species, we appear to be acutely aware of who is the "Them," because that helps us know the boundaries of where the "Us" begins and ends.

The Construction of the "Us" and "Them"

Berreby (2005) proposes that we are at a period in our evolution where there is a recognition by most people that the categories we assign to people are not biological but instead are socially created. He suggests that, because of the global trend towards much higher degrees of interaction, we know there are multiple categories that encompass human action and we understand more of the complexities of human behavior. Is Berreby giving humanity too much credit? He claims we have evolved to the point that we can embrace a more nuanced understanding of the capabilities of persons, for good and harm. In speaking about the history of humanity's capacity for violence, he proposes, "It is now obvious that human-kinds violence belongs to no one religion, nation, race, culture or political ideology; it's equally obvious that a 'good man' at home can be a torturer at work and supposedly ancient hatreds can disappear, even as supposedly peaceful societies can turn genocidal. All of this leads to a hunger for new ways to think about human kinds" (2005, p. 31).

This chapter is positioned in a book on social constructionism and how this theory shapes how problems are constructed and understood, and how, for example, researchers, scholars, professors, therapists, and students understand how human problems can be addressed. The underlying assumptions drawn upon in writing this chapter are that human categorizations are culturally made up. They are constructed through a social, historical, and political prism. The construction of human categorizations does not mean that the effects of these artificial labels are insignificant or not worthy of study. In fact, the social groupings that people can be assigned to, have real effects on life choices and life chances. Some human categorizations can result in life-or-death consequences.

A Society of Immigrants

Nowhere is the role played by the construction of human categories more apparent than in the categorization of "immigrant." There is considerable attention paid to the meaning of immigrant in the United States and the status that immigrants are permitted to have. It is clear that we are, as a human species, all originally migrants or immigrants, having left one part of the planet to move to another. In the continents of the Americas, the first migrants, who we often refer to as the indigenous people of the Americas, were made up of diverse ethnic and tribal groups. The early migrants arrived over a period of 16,000 years. It is only in the last 500 years that people from European origins began continuous (colonizing) settlement (Cordell, Lightfoot, McManamon, & Milner, 2008; Pauketat, 2015). In the United States, some of the sharpest lines dividing people are drawn between group categories associated with the construction of immigrant status and who does and does not belong. We, in the

United States, are made up of extraordinarily diverse groups who have come from many parts of the world. We have been brought together as a result of very different historical processes—voluntary migration, refugee migration, conquest, colonization, the slave trade, and territorial acquisition. Since the United States became a country in 1776, there has been almost constant migration (Gerber, 2011). In Chapter 4 we discuss in detail the impact and movement of enslavement of millions of enslaved African people, and the effects of forced slave migration on the Black community in the United States spanning more than 300 years. In recent times, the largest number of immigrants has come across the southern U.S.–Mexican border without U.S. immigration documentation. Categories drawn around race are interwoven into the story of immigration to the United States. These categories are socially, politically, and historically situated. Immigrant populations, such as the Latinx and Japanese communities, have suffered from horrendous racial trauma at the hands of the resident White population and have been harmed as outgroups across social, economic, and political contexts (Chavez-Dueñas, Adames, Perez-Chavez, & Salas, 2019; Gerber, 2011; Nagata, Kim, & Wu, 2019).

Negative judgments and prejudices about particular categorized and minoritized immigrants have been weaponized and created intense divisions between groups of people in our communities. Gerber (2011) labels the group who identifies and categorizes immigrants as a threat, and struggles with the presence of new foreigners, as "nativists." This group, which is made up of ethnically diverse groups and some labor unions, argues that wages and living conditions deteriorate when mass immigration occurs, especially by migrants without proper U.S. work authorization. Those that see immigrants as a threat tend to obsess about a proliferation in crime, resource allocation and depletion, the non-English languages spoken on the streets and in stores, and the expanded population growth. It is worth noting here that numerous studies show immigrants are less likely to commit crimes or be imprisoned than native-born U.S. citizens (Gerber, 2011).

One group that seeks to embrace all new immigrants fleeing violence, torture, death, grinding poverty, and hopelessness have been defined by Gerber (2011) as the "pluralists" (in whatever way they got to the United States). This group pays attention to the history of the United States and thinks of this country as a place that honors our immigrant ancestors and their contributions to U.S. society, and thus welcomes new residents. The pluralists are often allied to employers who may not be at all interested in ethnic diversity but are very motivated by cheap labor. Gerber notes that U.S. employers are dependent upon undocumented workers because of the low wages they can be paid and the working conditions they are prepared to tolerate. For example, Mexicans with or without U.S. immigration documentation feature prominently in the workforce in agriculture, light manufacturing, construction, meatpacking, and garment manufacture; initially in the Southwest of the United States but now in many other states. Anna Crosslin (2010) says that what feeds many U.S. cities is the arrival of new immigrants, where they often end up renewing decaying inner-city areas.

As Gerber states, there are unlikely coalitions that group people together as nativists and pluralists. The nativists may be social conservatives and some labor unions, while the pluralists are a mix of conservative capitalists and democratic idealists. These groups do battle over the legitimacy or illegitimacy of allowing new immigrants into the United States in much the same way these various stakeholders have during every wave of migration going back to the first massive migration in the 1840s and 1850s (Gerber, 2011).

Given that we have millions of people living, working, and going to school in this country, most of whom are unconnected, Gerber (2011) poses the questions: "Who are we as a people?" and "Who am I?" Gerber answers his own question: "We are everyone. Many cannot accept the answer. They do not want to consider themselves to be like those who represent, whether on the basis of visible traits like skin color or of the sound of a language they cannot understand, the antithesis of their ideal image of themselves" (2011, p. 6).

Our Purpose for This Book

As you read this chapter, you might pay attention to categories that you and your family and friends (and the people you do not like) belong to, and those categories you are excluded from. Some human categories you get to choose to belong to. Others are already decided for you by the communities you live in. New human categories get invented all the time, and we are all keenly aware of whether we are in the ingroup or the outgroup. We know every moment of every day whether we are living our lives as an "Us" that belongs or as a "Them" positioned on the periphery, at the margins, on the border, and excluded (Berreby, 2005). Of course, in our lived experience, we have periods of being in both ingroups and outgroups, and this can happen at the same time and all in the same day. At any one moment we are living in different categories of persons at different identity intersections. In a single conversation, we can rapidly cycle through multiple human kinds, or identities. In one moment, I (Gerald) am a man in my sixties talking to a woman in her twenties, and the next moment my accent shows I am a foreigner and from somewhere else. In a space of a couple of minutes, we cross multiple intersections, experience multiple representations in multiple categories. Some of these categories feel welcoming and enjoyable and others may feel uncomfortable or even distressing. Even if the categories are not highly distinguishable, there is a network of human allegiances, connections, and affiliations.

The human categories in which we find ourselves have an extraordinary influence on our well-being as we move through the world. The cultural processes that create and shape human categories are not always benign ones. Every human category has an effect on the members of that group and across groups. The categorization of humanity dislocates experiences. It makes it challenging to relate interculturally when such categories are created by powerful hierarchical cultural forces that typically emerge from Eurocentric origins. When living in some categories, there is a lot at stake for us. In others, the stakes are not so high. For example, living in the United States as an undocumented student brought to the country as a young child is a category that has a person living daily under threat of being captured by immigration authorities; torn away from studies, career prospects, friends, and family; and brought into a country and town or city that is completely foreign. If that person gained immigration status, the fear of incarceration and being taken away from loved ones disappears and one can participate in life without being hypervigilant of the moves made by any authority figures that come into one's vicinity. Participation in an ingroup can provide joy, happiness, well-being, and fulfilment. Being in an outgroup can mean we are made to suffer, demeaned, silenced, threatened, and, potentially, fighting for survival. The quality of our mental health can depend on the extent to which we belong to human categories where we are accepted, respected, recognized, represented, and known, and to the extent that we have a voice that can be heard. Our physical and psychological well-being can be threatened by the cultural forces swirling about us that create sharp binary divisions of category membership that set us up to attack, defend, dehumanize, stigmatize, and talk past one another. These wider macrolevel forces that originate outside of ourselves have the most startlingly intimate effects on our daily mood, familial and community interactions, rituals, and routines. We are in touch with the feeling of belonging and connection, or the effect of being shut out and shut down.

There are strong biocultural forces that can hijack us to pay attention to difference rather than similarity. In our classes, we sometimes hear students say, "I don't judge people." Some students were trained to say that as the polite thing to do. "Don't be quick to judge until you know people," is another common refrain. What happens, according to some contemporary social science theories and research today, is the opposite. In the United States, there are a lot of studies that show human beings seem to make rapid judgments of one another, first in terms of whether to move towards this person or move away. Only after the initial judgments are people ready to make new decisions on learning about who this person is and what they are about.

Going forward, we can live in our corners and only interact with the Other if we have to. Alternatively, we can move toward interculturality by being suspicious of the lines that categories draw among us to separate us. We can do so with curiosity, open-heartedness, and empathy, seeking to understand one another and make a connection—to build a bridge that, among other things, can change the very same practices that have categorized our humanity. The reality in this globalized and interconnected world is that we have the capacity to find interculturality when discovering commonalities, and shared purposes when we pay attention to the intersections of our identities. At those intersections, we find points of connection with others and then build on those rather than being consumed by the bifurcations that alienate and divide.

This book is an effort to support people training or working in the counseling professions to better manage initial split-second reactions or early judgments when detecting difference that can propel people away from one another. When clients or therapists immediately register difference between each other, the therapist's job is to bridge across that difference. What we have attempted to do in this text is provide a variety of resources for therapists to expand their relational repertoires and create more varied ways of connecting, to work together with the people they will serve. Effective counseling or psychotherapy occurs when a strong relationship is forged between client and therapist across cultures and shared identity intersections. Providing effective counseling is not an easy thing to do when we are living in an Us and Them world—especially when clients that seek our services, or are directed by some outside organization to work with us, perceive us to be part of the ingroup and they feel part of the outgroup, or vice versa; or when they belong to outgroups that have been minoritized, criminalized, or discriminated against. Alternatively, if we feel part of an outgroup as counselors, there can be a lot of constraints working against us, as we struggle to provide services to those who are seeking our help.

To deliver more effective therapy, we think there is value in looking more closely at the Us and Them phenomenon and how these human categories operate, with the intention to search for ways to interrelate beyond these socially constructed categories. Looking at this human landscape from a number of perspectives, our hope is will set you up to take full advantage of the material laid out in this book, and ultimately prepare you to practice as intercultural counselors and build across the intersections between the Us and the Them.

This chapter is an effort to begin the process of looking at how problems—the problems that bring clients to us—get to be problems in the first place. We feel confident that examining the historical, social, political, biological, and cultural processes that are at work in shaping our lives will render the approaches and practices laid out in this book both relevant and effective in supporting your personal and professional journey as healthcare professionals. Now let us turn to the mechanisms that invite us to attend to Us and Them.

Tuning into Us and Them

Human beings are primed to tune in to one another. Researchers find that newborns that are a few hours old are already paying attention to human faces (Berreby, 2005). Very early on we become highly sensitized to people's nonverbal behaviors. We notice the subtleties of voice tone, a faint smile, a shrug, a flash of disgust. We are tuning in to figure out, "Who is this person?" As we get older, we track the emerging social codes we become sensitized to. Is this person like me? Do they eat like me? Do they talk like me? Do they have my interests? Do they get "who I am"?

When studying the Us and Them phenomenon, Black and White participants in a research study conducted in Europe, more specifically Italy, observed videos of hands being pricked by pins by their participants, White, Caucasian Italian and Black African born in Africa and living in Italy. Avenanti, Sirigu, and Aglioti (2010) found that the observer's hands would sometimes unconsciously twitch when they saw a hand that was a similar skin color grouping to their own. If the pricked hand was a different skin color, there was less or no reaction. Sampasivam, Collins, Bielajew, and Clément's (2016) study from Ottawa, Canada, found that when a group of research participants identified with a person who looked like them, and who seemed to be threatened, the research participants secreted higher levels of stress hormones, such as cortisol, in their saliva. Their participants were in the majority women (102) and men (16) with an average age of 19 years old. Scheepers and Derks (2016) found it was possible to observe changes in brain activity within 200 milliseconds when a face was shown to a person who belonged to a different or similar social category. They found individuals who identified with a group used certain parts of their brain to process ingroup-related information and a different part of the brain to process outgroup-related information. These studies demonstrate that, among individuals who identify as European and European American, their autonomic (automatic) nervous systems' responses depend upon social context. In this way, there is significant interplay between biological responses and social ones. We believe that, in spite of these findings, being as they are particular to the politics of the researchers and experiences of the social locations of their participants, as in any research, there can be value in their claims from which we can learn.

We tend to take the judgment of the Us and the Them for granted, as though all of our categorizations are common sense. If that is so, then as Gilles Deleuze (2004) argued, common sense is not to be trusted, because it contains opinions that are not reflected upon or carefully considered. Nevertheless, we often feel like our categories have always been there and are essential, nonnegotiable, stable, true, and real. Instead, we are many different human kinds at the same time that are overlapping and even contradictory and conflicting at times. In the chapters that follow, we will show how our human categories, or identities, are created and further shaped by powerful cultural forces that contextualize our lives. Human beings are swept up in the cultural forces that shape us from as early as we can remember. We often do not feel we have a choice about being categorized and what kinds of categories we belong to, just as we often are unaware of the culture we "swim" in. The social practice of categorization and social categories seem to be already there, pre-made, and we may not even know that we can contradict them. The cultural forces that seem to be most influential and defining across the world appear in hierarchical categories of language, ethnicity, gender diversity, sexuality, relationship status, body appearance, class, religion, occupation, status of mental and physical ableness, political affiliation, nationality, immigration status, and geography. These categories that can define our lives are not just intellectual ideas. They affect many areas of our lives, including our physical and psychological safety, emotional well-being, and the practical and logistical elements of our day-to-day lives, including how we relate to one another. Sapolsky (2018) discusses different human kinds or human categories as emotionally "sticky." When our category is visible to others, such as skin color, we are subject to all of the dominant cultural ideas that accompany our category in the different settings we may be inhabiting. These categories stick to us. This all feels extremely personal and we might experience an emotional reaction. Living inside of specific categories is "identifying." Unless we deliberately choose to counter them, we become these identifiers that we carry with us. Our identifiers or our identities become our touchstone for belonging. They define the boundaries of our "Usness" and "Themness." Our identities inform us about what we should be doing, and whether we are aligning with the right things for our kind. Our identities also tell others about what we should be doing. We learn to measure the value of our lives and our identities and the value of others and their identities; which, in turn, impacts our disposition toward intercultural connections or the lack thereof. Again, unless we gain awareness about them and deliberately choose to counter them, we are pulled into what we feel and must do. These cultural forces constructing our identities are like maps, which tell us what humankind we should be. We are knitted to these identities, from which we derive our sense of well-being, and of what behavior feels right. The consequences of the identities that are imposed upon us can be welcoming and supportive or vile and destructive to our lives. In this book, we will look at the roles that both biology and discourse play to form these identities and how they impact intercultural possibilities.

Defending Our Categories

When we are living in accordance with our identities, things appear quite clear to us. Life looks normal within our frame of reference, even though for some of us this state can be highly aversive or distressing. Our behavior is explained to our satisfaction in nuanced ways by the circumstances in which we find ourselves. The well-established psychological concept, described by Lee D. Ross (1977), called "the fundamental attribution error" is very helpful in explaining the Us behavior and the Them behavior. As Berreby (2005) says, we explain our own behavior in relation to external circumstances and understand others through internal categories. For example, if someone is late to an appointment, we may be quick to judge them as selfish, but if we are late, we are quick to point out situational reasons, such as traffic. Berreby writes, "One way you can tell if it is an (attribution) error is that you would never apply such a crude generalization to yourself" (p. 6). When we assign people to categories, we generally classify the diverse individuals that make up the category as all the same. The categorization and generalization of people is often a "common sense" approach. Many researchers (Berreby, 2005; Gladwell, 2007) claim that we engage in categorizing human beings as a quick way to make sense of who a stranger is. It falls into a known thought practice and does not require much effort to go along with it.

Human beings often pigeonhole others by deciding what traits apply to them and then deciding whether they fit that category or not, based upon the cultural information available to them. Berreby (2005) cites the classical definition left by Aristotle, who derived the term "category" from the verb that meant "to accuse." Berreby says that categories are not just lists of things. They are explanations for making meaning. Categories are generally constructed and understood by large numbers of people. So we can usually easily find others who will confirm our categorizations. Other times they get to be quite narrow. Thus, categories emerge from the needs of the categorizers. They are not separated from the purposes of who is using them. Categories get made to serve particular needs of the time. The categorizing of persons has real effects both on the categorizer and the categorized; and, consequently, on the possibilities to connect across them, interculturally. In the first two decades of the 21st century, a highly polarized political climate has existed. It is evident that categories such as Democrat and Republican, or liberal and conservative, serve particular purposes and have real effects.

Leach, Spears, Branscombe, and Doosje (2003) describe the phenomenon of Schadenfreude, where people have the capacity to gain some pleasure in the suffering, pain, and troubles of the Them categories. Schadenfreude is the opposite of empathy. Leach et al. liken this phenomenon to sports fans who are vested in their team's success, so when the rival team fails, schadenfreude occurs. The political landscape in the United States is set up around schadenfreude and appears to drive responses from the winning or losing political side. Policy decisions are often made on the basis of reactions to losing in an earlier round when the current political party has the chance to avenge an earlier defeat. Leach et al. suggest this state emerges when one humankind has inferior feelings about the treatment they have experienced at the hands of the other, so when the rival is defeated, schadenfreude is felt as a form of emotional revenge.

The Production of Us and Them

The Primacy of Fear

Many scientists from diverse disciplines, such as anthropology, psychology, political science, evolutionary biology, history, and sociology, recognize that a community's sociocultural and sociopolitical landscape is heavily influenced by the extent to which people feel secure in their communities, and safe from physical or psychological threat. Hetherington and Weiler (2018) report pessimistically that, as we become more consumed by fear, survival instincts are mobilized and our high-minded, more ethical viewpoints retreat. In fact, our level of fear, a primary emotion, tends to drive our beliefs about the nature of things, unless we actively work against it. Research shows that we register fearful and/ or threatening faces more quickly than we register happy faces (Yang, Zald, & Blake, 2007). There is a powerful drive that underpins our desire to organize ourselves into categories and to sort out who is "them" based upon how dangerous the world is perceived to be. We seek to avoid connection with the other, in part because of fear. Brene Brown (2017) suggests that, in the post 9/11 United States, fear has become exacerbated in our daily lives. She says, "our national conversation is centered on, 'What shall we fear?' and, 'Who should we blame?'" (p. 56). As life feels more unpredictable, stress increases and people become more suspicious of the other.

Inglehart's (2018) extensive research on societal systems all over the world came to two rather simple conclusions that are relevant here. Communities that grow up with their members feeling that their lives are insecure and are centered upon ensuring their survival take on a different shape than those whose members tend to take their security for granted. These two life positions have a shaping influence on people's identities. People who are confronted with scarcity or feel the threat that all will be taken away from them tend to be more afraid of the other. It becomes easier to believe that life is organized around a zero-sum game, where there are exclusively winners or losers. Inglehart's research on many societies found that, when communities are mobilized around survival, they are drawn to authority figures, and that authoritarian populism flourishes in this context. He describes these communities as existentially insecure and much more concerned with economic survival and physical security.

So if fear is one powerful driver, we should ask what might counter it. In Inglehart's research, the counterpoint is the communities that tend to be more existentially secure, taking their security needs for granted. They are likely to be more outward looking, more embracing of diverse ways of life, and more attentive to new ideas. He calls these communities who have had intergenerational stability and security, and who put value on choice and self-expression, post materialists. Because of the consistent and more predictable sense of longevity, people's lives are more emotionally stable, making it more possible to invest in more culturally diverse, long-term, trusting relationships.

Cultural psychologist Michele Gelfand (2018) lays out a similar dichotomy in her book *Rule Makers, Rule Breakers*. She spent two decades conducting research in dozens of countries on many characteristics, including age group, class, and family organization, and concluded that human behavior was shaped by fear or the perception of threat. She described two different types of cultural communities: one which was "tight," and leaned towards a more hierarchical and autocratic way of organizing itself, and one which was "loose," with more open norms. She says tight societies are top-down, and tend to shut down dissent and be more religiously oriented. Cultural norms that characterize tight communities tend to be more rigid, dogmatic, and intolerant because they perceive greater threat. Loose cultural norms emerge when communities feel economically secure. There is less need to turn to what fear might offer.

Hetherington and Weiler (2018) have developed a similar analysis to the "tight" and "loose" communities described by Gelfand. Their research is based primarily upon understanding how U.S. democracy becomes vulnerable and potentially threatened by populist and authoritarian undercurrents. Through examining the political impulses of the U.S. electorate, they hope their research will clarify the social and cultural forces that will influence the future political landscape of the United States. From their research on political beliefs of voters in the United States, Hetherington and Weiler conclude that there are three categories of persons: fixed, fluid, and mixed. People described as "fixed" are more set in their ways, more suspicious of strangers, and more comfortable with the predictable and familiar. So-called "fluids" are more open to changing cultural attitudes and more comfortable with diversity. Of course these are arbitrary, binary descriptions and Hetherington and Weiler found that two-thirds of people polled were a mixture of fluid and fixed. Both Inglehart (2018) and Gelfand (2018) note that religious activity typically declines when economic security has been intergenerationally established. They note too that richer communities lean more democratic than poorer ones. Inglehart (2018) shows that, with rapid social changes and the increase in robotics and artificial intelligence in wealthy industrialized societies, the less technologically prepared will experience greater existential threat and insecurity, which fuels the fear of threat by the "Them" and greater attraction to authoritarian systems of community organization. When there is a deterioration in income levels and heightened job insecurity, combined with mass immigration, a cultural backlash among older and less economically secure individuals often occurs and is directed against new immigrants, as well as against the post materialists that support them.

It is reasonable to start thinking about who the secure and insecure communities are and who the materialists and post materialists are. You may be thinking, who are the fixed people and who are the fluids? Any classification system of this kind is usually dangerous to hold fast to, because we are often drawn to tidy and simplistic binaries to help us make meaning of complexity, confusion, and contradiction. As mentioned previously, the reality is that categories can change, sometimes quickly, and other times hardly at all, even across centuries. We also know that people categorized as one way at one point at time and space may enter completely new categories and exit old ones.

Nevertheless, thinking about the different kinds of organizations of humankind can disrupt our tendency to rely on old pathologizing descriptions of individuals or resort to old familiar categorizations around race, ethnicity, social class, gender, and sexuality to make meaning of who we are and who they are. New ways of looking at how we can make meaning of groups of people and their actions may help us grapple with the multiplicity and complexity of our lives, and the possibilities whereby intercultural relationships are possible, respecting the integrity of what makes us different. There are so many ways we can make meaning of ourselves, others, and how we relate to one another. The main point here is to notice that these categories arise from macrolevel economic, political, social, and historical forces within which people's lives and relationships are swept along in ways that are beyond individual choices and proclivities. It would be a mistake to think that post materialists are a psychological type or that somebody had a fluid character. Once we are starting down the track of psychologizing individuals who are caught up in something much bigger than themselves, we are moving towards pathologization, a practice we are arguing against in this text.

The Biological Processes of Us and Them

As you are aware from the Foreword and Introduction, this book is largely written from a social constructionist perspective. Put simply in this chapter, social constructionism attends to how we make meaning of any phenomenon through a collective set of assumptions about what we name as reality. In any particular era, we build out a set of social constructs that come to be regarded as true and that are taken for granted among large sections of the population. Social constructionist texts typically focus on the social and the cultural, not on the biological (here referring to the body and the brain). From a social constructionist perspective, the cultural and the social dimensions of human behavior are inextricably interwoven together with biological dimensions. All of the human senses, while biologically driven, function through a cultural lens. To parcel out biology, the body and the brain, from the social, cultural, and relational is an old, dualistic, Cartesian practice that immediately draws artificial categories that do not exist in our lived experience. Everything is connected.

Nevertheless, there is a growing number of textbooks on cross-cultural communication, multiculturalism, and cultural diversity that dedicate chapters to studying the applications of neuroscience in making meaning of cultural encounters, and how to better manage cross-cultural interactions while considering the biological dimensions at play (Choudhury, 2015; Prinz, 2014). In contemporary psychotherapy, many theories have been developed in the last few decades that describe how we understand the role of the body and brain when doing therapy. Considerable attention is now being paid to the contributions of neuroscience in understanding how the neurological structures of our brains influence therapeutic interactions between counselor and client. Despite the extraordinary growth in research on the brain and how the biological dimensions of human interaction occur, the research is still in its infancy in determining how exactly our brains function within the relational spaces humans occupy. There has, however, been increasing awareness that *both* biology *and* culture (nature and nurture) matter. To ignore biology and the influence it has on us in this text would contribute to the othering that we argue is so damaging. We are committed to not positioning biology as "Them" and culture as "Us."

We do argue here, though, that we should be cautious in blindly accepting popular theories about how our bodies and brains affect the Us and Them dynamic. It is a slippery slope to start explaining that it is exclusively our brains and our internal, biological mechanisms that influence the division of Us and Them. It would be a terrible mistake to suggest that the ugly elements of bias, stigma, and prejudice that we discuss in this chapter have distinctly biological origins and are somehow therefore devoid of the historical, social, and political forces that produce these painful relational dynamics.

You will find in the counseling and neuroscience literature some widely accepted ideas about body/brain relationships and psychological well-being. A great deal has been written on the impact of traumatic stress on neurological functioning, especially when human beings are under threat or are in danger (Griffith & Griffith, 1994; LeDoux, 1996; Siegel, 2007, 2009, 2010; Van der Kolk, 2006, 2015). We can speculate that our limbic system and autonomic nervous system (ANS) are primed to try to control our environment. Vigilance to threat is heightened and attention is focused outward and mobilized to predict, contain, and try to manage the aversive environment. The ANS, with its control centered in the limbic system, is an evolutionarily old part of the brain, made up primarily of the hippocampus, thalamus, hypothalamus, and amygdala. The significance of this brain system is that when it experiences danger, the body reacts rapidly, and then the brain/body system is essentially functioning on autopilot and beyond conscious control (Van der Kolk, 2006). The amygdala is a part of the brain that scans for threats. Hanson (2009) says the amygdala registers both what is a threat and what is pleasurable, even though this perception could be incorrect. By the time a signal of danger arrives via the amygdala to the neocortex, which is the conscious, "thinking" part of the brain, the body is already flooded with adrenaline and cortisol. The heart rate immediately increases, breathing becomes shallow, the visual field is narrowed, and the gut and liver are activated for some form of immediate response. Cognitive responses in the neocortex take a while to catch up. When overwhelming danger is perceived, the body's first job is to survive; analysis comes later. According to Van der Kolk (1998), as a consequence of sustained levels of stress caused by a physical or psychological threat, the verbally based system of memory goes "offline."

Sydney psychiatrist Russell Meares (1999) offers a different account. His clinical research suggests that a traumatic memory can do what Van der Kolk describes by taking memories "offline." But his is a more nuanced account than a simple on–off mechanism. First of all, he documents a series of different types of memory, which are sequentially learned as a child grows. The earliest is a perceptual memory that infants master in the first few weeks of life. Next comes procedural memory, which involves remembering a sequence of movements that make up an action. Then comes semantic memory, which appears around the end of the first year of life. It becomes "declarative" with the advent of language. The next form of memory is called episodic memory. It appears around three years of age and involves a recounting of simple and recent events in a child's life. Autobiographical memory allows a child to remember events in one's life and to recount them. It is found in children at about five years of age. It connects with what 19th century psychologist William James called the stream of consciousness. According to Meares (1999), the autobiographical memory is necessary for a person to "double" consciousness through reflecting on experience.

Now let us look at what happens when a traumatic experience occurs. Russell Meares (1999) argues that memory fails, much as Van der Kolk suggested, but it does not fail all at once. Instead, the most recently developed form of memory, autobiographical memory, fails first, followed by episodic memory, semantic memory, procedural memory, and finally, in the most serious cases, perceptual memory. When a particular kind of memory fails, the person experiences traumatic memories as if they are happening right now. This occurrence is very frightening. The other implication for therapy is that the person's memory system can be reconstructed piece by piece. Michael White (2006) references Russell Meares (1999) and shows how this is achieved by seeking out what a person gives value to and using that to overcome fear. The point is that fear may be very powerful, but it is not all powerful, and it can be countered.

Levels of cortisol increase, however, as fear increases, and this impacts the language centers in the brain. In a high-fear situation, the ANS creates a hyper-vigilant response to the sensory cues in the environment, with the nonverbal systems—visual, auditory, olfactory, kinesthetic—all activated. In general, most of us are not fighting off some physical life-threatening situation when the physical sensations in our body and the accompanying strong emotions are on red alert. However, we are experiencing stress caused by a perceived threatening encounter that can potentially occur in all contexts we live in. Our bodies are attuned to seeking psychological safety. We also strive for recognition and acceptance.

Lewis, Amini, and Lannon (2000) have documented significant research showing that our heart rates, blood pressure, and mood are synchronized with others close by, and those who are emotionally influential impact ours and others' mood, even without any words being spoken. Lewis et al. noted that we regulate or dysregulate with others, and this occurs at a deep biochemical level. When the collective physiology becomes synchronized with others, emotional resonance occurs between one another. This is the biological experience of feeling that comes when we are "Us." When we are part of a cooperative group, we feel safe. Lewis et al. (2000) state that our brains automatically process relational dynamics in our environment, sometimes unconsciously, preferring experiences with others who are most like us.

When human beings feel safe in their relationships and in their physical environment, Griffith and Griffith (1994) say we demonstrate an emotional posture of tranquility. In a nonthreatened body state, one is well-placed to care for others and oneself. Humans in a tranquil state are found to be loving, trusting, reflecting, and affirming. In a state of tranquility, we are not focused on managing our external environment, as we perceive there to be minimal threat. In this state, we pay attention to others who contribute to our well-being.

However, when the emotional landscape is discordant or out of step, and when things seem awkward and challenging, we are more likely to pay attention to "Them." Now we are in a state of emotional dissonance with the "Them" that are around us. Wilkinson (2001) said that our stress response is triggered most intensely when we feel our sense of belonging is threatened. The human nervous system is set up to pay acute attention to others' physiological reactions. Griffith and Griffith refer to the emotional posture of a zone of alarm when the body prepares to defend against an attack. When the body is under threat, this emotional posture shows a range of protective reactions, such as scorning, shaming, justifying, ignoring, criticizing, and mobilizing for action. A fearful body does not experience joy or feel confident. Nor will somebody stand tall and proud when experiencing fear. Lieberman (2013), a neuroscientist, said that when there are threats to our social bonds, "the brain responds in much the same way it responds to physical pain" (p. 40).

In alignment with this discussion on the physiology underpinning the construction of Us and Them, Myers (2007) noted that we have an inherent tendency, which he calls risk intuition, that assesses threat in our environment; further, because of repetition in our neural networks, our brains do not have to be as actively assessing threat with those that we perceive as most like us. Of course, this information is critically important to consider within the counseling context. A client is meeting the counselor for the first time. Imagine the physiological experiences that the client may be going through in relation to a stress response. In this early encounter, the client is scanning for clues from whatever source is available (including the physical environment where the counseling meeting takes place) to determine psychological safety. If the physical environment is within the counselor's physical context, the client may be looking at the decor, the pictures and art on the walls—studying the people in this location with the intent of determining whether this going to be an "Us" place or a "Them" place. Then, in those first moments of the client meeting the counselor, the client is scanning every microlevel interaction of the counselor from a smile or neutral expression on their face, to a formal greeting, noting how the counselor is dressed, noticing skin color, sex, gender, age, all in the process of determining: is the counselor an Us or Them? Of course, all of these same observations are going on in the mind of the counselor in determining if this person is "my people."

These rapid-fire biological processes at play become extremely important when we consider those early human reactions to a stranger. And while we are attempting to describe these experiences and the ways they take shape within a biological framework, it's important to maintain that the same experiences are shaped by cultural knowledge that shows up as bias, and "common sense." We will take a look in more detail as to what happens when strangers meet.

Bias, Stigma, and Dehumanization as a "Them"ifying Action

In this section, we will map out some of the biological forces at work in the creation of bias and dehumanization. As we do this, it is important to remember that bias and dehumanization are not inevitable. People every day do things to counter these forces. Biological forces can incline us in a certain direction, but discursive forces hold an immediate influence and an interlocking relationship with these inclinations.

Bias

Bias is normally defined as a judgment made in favor of something based on a comparison between things, persons, or groups. The judgment of bias is normally considered negative or unfair, but not always. There is some disturbing research that suggests that, despite our best efforts to avoid favoring one group over another group, we actually are inclined to have a hidden or unintentional preference for specific groups of people (Greenwald & Banaji, 2017; Kurdi et al., 2018).

Banaji and Greenwald (2013) and their colleagues have conducted hundreds of studies over more than 20 years investigating unconscious bias and stereotyping. A stereotype is an oversimplified image or idea of a particular type of thing, person, or group. The results from implicit bias research, using the Implicit Association Test (IAT), is compelling: it is clear that human beings show bias towards particular groups, and can be completely unconscious of doing so. The bias we exhibit can be in stark contrast to our stated beliefs. Even when people vehemently deny negative feelings toward an identified other, in test conditions they almost always display a bias. Berreby (2005) suggested that the largest sample of students from the United States (presumably White) showed unconscious favoritism for White over Black and male over female using the IAT. Associations to an outgroup that have already been made in a person's background are internalized to such an extent that the bias happens automatically. When people are distracted by some competing stimulus, the bias is even more in play. The social psychologist Siri Carpenter (2008) said that responses outside of our awareness show that we have biases that we abhor, and that the worst aspect of this is that we act on our biases. The IAT results show that we negatively judge others for no good reason. Still, test conditions are different from real-life ones.

The data produced suggests that we are biologically primed to give the benefit of the doubt to people like Us in our reactions. Those that look different to us we judge more harshly. This occurs most commonly with those that are phenotypically different to us. Historically, identity groups who have been culturally deemed to have a higher status in our communities, such as middle class, White, male, able-bodied, formally educated, rich, stereotypically attractive persons, for example, tend to be judged with greater favoritism. Identity groups that have been traditionally associated with lower status, such as people of color, sexual minorities, the working class, poor, or people with disabilities are judged by high-status groups with more negativity. The surprising result from the IAT research is that not only Whites demonstrated a strong pro-White bias. Latinx and Asian identity groups also exhibited strong pro-White biases. Disturbingly, even when members of so-called low-status groups explicitly say they prefer to connect with their own group, the first responses on the IAT for many non-dominant groups favor the dominant group (Nosek, Banaji, & Greenwald, 2002).

As has been already discussed, our unconscious mind operates out of awareness and reacts to the oceans of stimuli that are bombarding us. Wilson (2004) states we can only keep a handful of items in focus at any one time. Those of you who drive a car may recall experiences where you have been on autopilot, driving down the road and having no conscious awareness of the ground you have covered, because you were thoroughly distracted by some other stimulus that caught your attention. Perhaps it was an argument you just had with a friend or colleague, or thoughts of an exciting vacation you are wanting to have. This autopilot function can occur when we are preparing a meal, playing a sport or musical instrument, or when we are just doing things without conscious awareness. When we give something our attention, we can override this automatic pilot. Bias often occurs when we are in autopilot and we are just reacting to a multitude of information coming at us. As Ross (2008) says, "As a result of … pre-established filters, we see things, hear things, and interpret them differently than other people might. Or we might not see them at all!" (p. 3).

Bias is most prominent in decision-making circumstances where time is limited or there is some perceived threat, because what is happening is occurring faster than we can think about it. Client and counselor encounters in the high-stakes environment of therapy are ripe for interactions that are affected by bias. Negative implicit bias occurs against people of color in job interviews, leaving them at a serious disadvantage. Black patients in hospitals are at more risk of not receiving the care they should get, and are at risk of suffering physical harm, because of bias from healthcare professionals (Green et al., 2007).

Siri Carpenter's (2008) research shows that in the police force in the United States, where individuals show high levels of anti-Black bias, police mistake day-to-day items such as a wallet or cellphone for a gun when it is in the hands of a Black person rather than a White person. There are dozens of Black men, women, and children who have died in recent years, and whose stories are known in the mainstream media, because of the availability of witnesses with cameras in smartphones to document the violence (Dukes & Gaither, 2017). There are many more Black men and women who have died from police violence and brutality during this same period, and whose names are not known at all (Davis, 2017). Payne (2006) described the phenomenon of "weapons bias" as an example of race bias, in the context of policing. Of course, these findings are disturbing, and add more weight to concerns of groups such as "Black Lives Matter" who protest against police brutality. Police in the United States consistently maim or kill Black men, women, and children in much greater numbers than White equivalents (Lopez, 2018).

Stigma

A stigma can accompany a bias and stereotype, and is a negative response made to a constructed category of persons. In addition, stigmatization is an essentializing process, which negatively marks a category of person. In fact, "stigma" in Greek means to "mark," which was an activity in classical Europe where a criminal or a slave was identified by a branding or specific cut and scarring to their body. The act of marking is a permanent, indisputable sign of not belonging that could always be seen no matter what the person did (Berreby, 2005). Note that in recent human history, African slaves and Jews were physically marked to be designated as other. Displaying stigma today is an act that essentially paralyzes people's efforts to view a person or an entire population of human beings as anything other than a negative attribute associated with that category of persons, across all contexts. In reality, in most contexts, human beings can show up in multiple contexts and perform as different human kinds. For many of us, while it is interesting, enjoyable, and a novelty to team up with other human kinds who belong to different categories, there are also powerful prejudicial, cultural processes at work that blind us to the ways we might join with others. Persons who are stigmatized can only be one kind of a person and that person is always bad (Goffman, 1986).

Human beings have a history of defining categories of persons as "bad" and using words, images, and symbols to shore up the categories to mark certain people as despised and assigned to the "Them" tribe. While most communities do not employ branding to target the recipient of the stigma, the signs, symbols, and what are called "dog whistles" (coded messaging that appears to be benign in intent but has a veiled, more malevolent message targeted against a subgroup) ensure there are persons who are clearly marked as Us and Them. These are crude mechanisms employed to stigmatize and objectify persons as not truly human.

Stigma is psychologically and physically harmful to the target of the stigma.

"There is now abundant evidence that stigma is physically bad for people. It shortens lives, lessens their abilities and increases the allure of false consolations, like drugs and drink, that do harm. ... Stigma drives up blood pressure, scrambles sleep, and increases your chances of dying young. Its effects are transmitted to the next generation too: a stigmatized mother is under stress, and a stressed mother is more likely to give birth to babies with physical and emotional difficulties" (Berreby, 2005, p. 257).

Some people have had to live with stigma their whole lives, because of the categories they were born into. For other people, when life circumstances change dramatically, they can be suddenly confronted with stigma. It is a terrible shock to go from the status of an "Us" to a "Them." For instance, when people's economic circumstances collapse and they end up shelterless, they come to know stigma as they now become a "Them" on the street. Take, for example, a young, successful person full of promise who then is suddenly subjected to a series of delusions and hallucinations. Within a short moment, they can become stigmatized as mentally ill and crazy. Somebody who was an upstanding citizen in one moment and then finds themselves in prison the next is fully subjected to the pain of stigma.

Dehumanization

Smith (2012) reflected that, when we want to harm a group of people, we have to overcome inhibitions and values against harming, killing, torturing, and degrading others. To overcome the inhibitions against demeaning others, the first move is to dehumanize them, to subvert the inhibitions to harm. Dehumanizing starts with seeing others first as less than human, and then second, deserving of inhumane treatment. We solidify an image of the person as the enemy who is dangerous and morally inferior. Once demeaning of the other has taken hold, we are more comfortable with our violations against them.

Brown (2017) suggests that dehumanization first starts with language, with the assigning of signs, symbols, and images. Nazis described Jews as Untermenschen—subhuman or Jewish disease-carrying rodents—and even in this era, social media is used to drive the dehumanizing process. Even children's books in Germany in the 1930s and 1940s were used to further categorize and dehumanize persons. Dehumanizing and objectifying symbols are most effectively employed when one humankind is being mobilized to destroy another humankind. History is laden with the dehumanizing actions of one group of people—more typically the dominant group—who have mobilized to vilify and often destroy the spirit, if not the person, of the subjugated group. This is most clearly depicted in the actions of colonizing people mobilizing against indigenous people, and this book is replete with examples of this form of subjugation and vilification. Even in the 21st century, the U.S. military in its darker moments has participated in dehumanizing actions against the identified enemy. Berreby (2005) cites contemporary examples of dehumanizing instructions given to U.S. junior army officers by senior army officers regarding the prisoners in Guantanamo Bay in Cuba. "They are like dogs and if you allow them to believe at any point that they are more than a dog then you've lost control of them" (p. 235). The infamous graphic image of a prisoner in Abu Ghraib in Afghanistan with a leash around his neck being led around like a dog provides gross evidence of this phenomenon of dehumanization.

Michel Izard (1975), cited by Berreby (2005), coined the term social death to describe people who had been enslaved following war in a West African society. Losers in battle were viewed as living without human attributes. Those who were vanquished were physically alive but socially dead. The concept of social death is a final result of dehumanization. Mental health professionals understand how this construct of social death can be helpful in working with people who have been victims of torture, terrorized by psychological and physical abuse in the home, or who have escaped from a kidnapping or a cult. Berreby (2005) talks about the Us–Them code that produces social death. The rhetoric of stigma and dehumanization essentially is the construction of "Them" through the code of "words, actions, commands and organized behavior" (p. 269). Therapists work at undoing social death by reversing the social coding that led to the that can accompany prostitution and how it can be a version of social death for many women. Elements of social death can occur for people starting military service boot camp or being hazed when joining a fraternity.

Contemporary politics in the United States is edging towards practices of dehumanizing the opposition. Social media is a powerful conduit for starting the dehumanizing process, as the other is easily portrayed as a potential threat to humanity's survival. While the realities of membership of political parties are extraordinarily diverse, the outgroup get binarized. Republicans become "baskets of deplorables," and "Democrats are not even human." As Brown (2017) asserts, dehumanizing works as a tactic, because those who seek to oppose it are then attacked, vilified, and branded with the same dehumanizing rhetoric that the protesters are challenging. The dehumanization process sets up the idea that you are either With Us or Against Us. And people get caught in this false binary, with strong pressures to choose a side. They become vulnerable by not taking a stand against simplistic accounts of what is going on, as the social pressures prey on our fears of not belonging to an "Us".

In 1954, social psychologist Muzafer Sherif and his coworkers created an experiment that is arguably an extraordinary window into understanding human behavior, culture, and identity, and the tribal pull towards Us versus Them. Sherif recruited 22 boys from Oklahoma City and sent them to two different campsites adjacent to one another at Robbers Cave State Park. The boys were of the same class, ethnicity, and religion: middle class, White, and Protestant. They were all deemed to be nearly identical in education and physical and emotional fitness. None of the boys had met one another before. They were divided into same-sized teams; one group came to be called the Rattlers, and the other, the Eagles. Without their knowing, they had entered into a three-week experiment on group behavior. In the first week the groups were kept separate.

Right from the beginning the boys grew to know their own group members and formed a strong sense of themselves as a group. In the second week they learned about the existence of the other group. Immediately they started referring to the other group as "outsiders" and "intruders" and "those boys" even though they had not met yet. The teams grew impatient for a challenge, as the experimenters had set the stage for a tournament. In their first interactions in a baseball game, one of the boys in the Eagle group called a member of the Rattlers group "dirty shirt." By the second day, the boys were name-calling the other group, using negative terms such as "cheaters," "bums," and "pigs." Each of the team members was reluctant to spend time with the other team members.

Shortly after, things deteriorated and the Eagles burned the Rattlers' flag. The Rattlers raided the Eagles' cabin in the middle of the night. The Eagles raided the Rattlers' cabin the following night. Things got worse as the boys collected rocks for combat and fistfights broke out. The experiment had to be interrupted as things became dangerous and the boys' safety in both groups was threatened. By the end of the second week, the boys who had only met two weeks previously were acting like hostile tribal members to one another. In the third week, the boys were given tasks to see how much tribal affiliation would distort their view of simple experiments. In one experiment, the boys were to observe the other group's effort to collect as many beans off the ground as they could, then had five seconds to determine the number of beans picked up. Each boy estimated more beans for their own group than the children in the opposing group. The experimenters had shown the boys the same number of beans every time.

Many other similar experiments followed from this first Robbers Cave Park exploration of human group interaction. What became consistently recorded was how each group overestimated its own abilities, morality, and worthiness and how the other group was so easily stigmatized, viewed as morally suspect, and underestimated for their contributions.

Mason (2018) reflects that, while people in the United States might see themselves as sophisticated and tolerant, in this 21st century, we are all aware of the deep tribal affiliations that have existed and still exist across the country. We notice the behaviors and attitudes that accompany these tribal groups and how they shape the human landscape of the United States. Mason speaks of the political tribal formations that have formed:

> The norms of racial, religious, and cultural respect have deteriorated. Partisan battles have helped organize Americans' [sic] distrust for the "other" in politically powerful ways. In this political environment, a candidate who picks up the banner of "us versus them" and winning versus losing is almost guaranteed to tap into a current of resentment and anger across racial, religious and cultural lines. (p. 3)

Given these recent hostile tribal political affiliations, we, as a society in the United States, are at risk of amplifying our stereotypes, deepening our negative biases, and stigmatizing those we deem to be different than ourselves. The ultimate danger is the act of beginning to dehumanize others based upon these tribal sensibilities.

Atrocities Created by Us and Them Categorization

We have been discussing the effects of bias, stigma, and dehumanizing actions that occur around the markers of Us and Them. The stakes are high for all of us, if we are not able to disrupt the tendency to stigmatize and dehumanize. Many human categories of "Us" and "Them" are associated with human atrocities on the ugliest of scales. Here's a graphic example of one form of dehumanization that occurred in England more than 500 years ago, and that highlights the completely arbitrary construction of Us and Them.

The Lethality of Human Categorizations

Witchcraft in 15th-Century England

Federici (2018) described a tumultuous period in early 15th-century England in which many people who had previously benefited from the relative economic stability of feudal life became impoverished. This context of economic instability and the unleashing of misogynous religious and secular forces drove many poor, single, or widowed women into subordinate social positions. Women who disrupted the tightly wound, oppressive religious systems of the day, by displaying any form of assertiveness, or who voiced resentment towards injustices suffered, were perfect targets for being charged with membership in the most despicable of categories of persons in this era—those who practiced witchcraft.

In England it was almost always women who were assigned to the category of witch. They were accused of becoming servants to the Devil who threatened the very foundation of community life. Witches were said to kill children, maim pregnant women, and steal men's genitals to make them impotent. In an earlier era, some of these women might have achieved a certain degree of status in the community as folk healers, herbalists, or midwives, and held certain knowledge transmitted from mother to daughter; or perhaps they might have been held in esteem for possessing certain magical powers. Older women in this earlier period may have asserted authority in the community by tracking economic activity in the township. During this religiously tumultuous period, fueled by the Reformation, such a woman could be charged with witchcraft. The witch was a woman of "ill repute." If a woman had a child out of wedlock, or displayed behavior that went against the community norms of femininity imposed by local laws or religion institutions, she became a potential target for the charge of committing witchcraft.

According to Federici (2018), certain religious doctrines imposed on women during this period expected women to live as sexless, obedient, and submissive members of the community whose primary purpose was to procreate. The witch hunt became a regime of terror forced upon women, and driven by the social and ethical code of the period, where the church and the state possessed significant authority over what was deemed evil. Fantastic accusations were devised, horrendous torture and public executions became the order of the day. The ingroup was maintained by torture or the threat of it, by women having to denounce their friends as witches, and even daughters turning in their mothers, as they were assigned to the outgroup category of witch.

Matthew Hopkins' (1647) "authoritative" text, *The Discovery of Witches*, recorded the techniques that led to the conviction of hundreds of witches in just a couple of years. Elaborate tests were employed to categorize who was a real witch. Women were stripped naked and shaved in public so the witches' mark could be located. The witches' mark could be a particular scar, mole, skin tag, birthmark, or natural blemish. If the mark could not be located, then the "pricking the witch" technique was employed, in which pins were driven into the body. Once an insensitive part of the body had been located and the person was no longer recoiling in pain, this proved the person was truly a witch (Hart, 1971). The most well-known technique of all for finding a person belonging to the witch category was the swimming test. Popularized in the witch hunts of the 16th and 17th centuries, the accused was tied to a wooden chair and thrown in the water. If the accused woman sank, she was considered innocent. If the woman floated on the surface, this proved witchcraft. It is estimated that as many as 50,000 women were tortured by all kinds of devices and then executed, because they were "proven" to be witches. The assignment to a category such as witch is a disturbing illustration of how human categories are socially constructed and how ingroups and outgroups can function.

Ian Hacking, a philosopher from the University of Toronto, talks about how categories get made in the first place. Where there is a random and accidental pairing between some easily identified feature and some action displayed by a group of people, this pairing sets the stage for the beginning of a category. Berreby (2005) calls this a Founder Effect. They start out being invented by somebody who convinces others that they are meaningful, and then it spreads to others. When the category begins to guide behavior and becomes a reference point for people to make meaning of what is going on,

Hacking (1995) describes this as a Looping Effect. When the Looping Effect takes hold and occurs over a substantial period of time, the category morphs into a tradition, leading to a hardening of a category. Shockingly, human beings are capable of creating and maintaining harmful categories of persons who are part of a "Them" group across centuries.

Contemporary Examples of Atrocities in the Name of Us and Them

The disturbing example of witch hunting, which so graphically illustrates the arbitrary creation of Us and Them, is a modern-day activity in certain parts of the world. Federici (2018) has researched atrocities in Africa and estimates that approximately 23,000 women were categorized as witches and killed between 1991 and 2001 in Benin, Cameroon, Tanzania, the Democratic Republic of the Congo, and Uganda. Federici reported that, in recent years, the murders of women have increased, with an estimated 5,000 women murdered every year in Tanzania by being macheted to death or being burned and buried alive. Women found to be no longer economically productive and perceived as being a drain on resources are vulnerable to being categorized as a witch deserving of death. Alternatively, women who attain success as entrepreneurs in creating small businesses and asserting influence in a community may be labeled a witch and summarily killed. Today, witch finders may be young single men turned into mercenaries by politicians, or enlisted from rebel armies. In 2016, in the Central African Republic, more than 100 women were executed and burned at the stake for witchcraft. People continue to use a 16th-century rationale for locating and threatening the execution of witches in Nepal, Papua New Guinea, and Saudi Arabia. Witches might be marked by a woman's red eye color, which is a consequence of decades tending to smoky cooking fires. Witches can be found in all locations to explain infant deaths, the failure of crops, and even an epidemic outbreak of meningitis, as occurred in Ghana two decades ago. There are records of ISIS executing witches, too. Federici cites examples of witch finders using computers as a tool to unmask witches. The construction of categories of human kinds begins as an arbitrary process, but as the Founder Effects and Looping Effects become manifest, the systematic cultural forces that can be unleashed threaten the very survival of humanity.

One of the most lethal categorizations began in the 19th century when social scientists used the Sanskrit word for "noble," changing the word to "Aryan" to describe a collection of ancient languages (Berreby, 2005). Originally, the name had a benign association. In Germany, the term Aryan was weaponized; it developed a certain status and was co-opted by National Socialists under Hitler, who turned a large, impressionable citizenry into a so-called "Aryan race." This Aryan race was transformed by Nazi propaganda into a lethal and brutal army, enslaving, torturing, and then killing more than 6,000,000 members of the Jewish community, as well as homosexuals, Roma, Poles, Afro-Germans, and people with mental health issues and physical disabilities. Today, the term Aryan is still used as a tribal category to commit racist acts of violence, such as by the Aryan Brotherhood, which continues to make its presence felt in the United States.

Further contemporary versions of human categories were created in Africa by European colonization. In the 1920s and 1930s, Belgian colonists had created their own theories of racial origins of tribal groups, and used the descriptions Hutu and Tutsi to establish schools, churches, and governing bodies. This colonizing categorization of peoples in the Rwandan region became the grounds for horrific genocidal killings in the early 1990s. This seemingly ancient tribal rivalry was largely a product of the Belgian organization of Rwandan society to coordinate its colonial activities in this region (Mamdani,

2001). Once a humankind creates a set of distinctions, its own members participate in concretizing its boundaries. Categories of persons become essentialized (this term is explained further in Chapter 2) even if the traditions are invented. Rwandan political figures in the early 1990s used these colonial constructed divisions Hutu and Tutsi to organize the mass slaughter of the Tutsi. Human beings have a strong history of essentializing characteristics and then basing the categorization of our humanity on them. Put simply, essentializing is an action of making decisions about categories, including people and how we should engage with them. Essentialist categorization of our humanity could easily facilitate intercultural encounters that further replicate biases and dehumanizing practices. For example, in multiple places around the planet, human categories have been constructed with hierarchical value using religion, nationalism, political and economic systems, ethnic identities, and phenotypical characteristics. Countless human atrocities that have occurred in recent decades constructed around fixed, essentialist categories. Here is a very small list of examples:

> Contemporary atrocities occur among religious ingroups and outgroups, such as Protestants and Catholics in Northern Ireland, the Shia and the Sunni in Iraq and Iran, and the Jews in Israel and the Palestinians in the Gaza Strip and the West Bank.
> The decades-long conflicts between the capitalists and communists in China, Vietnam, North and South Korea.
> The genocide of the capitalist urban elites by the socialist rural poor in Cambodia and China. The systemic violence against groups of Blacks and coloreds by Whites in apartheid-era in South Africa.
> The ethnic/religious/nation-state wars between North and South Sudan.

The Failure of Us and Them to Capture the Complexity of Our Lives

We Belong to Multiple Humankinds at the Same Time

Mason (2018) confirmed, as have many other social scientists, that we are, of course, made up of multiple identities or categories. Because all of us belong to more than one humankind, we pay close attention to who "We" represent and notice the symbols that convey categories. Take, for example, a person who identifies as a cisgendered, single, Democrat, sole parent, cyclist, Muslim, plumber living in a middle-class neighborhood. Immediately we can imagine a multitude of symbols and signs that would be illustrative of who this person could be. We also classify and reclassify people we know and ourselves as situations change. Sometimes it takes a few moments to switch our understanding of who the person "is" when we see them in a new context.

Roccas and Brewer (2002) researched how our multiple social identities work together. They identified how some people have their identities overlap or align, and how others have unaligned identities. When identities align and a large portion of the members of one group have identities that overlap with another group, intolerance tends to be in abeyance. Intolerance of others increases due to a lack of exposure to people that are different from you in multiple ways. For example, someone who identifies as White, middle class, cisgendered, rural, religious, and Republican may struggle with understanding the lived identities of somebody who identifies as queer, secular, Black, of lower socioeconomic status, urban, and Democrat. The opposite of course is also true. Roccas and Brewer (2002) found that people tend to be more biased, less tolerant, and more angry at people in outgroups. Mason (2018) observed that when multiple social identities are threatened by an outgroup, anger, prejudice, and intolerance thrive. In times of hostility and in life-threatening situations, if a person is a "Them," the multiple categories that that person belongs to shrink to a unidimensional categorization—a paper cut-out version of the Other. We become oblivious to all of the other categories of person they belong to. Mason (2018) comments that, without exposure to people of outgroups and identities that are not known personally, prejudice towards others can increase and other people's positions, attitudes, and beliefs can be viewed as wrong. He argues that when people live cross-cutting identities, their emotional reactions to an outgroup are less reactive. Nations thrive, people thrive, and families thrive when they live with multiple contrasting and cross-cutting identities.

Humankind Categories Can Change, Disappear, or Be Reinvented

Human categories and the humankinds they invite arise, fade, disappear altogether, or can be reinvented when social contexts and circumstances change. For example, in the United States in the 1960s, some researchers determined that people who adorned their bodies with tattoos were likely to engage in deviant behavior. During this period, in the United States, tattoos were prominently displayed by sailors and motorcycle gang members. Some people in the criminal justice system adorned themselves with tattoos. Older generations in the United States tend to associate tattoos with that period of symbolism. However, younger and older generations today all over the world adorn their bodies with tattoos with colorful signs and symbols demonstrating certain family connections, meaningful memories, value systems, ethnic associations, or just fashionable interests. The symbolism of tattoo to categorize kinds of persons has significantly changed in a handful of decades.

The categorizations of the U.S. Census Bureau illustrate perfectly the creation and reinvention of human categorizations. For example, Mexicans were categorized as a race in the 1930 census and never before or after. The category Hindu in the 1930 and 1940 census included Muslims and Christians. It was a category of persons intended for all people from the subcontinent. Armenians were not White until a court decided they were in 1909. In the U.S. courts in 1854, it was judged that Chinese people were Indian under American law. In 1893, people from Japan were classed as Mongolian (Rodriguez, 1999). We are not used to thinking about human categories as subjective and fluid. Neither do we have traditions of viewing races, ethnicities, tribes, and even nations as manufactured sociopolitical, sociohistorical, sociocultural creations. We tend to assume that the category "race" is based on biological facts, and therefore treat racial categorizations as real, because humanity is sometimes trapped by historical, social, political, and economic forces that keep operating upon us, keeping us in check and demarking the category perimeter. These cultural forces have real effects in demarcating human action. It is not that they are impenetrable categories that cannot be redefined; rather, some human categories align with powerful cultural forces and appear extraordinarily stable and difficult to shift. Some of us are living in human categories we have not consented to be in, and neither have we consented to be subjected to the social injustices that accompany those categories. Living in the United States as an undocumented farm worker with one's undocumented family contributing hundreds of thousands of dollars to the U.S. economy over many decades is an example of a category that inflicts harsh penalties when wages are barely enough to survive on and the threat of deportation remains a clear and present danger. Berreby (2005) gives an example of a White person and Black person meeting in a coffee shop in New York City. They might agree that race is a made-up category to describe persons; yet, when they depart from the meeting and each hails a cab, the White person is more likely to get a cab first. In that situation, racism is awfully real. Race is real in some places in some times, while in other places and at other times, it is not significant.

Categories constructed around sexuality can be illustrative of boundary drawing that can shift overtime. Somerville (1994) reported that only in the late-19th century did categorizations of sexuality emerge in which sex acts and desires were at first constituted and then interpreted through the construction of a homosexual identity. Somerville explained how sexual identity is a construction of historical and cultural forces brought by 19th century White, middle-class gender sensibilities. For example, "a model of homosexuality, [became] defined as deviant sexual object choice. These categories and their transformations, … reflected concurrent shifts in the cultural organization of sex/gender roles and participated in prescribing acceptable behavior, especially within a context of White middle-class gender ideologies" (1994, p. 244). The fields of psychiatry and psychology colluded in defining homosexuality as a mental illness—as further discussed in Chapter 10.

Berreby (2005) suggests that categories are going to persist, and the high-stakes ones sometimes seem immovable. Behaviors associated with categories that do no good and are harmful to many people should be done away with, but that is not going to happen by magic. George Lakoff (1987) said the way to start disrupting unhelpful categories is to pay attention to asking questions that get different answers. If we create descriptions like "New Zealanders are peace loving," "Californians are laid back," and "Catholics are attached to rituals," and we say them enough, we come to believe them. These categories gain momentum and the Founder Effect is started and reinforced by interactional feedback loops.

New Fault Lines in Human Categorization

Identity and Identity Politics

In most of this chapter so far, we have been using the terms *human categories* and *humankinds*. You will find throughout most of the book that we shift to using the terms *identity* and *identities*, within their cultures, to describe who we are, how we identify, and how we might like to be represented or how others like to represent us. Identity is what is both internally and externally a driver in guiding our way of being in the world. Our own connection to identity is a powerful organizing filter in influencing how we see ourselves in relation to others, and is a vibrant organizing code to help us decipher which others share one or more of our multiple identities. Fukuyama (2018) talks about identity and identity politics as coming into view in the 1980s and 1990s. Because we as a society crave recognition, Fukuyama says that the focus on identity quickly evolves into identity politics. Identity politics is typically associated with the struggle to be recognized, to achieve equity and to be heard in shaping our lives and accessing resources that others appear to have access to, but that are denied to our own group.

Fukuyama (2018) says that the lived experiences of identity groups are not the same, and are often shaped by different social forces. Members not part of the identity group are often oblivious to the identity group's needs. A recent example of an identity group that has captured a lot of attention is the

Me Too movement. The identity politics that drive the movement have brought prominent attention to many men's actions, primarily White men, who were ignorant or discounting of the sexual harassment and sexual assault perpetrated by men. The political actions of this movement have been critical in helping to shift the cultural landscape of gender relations that will benefit all our communities. The identity politics that mobilized people around the Black Lives Matter movement is another example of a robust and effective response to injustice in our communities. One of the unanticipated negative effects of the expansion of identity groups and identity politics is that, as causes have become more narrow, and lines have been more sharply drawn, formerly aligned groups have fractured. An example of such an unanticipated negative effect is the unfortunate shift of progressive Whites and Blacks toward a more conflictual stance over cultural appropriation (Shriver, 2016). Fukuyama (2018) points out another example, that of rich White women striving for greater equality in Silicon Valley and Hollywood and becoming disconnected and perhaps alienated from poor and working-class White women and women of color struggling with income disparity and the opioid epidemic.

Identity politics, which were movements originally motivated by left-leaning communities, has now been co-opted by right-leaning groups. Fukuyama argues that identity politics marshalled by groups on the left legitimated some identities while dismissing and even denigrating others. For example, he sites Christian religiosity, rural residence, beliefs in "family values," and European ethnicity as groups that are sometimes vilified by left-leaning elites. Political correctness has now been used as a denigrating phrase by right-leaning groups towards left identity political groups fighting for justice for their respective causes. Right identity groups are forming around their cultural identities and seeing the left cultural values of political correctness as a threat to their way of life. The disturbing fissures opening up around right identity politics is largely fueled around racial dividing lines. In the last few years, right identity politics is moving towards embracing White nationalism that was more at the fringes a few decades ago. Leading right activists are arguing that if there is a Black Lives Matter movement, it is time for a Whites' rights movement, which White nationalists argue will be decried as racist and bigoted by the left.

Haider (2018) makes the point that one of the downstream effects of identity groups making demands about their rights is that the whole landscape of their adopted political position is defined by a defensive posture. One's own identity category ends up needing to be defended. The right's response reduces all the members of that category to victims. Haider suggests that confronting White identity politics involves offering an alternative vision and language. Fukuyama (2018) argues that with the shift to narrower and narrower identity groups, the possibility of open dialogue gets shut down. He says, "The remedy for this is not to abandon the idea of identity. … The remedy is to define larger and more integrated national identities that take into account the de facto diversity of existing liberal democratic societies" (p. 122–123).

Identity and identity politics are now integrated into the fabric of how we organize our activities in the United States, and we cannot escape these groups that form around their specific concerns. It is also true that identity politics exacerbates the Us and Them categorizations. Fukuyama says, "We need to remember that the identities dwelling deep inside us are neither fixed nor necessarily given to us by accidents of birth. Identity can be used to divide, but it can also be used to integrate" (2018, p. 183).

Clients are acutely tuned in to the extent to which a counselor lives or performs identities that clients can recognize. The greater the extent that clients feel their and the counselor's identities and cultures overlap, the greater likelihood clients will feel recognized by their therapist. This recognition will immediately build trust, a critical feature of a therapeutic, intercultural relationship. There is less work to do in building a bridge with the client when multiple identities overlap between therapists and clients; yet much more work is required to sustain their differences within their shared similarities.

Intersectionality

The concept of intersectionality and the body of work that accompanies it is a great resource to counselors when they think about how the therapeutic process involves the commingling of cultures, categories, and identities. We discuss intersectionality in more detail in Chapter 13. Collins and Bilge (2016), in their book titled *Intersectionality*, describe how the conditions of human life are shaped by many intersecting axes that influence each other. As we have argued in this chapter, people fit into more than one category. The intersectional research is especially interested how the major social divisions that exist in the community do not operate as exclusive entities, but build on each other. Most intersectional researchers, like Collins and Bilge, and Moradi and Grzanka (2017), target ethnicity/race, class, gender, sexuality, dis/ability, and age as the more influential axes of social division. When these intersections contribute to social and economic inequality, the collective result can produce a shared human experience of exploitation, domination, and marginalization; elements that have tremendous bearing on mental health and well-being. For example, in the last three decades, inequality in income has grown exponentially in most countries. Collins and Bilge (2016) reported that nearly half of the world's wealth is owned by 1% of the world's population, and if we examine the intersectional identity points, we find that the structure of this inequality gap tends to be simultaneously racialized and gendered. It is often women of color who end up being the most marginalized across these intersections. Collins and Bilge argues that bridges can be built to mobilize and grow a complex social movement that draws together the intersectionalities of ethnicity/race, gender, class, nation, and sexuality to harness the multidimensional lived experiences of domination, exploitation, and marginalization. When therapists are able to identify with clients and recognize the powerful intersectional social injustices that accompany certain identities, the therapist is better prepared to advocate with the client against these systemic injustices.

Where the counselor fails to grasp intersectionalities that drive social inequity, it is much more difficult to build a robust therapeutic relationship with the client and be effective. A young Muslim, Mimo, a woman born in Somalia who came to the United States while a child, and then later trained as a therapist (and who currently practices in an ethnically diverse community), said she would never go to a counselor who identifies White and middle class. She said one of the most painful elements of adjusting to life in the United States was not feeling like her identities were understood, recognized, and respected, and that this was most prominent in college life. She said she will approach therapists who identify Black, African or African American, and female, as she feels there is much greater likelihood that her identities will be understood and embraced—this is especially the case for her, due to her worries about the growth of White nationalism in recent years and the prejudices that have deepened towards Muslims.

White Working-Class Identity

Brammer (2012) points out that White people are in a state of transition. They are made up of many different ethnicities of Whiteness. As a group, they are less cohesive than in the past. More than ever before, a deep chasm has emerged between the White middle class—the professional managerial elites—and the working class. The White working class are experiencing a sense of alienation in a country they feel their families have contributed to building with a history of back-breaking work, whether laboring in the coal mines of the Appalachians or keeping the sewers working and power grid functioning all over the United States.

White working-class household earnings relative to inflation have deteriorated since World War II (Teixeira & Rogers, 2000). In 1970, only a quarter of White children lived in neighborhoods with poverty rates of 10%; this had increased to 40% by 2000 (Case & Deaton, 2015). Also, for White working-class men and women aged 45 to 54 between 1993 and 2013, death rates have increased, not decreased, over time, in contrast to most death rate trends in the United States.

Who are the White working class? We use Williams' (2017) definition of Whites who are below the top 20% of income earners and above the bottom 30%, which accounts for 53% of all U.S. income earners. This is not the poor class, who had a median income of $22,500 in 2015 (30% of U.S. families), a group which the working class want to draw sharp distinctions from (see the box on the precariat in Chapter 10). The working class also draw demarcations, both financially and culturally, between themselves and the top 20% of income earners—the elites, with a median income of $173,175 in 2015, representing nearly 17% of U.S. households. The sharp distinctions drawn among the working class and the poor class, and the working class and the professional elites, reveal a great deal about the "Us" and "Them" barriers for this population.

Williams (2017) offers some unique cultural insights into working-class culture that affects all ethnicities in this community. She comments that many workers in this class are having to work either in very physically and psychologically demanding jobs, or working in roles that are highly supervised. Many of these people feel like their whole working lives are under a form of surveillance in a manner that is similar to life in some prisons. Their employment activities are tightly controlled and often involve mindless and repetitive work. Think, for instance, of the demands on technicians in healthcare, construction workers, factory workers, bus drivers, long-haul truckers, and those who work in customer service. Williams comments that some occupations in the working class involve a high degree of self-monitoring in the face of menial work, and people have to stay in the job for years at a time, otherwise they face the risk of unemployment. The working class often have to submit to authority and not challenge those in charge, or they are at risk of losing their job. Hochschild (1983) talks about the demands of service industry employees, who must placate, restrain, suppress, produce, and project emotions for the benefit of those they serve. Workers are expected to feign pleasantness and even happiness in the service of their customers, even in the face of violating interactions.

In many ways, Williams (2017) identified how Whites in the working class resent the poor, because there is an attitude among this White population that the poor are the recipients of unearned handouts from the government, despite the fact that the White working class also get governmental benefits. According to Williams and Boushey (2010), poor, White, married mothers are more than twice as likely to be at home full time in comparison to married mothers in the working classes. These authors suggest that nearly 60% of working-class mothers work full time, compared to slightly more than 40% of poor mothers. In terms of child subsidies, according to Williams and Boushey's research, poor families get three times the amount of subsidies as working-class families. For many Whites in the working class, this drives an attitude of disdain for the poor, who they see as receiving unearned government handouts.

Williams (2017) argues that working class Whites' dislike for the poor and what are viewed as undeserved government subsidies is matched by the deep resentments held towards the professional management elites. She presents the popular working-class phrase: "Born on third base; thinks he's a triple" (p. 6). This is a sarcastic dig at the elites who attain a great deal of unearned privilege yet believe that their wealth and success is based upon merit. Surprisingly, the resentment towards the professional elites is not always projected onto the truly wealthy. If the understanding is that the wealthy worked for it, then according to Williams (2017), the working class believe the rich deserve it. The wealthy can symbolize what might yet be attainable when someone has earned their independence, can give their own orders, and run their own business.

Pierre Bourdieu (1980) studied how class is a powerful influence on the creation of cultural aspirations. The cultural expressions of class are most fully on display when it comes to education. Williams (2017) comments that the elites view college as a prerequisite that creates the opportunities for the children to attain their parents' professional status. For working class parents, however, college may be an undesirable thing for their children to embrace. It might not pay off. The family may be saddled with large bills and their child might receive a degree but still end up being unemployed. Children from privileged families are educated in ways that produce them as members of the ruling class, while children from poor and working-class families are schooled to learn to do what they are told and not buck against authority. The psychological and material injuries felt by the White working class fuels the sense of marginalization and an experience of being left out in the cold. They believe they have worked hard their whole lives and feel that their share of the American dream has been snatched out from under them. Many feel that the new immigrants have jumped the queue, taking from them what was rightly theirs. Mutz (2018) presents a case that White disenfranchisement is more about loss of status than financial hardship. Conservative *New York Times* columnist Ross Douthat stated that this community wants to "protect the once dominant majority to restore its privileges and reverse its sense of cultural decline" (cited in Hetherington & Weiler, 2018, p. 220.)

Because of the way the Electoral College is set up in the U.S. political system, the White working class carry a strong voice, and they are increasingly using it in the politics of the rural United States. For 112 years of U.S. elections, the candidate who won the popular vote also won the Electoral College vote. Today that has changed. The U.S. electoral maps show the rural interior that leans heavily red (conservative) flanked by a thin blue (liberal) ribbon on the East and West coasts. Williams (2017) points out that liberals care about diversity and equality but somehow ignore the needs of the White working class. She notes that, to the White working class, elite truths do not make sense, while their own truths do. Until the White working class feel like a "We" in the United States and have jobs that lead them to be upwardly mobile, their suffering will continue to be expressed in seeking political leaders that recognize their needs and understand their inequalities.

Political Tribal Identities

There is a growing recognition in political science that identity has become a crucial element in U.S. democracy and social life. For example, partisan identity in the United States, most commonly Republican or Democrat, is a powerful motivator in relation to human action, judgment, emotion, and behavior. There is an incentive—especially when this is tied to winning or losing—to see life through a partisan lens, associate exclusively with people of your own group, believe one's own views are superior to others' perspectives, and interpret the actions and characteristics of others with intolerance and bias, and sometimes hatred and loathing. A lack of engagement with other groups and social identities can have people view others as foreign and extreme, when in reality there are far more connections with outgroups than people would realize. Sasse (2018) reports that political partisan tribalism is now statistically higher than at any period since the Civil War. The Us versus Them rhetoric has reached a deafening pitch. The political parties have become so polarized in the United States that ethnicity, class, geography, and attitudes to immigration are dividing the country into binary mega-identities forming around politically partisan lines. Mason (2018) suggests a "single vote can now indicate a person's partisan preference as well as his or her religion, race, ethnicity, gender, neighborhood, and favorite grocery store" (p. 14).

Red and Blue Tribes

Today, Democrats (the blue tribe) and Republicans (the red tribe) are now social and partisan enemies who have little reason to find points of connection. At first glance, the tribal appearances look uniform and homogenous. Within the blue tribe are identities that might be secular, liberal, urban, and ethnically and linguistically diverse. The blue tribe resonates with a fluid identity, is drawn to cities, and is often secular in orientation (Hetherington & Weiler, 2018). The red tribe is made up of identities that are likely to be church-going, fiscally and/or morally conservative, rural, and more ethnically White. The red tribe tends to have a fixed identity, often finding their strength through prayer and favoring living in small country towns and rural areas (Hetherington & Weiler). The tribes are now so distinct, they seek their social media from different sources. TiVo Research and Analytics released the top 20 shows that Republicans and Democrats tend to watch, and not one network show appeared on both lists (Mason, 2018).

According to Hetherington and Weiler (2018), the red tribe is influenced by an idea that "our lives are threatened by terrorists, criminals, and illegal immigrants and our priority should be to protect ourselves. The blue tribe is influenced by the idea that the world is big and beautiful, mostly full of good people, and we must find a way to embrace each other and not allow ourselves to become isolated" (p. xi). These world views have real effects on where people live, what work they do, and where they go to school. Hetherington and Weiler (2018) cite a Pew Research Center Poll taken in 2016 that found that both Republicans and Democrats surveyed reported that the other party caused them to feel "angry" and "afraid." The red tribe cannot figure out why the blues would make the country so unsafe and not support travel bans and border walls from potentially dangerous strangers and thereby fend off a potential catastrophic threat. The blue tribe cannot figure out why the red tribe would be so callous and unfeeling as to see Syrian refugees and Central American immigrants denied entry into the United States as regular people wanting to feel safe and secure and seeking a better quality of life, like everybody else. Each tribal group views the other as a potential threat to their security and survival.

Verdant Labs (2015) studied 50 occupations and found strong representations of red and blue world views in the workplace. For example, pilots typically lean red, and flight attendants blue. Beer wholesalers, car salespeople, home builders, exterminators, insurance agents, and Catholic priests tend to lean red, while midwives, yoga instructors, gardeners, architects, and Episcopal priests blue. Judis and Teixeira (2004) remarked that White-collar workers are made of a mix of both red and blue. Yet, most traditional managers and business executives lean red, while academics, engineers, nurses, teachers, computer analysts, and therapists lean blue. University students also have been identified as having red and blue leanings. Red-leaning families are tuned into the biases their children might face if they attend universities that are perceived as liberally focused or associated with Ivy League elites. A clear example of tribal distinctions on display was identified in two contrasting universities. At Auburn University in Alabama, students surveyed in 2016 aligned overwhelmingly with the red tribe. At Vanderbilt University in Tennessee in that same year, students surveyed were heavily in favor of the blue tribe (Hetherington & Weiler, 2018).

Feldman and Zaller (1992) conducted research on political opinions related to the kind of parenting goals voters aspire to. He discovered that, in general, more strict parents who favored strong hierarchies, obedience, respect for elders, good manners, and good behavior for their children also favored strong, unwavering political leaders who mirrored the more authoritarian structure of their home life. The opposite was also the case. People raised with more egalitarian parenting styles tended to be attracted to a more democratic leadership style.

Much of the research that has been presented so far is based on predominantly White participant survey data. People of color are not reflected accurately in this data set. Hetherington and Weiler (2018) cite evidence that people of color identify overwhelmingly as Democrat and in many ways fit the characteristics of the blue tribe; yet, many communities of color also support traditional family hierarchies and top-down authority. Based upon so-called fixed views, one would think African Americans and Asian Americans would place themselves in the red tribe. However, Hetherington and Weiler muse that when minority ethnic communities feel under attack, self-protection trumps world view.

Hetherington and Weiler (2018) suggest it would be easy, based upon these fixed and fluid categorizations, to say that the fixed group is more racist and the fluid group is less racist, but their research did not support this simplistic generalization. They concluded that the fluid group do fear racial and ethnic differences, but they are more secretive about it and it is "less cool" to acknowledge it in front of their fluid friends.

As we have already discussed in this chapter, multiple identities of persons are often accompanied by elaborate cultural signs and symbols that are used for demarcation of identities that are Us and Them. This is prominently on display for blue and red tribes. The signs, symbols, fashions, food, entertainment, music interests, sports watched, the animals they are drawn to for animal companions, and even forms of transport often line up with particular tribal displays. For example, the beer that people drink, the restaurants they go to end up being symbols of their world views. For example, the blue tribe are much more likely to go to Starbucks, whereas the red tribe tend to favor Dunkin' Donuts. reported that people they identified as "fixed" tended to buy U.S.-made cars (64% of cars purchased by this group), with the Dodge Ram pickup being the most popular vehicle. By contrast, 60% of the vehicles bought by people identified as "fluid" were built overseas, with the vehicle of choice being the Toyota Prius. A conservative blogger captured the significance of signs and symbolism of these cultural artefacts. "They (Toyota Priuses) are as much a political statement as anything. By driving one of these cars, these folks are saying, 'I care more about everything than you, and you hate the environment and support torture.'" (Hetherington & Weiler, 2018, p. 99).

Perhaps tellingly, red tribes and blue tribes now have so much antipathy towards one another, their prejudices and biases are beginning to supersede even more traditional, deep-rooted prejudices. In

2010, when the situation was even less partisan than it is now, almost half of red tribe members surveyed said it would be very concerning if their son or daughter married a blue tribe member; and among blue tribe members surveyed, a third of the respondents said it would be very concerning should their child marry a red tribe member (Graham, 2012). This contrasts strongly with 1960 data, in which only 5% of members of each of the tribes would be concerned by intermarriage across red and blue lines. Iyengar and Westwood (2014) report research findings that partisan bias and loathing between the red and blue tribes is even stronger than the racial biases that Whites possess about Blacks or Blacks experience about Whites.

Many families all over the United States are made up of opposing red and blue tribal members. These differing tribal affiliations put tremendous strain on family relationships. The animosity can be so great between some family members around blue and red affiliation that these contrasting identities have fractured family relationships, leading to sharp divisions among brothers and sisters, sons and daughters, parents and grandparents, who may cut off communication, leading to painful family alienation.

These issues play out in the workplace, too, among colleagues and acquaintances. Partisan lines get drawn within the workplace and both nuclear and extended families around topics such as women's rights (White women and women of color) to choose what happens to their bodies, and whether there should be transgender bathrooms in schools or whether transgender people should be allowed to serve in the military. These topics go right to the heart of matter regarding human rights, equity, and safety. For example, tensions and conflicts arise around how security issues should be addressed at the U.S. southern border; how immigration rights should be responded to; whether there should be travel bans on particular groups based upon religious affiliation; and whether there a place for gun control, and/or racial profiling. These topics become hot-button issues that are processed within the context of identity politics. For families and work colleagues to remain connected and interact across these cultural constructions, in the face of red and blue tribal hostilities, there must be delicate maneuverings made by everyone to not stand on these contentious landmine topics. These intensified divisions pose challenges for therapists seeking to promote intercultural bridges across the red and blue divide with clients to help address family and workplace conflict.

Fake News: What Is Really Going On?

Fifty years ago, media was one of the most trusted institutions in the United States. The iconic news anchor of that era, Walter Cronkite, who reported the landing on the moon, was the most trusted figure in the media in the United States during that time. In a 1972 poll, 72% of people surveyed said they expressed confidence in his reporting (Ladd, 2011). There has been a rapid change, especially in the last few decades, in the level of trust of sources of social media. The Pew Research Center in 2014 found that the only overlapping sources that television watchers received their news on was local television news, and that was only 5% of all people polled. Forty percent of conservatives surveyed got their news from Fox News, and the remainder from multiple other online, newspaper, television, and radio sources. Liberal respondents got 15% of their news from CNN, 12% from MSNBC, 10% from *The New York Times*, and then multiple other sources. Since that survey, trends have shifted even further. Ninety percent of people in the United States are online and get some of their news from social media, including Facebook and Twitter. According to Hetherington and Weiler (2018), 80% of people in the United States have Facebook accounts.

Inglehart (2018) reported that 2010 was the year when the world had attained its highest level of prosperity. Sasse (2018) cited criminal record data that show U.S. child kidnappings and child abductions were at all-time lows. Violent crime was at a 40-year low. Yet, Sasse reported that the anxieties about abductions and violent crime have risen because of the kind of media coverage occurring. Krook (2014) similarly reports that crime coverage seemed to consumers to have increased by 600%, but in actuality it had fallen by 20% during the same period. News media often identifies the perpetrator of a crime by their ethnicity or a category of persons is deemed to be potentially threatening to U.S. society. The 24-hour news cycle repeats the human categorization on multiple occasions, serving to reinforce fear of the other. Perhaps the assailant is an undocumented immigrant, had a Middle Eastern appearance, and they were Black or Brown. This distortion of coverage perpetuates more fear, causing greater social isolation and strengthening the notion that strangers are dangerous.

Sasse (2018) comments that we now use social media as a site for confirmation bias. For example, research at Ohio State University found that, from a sample of 156 people, research participants read articles that either confirmed or contradicted their political ideas. Participants spent far more time reading articles that confirmed what they already thought than articles that might have taught them something new (Hsu, 2009). Fukuyama (2018) argues that social media is fragmenting liberal societies by amplifying very narrow identity groups' messages. It serves to wall off one group of people from another and create "filter bubbles" (p. 180). Social media in its present form often facilitates the circulation of "fake" information intended to undermine and attack opponents, and its anonymity allows people to post without fear of reprisal or accountability, sabotaging efforts at civility.

Sasse talks about the dangers ahead, where there is a new media appearing on the Internet that looks real but is artificially manufactured or digitally constructed. This constructed media is described as deep fake videos. In the future, real footage on video is going to be more and more difficult to decipher from digitally manufactured footage, creating even more disruption and free-floating anxiety. In the last two years, 126 million members of the general public in the United States have been exposed to fake material on Facebook produced by Russian bots and fake Russian accounts (Sasse, 2018). During 2016, Guess, Nyhan and Reifler (2018) found that 65 million people consumed fake news, with 40% of conservatives reading at least one fake news site, and 6% of conservatives getting their news from completely fake news sites. One percent of liberals was getting news from fake sources (Hetherington & Weiler, 2018). To make matters worse, a 2018 Gallup/Knight poll found that 40% of conservatives believe that fact-checked accurate information is fake. Fifteen percent of liberals thought the same information was fake. There is now a very muddled perception among news consumers, who can be confused about the veracity of news items that are fact-checked, and news items which are opinion pieces or are completely made up. Collectively, we are being overwhelmed and struggle to discern factual reporting in the face of this avalanche of news and social media coverage. We retreat to locations of social media that feel true and right and reinforce who we are, who our people are and who is our tribe. Yet our identities are being actively constructed from realities that are not born out by lived experiences. Rather, our experiences are being completely manufactured or seriously distorted with very tangible consequences on our lived experience. The consequences are that we occupy spaces that create a greater rift among the humankinds comprising the collective us, and limit our intercultural, overlapping, and shared identity experiences.

Cashing in on Tribal Affiliation and Social Media

The neoliberal systems that dominate Western societies and how they organize our communities are exponentially more effective in shaping individuals' appetites as material consumers in the age of the Internet. The relationship between consumerism and social media has become completely fused. And this has occurred under our noses, especially in this last decade, when the smartphone has become a most dominant tool for engaging with social media. Most of us who use the Internet are quite oblivious to how our humankinds are more than ever being sculpted to feel, think, and behave. Interestingly, the designers of the most sophisticated tools to harness social media were aware from the beginning of how powerful the technology could be in shaping our day-to-day lives. For example, it was reported that Steve Jobs refused to allow his children to have an iPad. "We limit the technology that our kids use," he told *The New York Times*. "We think it is too dangerous for them" (Bilton, 2014). It is difficult to know exactly what danger Jobs was referring to. In her landmark book, *The Village Effect: Why Face-to-Face Contact Matters* (2015), Pinker notes that, within a very short space of time, human beings are changing from group-living primates, using our skills at reading one another's gestures and intentions, to a solitary species, captivated and preoccupied with a computer screen. Now that so many of us are online, large multinational companies are increasingly controlling what we come to know about ourselves and others in this age of the smartphone and laptop computer. For those of us who go online (which is nearly every child, teenager, and adult) we are being measured by what we are worth as a consumer. Media companies know a great deal about us and our habits and what we care about. They drill down to what emails we open and what we read. With the sophisticated abilities of large companies to track our movements in real time and in digital spaces, algorithms are devised to provide rapid feedback loops, enabling news organizations to determine not just what headlines will be written but what articles will be written and for which audiences. Many news outlets concentrate less on providing some balanced overview of current events and more on providing what Sasse (2018) calls polititainment. Companies are delivering what the consumers want, because this is what drives revenue. It is all about capturing your attention as advertisers pay for access to engaged consumers who spend their time online. The number of clicks your webpages receive translates directly into cash flow. The job of social media managers and web designers is to keep you clicking and captured by information content in the same way that a videogame designer strives to keep you coming back to the same game. For example, analytical tools measure how long you stay engaged with a news item. If they click for more content within an article, you are worth a lot more to the media companies that are rewarded by your presence.

Media companies on the Internet, radio, and television are getting better and better at tailoring content to match people's specific interests and concerns. Media managers have figured out that the best way to build a committed group of core followers is to stir people's emotions. The more anger and rage that is evoked, the more likely it is that people will share their reactions with others and share news stories. Anger magnifies the impact and increases the number of clicks, increases revenue generated from advertising and increases profit, all at the expense of the manipulated, stressed-out, and fired-up consumer. Radio and television talk show hosts are masterful at whipping up hysteria. The ability to create righteous anger and indignation are big revenue generators for the news anchors as well. Readers and viewers are generally attracted to more outrageous, sensational, salacious headlines. Online news feeds are tailored by editors to target the places you get your news and the sites you visit. You will find different versions of an article online with different headlines designed to cater to your own proclivities, reinforcing your version of reality.

Sasse (2018) talks about the news organizations that are set up for different political persuasions and how they cash in on insult. "It is simply a matter of capitalizing on the outrage feedback loop: spot something stupid an obscure liberal/conservative said; use it to malign all liberals/conservatives; watch your profile rise as you become a hero to the people on your side and a villain to people on the opposite side; rinse and repeat" (p. 110–111). Outrage keeps consumers engaged with a news outlet and increases tribal following, thus exacerbating the Us and Them phenomenon. Because there are now no media outlets that capture large and diverse consumers, executives see their task to be keeping an audience involved and understand that getting attacked is worth as much as being embraced by devoted viewership. Hetherington and Weiler (2018) commented that we are living in our own echo chambers that reinforce our pre-existing beliefs, exacerbating hatred for the other while media outlets stoke hatred. Duhigg (2019) suggests that the main cable networks focus on tapping into our reservoirs of moral indignation. "The point is to keep viewers tuned in, which means keeping them angry all of the time. No reconciliation, no catharsis, no compromise" (p. 71). This fuels further rage, which serves to create more distance between the red and blue tribes while increasing the profit margins of the social media companies.

Digital Identities

Online Identities and Aloneness

Today, the masses in the United States and pretty much everywhere else all over the world are hypnotized by computers. Take any moment when you are in a public context and scan your surroundings. If you are in a park, on a university campus, on the bus, train, airplane, car, waiting room, beach, rock concert, and even in the restroom, children, adolescents, and adults all around you are transfixed by images moving on the smartphone screen. In this age, we are the most digitally connected people in human history. Perrin and Jingjing (2018) found that 26% of us admit to a high frequency of being online, up from 21% three years ago. Median data shows people who live in the United States check their phone every 4.3 minutes. Nearly 40% of young people in the United States from the ages 18 to 29 are online virtually every minute they are awake.

Many of us spend this time online for comfort, connection, entertainment, education, and excitement. For some, online platforms create solace for us to perform our identities and digitally live in our "Us" communities. Many of us form lifelong relationships that were found online. Increasingly, we are finding our future marital partners on dating websites. A multitude of users are looking to come out of isolation and find in the digital world people who are "like me." Cho (personal communication, January 20, 2019) commented that there are many communities that find hope and a sense of empowerment within online communities. The Internet and social media have created global communities all over the world where people can gain free access to advance their knowledge, their careers, and their networks. She reported on how much comfort people can receive from applications (apps) on social media. "There are apps that remind us to go to sleep, check our physical movements and remind us to be active or take a deep breath" (Cho, personal communication, January 20, 2019). We use apps to check on our physical and psychological well-being. There are apps that help us navigate both the physical world, using satellite navigation, and our cultural worlds, as we connect to online communities—today it is Reddit communities, Tumblr forums, YouTube channels, or Twitter, Snapchat, and Instagram followers; and tomorrow, there will be new social digital platforms.

Social media have extraordinary power to motivate people to gather and protest against the many social injustices and inequalities happening in our communities. In the United States, many live-streaming sites expose hate crimes and bring attention to violations that are occurring, thereby challenging those who are in denial about problem issues that need addressing. Organizing Women's Marches, mobilizing the Black Lives Matter community, and bringing together teachers to improve the school environment are small examples of the effectiveness of mobilizing a "We" online. One powerful international example of connecting via social media was the mobilization of people in a fledgling democratic movement in Egypt. The Arab Spring that occurred in late 2010 in many parts of the Middle East was launched on social media.

Despite the all-encompassing power of the Internet to shape almost every aspect of our lives, Sasse (2018) argues that a staggering level of cultural disruption is already on its way as a result of an addictive engagement with digital materials. He says we are hyperconnected and yet in many ways disconnected. Tony Reinke (2017) observes that the more time we spend connected to our computer screens, the more we tend to become depressed, anxious, and detached from those we care about.

Consider the lives of many middle-class families in the United States today, and their use of smartphone technology. What is becoming common and acceptable is for individual members of a family to regularly be by themselves (on their electronics) while together. Generation Z have lived with this reality for a decade or longer, and for many this has totaled half of their life. For them, this is life is normal. When there are multiple electronic devices available to family members in the home, we may be partially aware of interactions happening around us, while at the same time having our eyes glued to a screen. Turkle (2015) observes in the United States that we are moving to "post familial" lives, in which the tradition of having family meals is rapidly disappearing. There is a paradox, in that electronic connections help us to feel close, but for many of us, the reality is we are spending more time connected with a screen than with human, face-to-face contact. Clearly there is a generational angst related to this analysis. For the teens and twenty-somethings, this is the natural order of things, and for many people of Generation Z this is in fact preferable. For older researchers, Sasse makes a case that smartphones are making us progressively more unhappy. Heid (2017) quotes Shakya from the University of California, San Diego, who says, "Lives are always more spectacular on the other side of the filter. … We found that the more you use Facebook over time, the more likely you are to experience negative life satisfaction" (para 6). Vannucci, Flannery and Ohannessian (2017) who studied anxiety levels of 18- to 22-year-old social media users, found that the more time spent on social media, "the greater the association with anxiety symptoms" (p.163).

Twenge (2017), in her research on the IGen generation (people born after 1995), found large upticks in anxiety and depression, especially for girls. The I-Gen, or Generation Z, who have grown up for most of their lives with ready access to a computer, or more likely, a smartphone, are even more addicted to the smartphone and what can be viewed on it than older people. Not being online for even a day means to this generation that you are becoming invisible to your online family. Things happen in the digital world really fast, and if you are not online there is the experience of fear of missing out (FOMO). Other challenges are amplified for the younger generation. Many young people suffer, get down, and feel rejected when people are not responding to their online postings. Today it is the Instagram story and tomorrow, there is no way of predicting the software choices that will be available to us. Receiving no feedback on carefully crafted photos and storylines on what is going on in your life can range from disappointing to devastating, as can having unappreciative followers as an audience to your digital life. For example, young people can become quite down as they view social media, comparing themselves to what really is an imaginary perfect person with the perfect picture, the perfect story, and perfect life. Of course, these digital postings are carefully manufactured by the creator and often not illustrative of their day-to-day real lives.

It is so easy to be seduced by the latest digital stories, Facebook postings, and YouTube uploads of friends, acquaintances, or people we aspire to be like. The age of the YouTube influencer speaks to the impact of people online who have been found by millions of followers to be desirable. Often the younger viewer is looking at all of these images and feeling like they are a member of an outgroup. What intensifies the anxiety, depression, and isolation is the experience of cyberbullying, which is terribly destructive and a powerful predictor of increased suicide risk. Teens who are being cyberbullied find it difficult to avoid their tormentors, when nasty messages and images can be posted online in any 24-hour cycle.

According to Sasse (2018), on average a person in the United States has 330 friends on Facebook. That is a lot of people who can show us digitally what great lives they are leading. App designers are highly skilled at keeping us online to keep scrolling and clicking. Being online can distract us from the boredom, dullness, and monotony that we might be experiencing in the moment. It is a form of escape, as we find ourselves comparing ourselves to others who seem to be so much happier with their better holidays, better clothes, better friends, better families, and better living situations. For young people and adults alike, is it is easy to feel like we are living in an outgroup, as our lives seem drab, boring, or even meaningless in comparison to the ingroup, who seem to be living this amazing life as portrayed on digital media. Sasse (2018) states,

> Tragically, Americans [*sic*] are losing their real families while chasing images on smartphones that often turn out to be nothing at all. We abandon real places and neglect real people—and for what? The undermining of local familial and friendship ties never ends up being worth it, as the substitute virtual family we eventually join are generally much better at being against things than being for things. The end result is aching loneliness (p. 188).

Turkle (2010) notes that while we might feel connected online with digital friends, in reality, we can feel very isolated. She comments, "The ties we form through the internet are not, in the end, the ties that bind." [They are] "ties that preoccupy" (p. 178).

For generation Zers, this is a rather harsh and judgmental analysis. There is a literature that is "in defense" of the contributions of social media (Abramian, 2018). For example, Robyn Treyvaud's (2017) research reports that 68% of teens seek solace in social media during difficult times. Forty six percent of young women agree that some social media platforms support them to speak out about challenging topics to others. The largest majority of young people surveyed by Treyvaud said that social media facilitates greater connections with friends.

There is clear evidence that people have gained great fulfillment connecting with others across the globe. Many marriages, friendships, and communities have formed meaningful connections online.

In contrast to the surveys on the favorable elements of social media, one of the impacts of this new digital age is that our human, face-to-face networks are getting smaller. In his book *Bowling Alone*, Putnam (2000) comments that our social capital of human connection is rapidly diminishing, and we have fewer nonvirtual friends, since data has been collected on this subject.

Olds and Schwartz (2010) studied the research literature on friendship and found that the average U.S. citizen has reduced their flesh-and-blood, actual friends to less than two over the last three decades. There is no doubt that social networks, connections with others, and relationships of reciprocity built on trust have deteriorated dramatically, and social media has had a part to play in that trend. The Internet can be a lubricant for intensifying human connection as much as it can be a technology that contributes to disconnection we feel as a society and as a country. Perhaps more than ever before, we are digitally connected; yet, many of us feel existentially alone and isolated. We are living the life of an outgroup while everyone else seems to be passing us by. For a few of us, the desperation, isolation, the sense of not belonging in an ingroup leads us down a track of getting numbed out with prescribed and nonprescribed medications, other drugs, and alcohol, or wanting to die. In fact, the suicide rate in the United States has been trending upward in the last fifteen years. From 2000 to 2016, the suicide rate has jumped 30% (Centers for Disease Control and Prevention, 2018). For girls between the ages of 10 and 14, the suicide rate increased dramatically; it went up for females in every age group and for men under 75. Death by suicide is now the second leading cause of death for males and females from the ages of 10 to 34 (Brueck, 2018). Now, more than ever, it behooves us to figure out how we cross the abyss between "Us" on one side of the chasm and "Them" on the other side.

What's Next

Our effort in this chapter is to provide some contemporary cultural context and a backdrop for the challenges and possibilities of interculturality for what follows in the remaining chapters in this text on practicing counseling from an intercultural stance, with a highly diverse population, made up of the many tribes, including those constructed in the digital realm. In this chapter, we have given a brief overview of some the biological, historical, social, and political forces occurring within the United States in this early phase of the 21st century that have real effects on shaping people's identities and cultural practices. These powerful forces shape people's sense of belonging or sense of alienation, their sense of hopefulness or hopelessness in what is happening in their lives now and what is around the corner. We have provided a cursory view of some of the basic biological features of the body and brain that affect people's experience of safety or fear in how they are living their lives. Effort has been made to briefly show the harmful effects on people as they are constructed within outgroups through negative bias, the stigmatization of identity, and the terrible dangers that can arise when we as a human species descend down a path of objectifying the other and embrace the signs and symbols and cultural practices that can dehumanize and pathologize others. Lastly, we described some of the effects of contemporary applications of social media and how digital technologies can construct our identities as commodities, so that we become economic units serving the needs of the neoliberal and neocolonial machine. And finally, we noted how the Internet, while providing opportunities for information, entertainment, and connections to others, sometimes sets in motion, with no deliberate or malicious intent on the part of any one group, a culture that has the potential to deplete meaningful human connection with others.

The implications of Us and Them for the practice of counseling with intercultural intentions that respect the integrity of our differences and dignify our humanity will be woven through the chapters that follow.

Make a list of all the ingroups and outgroups you have been a part of in the past (or are currently a part of) within family, school, and community contexts.

Discuss the following in groups of three.

1. How did you get placed in those groups?
2. Which groups were you assigned to and which did you choose to belong to?
3. What were the effects of being in those ingroups and outgroups?
4. Did you move in and out of those ingroups and outgroups?
5. Once in those groups, what led to the change when you left one (or more) of them?
6. Did you ever want to get into one of those groups you experienced being barred from? What happened?
7. What advantages are there from being in an ingroup? What are the disadvantages?
8. What are the counseling implications for counselors working with clients in an ingroup?
9. What advantages are there from being in an outgroup? What are the disadvantages?
10. What are the counseling implications for counselors working with clients in an outgroup?

EXERCISE 1.2

This book emphasizes how we simultaneously occupy multiple identities in particular moments and contexts. A therapist is exposed to diverse presenting issues by diverse clients, and on many occasions we can be very conscious of the differences and similarities we have with our clients. At other times, we can be completely oblivious to the similarities to and differences from our clients, but our clients may be astutely aware of these similarities and differences.

Take five minutes and identify **your identities** that could be noticeable and significant, to you and/or your client(s), if you are working in the following circumstances.

1. A woman is seeking counseling who is recovering from violence (has visible physical markings around her throat and a broken arm) caused by her same-sex lover.
2. A young, White male from a lower socioeconomic family is wanting to address trauma following being released from prison, recounting a trauma of being gang raped by three White inmates.
3. A distressed mother is seeking counseling for her angry 14-year-old son, who was molested by a favorite uncle from the ages of 6 to 10 years of age.
4. A Black student reported being disrespected and treated unfairly by a young, female, White teacher, who said she was being cussed at. The student was sent to the counseling office by the White teacher.

5. A distressed, terminally ill 32-year-old African American woman with cancer received a delayed diagnosis (if the cancer could have been treated earlier, she would have had a chance to have it treated before it became so lethal) and she is upset due to the second-rate treatment she received by White male and Asian male doctors.

6. A suicidal 12-year-old is being bullied at school for "dressing like a girl."

7. A frightened 71-year-old man is trying to hold onto a 30-year relationship with his wife, who states she has had enough and is going to leave him.

8. A 16-year-old, newly arrived Karen refugee from Myanmar is experiencing suicidal ideation and struggling to speak English in the high school.

9. A 22-year-old young woman is struggling with managing her jealously in a one-year polyamorous relationship.

10. A distressed father is seeking help after his 11-year-old threatened to hurt the mother after getting a knife out of the drawer and then carving their name into the refrigerator.

11. An overwhelmed mother is a sole parent and struggling to handle the intense out-of-control sibling conflict of 6-year-old twins.

12. An adopted, Black, non–gender binary 16-year-old is experiencing verbally abusive interactions with their 60-year-old White parents.

13. A 14-year-old Somali teenager, born and raised in the United States and attending a public school, is in full-blown conflict with parents who moved to the USA from a rural village in the Horn of Africa. The Muslim parents speak very little English.

14. A White Vietnam vet, who is homeless and staying in a temporary shelter, with newly treated psychosis, is trying to address long-standing drug and alcohol problems.

15. A family has a 14-year-old child who is refusing to go to school and is wearing a MAGA (Make America Great Again) hat in the in-home counseling session.

16. A heavily depressed and suicidal 45-year-old male, White automobile worker, unemployed due to a recent automobile plant closure, is in a 51/50 hold in a residential treatment facility for suicidal ideation.

17. A young 19-year-old, middle-class, White college student is seeking counseling after being date-raped by an African American male college student.

18. A 12-year-old White female is depressed and frightened. She lives in a car with her mother and younger sibling and is struggling to have access to adequate food and clothing. Her mother has mental health problems.

19. A 15-year-old Vietnamese female is worried about the gambling habits of her father. Their family finances are now depleted, and the family are about to be evicted from their home.

20. A 15-year-old White female is struggling with anxiety and depression following the acrimonious breakup of her parents' 20-year relationship, and is struggling to adjust to the presence of her father's new African American boyfriend.

Discuss this exercise in pairs and review with your partner your identities that might be significant in these counseling sessions.

How might your identities pose either challenges or strengths for building connection with these clients described above?

In what ways can you build bridges with your clients to better serve them?

SARAH Z. KAHN, PHD, LMFT

Sarah Z. Kahn is the director of the Counseling and Social Change undergraduate minor at San Diego State University (SDSU), and has been teaching at SDSU at both the undergraduate and graduate level. She received her MA in Marital and Family Therapy from Alliant International University and earned her PhD in Multicultural Education from the Joint Doctoral Program at Claremont Graduate University and SDSU. Sarah's research focuses on narrative approaches to pedagogy, the clinical supervision process, and mentorship. In particular, she has a developed a keen interest in the supervision process and has written and presented on narrative supervision as a social justice practice. Her teaching addresses intersectionality, the social construction of identity, and applied clinical training. Sarah maintains an active therapy practice, supervises, and co-leads a community-based narrative consultation group for both licensed and unlicensed therapists in San Diego, California.

The authors present a robust discussion of some of the most shaping historical, political, sociocultural and biological forces that constitute cultural engagement. At the heart of this analysis lies the construct of Us and Them; a discursive product positioned to reduce the complexities of intercultural engagement to singular, fixed, and essentialist understandings of self and other. This chapter provides an entry point to consider the many seen and taken-for-granted influences that impact our quest to engage in counseling practices that support culturally responsive and respectful care.

The ways in which I make sense of this chapter, and the concepts of Us and Them, are directly tied to my own social location. I have been shaped and continue to be shaped by my personal history, community connections, and how I am positioned in the politics of the larger sociopolitical world. All of this matters, as it produces the interpretative lens through which I make meaning of my life and of the larger world in which we all exist. I am a White, cis-gendered, heterosexual Jewish mother of two young children. I have dedicated much of my life to studying how counseling practices intersect with and can support social justice pursuits. The therapy room is not a neutral locale, and must be critiqued and investigated for the potential harm that can occur, as well as the potential for hope, agency, and social change that can arise from critically informed intercultural counseling conversations. I am heavily influenced by poststructural thought and narrative approaches to therapy and supervision. I continue to learn from my every interaction with clients, supervisees, and students, as these have formed some of my most humbling moments, greatest joys, and sources of growth. It is from this position that I share my thoughts on this chapter.

An important entry point into exploring the constructs of Us and Them is to investigate the process through which bifurcated understandings of life are constituted, and how they are negotiated within relations of power. In reference to binary pairs, Jacques Derrida (1978) argues that the meaning of a particular word exists in direct relation to what it is not. As applied to the phenomena of Us and Them, the identification of Us therefore means, by its very definition, that you are not "Them." Perhaps readers of this chapter will have had their own lived experience of engaging within a binary frame. Perhaps some will have found solidarity with those who join them on the "right" side of the divide, while simultaneously being villainized by and villainizing of those who are positioned as "other." The relationship between the two sides is always connected. The existence of Us is dependent upon the existence of Them.

It is important to remember that these are not neutral categories, but are produced through relations of power, where one side is privileged, and the other side subjugated. Deconstruction (see Chapter 5) of these bifurcated understandings of life present a particularly hopeful path towards the possibility of intercultural engagement. Moreover, frameworks that address the complexity of intersectionality (Crenshaw, 1989) and the politics of representation are of central importance here. There is value in uncovering the dimensions of life that fall outside of our experiences of Us and Them in order to find alternative and varied ways of working as counselors alongside persons and communities we are positioned to serve.

In reading this chapter, I am compelled to reflect on how my own life has been both created by and creating of division and categorization. As a Jewish American woman, the dehumanization of Jewish people during the Holocaust and the atrocities that resulted from such still reverberate in my family, my community, and in Jewish people all over the world. I have historical knowledge of how these divisive categories brew fear and hatred, and can result in grave acts against humanity. Foucault (1978) theorized that patterned applications of dividing practices can consistently privilege or disadvantage certain groups throughout time. These divisive practices can have catastrophic effects. Social justice concerns are imbued with the construction of these divisions as well as the ways in which our lives traverse through the various intersections of these divides. On any given day, I may find myself working alongside a group of students at a community protest, and then later that night at dinner with extended family who fall on the "other" side of the red/blue political divide. The conversations that ensue within these points of intersection can be painful and alienating. We can so easily be positioned and position others as enemies and yet I also have the experience of knowing that there is more to our relationships and ourselves than that which divides.

As a narrative therapist, I have come to believe that the breadth and complexity of people's lives cannot be contained within the deductive framework of categorization and the normative assumptions that they produce. There are always aspects to people's lives that are not included within the dominant stories that they tell or that others tell about them. This encourages an exploration of the messiness of life. It requires a commitment to engaging with the world, not only within and between the categories that have been laid out before us, but also with the dimensions of life that defy division. The aspects of life that do not fit within the dominant frameworks hold potential for new understandings of self, other, and the world in which we exist.

If there is more to lived experience than what can be contained within these divisive categories, then we must ask ourselves, how are we being produced to fit these molds and how are they governing our lives and the lives of others? Foucault's (1980) analysis of modern power feels particularly relevant here. Considered constitutive versus merely repressive, Foucault was interested in the way that modern power operates to get people to act, think, feel, and identify with particular stated norms. Power within this framing is not centralized, but is inherent within our relations and is spread across all aspects of life. However, this power is never total in it effects. It can be rendered fragile, subject to change, or even overthrown, as its existence remains uniquely dependent upon people's active participation. Therefore, there remains the ever-present potential to cultivate acts of resistance.

I find this chapter a welcome invitation to critically engage with current divisions and further expand counseling practice to encompass intercultural considerations. I would also encourage readers of this text to reflect on the rich and uniquely positioned discussion the authors present on the interface between our biology (described as brain and body) and the sociopolitical processes that construct identities and cultural engagement. The text invites us to explore an embodied experience of cultural division and exchange. More specifically, how our biology is in constant interaction with the socially constructed world, and how these embodied experiences impact social engagement practices. This discussion is unique in that it resurrects traditionally understood biological discourse from essentialist thought, inviting new considerations with the realm of social process, power, and intercultural engagement.

We cannot remain complicit with the assumed objectivity and neutrality toward the categories of Us and Them. Black Lives Matter, transgender rights, and the Me Too movement serve as powerful examples of the injustice and violence that continues to occur through the consistent application of racist, heteronormative, and sexist discourse. Counseling conversations are not isolated from these larger social–political discourses and the resultant dividing practices that construct our world. I encourage readers to continue to critically reflect on the ideas presented in the chapters that follow and reflexively investigate how their own social location is impacting their embodied experience and personal understanding of cultural engagement and counseling practice. It is through this critical reflection that we can begin to move beyond that which divides to better serve our clients.

Chapter 2

Culture and Cultural Identity

Beyond the Binary—A Social Constructionist Lens for "Culture"

One way we want to ground this book is by making explicit the particular perspective we are starting from. If you don't share the same world view, that is okay. We respect that. But at least you know where we are coming from and can make allowances in how you read what we say here. We call the position we write from *social constructionist*, which we have alerted you to earlier. That means something specific to us, which we shall explain, but it is far from an agreed-upon term. Even many people who share a number of the ideas and concepts that make up what we call social constructionism (see Box 2.1) choose to use other terms to describe what we are referring to. We are also not the only writers who have used the ideas of social constructionism in the area of culture and counseling. Recent examples include the work of Lisa Tsoi Hoshmand (2005) and Garrett McAuliffe (2019).

BOX 2.1 SOCIAL CONSTRUCTIONISM AND DISCOURSE

Social constructionism refers to the processes by which people use language, or more precisely, discourse, to construct their lives. Kenneth Gergen (1994, 1999, 2009; Gergen & Davis, 1985; McNamee & Gergen, 1992; Shotter & Gergen, 1989) has been a major contributor to the development of social constructionist ideas in psychology. He summarizes the constructionist position in these words: "In the end all that is meaningful grows from relationships, and it is within this vortex that the future will be forged" (Gergen, 1994, p. ix; see also Gergen, 2015).

One of the central conceptual tools that underpin social constructionism is the term *discourse*. Discourse refers to the assumptions that develop in a given cultural context to guide people's thinking and acting. Without general agreement on which discourse counts in that context, words and actions remain meaningless. In the process of using discourse, people must wrestle with the ways in which the very language they use presupposes many things and exerts a shaping or structuring influence on what they can think. For example, in contemporary U.S. culture, the term feminine typically suggests modesty, gracefulness, nurturance, weakness, passivity, or timidity. The taken-for-granted assumptions that accompany the word in turn influence the behavior of men and women alike. From our position, the role that language, or discourse, plays to represent or stand in for things is critical to cultural experience. Hence, we aim in this book to develop an understanding of the concept of discourse and to use it often as almost a synonym for culture. It is our belief that the concept of discourse has much to offer, not only to the practice of counseling, but also to the task of sorting out the confusions and finding a way forward in the many stalled conversations around issues of culture. Discourse is a wonderful bridge across the divide when people get stuck in essentialized, rigid categories of personhood. A wonderful way to expose the presence and actions of discourse is to use the methodology of deconstruction.

BOX 2.2 DECONSTRUCTION

Deconstruction, a philosophical inquiry into the meanings of words and experiences, was first articulated by the French philosopher Jacques Derrida (1976). Derrida suggests searching for the meaning of a word, not so much in a precise capturing of its essence as in a careful tracing of its relation to other words and concepts used by people in particular social contexts throughout history. Each word carries with it a trace of meaning from its other significant usages. It participates in the general exchange of discourse and develops overtones of usage from those who have deployed the word for particular purposes. Derrida also seeks to uncover the meaning of a concept in its relation to other concepts around it. In particular, he wants to drill a philosophical mine shaft into the relationship of binary conceptual opposites. For example, he argues that the word light has meaning only in relation to its opposite, dark, and carries the meaning of the opposite as a hidden referent in its own meaning. In other words, the meaning of a term or concept can be made clearer by searching for the meaning that it negates as much as in what it asserts. In this way, the meanings of binary concepts are always bound to each other in a relationship. There are a series of binaries pertaining to the subject matter of this book that are bound together in this way. White/Black, nonbinary gender/binary gender, rich/poor, educated/uneducated, normal/abnormal, Republican/Democrat, problem/solution, and Us/Them are binary pairs. These binary distinctions are important because they become headings under which much of our thinking gets organized in either/or terms. Derrida proposes opening up the relation between these binary opposites and then identifying the surpluses of meaning that escape such binaries. The intention of the deconstructive endeavor is not to render everything so relative that it is meaningless. Derrida has been very strong on that point. Rather, it is to open up new possibilities for meaning and fresh openings for living. Therefore, we think that deconstruction has a useful part to play in the process of addressing problems, be they social problems or personal problems, in counseling. Those who have argued explicitly for the value of a deconstructive spirit in counseling include the narrative therapist Michael White (1992) and the psychoanalyst Jacques Lacan (1977). The general spirit of deconstruction, however, is implicit to some degree in many other approaches to counseling.

What Is Culture?

"What is your culture?" People answer that question in lots of different ways, illustrating the confusion we have about what culture is and what it means to us. Some people answer by referring to a political entity, such as their country or state of origin. Others refer to a geographic location, such as the continent they belong to or migrated to or from, or to a region or locale with which they identify, or to their ethnicity or tribal origins. They answer, "I am American," "Cuban," "Indian," "Canadian," "Mexican," "Caucasian," "Asian," "Californian," or "a New Yorker!" Sometimes they mix geography with ethnicity, calling themselves, within the context of their migration experience, "African American," "Arab American," or "Caribbean American." Or they might say "Black," "Brown," or "White," drawing attention to physical characteristics over geography or ethnicity. In some parts of the world, people more commonly answer in terms of religion, saying, for example, "I am Jewish." Or they might reference a linguistic heritage or mother tongue, calling themselves "Hispanic." You have probably also heard people say they either don't have a culture or wish they had one. Some individuals are referred to (usually by others) as "really cultured." It is not uncommon that people who have had no access to formal education are unfamiliar with the term all together.

These differences in response are not trivial. We believe they reflect differences not just in individual thinking but in the general discourse about culture. These differences also frequently have painful and quite real consequences. As a result, it is easy for others who have not attuned themselves carefully enough to the nuances of these terms to ascribe cultural identity in ways that create offense. We want to explore the possibility that these exchanges illustrate the limits of understanding produced by many prevailing concepts within dominant ideas about culture and the potential frustrations and pain that can result. We do so to illustrate at the same time possibilities that can be opened for intercultural encounters when discerning experience within its cultural contexts. Indeed, what suffers from our different responses to the question "What is your culture?" is often the conversation itself. This book represents our effort to find ways forward in such conversations and to stretch the limits of current thinking about engaging interculturality in counseling.

As we traverse the territory of culture in this book, we need to remember that the very concept of culture is not stable or straightforward. We shall take the attitude that an appreciation of this complexity enriches us with more possibilities for making a difference in the world. The study of interculturality is an effort to embrace diverse epistemologies, paradigms, knowledges, and practices, from which new learnings can emerge and generate fresh opportunities for promoting well-being at an individual, family, and community level. At the same time, we believe that, if we explore the complexities of interculturality as applied in therapy, we are more strongly positioned to start building the bridges of the Us versus Them divide. We therefore invite readers to join us in some careful thinking, and cultural analysis, about many of the complexities that the concept of culture entails. We shall explore some of the various contemporary definitions of culture and the different meanings of, and historical associations accompanying, words like race and ethnicity, paying close attention to the social context out of which these terms have arisen.

The Context of Culture

Becoming "cultured," from the 18th to the mid-20th century, was a process of intellectual-spiritual formation (Arnold, 1865; Appiah, 2005; Benhabib, 2002; Kroeber & Kluckhohn, 1952). It was sometimes contrasted with a meaning of "civilization" that referred more to the material and technological practices characterizing a particular way of life. This meaning of "culture" persists in some modern usages and is to some extent echoed in recent formulations of the process of "acculturation." According to this idea, a person's relationship to a culture emerges through a process of evolution as she moves toward a higher stage of enlightenment.

Gradually, the word culture began to be applied to the masses, rather than just to sophisticated and educated elites. It became more synonymous in some usages with the colonial idea of civilization and delineated stages of evolutionary social development, from lower, "primitive" civilizations to higher, "civilized" ones. Some Latin American scholars called this analysis "developmentalism," seeing it as directly linked to a global liberal ideology that sustains the capitalist world economy. It promotes an idea of progress in which anything new is necessarily good and desirable (Grosfoguel, 2000). As Clifford Geertz (1995) notes, the concept of culture was used to mark off the colonizing West from the non-West, amid assumptions that all cultures were engaged in a process of evolution to some higher form. Western cultures were, as a matter of course, considered more highly developed along this evolutionary path and assumed to exhibit characteristics of more rational, progressive thought, with their correspondingly prosperous economies, than the more superstitious, magical, and archaic characteristics of non-Western cultures, considered stagnant. This view of culture served to provide a justificatory rationale for the imposition of European political authority over other cultural and political systems. It was "for their own good" that such "backward" cultures had been or were being colonized. We would now call such assumptions racist or Eurocentric, but traces of these assumptions linger in the discourse that is available to frame the way we think and speak. If we want to separate ourselves from such assumptions, we sometimes have to work actively to challenge them in our own and in others' words. Therefore, the very concept of culture itself, even when we use it to criticize racism or other injustices, carries with it traces of the very assumptions that drove the process of Western cultural domination and colonization.

Current dominant understandings of the term culture are usually closer to the scientific, anthropological meaning that Tylor's (1871) definition began to articulate, namely, a set of attributes of a group of people. This set of attributes is assumed to be stable and knowable. As social scientists developed the study of culture, they treated these attributes as if they had enough coherence to provide the basis for scientific prediction. During the late-19th and early-20th centuries, this meaning became widely accepted and evolved to be less and less associated with judgments about the degree of civilization of any particular culture. Culture became more relativistic (rather than hierarchically ranked) and more inclusive. In 1952, A. L. Kroeber and Clyde Kluckhohn wrote the most thorough examination to date of the history of the concept of culture. Here is a summary of the range of aspects emphasized in the definitions they found.

Culture can be taken to refer to a social group variously in terms of their

1. knowledge, beliefs, points of view, world view, values, ethics, laws, norms, morals, burial practices, and religion;
2. customs, behavior patterns, acquired habits, food habits, and rules of etiquette;

3. art, artifacts, crafts, consumer goods, and products of human industry, and the treasury of their creations (including books, paintings, buildings, and music);
4. patterns of organization of social relations, sexual relations, and family relations;
5. language and means of transmitting information from one person to another through education, instruction, or imitation; or
6. social groupings, institutions, and processes of granting sanction to persons' endeavors.

The objective scientific perspective introduced a sense that all cultures were relative and should not be judged against external criteria. The classical anthropological studies of culture performed in the old British colonies emerged from this perspective on culture. Clifford Geertz (1995) calls it the "cookie-cutter" version of culture. Many confidently definitive "people studies" (Geertz, 1995, p. 43) were written about the Nuer, the Trobriand Islanders, the Kwakiutl, the Tallensi, and so on. The objective scientific method reigned triumphant and was able to pronounce the truth about tribal peoples in ways that made them seem exotic but known, summarized and packaged into a parcel of established truths. We believe that some multicultural trends in the United States have been founded on this "cookie-cutter" version of culture, in the name of the European discourses of "progress" and "development" of the counseling profession. In addition, counseling practices have been mostly founded on "new" or the most recent available research literature, which is typically considered "good" or "better." It is our interest here to introduce interculturality as a decolonial means by which cultural differences are honored and engaged for purposes of social transformation. For example, we could envision practices that might borrow from both Western and non-Western cultural traditions to reimagine what can count as a legitimate counseling practice.

Discuss

1. What examples do you notice in everyday life where people use a cookie-cutter definition of culture?
2. How often does this definition of culture feature in textbooks and teachers' lectures?
3. How do these definitions of culture either inform or limit people's ideas about the diversity of human behavior and engagement?

Context of Culture in Modern Psychology

The modern history of therapy and counseling can be said to have begun with the psychoanalytic work of Sigmund Freud, so let us look at some comments Freud wrote that indicate some of his assumptions about culture.

> Primitive man is known to us by the stages of development through which he has passed: that is, through the inanimate monuments and implements which he has left behind for us, through our knowledge of his art, his religion, and his attitude towards life, which we have received either directly or through the medium of legends, myths

and fairytales; and through the remnants of his ways that survive in our own manners and customs. Moreover, in a certain sense he is still our contemporary: there are many people whom we still consider more closely related to primitive man than to ourselves, in whom we therefore recognize the direct descendants and representatives of earlier man. We can thus judge the so-called savage and semi-savage races; their psychic life assumes a peculiar interest for us, for we can recognize in their psychic life a well-preserved, early stage of our own development. (Freud, 1938, p. 775)

It is noticeable here that Freud conceived psychosocial developmental processes in terms borrowed from the dominant European discourses that drove the processes of colonization. He also echoes the social Darwinism that was very influential in 19th-century European academic discourse, whereby "primitive" people were considered to be on an evolutionary pathway toward the kinds of civilization for which "superior" European culture could serve as the model. "We" are already civilized; "they" are stuck in cultures that, while backward, are evolving toward civilization.

The work of Carl Jung has been very influential in the counseling field. His interest in the study of spirituality led him to many inquiries into the beliefs, practices, and rituals of different cultures around the world. One thing he sought to establish was a series of archetypal symbols that could be found in the waking and dreaming life of all of "mankind."

Like Freud, he was interested in "primitive" culture for what could be extracted out of it by the trained scientific mind; he was looking for what it could teach the civilized European scientist about a universal human nature. As he talks about the force of his "archetypes" in shaping psychological experience, he makes the following comment:

> We carry our past with us, to wit, the primitive and inferior man with his desires and emotions, and it is only with an enormous effort that we can detach ourselves from this burden. (Jung, 1983, p. 88)

In the next generation of psychological writers, the divide between modernist scientific behavioral psychology on the one hand, and the more Romantic vision of humanistic psychology on the other hand, became manifest. Our question is not so much about the theories and practices that emerged as about what happened to concepts of culture in the process of these developments. If we look at the work of the most prominent behavioral psychologist, B. F. Skinner, we find evidence of the shift to a more universal view of culture made into a subject of scientific analysis. Take the following comments:

> Culture has constructed mediating devices in the form of conditioned reinforcers: the student studies because he is admired for doing so, because immediate changes in his behavior make progress towards later reinforcement, because being educated is "a good thing," because he is released from the aversive condition of not-knowing. Cultures are never particularly successful in building reinforcers of this sort; hence the importance of a direct attack on the problem in a technology of teaching. (Skinner, 1968, pp. 155–156)

Culture is reinterpreted as a set of "conditioned reinforcers," but they are described as "never particularly successful" in comparison with the superior reinforcers that science can offer. Skinner's remarks assume the position that most modernist social science and professional practice did during the mid-to-late-20th century: we all have culture, but it is not particularly to be celebrated.

Cognitive-behavioral counseling has achieved enormous influence and popularity in North America as a result of the bringing together of behavioral scientific principles and the therapeutic practice ideas of Albert Ellis. In Ellis's pugnacious writing, we find references to the same commitment that Skinner has to modernist social science standing in opposition to cultural traditions. Consider his comments on religion, for example:

> In the final analysis, then, religion is neurosis. ... [R]eligion goes hand in hand with the basic irrational beliefs of human beings. These keep them dependent, anxious and hostile, and thereby create and maintain their neuroses and psychoses. ... Obviously the sane and effective psychotherapist should not—as many contemporary psychoanalytic Jungian, client-centered, and existentialist therapists have contended he should—go along with the patient's religious orientation and try to help these patients live successfully with their religions. (Ellis, 1985, p. 15)

For Ellis, therapy is about the application of rational, scientific thinking to the problems of individuals' lives. Like Skinner, he believes (you could say he has faith in) the possibilities that thinking more rationally can bring, in contrast to the inferior options for making sense of life offered by religious commitment. He is talking here about the relationship between science and religion, but if we consider religious commitment to be an important aspect of a person's cultural identity, then it is reasonable to conclude that Ellis does not place much value on cultural formations other than those produced out of modernist science. He does not even advocate communicating respect for a patient's religious beliefs. In the cognitive behavioral literature, it is uncommon to find much in the way of references to the concept of culture at all.

A similar scientific universalizing of the relationship between culture and science appears when we look at Carl Rogers's humanistic account of culture; he did not often refer to persons as members of cultural groups. His interests were more in the individual's personal experience of life. However, here is a passage in which he refers to the relationships between individuals and their cultural environment. Speaking of what he saw as the clash of values between young people and their elders in the 1970s, Rogers (1973) says,

> The world culture, in all its aspects, seems increasingly scientific and relativistic, and the rigid, absolute views on values which come to us from the past appear anachronistic. Even more important perhaps, is the fact that the modern individual is assailed from every angle by divergent and contradictory value claims. It is no longer possible as it was in the not too distant historical past, to settle comfortably into the value system of one's forebears or one's community and live one's life without ever examining the nature and assumptions of that system. (p. 13)

In this passage, Rogers refers to a new science-dominated "world culture," which is in contest with the traditional, more local cultures of one's "forebears." This is clearly a reference to the cultural influences of what we would now call the modernist world. But Rogers does not pay great attention to these influences. He is more interested in the existential struggle of the individual to free himself from the restraints of both the unexamined and perhaps primitive cultural world and from the scientific world culture. This is the struggle for self-actualization that Rogers articulates more fully elsewhere. The struggle of the individual in Rogers's thinking is primarily a struggle to free oneself from culture, whether it be modern culture or the culture of forebears. He is, therefore, no multiculturalist, let alone an interculturalist, because the multicultural movement by its very nature seeks to situate the individual more strongly back in the world of cultural influences, rather than to free him from them.

We have seen, therefore, that the place of culture in some of these works by significant contributors to the therapeutic field has evolved through the last hundred years. The version of culture that once was a preserve of savages dripping with raw emotion and standing in contrast to civilization gradually gives way to a more modernist version of exotic culture. In the more modern version, culture is something that we all share, although there are still hints that a civilization based on science can do better for the individual than culture can. This is what we have been calling the cookie-cutter version of culture. The differences between different writers relate more to the role of science than to the role of culture. Science either provides the model method for rising above cultural influences and improving on them, or it is part of the stifling and sterile environment that individuals must free themselves from.

Culture and Colonization

As we explore these historical influences on our current ideas about culture, we cannot help but do so from a vantage point constructed on the foundations of the overarching influences of European colonization. The concept of culture cannot be thought of as a timeless, abstract, decontextualized, apolitical, or universal phenomenon. The modern world has been founded within coloniality. For decolonial scholars Quijano (2010) and Mignolo (2007), modernity and coloniality are inseparable concepts. Mignolo wrote that "modernity is a European narrative that hides its darker side, 'coloniality'. Coloniality, in other words, is constitutive of modernity—there is no modernity without coloniality" (p. 39). Here, the term coloniality is considered as a secular, political, and economic world system of power that remained after military colonization was discontinued. It's social, political, religious, educational, and economic influences continue to this day in contemporary North America and around the world. Like it or not, our current understandings of culture have also arisen in the context of this history. Even as we might seek to escape the bounds of this history, our consciousness is still profoundly shaped by it. To study the understandings and influences of culture in our own and in other people's lives, we must wrestle with the effects of history, sometimes grieving over its legacy of pain and injustice, but at the same time identifying juxtaposed decolonial points of resistance where ruptures of this legacy have been created, and sometimes celebrated. We believe that much can be built from these ruptures for possibilities of intercultural developments and understanding to grow out of this unfortunate legacy.

Essentialist Thinking About Culture

One particular habit of thinking that has been so strong in European "cookie cutter" traditions of thought about culture, for so long that it finds its way readily into modernist assumptions, is the habit of *essentialism*. One of the main purposes of this book is to suggest ways of shedding the assumptions of essentialist thinking in order to advance an intercultural practice in counseling. In the next section, we shall address some of these complications and also define what we mean by essentialism and essentialist thinking.

A social constructionist perspective raises many questions about essentialism and seeks to open up alternatives to essentialist ways of conceptualizing culture and personal identity. This is not easy to achieve on a consistent basis, because essentialism is built into the very fabric of much of our philosophical history and into the academic disciplines, such as psychology, that counseling draws upon. We need to spend a little time here explaining what essentialism is and what the alternatives to it are, because this will equip us to ask questions about many other concepts throughout the rest of the book.

Essentialism is the habit of thinking in which one seeks out the truth value of a concept by searching for its core or central meaning. If we are talking about the meaning of a word, essentialist thinking would have us search for its true underlying meaning. If we are talking about a person, essentialist thinking has us peeling away the layers of the onion to discover the core truth of that person's nature. The assumption of essentialist thinking is that there is a stable, reliable core, or a hidden truth, to be found in the meaning of a word or in a person's life, and that it is indicative of what is true and trustworthy. From an essentialist perspective, if we can come to understand the central "nature" or "essence" of given individuals, that which is born or programmed early into them, we can predict how they might behave (Burr, 2015). Examples of essentialist ideas in counseling include Sigmund Freud's idea of the unconscious, Carl Rogers's self-actualizing tendency, and Carl Jung's extrovert and introvert personality types. The *Diagnostic and Statistical Manual of Mental Disorders* (American Psychiatric Association, 2013a) is replete with essentialist thinking. You are all probably used to hearing things like "Homero is ADHD," "Sarah is borderline," and "Hein is narcissistic." Lay examples of essentialist language include "I am shy," "She is depressed," and "He is bulimic." In all these instances, there is no attempt to separate out the complex contradictions of a person's life from the supposed determining essences of ADHD, borderline personality disorder, narcissism, and so on. Neither is there any recognition of the diagnostic labels as culturally produced metaphors that might have effects on a person's life. They are assumed to allow us to see through to an unquestioned natural truth about the person. The characteristics referred to by the metaphors are seen as residing within the individual in an essential or natural way. The assumption of nature underpinning essentialist thinking undermines curiosity. That is, the risk of arrogance accompanies the certainty embedded in essentialist descriptions. Common assumptions that women are good child caregivers because they are women, or that Black people are good at sports because they are Black, or that Asians are smart, are founded on essentialism. In recent times, political descriptions, such as "freedom lovers" or "evildoers," and implications that "you are either with us or against us," are indicative of essentialism and the divide it invites between Us and Them. Despite the familiarity of essentialist thinking, you cannot prove the existence of such essences; you can only proceed on the assumption that they exist. The social constructionist perspective asks the question, "What if they do not exist?" Or, more accurately, "What if they are not consistent in their truth value?" "What if the meaning of a word is less straightforward than that and depends on many things in the context in which it is used?" "What if the core or heart of a person is not as stable and singular as we often assume, but instead is made up of many fragments that we are always seeking to organize into some picture of coherence or pattern, but that never stay still from one moment to the next, or from one context to the next?" In other words, social constructionists challenge essentialism's oversimplification of human beings' attitudes, feelings, and behaviors.

Essentialist views of culture promote close identification of individuals with cultural norms and have the function of promoting the stability of cultures. They tend to emphasize cultural preservation and sometimes hold back cultural change. While individuals may identify with discrete cultures and represent themselves by certain cultural traditions as if they existed in some stable and static form, people outside these groups can constantly stereotype such individuals as people belonging to static and uniform cultural groupings. Native Americans, for example, continue to be stereotyped and caricatured by depictions of them wearing a feathered headdress, a shawl, and moccasins in front of a tepee, as if their tribal groups had not evolved over a few hundred years. A glossy magazine advertisement skillfully challenges these essentializing stereotypical descriptions by showing two Native Americans, one dressed in a surgeon's garb and the other dressed as a judge in a professional Western-style suit, with the words, "Have you seen a real Indian?" written across their portraits.

What an essentialist view of culture does not do so well is accommodate intracultural differences, except as diluted versions of "true" culture. Essentialism plays down the political struggles and conflicts between groups of people who claim the same cultural membership. Kenneth Gergen (1999) goes as far as to say that essentialized identity categories actually "destroy differences" and "suppress enormous variations" (p. 45). For example, essentialism assumes that all African Americans or all middle-class White men share the same preferences, values, and ways of thinking and behaving. It does not help us notice how often so-called cultural norms are products of political debate and reflect current compromises in those debates. A social constructionist perspective, by contrast, asks us to always look for the social and political contexts by which cultural worlds get established in fluid and unstable forms. Social constructionists ask questions about how the boundaries of cultural membership are policed and who gets included and excluded. From this perspective, cultural traditions and norms are not just natural or stable givens, but they have become emblematic of a culture through the situated decisions made by people in particular times and places. And they are always changing accordingly.

Most of us exposed to culturally diverse communities are quickly confronted with the immense diversity in communication styles within identifiable ethnic groups. Stereotypical generalizations can still persist, and these perspectives are granted authoritative status in the multicultural literature; we discuss the implications of this in Chapter 14 on the idea of competency. For example, in multiple choice licensing exam questions, examinees might still be asked to identify how you would counsel a newly emigrated Egyptian client or a gay client recently infected with the HIV virus, or choose the best approach for counseling African American clients. The simplistic and naive nature of these questions can be deeply offensive. It is as though candidates were being asked how to treat a particular character disorder or psychological problem rather than a person. Treating another culture as an object of study risks promoting the objectification of individuals who draw from that culture. Additionally, the value of the knowledge produced through such descriptive study may be, as Lisa Tsoi Hoshmand (2005) suggests, severely limited because of cultural trends such as "assimilation and hybridity resulting from migration and globalization" (p. 5).

While there is value in specific cultural communities gathering together and subjectively asserting some of their shared characteristics and understanding their unique histories, we emphasize caution in how a professional field might represent such a group in an objectifying way, and then make assumptions about their counseling needs. Some categorizations may be experienced as offensive. For example, some people are opposed to being categorized as Asian Americans because they come from a country such as Laos or South Korea. Essentially, the description "Asian American" is a fiction constructed by the official designations of race in U.S. government documents and represents diverse communities in homogenous ways, in turn. It does not represent the life experience or the preferred identities of people themselves, but the institutionalization of identity. Asia is a geographical reference to a continent, not a race or ethnic group, yet it has gained racial meanings in social discourse. The racial category *Asian* is seldom one that people from the various countries on the Asian continent use to describe themselves. If we use the term *Asian*, we gloss over the fact that there are at least 29 distinct subgroups represented under that label (Moy, 1992; Ridley, 2005). Each of these subgroups has its own traditions, languages, and customs, which vary tremendously from those of the other subgroups.

Similar arguments can be made on Latin Americans, Latinx or Hispanics, as well as Native American populations, which are extraordinarily diverse in their languages and identities. It is impossible to make general recommendations regarding counseling interventions for those who identify as Native American (Thomason, 1991). Different customs and languages among Native Americans, in addition to the individual differences within tribes, produce huge variation in the lives people live. Perhaps even more significant than these intertribal and within-tribal variations are the differences that most ethnic minorities in the United States experience because of the degree of acculturation to mainstream U.S. culture. As Timothy Thomason (1991) suggests, there is a significant continuum extending from those Native Americans born and reared on a reservation, perhaps even speaking their mother tongue, to persons identifying as Native American who live in a city and have completely lost touch with any tribal ancestry.

Culture as Heritage

Another subtle variation on the way in which culture is conceived is associated with the links made between culture and the past. In this usage, aspects of culture that refer to what is traditional and unchanging are emphasized. Culture is viewed at times as a repository from some golden age in the past that is remembered nostalgically but diluted into impure forms in the ways that people live in the present. Margaret Wetherell and Jonathan Potter (1992) have described this perspective as an emphasis on "culture as heritage" (p. 129). From this viewpoint, culture is ancient, constantly under threat, and deserving of preservation. It is frequently associated with indigenous people, or non-Western cultures whose ways of life have been modified and overtaken by modernism.

Wetherell and Potter show how this emphasis has consequences for Maori people in New Zealand, who are portrayed, or may portray themselves, as seeking to "hang on" to their culture in the face of threats to erase it. They must avoid at all costs the danger of "losing" their culture. In this formulation, however, culture is assumed to be like a museum piece rather than an articulation of how people live their lives in the present, and indigenous people are characterized as museum keepers. The cost for Maori and for others who are described in this way, Wetherell and Potter argue, is that culture becomes frozen in an archaic, pure form right out of a romantic past and separated from the lives of people in the present. Only those who have stronger connections with the past (usually traditional cultural elders) are considered authentic enough to speak as spokespersons for Maori culture. As a result, the issues of power and privilege that might be shaping the lives of minority groups in the present are rendered invisible and less than relevant. Those who contest such issues might be criticized by the dominant cultural majority as out of tune with their own culture or as abandoning their culture. For example, African Americans are accused of "selling out" or being an "Uncle Tom" when they act in ways that contradict traditional customs or expectations.

Equating Geo-Culture and Nationality

During the 20th century, many efforts have been made to establish political and geographical boundaries on the basis of cultural groups and to whip up nationalistic fervor around cultural membership. The result has often been the exclusion of others who are defined as cultural outsiders. The worst examples are the ghastly results of the assertion of "Aryan" culture in Nazi Germany, but similar patterns of thinking have led to many other examples of ethnic cleansing and xenophobic nationalism in recent history, to massacres and genocides. Nationalistic causes often portray certain cultural features or perspectives as essential to a nation, and which all patriotic people must affirm on pain of sometimes dire consequences. In some instances, national citizenship is accorded only on the basis of an assumed ethnic essence and all others are excluded. Insistence on the coincidence of a person's nature with his political identity is an essentialist premise.

Moving Away from Unidimensional Notions of Cultural Groups

In the early application of multiculturalism in counseling, culture was treated as an add-on to general theories of the individual rather than as a challenge to the many individualistic assumptions that have been built up in conventional psychology. Today, there is a more comprehensive and rigorous view of culture and counseling that not only pays attention to the effects of power in the construction of psychological problems, but also raises serious questions about many existing theoretical concepts in the counseling field. In Chapter 1, we began to scrutinize more closely the relationship between psychology and culture; in Chapter 14 we critique how unidimensional understandings have supported counselors' idea of achieving a competency to work with communities who subscribe to different cultural backgrounds, essentializing them in turn.

Like many of our colleagues in the multicultural movement, we are seeking to acknowledge complex counseling needs and requirements, to understand clients' experiences within their unique, culturally negotiated contexts that may have, in part, resulted in their minoritization and marginalization. This is a departure from the stereotypical and academic racism format employed in multicultural books at an earlier stage in the multicultural field. Cecil Patterson (1996) argues that knowledge of cultures other than one's own can lead to facile stereotyping and that attempting to fit counseling techniques with clients' cultural background is very much a hit-or-miss business.

We have underscored the contemporary complexities of understanding and addressing culture with their relevance to the practice of counseling and therapy. Our primary purpose here is to outline the ramifications, challenges, and nuances of adopting a particular understanding of culture and cultural identity, or lack thereof, when working in a way that respects cultural integrity and sustains cultural difference. We believe that this requires from us careful consideration, not only of the complexities of the multiplicity of cultural self-identifications, but of how we can interconnect across difference to work together. As we have already suggested, culture is a production of complex social processes through which, for example, race, ethnicity, gender, sexuality, class, and religion are constructed. It is also the representation of these processes that we form in our heads. These complex processes make it difficult to identify unambiguous and noncontradictory themes, despite the best efforts of multicultural scholars. Empirical studies of cross sections of populations should always be treated cautiously in this regard. In the first place, such studies always predetermine the "populations" to be studied and, therefore, to some extent produce what they are looking for. Second, the results of these studies can only ever best be understood as probabilities that can never account for the all of the particularity and variability in human cultural experience. Wise heads in the culture and counseling field are increasingly cautious about naming certain therapeutic practices that best cater to Whites, Blacks, Asians, Latinx, and others.

Culture and Postmodernism

Today there is a shift to new ways of thinking about culture, partly in response to philosophical shifts introduced through postmodern social theorizing and partly through the development of a new academic discipline of cultural studies. This shift has been marked by a series of critiques of the modernist view of culture and by the gradual emergence of some new ways of looking at culture. Stuart Hall (2005) characterizes this shift simply as a shift to an understanding of culture as "shared meanings" (p. 295). This emphasis focuses our attention much more on the work done in language to represent ways of living rather than directly on the ways of living themselves. A culture is a way of interpreting life as much as it is a way of life. As Hall notes, however, meanings and interpretations are slippery; they move about, they are contestable, they are seldom singular or fixed. Moreover, from this perspective, the understanding of culture becomes a matter of understanding how people give meaning to things. Kwame Appiah (2005) also notes a turn to a more linguistic and interpretive understanding of culture as well as an expansion of the kinds and numbers of groups to whom the concept of culture has been applied.

Seyla Benhabib (2002) summarizes some of the major ways in which recent scholars have come to be critical of the conventional concept of culture. She suggests that there are three false premises in modernist conceptions of culture. The first is that cultures are "clearly delineable wholes" (p. 4). It is notoriously difficult in practice to define who is a member of a cultural group and who is not. Arguments develop about whose membership is valid and whose is not. The second false premise is that a "non-controversial description of the culture of a human group is possible" (p. 4). For many assertions of what is a cultural norm, there are conflicting practices by other members of the same group, so much so that many would argue that divisions and differences about cultural patterns are more common than uniformity. The third false premise is that there exists a one-to-one correspondence between groups of people and cultural practices, and that political decisions can be made with a degree of certainty about how members of a particular cultural group will respond. Think of how difficult it might be to plan a policy or a counseling program that will meet the needs of women, for example, given that there are vast differences among women with different backgrounds, lifestyles, beliefs, and experiences.

Benhabib calls the modernist version of culture "reductionist" because it reduces groups of people and descriptions of culture to each other without thinking about the problems of doing so. Others have echoed these problems with conventional views of culture. The overemphasizing of the boundedness and distinctness of culture has been criticized by anthropologists such as Terence Turner (1993) and Renato Rosaldo (1994). It is just not as easy as many people think to define who is Latinx or what Japanese culture is about. Any definition of cultural membership you come up with will leave some people out, and any description of a cultural belief or norm will encounter immediate contradictions from many who would claim membership of that culture. Being too definite about cultural characteristics has the effect of sidelining those who live on the "borders" of any particular cultural group. In Chapter 3, we shall explore the concept of border and hybrid identities further. Newer conceptualizations of what culture is make it a much more fluid concept.

Culture is not so much a fixed orthodoxy as an open field of meanings. It is always emergent, always in process and always changing. Therefore, fixed accounts of what a culture means appear inadequate. From this perspective, cultural groups are noticed to be constantly negotiating ambivalences or tensions among themselves as well as in their relation to other cultural groups (Yon, 2000). Claiming that someone is an "authentic" group member becomes less and less possible, because any definition of what is authentic can be disputed. The search for "indigenous authenticity" is more realistically represented as a "tangled multiplicity" (Geertz, 1995, pp. 52–53). As the concept of culture has itself become more elusive, it has become harder to make straightforward statements of cultural identity. Daniel Yon (2000) researched in a compelling way the cultural identifications of young people in a multicultural high school in Toronto and used the word "elusive" to describe the young people's culture.

Consider, for example, the enormous shifts in gender identity descriptions that have arisen in the last decade, especially in Western contexts. There are increasing numbers of people describing themselves as having a nonbinary identity and not wanting to be categorized or addressed as a man or a woman. While there are both poststructural feminist academics (for example, Butler, 2011) and a small number of laypeople, who, for many years in the United States, have railed against the cultural construction of binary gender, in many classrooms in high schools and universities today, students are seeking to be addressed as "they" rather than she or he. At this time of great cultural flux, people still strive for coherence and seek to maintain stable reference points for themselves as much as they can, even while the forms of life around them are shifting and changing. A particular kind cultural identity does not mean the same thing it did a generation ago. Cultural descriptions shift beneath our feet as we walk through life.

From this perspective, a culture needs first to be understood as a construction imposed onto the lives of a group of people by whoever is describing it. The person doing the describing, therefore, comes much more into view, whether this person is describing himself or is an anthropologist, a politician, a journalist, a psychologist, or a counselor. Whatever we might say about another person's culture is now viewed as an interpretation much more than as a simple description. So whose interpretation is it? What assumptions from the world view of the person doing the interpreting are unwittingly included?

BOX 2.4 MINORITIZED GROUPS

A recent development in the literature on cultural issues is the use of the concept of "minoritized groups" instead of the term "minorities." It is worth asking why some prefer this term, particularly since it is the less economical term. In an article aimed at school leaders, Khalifa, Gooden, and Davis (2016) define the concept this way: "We consider minoritized students individuals from racially oppressed communities that have been marginalized—both legally and discursively—because of their nondominant race, ethnicity, religion, language, or citizenship" (p. 1275).

It is worth noticing here the shift from a simple noun ("minorities") to a verbal construct ("minoritized"). It suggests a process that is done to groups of people (they "have been marginalized") and takes the emphasis away from a numerical calculation of who is actually in the majority or minority. It also connotes a historical time in which this process of minoritizing happened. It is done by some people to other people. Power relations are located, in theory at least, in a time and a place—that is, in history. In this way it asks us to consider when this process might have taken place, rather than assuming that being a member of a "minority" is a historically static, more essentialized state of being. If we are talking about a process that took place in history, then the implication is that history can take other turns and change what once happened. This is a recognition that discourses shift. They do not always remain the same.

The person making the interpretation is always speaking from a cultural position and, in speaking about others, is always revealing something about himself. This is one reason why we want to be transparent about our own theoretical leanings in this book. In other words, "the study of culture is culture" (Wagner, 1981, p. 16). Objectivity is, in principle, one of the cornerstones of modernist social science, but it has started to look a lot more difficult to achieve. How can a description of someone's culture be objective if it is infused with the cultural perspective of the person doing the observing? Thus, studying culture has in recent times become a matter of studying relations between the subject and the object of the speaking, that is, between cultural positions, rather than a simple objective study of the Other. In recent decades, the academic study of culture has grown a new branch that has opened up different perspectives from those championed within the discipline of anthropology. It is called "cultural studies" (see Box 2.5), and it has developed many new postmodern concepts and perspectives on culture. For a start, it has often been written not so much from the point of view of the colonizing people as from the position of those seeking to shrug off the yoke of colonization.

Thus, this field of study has at times become known as postcolonialism. Shifting fields of study reflect shifting experiences of life. Hence, the emergent view of culture and cultural identity is less solid and increasingly a more fluid concept. Culture and cultural identity are considered less as finished products and more as ongoing processes of production (Yon, 2000). Cultural identity, which might have been regarded as a discrete and stable category, now appears always risky, because it blinds us to processes by which people are continually remaking cultural identity and belonging in daily life. Rather than homogeneous essential characteristics, cultural identities appear to be much more hybrid. People's cultural identities are in a constant state of revision as they respond to the changing circumstances around them, and this occurs more than is often recognized.

BOX 2.5 CULTURAL STUDIES

Cultural studies does not just focus on cultures as if they could be studied directly without problem. It also focuses on the field of representations through which our knowledge of other cultures must pass. It is a field of study that has rendered problematic conventional understandings of culture. It seeks to represent culture as more complex, more contested, more driven by politics and power relations than traditional cultural anthropology commonly holds it to be. The discipline of cultural studies is multidisciplinary in its focus and its methodologies. It has even been called "antidisciplinary" (Grossberg, Nelson, & Treichler, 1992) in the sense that it actively resists being caught in the conventional disciplines of the traditional academy. It has turned the focus of the study of culture away from exclusive attention to the cultures of exotic Others and onto the intercultural trends in all parts of the modern world. It pays serious attention to the products and texts of popular culture as cultural formations worthy of interpretation. The cultural studies field has thus granted a new "authenticity" to aspects of culture that were previously not studied.

Thinkers in Cultural Studies

Edward Said is considered one of the most influential figures in the development of the field of cultural studies, as is Raymond Williams. Other well-known writers who dominate the reading lists in cultural studies include Stuart Hall, Donna Haraway, bell hooks, and Cornel West. South American cultural studies scholars have become increasingly influential in their study of decoloniality and post-development theory. Nestor Garcia, Beatriz Sarlo, and Jesus Martin-Barbero have gained international recognition for their work in the cultural studies field.

The Case for Interculturalism

This has been only a brief survey of the recent evolution of the concept of culture. The practice of cultural counseling must be based on some such foundation. Increasingly, writers and practitioners are embracing postmodern ideas of culture and tracing their significance into the domain of intercultural counseling. Cultural categories are unlikely to remain stable and will continue to change in response to the evolving complexities of people's lives. Cultural worlds themselves are made up of the thousands and millions of interactions between people and between human beings and the physical environment that take place on a daily basis. It is therefore not surprising that among these many events there will be many differences in the patterns of life that people live out.

The simple fact of cultural belonging does not say all that can be said about an individual person's identity as it moves through time. Cultural identity is produced not so much out of singular formations as it is out of a series of layers. Tracy Robinson (2017) refers to this process as one of "convergence," referring to the ways in which the different identity formations converge in an individual person.

If these postmodern critiques have disturbed the comfortable assumptions about culture that have become commonplace, then they are gradually giving way to a new view of culture that is more fluid and less essentializing. Rather than stressing the homogeneity of a people, the postmodern concept of culture has become pluralistic or "polyphonic" (Geertz, 1995, p. 48). Most of us are familiar with how people borrow from different cultural traditions and cannot be defined within one cultural box. We also see that they discard cultural practices when they no longer fit (Narayan, 2000; Yon, 2000).

We would like to emphasize the value of speaking in terms of cultural narratives that run through people's lives, rather than thinking of people as identified in a one-to-one correspondence with a particular cultural identity. Renato Rosaldo (1994) suggests thinking of one's life as an intersection through which cultural narratives are always traveling like vehicles. Kwame Appiah (2005) argues for thinking of identity in terms of a "narrative arc" (p. 23). Seyla Benhabib (2002) suggests that the nature of a culture exists much more in the accounts we give of it, that is, in our interpretations, than in a simple observable reality. Lisa Tsoi Hoshmand (2005) notices how in cultural psychology the concept of narrative has taken on the character of a root metaphor. Critical race theorists, such as Derrick Bell (2000), also argue for the use of narratives to uncover the modern workings of racism. And Edward Said (1978, 1994) suggests that we are always required to take account of the narratives that other people from other cultural backgrounds tell about our People. As a result, the actual lives that people lead are much more fragmented than simplistic uniform accounts of cultural coherence can admit.

Social constructionism enables us at times to ask questions about movements for cultural preservation that would be forbidden by an essentialist perspective. From a constructionist view, such movements appear advantageous to certain people in the power relations among groups within a cultural context. Sometimes it is certain persons' positions of power that are being preserved, rather than the cultural advantages for all cultural members. For example, dominant groups within a culture may seek to preserve selected cultural elements to preserve their own cultural power. Indian feminist Uma Narayan (2000) calls this the process of "selective labeling" of "essential" cultural norms. It ignores, she argues, the ways in which cultural groups have frequently discarded cultural practices in response to changing circumstances.

Essentialist thinking invites people to judge each other's cultural worthiness in relation to established essential norms. You may have heard or even been caught up in arguments about who is a real Native American, who has an authentic right to speak for African Americans and who does not, who is more oppressed than someone else on the basis of cultural membership, who is betraying the essential cause of feminism and who is not. Such arguments can never be resolved. The danger is that they fragment people more than create understanding. Polarization is frequently a direct outcome of such essentialist assumptions. The problem lies in the very idea of seeking to establish a "natural" basis for claims of cultural authenticity, which sets up needless competition for the right to speak and works against a more inclusive and complex approach to the diversity of experience. An important danger of essentialist thinking is that it invites a polarizing stance and tempts people to judge the worthiness of others' experiences, including their experiences of discrimination and oppression. What can result from these kinds of essentialist encounters is that particular voices are not recognized as valid, or as having a right to speak. The conversation then quickly deteriorates and groups retreat to our familiar Us versus Them binaries without any additional understanding.

Interculturality as an Option for Counseling

The multicultural counseling movement has itself shifted the ground on which we stand. It has had a powerful effect in placing culture on the agenda much more strongly than any of the counseling theorists cited above ever envisaged. However, the mainstream practices of counseling have still not strayed far from their origins with regard to taking the more nuanced versions of culture into account. The cookie-cutter version of culture is still dominant in many counselors' thinking and their practices. In this book, we introduce interculturality as an option for counseling to revise its procedures when recognizing, sustaining, and revindicating cultural difference as an absolutely necessary consideration for therapeutic change in a pluricultural world. While multiculturality has done an excellent job in helping us recognize and address the culturally diverse needs of people within a counseling context, interculturality takes us a step further by explicitly examining the effects of the power relations that are present in all counseling communications in diverse contexts. Interculturality requires us to pay attention to how suffering and healing is understood in different communities and requires us to expand our approach to therapy beyond mere adaptations of Eurocentric counseling approaches to fit culturally different needs. The practice of interculturality embraces the legitimacy of diverse ideas, experiences, and practices emerging from a wide range of cultural traditions that can serve an essential purpose in facilitating change. Knowing diverse oral traditions, languages, and indigenous practices of healing are critical in promoting the global mental health needs of diverse communities. Interculturality alerts us to the value of counseling interventions that are drawn from different cultural paradigms (European, non-European, and otherwise), providing new ways to practice that contribute to genuine transformative change. The practice of interculturality means that not only does the content of our therapeutic conversation change by addressing the cultural context of the client's experience (which is emphasized in multiculturalism); more importantly, the fundamental assumptions and terms in which therapeutic conversation occur also change.

The vision of counseling that displays a serious commitment to engaging cultural difference at the forefront of its practices rests on a belief in some form of social, cultural, and linguistic justice. In this sense, it is a political vision. It is not enough to just celebrate the rainbow colors of diversity without taking seriously the ways in which pluriculturality leads to differential opportunities for the development of new intercultural alternatives that further advance social and personal change.

It is heartening to witness the multicultural counseling field develop a sophisticated understanding of how power works to shape relations among groups of people and how this plays out in the personal lives of individuals. Lisa Tsoi Hoshmand (2005) refers to this as "the politics of culture" (p. 1). If counseling practice is not based on addressing the effects of power relations, we do not believe it adequately addresses the complexities of cultural differences, given that these are embedded in hierarchical structures and meanings. Not all cultures are socially valued as equally legitimate in their practices and traditions. Hence, many of the culturally negotiated problems people bring to counselors, as much as the practices with which counselors respond, need to be understood as effects of power relations. The postmodern move in multicultural counseling has more radical consequences for the theory and practice of counseling than has sometimes been acknowledged. We believe that decolonial interculturality brings a critique to systems of power, more specifically colonial power. We discuss this more in depth in Chapter 14. Decolonial interculturality critiques and challenges many of the comfortable assumptions of counseling theory, assessment and diagnostic processes, and practices that are based on largely monocultural traditions of thought. We want to add to, as well as critique, these multicultural developments. Here we borrow heavily from Andean decolonial academic and social activists' perspectives on interculturality with this in mind.

According to decolonial academic and social activists, interculturality is a decolonial activity (Walsh, 2009) that contests ethnocentrism, Eurocentrism, universalism, or any other expressions of singular cultural understandings about experience and the world in which it takes place, as discussed at the beginning of this chapter. Interculturality challenges the denial of the existence of different juxtaposed paradigms (European, Indigenous, African, and so on) by emphasizing heterogeneity and pluriversality (Quijano, 2010) instead of universality. The indigenous sociologist and activist from Bolivia, Silvia Rivera Cusicanqui (2018) borrows the Aymara term *ch'ixi* to articulate an intercultural posture that illuminates juxtaposed differences that are not reduced to hybridities or melting pots. Cusicanqui offers an alternative understanding that keeps from transcending differences, as in hybridity, where an overarching third option is developed. Instead, she insists on the importance of not blurring differences so that an ongoing exchange, and hence a learning process from each culture, can remain. *Ch'ixi* sustains heterogeneous elements, *abigarrados* or mottled, that do not fuse but recognize contrasting, contradicting, or complementary cultural differences as sources of interchange of knowledges, ethics, aesthetics that expand pluricultural threads. This approach seeks to build alliances that sustain what they are and are not, never mixing or melting, but shaping pluricultural experience to respond to ethnocentric, colonial hegemonies.

The adoption of both multiculturalism and interculturalism assumes a commitment to social justice in counseling and therapy, or engagement in some kind of political enterprise. To consider the politics of counseling and the politics of culture, we need some overarching theory of democracy, within which a vision of social justice can be materialized. Most multicultural theorists and practitioners acknowledge that counseling is not a politically neutral process, and certainly decolonial scholars assume the same position. Counseling is profoundly democratic in its ideals (see, for example, Rogers, 1970). That is why some people who are not committed to the noblest traditions of democracy, including a vision of fairness of opportunity for all people in life, are either suspicious of counseling or want to make it fit dominant cultural practices. Counseling practice is, in itself, a cultural force that has produced social effects.

Democracy is not just about electoral politics, however. It is about people having a say in the creation of the conditions of their own lives. It is about social inclusion rather than division. And since the necessary conditions for such democracy are frequently not achieved, it is about promoting social change. In the end, interculturalism is about improving democracy, and interculturality in counseling is about envisaging ways in which counseling practices can play a part in improving the experience of democracy in the everyday personal lives of our clients. We discuss further the notion of democracy in Chapter 14.

Current conceptualizations of multiculturalism or interculturalism, which is our preference in counseling, are, we believe, aimed at this kind of vision. But there are places where multiculturalism has conceptual limits that hold back the advance of practice. There is strong support in the multicultural movement for the notion that the essentialist, cookie-cutter view of culture, so popular in modernist social science, holds back the development of cultural counseling. Essentialist assumptions of all sorts do not help us notice the sometimes subtle cultural components of our identity narratives or the opportunities for social change that lie around us, particularly when engaging others within the cultural components of their identities. It is our aim here to stretch the limits of both theory and practice as an intercultural praxis in counseling. To do this, we are consciously drawing on social constructionism and decoloniality, because we believe they not only open up new questions about both personal and cultural essentialism, but transcend them to consider the engagement of difference for the construction of alternatives geared toward social, communal, family, and personal transformation. As you read this book, we invite you to envisage a counseling practice based on the following assumptions:

It is more useful to think in terms of people being shaped and influenced by cultural narratives than it is to simply identify individuals as members of a culture.

The concept of discourse enables us to think in a more discriminating way about how certain cultural influences become dominant and others remain subjugated.

Cultural identifications always exist in the context of cultural power relations that are constantly shifting and changing.

Counseling knowledge itself needs constant reexamination with regard to its cultural assumptions and its colonizing potential.

Personal identity is not an essential given on the basis of naturalistic versions of either personality or culture but something that is best considered as an achievement of living through the process of engagement with cultural narratives.

There are always competing axes of cultural membership and we cannot reduce these to singular dimensions without creating distortions.

We need to make room in our conceptualizations of culture for the contradictory positions that people take up in response to cultural narratives and not expect that people will fit neatly into cultural boxes.

Response to Chapter 2

ALLEN E. IVEY, EDD, ABPP

Allen E. Ivey is distinguished university professor emeritus at the University of Massachusetts Amherst, and the founder of Microtraining Associates, who produced the first multicultural therapy training video in 1980. This group went on to market a long list of social justice videos, and he continues this tradition as a consultant to Proquest/Alexander Street Press. Ivey originated the influential microcounseling framework and the integrative theory Development Counseling and Therapy (DCT). More recently his writing and presentations have focused on neuroscience and its implications for counseling and therapy. Dr. Ivey has won wide recognition and national and international awards, including the American Counseling Association's Professional Development Award. However, he is most pleased and honored by being named a Distinguished Multicultural Elder at the National Multicultural Conference and Summit. He is the author or coauthor of over 50 books and 200 articles and chapters, and his work has been translated into 20 languages.

Our clients come to us with many voices.

—Paul Pedersen

First, it is an honor to respond to Gerald Monk, John Winslade, Stacey Sinclair, and marcela polanco's brilliant work in this chapter. What they are saying elaborates and makes specific the ideas that I express here. What they have done is present a true "culture-centered" approach to our helping fields that will enable us to become aware of the unique background and many voices our clients present to us. Moreover, they provide specifics for action in the session and community.

"I do not speak. Rather, I am spoken." French psychoanalyst Jacques Lacan points out that our socio-historical background (our culture) influences us so deeply that even our thoughts are not our own, but the outcome of our forebears and developmental history. The "feeble ego" is a construction of the past and our present interactions. In effect, we seldom speak for ourselves. Our language and very way of thinking are given to us. As theologian Paul Tillich says, "We are thrown into the world." This "thrownness" determines so much of who we are, perhaps all. Much of who we are and how we think is determined by the immediate family, community, religion, and national world into which we are born.

Our interviews, sadly, do not begin with this awareness. The focus on individualistic psychology produced by White males is no longer sufficient or adequate. Research in cultural-oriented neuroscience reveals clearly that our brain is shaped from birth to what we are now. The external environment and sociocultural interactions plus genetics determine who we are and the nature of our "being-in-the-world." However, genetics turn out to be much less powerful and influential than we have thought—environment typically trumps genetics, although genetics remains important knowledge for our profession. Now even those with two APOE-4 genes may be found to be predisposed to dementia. But many without awareness beat the challenge of genes through lifestyle.

Let's consider a bit more theory. Consider the multicultural cube presented below (Figure 2.1). As you examine the figure, are the categories real or imaginary? Are they as separate as the diagram might suggest? Are all "dimensions" really covered? The answer is no! Missing are family, school, and communities, which shape each individual in vastly different regions, cultures, and nations, some with challenges of flood and earthquake. Can we really divide multiculturalism into a few discrete boxes? I think not, but perhaps this is a beginning to help us all think about ourselves and our clients.

More important, consider the web of interacting dimensions. Which one is most salient for which client? Which approach is likely to be effective with different backgrounds of race/ethnicity, gender, language, sexual orientation, or community experience in a certain nation at a certain time (e.g., war, climate change, migration)?

Like my coauthors, Mary Bradford Ivey, Paul Pedersen, and Carlos Zalaquett, I'm one of those who believes that all counseling and therapy is ultimately multicultural and that failing to be aware of and being unwilling to deal with the broad base culture-in-context is literally unethical. There is no immaculate construction! We are constructed out of many people—both dead and alive. Our very landscape impacts our conceptions of self and others (e.g., Mississippi, New York, Colorado, Sweden, Turkey, India). And note the different conditions for thrownness in each of these settings.

Thinking multiculturally requires us first to think of ourselves as multicultural beings and to consider how life experience affects our language and our being. The authors of this book present important exercises at the end of this chapter in which they ask you to think about past experiences that help define who you are now. I'd like to follow along and give a brief analysis of myself as a multicultural being.

I come from a solid fundamentalist Baptist background, which was first challenged by a wonderful biology course in my university that revealed that all I had been taught was not necessarily true. The

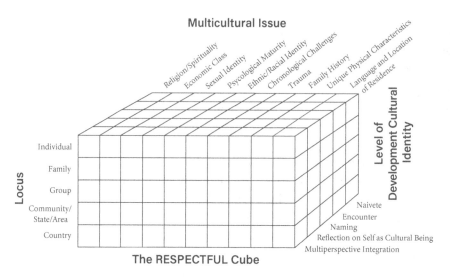

Multicultural Issue

Religion/Spirituality
Economic Class
Sexual Identity
Psychological Maturity
Ethnic/Racial Identity
Chronological Challenges
Trauma
Family History
Unique Physical Characteristics
Language and Location of Residence

Level of Development Cultural Identity

Locus

Individual
Family
Group
Community/ State/Area
Country

Naivete
Encounter
Naming
Reflection on Self as Cultural Being
Multiperspective Integration

The RESPECTFUL Cube

FIGURE 2.1   The RESPECTFUL cube is used by permission of Allen E. Ivey. The RESPECTFUL concept was developed by Michael D'Andrea and Judy Daniels (2001).

university culture interacted with my Baptist foundations, and change quickly occurred. Yet "a boy can leave the Baptists, but the Baptist in the boy will never leave." There is still much in this cultural tradition in my thought and language that I treasure. Interacting with Catholics, Hindus, Latter-Day Saints, and many others constantly changes my thoughts and causes me to think and speak differently. My "discourse of the Other" constantly changes as my brain is rewired.

Born into a working-class family and community, as a professor I now find myself in the so-called middle class. It is not so easy to forget those early origins and the racist and narrow community in which I grew up. But I have had to work hard to eliminate as much prejudice and racism from myself as I can. Nonetheless, racism (and other "isms") are so deep in our society that I consider any White person who claims to be nonracist is both naive and dangerous. This awareness has enabled me to write books and articles, as well as make presentations. My commitment long-term has been and still is to multiculturalism and social justice. My first anti-racism workshop was over 50 years ago, and I am still delivering these workshops.

As a heterosexual, the discourse, church, and the language/behavior of those around me originally led to homophobia and heterosexist thoughts and actions. My rural background had a deep impact on me, and here we see the intersection of sexual orientation, gender, economic class, and even race. It was a challenging learning experience to clean and remove my many deeply held biases. Can you imagine how my Baptist congregation responded in 1970 when I brought a lesbian couple to speak to the teenage Sunday School class I was teaching?!

Psychological maturity speaks to cognitive and emotional self-development, always changing and moving. Becoming aware of myself as a privileged White person took a lot of time. For example, I never personally met an African American until I worked with a student in my third year of university teaching. Talk about segregation and a limited cultural experience! I needed a lot of learning and growing.

Still active and semi-retired, I now occasionally feel the oppression of society on the elderly. But, even more, I am aware of the oppression of poor children who don't get the same benefits for medical care that I receive from our nation. I have learned the Therapeutic Lifestyle Changes (TLC) such as exercise and strength training, diet, sleep, and so on. Two other TLCs need to be stressed—socialization and pride in my family and culture, but with awareness of the many limitations that background has thrown me into. Socialization, by the way, has been found in some research to be the most important TLC of all for brain and body. Finally, I often ask the question—why do I receive good, relatively inexpensive medical care, while a poor child has to go to the emergency room?

Trauma survivors also compose distinct cultures. Whether it is cancer, heart disease, war, rape, or even divorce or a serious auto accident, trauma creates distinct cultural groups that impinge on the way people think and speak.

My family history is clearly bicultural, even though I am White. Put together a Celtic father with an English mother and you may sense the confusion I experienced ethnically. My history is replete with my dealing with those differences at war inside me. My physical self deals with issues of lookism and the physical ideals of our culture.

Language is central and I can speak only English. This makes me disadvantaged, as I lack skills in another language and culture. Location makes a difference. Raised in Washington state, I've lived in California, Colorado, New England, and Florida. Yet it was time spent learning in Denmark and teaching in Australia and Japan that most changed the way I think. I grieve that more U.S. citizens don't spend significant time abroad so that they can learn how narrow this one U.S. culture is. Not that it is necessarily bad, but we take an extremely limited view of the world.

So, I speak from a multicultural and global base. White and economically privileged, I face the challenges of old age and a society that increasingly wants to ignore me, but somehow, I find that most are still listening, and my writing is encouraged. So far, my physical self is holding together. But all of these intersecting multicultural dimensions remain and define me. *I do not speak. Rather, I am spoken.*

Discuss

1. Can you think of examples of essentialism in how we think of cultural issues?
2. Consider your own experiences of cultural identity. Then consider others who are close to you and imagine how they might answer this question. In which instances do you find yourself fitting into the center of a cultural identity, and in which instances do you find yourself having a border identity?
3. What implications for counseling practice might flow from these ideas about culture? Do you see yourself straddling the borders?
4. How might Allen Ivey's RESPECTFUL cube help you make sense of the complexity of cultural experience? Look for the most salient contextual issues underlying specific client concerns?
5. Do an online search and find instances where culture is talked about principally as a repository of the past rather than as a vibrant and living force. Do the same for subcultural lifestyles and culture as equated with nationality.
6. As you read about the questions raised in this chapter, what concerns do you have, or what problems do you see within these ideas?
7. How do other texts that you have read treat these issues of cultural complexity? Where would they agree or disagree with the ideas presented in this chapter?

Chapter 3

A Short History of Colonization and Decolonization and Why It Matters

If we assume that a person who seeks out the help of a counselor is living a life caught in a web of cultural patterns, it is useful for us to pause and consider the historical trajectory that has given rise to those patterns, rather than assuming that the patterns began in the psyche of each individual. This is one of the chief contributions that a cultural approach has to offer the practice of counseling. It helps counselors understand the lives of their clients as produced in a cultural context, rather than as isolated, singular, peculiar events.

The cultural patterns that have a shaping effect on the lives of individual people are not arbitrary, however. They exist as a product of history. They partake in the connections and clashes that have occurred among peoples across the ages and across the oceans and continents. These histories are materialized in the shifting details of everyday, contemporary life. What has happened in the past often places us in a limited range of positions from which we can live. Ulrich Bonnell Phillips (1968) said, "We do not live in the past, but the past lives in us" (p. 269). This statement suggests that history is worth studying not just so we can learn about the past but also so we can obtain rich accounts about our present cultural life. It helps us understand ourselves and each other today—economically, intellectually, and spiritually. So let's now place the cultural worlds in which we live in some historical context. Why, you might ask, should a counseling text focus on processes of colonization and decolonization? Our brief answer is that counselors will fail to understand fully enough the problems that people experience in their day-to-day relations with others if they don't take into account the shaping forces that give structure and substance to the backdrops against which individuals speak and act. Perhaps it is becoming more common to focus a cultural counseling text on colonizing history in this way, but we do not want to do this in a manner that is too abstract and separate from the influences that have shaped it. In this abstract version, cultural influences appear to be free-floating ideas rather than concrete products of the people who formed them in actual places and times. Ahistorical versions of culture also seem fixed and static rather than susceptible to constant debate and social change. Focusing on history is another way of disrupting the essentialized understandings of culture that we raised questions about in Chapter 2. In order to practice our craft with respect, understanding, and effectiveness, it is necessary to understand the links between the world's recent history and the issues and challenges that face counselors and therapists today. To understand the counseling of diverse populations in contemporary times and to advance the practice of cultural counseling in the future, we must grapple with our histories and their expression in our current social, educational, and political systems.

This is not a history text, so we shall necessarily offer a brief overview rather than a thorough examination. Our scope will be limited to the historical influences that have shaped cultural relations in the modern world, and we shall concentrate on the last 500 years to capture these shaping influences. Our contention in this chapter is that the process of colonization of most of the earth's territory by Europeans between the 16th and 20th centuries has had a significant impact on the lives of all people everywhere. It is not possible to live in the modern world without somehow engaging with or being engaged by these influences. It is not that this is the only colonization that has happened in history. There have been many of those influences, and the European people who perpetrated modern colonizing were no different in their intent from many other colonizers of diverse cultural backgrounds at different times and in different circumstances. What has been different, however, has been the scale of this colonization. By the 20th century, it had achieved a greater scope of political control than any previous colonizing process.

Colonization has been a major shaping influence in the modern world on the entitlements that people claim, the privileges or disadvantages that they enjoy or suffer, the expectations of life that they can "realistically" expect or not expect, the shape of family relations that they might grow up in, the identity stories that they might enact in life, the careers that are possible for them to enter, the ways in which they might make sense of adversity and respond to it, and the feelings that accompany all of these experiences. In other words, it was not just land that was colonized.

Part of the experience of colonization was psychological in effect. The psychological effects of colonization that persist to this day cannot be fully understood by counselors and by their clients without taking account of the history of the cultural relations produced by colonization. Gregory Cajete (2015), a Pueblo indigenous educator, comments that it is critically important to learn the histories of the indigenous communities and colonization to understand what is taking place today among indigenous peoples all over the world. He states: "We must confront the modern and widespread denial of colonization because it leads to blaming the victims of colonization for their victimization" (p. 127). However, the process of colonization has never had things all its own way. From the inception of the modern process of colonization, it has been called into question and often actively opposed. People have found many ways to resist the loss of sovereignty that colonization thrust upon them. Cajete (2015) describes how each indigenous community has responded in different ways to colonization. Some communities have been forced to assimilate to survive. Other indigenous peoples have outwardly conformed to the forces of colonization while covertly resisting the attack on language and all cultural aspects of their way of being. A few communities have managed to largely keep intact the cultural fabric of their community because of geographical isolation and their ability to dodge the full-throated exposure to colonial forces. However, for the most part, across the world, indigenous communities have suffered in incalculable and unimaginable ways. Cajete points out that the challenge for the indigenous peoples around the globe is to rebuild the social fabric and ecology, reasserting self-determination, following the example of Maori in Aotearoa, New Zealand, and Native Hawaiians in Hawaii. Kaupapa Maori was a decolonizing movement that began in the 1960s. It was a grassroots movement inspired by community leaders to rekindle the indigenous knowledges and life practices that were fast disappearing through the colonizing forces brought forth by predominantly English settlers in the 1800s. Kaupapa Maori reinvigorated the indigenous world of Maori language, spirituality, education, and tribal knowledges to set a new vision and community vision for the Maori community (Tuhiwai-Smith, 2012). Integrating contemporary knowledge that complemented traditional Maori knowledge set in motion a transformative movement that became a conscious intervention on Western education and taken-for-granted colonizing doctrine that pervaded all aspects of life in Aotearoa, New Zealand. Kaupapa Maori and the de-colonizing accomplishments it has led for nearly 50 years have become a guiding vision for indigenous people everywhere and a source of aspiration and inspiration.

Political movements have been spawned, protests have been made, violent and nonviolent resistance has been offered, and gradually, in many instances, political independence has been won. The European political colonization of land and territory has been steadily reversed during the last hundred years in most parts of the earth, a movement that has become known as decolonization. Just as colonization has produced psychological effects that can be traced into the problems people present to counselors, so too does the process of decolonization require psychological as well as political resistance. Counselors who understand this well are in a much better position to make sense of the cultural positioning of their clients and to help them articulate their lives in relation to the psychological resistance in which they choose to participate. Because decolonization is psychological as well as political, it is associated with the production of good mental health.

With this introduction, let us now turn to a brief account of the modern history of colonization and decolonization.

A Review of the History of Colonization

Domination and Subjugation

In the history of human civilization, many societies have sought to dominate others, and those societies threatened with domination have struggled to resist. Our human history is full of examples where more powerful societies with technological advantages or greater numbers have wrenched physical and economic resources away from less powerful societies. Domination in human history has usually occurred through wars of conquest, which typically lead to the colonization of the defeated peoples by those who are militarily successful. As a result, the colonized may have their entire moral and physical universe destroyed and subsequently reshaped and restructured.

Colonizing societies don't usually stop at dominating and controlling the geography and the available physical resources. They typically impose their own language, their own religion, and their own social and political systems of governance on the colonized. In the process of overpowering and dominating another people, they regularly claim that they are superior to those they have defeated. The victors represent themselves as possessing all that is worthwhile and those that have been vanquished as generally inferior or barbaric.

Christopher Columbus was conscious of this intent from the beginning of his explorations of conquest in the New World. After his first contact with the Arawak people on the island of Hispaniola, he wrote in his log the following comments about the culture of the indigenous people:

> They do not bear arms, and do not know them, for I showed them a sword, they took it by the edge and cut themselves out of ignorance. They have no iron. Their spears are made of cane.... They would make fine servants.... With fifty men we could subjugate them all and make them do whatever we want (Zinn, 2003, p. 1).

Important aspects of the history of the next 500 years are prefigured in these words. Europeans and indigenous peoples in many places are still working through the implications of the desire for cultural power that Columbus expressed. Contemporary social configurations around the globe need to be understood as shaped largely by events that have occurred over the last five centuries, featuring generations of dominance, subjugation, and frequently, genocide. In particular, wars, famines, disease, technology, and religion over this period have shaped contemporary patterns of relationship across diverse cultural communities. On Hispaniola (which we now call Haiti), there were an estimated 250,000 Arawak Indians when Columbus arrived. After two years, by a combination of wholesale murders, mass suicides, and disease, half of them were dead. Fifty years later, there were none of the original Arawak people left on the island (Zinn, 2003).

The devastating effects of colonization of the indigenous peoples of the Americas initially came in the form of loss of land, deadly European diseases, forced dislocation, genocide, and the subsequent destruction of language and community. Cajete (2015) states that the socially destructive forces that occur at this present time that negatively affect Native American communities have their roots in the colonizing forces of oppression causing "ethnostress" (Cajete, 2015 p. 224). *Ethnostress*, originally described by Antone, Hill, and Myers (1985), is a complete disruption of the entire meaning-making systems of a people, leading to internalized oppression that drives hopelessness, self-abuse and apathy. Cajete comments that many indigenous peoples who are unaware of these colonizing forces negatively and unconsciously act out destructive behaviors brought through the consequences of colonization, even when the actual conditions that began the colonizing efforts have all but disappeared.

Acting out behavior, blaming, playing the victim role, self-medication, and self-abuse are prevalent in many native communities. This behavior alienates us from ourselves and communities in various ways. We act out our feelings on our family, our friends, our community, and ourselves. Distress reflects the ways we invalidate ourselves, isolate ourselves, act out our feelings of fear, anger, and hopelessness. We fail to trust our thinking about situations we know are wrong. We live in a world of fear and anger. As a result, our thinking becomes paralyzed, our emotional ability is affected, our relations disrupted,

BOX 3.1 THE BRITISH CIVILIZING MISSION

Modern anthropology grew out of the tradition of studying "the natives," and Said (1978/1994) shows how many other academic disciplines joined in the production of knowledge about "other" cultures. He also shows how many of the great books of the established canon of English literature, including works by Jane Austen, Charles Dickens, William Thackeray, Joseph Conrad, and Rudyard Kipling, simply assumed this civilizing mission as a natural truth. He adds to this list historians such as Thomas Carlyle and Lord Macaulay. And he traces the discourses of "Orientalism" into the foreign policy statements of politicians and political theorists as disparate as Napoleon Bonaparte, Karl Marx, T. E. Lawrence, Benjamin Disraeli, and Henry Kissinger. "Orientals," or "natives," goes this argument, can never be expected to understand the principles of democracy or the advantages of civilization the way "we" do, unless we teach them through the process of colonization.

and our ability to help ourselves is significantly affected (Hill, Antone and Myers 1986). These are the results of multigenerational experiences of trauma.

These "civilizing discourses," with the accompanying aesthetic production of "high" culture, proceeded to assert their authority over colonized groups with little regard for the violence and injustices inherent in the political and social institutions they established in these communities. Assumptions about the inherent inferiority of colonized peoples were intimately interwoven into the dominating discourses of colonization and provided the rationale to energize and drive these movements. In the fabric of contemporary life in the West, these forces continue to operate. However, there is also an implicit irony here. The civilizing mission of European colonization can be argued to contain within it the seeds of its own failure. If it were actually to be successful in its civilizing mission, it would produce leaders among colonized people who would stand up to the forces of colonization on its own terms and challenge its whole rationale. Perhaps it is not surprising, therefore, that many leaders of anticolonial movements, such as Mahatma Gandhi, Martin Luther King, and Nelson Mandela, or scholars like Edward Said and Frantz Fanon, were professional men, well educated in the discourse of the colonizers, and knew intimately its points of weakness. Because these leaders spoke eloquently in the discourse of the colonizers, what they had to say could not so easily be dismissed.

A parallel can be found in the counseling field. One of the most significant efforts that has occurred in the multicultural counseling movement is the attempt to develop a set of multicultural counseling competencies in order to thwart the extent to which the dominating influences of Anglo culture subjugate the discourses of other cultural communities. Or, to put it another way, to provide a set of standards for the multicultural community so as to give voice to persons and communities otherwise rendered invisible, disenfranchised, and isolated. But it has been written in the discourse of "competencies" to connect with the dominant discourse of counselor education. We focus on these competencies in Chapter 5. In all the colonizing powers of the modern era, there was a deeply embedded assumption of the superiority of the colonizer in all aspects of life, and the inferiority of the colonized. A French advocate of colonialism spelled out all too eloquently the spoken and unspoken assumptions of colonizers of 18th and 19th century Europe:

> It is necessary, then, to accept as a principle and point of departure the fact that there is a hierarchy of races and civilizations, and that we belong to the superior race and civilization, still recognizing that, while superiority confers rights, it imposes strict obligations in return. The basic legitimation of conquest over native peoples is the conviction of our superiority, not merely our mechanical, economic, and military superiority, but our moral superiority. Our dignity rests on that quality, and it underlies our right to direct the rest of humanity. Material power is nothing but a means to that end (François-Jules Harmand, in Curtin, 1971, pp. 294–295).

It is within this cultural discourse that the early European settlers established their residence in the Americas. These cultural assumptions about their identities and their understandings about their supposedly rightful place in the world were fundamental to the way they engaged the inhabitants of the "New World."

The Expression of British Colonization in North America

In many ways the majority culture of the United States continues to be an expression of British colonial discourse. The settlers who created the colonies along the American Eastern Seaboard had a decisive and lasting impact on the culture and institutions of that society. The United States as we know it now is a society founded by 17th- and 18th-century settlers from the British Isles. Thus, the dominant cultural ideas and dominant discourses in America arise from the culture of 17th- and 18th-century English settlers. The Christian religion, Protestant values, moralism, work ethics, the English language, British traditions of law and justice, the limits of government power, and the legacy of European art, literature, philosophy, and music all arise from the imposition of British colonization on the peoples of the land known as North America (Huntington, 2004). Out of this culture, settlers developed the American creed, with its principles of liberty, equality, individualism, representative government, and private property.

While subsequent immigrants modified this culture, they did not change it fundamentally. There are rich historical descriptions around the world of how colonizing groups tend to preserve habits of life or speech that are no longer current in their home country. In 1760, Benjamin Franklin declared proudly, "I am a Briton." Sixteen years later, Franklin signed the Declaration of Independence and thus renounced his British identity. In the intervening years, settlers in North America made efforts to carve out a new cultural identity as relations with Britain deteriorated over trade, taxes, military security, and the extent of parliamentary power over the colonies. In terms of race, ethnicity, and language, White Americans and the British were nevertheless essentially one people. Hence, U.S. independence required a different rationale—an appeal to political ideas. According to Huntington (2004), White Americans argued that the British government was deviating from English concepts of liberty, law, and government by consent. White Americans began to invoke universalistic self-evident truths concerning liberty, equality, and individual rights, which ultimately led to the Declaration of Independence. Their enemies were tyranny, monarchy, aristocracy, and the suppression of liberty and individual rights. Paradoxically, while the Anglo Americans stood with great pride alongside these high-minded ideals, the reality for all others was anything but liberty, equality, and any form of basic human rights.

Despite the breach with Britain and the establishment of the declaration, the underlying cultural discourse of British colonization, which perhaps could now be termed American colonization, continued to guide and shape the fundamental identities of Anglo Americans. During this period, certain Anglo Americans took pride in their high-minded ideals that spoke to human dignity, equity, freedom, and justice, but these values barely extended to even members of their own ethnic group. At the same time that the founders of these new political and moral institutions, constructed upon British law, were articulating their vision of democracy, they were betraying their own principles with peoples who were not members of this Anglo American or White race. Neither did they include women.

The Role of Slavery in European Colonization

An account of European colonization in the Americas cannot be complete without acknowledgment of the transportation of many millions of Africans from the sub-Sahara on slave ships to many destinations in the Americas. European trade in African slaves had actually begun 50 years before Columbus, when slaves were transported from Africa to Portugal (Zinn, 2003). There is no doubt that much of the accumulated wealth of the European empire, generated from the extensive sugar and cotton plantations

BOX 3.2 CULTURAL APPROPRIATION

Cultural appropriation happens when members of a dominating culture take up aspects of a minoritized culture and use it or mimic it without the consent of members of that culture. What is appropriated may be customs, symbols, words or expressions, songs, dances, artifacts, or religious traditions. Appropriation is taking or borrowing something that does not belong to you. It may be either illegal or legal but unjust. It signifies an imbalance of power, such as the exploitation of an indigenous culture under colonization.

Cultural appropriation has to be carefully distinguished from normal cultural exchange. It constitutes appropriation when disrespect, or even desecration of the original significance is involved, when what is taken is, say, sacred and sensitive, or when the direct opposition of members of the indigenous culture is ignored. It amounts to cultural appropriation when a serious element of a cultural tradition is trivialized or incorporated into a fashion or toy which fails to honor its origins.

An example might be the use of Native American headdresses as fashion accessories or to symbolize a sports team, for example, as a mascot, in an isolated way. When members of a dominating culture use cultural symbols without any experience of the subjugation experienced by the colonized culture, they may be said to have appropriated these symbols.

It should be recognized that particular instances of cultural appropriation are often controversial, and the usual defense is that paying homage to the culture was the intention, but there are clear instances where a line is crossed and the accusation of cultural appropriation is justified. It was only in the 1980s that cultural appropriation was first studied academically. Yet it has been recognized by the United Nations in the following way. Article 31.1 of the United Nations Declaration on the Rights of Indigenous Peoples states the following:

> Indigenous peoples have the right to maintain, control, protect and develop their cultural heritage, traditional knowledge and traditional cultural expressions, as well as the manifestations of their sciences, technologies and cultures, including human and genetic resources, seeds, medicines, knowledge of the properties of fauna and flora, oral traditions, literatures, designs, sports and traditional games and visual and performing arts. They also have the right to maintain, control, protect and develop their intellectual property over such cultural heritage, traditional knowledge, and traditional cultural expressions.

of the American Eastern Seaboard and the Southern states, was gained at the expense of the suffering of African slaves. There are no exact statistics covering all the places that African men, women, and children were sent. Howard Zinn (2003) estimates that during the centuries of the modern slave trade, Africa lost some 50 million people to death and slavery. There were an estimated 14 million slaves sent to Islamic nations in the Middle East alone (Sowell, 1998). Hundreds of thousands and possibly millions of people perished in transit, whether it was on the desolate slavery trails in North Africa or on the hundreds of slave ships that crossed the Atlantic. Shockingly, as widespread as slavery was in North America, Brazil alone imported six times as many slaves as did the slave traders in the northern continent (Sowell, 1998). By the end of the 17th century, most African slaves in the American (U.S.) colonies had been born on American soil and were losing many of their customs and traditions. In the slave societies of Brazil, the slaves' African customs and traditions stayed more intact, because the slave trade in this country continued right through until the 1880s.

The brutality that accompanied being captured in one's African homeland and transported to the Americas was matched by the brutality of the foreman in charge of the plantation slaves. Many of the working-class Whites who traveled from Britain and Ireland in search of employment in North America served the higher-class slave owners as foremen, who would control, discipline, and punish the slaves. The individuals wielding the whip and lash were often immigrants from the fringes of British civil life. They themselves had come from violent communities dominated by poverty and lawlessness. Many of them were ruthless men used to settling differences with violence, sometimes as graphic as the biting off of ears and noses. Thus, this pattern of ruthless violence was brutally transferred on to the slave societies.

A significant irony in the history of British colonization is that Britain, the leading slave-trading nation, ultimately became the leading advocate for the end of the slave trade and finally eliminated slavery altogether. This was no mean feat, since England and America had economically benefited so greatly from exploiting slave labors. The significance of this achievement is also hard to understand without appreciating that slavery was a worldwide institution that had been conducted by dominating institutions and nations on every inhabited continent, subjugating people of every color, language, and religion, for thousands of years. Sowell (1998) states, "The dogged persistence of the British in that struggle was a key factor in the ultimate destruction of slavery around the world" (p. 91).

However, the Anglo American culture of the slavery era established laws and systems of education that were in stark contrast to the high-minded ethical principles they had established on that important day in 1776. Through the lens of British American colonial discourse, Anglo American Protestant values were reinforced in schools, which also served to undermine the capacity of immigrants, indigenous people, and African American slaves to transmit their own cultural histories and cultural fabric to their U.S. born children. The pressing question from the perspective of the 21st century is, how could the founding fathers appear to stand so proudly by their newly made constitution that espoused life, liberty, and the pursuit of happiness, and yet treat so despicably all other groups of people who were not permitted to identify as White? A large part of the answer to that question must surely rest with the construction of race. We shall address the construction of race more fully in Chapter 4.

Europe received all its major technological innovations via the Middle East and China. Even as late as 1450, the flow of science and technology was primarily emerging from Islamic societies stretching from India to North Africa. Jared Diamond's (1999) argument carefully documents how the Europeans were able to conquer other peoples. A combination of serendipitous factors led them to develop European guns, steel tools, and manufactured products, and to carry powerful infectious diseases against which they had themselves developed immunity. Diamond meticulously outlines how the most ancient agricultural and horticultural belt of the Fertile Crescent (now Syria, Israel, Palestine, Lebanon, Jordan, Turkey, and Iraq); the early domestication of animals, such as the horse, pig, sheep, goat, and cow; and the centuries-long opportunity for Europeans to develop immunities to diseases carried by domestic animals became of central importance to Europeans in developing powerful armies that could defeat indigenous hunter-gatherers and newly emerging farming cultures. A combination of these outgrowths of thousands of years of Eurasian development led to immunities from influenza, whooping cough, measles, mumps, and chicken pox. These diseases became more effective than military weapons in weakening and ultimately destroying any potential threat to the success of European expansionism in the Americas and the Pacific. For example, in what is currently Mexico, there is wide agreement that these new European diseases were the most significant contributor to the decline of the Mayan, Aztec, and other Indian tribal populations from 22 million to just 2 million (Coe, 1996). The population of the Incas of Peru declined by approximately 90% after the Spanish arrived (Cook, 1981), and the majority of those deaths are attributed to European diseases.

In North America, the spread of European diseases decimated the Indians with whom the British came into contact. For example, the Wampanoag on the East Coast lost a staggering 90% of their tribe (Steele, 1994). Small Indian populations that were left after the epidemics required less land, so these Indians traded cultivated land to the European settlers. In this manner, the small European settler population began to gain a stronger foothold on accessible fertile land. The Cherokees living in what is now western North Carolina and eastern Tennessee were the largest tribe east of the Mississippi, and numbered 20,000 in 1690. Within 50 years there were just 10,000, mostly because of the toll of European diseases (Goodwin, 1977). Indians in the west, such as the Blackfeet, the Comanches, and the Mandans, died of the newly introduced smallpox and cholera in such numbers that their tribes' very survival was threatened; in some instances, they were virtually annihilated (Hagan, 1993). Disturbingly, there is documentation that European settlers traded with and donated blankets—an item sought by the Indians—knowing that the blankets were riddled with the smallpox virus (Sowell, 1998). Human death from the introduction of European diseases occurred at a magnitude that is difficult to grasp.

The devastation of indigenous peoples was to be repeated countless times in many lands and continents around the world. In New Zealand, for instance, where two of the authors (Gerald and John) are from, the arrival of the European settler led to a devastating loss of Maori life after they were exposed to European diseases (influenza and whooping cough). These diseases introduced a vulnerability to this people that they had not experienced since their migration from Eastern Polynesia. By 1896, the Maori population had declined from 110,000 in the early 1800s to slightly more than 40,000. The British sentiment at the turn of the 20th century was to "smooth the pillow of a dying race" (King, 2003, p. 258). How familiar this history sounds when we consider the plight of the American Indian, the Australian Aborigine, and many other indigenous peoples around the planet too numerous to mention!

Colonization in Pre-European Societies

Terrible indeed were the consequences of European expansion and empire for indigenous peoples around the globe. It is easy to vilify and hold 16th-to-19th-century Europe responsible for all of the large-scale human travesties that have occurred in the records of human history. However, what we must remember is that over thousands of years many human societies have exploited technological or organizational advantages to conquer other societies. Virtually all societies on the planet, small or large, have, at some time in their history, been either conquerors or victims of conquest. Sometimes they have been both at different times. In the continent of Africa, where human ancestry can be traced back approximately 8 million years, there were colonizing empires that arose and declined in the sub-Saharan area of what today would be called Nigeria and Ghana. Evidence suggests that the Oyo empire (founded sometime before 1400 and slightly smaller than Colorado) and the Songhay empire (about the size of France) were huge states in this continent. As in other parts of the world, those with superior strength in organization and well-equipped fighters used their colonizing prowess to subjugate and enslave others, including their fellow Africans. These events occurred completely independently of the Ottoman, European, and North and South American slave trade. According to Martin Klein (1998), most enslaved African peoples remained in Africa, in the Sudan and Nigeria, despite the enormous numbers of people enslaved beyond African shores.

We know that when the first Europeans arrived in North America, they behaved badly toward the indigenous people they found there. Sadly, as Thomas Sowell (1998) describes it, they behaved as conquerors have behaved all over the world for thousands of years—which is to say, brutally, greedily, and with arrogance towards the conquered peoples. Indeed that is very much the way Indian conquerors behaved toward other Indians, long before Columbus's ships first appeared on the horizon (p. 255). In southern North America, in what is today Mexico, the sophisticated civilizations of the Mayans and Aztecs considered hunters and gatherers to be no more than barbarians. These technologically advanced societies disdained, enslaved, and exterminated or sacrificed hundreds of thousands of people who were less equipped to protect themselves. Before European invaders arrived in the Americas, the Incas developed one of the largest empires in the world. It stretched for 2,000 miles, crossing what today is Peru, Ecuador, Chile, Bolivia, and parts of Argentina and Venezuela. The Quechua-speaking people who lived in the heart of the Inca Empire spread their hegemony to all those within their reign. Equivalent to the Mayans and Aztecs in their technological superiority over hunters and gathers, they built stone cities with sophisticated canals, suspension bridges, and irrigated agricultural terraces (Hemming, 1970). Immediately before the Spaniards arrived in what is now Peru, the Incas were entrenched in a bloody and devastating civil war between the forces of Huascar and Atahualpa. Atahualpa instituted a mass slaughtering of Inca nobles, accompanied by hideous atrocities against the wider population (Davies, 1995).

Psychological Effects of Colonization

Edward Said was keenly interested in how the colonized were portrayed by colonizing Western powers. Box 3.3 represents, from the viewpoint of European writers, his characterizations of people of the West in comparison with people of the East, who were to become part of subordinated communities dominated by Western imperialism. Such descriptions detail the psychological contours of the landscape of colonization. These comparative descriptions portray Westerners as morally superior, wise, even handed, virtuous, and self-disciplined. An Easterner or Oriental, by contrast, is consistently characterized as undisciplined and unruly, lacking wisdom, rationality, maturity, and morality. Westerners' assumptions of their own superior virtuous qualities fortified them in both their conquering and their civilizing missions, and justified their psychological domination of those living in the East. They sealed off the Western mind from caring about the human costs paid by indigenous people for the acts of conquest and colonization. In some measure, the people of the East were assumed to deserve what was happening to them and were, therefore, less to be pitied.

As it developed, British colonization became not just about the exploitation of the physical resources of a foreign territory, but also about imposing the colonizing power's political, moral, religious, and economic will on the subjugated societies. When the meaning-making frameworks central to the organization and structure of a community are removed, together with the physical resources that sustain them, people experience a profound sense of dislocation, isolation, and alienation. Their physical,

East:	West:
Mysterious	Obvious
Mystical	Sensible
Childlike	Mature
Silent	Articulate
Weak	Strong
Dark	Light
Irrational	Rational
Depraved	Virtuous
Tyrannical	Democratic
Sensual	Self-controlled
Incapable of self-government	Capable of self-government

Source: Adapted from Baldwin, Longhurst, McCracken, Ogborn, and Smith (2000).

psychological, spiritual, and social fabric is damaged or destroyed. The resulting degradation steadily becomes internalized among its citizens, and leads ultimately to their loss of belief in their own worthiness. Ironically, the internalized degradation sometimes mirrors the attitudes ascribed to them by the colonizing power. Even the highly negative assumptions of racism can be psychologically internalized in the thoughts of the very people who are subjected by them. If we hold this story in mind, it becomes easier to understand how the effects of colonization can show up in the kinds of mental health problems many people present to counselors even today. Native American, African American, and Latinx communities in the United States are overrepresented in the statistics of people suffering from mental health problems, drug and alcohol problems, and incarceration.

The same disproportionate indicators of personal suffering can be found around the world among other colonized peoples. These figures can be ascribed, in no small part, to the ongoing deleterious effects of colonizing actions of the Western European culture over 400 years. It takes many generations to work through the effects of such damage, especially when the power relations that produce these effects have not disappeared, even though they may have been considerably modified. Through the potent mechanisms of colonizing culture, subjugated peoples come to abandon the very foundations that give meaning to many of their own cultural practices and identities. As a result, great harm and suffering occurs. The effects of colonization have been eloquently elaborated by Albert Memmi (1967), who describes the bond that creates both the colonizer and the colonized. It is one which destroys both parties, although in different ways. Memmi draws a portrait of the "Other" as described by the colonizer. In dominant colonizing discourse, the colonized emerges as the image of everything the colonizer is not. The colonizer is represented as civilized, hardworking, resourceful, intelligent, moral, and compassionate, while the colonized is positioned as lazy, wicked, backward, immoral, and in some important ways, not fully human. Memmi points to several conclusions drawn about the artificially created Other. First, the Other is always lacking in the valued qualities of the society, whatever those qualities may be. Second, the humanity of the Other becomes mysterious and unknown. Third, the Other is not a member of the "civilized" human community, but rather part of a chaotic, disorganized, and anonymous collectivity. Finally, the Other carries the mark of the plural. Whereas "we" are all unique, differentiated individuals, "they" all look alike and can be treated en masse. The colonizing discourse is dehumanizing, because the ultimate positioning offered to the recipient is an existence which serves the needs of the colonizer.

What are the psychological effects of this process of "Othering"? We have already spoken about the danger of internalized degradation. It is achieved through the colonizer's imposition of an image of the colonized groups onto those who have been subjugated. They are required to see themselves through the same deprecating lens through which the colonizer views them (Fanon, 1963; Taylor, 1994). In the modern world, this process is frequently replicated by encounters with mental health professionals who fail to take the processes of colonization, still expressed through racism, seriously in their diagnostic assessments. They seek primarily to understand a person's psychological distress in individual, intrapsychic terms. Healthcare professionals can be seduced into ascribing problems to personal deficits rather than to cultural positioning in the drama of colonization. They can proceed to work on solutions that address only the limited dimensions identified by their diagnostic procedures. In these ways, counselors and therapists often fail to take into account the historical and cultural trauma suffered by multiple groups, such as indigenous peoples all over the world.

The vile abuses that occurred against these peoples and the subsequent destruction of kinship and community have left serious intergenerational wounds. Drug and alcohol abuse, mental health problems, violence, alienation, and economic hardship can be directly related to 500 years of European colonization. Rather than seeing these problems as hangovers of a historical context, traditional counseling focuses on challenging individuals to be responsible for themselves. It ascribes diagnoses of deficiency and pathology to those who cannot maintain this sense of rational responsibility and fails to take into account how the very ability to be self-governing was targeted and undermined by the colonizing process. Neither did these processes all cease centuries ago. Further layers of these hardships are experienced by people from former colonized countries who in recent times have sought to escape harsh living conditions and immigrated into modern European and U.S. cities, and then often been subjected to further harm and distress. Once in their adopted country, they often take up positions only on the margins of their new social world, finding themselves in socially and economically deprived ghettos. There they experience the same internalized abjection their forebears felt.

Decolonization

People in colonized lands have struggled to overthrow colonial political systems for centuries. They have their seeds in the expressions of resistance to modern colonization as far back as its very beginnings. Indigenous people in many places fought against the invading armies of the colonizers, sometimes winning but more often losing these battles. People captured into slavery made desperate attempts to run away. Organized rebellions took place on the slave plantations. Howard Zinn (2003) counts 18 uprisings aimed at the overthrow of colonial governments, 6 Black rebellions, and 40 riots that occurred before 1760 in America. In some cases, poor White people, many of whom came to America as indentured laborers and whose conditions and rights were only marginally better than those of Black slaves, joined forces with the slaves in resistance. Bacon's Rebellion was a case in point. Also, some slaves were freed early in the slavery period.

From early in the history of slavery there were also White people who stood against the practice of slavery. The abolitionist movement in Britain developed a large following around the period of the Enlightenment, and this continued through the 19th century. Even that was not the beginning of the antislavery movement in Britain; slavery and enforced servitude in England had once been abolished way back in 1102. But as the African slave trade began, many slaves entered Britain from the Americas with their masters. They were freed by a decision of the chief justice of the Court of King's Bench in 1772, at which time there estimated to be 10,000 to 14,000 slaves living in Britain. In the rest of Europe, other movements to make slavery illegal sprang from the Enlightenment. One hero of this movement was the French bishop Abbé Grégoire, who had considerable influence in the revolutionary government after the French Revolution. He was immensely popular in France (although hated by the Pope) and led the revolutionary government in a policy of religious toleration for Jews and granting freedom to Black slaves in France. In 19th-century Britain, the Aboriginal Protection Society campaigned for the rights of colonized people and was responsible for influencing the Home Office to make treaties with indigenous peoples in New Zealand and elsewhere (Orange, 1987).

Throwing off the yoke of colonization is not just a matter of a change of government. In many places around the world, systems of social organization and systems of thinking have continued to maintain privileged opportunity for White people and the racist assumptions of the colonizing era, long after the politicians and colonial administrators have left. The process of decolonization has likewise focused not just on regime change but also on the development of ways of thinking that depart from the assumptions and practices of racial and cultural superiority. Decolonization is necessarily, in part, a psychological struggle, since the colonizing assumptions have penetrated deep into the psyches of people in the modern world.

Hence it is important for counselors to understand the psychological process of decolonization and its effects in order to work with people who are affected by it. Counseling can help throw off the internalized images of abjection that have resulted from colonization.

By way of example, Mikela Jones's narrative contains twin stories of colonization and decolonization. As you read it, keep an ear out for the ongoing effects of the atrocities committed by Anglo Americans and settlers in their colonizing quest. And also listen for the decolonizing assertions of resistance and the effort to maintain cultural resilience in spite of the effects of colonization.

Mikela's Writing

Sin ta yabe machi na, ke sheeyay Mikela Jones, ba tenik xabe. Ke nahpo, che ya ta kai casil. My name is Mikela Jones and I am Pomo Hinthil from my mother's side. My people are the indigenous inhabitants of what is known today as northern California. We are the Little River Band of Pomo Indians. I am also Paiute Shoshone from my father's side.

My people currently reside in northern Nevada. We are from the Duck Valley reservation. I am che ya, which in my language means people of the earth and father sky. Today I have grown comfortable calling myself Indian. Not all Native people are, but I don't mind it. My mother knew what it was like being Indian growing up in a Westernized world; therefore, she felt it was critical to teach me, to arm me with the tools necessary to defend myself against critics and racist people. I was told the real story around that term Indian, and it is a bit different from what most people believe. During the 1490s, when Columbus arrived, the word "Indian" did not exist. When he landed, his first observation of these indigenous inhabitants was how very religious they were. His exact words were "en Dios," which translated means "of God." He was saying that these people were of God. The term evolved from En Dios to Endian and continued to evolve to what it is today. I am a child of the creator, which is why I have no problem saying that I am an Indian. My Indian-ness has not only been instrumental in shaping my life, but it has also been monumental in shaping my family's history and their present and future status as a people. I am empowered today because of the terrible sacrifices made by many of my people. Everything follows from my being Indian—my culture, economic class, life choices, and so on. It dictates a starting place, but where I finish is up to me and what I do with this life. But in order to know where we are going, we have to know where we are, and to know where we are, we have to know where we have been. We must look at the history of our people to find its influence on all of these factors and its impact on me. Indian is not an ethnic group, nor is it a race. It is a political organization. Indians are the only group in the United States that have their own federal agency. That agency is the Bureau of Indian Affairs (BIA). The reason is partly political status, but how did we get that political status? We need only to look at the history of my people. Tribes are sovereign nations to the extent that the government allows them to be. That statement doesn't really make sense, considering the definition of the word sovereign, but regardless of its confusion, that is exactly how it is when we consider the relationship my people have with the United States.

It all began in 1492 when Columbus landed on Turtle Island, followed by others leaving their homes to seek a place where they would not face any religious prosecution—their freedom meant the loss of another's. In the development of the United States, early leaders saw native people as animals, not human beings, which allowed them to treat them the way they did. This perception of "savage" is still around today. Countless legal inequities were imposed on my people at the highest levels of government. The brutality and disenfranchisement arising from the United States' treatment of the Indian over these last few hundred years is too enormous to mention here. However, part of this history led to the emergence of the BIA. This institution has played a part in the shaping of native sovereignty and its relation to the state and federal government. Because the Supreme Court gave us the title of a distinct dependent nation, we now have a unique relationship with the United States. Even more troublesome is our relationship with the States that were created around Tribes. States are like our siblings, requiring us to work together even when states and their leaders do not agree with Tribal Sovereignty. By making this precedent-setting decision, the United States has a responsibility to be that guardian, but there *is a disquieting contradiction: Tribes wanting self-determination are also being treated as a dependent. That is why we have a quasi-definition and status of sovereignty. I continue to ask myself this question as I tell you the history of my people: how does this affect my family and me? Sovereignty is a power that has been given to us. It is something that unites us. It seems to me the only power we have in a country that wants to keep all the power to itself. My Tribe and all Tribes are working at exercising this power in any way that we can. Casinos are one way, but there is a lot more that Tribes can do to be economically self-sufficient. Sovereignty means self-determination, and for my people self-determination takes us one step closer to the way we used to live and one step away from colonialism. Self-determination allows us to guide each other using traditional philosophies and ceremonies, and not live solely by the Westernized ideologies that at one time were forced down our throats. The year 1887 gave rise to the Dawes Act. The goal of this legislation was to acquire more Indian land by a policy of assimilation. The government enacted the policy of "allotment," which took Tribal land and broke the reservation into parcels of land, or allotments. Prior to this, Indians had been dispersed throughout the land. Allotment put them in distinct area, limiting their ability to live in their own vast lands. Each member was given a parcel of land that was theirs. Surplus land went to the government to open up for homesteading and the growth and expansion of the United States.*

The settlers' movement west took our indigenous people out of their traditional homelands, removing them from sacred sites where their ceremonies had been practiced. In many instances, my people were separated from their traditional food resources. This made them rely on government-supplied food, which they were not accustomed to eating. Prior to contact with European immigrants, Native people had been extremely healthy. What is the situation today? Diabetes is an epidemic for Indian people, and this is due to the diet. Our bodies are not used to the processed foods consumed in our communities today. From the 1800s to the mid-1950s, the government used boarding schools to assimilate Indians. Children were taken from their families by force and sent away to schools designed to force young people to become assimilated and estranged from their cultural roots. The government had a saying at this time: "Kill the Indian, save the man." The purpose of these boarding schools was essentially to kill the Indian. At these schools, children were abused physically, mentally, emotionally, and spiritually. Some were sexually abused and beaten for speaking their language. They were forced to learn positions of servitude, to forget what it was to be an Indian. They were not allowed to go home. They weren't allowed to nurture each other, nor were they nurtured by the staff. They were no longer allowed to practice their traditional ceremonies. Everything was taken, and what replaced that void was the compulsion to be servants to a Western ideology.

Even on the reservations, genocidal and assimilation tactics were being practiced. My ancestor, Wavoka, a Paiute medicine man, had introduced the Ghost Dance—a dance that was supposed to bring back those who had died and make all the White people go back to where they had come from. When practicing this ceremony, Tribal people were shot down, including women and children. Tribes had no religious protection and were killed for practicing their ceremonies. It was not until 1978 that Tribal people were allowed to practice their religion and it was protected by the United States. Today, when I am asked, "Do you speak your language?" I almost want to cry. I think about what my people went through and why I cannot speak my language fluently. Many people, including other natives, judge you in a negative way if you do not speak your language. There was a time in my life when I really struggled to figure out what made me Indian. The only thing I could think of was that I had long hair, brown skin, high cheekbones, and a big nose. Oh, and I had Indian blood, but was that it? I didn't know my language, my songs, my dance, or my ceremonies. They were gone because of what had happened to us, the genocide my people had endured. I had to go through a lot of traditional and nontraditional counseling methods. I had to pray to bring those things back into my life. The acts of the past impact me and my family today. We struggle to find our songs, our language, our dance, and our ceremonies. It is now our life's work to bring back the Indian within us, for it is the only way we can be whole again. Part of the healing comes with an understanding and education for all people. Both the colonizer and the colonized. It is a history that doesn't want to be told, nor heard. The late 1840s marked the era of the gold rush. Many history books talk about the development aspect of the gold rush, the building of cities and the histories of the miners. Seldom is there anything written about the original inhabitants of this area, the Pomo, as well as the many other Tribes living in California at the time. California has the most diverse of native populations across the country, and they all have a history that is rarely discussed in the textbooks of our schools. Would it be too violent to talk about in school, or is this a history that people are trying to forget? Federal bounties were placed on the heads of my people: 20 cents for men, 15 cents for women, 10 cents for children. In a period of just 20 years, the United States paid over 2 million dollars in bounties. Tribes in California were decimated. It is estimated that more than 20,000 bounties were claimed. That means that 20,000 of my ancestors were killed by bounty hunters alone. The way they collected money for bounties was by turning in the scalps of their victims. These bounty hunters were so money hungry that they started killing non-Natives and turning in scalps of dark colored hair. This is where the term redskin was developed; the United States said they would only pay bounties for scalps with "red skin." Now that is a name of a team, a mascot. Not only it is a derogatory term, it is despicable to use a group of people as a mascot. We are not mascots! Indians that were not killed were taken into a kind of slavery, known at this time as indentured servitude. My people also have the story of the bloody island massacre, which occurred in the early 1900s. Some of my people who were indentured servants rebelled and killed a wealthy White man for enslaving and abusing the people. This man also happened to be the brother of the governor of California at that time. All the women, elders, and children fled to an island for safety, while the men, the warriors, stayed behind and prepared for the consequences of their actions. The governor of California returned with the United States Cavalry, not to fight the warriors, but to the island. They slaughtered dozens of elders, women, and children, almost annihilating the whole village. There were few survivors. Those that did survive hid in the water breathing through Tule reeds. The island was red with their blood. These things were happening to my people not that long ago. That man that enslaved, murdered, and raped native people, Andrew Kelsey, had a town named after him: Kelseyville, California.

Forced assimilation and genocide have left my people in an unhealthy place. Today, many are in a state of poverty, have lost their identity, are in poor health, and have poor living habits. Today, many are in a damaging cycle of abuse and have negative self-medicating habits. That is why I feel it is my responsibility to counter the efforts of this abusive cycle. Even though these events happened long ago, we are all still being impacted by them. Posttraumatic stress syndrome is one way that it is impacting us. Historical Trauma; traumatic experiences through history have sent us into a cycle of depression and anger. I had to heal myself in order to see clearly, to forgive and move forward. Once I began to see the history, I began to put together the puzzle that shaped my actions and my people's actions. It became evident why my people are in the place they're in, why we are poor, why we drink, and why we have lost our history and cultural fabric. Understanding this gave rise to my pursuit to find the Indian within. I struggled with substance abuse when I was younger because that was what I was taught—that's what I thought it was to be Indian. I went through a healing process and began to pursue my culture. I also began to think about self-determination and how I could contribute to that. My answer came with the idea that we need more professionals, because the reality is that each day our sovereignty is getting weaker. We are losing it in the court systems. Most people do not think Indians should get any special treatment. We need people to learn the language of the courts and fight for our people with pen and paper. To hold the United States accountable for the treaties they signed with all Tribal nations. That is why I pursued a college education. I became the first male from my Tribe to graduate from a four-year university and the first from my Tribe to receive a graduate degree. My history influences my behavior as well as motivates me to be successful, to help my people. My cultural group is not just something I belong to; it's a way of life for me, a way that guides my choices and my ethics. It is something that I live by and protect, something that my people live by and protect. Our history brought us to where we are today. It does not define us; it can if we do not address it, therefore we have to make the conscious effort to make a positive change.

In my family, we have generations of men being raised by women alone. Could this be related to the acts of oppression and genocide my people endured? I believe so. Of all the things that have been taken away from my people, I think the status of "warrior" is one of them. There is also some shame there. Shame that we couldn't defend our people the way we wished we could. Though we are still alive, there is a sense of loss, and many of our warriors are in the negative cycle. When I was with the men of the reservation, I was given a role, a responsibility, though it was hard at times. I was independent and expected to handle things on my own. When I was with the women, I was nurtured and cared for; it felt good. I was also taught a lot about what it means to be a good man. Today, as Indian men, we are in need of developing healthy roles in our families. One that is a combination of traditional values and the latest best practices. We are redefining warrior and the ownership of that role. Our community is violent because our young men don't know their role. It is part of our history and trauma. There are not a lot of people there to teach them about the source of their anger, healthy coping mechanisms, and their own war-rior-ness. Domestic violence and infidelity are just some of the issues that come because of this loss. Indian men need to learn about their healing issues. They need to not feel guilty. We are still alive, capable, and beautiful people. In reflecting on these events, I am able to see how far we have come. I am able to see what my people have done to make it this far. I honor my ancestors and what they endured so that I can live today. Even today, we live in some of the most beautiful areas. We still know our songs, our dance, and our language. It is coming back, and not only is it coming back, but we are taking responsibility for our self-determination. I am not the only one doing this. This renaissance is happening all over.

Many Tribal people are stepping up and becoming professionals. Accepting that respon-sibility and becoming present-day warriors, fighting for sovereignty with the pen. We are walking in two worlds, still adapting, but accepting the beauty in both and trying to bal-ance the inequities in one. Please understand the challenge that we face. The challenges that history brought us. Understand that the more we grow as a professional, the more we move away from our traditional side, roles and responsibilities. Although as we develop professionally we become more credible to academia, we step away from our roles as Natives. That is why the effort is two-fold, developing the knowledge to live in the West-ern world while maintaining the commitment to the Natural world.

Ke sheeyay Mikela Jones, ba tenik xabe. I am Pomo Paiute Shoshone Hinthil, che ya. Kadi ho kaline ya nake nake. Yaqui kooto.

FIGURE 3.1   Photograph of Mikela Jones

Mikela Jones identifies as Pomo Hinthil and Paiute Shoshone.

Discuss

1. As you read Mikela's story, how did it touch you?
2. Were there places where you were saddened, enlivened, angered, dismayed, or excited, or felt any other response?
3. What did you find surprising in it?
4. What difference did it make to you?
5. How were the psychological effects of colonization evident in this story?
6. How was the theme of resistance and decolonization present in this story?
7. What are the counseling implications of Mikela's story?

It would be a mistake to think of the forces of colonization as inevitable and inexorable. If we look closely at history, we can trace the development of an alternative story from the beginning of the colonizing process. Colonization was resisted, with varying degrees of success, by many people all around the world. Subjugated groups always sought to maintain the integrity of their cultural perspectives and sometimes organized their sense of cultural belonging around their projects of resistance. They also always made accommodations to the European way of life, adopting practices that they found attractive from the colonizers and discarding some of their own traditional practices. The political forms of 19th-century colonization no longer apply. The general consensus of world politics, as expressed by the United Nations, is now opposed to colonizing practices, and international law, such as it exists, and has outlawed them.

Through the 20th century there has been a steady movement toward the reestablishment of independent status for nation states around the globe. The old British and French empires no longer exist in the form that they did a hundred years ago. German efforts to establish political dominance in Europe were turned back in World War II. The Russian rule over vast territories in Europe and Asia ended with the overthrow of the Soviet system in the 1990s and the breakup of the Soviet Union into many different countries. While present-day Russia under President Putin wishes to resurrect elements of the old Soviet Empire, illustrated by invasions of Georgia and Ukraine, major political and military forces in Eastern and Western Europe and North America have pushed back and substantially constrained these predatory efforts. The ugly outcomes of the Iraq war and the brutal emergence of ISIS and the carnage of its defeat that followed are a sore reminder that the United States, while capable of defying international law and invading other countries to bring about "regime change," has no stomach for colonial actions of this kind.

Today, the United States feels the constraint of anticolonial discourse and its own rhetoric of democratic independence and history of the overthrow of colonial rule. The U.S. public would not accept the political intention to colonize as an acceptable goal of U.S. power in the way that the British public did a hundred years ago. In other words, there has been a worldwide shift in discourse against the practice of colonization.

The colonizing impulse to take control of others' resources has by no means disappeared. With the extraordinary economic and military growth of China in the last three decades, and its coordinated efforts to use its economic might to gain leverage over the natural resources in many countries around the globe, it is positioned to push for a colonial presence of the kind that Britain asserted a few hundred years ago.

BOX 3.4 DECOLONIZING EFFORTS AT STANDING ROCK

The Standing Rock Sioux tribe's and other indigenous tribal groups' efforts in 2016 and 2017 attempted to stop the Dakota Access Pipeline (DAPL) being routed through tribal properties. The construction and subsequent operation of the pipeline risked an oil spill on tribal water, treaty fishing, and hunting rights. The protests were an example of a decolonizing effort to stop big business and prominent political forces from imposing their financial interests on indigenous land and water rights and environmental protection. The protest is reported to have been the largest gathering of Native Tribes in the past 100 years (Northcott, 2016). It was reported that there were over 300 federally recognized Native American tribes and an estimated 3,000 to 6,000 pipeline resistance supporters participating in the protest (Medina, 2016). More than 9.2 million United States citizens signed the petition against DAPL. This protest against DAPL was more than just a protest about an oil pipeline. It was emblematic of an indigenous effort in cultural preservation and spiritual resistance. On February 7, 2017, president Trump authorized the Army Corps of Engineers to proceed with the pipeline construction, effectively closing down the environmental impact assessment reports and finally disbanding the remaining protestors.

It can be argued that colonizing forces now take on new and more sophisticated forms, and this process is now not so much about occupying land as about economic control held by multinational corporations and international banking systems. These continue to actively produce both privilege and poverty in systematic ways around the globe, with much the same effect as previous practices of colonization. For accounts of these modern practices of what has been called neocolonialism, look at the work of Noam Chomsky (2003), Arundhati Roy (2004), and John Perkins (2004).

This shift of general discourse against colonizing practice has, however, produced a strong counter theme of decolonization that has sought expression in numerous ways in different parts of the world. In later chapters we shall explore this discourse of decolonization and some of the expressions it has taken. We shall also relate these to the worlds of counseling and education in order to show that it has had an effect in the lives of ordinary people in many places.

Despite the development of an anticolonization discourse, however, it is important to remember that the effects of the processes of colonization are still being worked out. They are still pervasive in the assumptions of "culture," as we outlined in Chapter 2. And they continue to have material effects in people's lives, constructing their lifestyles and constraining their life chances. We should not expect otherwise as long as we remember that shifts in discourse are not mere acts of personal willpower.

We all must live in a world that is still shaped by the era of colonization in many ways. Its assumptions are woven into our language, our political rhetoric, our academic and social science concepts, and our identity categories. Kawagley (1995) captures the impact of colonizing discourse and the blistering effects of Western institutionalized cultural transmission on indigenous peoples in which they continue to be forced to live in "a psychic world not of their making."

As we conclude this chapter, we hope we have made it clear why a review of colonization is important to the practice of counseling. These practices of colonization can be recapitulated by counselors in the practice of counseling if we are not careful. Specifically, counselors must be acutely aware of how the very counseling theories they adopt may embody certain colonizing legacies constructed upon a Eurocentric vision, as discussed in Chapter 2. Counselors must guard against using a solely intrapsychic focus in evaluating and intervening in people's lives when their clients have been victimized by cultural trauma produced by colonizing forces. It is also important to acknowledge that some personal traumas have been caused by the dislocation or destruction of kinship and familial support systems.

Some of this fragmentation is relatively recent, given the welfare policies in the United States, Canada, and Australia, where the federal government, even until the 1960s, promoted the policy of removing Indian and Aboriginal children from their parents and placing them in boarding schools to better socialize them to a Eurocentric lifestyle. Many people continue to suffer from the ongoing social and psychological dismemberment of their familial systems. There are many more psychological effects produced by colonization inequitably affecting those who are the benefactors of colonization and those that have suffered because of it. On the other hand, counselors can exercise the choice to apply counseling theories and practices that explicitly support the resilience and courage exhibited by individuals, families, and communities who have suffered the full negative effects of colonization and who have not only survived but have even restored their communities in the face of the demeaning impact of Western ideologies. When counselors appreciate fully the extent to which their clients' experiences are produced within a particular sociocultural and historical context, they are in a better position to intervene in culturally respectful ways.

Response to Chapter 3

CAROL ROBINSON-ZAÑARTU, PHD

Carol Robinson-Zañartu is an emeritus professor of the Department of Counseling and School Psychology at San Diego State University, and director of the Native American Scholars and Collaborators Projects. An educator and psychologist concerned about social justice, her primary professional affiliation is school psychology. She is Scotch-English by ancestry, has raised two bicultural (Chilean American) children, and has been mentored by numerous indigenous teachers. Her research and scholarly activities focus on issues of social justice, especially Native American issues, systemic approaches to change in education, and dynamic intervention-based assessment.

I have come to believe that to treat or even to claim to educate indigenous peoples and others whose lives have been shaped by the profound implications of colonization and historical trauma without grasping more than a brief history of colonization and its implications is truly unethical. Thus, the authors of this chapter provide a much-needed introduction to some of the concepts and consequences of colonization, its historical antecedents, and current attempts to address these issues. This chapter should whet the appetites of mental health and educational professionals for more in-depth treatment of both the theory and practical implications of colonization and decolonization (see, for instance, Battiste, 2000; Cajete, 2015; Cleary & Peacock, 1998; Duran, 2006; Smith, 2001).

The effects of colonization for many indigenous peoples reflect the inseparability in world view of the physical (land/body), the psychological (mind), the spiritual (spirit), and the emotional (heart). For instance, the land base is central to many creation stories, and when it is defiled or stolen, a profound spiritual hurt is coupled with emotional and psychological consequences. For many indigenous peoples, colonization and attempts at cultural genocide, in acts ranging from the forced removal of children to brutal murders of the innocent, the breaking of treaties, seizure and defilement of sacred lands, and degrading government policies designed to remove all vestiges of culture, resulted in traumas that have been passed from generation to generation. Not unlike some of the effects described in the literature on posttraumatic stress disorder, neurological, behavioral, and emotional symptoms, such as acting out against peers, underperformance, depression, alcoholism, lack of focus, and executive function difficulties, may be displayed by survivors of historical trauma, who can well be the hidden victims of traumas gone unrecognized, untreated, and unresolved.

Adult survivors demonstrate additional and often debilitating mental and physical health issues which have been directly linked to trauma exposure (cf. Felitti et al., 1998). Many of the youth are mistakenly identified as incorrigible, unmotivated, or just "bad kids." Too many school and community counselors, psychologists, social workers, family therapists, and teachers are unaware of the complex dynamics of traumatic stress, and thus misdiagnose, mis-place in education settings, and miss the opportunity to intervene.

Therefore, we must take care not to name such behaviors as typical characteristics of people from indigenous or colonized cultures, but must instead consider the possibility that we are seeing the effects of colonization. Eduardo Duran (2006) discusses this intergenerational effect of the attempts to conquer land, heart, mind, and spirit as a "soul wound." Healing that soul wound at the individual and collective levels requires some depth of understanding, not only of the antecedent actions but also of the traditions that guide healing within the appropriate culture. Because decolonizing goes beyond voice and reflects the reclaiming of a cultural lens, cultural identity, and world view, individuals and communities will begin to provide new perspectives, new social structures, new ethics, new actions, and new demands as outcomes of decolonizing work. Counselors and therapists can also begin to work more effectively from strength-based or resilience models, recognizing the assets of the cultural world views and histories from which these populations come, and using those to support the alternative narratives.

I have been privileged to participate in projects with Filipino, African American, Japanese American, Puerto Rican, and Mexican American people engaged in decolonizing work, as well as with individuals from the Hopi, Pomo, Tohono O'odham, Zuni, Cree, Yaqui, Creek, Choctaw, Seminole, Caddo, and Diné (Navajo) nations. As the histories vary, so does the work. For instance, Jennifer Gorospe (2007) confronted such issues as high depression rates among Filipino Americans, a passive response of some families linked to their belief in bahala na ("come what may"), and "the resignation of a people to a history of repeated colonization." This decolonizing work has been a path marked at times by tears, anger, and argument, as well as empowerment, voice, and the emergence of compelling perspectives and ideas.

Certain phrases will linger with me for many years: Why didn't they tell us this? This makes me struggle with everything I believed was the truth! I have such a newfound respect for my grandparents. I want to know my history. I am proud of who I am! Traversing the annals of an alternative view of history, my graduate students have grappled with information on colonization and the depths of a new reality. Their work will transform future generations, and has also been said to help heal the wounds for former generations.

Those of us typically empowered by the mainstream system must learn this well enough not to recolonize unawarely through such patronizing actions as "giving" to the disenfranchised a place at "our table" with expectations that "they" will now become leaders, thinkers, and writers "like us" with stronger voices than before. Rather, we must be prepared to have our knowledge bases and perspectives augmented as we become learners, collaborators, and followers. We must do our own decolonizing work, letting go of the entitlement that has become a historical legacy of the colonizer mentality.

Discuss

1. Think about your own family histories. How have they been shaped and affected by the history of colonization and decolonization? Share stories of what you know.
2. How have these histories shaped your own life, your own social location, your own values, your own commitments?
3. As you think about these histories, what difference do they make to the work you are doing, or would like to do, as a counselor, psychologist, social worker, or other professional?
4. Do an online search for statements in the public discourse that support colonization or that support decolonization.
5. What are some examples you can identify of the current ongoing psychological effects of colonization?
6. What are some examples you can find of inspiring stories of resistance and resilience in the face of colonizing practices?
7. Read modern newspapers and find traces of assumptions about the moral inferiority of colonized groups that still persist.
8. What are the most useful roles that counselors, psychologists, and social workers (or other professionals) can play when faced with the effects of colonization?
9. What are some strategies that you know of that would assist in this work?

Race, Ethnicity, and Identity

Race has played a dominant role in shaping contemporary life throughout the world. The history of race and its role in European colonization has powerfully shaped, and continues to shape, how we perceive ourselves and others in relation to particular defining physical features. (We discuss further the connection between race and colonization in Chapter 14.) Racial categorization has meant for some groups continuous and systematic unearned access to opportunity in important aspects of day-to-day life. These opportunities lead to quality housing, education, healthcare, political authority, and overall psychological well-being. For less-favored racial groups, racial categorization produces systematic denial of opportunity and access to quality essential services.

Access to societal resources, or the denial of access to them, has a profound influence on people's quality of life. It also impacts on what can be accomplished within a counseling and therapeutic process. For example, if a client has privileged access to opportunity and resources, it is easy for a counselor to confront him about taking responsibility for his own choices in life. After all, if systematic advantages are in your favor, it is more plausible to argue that what holds you back in living a satisfying life is what you as an individual make of those circumstances. When those same choices are systematically denied to people along racial lines, such confrontation can have a much more negative impact. In fact, a counselor's insistence on individual personal responsibility may make experiences of frustration and depression in the face of difficult circumstances considerably worse. In a counseling or therapeutic relationship, the issue of race tends to be most salient when the therapist is perceived to be from a more privileged racial background than the client. We will discuss the significance of this issue in counseling in this chapter. Without constant awareness of these themes, they can negatively impact both the counseling relationship and the value of the therapy.

Our dreams, aspirations, long- and short-term goals, passions, attractions, loves, and losses are all experienced through multiple ethnic memberships and racial categorizations. Many of our meaning-making functions are constructed within ethnic history and ethnic membership. Often, our successes and troubles are understood through an ethnic lens. Many counselor and therapeutic exchanges occur within the context of multiple ethnic understandings and misunderstandings.

Race as a Defining Domain

Let us begin with the subject of race. We shall explore the implications of this historical and contemporary cultural formation on the practice and delivery of intercultural counseling in the United States and elsewhere. Like the concept of culture, the concept of race has evolved in particular historical contexts, and it cannot be understood without investigating those contexts. Like the concept of culture, race is not a stable concept. What we mean by it now is not what it has always meant.

British and European colonization is implicated in the ongoing discursive legacy embodied in the concept of "race." The very use of this word carries with it the idea that there are biological differences among groups of people that can be used as markers for organizing our perceptions of and attitudes toward each other. This idea of distinct, biological differences among peoples, usually with a special focus on skin color, is intimately associated with British and European colonizing discourse.

A race is generally defined as a human group distinguished by common phenotypical characteristics that are held to be natural and genetic in origin. The modern notion of race, constructed around biological differences, has its origins in pseudoscience, popular culture, and history, rather than in any scientific evidence that is recognized as valid today. There have been many attempts to develop a scientific account that incorporates the concept of race. There is general scientific consensus that these attempts all lack credibility when examined closely. However, the concept of race is so deeply entwined in contemporary consciousness that it is not possible to avoid discussing it. Everyone thinks she knows what race means. Yet it remains a problematic concept. We shall investigate the concept a little by asking some questions about it.

What Is the Genealogy of the Term *Race*?

The term *race* first appeared in the English language about 300 years ago (Smedley & Smedley, 2005). The notion of race originated from the French language, meaning breed or lineage as defined by physical markers. The markers include skin color, facial and bodily features, and hair type. Categories of persons were invented based on these physical markers. We shall argue here that there is no inherent meaning in these categories. The meanings were simply devised by members of the English aristocracy who were in the position to do so.

The genealogy of the term *race* as we know it can be traced back to the period when Europeans began to develop extended contact with non-Europeans (through their colonization). In the late-15th and early-16th century, Europeans started expanding beyond their national horizons in search of wealth and conquest. Noting how others in the faraway lands they visited were different from themselves, they determined that these differences were indicators of some fundamental difference in the nature of human beings. It was a small step for early European explorers to conclude that, since the indigenous peoples of these continents did not have technological developments equal to those of the Europeans, they must be either an inferior kind of human being or, in Franz Fanon's (1952) terms, beings with nonexistent humanity. Usually, they assumed that Europeans were in sole possession of the attributes of "civilization" and frequently referred to other peoples as "savages." Savages, by the logic of the time, did not need to be accorded the same rights and respect as civilized human beings (Huntington, 2004).

As the Enlightenment scientific project developed, one of its major aims in the field of biological study was to document, classify, and categorize all species of plant and animal life on earth. The categorization of types (genus types, species types, subspecies types) through the analysis of characteristics was the dominant scientific emphasis. The analogy of species "type" was readily extended by the European mind, with its assumptions of superiority and manifest destiny, from animal species to human beings who looked different. The concept of the "human race" is actually an older concept than the modern term *race*, which refers to human beings of different physical characteristics. It was the application of the idea that the people the colonizers encountered were not fully human that led to the development of the idea of racial type and therefore the modern concept of race. There were many efforts to categorize racial types according to "phenotypic characteristics," to measure the skulls and brain sizes of people of different "races" in much the same way that the skeletons and skulls of extinct animals were investigated.

Racial discourse of the time assumed that differences among races related to fundamentally different types of blood, a concept that persists in both popular and official discourse through the descriptions of people of color (but not White people) as "full blooded," "half blooded," and so forth. The science of racial types has long since been discredited, and modern geneticists have replaced the idea of blood type with the idea of populations that share a genetic stock (Lévi-Strauss, 2001). Still, the idea of inherent biological differences of different races has lingered.

As Darwinian ideas about evolution became popular in the 19th century, the assumption of "advanced" and "more highly evolved" races took hold. Although it bore little relation to Darwin's biological project, social Darwinism created an analogue that was readily adopted by Europeans already bent on establishing positions of power over the people who inhabited the lands they wanted to conquer. The concept of superior and inferior races was a welcome intellectual tool that could serve to rationalize and justify the treatment of colonized races as less than fully human. If it had scientific backing, then it had even more authority. It eased the European conscience with regard to moral questions about the treatment of non-White people, making it possible to regard them as children to be ruled over for their own good and punished when they were naughty. After all, "they" were not like "us." Their inferior minds meant that they were not really fit to govern themselves.

You can still hear traces of this logic when people talk about the reasons that some countries in Africa and Asia struggle with political turmoil. After all, goes the racial logic, "they" cannot be expected to have the minds that would appreciate democratic and peaceful social systems. It's just not part of their mind-set, meaning their natural mental capacity. The concept of race was deployed to make it seem normal that White people, by their very nature, are superior and deserve to be rulers, and that people of color are naturally inferior and deserve to be ruled. The concept of race thus served as a justification for policies of colonizing conquest and economic exploitation and for practices of enslavement and even genocidal extermination.

The whole idea of the existence of race needs to be understood first and foremost as a construction of European colonizing discourse. It is a modern construct and has not always been around, as some people assume. It is more correct to say that the concept of race has become naturalized in our understandings than it is to call it a description of a natural phenomenon. In the story of European colonization, Europeans created the notion of distinct and identifiable races and by some definitions created categories of subhumans or nonhumans. In the first English settler communities on North American soil, begun in 1607, 1620, and 1630, contact between the English and the indigenous peoples of North America was generally cooperative (Huntington, 2004). However, relations deteriorated in response to settlers' expanding demands for land. Indians developed justified fears that prospects of coexistence were being replaced by the prospect of domination. The result was a long and bloody engagement between settler and Indian.

By the 1660s, European Americans had categorized Native Americans as a race of people who were backward, savage, and uncivilized. In the early-19th century, President Andrew Jackson persuaded Congress to pass the Indian Removal Act, and principal tribes in six Southern states were forcibly moved west of the Mississippi in a process that would be described as ethnic or racial cleansing today (Huntington, 2004). At the same time that Indians were being taken from their homeland and killed in devastating numbers, Africans were being imported and enslaved until the cessation of the slave trade in 1808. According to Samuel Huntington (2004), the founding fathers required high levels of racial, ethnic, and religious homogeneity. At the time of the first naturalization statute in 1790, when citizenship was made available to "free White persons," the first U.S. attorney general, Edmund Randolph, stated that Black people were not "constituent members of our society." At this time there was a total U.S. population of 3,929,000, of whom 698,000 were slaves (Huntington, 2004, p. 54).

Thomas Jefferson, along with other political and religious figures of the day, while stating that Whites and Blacks were "equally free," also stated that they could not "live in the same government." During President Jefferson's term of office, the country of Liberia was created in Africa so that all the Blacks brought as slaves to North America could be transported back to the continent from which they had been captured and enslaved. Between 11,000 and 15,000 Black people were transported there. Abraham Lincoln wanted all Black people to migrate to Africa (Huntington, 2004).

Similar forms of oppression and marginalization were suffered by early Chinese immigrants to the United States. The Chinese were also perceived by the Anglo Americans to be an inferior race. In 1875, after a wave of Chinese workers came into the country to help build the railroads after the Civil War, the first laws restricting Chinese immigrants from entering the country were enacted. In 1882, the Chinese Exclusion Act was implemented, with Justice Stephen J. Field defending this new law on grounds that "Chinese were of a different race, and it seems impossible for them to assimilate." If their migration were not restricted, he said, it would lead to an "oriental invasion [that] would constitute a menace to our civilization." (Huntington, 2004, p. 56). This legal barrier to Chinese immigrants entering the United States was lifted only in 1952.

Even as the European empires as political entities began to break up during the 20th century, the idea that Whites could be deemed innately superior to non-Whites has persisted. In North America, by the early-19th century, the concept of race was playing an increasingly important role in scientific, intellectual, and popular thinking among White Americans. Reginald Horsman (1981) suggested that by the middle of the century the "inherent inequality of races was simply accepted as a scientific fact in America" (p. 134).

From the 19th century to recent times, it was widely believed that humans are divided hierarchically into four major races, with the Caucasian at the apex of the hierarchy followed by, in descending order, the Mongolian, the Indian, and the African. A further differentiation among some Caucasians placed Anglo-Saxon descendants of Germanic tribes at the top (Huntington, 2004). Madison Grant, president of the American Zoological Society and a trustee of the American Museum of Natural History, wrote a bestselling book in the 1920s in which he said,

> Neither the black, nor the brown, nor the yellow, nor the red will conquer the white in
> battle. But if the valuable elements in the Nordic race mix with inferior strains or die

out through race suicide, then the citadel of civilization will fall for mere lack of defenders. (Grant, 1921, p. xxxi)

This confident assumption of the superiority of the "Nordic race," referring to those whose ancestry can be traced to northern Europe, along with the assumption of the importance of preserving racial "purity," was later taken up by Adolf Hitler and the Nazi party and pushed to grisly extremes. This same concept of race buttressed White America's comfortable position of assumed superiority. It further legitimated the conquering and ruling of Mexican Indians and numerous other groups. In addition, the hierarchical categorization of people as belonging to particular races based on some innate characteristics served to maintain the racial purity of a White society.

During the 20th century, the concept of race continued to remain important. In the first half of the century, the eugenics movement gained considerable sway. It was popularized in books that sold widely, but it also developed substantial respectability in academic circles and was taught to a generation of students of education and psychology. Eugenics was founded on the assumption of the prime importance of genetic inheritance and concern about the "contamination" of the "race" (meaning the human race) by people with "weak" genes. It was closely linked with the idea that those born of an "inferior" race were to be automatically considered a burden on society. In other words, eugenics was closely intertwined with racist thinking.

What is important for modern students of counseling and psychology to realize is that the people who popularized eugenics in the early part of the 20th century were not extremists or crackpots. They were centrally placed in the psychological sciences and in education (Selden, 1999). They include names that we know today as founders of many branches of study. For example, Francis Galton coined the name *eugenics* and was honored by the Galton Society (which existed to promote eugenics). His work was foundational in starting what we know today as the study of human development. Other eugenicists include G. Stanley Hall (the originator of the child study), Charles Spearman (known still for his method of calculating correlational statistics), Lewis Terman (the early developer of intelligence tests), and Leta Hollingworth (who launched academic interest in the study of gifted children). Theodore Roosevelt was an enthusiastic supporter of eugenics, and it was the basis of several immigration laws passed by Congress.

The point is that the assumption of the primacy of certain hereditary factors, including race, and the ready assumption of a hierarchy of races were commonplace features of citizens in the U.S. thinking during the first half of the 20th century.

Are There Biological Differences Among Different "Races"?

There has, in fact, been little agreement about the nature and number of human races. If there were clear biological differences, we might expect to find greater agreement about what these differences are. Any contemporary scientific study that attempts to tie down the distinguishing biological differences among racial categories of human beings has been doomed to failure. With the completion of the human genome project, in which the genetic makeup of the human being was mapped, there is yet further evidence of the difficulty of drawing genetic or biological distinctions among groups of human beings that could be said to be racial differences. In fact, in genetic terms, the human being shares 92%

of his genetic structure with the fruit fly and 99% of the same genetic makeup as the chimpanzee. As discussed in Chapter 1, genetic differences between any two people in the world is infinitesimal. In fact, as critical race theorist Ian Haney Lopez (2000) states,

> There are no genetic characteristics possessed by all Blacks but not by non-Blacks; similarly, there is no gene or cluster of genes common to all Whites but not to non-Whites. … Greater genetic variation exists within the populations typically labeled Black and White than between these populations. (p. 166)

Modern genetic science, therefore, does not support the existence of race as a biological category. Scientists and scholars over the last few hundred years have nevertheless attempted to categorize and class groups of people on some kind of biological basis. Agreement among scholars is hard to find, even on the names of different races (Atkinson, Morten, & Sue, 1993), let alone on just what the biological differences among them are.

> Linnaeus had found four human races; Blumenbach had five; Cuvier had three; John Hunter had seven; Burke had sixty-three; Pickering had eleven; Virey had two "species," each containing three races; Haeckel had thirty-six; Huxley had four; Topinard had nineteen under three headings; Desmoulins had sixteen "species"; Deniker had seventeen races and thirty types. (Gossett, 1963, p. 82)

Over the last thousand years, there has been even greater variation in human characteristics such as blood type, hair texture, skin color, and body type than there was in previous times. There is dramatic variation in physical characteristics within so-called racial groups. As we have suggested, the genetic variation is so tiny between persons that it can be greater among individuals within a racial group than it is between individuals belonging to different racial groups (Atkinson et al., 1993; Cornell & Hartmann, 1998; Ferrante & Brown, Jr., 2001; McAullife, 2019; Ponterotto & Pedersen, 1993; Ratts & Pedersen, 2014).

The problem with racial categorization is that an unfounded biological argument has served as the basis for political, social, and economic hierarchies to organize the nature of how the world is understood and simultaneously deny large portions of humanity accessibility to human rights. These are assumptions with no scientific basis at all; yet, even if science was a defining factor and evidence could be demonstrated, the problem is the racialization of identity and its categorization. Efforts to distinguish and then categorize differences among human beings based on biological makeup are, in fact, founded on the European colonizing discourse of White superiority rather than on empirical biological data. The adoption of scientific means for the "production" of Eurocentric truths, here to define different races, was directed toward legitimating the dominant discourse of the day. The idea of systematic, inherited, distinct biological differences just cannot be made to hold up. Janet Helms (1994) calls it "irrational" (p. 295). Historian Barbara Fields has summed up the current scientific consensus on race in this way:

> Anyone who continues to believe in race as a physical attribute of individuals, despite the now commonplace disclaimers of biologists and geneticists, might as well also

believe that Santa Claus, the Easter Bunny and the tooth fairy are real, and that the earth stands still while the sun moves. (cited by Lopez, 2000, p. 167)

And yet the biological concept of race, scientifically flimsy as it is, continues to persist. Not only do notions of race continue to be alive and well in our communities, but the factor of race is intimately involved in shaping the relationship between client and counselor. For instance, some multiculturalists advocate racial matching between client and counselor to maximize cultural empathy between the two. There are significant issues of trust that arise on the foundation of racial difference that need to be worked through for effective counseling to occur. A Black client may have significant concerns about trusting a White therapist because of the historical legacy of European colonization that we have described. Therefore, if race is not a biological category, we need to focus more on the social process of categorization. Alternatively, a Black therapist may have to gird themselves in managing dynamics with White clients when the pervasiveness of racism can impact any interaction.

What Has Been the Social Function of the Term *Race*?

Whether or not the concept of race corresponds with any real biological differences other than at the level of the epidermis, we know that it has real effects through its social consequences. It is in practice a sociopolitical construct rather than a biological one (Ferrante & Brown, Jr., 2001; Helms & Cook, 2007). Race has served as a major dividing tool among people throughout most of the colonized world. Ascriptions of race have been used to mark people out for entry into privileged opportunity or to limit their access to such opportunity. On the basis of racial divisions, the social practices of discrimination have been, and in many instances continue to be, legitimated.

As discussed in Chapter 1, race is not the only dividing tool, however. There are other dividing lines based on religion, language, social class, and gender, for example. In some contexts, race is not even the most salient dividing line. Northern Ireland is an example. It is a territory colonized about 400 years ago by the English, and the division between the colonizers and the colonized has been marked on the basis of the Catholic/Protestant religious divide more than on a concept of race. The point is that, while race has frequently been marked out as the basis for social division in ways that lead to oppressive practices, it has not been the only basis. Within England itself, although dividing practices built on race are of growing importance, markers of social class, such as accent, have been traditionally more strongly employed in the dividing practices that exclude groups of people from access to opportunity.

Throughout the Americas, Africa, Asia, and the Pacific, however, race has usually served as the prime marker for social division. Despite efforts to promote greater equality, racial markers remain in our consciousness. It remains a salient category of thought in our daily lives—for example, in the forms that we fill out for a hundred purposes. Try to fill out the form in Box 4.1 and discuss its implications.

Skin color and other physical characteristics get selected out and tend to obscure an emphasis on cultural distinctions because of race's assumed biological authority. But how are race categories decided upon? The physiological differences that serve as racial markers change according to which cultural constructions are dominant. Defining the boundary between one race and another is more complicated than most people think. In fact, there are no consistent differences among racial groupings. People whose physical characteristics are at the borders or margins of the group are often made into new races.

BOX 4.1   PLEASE FILL OUT THIS FORM

Name:

Gender:
- ☐ Male
- ☐ Female

Age:
- ☐ 0–15 years
- ☐ 15–25 years
- ☐ 25–35 years
- ☐ 35–45 years
- ☐ 45–55 years
- ☐ over 55 years

Race (choose one):
- ☐ Caucasian
- ☐ African American
- ☐ Hispanic
- ☐ Asian or Pacific Islander
- ☐ Native American

Nationality (choose one):
- ☐ American citizen
- ☐ Foreign-born U.S. resident
- ☐ Legal alien

Ethnicity (choose one):
- ☐ European
- ☐ Latino
- ☐ African American
- ☐ Native American
- ☐ Jewish
- ☐ Arab
- ☐ East Indian
- ☐ Chinese
- ☐ Japanese
- ☐ Other (please specify):

Income (Estimate your yearly household income. Include your spouse's income.):
- ☐ $0–$15,000
- ☐ $15,000–$25,000
- ☐ $25,000–$40,000
- ☐ $40,000–$60,000
- ☐ $60,000–$80,000

- ☐ $80,000–$100,000
- ☐ Over $100,000

Discuss

1. What was your internal experience while filling out this form? What internal debates did you have to settle in order to choose an answer? What difficulties did you encounter?
2. At which points did you find yourself making a forced choice?
3. What aspects of your experience of life or identity were excluded from visibility through the construction of this form?
4. Who else can you think of whose preferred identities might not fit with the identity categories listed in this form?
5. Speculate on the reasons that the categories used on this form are there. What perspective do they represent?
6. In what sense might data collected from this form be objective or not objective?
7. Where have you been asked to fill out forms like this? What experiences have you had in doing so?

BOX 4.2   MICROAGGRESSIONS

The term *microaggressions* was developed to describe everyday slights, insults, or indignities that may be casually and briefly delivered but which add up to the denigration of people for their membership of a group. It was first used by a psychiatry professor at Harvard University, Chester M. Pierce, in 1970. Microaggressions may happen below the awareness of those who use them and they are different from outright bigoted statements or hate speech. They are more subtle and yet they cause harm by reinforcing stereotypes.

Originally, the concept was used to describe the put-downs that were constantly given to African Americans, but it has by extension been applied to other racial groups and to those who are marginalized by other forms of social discrimination, such as the poor, women, the sexually diverse, or the disabled.

Microaggressions are frequently unintentional, may appear banal or trivial and may be vigorously denied by those who utter them. They feel offended by the idea that what they say may be experienced as an expression of racism, for example, by others. Moreover, those on the receiving end may struggle to identify exactly what they are affected by. As a result the targets of microaggressions are frequently called over-sensitive or paranoid. Yet the effects have been shown to be sometimes more intense than outright hate speech, which may be more easily dismissed.

In the terms advocated in this book, microaggressions may amount to the assumptions of a discourse of superiority. They position people who have become targets in a place of inferiority, abnormality, or exclusion. Typical microaggressions are insulting or invalidating. For example, the experience of being watched closely in a department store may unsettle African American shoppers. Like other microaggressions, it may undermine the sense of well-being of the target, create a hostile environment, and perpetuate stereotypes.

We might expect the official discourse of government to be more stable, but even here the categories and boundaries are constantly being revised. In 1970, the United States government listed five races in the United States: "White, Colored (Blacks), Colored (Mulattoes), Chinese and Indian. … In 1950, the census categories reflected a different social understanding: White, Black, and other" (Spickard, 1992, p. 18). In the 1990s, federal programs, responding to challenges from groups having nothing to do with biological theory, required various community structures to report racial data in five categories again, although by now they had changed the categories to White, Black, Asian, Hispanic, and Indian (Cornell & Hartmann, 1998).

The Hispanic category arose only as a result of political developments, and has been used to include people of many different nationalities, ethnicities, and cultural traditions, without any consistent physical or linguistic markers (Birman, 1994). However, it is still primarily focused on immigrants to the United States from Mexico. In the early 1800s, Mexican people were variously categorized as White, Indian, Black, or Asian (Lopez, 2000). When Mexico gained independence in 1821, its citizens were not thought of as a race. As the Anglo-Mexican battles over territory intensified in the 19th century, Mexicans were considered a mixed race (a mixture of White and Indian "blood") and later were explicitly designated as a distinct race (Hispanic) in their own right. Many people who are now classified racially as Hispanic share physical characteristics that are indistinguishable from those classified as White (Cornell & Hartmann, 1998).

The category of Asian is in fact such a catchall that there are no physical features that apply to all people whose ancestry hails from places like Iran, India, China, and Japan. Pacific Islanders are lumped in with Asians despite the vast differences between people from China and people from Polynesia. The determination of which characteristics constitute race is of course a selection of physical characteristics chosen to be salient at a particular point in history. But the determination of salience is not predetermined by biological factors. The categories appear to change not so much in response to the characteristics of the people they categorize as in response to the dominant discourse of the day.

Associated with the concept of race is the concept of "blood," which originated in the completely fallacious idea that racial differences are the product of differences in the blood that courses through the veins of people. This hypothesis has long since been dropped, but the metaphor remains in usages like "full blooded," "half blooded," and so forth. It has even been used in the United States Supreme Court as recently as 1991. In that year, Justice Antonin Scalia rejected a claim in favor of minority broadcasting licenses by charging that the policy "reduced to a matter of blood … blood not background and environment" (cited by Lopez, 2000, p. 168).

"Blood" is still used to describe interracial progeny. Seyla Benhabib (2002) points out, however, that it has been used differentially in the United States. The idea of "mixed blood" is little used in reference to people whose ancestors all had the same skin color. Ask yourself if you have ever heard of a person whose parents were, say, Anglo and German, being thought of as half blooded. But the minute the Black/White skin divide is crossed, the concept seems to come into play. Historically, the "one drop of blood" rule meant that a person was defined as African American or Native American if she had one ancestor among eight who qualified, even if all her other ancestors were White (Helms, 1994). But the reverse did not apply. One drop of White blood did not qualify a person as White.

Here are two examples showing racial categories to be historical social constructions. Virginia Dominguez (1986) describes a well-known case in which a Louisiana woman went to court to dispute the state's conclusion that she was Black. She claimed her ancestry was White. The state's argument was that her ancestry was at least 1/32 "Negro," which, according to state law, meant she was Black. This woman lost her case because of the one-drop rule (Davis, 1991). These rules have a history. They emerge in particular historical contexts—in this case, the history of slavery in the United States. It is interesting to reflect on the notion that being 1/32 Dutch, Irish, or Japanese does not mean belonging to that grouping, but one drop of Black blood has long been considered sufficient for racial categorization. Since the era of the Civil Rights Movement in the United States, many individuals with "1/32 Black blood" proudly identify as Black (Cornell & Hartmann, 1998). However, such people are often queried about their membership in this category, because they are perceived by others who have darker skin pigmentation to benefit from a lighter skin and are thus deemed to not really know or feel the systemic effects of oppression felt by darker-skinned people. Racial categories change over time as they are revised, contested, interpreted, and reinterpreted.

Societies such as the United States pour substantial resources into policing the boundaries of racial groupings, and the outcomes of classification have significant consequences for the individuals involved. An illustration of this occurred in 1922, when Takao Ozawa applied for United States citizenship (Lopez, 2000). In accordance with the Naturalization Act, he asserted that he was White because, born in the northern part of Japan, his skin was as White as most Europeans'. The Supreme Court rejected his claim and in their ruling stated that race could not be defined by "mere color of the skin" (p. 167); otherwise, it would have to exclude from the category of White many Europeans of swarthy complexion. Even the common assumption of skin color as a racial designator can be set aside when it suits the purposes of governing authorities. This paradox (that skin color is sometimes and sometimes not the primary indicator of one's race) gets played out increasingly in our contemporary, globalized world. In our classrooms, we frequently hear conversations and debates about the supposed legitimacy of a person's self-proclaimed race. Consider, for example, the student who is challenged about the amount of "Blackness" he possesses, given his biracial genealogy and light skin.

Brazil, because of greater intermarriage among different peoples with different physical characteristics, has officially given up on the notion of distinct races. Overlapping categories have been established that recognize the various mixtures, usually based on a person's appearance but relating to skin color from lightest to darkest. However, the legacy of European colonization continues to play a prominent role in Western society, promoting the definition of the relative merits of a people's status based on how close their skin pigment is to White. Think of all the television shows broadcast from Latin American countries where the popular television characters are almost always very light skinned and the maids and servants are typically darker skinned.

Racial categories are always relational (Lopez, 2000). They exist only as points of distinction from other races. The category Black relies on the assumption of what *White* means in order to make sense, and vice versa. These categories of difference were originally produced in relation to the politics of conquest, colonization, and subjugation. As these politics have shifted and changed and new forms of distinction have become required for the purpose of ongoing subjugation, the racial categories have shifted and changed with them.

Henderikus Stam (1998) states that Brazil's complicated racial categories based on skin pigment do not match other racial typologies. Francis Deng (1997) points out how the South African apartheid system's *Black, White*, and *colored* categories were different from those of other colonizing classification systems. Koreans and Japanese regard each other as belonging to different races, even though these two peoples are perceived by outsiders to have similar phenotypic characteristics. Within Brazil, the socioeconomic status of an individual frequently affects her racial category.

It is heartening to see that some geneticists consider race to be culturally determined. James King (1981) comments that, within the British colonial framework, skin color, hair type, stature, facial structure, and other bodily features became physical markers that identified the limits of group boundaries. Categories were invented according to phenotype but appear to have no inherent meaning. They were endowed with particular cultural meanings that became the basis for how we conduct our relations with others, and in that sense they seemed to become real and true.

What Are the Effects of the Construction of Race?

Race is institutionalized into U.S. culture, and significant levels of human social interaction take place around race. In fact, race is a central organizing principle in most modern nations. The racial category *White* is a highly privileged status in most Western countries, while the racial category *Black* generally describes a less privileged status. The great German sociologist Max Weber, when he visited the United States in 1904, was struck by the intensity with which Black Americans, more than Native Americans, were objects to be despised (Stone, 2003).

As Stephen Cornell and Douglas Hartmann (1998) outline, "race has been first and foremost a way of describing others, of making clear that they are not us" (p. 27). The purpose is usually to create populations of people who can be governed and managed. Racial designation is always linked to practices of power. Michel Foucault (2000) identifies the designation of people into "populations" as a technological invention in the modern world to make the governing of people's lives easier. Racial categorization serves to distinguish "us" from "them." Mainstream cultural assumptions held by large groups of people do not like to allow movement across racial divides. For example, David Hollinger (1995) points out that "a Cambodian American does not have to remain Cambodian, as far as non-Asian Americans are concerned, but only with great difficulty can this person cease to be an Asian American" (p. 28).

The power that derives from racial categorizing can go both ways. Today, racial categories are used not only for oppressive purposes or to further the cause of a European colonizing agenda. Many state, federal, and private institutions in the United States track people by racial categories. Some of these institutions use racial dividing practices to identify when services are not being provided to specific racial groups and when the government is being successful in catering to a particular group's needs. For example, in education, authorities can track whether the educational needs of African American, Filipino, Latinx, and other groups of students are served in the public education system. When a group's needs are not being responded to, advocate groups can use statistics based on racial categorizations to point out to politicians and decision makers the failure of particular practices and campaign for increased resources. Statistics of this kind are used to track many issues in North American society. For example, statistics are gathered on specific racial groups in the domains of mental health, criminal justice, housing, and employment with a view toward resource allocation to promote equity and social justice.

In the last few years in California, many people from majority culture have wanted to change the way that California collects statistics and have promoted doing away with racial categories. The defenders of racial equity and social justice have come out in strong support for keeping racial categorizations intact, recognizing the leverage that can be gained to attract state, federal, and private resources. Advocates for policies of affirmative action in education and the workplace are dependent on the maintenance of racial categorization. These are examples of employing decolonizing moves to systematically undo the injustices perpetrated against groupings of people who have historically suffered the discriminating effects of European colonization.

In Native American communities that have access to casinos, tribal authorities carefully monitor blood ties to determine the level of access tribal members have to the significant financial resources produced by gambling. While these uses of the concept of race are aimed at helping people who are disadvantaged by the very distinctions that historically have been made on this basis, these processes of gathering and keeping statistics also help ensure that the categories of social division remain in place.

The History of White Identity in the United States

During the era of British colonization, colonizing groups created the justifying assumption that human groups are inherently different and that these differences constitute natural physical, moral, and religious hierarchies. Being at the top of the hierarchy legitimated using those at the bottom of the hierarchy as a resource to be exploited. Interwoven with hierarchy is the insidious and widely held belief that some races are inherently more intelligent than others, and that those at the bottom of the hierarchy have reached a lower stage of human evolution. All social groups, including those constructed by the identity "race," can make their own hierarchies. However, over the last 400 years, it has been White racial groups who have had the power in the United States to create racial categories that organize the institutions and social relations to which we are obliged to conform.

From a colonizing perspective, Whites generally represent what is normal while others are "them" and not "us." Ruth Frankenberg (1993) notes that "the White Western self as a racial being has for the most part remained unexamined and unnamed" (p. 17). That is why it is so common for students who come from an Anglo American heritage to report that they don't identify as belonging to a race or don't have a distinct culture. Whiteness conforms so much to the characteristics of dominant modern culture that it is difficult for Whites to distinguish their lives as belonging to a racial group or to have the words to name the way they live their lives as a culture. Failure to register Whiteness as a racial category is sometimes assumed to result from an individual lack of awareness, but we would argue that it is more a product of shared discourse than it is of individual consciousness. This point has implications for the intercultural counseling movement and those who advocate self-discovery and self-awareness as the foundation for multicultural competency. That is, there are real, material limits to how much self-understanding can be accomplished (and thus how much multicultural competency can be achieved) within the larger cultural background dominated by a narrow, privileged perspective.

There has been an interesting shift in what we could term the racialization of Whites (Cornell & Hartmann, 1998). In the United States, not only were non-White categories established, but the category *White* was assigned to certain persons. A distinct set of statuses followed. In the early history of the United States, English, Dutch, and a few others shared the White category. The Irish, Italians, and some Jews were not classified as White. In fact, the Irish, even though they had the same skin pigment as the English, were regarded as a distinctly inferior race. Michael Hechter (1975) quotes a Cambridge University historian's description of the Irish about 200 years ago:

> I am haunted by the human chimpanzees I saw. ... [To] see White chimpanzees is dreadful; if they were Black, one would not feel it so much, but their skins except where tanned by exposure, are as White as ours. (p. xvi)

At this time, the Irish were assigned to a non-White category. Heather's story of her family's early history clearly illustrates the attitudes of the time.

> *Growing up, I remember stories of the oppression that my descendants faced on their arrival in America [sic]. Dates and generations seem to have been lost; however, the oral tradition of our family's oppression still remains. When my ex-stepfather's Irish descendants stepped off the ship on which they had traveled over, they changed their surname to a slightly less Irish-sounding name—from McNeelis to McNellis. The reason my ancestors had to change their name was the oppression that Irish immigrants received in terms of employment in America [sic]. Although my ancestors looked much like the White Americans [sic] they encountered, they were singled out and discriminated against if they spoke with too thick an accent, or had a last name which sounded too "foreign." Immigrants were forced to assimilate as fast as possible, sometimes dropping all of their traditional values and customs as well as their last names, in order to make it in America [sic]. My ancestors shunned their cultures and assimilated to the American [sic] way of life to survive and flourish in America [sic].*

The Irish side of Sarah's family faced similar challenges.

> *My great, great grandfather was Black Irish Catholic. This meant that he had an olive skin tone and wavy Black hair. He therefore did not fit the mainstream European look. Coming to escape the potato famine, my Irish grandfather was not as welcome as my Scottish ancestors. A large part of this had to do with his being not only Irish, but Irish Catholic. Many Irish immigrants were forced to do jobs that Anglo Americans were not willing to do, like digging canals and working on the railroads. The strong Protestant beliefs in the United States meant that the Irish way of life was not warmly accepted. Having an Irish accent was difficult for immigrants from Ireland, especially since the Anglo population looked down on them.*
>
> *This was later to change. This example again shows the socially constructed nature of race and how categories can shift. In different periods in U.S. history, Whiteness has included some other groups who have, for a short period, been embraced as White and then shortly after been recast as non-White. Briefly, some Native Americans and later Latinx were included under a "White" umbrella.*

Is *Ethnicity* a Better Term Than *Race*?

Racial classification assumes that pure phenotypes exist. This premise cannot be proven, even if one accepts the conjecture that pure phenotypes existed at some point in history. Ethnicity, as we understand it in the modern world, is a much more recent term. It developed its current meanings around the middle of the 20th century through the work done by anthropologists. Originally a Greek term for Gentiles, it derives from the noun *ethnos*, meaning "foreign people." For many centuries, the term *ethnic* in English meant "heathen." The general consensus now is that ethnicity does not refer to physical characteristics as much as the term *race* does, although there is some overlap. Ethnicity is a group identity based on a common history, a shared set of cultural symbols (which usually means a shared language), and sometimes shared nationality, tribal affiliation, and religious faith. Its historical markers are more identifiable and tangible than those associated with race. Whereas racial groups are considered to be few, there are hundreds or thousands of possible ethnicities.

Max Weber defines ethnic groups as "human groups (other than kinship groups) which cherish a belief in their common origins of such a kind that it provides a basis for the formation of a community" (cited by Stone, 2003, p. 32).

Notice the emphasis here on what we might call discourse in this definition. Weber sidesteps an essentialist definition of ethnicity and privileges the role of *belief* in common origins, rather than the role of those origins themselves.

Like race, ethnic identity produces social boundaries that define how people distinguish themselves from others. The boundaries, however, are much more porous and complex. As with race, a particular ethnic membership has meaning only within a social context in which individuals can contrast themselves with others to produce a "them" and an "us." In the United States, many people use the word *ethnic* to describe a minority population that is different from the dominant culture. For instance, "ethnic foods" are non-European cuisine. The expression "That's really ethnic" is used to describe something unique or exotic and not found in European American middle-class culture.

However, ethnicity is not really encompassed by these colloquial uses. As a categorizing label, ethnicity is not tied as closely as race is to physical markers. A shared ethnicity is more of a fluid association and is less essentializing than the category of race. It is also not tied to the fallacious analogy of blood. Neither does it make any sense to calculate percentages of ethnicity. When communities generate their own categories on the basis of particular collective histories, they are engaged in the production of an ethnicity (Cornell & Hartmann, 1998).

Another distinction between race and ethnicity is which people have the power to name the categories. A shared ethnicity is not just assigned and defined by an outside group. Belonging is typically named and asserted by group members themselves on the basis of shared experiences. Over the last 300 years in the United States, it has been only Anglo American people who have assigned themselves the role of constructing racial categories for their own purposes. When categorizations that accompany race are invoked, assumptions about biological inferiority or superiority are immediately drawn. All ethnic groups are certainly capable of believing they are superior to others, but the reference point is not biological inferiority or superiority as it is with race. Thus, the moral force of the categories *ethnicity* and *race* operate at different degrees of magnitude. This is why, when a person of color utters a racial slur against another group, it might be racist but does not mean the same thing as it does when a White person utters it, since it does not have the force of the history of racial categorization behind it.

The anthropologist Ashley Montagu (1962) presents an argument for choosing to use the concept of ethnicity instead of the concept of race:

> The term "race" takes for granted what should be a matter for inquiry. And this is precisely the point that is raised when one uses the noncommittal "ethnic group." It encourages the passage from ignorant or confused certainty to thoughtful uncertainty. For the layman, as for others, the term "race" closes the door on understanding. The phrase "ethnic group" opens it, or at the very least, leaves it ajar. (p. 926)

While race is the fundamental organizing dimension in most of the colonized world, it is not so in all countries and continents. For example, in Belgium, ethnicity has overshadowed race as a basis for categorizing people. In Canada, French-speaking Quebec places greater weight on a French Canadian linguistically based ethnicity than it does on racial categorization. The concept of the Polynesian race refers to the genetic similarities of many people around the Pacific. But the ethnicity of these peoples is much more diverse and is divided into Hawaiian, Tongan, Samoan, Cook Islander, Tahitian, Maori, and the like (Cornell & Hartmann, 1998).

The terms *race* and *ethnicity* are not mutually exclusive. For example, many American Blacks have come to adopt both race and ethnicity to define themselves. They identify themselves as a distinct race by color and bodily features. While using a classification system devised by 16th-century Europeans, many Blacks have embraced the physical markers as defining characteristics of their group and are redefining race by attempting to remove it from its historical associations with inferiority and superiority. Many Blacks who are confronted with historical and day-to-day discrimination based on physical markers embrace these markers as points of shared oppression. Joining together around a history of shared oppression has provided a powerful impetus to build resilience and strength, as exemplified by the Black Lives Matter movement. In addition to identifying themselves as belonging to a race, many Blacks embrace a common ethnicity as a self-conscious population who share a homeland, a history dominated by slavery, a religion, and a language.

Categorizations based on physical markers continue to dominate the way our global society operates. Many Blacks and people of color continue to be systematically disadvantaged when it comes to jobs, social resources, and political sway. These factors have a huge impact on how problems for which people seek counseling are created. To not acknowledge the significance of race and ethnicity in shaping client problems and in raising important challenges for counselor effectiveness would be to neglect essential counseling dynamics. Most multicultural counseling texts comment on race and ethnicity as central domains to address when they suggest that counselors must be multiculturally competent.

The colonizing code that directs many Whites to treat Blacks and other people of color as inferior continues in covert and overt ways across the globe. Unfortunately, focusing on the construct of race, in our view, maintains essentializing and static categories and keeps our attention on physical markers as the primary site of dividing practices in a multicultural society. The problem with the construct of race for counselors is that it can seduce them into believing in stereotypical, unitary conceptions of who and what a White person is, who a Black person is, or who an Asian person is, and thus lead them into simplistic therapeutic directions.

Therefore, we prefer the term *ethnicity*, which, by definition, acknowledges more directly the constructed and fluid nature of human organization while at the same time acknowledging the defining power of physical markers in a person's identity. The term *race* is associated with colonization and is produced out of a colonizing analysis of characteristics of human beings, while the term *ethnicity* does not have such a problematic legacy. Ethnicity more consciously groups human beings by historical events and collective meaning making. Race, while constructed by these same social processes, is understood by many to be natural and inherent. Ethnicity acknowledges more the construction, reproduction, and transformation of social identity, a concept congruent with postmodern thought. As Richard Jenkins (2003) observes, race is more a category to which people are assigned without choice, while ethnicity is a group of people who usually have some degree of choice about their own belonging.

On the other hand, the concept of race cannot just be wished away. It is a highly problematic concept, but it exists in the general discourse and everyone acts daily on the basis of shared assumptions of what it means. Race still has official authority behind it, too. Power relations are constructed on the basis of these assumptions, and these power relations have very real material effects on people's lives. In this sense, the notion of race is by no means illusory. It produces an all-too-real impact on people's lives. Even though it is a social category ascribed from the outside, it becomes internalized into strongly felt identities (Jenkins, 2003). Therefore, we do have to engage with it. But we can best engage with it as a politically charged social construct that can be contested, rather than as a straightforward biological reality. And we can choose to use the term *ethnicity* where it seems to more accurately and respectfully refer to the cultural differences that groups of people themselves regard as salient.

One of the other difficulties with the concept of race is that, through evolution and interracial unions, new generations have physical markers different from those of earlier generations. With greater levels of intermarriage and the changing phenotypic shapes of human beings around the globe, it is becoming more and more difficult to police the boundaries where one race begins and another ends. As a result, it is also more difficult for people to embrace race as a criterion for social division. Decolonizing movements in opposition to racist practices have also made it more difficult to sustain as a dividing line.

Some Blacks in the United States struggle with determining whether someone deserves to be considered Black if his skin color is too light, his hair is not kinky enough, or his eyes are not brown. Conversely, some individuals self-identify as White but have a skin color that is darker than that of many who identify as Black. There is also an emerging challenge to the view of race as something fixed, natural, and inherent in the growing numbers of children whose parents form combinations such as Samoan-Chinese, Portuguese-Filipino, and Korean–African American. As growing numbers of people claim multiracial or multiethnic identities, to what extent will federal racial categories hold up? Currently, if a Black woman and an Anglo American man bear a child, the child will be considered Black. American (U.S.) society still largely employs the one-drop rule, where if you have any Black ancestry you are automatically Black. It is more difficult to predict what racial classification will be used when Anglo American–Native American or Asian–Anglo American couples bear children (Cornell & Hartmann, 1998).

Ethnicity and Context

Context and situation play a very big part in the ethnicity and identity people present to others. For example, in New Zealand, the indigenous people belong to various tribal identities. When the Ngapuhi and Tainui tribes meet, they engage in ritual greetings that honor the traditions and ancestors of each of those tribal communities. Tribal organization and tribal customs and practices take precedence. However, when these two tribes are threatened by some political or economic action instigated by the dominant Pakeha (White) ethnic group, they invoke their ethnicity as Maori. They will join to identify themselves as the *Tangata Whenua*, or first indigenous people of the land. This contextual organization and situational change of ethnicity doesn't happen at just the community level. It often takes place within extended families. The promotion of one identity and the submergence of another is dependent on a number of factors. For example, when Belen is with her Mexican community, she identifies with that ethnic group and participates in the Cinco de Mayo celebrations. When she travels to Flagstaff to be with her Indian side of the family for Native Heritage Month, she participates fully in Diné drumming and dance activities. Paul Spickard and Rowena Fong (1995) describe a similar scenario with a young woman who lives multiple ethnicities in Hawaii:

> If I am with my grandmother I'm Portuguese. If I'm with some of my aunts on my dad's side I'm Filipino. If I'm hanging around, I'm just local. If I'm on the mainland I'm Hawaiian. (p. 1370)

Due to increased rates of movement, migration, and interethnic marriage, ethnic boundaries can become less obvious, less compelling, and more difficult to maintain. When people are living with multiple ethnicities and multiple heritages, what starts to matter more is not the boundaries that separate one group from another but the sites within these ethnic domains where they will find acceptance. Paul Spickard and Rowena Fong (1995) suggest that when the boundaries around ethnic definition become more permeable, what might matter more will be the potential connections between ethnicities. Boundary policing based on historical orientations to past abuses and violations will then diminish.

Stephen Cornell and Douglas Hartmann (1998) envisage one possible future scenario as a result of patterns of global migration in which there will be fewer identifiable ethnicities but more multiethnic individuals. They suggest that brothers and sisters will share combinations, but "each combination will last only a generation before some other set of ancestries joins in to produce offspring whose ethnic lineages are more complicated still" (p. 245).

The fluid and complex quality of ethnicity reminds counselors that they cannot assume that a person has one particular ethnicity. Counselors and therapists need to be respectful of and curious about the meaning-making systems with which *every* client is engaged. Ethnic understanding is vital to successful and effective counseling, but it is impossible to know by looking at people, or by hearing or viewing a label that describes an ethnicity, what these important defining characteristics might be. Only through conversation can these characteristics be understood. Because of the fluid and dynamic quality of ethnic membership, one cannot even assume that all the members of the same family will share the same identities or ethnic categories. In all counseling interactions, open curiosity and naive inquiry are essential to understanding the complexity of a client's multiple identities and ethnic histories, and the client's construction of her various problems. What's more, multiple ethnic sources of identity can provide clients with a richer resource bank for use in overcoming problems.

Just as it may be possible for ethnic boundaries to become more permeable and dynamic, it is also possible for ethnic boundaries to harden. There is every prospect that racial categories will continue and thus permit the alienation, separation, and conflict that are founded on these socially constructed barriers. These dynamics play out in very different ways in popular culture and in the media. Ishmael Reed (1989) talks about the well-publicized book and movie *Roots*, in which Alex Haley (1976) traces his genealogy for many generations on his mother's side through the period of slavery and finally back to Gambia in Africa. Reed comments that if Alex Haley had followed his father's ancestry, he would have traveled back 12 generations and ended up not in Gambia but in Ireland. The historian David Hollinger (1995) points out that Haley never had any real option to place any weight on his father's bloodline. American (U.S.) social conventions classify him as Black, and his White, Irish ethnic heritage is perceived as unimportant. Haley could hardly choose his Irish heritage, as he would be crossing a racial divide and would be perceived to be siding with those historically responsible for the oppression of his mother's bloodline.

Constructing Ethnic Identities

There is good evidence to suggest that the more one possesses physical features of the majority White cultures, the more choice one has to inhabit, experiment with, and claim a variety of ethnicities and identities. The farther removed one's physical characteristics are from White, Anglo American facial features, such as a White complexion, straight or wavy hair, almond-shaped eyes, a pointed nose, and certain chiseled features, the less one can claim an ethnicity unaffected by racial classification.

To illustrate, we shall use an example from New Zealand, which has been just as influenced by European colonizing values as has North America. A Pakeha, or White, mother adopted Karen, who had physical features that were Maori, including the classic Polynesian brown skin, brown eyes, and Black wavy hair. The child was not exposed to any Maori or Polynesian people, nor did she have any knowledge of Polynesian history or ethnic ancestry. Karen did not eat the traditional foods, know the popular Polynesian music forms, or learn the linguistic subtleties of Maori communication styles. Karen was very confident in a middle-class English register. When she was nine, Karen's White peer group began to communicate to her that she no longer belonged with them because she was Maori. The child had no conception of what it was to be Maori. By the time she was 14, her peer group was Maori. To gain membership as Maori, she had to learn all of the significant cultural meanings of this peer group. Since she looked like them, the assumption was that she belonged to the Maori group.

Karen clearly had limits imposed on her as far as the ethnic reference group she was allowed to belong to. Most often, middle-class Whites have genuine ethnic identity choices. They can choose to be Irish or Italian, French or Polish. They can choose cultural identities pertaining to religion, urban versus rural orientation, and even class. A gay or lesbian person can decide to come out or not. A person with an accent that distinguishes him as, say, lower class can sometimes change his accent to show that he belongs to a higher class. However, bodily markers and the dominant meanings that accompany them cannot be so easily changed.

Many Asian, Latinx, and Native American communities, but much more obviously Black communities, have fewer ethnic options because of dominant cultural assumptions formed around physical markers. These markers make it difficult for people with non-White physical features to embrace their forebears' Italian or Irish ethnic heritage. Of course, the same can occur for those that look White but wish to claim a heritage that includes slavery and an African ancestry. Yet the consequences for White-skinned individuals wishing to identify as Black are very different from those of Black-skinned individuals wishing to identify as White (Cornell & Hartmann, 1998).

Natasha reminds us of the contemporary versions of racism in the United States.

> *Throughout my life I've heard many Blacks say, "I'd rather live in the South than in the North. At least you know where you stand." The South has a history of overt, in-your-face racism. If people are going to discriminate against me because of skin color, I know it. It's apparent in their attitudes, actions, and words. There is no question about it when you encounter it. In the North, however, there is a history of subtle racism. It will come out in racial proofing, hiring practices, being passed up for promotions, and unfair housing practices. You'll just be told, "There are no more apartments available," not, "We don't allow_____ [fill in the blank] to live here." I have to constantly question whether someone's actions against me are racist, or whether the person is just being rude. I become hypersensitive, dare I say paranoid. When it's overt, you know how to avoid it, what neighborhood not to go in. When it is subtle, I am forced to live a life of wonder: Was that a racist act? Did I just get discriminated against? It would be nice if the options were (a) overt racism, (b) subtle racism, or (c) no racism. I know which one I would choose.*

Veronica talks about some painful recollections in her own family.

> *In my family, we African Americans favored narrower noses, big lips, neutral eyes, and being tall and skinny. Having lighter skin was also favored. The darker the skin that people had, the more unfavored they were. Darker-skinned people did not get paid as much as the lighter-skinned people. In the 1960s, it was known that the lighter, the better.*
>
> *My father (Don) had darker skin than his sisters and he was not shown favor. Jacqueline, among other relatives, did not favor Don because of his skin color, and he was aware of it. Jacqueline would take Bruce and Frank out to different places and leave Don at home. My mom told me that Don knew he could not go out with his mom, because he had picked up the fact that he had darker skin and his mom told him that he was too dark. My father tried to commit suicide because of the way everyone was treating him on account of his skin color. Some of the stereotypes that Don believes others have of African Americans are that they have big noses, are lazy, and are not smart. Some stereotypes that Don said he had of African Americans, which is an example of turning racism on ourselves, are that they eat fried chicken and that the women are overweight.*

According to U.S. colonization, the physical features (such as eye shape, stature, and hair) of Whites are deemed superior to those of Asians. Since skin color has been enlisted as a powerful dividing practice for 400 years, it is not surprising that ethnicities form around the privileges associated with being White and the oppressive experiences associated with being Black or yellow. We are slowly working out the consequences of this history, but it will probably take much longer for it to be consigned to distant history.

Some ethnic groups strategically use the essentializing of ethnic bonds as a basis for organization and purposeful action. Originally, the markers of race and ethnicity were used by the colonizers to identify, separate, organize, and subordinate groups. In the last few decades, some ethnic groups have essentialized and reproduced the rigid boundaries of the colonizing cultures to build a base for struggle and empowerment. The Maori in New Zealand are a good example of this. The move by disadvantaged groups to wholeheartedly endorse race as a meaningful construction has been largely fueled by ongoing disparities of status, wealth, and well-being.

As Stephen Cornell and Douglas Hartmann (1998) suggest,

> There is little inherently good or bad about ethnicity and race. … What makes them significant is what human beings do to them. … The critical issue for the 21st century is not whether ethnicity and race will continue to serve as categories of collective identity but what kinds of ethnic and racial stories groups tell and how these stories are put to use. (p. 252)

Counseling Implications of Race and Ethnicity

"Why can't we just treat everyone as a human being? Why not just treat everyone equally, and surely the problems of race will disappear!" This cry is not infrequently heard from many counselors (usually White). Nor is it very surprising. Many counselors want to believe that all human beings start on an equal footing and have the same life chances. They are supported in this assumption by the dominant ideology in all modern Western economies, which endorses and supports the practices of universalism and individualism. This ideology is built into the legal system, the organization of capitalism, and political systems.

One corollary of this ideology is that if people are not thriving, it is assumed that there is something wrong with them as individuals. Such a person must possess some dysfunctional personality trait, such as laziness, idleness, or lack of motivation. On the basis of these assumptions, widespread attitudes are built that either deny or completely underestimate the impact of powerful sociohistorical factors at work. Denial of the power of present-day colonizing practices protects those who are beneficiaries of the dominant discourse from confronting it in their counseling practice.

Counseling diagnostic practices that alert counselors to look first at the intrapsychic processes of the client to the exclusion of cultural and contextual factors will always risk blaming clients for their difficulties and problems. Some clients who are suffering from problems in gaining access to quality housing, adequate education, and basic healthcare, not to mention sustainable employment, may be struggling because of systemic inequities in the community in which they live. Clients subjected to these inequities may easily be invited to internalize their suffering and blame themselves for their plight. They may feel ashamed of the way they are living and direct their energies into self-loathing, depression, and despair. They may be convinced that their problems result from personal lack of assertiveness, irrational thinking, or negative feelings about themselves as individuals.

On the other hand, other clients in this same situation may direct their frustration, outrage, and anger outside of themselves onto members of their family, or onto community representatives such as teachers, the police, healthcare workers, and the like. A counselor or therapist can be an easy target for the client's outrage, particularly if the client is a person of color and the therapist is White. White therapists must be particularly careful to locate the causes of depression, self-hatred, anger, and violence in a wider sociohistorical context, rather than simply attributing these troubles to personal deficits inside people. The White therapist can come to represent for some people of color a modern-day version of a colonizing master by using practices that build on assumptions of individual deficit.

Yet the legacy of colonization might make it even more difficult for a Black or Asian therapist to work with a White client. Racist discourse can influence White clients to dismiss or minimize the expertise of the Black or Asian therapist, which significantly disrupts the therapeutic process. We don't believe therapists who are persons of color should have to educate clients or to sustain their therapeutic efforts in these circumstances. It is preferable that the client be referred to somebody of his own ethnicity who can challenge unjust and prejudicial behavior as part of the therapeutic contract.

Contextualizing and situating clients' problems in a social and historical context can help defuse any inclination of the therapist to blame clients for their own plight. Some understanding of the complexity of social relations can be generated, and this by itself can help shift the dynamics onto a positive footing.

Whites can also have their identities totalized and stereotyped when people of color accuse them of embodying practices of superiority and uncritically assume them to be benefactors of racism. Where such accusations are true, there might be massive constraints on the counselor's helpfulness. But it is not a given that White counselors are practicing in ways that perpetuate their own privilege. The White counselor or therapist is wise to pay close attention to any legacy of privilege and to be acutely aware of how this can play out in counseling sessions.

Issues of trust pertaining to the legacies of race and ethnicity can become critical in the counseling relationship. These issues are sometimes best addressed by making them explicit. Potential concerns can be raised as legitimate topics of conversation early in the counseling relationship. For example, the White therapist might begin the session by asking a person of color whether he has any misgivings about working with her. The counselor should be ready to acknowledge that ethnicity and race might be a factor in their work together. Not raising the possibility that sociocultural undercurrents might be present limits the prospect of effective therapeutic work. It makes it much harder for counselors to help clients situate the challenges that confront them within the history of cultural practices built on the assumptions about race discussed above.

A culturally aware White counselor can also help a client of color tease out the difference between the dominant cultural practices of race, which cause oppression, and the practices of this particular White therapist. Identifying contradictory experiences does not have to undermine the validity of experiences of racism. Instead, it can become the basis for hope that things can be different. For a client of color, seeing a White therapist committed to standing against racism could be enormously helpful in engendering trust and hope.

We have been discussing the counseling challenges that may arise between a White therapist and a client who is a person of color.

Sometimes it might be difficult for counselors of color to see past the White privilege certain clients have. They may underestimate the suffering White middle-class clients experience even while benefiting from particular racist traditions. It is not uncommon for people who have been subjected to oppression, when given the opportunity, to engage in subtle oppressive practices themselves, either intentionally or inadvertently.

Just because the counselor and client are of the same race or ethnicity does not mean that the socio-historical factors are not playing out in their therapeutic relationship. Within ethnic groups, established hierarchies can be built around physical markers but based on the underlying dividing lines of race. For example, many light-skinned Blacks may have access to privileges that are less available to darker skinned Blacks. They may be perceived as more attractive and benefit from being able to pass for White.

Natasha has lived her whole life being subjected to what she terms intraracial prejudice.

> *When I was growing up I was made to think that lighter is better. During the time of slavery, many of the light-skinned slaves, most often the illegitimate children of the slave owners, became house slaves and were spared from working in the fields. Even though they were treated badly, they were perceived to get better treatment than plantation and field slaves. Many light-skinned Blacks found it necessary to pass for White in order to succeed, which meant leaving their family. It was a better life. I recall when I was a kid being called "tar baby" by another kid who was the same shade as me. Many times I have felt "less than" because of my color. Those with lighter skin and "good hair" (meaning straight or wavy) always got all the attention in my community. I have experienced the desire to marry a light-skinned Black; it would help increase the chances that my own children will be lighter than me and won't be subject to feelings of self-loathing due to something they can't change about themselves. When I was younger I probably did have some negative feelings toward my lighter brothers and sisters. Now, sometimes it's envy.*

Sometimes, light-skinned Blacks can feel marginalized by members of the Black community because they don't possess the physical markers that truly define them as Black. LaShanda, a lighter-skinned Black with other racial heritage, describes such an experience.

> *My grandmother on my father's side has told me and my siblings that we don't love her as much as our cousins do because we aren't fully Black. My older sister has told me that I deny my African American heritage, based on her own opinions. I believe that I am who I am; I know and accept myself. I can't make myself more African American than I am.*

How do we make sense of the practices that Natasha and LaShanda experienced? Are they evidence that Blacks can be just as racist as Whites? We would argue that this meaning relies too heavily on the essentializing of racism in those who express it. A better way to think of such experiences starts with the concept of discourse. Racist discourse has been internalized in non-White people's consciousness just as it has in White people's consciousness for over 500 years via European colonization. Racist discourse is expressed in a variety of ways, and sometimes the practices of racism are used by people against themselves as well as against others.

Significant distinctions also occur among people of the same ethnicity as a result of social class differences, relative wealth or poverty, and level of education. These distinctions can strongly alter a person's experience of the effects of racial discourse. This discourse often exceptionalizes certain individuals as models of the "good Black person" and grants them special status within otherwise White worlds. An upper-middle-class Black therapist with a college education may sometimes really struggle to build trust and empathy with a client from a poor inner-city community. While they are similarly positioned in terms of race, the effects of poverty may feel much more foreign to the counselor. A White therapist who was brought up in a lower-class community may have more understanding of the problems that a person of color who is poor may face. Differences in sexual orientation or problems with heterosexism may also present barriers for a counselor and client from the same racial group.

There are many racist practices that take place among non-White ethnic groups. Some who are committed to a structuralist analysis of power (see Chapter 6) argue that this is not possible and that racism is solely a White phenomenon. But this argument does not reflect the many day-to-day, painful experiences suffered by members of diverse ethnic and racial groups. We believe it is more accurate to say that racist practices are expressions of power and that they can be employed by anyone who chooses to use them to gain some advantage for herself by hurting someone else. Whatever the background of the person using racist discourse, the background of the discourse itself comes from the history of colonization. It is still true that the origins of the ideas of racism lie in the stereotypical, prejudicial assumptions woven into the arbitrary European nomenclature of race. Individuals of diverse races can plug into this systemic discourse of race at the moment that they choose to deploy racist discourse for their own reasons. They can join in the game of innate superiority and inferiority.

The point we are arguing here is a subtle one, but we believe it is important. *Racism is a term that should be reserved for practices, rather than persons.* The assumptions on which these practices are built, however, are not invented by any one individual. They are products of the history of colonization and the justifications that underlie it. The practice of making racist remarks is, therefore, available for any individual of any race. At the same time, racist remarks are products of a systematic discourse that is White and European in its genealogy.

Natasha explains it this way.

> *Unfortunately, throughout the course of American (U.S.) history, those in power and in the media have perpetuated stereotypes of each group. Since many of us were segregated and may have had little interaction with those in other ethnic groups, the stereotypes were believed and passed down. Growing up, I was surrounded almost exclusively by Blacks and Puerto Ricans. I am sure that I had stereotypes of members of other ethnic groups. Even though we know better, we still assume all Asian Americans are smart, all Blacks are lazy, and all Latinx are dirty. We are afraid of one another. This hinders us from working together to educate the nation and the world about the wonderful contributions we have made to making this country what it is today.*

Sometimes therapists assume that because they belong to the same ethnicity, they will be able to empathize with their clients and grapple with concerns that only persons of that ethnicity could understand. Assumptions may be made about the client's experience on this basis when, in reality, the client's experience is very different from what the counselor imagines. Such assumptions undermine trust and empathy and diminish the effectiveness of an exploration of major client concerns. In practice, the degree of shared outlook between a counselor and a client of the same ethnicity may be minimal. We have outlined above many ways in which the concepts of ethnicity and race are much more complex than they are often presented. Their meanings are multiple, and thus it would be surprising to find empathic understanding to be a straightforward process of ethnic matching. Creating shared understandings of issues of race and ethnicity between counselors and clients always needs to be worked at, and we believe it needs to be founded on a clear analysis of the genealogy of these concepts and of the present-day cultural formations in which they are being lived out.

While we have laid out an argument explaining the genealogy of racism in the history of European colonization, the world is a complex place and many contradictory patterns are also occurring.

Within popular culture, there are frequent contradictions of the assumptions of racial privilege. Often they occur as a result of the inroads of decolonization into modern culture. The fact that we could have had a Black president and first lady in the White House was an astonishing event not only in the United States but on the world stage. More than ever before, we have successful and powerful Black, Asian, and Latinx political leaders, artists, and sportspeople featured in social media. These people of color have a huge following among Anglo Americans. They clearly are accorded positions of authority and privilege that contradict the history of race. A phenomenon occurring among middle-class White youths and young people from around the globe has been the idolization of Black music artists. These artists may embody in their art forms experiences from their own recent history of significant oppression that can clearly be attributed, at least in part, to race discourse. Many successful Black artists come from the poorest and most downtrodden communities and display the cultural symbols of those neighborhoods with their dress, dialect, and cultural accoutrements. They even use these symbols as badges of resistance and decolonization. Ironically, however, after becoming cultural icons, these artists assume the trappings of privilege, and White youths now mimic their dress and style of communication. They are now in positions of power and influence that apparently belie what they are saying in their music. The point here is that it is not easy to make generalizations about the patterns of relationship that form around some ethnic territories. These people are not being inauthentic in the process. They are merely illustrating the complexity of cultural positioning in the world that we live in.

Response to Chapter 4

ANGUS HIKAIRO
MACFARLANE PHD

Angus Hikairo Macfarlane has strong tribal links to Te Arawa in the North Island of Aotearoa New Zealand. He is professor of Māori Research at the University of Canterbury (UC), Director of Te Rū Rangahau, the Māori Research Laboratory, and Senior Māori Advisor (Kaihautū) for the New Zealand Psychological Society. His research focuses on exploring Indigenous and sociocultural imperatives that influence education and psychology. Avid about Indigenous advancement, he has pioneered several theoretical frameworks associated with culturally responsive approaches for professionals working across these disciplines.

In New Zealand, year after year, Maori students are suspended from school at a much higher rate than their non-Maori counterparts. While any number of reasons are cited for this anomaly, it seems to be the education system's version of the conflicts in New Zealand associated with prejudice, exclusion, and discrimination that have persisted over the generations. Out of these struggles, however, has evolved an awareness of the need for people to get along with persons of diverse backgrounds and to better understand each other's expectations and world views. The realization that this requires commitment and effort on the part of all of us is not insignificant.

An underlying theme of this chapter is the important role that race and ethnicity play in the lives of people and the implications of that role for counseling processes and approaches. In New Zealand, a number of programs have been developed in the education and health sectors to help professionals be more culturally responsive as they work with Maori clients and their families. One such approach is the *hui whakatika*, which literally means "restorative conferencing."

People from one ethnic background are likely to enter a conferencing situation with very different views and expectations from those of people who come from another background. Conferencing is not new to Maori people. Traditional Maori societies had this down to a fine art, and many examples are magnificently manifested in mythology, legends, and history. Contemporary Maori society has retained an abundance of what their *tipuna* (ancestors) had to offer, despite the infiltration of Western processes into their conferencing techniques. For Maori, oneness of *tinana* (body), *hinengaro* (mind), and *wairua* (spirit) is often perceived to be distinct from the rationality and logic that influence Western thinking. If the conferencing process is going to be of value to Maori students who find themselves in trouble at school—and at risk of being excluded from it—then it needs to embrace Maori philosophy and logic.

Four quintessential features illustrate pre-European Maori counseling. They are:

1. an emphasis on reaching *consensus* and involving the whole community;
2. a desired outcome of *reconciliation* and a settlement acceptable to all parties, rather than the isolation and punishment of the offender;
3. not the apportionment of blame, but *examination* of the wider reason for the wrong, with an implicit assumption that there is often wrong on both sides; and
4. less concern with whether or not there has been a breach of law and more concern with the *restoration* of harmony.

Let me recite a case where I facilitated a hui whakatika. The hui whakatika was convened to consider the plight of Piripi, a 14-year-old Maori student. The head of the junior school had referred Piripi to me because of his rudeness, absenteeism, nonadherence to rules, and bullying of other boys by intimidation, including the use of stand-over tactics. He was not willing to share his problems, and attempts by the school counselor to reason with him through conventional approaches had led to a dead end. Piripi had recently stolen a car belonging to a retired couple and had damaged it while showing off to his mates. Consequently, the police had become involved. He was in dire straits.

A number of phases had to be worked through in this hui whakitika, including the following:

> Setup. Determining who needs to be involved, preparing those involved for what will happen, and establishing Piripi's willingness to make amends.

The conference proper. Opening, conducting, and closing the conference, adhering to (Maori) rituals along the way. This involved clarifying the desired outcomes and declaring that the problem, not Piripi, was the problem.

Seeking out new possibilities. This involved the consideration of alternative stories, planning, monitoring, and reviewing. Where to now for Piripi?

The hui whakatika process is intricate and demanding of people's time. Many people attend, including school personnel, family members, and those who have been affected or offended by the individual concerned. Maori protocols apply, such as *karakia* (prayer), *waiata* (song), *kai* (food), and *copious korero* (discussion). People of all ages and backgrounds attend the hui whakatika and are encouraged to actively participate. This approach is not about stipulating who is to be in the room or what checklists should be attended to. It is about preparing to speak with one another about difficult things in a way that avoids regression into the dynamics that gave rise to the problems in the first place.

In daily life, it is commonplace to encounter the use of punitive and judgmental forms of speech, particularly where there is a desire to rein someone in. These habits of judgment are hard to break. In this sense, conferencing is about developing new ways of speaking. All instances of conferencing are, by definition, intended to promote discussion. Speaking respectfully does not cost a great deal, and it can be extremely effective in achieving desirable outcomes. The hui whakatika approach is particularly interested in the types of conversations that are able to turn people and events around, not frighteningly, but assertively. The outcome sought is the restoration of a person from a state of disorientation to a state of optimism. The conversations are constantly searching for ways of going forward and developing new directions.

For students in situations similar to Piripi's, new opportunities and directions are sought and the punitive measures of expulsion are, where possible, avoided. The counselor and all others present at a hui whakatika are required to consider all the relevant matters and then draw up a plan to address the concerns. A good plan obviously includes aspects that would benefit the school (e.g., nonviolence pacts, attendance undertakings) as well as aspects that would benefit the student (e.g., having him or her join a sports club or receive counseling). It may also need to include aspects that benefit the community (e.g., the removal of graffiti) or the family (e.g., active parental interest in the school community). These options were applicable in Piripi's case, and satisfactory outcomes, while not guaranteed, did ensue in this instance.

The hui whakatika places culture at the center. It opens and closes in a manner compatible with Maori processes; there is an order to who should speak and when. There is a place for talk and debate, laughter and tears, food and song. There is also a wairua, a spirituality, that exudes *mana* (authority)— and mana can move people! Many voices are heard as the English and Maori languages blend. The dignified presences of *kaumatua* (older Maori people) provide a net of safety to younger members of the conference. Throughout the conference, the feelings of *whanaungatanga* (relationships) and the intensity of the *kaupapa* (discussion) are the *taonga tuku iho*, the treasures of history and mythology that have been handed down from the past. The hui whakatika has traditionally been the focal point of Maori counseling—and for many, it still is.

Discuss

1. The topics of race and ethnicity are sensitive topics. What sensitivities were stimulated in you as you read this chapter?
2. When would you prefer to use the term *race* and when would you prefer to use the term *ethnicity*?
3. Can you think of instances in which the ways that people use the terms *race* and *ethnicity* have affected you personally? How?
4. Do an online search for articles on the validity of the concept of race. What did you find?
5. Search online for examples of official government documents that use the concept of race. How is it used? Which races are given official status?

Chapter 5

Discourse, Positioning, and Deconstruction

I n this chapter, we want to introduce some relatively recent concepts into the literature on inter-cultural counseling. We shall introduce and explain the concept of discourse and the idea of being positioned in relation to discourse. We shall also explain the approach to understanding discourse usage called deconstruction. These are not-so-new concepts in social theory (they have been used in the fields of philosophy, cultural studies, sociology, literary studies, and anthropology for three or more decades, even though not universally by all academics in these domains), but they have only to a modest extent been picked up by psychologists and are still not widely understood in the field of counseling.

We have reasons for introducing these concepts here. This isn't just a matter of keeping up with academic fashions, and we certainly don't want to add jargon for its own sake to the field of intercultural counseling. But we think these concepts help us get around some recurrent problems in our field. We think that using these concepts gives us a fresh perspective in the field of culture and on the work that counselors do within it. Fresh concepts can allow for new ways of speaking, and we ourselves have experienced these concepts as opening up productive ways to think about culture and about counseling. We shall introduce these concepts in this chapter so that we can use them in the rest of the book, in the hope that readers will be assisted in their practice. We should warn you that it might take a bit of work to master these concepts. That is because they are not always familiar. We would encourage you to persist, however, because we think that the ability to make clearer decisions about a range of issues can be gained from such persistence.

One of the main reasons that we want to use the concept of discourse is because it often serves as a sharper instrument with which to discuss things that are more problematic to talk about when we use the word *culture*. *Culture* is often a blunt instrument because of the history of essentialist thinking attached to it. Discourse, on the other hand, allows us to capture more of the complexity of the situations in which people often live as they are pulled in contradictory directions that can never be adequately described by the idea that each individual belongs to a single culture. The word *race* is an even blunter instrument than *culture* in this regard, as we have made clear in earlier chapters. We think that identity construction is always a complex process of being positioned by a swathe of competing discourses, established through large-scale historical movements but having a unique impact on each person at every moment of their lives. We are seeking to talk about these impacts and the struggles people go through to position themselves in relation to dominant discourse in ways that fit their own hopes and ambitions in life. This is the stuff that people see counselors about. To us, the concept of discourse seems uniquely suited as an explanatory framework for making sense of the diversity and complexity of human engagement, which multicultural counseling is all about.

Another argument that we want to mount for our use of the concept of discourse is that discourse is always a product of the social world in which we live. Therefore, thinking in terms of discourse always makes the social and cultural aspects of the problems that people bring to counselors more visible. This visibility is in contrast to the use of, for example, biological metaphors, which can render the social and cultural world invisible or irrelevant. We believe it is in the interest of the intercultural counseling field specifically, and of the counseling profession generally, to reexamine many of the ways in which people are thought of, problems are diagnosed, and counseling interventions are conceived. From our perspective, the concept of discourse provides a language to name the social processes operating in clients' worlds that is in stark contrast to the essentialist understandings expressed in many models of counseling. It also provides a way forward in a manner that isn't blameworthy.

Deploying the concept of discourse also includes a focus on the language used in the counseling profession itself, and invites us to pay closer attention to it. It may often be part of the problem that the multicultural counseling movement is seeking to address. This is where the other concept mentioned above, deconstruction, comes in. Deconstruction lays bare the work done by discourse, makes it visible, and leads to openings for change.

Let's now discuss each of these concepts in turn and explain them in more detail before outlining some examples of how they might be used to constructive effect.

Discourse

In a general sense, discourse is both the process of talk and interaction between people and the products of that interaction. The things that people say or write are examples of discourse. In the more precise meaning that has developed in academic writing, the term *discourse* refers to a set of meanings, concepts, images, and/or statements that produce a particular representation of an event, object, person, or other entity in the world (Burr, 2015). Such meanings tend to become patterned and well known through constant repetition in hundreds and thousands of conversations. This concept of discourse, influenced chiefly by social constructionist and poststructuralist theory, is based on the work of Michel Foucault (1972), who described discourse as a "social practice" disseminated through cultural space that exerts a dominating effect on what can be thought or spoken. That is, we speak from discourse, feel from discourse, and behave from discourse. In simplest terms, you can think of discourse as a cultural idea.

You can get a sense of a discourse by listening to any statement that someone makes and asking yourself, what are the background assumptions on which that statement rests? For example, consider this woman's statement: "When I am going through a crisis, I find that the first thing I do is take control of my weight and eating habits—one time I even came close to the edge of a devastating eating disorder." There are a number of assumptions that lie in the background of this statement. They are not things that are often said out loud, but at the same time everybody within the cultural world that the speaker comes from knows these assumptions and thinks of them as just normal, everyday truths. We can render these assumptions understandable by spelling them out as simple assertions of what is obvious and taken for granted just below the surface of the words. For example, some of these assumptions may be as follows:

"Thin is beautiful."

"Women should take care of their appearance and make themselves desirable for men."

"A successful woman measures her weight and brings it under control, mainly by dieting."

"Eating disorders happen to women who are too controlling."

These are examples of discursive statements that we may find by analyzing a given utterance in a discourse.

At any given moment, a variety of discourses will be in circulation in a particular social or cultural world. Notice that the last of these assumptions may have points of reference in standard professional discourse and may influence writers of academic articles and books as well as laypeople. Discourses can also compete with one another. For example, with regard to the above discourses, there are competing ideas around them:

"Fat is just as beautiful as thin."

"It is wrong for anyone to be subjected to judgment of her personal worth on the basis of her body's appearance."

"Eating disorders are produced by cultural pressure on women, not by individual controlling personalities."

Discourses are not simply abstract ideas, ideologies, or theories (although theories and ideologies must be talked about in language and, therefore, in discourse). They are not as formally constituted as theories. They are, however, implicit in social practices and often lie just beneath the surface of our understanding as assumptions that are necessary to make what we say or do make sense. In this way, discourses construct meaning and shape individuals' behavior, their perceptions of the world, and the sense they make of lived experience. Discourse is the realm in which what is "normal," what is "acceptable," what is "right," what is "real," and what is "possible" are constructed.

Dominant Discourse

One of the advantages that the concept of discourse affords is a view of the relationship among competing discourses. The concept of culture is more static and is usually assumed to be more universal, less driven by conflict. Different discourses, however, are often quite contradictory. They can be thought of as being like political parties, clamoring for your vote at election time. While there are always a range of discourses, however, they are seldom competing on a level playing field. Some discourses always

Here are some well-known conceptualizations of discourse:

[Discourses are] practices that systematically form the objects of which they speak.
　　　　　—Michel Foucault, *The Archaeology of Knowledge* (1969)

A discourse is a system of statements which constructs an object.
　　　　　—Ian Parker, *Discourse Dynamics* (1992)

Instead of gradually reducing the rather fluctuating meaning of the word "discourse," I believe I have in fact added to its meanings; treating it sometimes as the general domain of all statements, sometimes as an individualizeable group of statements, and sometimes as a regulated practice that accounts for a number of statements.
　　　　　—Michel Foucault, *The Archaeology of Knowledge* (1969)

A discourse is any regulated system of statements.
　　　　　—Julian Henriques, Wendy Hollway, Cathy Urwin, Couze Venn, and Valerie Walkerdine, *Changing the Subject* (1984)

Discourse is a mode of action, one form in which people may act upon the world and especially upon each other, as well as a mode of representation.
　　　　　—Norman Fairclough, *Discourse and Social Change* (1992)

Discourses should be understood as statements with a material existence.
　　　　　—Michel Foucault, *The Hermeneutics of the Subject* (2005)

Discuss

1. What different perspective does each of these definitions make clear about the concept of discourse?
2. How do these definitions compare with your previous understanding(s) of discourse?

come to dominate others. We can thus talk about dominant discourses and subjugated, or alternative, discourses. *Dominant discourse* refers to those cultural ideas that have a privileged and dominant influence on our behavior in the world. They are not inherently "good" or "bad." It is apparent that some dominant discourses can be very harmful. For example, a person who is starving themselves and is at risk of dying does not thrive on the discourse of "In order to be beautiful you must be thin." Many dominant discourses are benign and helpful. To a driver wondering how to drive on the roads in North America it is helpful to follow the dominant discourse of "When driving in North America you must drive on the right hand side of the road." That is, dominant discourses reflect rules, prevailing ideology, including popular norms, values, and beliefs. Sometimes they are embodied as law or have official authority behind them or are bestowed by the most prominent academic commentators of the day. As a result, they are often so persuasive in a community that their implications for how life should be lived are completely taken for granted (Hare-Mustin, 1994).

All these discourses reflect what is often considered common sense about how people should behave, and exert a powerful influence in day-to-day interactions. In fact, it is the familiarity and taken-for-granted nature of dominant discourses that seduce us to adopt these popular cultural views. That is, "their influence can most easily remain hidden and difficult to identify and, therefore, to resist" (Gavey & McPhillips, 1999, p. 352).

Consider how the dominant discourse of one woman's family shaped her own understandings and experiences.

> *My grandparents and parents have raised me to have a certain ideal for the family. The perfect family starts with a man and a woman who are married before they have children. Then they have two children, a boy and then a girl: a boy to pass on the family name and to please the father, and a girl to please the mother. The parents are not too old, so that they can still enjoy their kids. They are financially secure before they have children. They do not divorce, ideally. The perfect family keeps their problems private. Since my aunt married my late Uncle Steve in Vegas and my sister had a child out of wedlock, there is a lot of pressure on me to make my grandmother proud in the way that I choose to live that part of my life. I have really thought a lot about marriage and its importance, so my Nanny's ideals have had a huge impact on my life.*

What this woman is describing is a pretty ordinary picture of how family is imagined in the modern world. She speaks of this "ideal" in terms of how it has been passed down from her grandparents and parents, but there are surely many other people who have had the same messages. They were not invented specially for this woman by her parents or grandparents. They are actually drawn from discourse. Discourse theorists would argue that this picture is not just an image of an ideal family, but an image of what has been instilled into us by dominant discourse as a "normal" family, that is, one that we should all measure our own family against to decide whether it is normal or not. The speaker in this extract actually starts to register this pressure to be normal in the last few sentences. She mentions a couple of marriages in her family that did not fit the normal picture, and she is now personally feeling increased pressure to construct her own life to fit the designated norm.

These dominating discourses shape every aspect of human functioning, embracing thought, behavior, and affective responses. It is not as if our feelings are somehow part of an authentic world that is untouched by culture, as is often suggested by liberal humanism (see Chapter 6). Some counseling theories have suggested this idea and have argued that we should concentrate on helping people get in touch with their inner feeling worlds, that there they will encounter a sense of self that is free of cultural influence. This is of course an essentialist idea. From a social constructionist perspective, this quest does not work. Our feelings are also produced out of a world of discourse and culture, such that we do not have some responses that are "pure" or culture free. Even our dreams have discourse symbols in them, which is not surprising if they include language.

Discourse and Knowledge

One of the aims of modern science has been to establish a body of knowledge that can be relied on for its truth value. In the last 200 years, we have witnessed the growth of the role of the university in modern society as the principal institution where such knowledge is produced, taught, and disseminated. The foundation of the system of knowledge creation that the academic production of knowledge is built on is a set of rules that constitute recognized research methods. These are, first of all, the rules of systematic observation by observers who are separate from what they observe. These observers are neutral and unbiased. The rules are also the rules of scientific categorization, experimentation, and logical proof, embodied in the end in mathematical calculations.

The goal of research production within this modern framework is to produce knowledge of the world of nature. By definition, the world of nature is that which is free of cultural influence. Hence it is not too far a stretch to say that modern science has tried to eliminate as far as possible cultural material from the knowledge that it produces. All this makes a lot of sense in the fields of physics and chemistry and other "natural" sciences. You don't want the culture of the scientist to interfere with knowledge of how the atoms of the universe interact, although even then scientists have to use linguistic metaphors to describe what they are discussing, and language is a cultural product. When we are studying human sciences, the issues become more complex. Human beings studying cultural worlds are studying themselves. Hence the human sciences have developed methods to create distance between the observer and the observed (experimental methods, control groups, calculation of statistical probabilities, etc.).

This is where the concept of discourse becomes important. Early in his career, Michel Foucault (1972) wrote a book called *The Order of Things: An Archaeology of the Human Sciences*, which received extraordinary attention in France and eventually in other parts of the world. He used the concept of discourse to show that the human sciences, like psychology, constructed as they were in language, were full of cultural presuppositions. Foucault argued that social scientists were much less able than everyone believed to separate themselves from their own cultural perspectives and pursue objective knowledge. This is not just a matter of removing "bias," either. The whole academic exercise is located deeply in a set of philosophical, and, therefore, cultural assumptions and is used for purposes that are profoundly political.

The meaning of Foucault's work for our purposes here is that we cannot separate knowledge from the world where discourse operates. Knowledge is constructed out of discourse and for discursive purposes. Knowledge, then, is a cultural product. Indeed, to know anything is to know it in terms of discourse (Davies & Harré, 1990). If we look back through the history of knowledge about culture, this is not hard to see. Nineteenth-century anthropology is replete with assumptions about race and ethnicity that we would regard as at best quaint and at worst racist. If we extrapolate this experience of reading 19th-century human sciences, we have to be concerned about how the simple "truths" of today will look to people living in the culture of future societies.

This viewpoint is a challenge to the assumptions of simple empiricism. Facts no longer speak just for themselves. From their conception to the explanation of their significance, they are always interpretations of the world. Interpretations are made by human beings imbued with cultural world views, and they are spoken in discourse that embodies the dominant perspectives of an age, a locale, and a people. Therefore, not only do we need to ask about a given topic, "What are the facts?" We also need to ask questions such as, "Whose facts are they?" "Who benefits from this version of the facts?" "Under what cultural 'regime of truth' have these facts been produced?"

Counseling knowledge is of course no exception. It is always built on the discourse of the day. Thus, Michel Foucault posited that social practices, including therapeutic engagements, are informed by discourse. If we look at the various theories of counseling and read them as pieces of discourse, they reveal a lot about the cultural worlds inhabited by the persons who developed them. A social constructionist perspective encourages us to do this. Sigmund Freud's theories do not, therefore, just speak about the human mind. They speak about the discourses that dominated the thinking of medical professionals in late-19th- and early-20th-century Vienna. Carl Rogers's work can be read as a product of the discourse of the Anglo-Protestant, midwestern United States from the middle of the 20th century. Such readings do not necessarily mean that these counseling theories are wrong or are any less valuable, but it does change our relationship with them. We know that discourse changes over time, and in response to events in history, and through encounters with different cultural perspectives. Hence, treating knowledge as discourse enables it to come down off the pedestal of grand narrative (Lyotard, 1984) and be more reachable for all of us. We can also expect ideas about counseling to change in response to the discourse of our day and to not remain frozen in the grand narratives of the past.

For the cause of interculturalism in counseling, the concept of discourse has great importance. It enables us to ask questions about the relationships between counseling ideas and the particular cultural worlds occupied by those who speak them. It enables us to examine patterns of cultural dominance in the literature of counseling itself. It enables us, too, to open up the field of counseling to cultural perspectives that otherwise are kept silent by the dominant discourse of the day.

It is not only the theory of counseling that can be investigated in terms of discourse. Counseling conversations in practice contexts are, of course, also conducted in discourse because they involve language. The ways that clients present problems to counselors are imbued with discourse, as are the counselor's responses. For example, the following discourses commonly circulate and capture many clients in counseling: "I expect my partner to take care of me forever." "My partner is my true soul mate." "A good family consists of a nuclear family." "Divorce is not good for the sake of the children." "Families should not discuss private matters with strangers."

Discourse and Identity

Discourse provides the material out of which we form identity. Who we are depends on the circumstances we are placed in and the discourses available in the setting we find ourselves in. Identity is made up of both personal preferences and cultural specifications for the range within which we are allowed to form preferences. For example, gender specifications are one domain in which identity patterns are laid out by gender discourse. Both men and women learn to perceive the world, and their experiences in it, through such gender discourse. Categories such as *feminine* and *masculine* are organizing headings within gender discourse, as men and women define themselves with reference to this division. For instance, to be considered "masculine" or "feminine," men and women must conform to certain cultural standards endorsed and enacted through discourse. For example, masculine men do not wear makeup and are active and competitive and make jokes and emphasize strength and taking initiative. Feminine women shave their legs, wear makeup, spend hours talking with their friends about personal troubles, and are caring and nurturing.

In discourse theory, identity is thought of in terms of subject positions. However, "while all discourses offer subject positions that suggest particular ways of being in and experiencing the world, they vary in their accessibility and power" (Gavey & McPhillips, 1999, p. 352). The idea is that discourse sets up patterns of relationships among people, but rarely on an equal basis. Particular discourses are always being contested and debated, and groups of people typically seek to shift the discourse so that it tilts in their favor. As a result, the discourse that dominates always gives some people more entitlement to speak, to do things, and to be recognized in their social world. Other people, meanwhile, are always up against it to have their voices heard, to be recognized by others who matter, and even to feel justified in having an opinion in the first place. They have to find places to live on the margins of the dominant discourse. Hence, we may talk about their being marginalized by this discourse.

Here is an example of one such struggle between discourses that produce differential subject positions. Hong, a Korean woman, speaks about traditional Korean discourse as it specifies gender roles and family configurations. She also comments on how this discourse has impacted her own life.

> *Confucianism defines family members as descendants along the male line. The family headship system decrees that a baby boy becomes the family head if his father, the family's only son, dies. Even though sons are no longer entitled to inherit the bulk of their late parents' wealth, most fathers still hand over their fortunes to the eldest son before they die. There has been a lot of change in Korea, but these ideas still remain in Korean society. As an educated Christian woman, I refuse to comply with the gender roles of my family. However, sometimes I realize that I am affected by these gender roles unconsciously. For example, I take care of my parents-in-law more than my own parents because I feel more responsibility as a wife of the only son of the family.*

In this statement, Hong references a series of competing discourses—Confucian and Christian, traditional and modern, educated and uneducated—each of which alters the mix of subject positions she can choose from. She mentions efforts to change by legal decree the traditional dominant discourse that is tilted in favor of men, but indicates that there have also been widespread efforts to mitigate the effect of these reforms that have been designed to benefit women. The dominant patriarchal discourse thus remains dominant because it dominates the practice that actually takes place on the ground.

Notice, too, the subject positions Hong takes up and builds identity around. She claims for herself positions as educated, Christian, woman, and wife. She "refuses to comply" with some gender roles in her family. On the other hand, she finds herself unconsciously acting out practices specified by dominant discourse with her parents-in-law. Her final statement is an interesting one. It suggests how discourse works inside the minds of people, shaping what they do without precluding the possibility of agency. However, Foucault (Martin, Gutman & Hutton, 1988) also said in an interview late in his life that it was his purpose to "show people that they are much freer than they feel" (p. 10). In other words, it is possible to exercise agency much more often than people realize. Discourse practices are so ordinary and everyday that they often slip by unnoticed, because they are just what everyone expects.

These workings of discourse are the very material that makes up culture. They are also the material that makes up people's identities. Identity is formed partly out of personal intention and preference on the one hand, but, on the other hand, it is chosen and constructed in social exchange and dialogue that is beyond any individual's express control. For counseling, the work that discourse does in the construction of a person's problems in life is very important. The places where a person might experience painful problems are very often the places where he is refusing to comply with dominant discourse and experiencing consequences as a result, or they might be the very places where he is unconsciously complying with dominant discourse and feeling discontented as a result. Therefore, there is a sense in which counselors who are working with their clients about personal struggles are always working

BOX 5.2 AGENCY

In social science, there is considerable debate over where to draw the line between the determining effects of social structure and human agency. Agency is the ability to act, to make choices, on one's own behalf. To claim that individuals are completely free to do these things is to ignore the limiting effects of social forces that structure our experiences, such as social class, race, ethnicity, religion, cultural customs, and so on. Many of the chapters in this book explore these structuring forces and how they influence human independence.

Some take a strong position in the struggle between structure and agency and claim that people are completely free to make their own choices. In this book, we offer a social constructionist perspective interlaced with poststructuralist insights. From this viewpoint, people are not born with a limitless agency as of right. Instead, they are born with capacity for agency, but this capacity remains virtual until it is actualized (Deleuze & Guattari, 1994) as we encounter in our lives the impacts of a variety of social forces. These may variously be called lines of force, dominant discourses, or assemblages. They live in our language and in our cultural customs and they suggest to us what we should do. The language used by the dominant injunctions is often couched in terms like "you should ...", "it is normal to ...", or "the right thing to do is ... ."

Agency on one's own behalf, however, is more of a product than a right. It is produced by taking a position of difference from what is required of one. We might say it is achieved, or performed, rather than given. Sometimes this performance means engaging in active resistance.

Michel Foucault, who introduced a new analytics of how power relations work in the modern world, is sometimes wrongly assumed to have emphasized the corrosive effects of power relations and to have precluded the possibility of agency. However, as we mentioned above, Foucault (1988) also said in an interview late in his life that it was his purpose to "show people that they are much freer than they feel" (p. 10). In other words, it is possible to exercise agency much more often than people realize.

with the cultural dimensions of life. Our argument is that the concept of discourse enables us to see the swirling and changing forces at work, and not to pigeonhole Hong as a stereotypical Korean woman who thinks the way textbooks say Korean women think.

Positioning

The concept of positioning (Davies & Harré, 1990) is built on the concept of discourse. It can serve as a bridge between the personal and the social aspects of discourse. It is a metaphor used to describe the fluid and dynamic relationship between people and discourse. Positioning refers to the way in which every utterance in a conversation establishes, even for a moment, a relation that is made up of discourse and discursive assumptions. In this moment, a speaker establishes a position for herself in relation to a set of meanings, including identity meanings. She also positions other people in a place of meaning from which they are invited to respond. A conversation is made up of a series of position-taking utterances that install moments of "moral oughtness" (Linehan & McCarthy, 2001) based on particular discourses. Each utterance also issues a position call to listeners. It calls them into positions from which to respond. In this way, positioning enables us to examine the influence of discourse on individuals' lives, or how we come to take up certain identities and not others (Drewery, 2005).

Let's examine an example. In a conflict situation, someone says, "Look, I'm only trying to be reasonable here." At face value, this is a straightforward piece of communication. When we think of it in terms of positioning, it becomes rich and dynamic. The speaker is seeking to establish a position in a relation from which he will be taken seriously. The basis for the claim to be taken seriously is one of "being reasonable." If we ask what being reasonable means, we start to enter a world of discourse where certain behaviors will be regarded as reasonable and others will not. The dominant discourse of the modern world privileges a certain display of self as a rational person who can exhibit a degree of control, unless tested beyond reasonable limits. There is a small element of threat in the original utterance that suggests that if the listener does not respond with the same degree of rational behavior, then the speaker will not continue to be "reasonable." Along with the establishment of the position of being reasonable, there is also an implied opposite that is being ascribed to the listener. "You" are clearly being "unreasonable," or "overly emotional," or "crazy," and this is testing "my" long-suffering patience. In other words, the speaker establishes a position for himself, the rational and reasonable one, and calls the other person into a position from which to respond, that of the unreasonable and irrational one. In the background of both these positions lies a discourse and a history and a literature that specifies what will be taken to be rational and reasonable. Thus, even this simple sentence has a cultural world that it relies on to make any sense. It may also be a gendered world, in which men are assumed to be more rational and women more emotional by "nature."

The discursive concept of positioning has only recently begun to be described within the counseling literature (Drewery, 2005; Drewery, Winslade, & Monk, 2000; Sinclair, 2007; Sinclair & Monk, 2004; Winslade, 2005) despite the potential it holds for culturally and socially responsible work. In fact, we would argue that the concept of discourse is inadequate without incorporating the concept of positioning. Positioning points to the manner in which individuals are located in conversations as active participants in producing what they experience. That is, individuals always speak and act from particular contexts and in response to other conversational moves that have gone before. Therefore, discourses are manifest in how we go forward in our therapeutic engagements. There is a dynamic back-and-forth quality to how we are positioned by discourse and how these discursive moves influence the changing assumptions and expectations we have about one another and ourselves. As Carla Willig (2001) explains, "discourses make available particular subject positions (certain ways-of-seeing the world and certain ways-of-being in the world) that when taken up, have particular implications for subjectivity and experience" (p. 107). For example, sexist language provides exclusionary positioning for women to the extent that unequal conditions of possibility are created (Winslade, 2005). In the family counseling arena, this can look like a husband asking his wife (without any prior negotiation), "I'm going to the gym; when are you picking up the kids from soccer practice?" In this instance, the woman is excluded from any possibility other than engaging in the caregiving of the children.

In emphasizing the subjectivity that is produced through the positions we take up (or are positioned in by others), the concept of positioning helps direct attention to the dynamic aspects of interactions (Davies & Harré, 1990) and prevents a static and fixed understanding of discourse. Moreover, the discursive fields within which people live inevitably provide some degree of subjectivity and thus an agentic position. The emphasis on the subjective (as opposed to subjected) quality of positioning permits individuals to exercise choice in relation to the discourses available. As Bronwyn Davies and Rom Harré point out, "choice is inevitably involved because there are many and contradictory discursive practices that each person could engage in" (p. 3). From this perspective, then, the power of dominant discourses is not absolute and invitations to take up certain positions in discourses can be accepted or rejected. For example, sometimes an initial move by the therapist as the dominant identity in the therapeutic conversation will influence the other speaker, the client, into positions she may not have ordinarily taken up. However, this framework recognizes that positioning in discourses creates space for resistance and renders our interactions in therapy visible, contestable, and amenable to change. Moreover, the agency conceptualized here is distinct from the agency within liberal humanism (see Chapter 6 for more about this concept), since it exists between people rather than within the individual (Drewery, 2005). Vivien Burr (2015) talks about how agency is only possible when it occurs to relation to others.

This understanding of our participation in the creation of new discursive possibilities allows us to consider how invitations for incorporating dominant discourse (in a non-reflexive manner) can be challenged or adapted. In other words, positioning allows room to actively engage with discourses in a way that is liberating. To be exact, disrupting dominant discourses opens up spaces for competing discourses in which alternative ways of being can be constructed. Indeed, there are discourses that do not typically bear such a dominant and oppressive influence in people's interactions. These *alternative* discourses challenge the more dominant discourses and are often representative of marginalized cultural ideas circulating within a context or community. Examples of alternative discourses around families include the following:

"Husband and wives are equally suited for economic and domestic activities."

"Single-parent families raise successful and well-adapted children."

"Children's voices are an integral part of family life."

"Same-sex couples are legitimate and deserving parents."

Examples of Positioning

In order to make the concept of positioning more explicit, let's look at some examples. Here is an exchange in which a young girl is positioned in gender discourse. The speaker is Rieko, whose ancestry is Japanese.

> *When I was about 10 years old, I became aware of the fact that I was a girl. My mother used to say, "Help me with the cooking and cleaning the rooms. You are a girl." My brother did not have to do any work at home. We were not treated equally. When I was at home with my brother, I was given instructions to do dishes and prepare dinner for my father and my siblings. I would complain, and my mother would reprimand me and say, "You are a girl. This is your training to take care of your husband and children in the future."*

Rieko is issued an explicit instruction that positions her in the place of either refusal or compliance. She makes an effort to complain, using the word *equal* to indicate her awareness of the existence of an alternative discourse. In the end, however, the force of the identity position, "You are a girl," is too much and she has to comply. This is an example of a statement that has behind it a matrix of assumptions that are not spoken but that everyone knows. What is also of interest is that Rieko remembers this exchange as an adult and maintains within herself a sense of the injustice in this differential positioning of boys and girls. In other words, the dominant discourse still works on her, but she is not completely subjugated into acquiescing to this discourse inside herself. Counseling should help someone like Rieko to articulate more fully the objections she has to the dominant discourse and to grow places of resistance in her own mind and in her interactions with others.

Now let's look at an example of positioning, from a counseling session, that is focused on both abuse and social class issues (Winslade, 2005).

> **Janine:** *When I was seven, I just had to do one little thing wrong and my mother would beat me. She wouldn't hold back. It was awful. I used to hate her. We used to live in a trailer park and the neighbours used to hear me scream and then look at me funny for a few days. Then when I got to be a teenager she would tell me sometimes you're never going to be worth anything, you're not going to do anything.*
>
> **Counsellor:** *What effect did that have for you?*
>
> **Janine:** *It has stayed with me and when I am feeling down it comes back and haunts me.*
>
> **Counsellor:** *So it has wormed its way inside you and it affects you. What does it affect in your relationships with others?*
>
> **Janine:** *It makes me feel like I am different all the time and that I don't really belong with people who are smart or have a nice house or a good job.*

Counsellor: So it undermines your sense of being OK in yourself.

Janine: Yes, I think it's half the reason why my identity always seems to be lacking something, because of all the self-doubt that I have accumulated. (pp. 358–359)

Like the previous example, this extract from a counseling conversation shows how positioning works to create both social and personal effects. Janine's mother made comments that positioned her in a place of self-doubt and of inferior social worth. Such comments were supported by the conditions of her life, hence they are difficult not to internalize. Janine works hard to challenge these positions in her own mind and in how she is raising her daughter. Again, the counselor's job is to help her to counteract the pieces of cultural positioning that are still negatively impacting her and to reposition herself in an alternative discourse, one in which she is accorded a place of worth.

The importance and practical value of the dynamic concepts of discourse and positioning cannot be overestimated. The advantage of taking up these conceptual tools is that it provides counselors with a way to keep the cultural backdrop of contemporary life visible and invites clients to think and be otherwise, which can be extremely freeing (Drewery & Monk, 1994). In other words, an examination of the discourses and positions available to therapists and clients helps work toward taking up positions in discourses that are less personally damaging (Burr, 2015). In this way, the concept of discourse takes change for granted.

Deconstruction

One feature of discourse is that it often does its work right under our noses without our noticing. There does not have to be anything deeply buried that must be found by tunneling deep down in the psyche. It is more that the surface evidence is often being overlooked because it is so obvious. We have become so used to it that we have taken its truth value for granted. Still, it sometimes takes some effort to uncover the work being done by discourse behind our backs, as it were. This is where the concept of deconstruction becomes useful.

The process by which discourses and positions are unpacked is called deconstruction. Deconstruction refers to the practice of exploring and uncovering the taken-for-granted assumptions and influential discourses that underpin our conversation, behavior, and emotional expression. The term *deconstruction* derives from the work of the French philosopher Jacques Derrida (1978). It was introduced into the therapeutic literature by Michael White (1992). Derrida developed the concept of deconstruction in the context of literary theory. He was interested in the problem of how to understand the meaning of a word in a piece of text. The conventional answer is to consult a standard authority (e.g., a dictionary) on the meaning of the word, or to inquire into the intentions of the author who is using it. Derrida argues, however, that neither of these approaches will do. The reason is that there is no trustworthy authority that is not itself part of the discourse context that the word refers to. And the intentions of the author are not free of the influence of other texts produced out of that same discourse context. Derrida says that the use of a word is always bound within a social and linguistic context and carries with it the many other uses of that concept in the thousands of other conversations that have taken place in the history of a language. Mikhail Bakhtin (1986) argues a similar point and refers to the way in which a word or a meaning echoes down a "long corridor of voices" (p. 121). This corridor of voices is another term for what we have been calling discourse. It is also another metaphor that refers to the world of culture.

Derrida's concern in proposing deconstruction as a method of inquiry is not to make everything relative and meaningless, as some critics contend. It is not a destructive or nihilistic aim. Derrida has even asserted that there are some things that cannot be deconstructed. He cites a moral concern for justice as an example:

> If anything is undeconstructable, it is justice. The law is deconstructable, fortunately: it is infinitely perfectable. I am tempted to regard justice as the best word, today, for what refuses to yield to deconstruction, that is to say for what sets deconstruction in motion, what justifies it. It is an affirmative experience of the coming of the other as other. (Derrida, 1994, p. 36)

Deconstruction aims to break up rigidities of thought, particularly where they are having oppressive consequences, and to open up a field of inquiry to previously unnoticed possibilities. It achieves this by disassembling pieces of discourse that are actually "constructions" that pose as "natural" truths. In the modern world, natural truths are regularly accorded the highest form of truth status.

Giovanna Borradori (2003) has offered a summary of Derrida's deconstructive method that can be summarized as follows:

1. Identify the conceptual construction of a particular discourse. Find the key words on which decisions turn or identities are assigned.
2. Identify the conceptual pairs that make up the polarized options for thought around which a discourse is organized. This move is based on the idea that every concept exists not just as a positive identity but also as a negation of something else. Male is not female. Light is not dark. Educated is not illiterate. Normal is not abnormal. Healthy is not sick. Ideal is not material. White is not Black. Culture is not nature. Derrida contends that meanings rely on their polarized opposite and that the meaning of the positive meaning depends on the negation of its opposite. Hence, they are tied together in a binary relation. Moreover, the pairing is organized in a hierarchy that privileges one meaning over the other. The construction of race is a case in point. It consistently privileges White over Black.
3. Derrida invites us to play with this binary pairing and invert it so that the normally subordinated meaning is privileged. For example, we might ask, "What would it be like if Black were the privileged meaning?"
4. Derrida invokes a search for surplus meaning, for third and fourth possible meanings that escape our attention if we focus only on the binary pairing. The aim is to break down the structure of the binary pair by overloading it with new meanings. The result is that new choices about how to respond to a text or a situation might emerge.

The concept of deconstruction is relevant for counseling because counselors, like literary critics, are vitally interested in carefully making meaning of the things that their clients tell them. Clients are frequently caught in binary oppositions. They experience them as internal dilemmas or problems and they bring them to counselors. They are also living in circumstances prescribed within discourses that divide their worlds in binary ways. In the West for example, our lives have historically been constructed in ways that require a choice between two binary genders, male and female, out of perhaps four possible biological sexes that people are born into. Of the multiple ancestries and cultural influences that we grow up among, the binary pairing of White and non-White is selected out, not by nature but by social construction, as the major dividing line around which people are allocated opportunity and privilege or denied these things. Of the wide range of human sexual responses, two major identities are historically selected out as a binary pair: heterosexual and homosexual. Other binaries include Christian and non-Christian, able-bodied and disabled, intelligent and learning-disabled, law-abiding and criminal, sane and insane.

Michael White (1992) was the first to introduce the concept of deconstruction into the practice of therapy. His use of the term is, he admits (p. 121), a little looser than Derrida's. It is, however, directed toward the same objective: that of helping people overwhelmed by the effects of rigid discourses in their lives to identify how things might be otherwise. White uses the term *deconstruction* to refer to processes of therapeutic inquiry in which the counseling aims to "subvert taken-for-granted realities and practices" (p. 121) by "rendering them strange" (p. 122). He directs the deconstructive focus specifically on ways in which dominant cultural narratives work to produce aspects of a person's self-narrative or identity.

The use of deconstruction in counseling involves a tentative, curious, deliberately naive posture. It differs from a more oppositional social critique in this way. For example, it leads a counselor to ask of any problem story, "What was left out? What was covered over? What was paid attention to and what was not?" (Monk, Winslade, Crocket, & Epston, 1997). Counseling from a discursive perspective focuses on the contextual staging of problems rather than on essentialist aims such as personality change or symptom removal. It is also less preoccupied with seeking definitive and objective answers for individuals. Deconstruction is also not something that counselors do to clients. During counseling, clients are themselves invited to engage in the deconstruction process that challenges the ways in which cultural systems maintain the status quo. This is achieved especially through developing curiosity about the meanings that dominate clients' understanding. Deconstructive questioning asks where these meanings come from, whom they benefit, what discourse grants them authority, and what other preferences or competencies they mask. When deconstruction is applied successfully, the client questions his preoccupations and preferred points of reference, familiar habits, social practices, beliefs, and judgments, which are often regarded as common sense.

The practice of deconstruction is differentiated from other forms of counseling, including what can be considered "best practice," in that it appreciates fully the extent to which people are seduced by culture and its imperatives to behave in certain ways. It therefore avoids the assumption that a person's cultural background provides her with authoritative identity prescriptions that must only be respected and followed. Deconstruction rather suggests that the world of culture is always riven with contested meanings and that the dominant meanings are not necessarily optimal. Deconstruction practices are especially helpful in addressing some of the more subtle effects of dominant discourse on the client; "because dominant discourses are so familiar, they are taken for granted and even recede from view" (Hare-Mustin, 1994, p. 20). Furthermore, when individuals are unaware of the particular discursive influences impacting them, they have a much more limited range of discursive responses available to them. In other words, deconstructive analysis of very particular discourse usages opens up choice and frees up the position-taking that is possible.

Deconstructing Identity Stories

Having outlined the three concepts of discourse, positioning, and deconstruction, we are now ready to put them to use. To understand these concepts better and to see how they can be useful, let's look at a series of identity statements and consider them as pieces of discourse that can be deconstructed. They are also position statements that can be analyzed so that the work that they do to form social relations can be made more explicit.

Here is LaShanda's story. Her mother is Japanese and her father is African American.

> *The union of my father, coming from the lower–middle class, and my mother, coming from the middle class, did not make my Grandma Rochelle happy. Grandpa Graham said he did not want his children marrying anyone of color. Grandma Rochelle felt that my mother shamed the family, so she was disowned. Marrying out of the race was not acceptable. All of my uncles and aunts had married Chinese people or another type of Asian. Rochelle herself was not treated nicely by her mother-in-law, yet she treated my father wrongly. Grandma Tracy and her family were extremely happy to see Ron getting married, but my Grandma Tracy has said some really hurtful things to me and my siblings. She told us that, because we are not "full" African American, we do not love her as much as her sisters and their grandchildren do. My mother is dead to her extended side of the family; therefore, I do not know much about them. If my mother's relatives found out about me and my family, they would be shamed again, and it could lead to my Grandma Rochelle's being disowned from the family. The division of my extended family is due to the union between my father and mother.*

In La Shanda's story, many questions are raised about the meaning of race and also about social class. There is a background discourse in place that specifies that marriage with a person of another race breaks a rule in a social world where the dividing lines are sharply drawn around race. A similar discourse about marrying another of one's own "station" is also in place. If we were to take an essentialist approach, we might locate the source of the disowning, the hurtful comments, and the family schisms in the prejudiced thinking of individuals. If we deconstruct the motivations behind these actions, we might be more inclined to locate their origins in the discourse about race and class that circulates in the wider cultural background and that has exerted a powerful influence on the thinking of these people.

For example, the idea that there can be such a thing as "full" African American presupposes the opposite possibility of a person being "half blooded." We have seen already that the whole idea of full and half bloodedness is based on 19th-century biological discourse that has long since been discredited as unscientific, and yet it persists in popular discourse. It assumes the existence of racial "purity," a notion that has continued to operate as a piece of discourse that builds on efforts to divide people into discrete racial groups. If we were to invoke Derrida's principle of turning a dominant discourse on its head and consider for a while the possibility that being born to parents or mixed ancestry might be more the norm than is imagined and that, if we dig a little, no one is actually purely anything, then perhaps the meaning of this family conflict might look different.

None of the people who are playing out this family drama invented these divisions or these concepts of racial purity. Therefore, it makes no deconstructive sense to talk with them about their prejudices or their personally faulty logic. The discourse that has influenced their actions has enveloped them and shaped their working assumptions. As a result, LaShanda's parents and LaShanda herself have been offered positions from which to respond in conversations that are not those of fully legitimate members of a family. Such positioning is hurtful and engenders shame and anger. And yet, each of these people has choices about whether he or she will choose to join with the background discourses of race and class or not. LaShanda seems to indicate that she is aware of at least the possibility of a very different approach. Even though she does not spell this out explicitly, LaShanda's comments give a hint of an opening to some ways in which things could be otherwise in her family. Counseling that focuses on deconstruction can potentially open up these implicit surplus meanings for exploration and future decision-making.

Esmelda identifies herself as a Chicana. There are strong views in my family about women and their roles in marriage and having children. My brothers have had children out of wedlock, and, although my mother was disappointed about it, it was accepted and the family moved on. However, when my sister was pregnant before getting married, she was kicked out of the house and spoken of really badly by my father, and we all let her know how upset and disappointed we were with her.

It is important for the daughters to be married to be considered somebody. The stress on marriage is not as apparent for the males. In nuclear and extended family, the question of marriage pops up at almost all family gatherings. "So, when are you getting married? Your sister is already on her second and you haven't even had your first."

My question to them would be, "How many marriages are you supposed to have?"

Although getting a divorce is looked down on, being married equals success. To some of our more traditional family members from Mexico, having an education is not as important as marriage.

As my sister kindly put it the other day, "it doesn't matter that we graduated from college and are both doing our master's; we are nothing because we aren't married."

One of my father's sayings about my sister and me is, "Ya estan dejadas." ("They have already been left behind.")

This saying is often used in my culture to refer to women; no guy is going to want to marry them because of whatever reason. To my father and to his family, my sister and I, at the ages of 26 and 27, are already considered old for marriage.

Now I am all grown up, and unfortunately things haven't changed much. My family's beliefs are still the same. Because I am a Chicana, I am still expected to become married and have children. It has been hard for my father to say that he is proud that my sister and I have bachelor's degrees and are both currently in graduate school. For him and other members in the extended family, our educational accomplishments are mere awards. We will be considered successful the day we are married and the day we have children.

This struggle has had an impact on me for the longest time. I think about how I will raise my children and how I will attempt to keep some, if not all, of those beliefs out of my immediate family. It is a struggle to try to balance my family's beliefs with my own, and I can see how this has affected me and will continue.

In certain situations, such as at extended family gatherings or at events with my ex-boyfriend, I have felt the need to act differently. For instance, instead of being together with everyone, I feel I have to stay separated with the women. I have to serve my father and brothers, or ask my partner if he would like to be served. If I don't, my family or significant other will look bad, and that would be the last thing I'd want. At these times I feel as if I'm being a hypocrite because I believe these kinds of roles shouldn't exist.

Therefore, my biggest struggle is trying to keep the idea that women and men are equal without embarrassing my family or a significant other. How do I maintain my own beliefs while still keeping my values and respecting the family? It is as if I have to go along with the idea that women are less than men in order to not put the family to shame. I need to keep up with the cultural idea of the female gender role and still maintain what I consider to be right.

Esmelda is struggling to establish a position that she feels comfortable with in relation to gender discourse. Her own preferences are compromised by the strength of patriarchal discourse in her family. Within this discourse she has been positioned as "left behind" and therefore not normal or legitimate. This positioning gives her a narrow range of options from which to respond, and she experiences being squeezed. We can distill the dominant discourse from Esmelda's comments and represent it in statements such as the following:

"Marriage, more than education, defines a woman as a success."

"The right age for a woman to marry is in her early 20s."

"A man should be the primary breadwinner and more educated than his female partner."

"A woman can attain true happiness only after marriage."

"A good mother devotes her entire life to her children and family."

Deconstructive counseling with Esmelda might examine the cultural and gendered discourses at work and their effects on her. It might notice the places where she is willing to make compromises with the dominant discourse (we all have to do that on occasion) and also the places where she wants to exercise her own preferences and position herself in places of resistance. In those places, good counseling might encourage her to articulate more fully the alternative discourses she would like to draw on and examine with her the conscious positions she might want to take up.

In this chapter, we have introduced some concepts that we think of as tools to think with when discussing cultural issues. We believe that they can be used more extensively in the intercultural counseling field than they have been to date. These tools have potential for opening up the tensions and contradictions within cultural worlds, as well as the consistencies and commonalities. To us, they seem to make cultural worlds come alive as sites of difference, movement, and contest, rather than rendering them narrow and static. They enable us to understand processes of change, and since counseling is about the facilitation of change, we believe this is an important advantage.

However, the process of change in relation to dominant discourses will necessarily encounter obstacles. Dominant discourses, by their nature, seek to remain in positions of dominance. Many people who are committed to aspects of them in their daily experience will act to keep them in place, so there will often be struggles that take place in families, in communities, and in cultural worlds. To make sense of these power struggles, intercultural counselors need to develop an analysis of how power works, and that is the subject we shall turn to next. In the next three chapters, we will explore some alternative readings of power.

Read the following examples, and then discuss and identify the discourses at work in these examples as you respond to the questions that follow.

Rieko (Japanese)

It is true that some Japanese people have undergone plastic surgery to make their eyes appear round. Recently, a number of women have undergone cosmetic surgery in Korea, where cosmetic surgeries are more popular and cheaper. I understand their feelings and their reasons.

I believe that attractive people have more social power. They are able to exercise power on a daily basis and negotiate their lives more efficiently. Physically attractive women are more likely to get privilege than unattractive ones. In many situations, they seem to be treated better and get more opportunities. I had hoped to be an attractive woman. I wanted bigger eyes, long eyelashes, a higher and narrower nose, bigger breasts, and longer and thinner legs. If I had these things, I would have lived a different life.

FIGURE 5.1   Rieko Onuma describes herself as Japanese.

Sarah (heterosexual)

My family is accepting of heterosexual and homosexual choices. My aunt is bisexual and for many years dated only women. Although this took time for my grandparents to accept, they had sensed it before she told them, so it was not a complete shock. Being exposed to gay culture at an early age has positively affected me. I am comfortable interacting with individuals who are gay and strongly support gay rights.

Mandy (Iranian)

The woman's role is primarily based on maintaining innocence and purity. Virginity is imperative for a woman before she is married. Otherwise, she is considered worthless. Once married, women take on the roles of submissive wife, domestic keeper, and loving mother. Although education and a career are attainable prospects, women are more respected for their domestic skills than they are for their individual achievement. On the contrary, Iranian men are honored and tenacious. Sexism in the culture is ubiquitous, as men are not judged for engaging in premarital sex. Furthermore, Iranian law supports the claim that one man is equivalent to two women. This chauvinistic mentality tolerates no deviance.

Discuss

1. What are the major concepts around which identity can be built in each of these pieces of text?
2. Where are the dividing lines around which differences are marked?
3. What background assumptions do these stories rely on?
4. What discursive statements can you construct that represent the taken-for-granted assumptions of this discourse?
5. What examples can you find of persons being positioned in relation to a dominant discourse?
6. What examples can you find of people drawing on a counter discourse or of resisting the position calls they are offered?

Response to Chapter 5

DAVID PARÉ, PHD

David is a counselling psychologist and director of the Glebe Institute, A Centre for Constructive and Collaborative Practice in Ottawa, Canada. He has written widely and presented internationally on the subject of narrative and collaborative therapies, as well as offering training and supervision in these areas. He is the author of The Practice of Collaborative Counselling and Psychotherapy *(2012), and co-editor of* Collaborative Practice in Psychology and Therapy *(2004);* Furthering Talk: Advances in the Discursive Therapies *(2004); and* Social Justice and Counselling *(2018).*

There was a time when there were no words for the complex interplay of ideas and beliefs, symbols and social rituals that constitute the ways of being in the world that we call "culture" today. Culture was just people living their lives and expressing their humanness in familiar patterns. But as homogeneous local communities expanded outward, they encountered others whose histories and values were unfamiliar, whose ways were strange. *Difference* became manifest, and the language of "culture" emerged to create distinctions never made before. This made it possible to talk about, to think about, and even to act in relation to each other in novel ways.

As John Austin (1962) reminded us, words help us *get things done*, not the least "thing" of which is what Nelson Goodman (1978) called "worldmaking." Language introduces distinctions to make sense of the "great blooming, buzzing confusion" that William James (1890/1981) described infants as perceiving until language helps them organize their experience (p. 462). This is all useful stuff when it comes to counseling and therapy. The dizzying complexity of persons' lives is organized in critically helpful ways through the language we bring to our work. Of that language, "culture" (along with many other words, meanings, and constructs that reverberate around it) has been eminently serviceable for alerting us that therapeutic conversations always take place across a divide. The introduction of culture as a key term awakened the field to its own traditional ethnocentricity. It reminded us that difference characterizes the social world and that homogeneity is an unattainable myth.

These reflections on words as tools for getting things done bubbled up in me as I read through Chapter 5. I see the chapter, indeed this book, as a generous offering of additional tools for practitioners to share with the persons who consult them as they construct new paths forward in complex lives. The chapter takes on theory of distinguished vintage but with a reputation for opaqueness and distills it to the point of transparent clarity. And it does so for some eminently practical purposes. Monk, Winslade, Sinclair and polanco suggest that the trusty tool that is the word *culture* may not always be enough to take on the increasingly complex task of counseling in the 21st century. They offer *discourse* as a valuable addition to counselors' repertoire of worldmaking implements. In what remains of my response, I would like to reflect briefly on three of the many aspects of culturally rooted lives that discourse helps us to engage, and to share an example to illustrate the ideas.

Discursive Multiplicity

While "culture" reminds us that the persons who consult us come from distinct backgrounds, it's been less helpful in illuminating the many strands of often contradictory ideas and practices that converge simultaneously, like threads of alternate histories, in persons' lives. This may be because the word *culture* has echoes of past meanings that located persons in one *or* another culture, usually separated geographically. In recent years, globalization has brought a massive intermingling of cultures, and contemporary uses of *culture* in counseling transcend the notion of a fixed geographic location. Not only that, but the word now encompasses categories like gender, class, and sexual orientation in addition to race and ethnicity, opening things up further. But *culture* falters in trying to capture how the myriad influences that surround us (as someone once said, "We are the fish; discourse is the water") are present *at the same time*, and recede in and out of the foreground as contexts shift. In "cultural" terms, this would be like saying we are both members and nonmembers of particular cultures concurrently: a confusing idea. Understanding persons as at the crossroads of multiple discourses helps to clarify things and opens conversational options not available when we view them as rooted in particular cultures.

Power and Dominant Meanings

I have leafed through the indexes of dozens of contemporary counseling texts in search of the word *power* and found to my dismay that it is rarely included. There is a rich thread of social analysis that comes with the introduction of the word *discourse* to the counseling lexicon. It makes it more possible to join with people in identifying how certain meanings (and the thoughts, feelings, and actions accompanying them) have taken hold because they are attached to powerful stories circulating in the broader culture. It trains the eyes and ears for alternative meanings obscured by dominant versions of "the way things are." And, equally useful, the attention to discourse leads counselors to turn a mirror on their practices and to consider the way that their theories and models, and the institutions in which they are embedded, can be at the service of maintaining normative standards versus opening the door to new possibilities.

The Co-Construction of Meaning

As this chapter reminds us, discourse refers to "both the process of talk and interaction between people and the products of that interaction." Here's another way to put it: discourse is both a verb and a noun (Strong & Paré, 2004). We don't just "draw on" existing meanings generated elsewhere when we talk with each other—talking itself brings new meanings into the world. The importance of this distinction may be easier to understand if we revert to the language of culture. The implication is that our work doesn't just happen *in* culture and isn't just talk *about* culture. Counseling conversations are in effect sites for joining with others in "culture making."

Alain is a working-class, 18-year-old French Canadian (known as a Francophone in Canada), self-identified as gay, enrolled in an English-speaking high school mostly attended by wealthy Anglophones. His slight French accent just adds to his energetic, extroverted charm, and he is popular among his circle of mainly gay friends at the school. Alain wants to speak to a counselor not because of problems associated with familiar "cultural" categories like sexual orientation, class, or language group. Rather, he has found he derives more joy in impersonating celebrities and making people laugh than he does in sitting still for hours reading, writing, and working out equations. Alain's gifts are invisible to his father, an electrician, who expects his son to take up the trade that he himself learned from his father. And they are frowned on in a school system that assigns merit according to its own scorecard. Increasingly, Alain feels like a failure.

The construct of "culture" in the broadest sense helps to locate Alain in society. But it is less useful for identifying the meanings that position him as not measuring up and thus unworthy. Those meanings are threaded through the wider culture he inhabits and can be traced intergenerationally through his family. They are a "dominant discourse" that exists alongside *other* versions of events that become more available to Alain as we explore his gifts, connecting them to his Uncle Jacques, who made a career as an actor. There is a multiplicity of stories in Alain's life, and our conversations help to foreground useful ones overshadowed by dominant meanings.

At the same time, it is important that we pay attention to the language of "attention-deficit disorder," which could be taken up in ways that position me as the expert assessor of pathology and Alain as the holder of the deficit. This is where the tool of discourse helps alert me to the risks of merely reinforcing normative prescriptions that Alain is already finding problematic. This is not to say we ignore the possibility that his learning style presents challenges in the school context. But it allows us to grab on to alternative threads and to construct new meanings. In asking Alain, "How have you been able to hang on to your creativity in the face of these messages that surround you?" I am not merely seeking information. This is discourse as verb: Alain and I are co-constructing culture as we speak, and over time it becomes a home for his abundant gifts.

Chapter 6

Power and Privilege

This chapter addresses the issue of power. It is a thorny issue in the helping professions, which are mainly oriented to working with one person at a time. When you are engrossed in counseling one person with regard to their struggles in life, it is often hard to conceptualize how the problems they are talking about are part of a larger picture of cultural relations. But that is what is required in an intercultural approach to helping relationships. An emphasis on culture invites us to see persons not just as individuals with their own thoughts and feelings about their lives, but as participants in discourse exchanges that shape what they think and feel, and as members of social groups that define and legitimate in important ways what they might feel and think about. Even seeing people as members of social groups, though, is not enough, because social groups, like individuals, never exist in isolation. They are always in some form of relation with each other. Hence, we do not really learn enough about a person by knowing about her group membership without considering how the social groups that she identifies with are drawn into relation with other social groups.

It would be nice if all the social groups to which people belonged were equally valued in our communities, and if members of all these groups had equal rights and opportunities in life. Then all we would have to do from a cultural perspective would be to appreciate and celebrate difference. In fact, this simple notion of appreciating and celebrating difference commonly appears in much professional talk about culture and counseling. From this perspective, counselors would only need to learn about and honor the experiences of each social group that they worked with in order for counseling to be socially just. A moment's reflection on life in the United States or anywhere else, however, is enough to see that this situation does not exist. There are clearly inequities and differential opportunities in many areas of life. Ideal social justice, while a noble idea, cannot be found on the ground in relations between social groups in any totally satisfactory form. You can find those who claim, usually from a position of privilege, that there is such a situation, but there are always others who object and protest that their chances in life are limited in some material way. Such protests may come from the African American community, who bear a disproportionate share of the negative effects of many elements of life in the United States. For example, one only needs to consider the large number of police shootings that kill many innocent African American people, which set in motion the Black Lives Matter movement. Women still do not command the same salaries as men. Organ transplants are given more frequently to White individuals. Large numbers of the poor do not receive adequate healthcare. Obese people are commonly overlooked for employment. Sexual minorities are sometimes targets for taunting and violent hate crimes. Prostitutes are arrested but their clients are not. These are just a random selection of injustices that can be traced back to power relations.

We need to develop an account of power relations to explain how inequalities between people and between groups of people are produced and how they shape and affect people's lives. An analysis of power needs to tell how persons influence and shape the lives of other persons and how institutional authority impacts the lives of individuals. We need an account of both privilege and disadvantage and of the ways in which these are not produced randomly, but systematically. An account of power relations needs to give us conceptual tools with which to make sense of the things that people say to counselors about the social limits they encounter. How we as professionals conceptualize these things will make a difference to how we respond to our clients, in how we conceive of their problems, and the remedial strategies we choose to engage with them. The task of this chapter, then, is to outline how we might conceptualize power.

As with many other domains of practice, simple consensus on these concepts does not exist. There are debates about the very terms in which power is talked about. We will outline the main ideas about power that have dominated the counseling literature in recent decades. We will also address recent postmodern developments in how power is conceptualized that offer promise for new forms of practice. Contemporary approaches to culture suggest that counseling is not neutral or objective. Especially in relation to questions of power, neutrality and objectivity can render us like the news reporter who photographs a drowning person instead of trying to save her. Our goal is not to be objective, but to represent the most useful ideas we have encountered and say why we prefer them, in the hope that you will be stimulated to develop your own thinking.

Three Approaches to Power

We will describe three approaches to the analysis of power relations. They arise out of three different views of the world and lead to markedly different orientations to social practice. The first is the *liberal humanist* view of power that has given rise to most of the world's democratic systems of government, the American (U.S.) Constitution among them. This view is based on privileging the individual as the prime mover in the social world. Advocates of this perspective, therefore, concentrate on how power is attached to individuals. In psychology, this analysis translates into an understanding of "personal" power.

The second view of power is based on structural thinking. It analyzes power as positions in an underlying social structure, rather than as the personal property of the individual. Hence, it is typical of what is sometimes called a *structuralist* analysis. A structuralist approach informed the social analysis of Karl Marx and the psychoanalytic theorizing of Sigmund Freud. This view of power has had an enormous influence on thought in many fields of academic study, such as politics, economics, history, and sociology. A structuralist analysis has spurred a series of social movements to address structural inequities and has been influential in cultural politics in social practice.

A third approach to the analysis of power is newer and based on the *poststructuralist* perspective, which has challenged both the liberal humanist and the structuralist view of life. Michel Foucault (1980, 2000) has made a major contribution to this way of thinking and offers some revolutionary tools with which to think about power relations and how they affect the lives of counseling clients. We want to explain each of these conceptualizations of power relations and explore their implications for counseling practice.

A Liberal Humanist View of Power

The liberal perspective focuses on individual citizens who are, in theory at least, born equal. Differences among people spring from the choices they make, the extent to which they use their genius or potential, and the accidents of genetic endowment. The idea of democratic equality in power relations had its modern origins in the 17th century in the work of John Locke who, in his "Treatise on Government," first articulated the theory of individuals having "natural rights," which he considered the economic right to own property and the intellectual right to freedom of conscience. These natural rights, forerunners of the modern idea of "human rights," were God given and superseded the rights of kings. As such, they constituted a challenge to the premodern idea that people were certainly not equal but instead slotted into a hierarchically organized Chain of Being, and that communities functioned best if everything was in order in this hierarchy (Taylor, 2004). The idea of these individual rights drove the English revolutions of 1642 and 1688 and eventually gave impetus to the French Revolution a century later. The American (U.S.) Revolution picked up the same notions of individual freedom and political rights in the American Constitution.

Free and equal citizens participate in the marketplace of life and influence each other to varying degrees as authors of their own decisions who act in their own interests. The idea of individual rights requires persons to be independent, rational, unitary beings who are freely responsible for their own decisions and fundamentally separate from the social and historical world around them. Personal change is initiated by the individual and dependent on his or her choice. Change occurs within the individual and is initiated by drawing on personal power. This focus is favored over any assumption that external sociocultural and historical influences might determine human action.

The emphasis on individualism as opposed to collectivity led to the modern tendency for liberal humanism to universalize human experience. Mainstream psychology has consistently maintained that its primary focus of study is on a human nature that represents the core functions of the universal human psyche, which is common to all people. However, this is an unusual emphasis in the history of culture. Anthropologist Clifford Geertz (1983) commented on the narrow, culturally prescribed person described by liberal humanist discourse.

> The Western conception of the person as a bounded, unique, more or less integrated motivational and cognitive universe, a dynamic centre of awareness, emotion, judgment, and action, organized into a distinctive whole and set contrastively against other such wholes and against a social and natural background is, however incorrigible it may seem to us, a rather peculiar idea within the context of the world's cultures. (p. 59)

In other words, the perspective from which we might analyze power in cultural relations is itself rooted in a cultural world view.

Liberal humanism has dominated the counseling field. From Rogerian psychotherapy in the 1960s, this perspective has consistently identified the individual as the agent of social phenomena. In 1998, Stephen Weinrach and Kenneth Thomas stated that counseling theories (all of them) are rooted in humanism, the individual being the center of any focus. They suggested that abandonment of humanistic counseling theories would leave counseling bereft of any viable theories. We would not agree. We can see a number of burgeoning counseling theories that are steadily abandoning the liberal humanist agenda.

Nevertheless, healthy identity has been consistently associated with the dominant White Western cultural norms of achievement, individualism, self-determination, and material success (Ivey, 1993; Maslow, 1956; Olssen, 1991; Ridley, Mendoza, & Kanitz, 1994; Sampson, 1989). Therapeutic goals such as self-actualization, independence, creativity, competence, and autonomy are all based on an individualistic ethic and orientation to therapy.

If power is about how people get others to do their bidding, then a liberal view of power seeks to explain how this is achieved through the internal attributes of the individual. Some individuals are strong and powerful and others are weak and powerless. Power is something that individual people "hold" and then exercise. It is an object that can be accrued and amassed over time in greater and greater amounts. If it can be held and accrued, there is a sense in which it can be measured and calculated. Whenever you hear someone say that one person is more powerful than another, there is a liberal humanist idea of power somewhere in the background.

You can accrue power by advancing to a position of greater personal authority and become a manager, a judge, a politician, a chief executive; or, for that matter, a gang leader or terrorist mastermind. You can make decisions that impact other people's lives. You can accrue wealth and buy more influence over others. You can threaten others with physical force and get them to do what you want. You can become more educated and develop the authority that comes with speaking with greater knowledge than others. You can develop a charismatic eloquence or conform to stereotypical versions of physical beauty that attracts others to you. Power in this sense is emblematic of a position in a social hierarchy. You get more of it by advancing up the ladder of the hierarchy. Where the specific hierarchy is more diffuse, social "status" is conferred on individuals by titles, leadership roles, ownership, recognition of achievements, academic degrees, or election to office.

The flip side is the idea that other individuals are not so lucky, or have not had the strength of character or foresight to accrue much of the various currencies in which power is measured. They have not worked hard enough or made good financial decisions and are not wealthy. They have not put time into study and acquired the knowledge that makes others defer to their judgments and opinions. They lack enough strength of character to assert themselves in conflict situations. They are physically weaker and less able therefore to back up their influence with force or the threat of it. In the discourse that developed during the 1980s, such individuals are described as "disempowered," in contrast to the powerful.

Simple accounts of power in the liberal humanist tradition have nevertheless developed greater sophistication. Those who do not have access to the main currencies of power are described (consciously or unconsciously) as resorting to covert means of "manipulating" others. Personal power has also been talked about in the counseling literature with reference to the concept of "assertiveness" (for example, Twenge, 2001). In the liberal humanist tradition, empowerment is often the action of a professional who teaches skills to an individual who lacks the ability to exercise power. They may be skills in "saying no," focusing on strengths, building individual resilience, or taking risks to stand up to powerful people. What is noticeable often is the equation of power with individual strength, rather than with, for example, group solidarity. The statement "He pulled himself up by his bootstraps" is a common metaphor to describe a person using their own efforts to succeed without any support from anywhere else and is illustrative of liberal humanism.

When racism is explained from the perspective of personal power, it is assumed to be a product of individual thought. Racism exists because some persons are racists. These individuals have thought patterns that are irrational, perhaps because of damaging early childhood experiences, or of being trained into authoritarian personality structures (Adorno, Aron, Levinson, & Morrow, 1950). In the popular media in North America there is endless examination of politicians' and celebrities' behavior to determine whether there is sufficient evidence to define them as racist or not. The rhetoric explores the extent to which there are flaws in people's character at such a level of pathology to be fittingly defined as racist. This analysis is embedded within a liberal humanist frame and the conversation is often completely devoid of sociocultural and sociohistorical considerations. The origins of racist practice are thus assumed to lie in the individual psychology of the person who exhibits it. Many research studies into racism start from this problematic assumption. Even when their findings are methodologically "valid," empirical data produced by such studies can still be faulty because they are grounded in inadequate starting assumptions.

A tendency toward essentialist thinking (Haslam & Whelan, 2008) lies in this theory of personal power, in the links between power and personal qualities such as charisma, physical beauty, intelligence, and personality. Freedom and autonomy of action are considered essential givens for the individual "man." (At the time of the origins of the liberal humanist account of individual rights, women, along with slaves, were not included.) "We hold these truths to be self-evident," said the framers of the American Declaration of Independence, "that all men are created equal." While all persons are theoretically born with equal opportunity, some have talents or develop abilities that make them more powerful than others.

What is the place of culture in this account of power? A liberal humanist account of power does not emphasize cultural belonging strongly, preferring to emphasize the individual's creation of his own life. Culture still has a place in this schema, as the collective exercise of many individual acts of initiative. Social groups are thought of as "collectives" made up principally of individual actors. Social privilege is often assumed to be earned largely by hard work, strength of character, or extraordinary genius, rather than conferred by one's social origins. Social structures and institutions are assumed to be products of the autonomous decisions of individuals.

Social change happens first on the individual level, too. A common catchphrase from this world view has been picked up by advertising campaigns as, "We are changing the world, one person at a time." Many counselors buy into this idea. The success of such change is measured by counting the number of individual changes that happen. So, changes in the social relations of privilege and disadvantage would be measured by counting, say, the number of African Americans or women entering positions of leadership, or the number of Latinx gaining graduate degrees, or the number of persons with disabilities earning a particular annual salary, or the number of openly queer people being appointed as CEOs.

All this emphasis on the individual is not, in itself, culturally neutral. Like most ideas, it comes from a cultural background, has a history, and fits into a matrix of other cultural assumptions. It originates in a Western view of the world and works best among people who hold other ideas in the dominant discourse of the European cultural tradition. For those who are not so culturally attuned to the Western world view, and who are more influenced by collectivist cultural narratives, this way of thinking makes less sense. For them, the liberal humanist version of power often does not fit.

There are other problems too with this liberal humanist idea of power. The emphasis on individuals as the source of power does not account well for the role of institutions in the construction of individual lives. It portrays persons as autonomous beings who are primarily responsible for their plight and easily turns into personal blame, even among counselors who profess to be nonjudgmental. What gets left out are the ways in which, for example, racism, sexism, and homophobia get built into the structure and practices of institutions like schools and courtrooms beyond what any individual ever intends. Culture is not just a matter of individual difference but of group allegiance, and cultural patterns act on the consciousness of individuals in powerful ways. It is, therefore, not uncommon for people to feel helpless in the face of the systemic forces that constrain them.

The dominance of liberal humanistic values has nevertheless been so taken for granted in contemporary counseling practice that practitioners regard it as the natural prescription for addressing human misery. Yet this stance has inadvertently blamed people who are marginalized for their very marginalization. It is a small step from taking a personal view of power to criticizing those who are victims for their lack of individual effort in addressing their problems.

Another problem lies in how people become individuals in the liberal humanist view. The process of subjectivation is at stake here (Ong-Van-Cung, 2011). It has to be learned rather than just absorbed in the process of development.

In contrast to the liberal humanist position, structural approaches reject outright the mainstream humanist assumption that the individual is both the source of all human action and the most important unit of social analysis. Despite these criticisms, a liberal humanist focus maintains momentum. Stephen Weinrach and Kenneth Thomas (1998) argue,

> Although it is clear that in the twenty-first century fewer and fewer clients (and counselors) will be White, there may be some reason to believe that widespread assimilation may reduce the urgency for radical modification of existing counseling theories. (p. 117)

However, the liberal humanist account of power relations is seriously limited to the extent that it can acknowledge systemic influences, hence the appeal for a more structural analysis of how power relations are formed. We shall look at this contrasting model of power next.

A Structural View of Power

Whereas a personal account of power relations focuses on the individual, a structural analysis constructs the individual as a product of her position in a social structure. Individuals are less than completely free, because their choices are determined for them by social structures, or by "the system." It therefore becomes more important to analyze the structures that shape and determine us and to work out how to change them. A structural analysis explains how some people seem to have unearned privilege and to have others do their bidding, not on any personal account of talent or hard work but on the happenstance of their position in social relations. People are often born into these positions, and the power they exercise precedes the entry of any one individual into such systems. From this perspective, power is a product of deep-seated social forces that produce structural sets of relations among groups of people. Individual power is the downstream effect, rather than the cause, of these intergroup relations. It is produced by virtue of individuals' membership in a group or by their position in a social structure not of their own making.

A structural analysis suggests that the conscious thoughts and intentions of individuals are not to be trusted as the primary sources of their actions. They are rather the surface effects of much deeper structural systems. People's thoughts, desires, motivations, and intentions are not just their own. They are determined by systematic forces outside of individuals, who are more like puppets of the system. When they open their mouths, they speak the lines of their position in an organized system of social relations more than they speak of their personal experience.

Below the surface of any social phenomenon lies a deep structure that gives shape to what is visible. This structure is hidden from view but is nonetheless real and determining. It can be deduced from its effects, rather than immediately sensed. The metaphor "structure" suggests an edifice as solid and permanent as a building. Models of social structures often argue that they are foundational for human experience and that many things that people talk about, or get upset about, are less important. These things are the superficial epiphenomena that shift and change, not through conscious persuasion but through fundamental shifts in the underlying social structure. For example, a structuralist argument about the reasons for a war would not concentrate on the explanations politicians articulate but on the underlying economic forces that produce the conflict, such as access to oil, competition for markets, or contradictory national interests.

A structural analysis is often compelling because it sees through immediate, confusing detail to more solid and enduring forces at work. It enables us to make sense of different events by reducing them to a single unifying explanation. The individual experiences of discrimination against women are explained better by a structural analysis of patriarchy than by an analysis of the negative oppressive intentions of individual men.

For example, male violence has been viewed in the mental health and counseling field as arising from patriarchal patterns of male power and control. Ellen Pence (1993) and her colleagues reported how male violence is promoted by an attitude of entitlement by men within their relationships with women. This view was backed by Jimmy Carter in a (2014) article in the Lancet. Men who are violent believe they have a right to be the sole authority in the home. With this authority comes control over family financial resources, decisions over whom their partners can associate with, and a belief that they are entitled to access to their partners' bodies. The counseling profession has been criticized for its failure to address issues of patriarchy and male violence in particular (for example, Drewery, 1986; Goldner, 1985; McKinnon & Miller, 1987).

The structuralist perspective on patriarchy and Eurocentric practices divides people into opposing camps of oppressors and the oppressed. Belonging to a defined group, rather than individual intention, is the main criterion for such division. The actions of professionals, however, may be analyzed for whether they collude with oppression or not. Many feminist researchers and practitioners have confronted mental health professionals for colluding with culturally oppressive practices and failing to attend to the structural inequalities that support racism and sexism (Adames, Chavez-Dueñas, Sharma, & La Roche, 2018; Grzanka, Santos, & Moradi, 2017; Hindmarsh, 1987; Lawson–Te Aho, 1993; McKinnon & Miller, 1987; Moradi & Grzanka, 2017; Smith, 1992; Tamesese & Waldegrave, 1993).

Karl Marx's analyses remain the most extensive theoretical accounts of social structure. Marx sought to explain the shaping of human consciousness by the relentless structuring power of economic forces. Within a given social system of organization, the structural economic base, that is, the means of economic production (including the social relations of production), determines social class relations (Tucker, 1978). On this economic base is built a superstructure of ideas and beliefs, but these are not independent of economic forces. They are determined and structured by the economic base. Thus, from a Marxist perspective, ideology, rhetoric, art, religion, fashion, and politics are all assumed to be products of social structure, rather than producers of it. In order to understand the ideological and political world, it is necessary to refer back to the economic or material base to understand the major organizing forces (Tucker, 1978). Political, religious, and philosophical ideas are thus relegated to the position of social effects and stripped of the possibility of originary force. As Vivien Burr (2015) points out, in Marxist analysis, ideology per se is always to be suspected as "false consciousness" and human beings are considered to be almost irrational and unwitting puppets of social and material forces beyond their control.

A feminist analysis of systemic patriarchy is often also structuralist in its orientation. It does not credit individual men with the oppression of women through the exercise of personal power as much as it stresses a systematic structural organization of life chances for men and women that grants considerable privilege to men and oppresses women. Hence, the feminist movement of the 1970s and 1980s worked by organizing consciousness-raising experiences for women. Paulo Freire's education work with the poor was based similarly on raising people's consciousness of structural conditions. Freire's "conscientization" was based on an educative and liberatory process that empowered subjugated peoples to recognize and ultimately challenge structural oppression (Freire, 1976).

A structural analysis takes the view that most people's difficulties are caused by social conditions over which they have little or no control (Poster, 1989). Indeed, from this perspective, counseling sometimes seems to have little point. At best, it might provide temporary relief from the ravages of systematic oppression, or place a Band-Aid over deep wounds. But it cannot alter a social structure by meeting with individuals one to one.

Structural theorists (see Hindmarsh, 1993) have concentrated on dealing with the outcomes of struggles around issues such as capitalism, patriarchy, and racism. The goals of a structural analysis are always structural change. Some kind of revolution, some universal law change, some mass transfer of wealth or power is often envisaged. The danger of this kind of analysis is that it always runs the risk of thinking in terms of the macro struggle and ignoring the particular complexities of personal experience in the individuals whose interests it purports to represent. In always focusing on the masses, it can sometimes be disrespectful to individual members of these masses. Individuals tend to be viewed primarily as members of groups, and their interests are considered to be the interests of the group rather than their own concerns.

A structural analysis shares with a liberal humanist analysis the understanding of power as a commodity, but the difference lies in how the commodity is obtained. Rather than being a product of individuals' talents, power is vested in individuals on the basis of their structural positioning or group membership. However, it is still viewed as a finite quantity distributed unevenly among groups of people. Since power is assumed to be accrued by those in structural positions of advantage, those who are the objects of the operation of power must be powerless. From this position, there seems little that the powerless can do to change things.

The Concept of Hegemony

A problem for a structural analysis of power is how to account for the times when people appear to be acting or speaking against the interests of their class, race, or gender. In response to this problem, the concept of hegemony was developed, first by the Italian Marxist Antonio Gramsci (1971), in his writings from prison. Jackson Lears (1985) defined Gramsci's hegemony as the

> spontaneous consent given by the great masses of the population to the general direction imposed on social life by the dominant fundamental group; this consent is historically caused by the prestige which the dominant group enjoys because of its position and function in the world of production. (p. 568)

The concept of hegemony is a move toward an understanding of how power operates inside the heads of those whom it oppresses. From inside their heads, power can get people to "voluntarily" give consent to their own oppression. Such practices are evident in the phrase, "Even when they say no, that might not be what they mean." Thus, unsuspecting oppressed groups consent to the definitions of their experience by social elites. Since they are participants in the operation of power, they are less likely to later object to it, even when it produces adverse effects. A marginalized person who has not been enlightened about hegemonic processes may not even be in a position to identify the source of his oppression and take any action. From a structuralist analysis, the liberal humanist analysis of power itself serves a hegemonic function.

There is, however, a trap in this structuralist analysis. It tends to end up with a self-appointed enlightened person knowing better about what someone else is saying and reinterpreting it for her. This in itself might be thought of as an act of power. Thus, when counselors practice from within a structuralist discourse, they run the risk of communicating profound disrespect to their clients. When an "oppressed person" gives an answer to a question, the counselor might recognize this opinion as a reflection of a colonized mindset and proceed to reinterpret events to the client. This has the effect of suggesting that colonized people cannot "know their own minds." Thus, a structuralist analysis ironically risks adopting a position of superiority and disrespecting even those it aims to support.

Gender, Race, and Class

Structural analysis often shares with a liberal humanist analysis the assumption that power is owned by those in structural positions of privilege. From the perspective of most structuralists, power is a commodity or property possessed by those at the top of the social hierarchy. Hence, social justice requires us to identify who owns the power when we respond to social injustice. Power is a finite quantity, distributed unevenly between groups, particularly on the basis of gender, ethnicity, class, and sexuality (Jones & Guy, 1992). This analysis of power views oppression as structured hierarchically, with those experiencing the worst oppression on the bottom and their oppressors on the top. Typically, White middle- and upper-class men are identified as accumulators of power on the basis of their membership in these identity groups. You can add to these oppressor identity categories heterosexuals, the able-bodied, and Christians. Oppressed groups, meanwhile, are made up of marginal categories: women, people of color, sexual minorities, the disabled, and non-Christians. Discussions about empowerment tend to view power as a property which can be appropriated and redistributed among these groups (Gore, 1992).

Julian Henriques, Wendy Hollway, Cathy Urwin, Couze Venn, and Valerie Walkerdine (1984) argue that the orthodox Marxist's position in relation to patriarchal power is that power is the property of men as the dominant sex class and that women are victims, the objects of power. Indeed, a structural analysis tends to make social change seem very difficult. It is suspicious of, and sometimes cynical about, any changes that do not significantly overturn structural arrangements. Anything less than a decisive transformation or revolution may be dismissed as cosmetic or token. Until such a moment, the role of helping professionals should be one of educating the oppressed about the nature of their oppression and producing an anger that might motivate change. Brian Fay (1987) suggests that "critical oppressive moments" are opportunities to educate those suffering from unjust hierarchical structures, to help them develop the necessary volition to produce a transformative experience.

The difference between a structural discourse of power and a liberal humanist discourse is the ability to critique the simplistic assumption that individuals are free agents with equal ability to extricate themselves from unjust circumstances. Unlike liberal humanists, who emphasize individual will, structuralists focus on the centrality of repressive social practices that contribute to oppression, marginalization, and powerlessness.

During the 1970s in the United States, the major structural emphasis in therapy was the recognition of the structural politics of gender relations and the idea that the therapist–client relationship should be structurally egalitarian (Gilbert, 1980; Rader, 2003). As a result of feminists' work on sex bias and sex role stereotyping, psychologists became more aware of the importance of informing clients about procedures, goals, and potential side effects of counseling. Some feminist therapists believed that limiting one's practice to counseling individuals was a form of treating the symptoms and avoiding the cause. They highlighted the need to work with the social disease represented by society. Edna Rawlings and Dianne Carter (1977) suggested that social action is an essential professional responsibility of therapists.

Much of the structuralist literature in the 1980s and 1990s, typified by a radical feminist analysis of patriarchy and male violence, focused on the variety of abuses perpetrated by men against women. Women were portrayed as trapped by patriarchy and believing that their role was to be subservient to men, and thus they were considered to collude with patriarchy.

Imelda Whelehan (1995) gives an example of the kinds of statements that were made by radical feminists in the United States around this time:

> All men are our policemen, and no organized police force is necessary at this time to keep us in our places. All men enjoy male supremacy and take advantage of it to a greater or lesser degree depending on their position in the masculine hierarchy of power. (p. 536)

From this analysis, male counselors were challenged regarding their ignorance of historical and contemporary institutional patriarchy and its effects on their practice. In order to counsel women in a respectful way, the counselor needs to first assess a woman's status in society relative to men and then encourage her to claim her own values, rather than be trapped by what a woman should be, according to patriarchal specifications. Counselors should encourage women to challenge the coercive authority of male privilege. Structuralists have criticized the individualistic focus of liberal humanism, which directed counselors' gaze away from the domination of patriarchy in the counseling profession. Mental health researchers adopting a liberal humanist position were tempted to pathologize the experiences of female clients.

Those advocating a structuralist approach to addressing gender issues in counseling note that women enter therapy more frequently and more often present with affective distress and anxiety-related disorders and relationship-related problems (Moore & Leafgren, 1990). Royda Crose, David Nicholas, David Gobble, and Beth Frank (1992) commented that women suffer from more debilitating chronic disease, whereas men suffer from more life-threatening illnesses, such as heart disease. They cited numerous examples of the psychological costs of patriarchal and androcentric culture to women. They suggested that women are more likely than men to receive a diagnosis of mental disorder by their physicians. Women are more often prescribed psychotropic medication and take more prescription and over-the-counter drugs. Women are also more likely to be informally labeled with a hypochondriacal, psychosomatic, hysterical, or dependent personality.

In studies of differential diagnoses by gender, men experience alcohol abuse and antisocial personality at a rate four to five times higher than women. Men who seek assistance frequently present with problems related to career, impulse control, and alcohol or other drug abuse, while women are twice as likely to exhibit depression, anxiety, or phobic disorders. According to Parker-Guilbert, Leifker, Sippel, and Marshall (2014), the PTSD prevalence rate for women across the lifespan is at least twice that of men. Parker-Guilbert et al. also reported on research showing that most individuals with signs of depression, anxiety, panic, anorexia, and phobia were women, and that they constituted a large percentage of the client population.

Structuralists make a link between patriarchal practices and an overdeveloped male gender role, which sometimes gets expressed by increased risk taking, self-destructive activities, high stress, emotional inexpressiveness, an emphasis on control, and the drive to accumulate money. O'Neill (1990) stated that men can display "rigid, sexist, or restrictive gender roles" because of the structural influences of patriarchal practice (p. 25). For both men and women, differences are attributed to group membership in structural relations.

To avoid further exacerbation of the structural inequalities between men and women, some counseling researchers have proposed that male therapists should avoid working with female clients. The commodity metaphor of power would make it impossible to attain equity, understanding, respect, or justice between counselor and client when a client is positioned in an oppressed group and the counselor in an oppressor group. Not only is it unlikely that a counselor from an oppressor group could empathize with a member of an oppressed group, except on the basis of an unequal relationship, but he might also have some unconscious investment in maintaining the oppressive status quo. To do anything else might undermine his privileged position. From this standpoint, it would be congruent to match counselor and client on the basis of a shared experience of oppression. Separatist developments in counseling, promoted by structuralists, use this commodity analysis of power in relation to understanding oppression and achieving the equalizing of power relations. In fact, radical feminists viewed gender matching for clients as a legitimate method of seeking justice for women in the counseling relationship. Female clients could achieve independence in counseling by being unencumbered by "male transference." In most instances, men should not counsel women (said Edna Rawlings & Dianne Carter, 1977) and women should work with a female therapist (Fisher & Maloney, 1994).

Structuralism views relationships between different groups as a hierarchy of oppression where the power relations are understood to be both monolithic and fixed. Wendy Larner (1995) identified how structuralist interpretations produce binary frameworks not only by gender but also by ethnicity, class, and sexual orientation. Binary distinctions are either/or distinctions that limit possible interpretations to two options only. You are either oppressed or an oppressor, for example. Such formulations do not allow gray areas, contradictory positions, or complexities in experience to be noticed. From a structuralist perspective, it would make sense that African American clients should work with African American therapists, and sexual minority clients should work with sexual minority therapists to balance the power relations. Using this analysis of power, it would suggest that White therapists for example, should not work with people of color, to avoid further oppressive practices, and heterosexuals should not work with sexual minorities to further exacerbate the oppressor–oppressed binary.

Barriers to educational achievement by those in poor, working-class communities are better understood as systemically produced economic disadvantage than as explained by the personal motivation to succeed of the individuals in those communities. Charles Waldegrave (2003) believed that many therapists address problems without reference to the real cause (which he suggests is often poverty and oppression). After therapy is concluded, people are sent back to the condition that created the problem in the first place. From this perspective, counselors are not benign helpers but rather functionaries of a system, there to help people adjust and adapt to the dominant group's values. Counseling practice is often concerned with adjusting people to the failure that is a product of a capitalist system. Counselors may be criticized for colluding with this system to pacify people with genuine grievances in unjust situations. A competitive society requires that there be failures despite all that might be done to minimize them. Saul Alinsky (1969) graphically illustrated a structuralist analysis in describing how appointed helpers adjust people to poverty:

> They come to the people of the slums under the guise of benevolence and goodness, not to help people fight their way out of the muck but to be adjusted so that they will live in hell and like it too. It is difficult to conceive of a higher form of treason. (p. 18)

For some, a structural analysis renders counseling virtually redundant. Counseling, so this argument runs, is much too focused on the superficial aspects of individuals' lives to ever get at the important underlying forces at work in the production of their oppressive experiences.

Derald Wing Sue and David Sue (1990), referring to counseling in North America, summed up the argument as follows:

> While counseling enshrines the concept of freedom, rational thought, tolerance for new ideas, and equality and justice for all, it can be used as an oppressive instrument by those in power to maintain the status quo. In this respect counseling becomes a form

of oppression in which there is an unjust and cruel exercise of power to subjugate or mistreat large groups of people. (p. 6)

Here, the exercise of power is at times not objectionable, and the effort to influence others is not essentially bad. It is just impossible for relations between people not to be also power relations. Therefore, the question of which practices of power are acceptable and which are not is an ethical one. If power relations are inevitable and are not always bad, then we need to think about which processes of power are acceptable and which are damaging.

A Poststructuralist Account of Power Relations

It is now time to introduce our third approach to power based on poststructuralist thought. We will draw heavily on the work of Michel Foucault, who has done the most to develop this account. Foucault (2000) argued that it is not enough to assume that power is basically about stopping people from doing things. He regarded it as curious that most analyses of power focus on its negative functions. The word *negative* does not refer to a value judgment as much as to how power *prevents* people from pursuing opportunities in life, *blocks* them from participating in decisions that affect them, *silences* them, and *excludes* them from social benefits. In other words, the usual focus has been on how power is used to

---

BOX 6.1 PRIVILEGE

In the social sciences, *privilege* refers to the unearned rights and advantages that accrue to a group of people as a result of their membership of a particular group. The group may be based on race, ethnicity, social class, gender, ability, religion, sexual orientation, and so on. It is often the basis of social inequality. For example, a group may have a greater opportunity than another group to pursue higher education. Therefore, this group of people can be said to be privileged with regard to educational opportunity. Privileges often go unnoticed by those who hold them and are also often assumed to be deserved or acquired through personal striving.

It was W. E. B. Du Bois who first wrote about privilege in 1903. He referred to the "wages of whiteness," which included being entitled to deference, having access to better schools, and receiving less punitive treatment in court. In 1990, an influential essay was published by Peggy McIntosh entitled "White privilege: Unpacking the invisible knapsack." She documented 46 examples of privilege that she enjoyed in the United States as a result of being White herself. These privileges were often unacknowledged and were not always discriminatory. When asked by Joshua Rothman (2014) of *The New Yorker* magazine why her article became so popular, she replied, "I think it was because nobody else was writing so personally, and giving such clear examples, drawn from personal experience, which allowed readers to understand this rather complicated subject without feeling accused" (p. 2).

McIntosh believes that everyone has either unearned advantages or unearned disadvantages. However, it comes as a shock to many to realize that there are systematic patterns that give shape to their personal experiences. She also suggests that the circumstances of our birth give rise to many instances in which we are placed ahead of or behind others without our having to do anything much.

create barriers that actively oppress people. Power is usually identified as "a law that says no" (Foucault, 2000, p. 120). In psychological language, this has become the repression of personal consciousness. Hence, we have counseling processes to help people get rid of internalized taboos, the influence even into adulthood of parents who said no, and the blocking of the expression of traumatic experiences. Foucault (2000) describes this negative emphasis on power not so much as wrong but as insufficient and "skeletal" (p. 120). It represents the bones of power without muscles and nervous system.

Foucault also challenges the common metaphor of power as a commodity. A commodity can be reified as an object to hold. This assumption is present in both liberal humanist and structuralist versions of power whenever individuals are thought of as holders of power. Membership of a structurally organized group is often described in terms of a person's amassing a certain quantity of power. Foucault prefers to speak of power as something inherent in a relation and associated with a set of discourse practices, rather than something held by an individual. It is a less essentialist idea and can lead to noticing greater complexity and nuance in how power works.

Foucault did not want to argue against the existence of oppression or repression. Far from it. However, he did not believe that this was the main way in which power works. Instead, he believed that power is primarily productive, rather than just repressive. In other words, he pointed to the ways in which power works to get people to do things, rather than just stops them from doing them. "It makes people act and speak" (Foucault, 2000, p. 172). His oft-quoted maxim describes power as "the conduct of conduct" (Foucault, 2000). It refers to what shapes and influences how people conduct themselves. The largest effort in all power relations goes into producing people in particular molds, rather than on repressing actions that do not fit the mold. Repression exists around the outside of the processes of producing people, as the backup system that deals with the failures of the productive processes of power. It is important, but secondary to the primary function of power.

This is a whole new domain of interest in social science. How do we produce people to feel the way they feel, think the way they do, act the way they act? You cannot even ask such questions, if you assume that power operates mainly to keep people from expressing their natural essences. The exercise of power must be understood in Foucault's terms much more as a technical question about how people's consciousness is constructed. It is about social processes that have effects on individuals' lives, their bodies, and their psyches. Once Foucault began to think in this way, he found all sorts of technologies of power that operate in the modern world and traced their emergence from premodern European practices.

It has also been customary in analyses of power to focus on the role of the "state" in the functioning of power. This domain we normally think of as political and is where we might look to notice the workings of power. Foucault does not overlook the role of the state, but he is also clear that power exists well beyond the places where we have traditionally looked for it. It is not just in the institutions of government that we might find how people's lives are governed. The governing of people's lives is much more widely diffused than that. Feminist analysis of gender power was one of the first places where this was made this clear. There is clearly no central cabinet or politburo where male dominance of women originates. Nor is it uniform. There are many places where women exercise power to govern their own lives and at times the lives of men and children. And yet there is still plenty of evidence of pattern and structure in the relations between men and women. In many contexts, many women do not enjoy all the same opportunities in life that many men routinely expect. A simple structural analysis of women's rights is not nuanced enough to account for ways in which women sometimes act against their own interests or are even oppressive toward men. Nor are all the techniques by which gender power operates embodied in legal rights.

The poststructuralist analysis suggests that power relations are based on the use of discourse. Foucault (1978) argues that "discourse transmits and produces power, reinforces it, but also undermines and exposes it, renders it fragile and makes it possible to thwart it" (p. 100). If power is constituted in discourse, it is vulnerable to shifts in discourse. Hence, it is dependent on the context in which discourse is used, rather than essentially tied to a person or to a group of persons. It cuts across individual lives in ways that entail privilege and oppression for the same person in different respects. Such fluidity, however, does not preclude the possibility of systematic and patterned applications of discursive power so that some individuals are more consistently disadvantaged than others.

There are discourses of family relations and of gender relations that underlie the decisions and actions of men and women on a daily basis. These discourses equip us with a matrix of assumptions that we repeat and reproduce each time we open our mouths. Where this discourse privileges life opportunities for men and diminishes these same opportunities for women, the repetition of this discourse in our speech patterns and in the media is likely to blind us to ways in which things could be otherwise. Hence, feminists have paid attention to the ways in which sexist discourse produced relations between men and women in lopsided ways. For example, the use of the word *chairman* carried with it the assumption that the leadership of a committee would be taken up by a man rather than a woman. The struggle for the substitution of the word *chairperson* ensued. Some people who do not understand how power works through discourse get impatient about these differences and dismiss them as mere semantics or complain about undue "political correctness." Often this accusation is a substitute for understanding quite substantive issues. Calling something "politically correct" and calling something "sexist" are both themselves efforts to exercise power. The task is always to figure out how a piece of discourse usage serves to govern the lives of others, what is at stake, who might benefit if these meanings gain ascendancy, and who might lose out. From a poststructuralist perspective, the decision between one version of events and another is, in the end, an ethical decision. It is a matter of deciding what is fair and just.

Power, then, is everywhere and pervades the social body. Foucault uses the metaphor "capillary" to describe it, referring to the tiny blood vessels that carry life to the extremities of the body. It does not simply accrue to some groups and not at all to others. We all exercise it to some degree, and therefore it makes no sense to describe anyone as powerless. Power is not centralized as much as structuralists would believe. However, it is still true that there are some places where power concentrates. There are those who more easily access the authority to shape the lives of others and those for whom the path to that access is overgrown with obstacles. Authorities in many places exercise the right to govern the lives of others, and their positions are not just organized around race, gender, and class, as a structuralist analysis has often emphasized. We often assume that the exercise of authority refers to the government, or the state. But there are many other places where authority is exercised over the lives of people. For example, bankers and credit agencies govern people's financial lives. Teachers govern children's lives in school. The fashion industry governs people's clothing tastes. Public health authorities govern people's bodies. Captains govern the crew of a ship. Employers govern the lives of their employees. Foucault uses the word *govern* in the sense of eliciting the desired forms of behavior in a population of people.

However, the world is not neatly divided between the dominant and the oppressed, or even between dominating and subjugated discourses. Things are not so strongly determined as that. There is always a degree of indeterminacy in the midst of power relations, where people govern themselves, individually and in groups. Hence, we need to pay careful attention to the microdynamics of power to make the most of opportunities for change. This is as true for counseling as it is for social change in a community of people.

In Foucault's analysis, there is a difference between power relations and domination. People often do not make a distinction between the two. According to Foucault, power relations are in a constant fluid exchange of relational expression. Whenever someone attempts to govern the conduct of others, he must engage in a strategy of struggle. There is always the possibility that the others may refuse to submit. There is always a reciprocal relation. Domination occurs from time to time when the usual exchanges between people in contests of power are frozen into patterns that are hard to even talk about, let alone contest (Foucault, 2000). Domination occurs when the reciprocal process of struggle and the ebb and flow of give and take is no longer possible.

Sovereign Power and Disciplinary Power

Foucault adds to this picture by making some distinctions between power as it is exercised in the modern world and power as it was in premodern times. He refers to these two forms of power as sovereign power and disciplinary power. He contends that the technologies by which people's lives are governed in the modern world can be distinguished from earlier times by the development of sophisticated new technologies of power.

Sovereign power was based on instilling in the general populace a fear of the authority of the sovereign. This was achieved through punishing wrongdoers or political enemies by enacting physical torture on their bodies or putting them to death. The long history of lynchings in the South of the United States served the function of keeping Black people afraid and docile. There is plenty of evidence that this form of power has not completely died out. The use of sovereign power continues today in some locations around the globe. Perhaps the most notable example of this occurring at a societal level is what has occurred in North Korea over the last 50 years, where any dissenters or political enemies and their families are executed, or incarcerated in brutal internment camps or gulags for decades. Sovereign power was at work in the horrendous crimes that were so publicly documented under ISIS-controlled territories. Despicable actions of sovereign power have occurred and continue to occur today in parts of Africa, South East Asia, and the Middle East, mimicking the acts of premodern times, when power was maintained by the person of the king. However, sovereign power is not restricted to the so-called "Third World." The United States in the 21st century continues to demonstrate vestiges of sovereign power when some police brutalize and sometimes kill crime suspects or innocent people. Some of the most documented acts of violence were in Abu Ghraib prison, where there was clear evidence of training for system-wide abuse and torture of prisoners by some personnel of the United States Military Police, who were acting on behalf of the CIA (Lankford, 2009).

Domestic violence perpetrated by many men against many women in order to maintain power and control can be understood to be seeking to use sovereign power to produce submissive behavior in women. Sovereign power is not outmoded. It still exists wherever the use of force is deployed. People are still tortured and put to death.

Disciplinary power, says Foucault, developed from about the 18th century on, and has become the chief means by which modern states get their citizens to be loyal, law-abiding citizens. Disciplinary power might, at first glance, seem more "civilized" than societies of old. Foucault would say we are not actually more civilized, but we have developed new technologies of power that often work far more effectively, and there is less need for the exercise of sovereign power to the degree that it was exercised formerly.

From the 17th century on, there has been a general movement (still accelerating today) to place the mechanisms of power inside people's heads, so that they have to monitor themselves and keep themselves in line, rather than be afraid of the power of the king to kill and maim. This shift began with the move to create modern prisons. Before this time, prisons were mainly places where people were held temporarily until they were put to death or were where torture took place. It was in the 17th century that the idea of holding people in prison to teach them to correct their ways and become law abiding again came into being. For this purpose, Jeremy Bentham developed the panopticon design for the modern prison. The panopticon design allowed the prison guards to be able to look into the individual cells of every prisoner at will. The prisoner never knew when she was going to be watched and so had to take care to monitor her own behavior and obey the rules of the prison all the time, just in case at any moment she might be observed. The prisoner became a new object of study. Her behavior was now a matter to be documented, and files were developed about it. Interviews of various kinds were developed to gather information for these files. Forms were developed with standardized questions that uncovered the information by which people were to be governed.

Foucault has suggested that Jeremy Bentham deserves to be recognized as the most influential thinker in the modern era, because of how this idea has contributed to the shape of people's lives everywhere. "Today we live in a society programmed basically by Bentham, a panoptic society, a society where panopticism reigns" (Foucault, 2000, p. 70). Bentham's panopticon has been taken from the prison and applied in every domain of modern life as the principal technology by which power operates. The same process of organization that began in the prison was copied in other institutions of modern life: the factory, the military barracks, the modern school, the government department, the immigration system, and the hospital. "Panopticism is one of the characteristic traits of our society" (Foucault, 2000, p. 70). It focuses on producing the individual in an acceptable mold through three main processes: "supervision, control and correction" (Foucault, 2000, p. 70).

By way of example, schools are organized by individualizing each student, and the main method by which young people are kept docile is not just from the threat of punishment. It is through the prescription of a curriculum that each child must learn and through the process of tests and exams by which children's progress through this curriculum is measured and calculated. Examinations serve the same function as the guard tower in the prison. They subject children to the gaze of the education authorities. Each child knows that sooner or later the truth about his learning will be accounted for and that he must produce himself as a successful student in order to access the privileges of the adult world. Learning is turned into an object of calculation. This enables norms to be established that specify rates of learning progress and enables distinctions to be made between different groups of students: those who are above average or normal and those who are below average and abnormal. Children must produce themselves in the identity categories laid down within the dominant system of schooling. Those who are deemed abnormal must be corrected.

Another feature of the modern operation of power is the role of norms. In the last 150 years, we have seen the rise of the normal curve. This statistical invention (Foucault points out that *statistics* are so called because they were developed as the science of the state, or the science of governing) has made it possible to map out a normal distribution of the population along a predictable bell-shaped curve. Those within two standard deviations of the norm are called normal. Those outside this range are abnormal and require some remedial treatment. In schools, children are routinely established in such positions by a large variety of tests. Most tests have been developed over the last hundred years and are usually assumed to be objective, neutral measures of personal qualities or abilities. Foucault would argue that such objectivity is a ruse designed to obscure the function of these tests, which is not objective at all. Their purpose is to create social divisions and to assign responsibility for those divisions to the persons who are being divided. You cannot object to being assigned the category *abnormal* if it is established by a scientifically designed, impersonal testing procedure. Instead, you must internalize the results of the test and adopt it as an aspect of your identity. This is the process of normalization. I *am* an average student. I *am* learning disabled. I *am* a nerd. The use of the verb *to be* indicates a powerful essentializing force at work. As a result of this normalizing judgment, a whole array of totalizing identities are assigned to young people to define who they can expect to be. These identities are then kept in place by surveillance and internalized monitoring.

Foucault also studied sexuality as a site of power relations. He describes how people's sexuality became a concern of the government of people, especially in the 19th century (Foucault, 1978). He argues that this concern arose through the conceptualization of "populations" in response to the population growth in the 18th century. Foucault maintains that the dramatic population increase during this time led to numerous health and housing problems. As a result, the government became much more interested in birth rates, age of marriages, illegitimate births, frequency of sexual relations, and the like. Those in authority became inquisitors into people's formerly private affairs. As Vivien Burr (2003) writes, "The practice of scrutinizing the population's sexual behaviour and of encouraging people to confess their sexual 'sins' developed into a powerful form of social control as people began to internalise this process" (p. 70). Scientific concepts of what is normal and abnormal developed and accounts of perversion became the focus of intense public scrutiny. The problematization of sexuality remains important today, especially for those who do not conform to heteronormative standards.

Through the modern discourse about sexuality, the body became a site for the operation of power. Western culture's current obsession with thinness can be understood as a manifestation of disciplinary power. Women especially, but increasingly men too, are placed under constant surveillance by such disciplinary power to look a certain way and encouraged to engage in whatever means necessary to fit the thin ideal.

Power can thus be at work inside us every time we look in the mirror or stand on the scales. We are incited to look at ourselves and measure ourselves against a "normal" ideal by advertising and the fashion industry, which work tirelessly to inscribe on women's bodies their expectations for attractiveness, including certain clothing and hairstyles. The most prominent standard for attractiveness for women is the cultural "tyranny of slenderness" (Chernin, 1981, p. 3). To prepare themselves for the evaluation of others, women must watch themselves with a critical eye and sometimes submit themselves to self-torture (diet and exercise regimens) to ensure that they conform to cultural body standards to avoid being judged negatively. Internalized bodily self-surveillance invites women to be preoccupied with physical appearance, to be concerned about deficiencies, and to see themselves as objects and to respond to other women as competing objects. In preparing for the inspection of others, a woman sees herself as others see her. "Through no small amount of labor, women within dominant culture are given the task of watching themselves from a position that is both inside and outside the body" (Spitzack, 1990, p. 34).

This monitoring and controlling of behavior begins with a governmental concern about sexuality and population but is eventually inscribed onto the individual body through a process of self-discipline. Thus, the ultimate success of the governing body's use of disciplinary power is when individuals take up the practice of self-discipline. These technologies of power are conceived by individuals and function through institutions, but it is important to notice that they are not owned by anyone, or any group, and that their effects are diffused through the actions of millions of people who all police themselves and each other. Anything that is so diffused through the actions of many people must therefore be understood as a cultural phenomenon and should be of interest to counselors who are working with individuals struggling with how to discipline themselves.

Power/Knowledge

The argument in the previous section illustrates another of Foucault's concerns: the close relationship between scientific knowledge in the human, or social, sciences and processes of social and political control. Foucault views the human sciences as far from maintaining a neutral or objective stance in relation to political and social issues. Rather, he charges medicine, psychiatry, psychology, and education (he was trained as a psychologist himself) with complicity in the operation of power. Psychologists have contributed to the elaboration of normalizing judgment with which to measure people's personal qualities and assign them identity categories. We discussed the process of identity categorization in Chapter 1. The human sciences, he says, have provided the tools for the modern governing of people's lives. They have developed the social categories to which we willingly assign ourselves membership. Race and gender are examples. Social scientists have developed vast knowledge about these populations, which make people more easily governed. They have elaborated the technologies of this government too, in the form of the psychological gaze and how it is applied by practitioners to produce citizenship.

Foucault also argues that knowledge in the human sciences consistently represents the interests of the dominant discourse of its day. Social scientists are, after all, members of a social world. They are influenced, as much as anyone else, by the ebbs and flows of discourse and sociohistorical trends, and these influences shape the knowledge that is produced in academic writing. Erica Burman (1994) elaborates on this point by suggesting that we cannot adequately understand psychological research without noticing "the circumstances in which the research was carried out, the social and political influences that made the topic seem relevant, and the role and impact of that research" (p. 5). Here are some examples: The development of psychological practices and knowledge has been influenced heavily by the wars of the last hundred years. World War I gave us new psychological accounts of trauma as a result of what was called in those days "shell shock." This was updated after the Vietnam War, which left scars in the American political discourse in many ways. One of them was the development of the individualized and depoliticized account of posttraumatic stress disorder to describe the suffering of soldiers who returned from that war deeply troubled by what they had witnessed. Posttraumatic stress renders the problem an individual abnormality rather than an understandably normal outcome of a political process. It blames the inadequacy of the individual soldier for his suffering, rather than the government that put him in harm's way. In this sense, no diagnosis of posttraumatic stress can ever be politically neutral, even though it claims to be objective. World War II left behind in Britain a large number of orphaned children who were cared for in orphanages amid political concern that they not grow up to become juvenile delinquents. It was the study of these children that led John Bowlby to develop his theory of attachment, which was connected with an associated discourse of motherhood (Burman, 1994). This was a response to a political issue of the day, and it served to create new worries for women about their responsibilities as mothers and encouraged them to stay at home rather than work.

Jeffrey Masson (1984) also argues that Freud's oedipal theory of early childhood fantasies of desire for the parent of opposite gender was influenced by the current discourse of his day. Masson shows how Freud probably founded his theory of the oedipal complex on stories of sexual abuse told to him by patients that at first he believed were true. Later, however, he was cold shouldered by his own professional community of doctors when he delivered a paper on the subject of the effects of traumatic experiences of sexual abuse. Disturbed by this rejection, or as we might say, by the dominant discourse of his day, he eventually shifted his thinking and began to explain the tales he was told by his women clients as sexual fantasies (to be understood as deep-seated oedipal urges) rather than as accounts of actual abuse.

Foucault's analysis of the relationship between power and knowledge in the modern world leads us to a different reading of much of the knowledge produced within the modern academy. Scientific studies, by Foucault's account, are not to be read as simple truths, in which empirical data can be trusted to speak for themselves. Instead, they are to be read as products of particular "regimes of truth" (Foucault, 2000). This does not mean that they are devoid of all truth value, merely that our reading of the truth that they offer needs to be understood more modestly than as universal truth about the essential human experience. Nor is Foucault suggesting that truth is completely relative. Scientific truth is rather grounded in the power relations of its cultural location.

The Confessional Society

One of the effects of the role of modern power/knowledge has been the development of what Foucault calls the "confessional society." In the government of people's lives, a strong incitement for people to bring their inner worlds into public scrutiny has developed. In modern life it is considered good to speak openly and honestly to designated others about deeply personal experience, to express feelings, to give personal testimony to one's failures and achievements, and to assign oneself identity categories. In short, we are incited constantly to produce ourselves to fit the dominant norms by confessing our inner deviations from these norms and then to align ourselves more fully with those norms.

This is not a new idea. It was developed originally in Western culture by the Catholic Church. The institution of the confessional, where people confessed their sins to a priest and were granted absolution and admonished to sin no more, was a major practice for the governing of people's lives in medieval times. It is aligned in Foucault's (2000) analysis with the development of what he calls "pastoral power" (p. 352). It is about governing people on an individual basis through knowing their innermost thoughts and inciting them to tell these to a person in authority. Foucault's argument is that this technique was taken over by the modern state and secularized. Every time in the modern world that we fill in a form (a daily practice) we routinely "confess" our identity in response to guided choices about who we can be. We are regularly interviewed by professionals who maintain files on our private worlds. We must confess our earnings and spending to the tax authorities once a year. We expect our politicians, movie stars, and sports heroes to make their personal lives available for scrutiny so we can compare ourselves with them and learn how to live. We watch endless talk shows and reality shows in which people reveal their inner lives before the camera and are taught moral lessons about how they should live while the rest of us vicariously watch and learn. We are incited by advertising to internalize personal lessons and then to perform the daily practices of living in line with dominant social norms (and of course to consume the products that will help us do so). Foucault's insight helps us see all this as the (somewhat hidden) operation of power that is shaping and producing people's lives. It constitutes personhood in patterns, including gender roles, ethnic identities, social class norms, and sexual orientations. Viewed from this perspective, the social structures emphasized within a structuralist view of power are produced and reproduced.

Counseling has had a special role to play in this endeavor. The general acceptance of counseling as a social practice has been built on its role as a place where people go to confess their private worries and explore their souls. It also brings these private worlds under the governance of a particular kind of rationality (Guilfoyle, 2005; Rose, 1990). It follows from this analysis that counseling has become part of the culture of modern Western democracies as a result of the growth of the confessional society. A trend to "send" people to counseling is assumed to fix many social ills. Counselors have seldom thought of themselves as governing people's lives, but a poststructuralist analysis of power invites them to consider this carefully. It has renewed interest in the operation of power in the counseling relationship, because it means that counselors should consider whether or not they are being used to adjust people to fit the social norms of the day.

Dividing Practices

Another concept necessary to Foucault's analysis of power is dividing practices (Foucault, 2000, p. 326). *Dividing practices* are those which define the categories in a social sphere that will be used to allocate status to individuals as legitimate or not, as having a voice that can be heard or that will be ignored. Dividing practices separate the mad and the sane, the sick and the healthy, the criminal and the law abiding, the good student and the poor student, the normal and the abnormal. This concept recognizes that, while everyone's lives are produced to fit within the specifications of dominant discourse, the process does not happen in the same way for everyone. As well as identity categories, dominant discourse also produces dividing lines. Some identities are produced to be recipients of social privilege and others to have limited access to privilege. Some are given ample opportunity to govern the lives of others and some are expected to submit to being governed.

What are these dividing lines? Every society has them, although their particular expression varies substantially from one context to another. In ancient Rome, there were dividing lines between patricians, plebeians, and slaves. In traditional Indian society, the divisions were constructed along caste lines. In Britain, there have been social divisions along social class lines that are marked out, in part, by the accents people use. In Northern Ireland, particular histories of colonization have led to divisions on the basis of Catholic or Protestant religious allegiance. The massive exercise of European colonization of many other parts of the world created the modern concept of race and its institution by sharp dividing lines. The practices of slavery, for example, were organized around sharp dividing lines between slave owner and slave. In other places, the dividing lines were organized around racial distinctions between farmer and indentured laborer, or between factory owner and waged worker. Dividing lines are not essential structures, as they are conceived of from a structuralist analysis, but are products of culture and discourse.

These dividing lines have persisted as organizing ideas for the social world, for personal identity categories, and for inequitable relations between those identity categories, despite the trends toward decolonization expressed in, for example, the American Revolution, the American Civil War, and the Civil Rights Movement. None of these events have succeeded in completely dislodging the concept of race to keep it from operating as a dividing practice that marks out lines of privilege and disadvantage for many people.

The concept of rights captures only a small part of it. Therefore, the modernist campaigns for civil rights have succeeded in democratizing some parts of the operation of power in the modern world but have also been restricted by the limited scope of their analysis. In other words, campaigns for human rights have not always produced the desired experience of freedom when practices of governmentality have leapfrogged over legal rights and manipulated discourse by operating inside people's heads to limit that experience of freedom.

Dividing practices along gender lines are a case in point. Campaigns for women's rights have succeeded in many places in giving women the vote, in granting property rights that used to be denied, in securing greater access for women to positions of leadership in workplaces and in the public sphere, in equalizing, to some degree, financial independence for women in situations of divorce, and so on. In other words, they have had effects in terms of the versions of power that are recognized within liberal humanist discourse. What has been left underanalyzed, however, has been how dividing lines of gender continue to be produced through the more subtle operation of discourse on men and women. It starts with the assignment of pink and blue to babies to mark their gender. It develops through the assignment of different kinds of toys and games for girls and boys. It trains girls to measure their worthiness in terms of their looks and body image and their ability to constantly attend to relational processes in ways that are not expected of men. Most of this is not set down in laws that can be changed through human rights campaigns. Therefore, the feminist movement has needed to analyze it by the slogan, "The personal is political." Differences between men and women have been produced inside our heads and then assumed to be natural.

Education has its role in dividing practices. In recent decades, around the world, education has become an increasingly sensitive political issue, reflecting the increasing role that education plays in the creation of social divisions more complex and sophisticated than simple exclusionary regulations along the lines of race, class, or gender. Nevertheless, parents and students implicitly know that their life chances to access material privileges hinge on success in school. In the United States today, going to college has become, although not uniformly, a marker of entry to privileged lifestyles. Going to Ivy League colleges marks a person as eligible for higher positions that have even more authority to govern the lives of others.

As a result, school counselors need to think of every conversation with students as about issues of power, because schools produce people's lives and the identity categories that dramatically affect life expectations. They need to study the particular microtechnologies of power in which children's lives are situated and to help children negotiate their own paths through this.

Resistance

It is easy to reach a mistaken conclusion when we start to understand power from a poststructuralist perspective, however. We can gain the impression that because modern power has developed these new capabilities and efficiencies by getting inside people's heads to produce docile citizens, it is therefore impossible to resist. We can reach conclusions of despair about the possibilities of social justice and change, simply because these modern technologies of power are so pervasive, and we can start to notice them happening everywhere around us and even in our own practices.

It can be tempting to give way to a cynical and deterministic view of the world. There is a danger here. Cynicism needs always to be examined for its contribution to the operation of power. It can easily be co-opted into the role of constantly viewing change as impossible and undermining the effort to bring about social change by convincing people that they cannot really make a difference. In this way, a cynical analysis can lead to what Michael White (2002) calls a "paralysis of will" (p. 37). An alternative is to adopt a position of optimism, not on the available evidence so much as an ethical stance.

There is a flip side to modern power. Its very strength is also its weakness. Foucault was at pains to point this out. He even went so far as to express concern that his earlier work had overemphasized a dark and implacable story of modern power. In his later work, he sought to correct this impression and to spell out the various ways in which people have considerable freedom to resist the operations of power.

The key difference between sovereign power and modern disciplinary power is that the sites from which power is exercised are multiplied and diffused everywhere. Power is not so centralized in the modern world. It is dispersed into every crevice of life, into every relation, into a myriad of dividing practices that are produced and reproduced on a daily basis. It works because it gets people everywhere to participate as the instruments of their own and others' oppression. The corollary is that so are the opportunities for change dispersed everywhere. It is no longer as necessary to mount a centralized structural revolution in order to effect change that makes a difference at the local level. Instead, opportunities for resistance are multiplied exponentially. They exist all around us wherever disciplinary power operates. In this sense, modern power has a fragile core. It is susceptible to challenge from within the very sites where it operates. If people produce themselves to fit a system of normalized judgment, they can understand this and refuse to participate. If modern power operates principally at the local level in prisons, schools, businesses, social service agencies, health clinics, and family life, then opportunities for social change exist in these same places.

Moreover, modern systems of power are never total in their effects. They are never completely dominant. There are always gaps in their ability to reach into every situation. Indeed, if a system of power ever succeeded in complete domination, we could simply not imagine change. There are always places where we can find people opposing practices of power. Even when such opposition is not organized, it might exist in the refusal to allow oneself to be defined by a power relation. For example, a 13-year-old boy who has been diagnosed by a psychiatrist with attention-deficit hyperactivity disorder announces to his school counselor, "I'm ADHD but I don't believe it!" (Winslade & Monk, 2007, p. 84). This is a moment of refusal of the operation of modern power, even though in the same breath this boy acknowledges the authority of the practices of power as he identifies with the diagnosis.

The close relationship in Foucault's analysis between practices of power and modern academic knowledge is also always open to challenge. There are always alternative knowledges that exist. People learn about and act on these "counter knowledges" (White, 2002) and make changes in their daily lives. Feminism is an example of a counter knowledge that raises questions about the operation of power along the dividing lines of gender. Many women have called on this counter knowledge to initiate changes in gender relations. Antiracism movements that develop counter knowledges about practices of race (e.g., Wise, 2005) offer challenges to the dominant practices in race relations. The literature on decolonization (Fanon, 1963; Said, 1993) serves to unravel many taken-for-granted "truths" of Western European superiority in ways that allow many people to develop an account of their own lives less defined by these assumptions.

It is not always the case, however, that resistance to practices of power is coherent or well strategized. Foucault (2000) talks about some expressions of resistance as "muddled" (p. 155). Such resistance might serve as an expression of rebellion without having a clear focus on bringing about change in the practices of power. This person who is expressing resistance instinctively recognizes herself as an object of power but can't quite determine how. In this case, the actions of resistance may be more damaging for the person herself than for the relations of power. For example, young people who instinctively realize that schooling practices are shaped in ways that will lead them to eventual exclusion from social privilege may develop a culture of resistance through breaches of dress code, through skipping class and smoking, or through extreme actions like taking weapons to school and shooting at other students. But these actions may only succeed in bringing down further operations of power on them that limit their opportunities for freedom. Good counseling may actually help these students articulate more clearly the particular operations of power that they object to and develop more targeted strategies of resistance that produce changes in their relations with others in their school community.

The key difference here between a structuralist and a poststructuralist analysis of power lies in the position of the individual person and his options for the exercise of personal freedom. Daniel Yon (2000) expresses this aptly when he argues that understanding the work of discourses of racism and cultural plurality from a poststructuralist perspective means noticing how they are being reworked on a daily basis in everyday experiences. This means that individuals are seen "not merely as objects of structures but as subjects who are producing and acting upon structures even as they are being constrained by them" (p. 126).

Advantages for Counselors of a Poststructuralist Analysis of Power

In counseling, Michael White has done more than anyone to translate Foucault's analysis into a practice of counseling. He describes his experience of first reading Foucault:

> Upon first reading Foucault on modern power, I experienced a special joy. This joy was in part due to his ability to unsettle what is taken-for-granted and routinely accepted, and to render the familiar strange and exotic. Apart from other things, I found that this opened up new avenues of inquiry into the context of many of the problems and predicaments for which people routinely seek therapy. (White, 2002, p. 36)

White's response envisages possibilities for professional practice rather than dwelling primarily on the reproduction of power relations. It gestures toward a vision of professional practice as a "counter-practice" (White, 2002, p. 37) based on a recognition of how modern power produces people's lives and on an appreciation of people's efforts to resist such power.

A poststructuralist analysis of power also directs attention to the counseling relationship on the assumption that it will always be a power relation. The exercise of power in this relationship will constantly fluctuate in response to discourse. Still, many discursive practices around the counseling relationship structure privilege for the counselor's voice (Guilfoyle, 2005). The ethical question is how counselors approach the exercise of power. Does a counselor stand on her own expert knowledge or make room for the client's knowledge? Does the counselor decide the topics of conversation or grant the client decision-making authority? Does the counselor name the problem (diagnosis) and decide on the "treatment" with reference to published psychological discourse, or does she share this authority with the client? An ethical counselor cannot remove the operation of power from the relationship and create some kind of ideal power-free zone by practicing in ways that are nonjudgmental, client-centered, and dialogic. But the counselor can conceive of the counseling conversation as an exchange in a power relation and ensure that the flow of power is mutual rather than unidirectional.

Less consistent with a poststructuralist analysis of power would be the claim that a counselor cannot possibly understand the experience of her client if she is from a different social group. The argument that men should not counsel women and that White counselors can never appreciate the experiences of disadvantage from which a Black client suffers are structuralist in origin because they fix identity in a structurally determined place.

Now that we have outlined a poststructuralist analysis of power, it is necessary to address its value. Let's list arguments for taking this analysis seriously.

First, it helps us see that power does not always operate in terms of structures. Therefore, changing the structures is not the only way to bring about change. Most people who emphasize a structural view of power claim a position exterior to the operation of power (White, 2002). They are helpless in the face of "the system." The poststructuralist account of modern power places us all where power relations are produced and reproduced—in daily conversation. We are much closer than we think to where social change can take place. This position can give counseling a more critical role in social change than it has ever assumed before. Sociologist Norman Fairclough (1992) has commented that counseling is an "ambiguous practice," not essentially either oppressive or emancipatory, but potentially either, according to how and in which contexts it is practiced. Foucault's analysis allows counselors to understand modern power, which they can easily reproduce in conversations with their clients. It also enables them to base practice on counter knowledges when they detect power in the production of oppression in their clients' lives.

Second, the poststructuralist analysis of power allows a more extensive vision of the operation of power. It is not as if the liberal humanist and the structuralist versions of power do not have places where they are still useful. But there is a much wider range of practices that can be included under the heading of power when viewed from a poststructuralist perspective. Counseling can produce personal and social change that makes a substantive difference if the analysis of power is more extensive. There are many ways in which new elaborations of the principles of modern power are being invented every day, particularly through the ever-widening deployment of computer technology to place people under surveillance. This analysis positions us where we can immediately understand some of the implications for people's lives.

The emphasis in a poststructuralist analysis of modern power is on *practices* that produce relations of power. Foucault talks about a "regime of practices" as being more foundational than the structure of an institution. Power is assumed to begin in social practices, not in individuals, nor in membership of social groups. A focus on practices is inherently practical. This is not to deny that people operate as individuals or that they are members of social groups, but to argue that they are produced as individuals out of social relations and that the social groups to which they belong are produced out of social relations, too. Practices produce structures. This difference requires us to focus on a person's participation in social practices rather than on their essential nature. Hence, the literature on cultural identity development that focuses primarily on either individual identity or on belonging to social groups is misguided. From a poststructuralist stance, it addresses the wrong question with regard to how power operates. For example, racism does not continue because there are too many White people who are unaware of their cultural identity or because there are too few people of color who are prepared to stand up for their cultural identity. It happens because we all participate in a range of daily discourse practices that set up relations among people along the dividing lines of color, and that privilege those who are White and disadvantage those who are not White. Racism is the ideology produced by this discourse and the justification for it. It reproduces itself over and over again through the repetition of its assumptions. A poststructuralist analysis directs us to pay attention first to language practices rather than to what lies in the hearts of people. The latter is assumed to be a by-product of the former rather than its source.

Another advantage of the poststructuralist analysis of power is that it spotlights the practices of power in counseling itself. It cautions counselors about becoming unwitting operatives of the confessional technologies of power that Nikolas Rose (1985) calls the function of the psy-complex. If these functions are illuminated, rather than remaining in shadow, their power can be used to different ends. An example is the trend within the modern management of persons for individuals to become thought of as "cases" (Foucault, 2000, p. 172). The language of counseling has often adopted this piece of discourse from the medical disciplines. If we recognize that such discourse usages are cultural pieces of the operation of power, then we can refuse to talk in this way. We can refuse to participate in one of the key steps in the operation of power, that of turning persons into objects first so they can be governed (treated) second. This can be difficult to achieve when counselors are required by their employers to fill out "treatment" plans couched in the language of objectification. However, creative counselors find ways to meet such requirements and still respect their clients by, for example, giving clients a say in what gets filled out on the form.

An acute sensitivity to the work done by power relations to construct people's lives also helps counselors hear what is critical to the experience of persons. Foucault (2000) has argued that "the most intense point of a life, the point where its energy is concentrated, is where it comes against power, struggles with it, attempts to use its forces, and to evade its traps" (p. 162). If this is true, then counselors should consciously direct their work to this place, where they can potentially have the most critical impact. They can help people discover different ways of governing themselves, not just of being governed by others. Foucault (2000) called this domain of practice "political spirituality" (p. 233).

If counseling is situated at this place, clients will seldom find counseling irrelevant or lack motivation to participate in it.

The poststructuralist analysis of power focuses our attention on its cultural nature. Power conceived of as a network of social practices that get stamped into our psyches emphasizes the role of culture in the production of psychological experience. This emphasis elevates the position of culture in the human sciences. It requires us to take more seriously the daily operations of power in cultural relations and gives us tools with which to do so. It also enables us to see that power and privilege are seldom monolithic and that cultural relations are often complex and nuanced. We can thus avoid the mistake of thinking people are powerless or completely lacking in freedom.

Discuss

Read these three transcripts. What do you think are the different approaches to power being used by the therapist when working with Daneesha? What are the advantages and disadvantages of applying the three different understandings of the operation of power?

Situation One: "So, in both of these situations you felt angry and powerless, right?" said the therapist. "Yes," Daneesha answered with resignation, and was silent. "So what could you have done this morning to claim more power for yourself?" "I could have told her that I was offended and to knock it off." "What would that have felt like?" Daneesha said that it would have felt good. "Would it be helpful for us to rehearse what you might say on other occasions when you experience this kind of silencing and lose your voice?" asked the therapist. "'Cause it sounds like in situations like this you want someone to know what's in your heart and to be assertive about it." Daneesha smiled, and they continued to discuss strategies for empowering her in this situation and others like it.

Situation Two: "Let me ask you something, though," said the therapist. "Were you responsible for the racist slur being spoken?" "No," said Daneesha, smiling through a few tears. "Are you responsible for the ways in which the *N* word has been used for centuries to keep African Americans oppressed?" "No," said Daneesha again. "Are you responsible for the ways in which Mexicans sometimes get tricked by racism into currying favor with Whites by putting down Blacks?" "Do you think that's what was happening? I never thought of it like *that*," said Daneesha. "Well, it's possible. What do you think?" "I suppose it makes sense," said Daneesha. "And no, I'm not responsible for that either. But I still feel upset about it."

"I guess I would too," said the therapist. "In fact, I've experienced something similar myself." The therapist went on to share with Daneesha her own experience a couple of years back. She had been in a situation where she was forced to overhear the *N* word, even though it wasn't directed at her. When she objected, she was told to lighten up and not take things so seriously.

"Thanks," said Daneesha, after listening to the therapist's story. "I don't feel so stupid when I hear you had a similar experience." "I'm glad," smiled the therapist. "We need to stand together against racism. It's too hard to handle on your own."

Situation Three: "Does that mean that when you encounter a racist remark, you are likely to take responsibility for the effects of that remark on yourself?" "It sounds dumb, doesn't it? But yes." "Well, I wouldn't call it dumb, but I am interested in whether you think that's what you would prefer to do in such situations." Daneesha thought for a few seconds. "No, I would like not to have to do that. I'd like to feel okay about standing up against racism and objecting to it when I come across it without getting all knotted up inside." "Okay," said the therapist. "So can we explore a bit how you learned to respond in a way that you don't want to keep repeating. Would that be of interest to you?" Daneesha was happy to engage in this conversation, and they talked about several experiences that had been similar for her. Eventually, during this conversation, she remembered something that had happened at a grocery store in Tennessee when she was 12 or 13. Her mom had asked for assistance from a young clerk. "I don't even recall what my mom wanted," she said, "but the clerk sneered and rudely said, 'I don't do anything for niggers.'" As Daneesha recounted this event, her eyes filled with tears. She told the therapist that her mom had told her to be quiet about the incident. Her mom had said that the godly thing to do was to pray for the young man, and they walked out of the store. "Did your mom's comment help the voice of responsibility taking or help your other voice of wanting to stand up against it?" "Well, it made me ashamed … and I didn't pray for that man. So I think I ended up feeling guilty myself, too."

"As you think about it now, do you think you were guilty of doing anything wrong?" asked the therapist. "No," said Daneesha. "So is it kind of like racism can trick you into feeling guilty even when you're not the one who's done something wrong?" Daneesha smiled at this. It sounded absurd and yet also strangely accurate. "Tell me," said the therapist. "Are there times you can remember when you didn't allow this to happen? Are there any occasions when you've chosen not to feel guilty and to stand in a different place?"

After some thought, Daneesha came up with a couple of instances. They related to more recent events in her life, particularly the discussion group on race and Christianity that she had attended at her church. "I guess I just saw how the whole racism thing works and is so powerful and I got mad about that," said Daneesha, "and that was just before the Black Lives Matter movement got started."

Share with your classmates your reflections on how you will work with managing power in the therapy room.

Response to Chapter 6

NAVID ZAMANI, MS LMFT

Navid received his BA in Psychology with a minor in Music from the University of California, Davis, and graduated from the San Diego State University Marriage and Family Therapy program. He is a licensed marriage and family therapist in the state of California, and has focused on supporting families experiencing domestic violence. He currently teaches in the Counseling and School Psychology department at San Diego State University, provides regular trainings on domestic violence conceptualizations and practices around San Diego County, and is actively engaged in writing and publishing scholarly work. He is also the head of clinical services and clinical supervisor at License to Freedom, a non-profit supporting Middle Eastern refugees experiencing domestic violence.

It has taken me a long time to wrap my mind around issues of power. Talking about and noticing power can sometimes feel like a disorienting and endless rabbit hole, similar to studying the brain or imagining the limits of the universe. And perhaps, as individual thinkers, it is a limited endeavor. This is where the diversity, complexity, and experiences of a community's thinking (versus individuals) becomes important.

It feels important to situate some relevant aspects of my background. I am the heterosexual son (cis-gendered male) of Iranian immigrants in the United States. For the first 20 years of my life, I visited family in Iran for two months out of the year, where I listened to stories of a country torn by a revolution. This is while growing up in a middle- to upper-class community in the United States. These experiences have been influential in my reflections on understanding the complexities and immediate fluidity of relational power. This early exposure to the multiplicity of human identity made me suspicious and critical of therapeutic pedagogical models that construct power as rigid and monolithic. Counseling models that offer step-by-step discrete "techniques" are widely embraced by counselor educators and therapists. In part, this is due to the straightforward nature of teaching and learning these models (such as emotionally focused therapy or cognitive behavioral therapy). I find counseling models built on reductionist principles limiting, when considering the supremely complex dynamics of relating and being in a conversation with somebody who has a drastically different world view than oneself. And while considerations of power, discourse, and identity discussed in this text can sometimes seem complicated and overly academic, there are emerging practices within an affective-discursive domain, such as recent applications from narrative therapy to domestic violence work (Augusta-Scott & Dankwort, 2002; Maerz & Augusta-Scott, 2017; White, 2009), neuro-narrative therapy (Ewing, Estes, & Like, 2017) and neuro-biological collaborative therapy (Beaudoin & Zimmerman, 2011), that offer ways to scaffold and explore these ideas with those who consult with us.

My practice is consumed by and requires a constant attention to issues of power. As a licensed marriage and family therapist in California, United States, I am in counseling contexts with families who have experienced domestic violence, which has occurred within an adult couple relationship. Part of my work I want to highlight here relates to my role working as a facilitator in a 52-week, court-mandated counseling group with Middle Eastern refugees and immigrants. As you can imagine, this context is a unique zone for exploring concepts and workings of power. This group is located in a city that houses over 15,000 refugees, originally residents from the Middle East who have been able to adjust to life in a large Southern California city, where they have developed a lifestyle that allows them to thrive in mainstream U.S. society (Alzendi, Zamani & Ashoor, 2017). This is while living and working within a large working-class, White community that is heavily influenced by an anti-immigrant, nationalist sentiment. The group I facilitate is multilingual, with group members speaking English, Farsi (interpreted by myself), and Arabic (with a dedicated interpreter). The group members are made up of Chaldeans (Christian Iraqi), Kurds, Afghans, Iranians, and Syrians. These refugee populations have been relocated to Southern California over the last 30 years (Alzendi et al., 2017).

The men are mandated to participate in the group and present with a diverse and wide-ranging set of concerns. The men are assigned to the group because the police arrested them and charged them with domestic battering. The court found them guilty and determined that a Domestic Violence Intervention Program (DVIP) would be the appropriate response to their harmful behavior. These groups require the facilitator to be trained in a 40-hour, county-approved program. The facilitator is required to teach the court curriculum, complete intakes and assessments, and provide progress reports to the court. My current research focuses upon understanding how this complex, quasilegal system impacts people mandated to participate in therapy. Here, I am calling attention to some of the nuanced, yet glaring ways that relational power influences the relationships in this group.

My observations come from poststructuralist, decolonial feminism, where I am interested in the critiques and analyses offered by both structural and individualistic approaches. I am cautious of the linguistic categorizations that shape our thinking and affective states. In my research and therapy work I pay attention to the contributions of feminism that acknowledge the influence of gendered histories and patriarchy in DV work. I also consider the histories of feminist activists in how they have constructed DV discourse. I notice, too, how much of what happens to men mandated to attend these 52-week groups is affected by the global influences of neocolonialism and neoliberalism. This perspective is important to me, as domestic violence work is a mosaic of various philosophical and theoretical approaches that often leaves practitioners with rigid understandings and typologies of violence that can further perpetrate harm on families during these moments of strain and crisis (Ferraro, 1996). For instance, men are often cast as dominating, powerful individuals who are actively seeking power and control, and women cast as victims who are subjected to a larger, patriarchal system that leaves them without agency or responsibility. What these typologies ignore is the influence of immigration due to U.S. military interventions in the Middle East and elsewhere, and the terrible effects of living in war on the group participants. The approaches to addressing violence in these DV programs pays little attention to the cultures of origin of the participants and the challenges of assimilation to very different norms and expectations of the United States.

It's important to note in this discussion that minority and marginalized communities are subjected to mandated therapy contexts more frequently than non-minority communities (Creek & Dunn, 2011; Dutton & Corvo, 2006; Ferraro, 1996). The curriculum used in these groups is constructed squarely within Western ideals regarding relationships, and developed within the confines of the Duluth Model and the Criminal Control Model. Violence is often perceived as an exclusively patriarchal behavior. Through the lens of patriarchy, it is men's "criminal behavior" that alone needs to be corrected, even though there are many other issues that are not being addressed (Dutton & Corvo, 2006; Ferraro, 1996; Schecter, 1982). Within these models, men are expected to be "accountable" to their violence, and thus, any statements that are outside of accepting full responsibility for their actions is understood as "minimizing," "avoidance," or "manipulation" (Augusta-Scott, 2001). The difficulty in this nuance is that these notions of minimization or manipulation can be very real processes that can occur or be used as techniques of power to gain and/or maintain control over women and others they deem to be "less powerful." The problem I am calling attention to is that these ideas have dominated the "best practices" in the field for working with these men, and are extraordinarily influential in shaping what a therapist does in these groups. If you find yourself uncomfortable with these ideas, then you are in that liminal space with me.

The difficulty here is that this system did not occur overnight, nor was it crafted by a single person with bad intentions. These DVIP groups were developed over the past half century, and DV understandings in the United States began in the late 19th century (Ferraro, 1996; Augusta-Scott, 2001). The current "best practices" that are applied to every "offender" mandated to these groups gives little space for considerations of immigration, exposure to war and violence, educational level, nonbinary genders, effects of neocolonialism, and/or other macrolevel experiences. These groups become a vortex in which cultural values and ideals get pulled in and mixed up, and are spat out as "evidence-based" truths where a collection of techniques and approaches are crudely thrown together and applied across a diverse group of people. In summary, the current status of DVIP groups in the United States reflects a heavily modernist, liberal humanist, neocolonial, and neoliberal American (U.S.) set of values that are hooded in progressive feminist values.

My own positioning in this group is often convoluted. In a moment where the idea of the "person of color" (PoC) holds political weight and is heavily discursively shaped, I find myself at odds with my own identity. In academic circles, I'm often referred to as a PoC and the assumptions that follow allow others to populate my history. However, in this group I am, by all means, White (Bouteldja & Valinsky, 2017). I am educated in the US, speak the language, understand the systems, do not have an accent, and so on. As far as the "knapsack of privilege" goes, mine is full of "Whiteness" in the context of this group (McIntosh, 1990). In other areas of my life, this idea of PoC does apply to some degree, but definitely not in this context. Furthermore, as a narrative therapist who is interested in allowing for space to explore the discursive landscape that informs actions, meaning, and identity, I find my values at odds with my relationship to the courts. In my role, I'm required to report to the courts. These are the same systems in which oppression towards minorities—my clients in this context—exist. This is not to mention my cisgendered positioning, where I am under the threat of being understood as inadvertently reinforcing patriarchy simply due to my "maleness." Within a structural, critical-theory understanding of these groups, I am situated to *always* reinforce patriarchy, despite my best intentions. Within a liberal humanist perspective, I can be understood to be able to make choices that can avoid such oppressive behaviors, with the assumption that I am (or can be) fully aware and in control of all the effects of my actions. Thus, my identity becomes a vulnerable location that either glimmers or darkens my work depending on the perspective, versus a complex person managing complex dynamics with other complex people, guided by values, intentions, and practices that are constantly adjusting and developing.

I can vividly recall the moment the complexity of my positioning occurred to me. One of the men was sharing about how Arabs are often perceived to be "loud," and how often his "[White] American neighbors" would call the police before "coming to talk to us to see if there is a problem." Per his story, the police arrived, asked him to step outside, and then proceeded to arrest him for domestic violence and "drinking in public." The primary issue is that he was inside his house with a beer in his hand, and when he walked outside with the beer still in his hand to talk to the police, he was arrested. Being influenced by the Criminal Control Model, and the need for accountability via the Duluth Model, I was certain that this story was intended to be "manipulative" and "minimizing" of the violence he had certainly engaged in! I came to find out over the next couple of weeks, via both the police report and other witnesses, that his story represented a truth held by most involved. Specifically, this client was arrested for "drinking in public" after being asked to step outside, when the original call and concern had been for "loud arguments" and "possible domestic violence." My conditioning to Western systems and domestic violence understandings had me commit a cardinal sin (in my opinion) of not hearing or acknowledging my client's lived experience. Furthermore, my client's presence in my group was understood as an admission of guilt, and any attempt to dissuade me from this was situated to be understood as avoidance.

Due to the privileges and opportunities that have been present in my educational journey, combined with my positionings and experiences, I have found some agency in the philosophies I want to discriminately draw on, and the practices I engage in. My entry into the field of therapy was squarely shaped within a poststructuralist framework. My work has also been influenced by discursive approaches to therapy and fortified by neurological and affective understandings of the brain and body, which have emerged with more prominence. In exploring this epistemology, I was able to recognize the possible positions of "domination" that I demonstrated in my role as a facilitator, when asking for and requiring that men conform their story to the narrative I needed to hear to "help" them. How ironic it was for me to identify that I was negatively affected by the workings of power within the criminal justice system, leading me to subjugate my own clients, all the while telling myself I was performing a role to help the men in the group recognize their abuse of power and manage it.

It's easy to feel frustrated, hopeless, and ineffective in the face of managing the negative effects of these larger systems, such as the courts, county curricula, and criminal control models. This is especially the case when these systems are riddled by harmful histories of oppression, particularly towards marginalized communities. It can be seductive to be drawn into anger towards perceived curators of these systems, and the human vessels through which injustice is funneled. I find comfort in knowing that many systems are comprised of various people (such as activists, lawyers, therapists, law enforcement, etc.) who are attending to what they believe to be the "cause" or the "solution" to domestic violence. Making sense of this complexity helps me recognize that the well-intended are limited by the cultural knowledges emerging from particular social and historical contexts that shape the behavior of professionals working in this quasilegal context. What has been enlightening for me is noticing that even asking the question of "What is the cause?" or "What is the solution?" of domestic violence is squarely located within Western, Enlightenment-era values of cause/effect and "rationality" models.

Power is complex. We should not be seduced into thinking we can understand power by taking a reductionist approach and compartmentalizing it to try and understand it. It requires a careful suspending of knowledge. Understanding power is as much a physiological process as it is cognitive one. It takes a particular physiological state to be able to stand within the "unknown" and explore it without the anxiety of urgency or "needing to know" (Ewing, Estes, & Like, 2017). Use your own limited knowledges and experiences to co-construct a curiosity with your clients—a curiosity that constructs a philosophical and physiological foundation from which your clients may benefit.

Addressing Racism

Failing to address racism is a form of racism itself. It is like having the ability to rescue a drowning child but failing to do so.

— Charles Ridley, *Overcoming Unintentional Racism in Counseling and Therapy (2005)*

This chapter addresses the destructive influences of racism—the ideological legacy of European colonization that has material impact on the lives of people across diverse cultures. Applications of counseling and psychology must not only deal with people from diverse backgrounds; they must deal with the effects of racist ideology on their lives. Combating racism, however, is not just a matter of agreeing that it is a bad thing and starting from there. It involves thinking through some issues in order to ensure that the work of combating racism is effective. Because there are some different approaches around, it also involves considering just how we will talk about the subject of racism. We suspect that some of these approaches are more helpful and less counterproductive than others.

This chapter considers a variety of approaches to addressing and combating the effects of racism in and through counseling practice. As we have been doing throughout this book, we shall highlight and explain some specific strategies that utilize the social constructionist metaphor and the application of discourse, deconstruction, and positioning concepts to more productively make racism visible to undermine its discourses and its effects. We also include a brief perspective of racism from a decolonial perspective.

Definitions of Racism

Among complex societies in an era of globalization, there is no single kind of racism or single definition of it. As David Theo Goldberg (1993) suggests, "there is no unified phenomenon of racism, only a range of racisms" (p. 213). Racism is fluid in nature and takes on both covert and overt forms. In part, this is why it is so harmful and dangerous to the well-being of all. Various racisms are tied up in all social conditions covering the gamut of economic, political, legal, and cultural realms. For a behavioral description, we could define racism as what occurs when individuals of one racial or ethnic group are denied access, on the basis of their race, to resources and opportunities that are available to and enjoyed by another group (Ridley, 2005). Charmaine Wijeyesinghe, Pat Griffin, and Barbara Love

(1997) invoke a commodity metaphor of power to describe racism as "the systematic subordination of members of targeted racial groups who have relatively little social power ... by members of the agent racial group who have relatively more social power" (p. 88). In both of these definitions, there is an underlying assumption (conscious or unconscious) of superiority of one racial group over another that is used to justify and support oppressive or paternalistic practices.

Here is another definition of racism from the anthropologist Ruth Benedict (1945):

> Racism is the dogma that one ethnic group is condemned by nature to congenital infe-
> riority and another group is destined for congenital superiority. (p. 87)

This ideological component is central. Any word that ends in *ism* refers to an ideology or a matrix of ideas. There can be little doubt that for different reasons one cultural group can develop specific aspects of superiority in certain dimensions of life. Among Inuits' cultures some could be considered to have superior ability to survive in cold climates. The same could be considered in Japanese cultures where sumo wrestlers may be superior than those from other cultures; and among Brazilian communities where soccer players train, being consistently superior to those who train in other countries. The racist assumption, however, is that such superiority is global and applies to all aspects of all people who belong to a racial group. A second assumption is that it is tied to biological inheritance in general and marked by skin color in particular (see Chapter 4).

Each of these definitions is founded on the assumption that racism is a cultural phenomenon. It is a product of cultural history and is shared among groups of people and aimed at other groups. It is not primarily an aspect of individual psychology, even though it takes on individual psychological formations and is expressed in individual behavior. If racism did not exist as a cultural phenomenon, any individual expression of it would not make sense and would be dismissed as irrational behavior. Its lethality lies partly in the way that individual expressions of racism line up with and reproduce cultural assumptions that many participate in.

Decoloniality and Racism

Academic and social activists who ascribe to the Andean understanding of coloniality and decoloniality, among them Ramón Grosfoguel (2012), consider that racism cannot be understood when devoid of a historical and political analysis. As we stated above, race is an ideology that emerged from European colonization that began in the 16th century. This colonizing history must be acknowledged if racism is to be grappled with. Decolonial activists situate racism as not only a cultural phenomenon or an ideology in itself, but constructed within social structures of power that reinforce practices, policies, and actions of discrimination against certain groups. Institutionalized racism occurs in the material everyday life of communities, which limits access to resources, and diminishes choices and rights.

Social structures are hierarchically arranged around power between those that are advantaged or superior and those disadvantaged or inferior. We take this to mean that racism is not situated only as individual biases or prejudices that lead communities to discriminate against others. Racism is not only in people's heads. It is a social practice. Grosfoguel (2012) notes that that if it wasn't for institutions that legitimize discriminatory practices within communities, racism would not exist.

This means that, when addressing racism in counseling, if we only address the personal prejudices, stereotypes, and biases that counselors may ascribe to and may introduce in their practice, it is not sufficient to eradicate racism. A decolonial perspective compels us to take a close look at the institutional practices within which counseling, psychology, and other related professions are situated. We must pay attention to how these institutional practices in these professions perpetuate discourses of racism that construct the superiority or inferiority of groups, particular epistemologies, practices, and ways of being, doing, and thinking. When taking a decolonial posture, for example, we would need to consider the operation of power relations at the base of training curricula in academia that favor some identifiable groups and not others. This is most commonly demonstrated within the knowledges and theories taught, who teaches them, who the recipients are of these curricula, and within what languages knowledge is delivered.

Decoloniality pays attention to the epistemological foundations of the curriculum as well as the social locations in which the people in positions of educational authority are embedded. Decolonial activists describe how professional institutions that determine policy, academic standards, and professional ethics in mental health are embedded within a kind of social racism. In the family therapy field, for example, the majority of faculty and supervisors are White, much like the authors of the most prominent Eurocentric family therapy theories. These ethnic histories of the developers of Eurocentric theories, and the personnel who teach the theories and work with them with clients, are vulnerable to the pervasiveness of racism that accompanies colonial Eurocentric racism.

Grosfoguel (2012) considers racism as an act of categorization of humanity in reference to various social markers not only on the basis of color as Black, White, Brown, and so on, but as including religious racism, gender racism, ethnic racism, and linguistic racism (this means that various expressions of racism exist among communities of the same color). From a decolonial perspective, racism is not strictly related to the idea of race, but extends beyond other referential points to discriminate against some communities and not others. Grosfoguel articulates this referential borrowing from the extensive work of the Martinique Franz Fanon (1963) on race. Fanon considers that racism is a global hierarchy of superiority and inferiority featuring prominently across a politically (Eurocentric, capitalist, patriarchal, modern, colonial) constructed line of what is deemed legitimately human and what is not. Grosfoguel speaks of a line that divides humanity. Above the line is a humanity that is recognized, deemed superior, and consequently has access to all kinds of important rights, including material comfort, employment, and social status and support. Below the line are those whose humanity, state of being, and existence is constantly contested, questioned, or even regarded as nonexistent. Although this line is embedded in Eurocentric practices of institutionalization, Grosfoguel is clear in stating that the line of division of humanity is not normally geographically situated (for example North and South), nor is it all encompassing or homogenous across the bifurcation. Above the line, or among those whose humanity is recognized, there still exists marginalization and oppression, which can be shared with others below the line. Even among those whose humanity is questioned, there exists superiority and inferiority. However, Grosfoguel adds, the oppression experienced among those whose existence is recognized is quite different than that experienced by those whose existence is not. This metaphor of humanity finds a lot in common with Latin American antiracist feminists (Curiel, 2007; Espinosa Miñoso, 2009) and Black feminists in the United States. These scholars critique White feminism, marking a tremendous difference between the experience of discrimination of White women in Europe versus the experience of Black women in the Favelas in Brazil. For Grosfoguel, there is privileged oppression among those whose humanity and existence is recognized, and aggravated oppression among those for whom it is not. For the former, political or legal options are offered and available where their existence is not at stake. For the latter group, when demanding their rights their life becomes at stake, which can occur through forced displacement, violence, or murder.

An example of privileged oppression is to have rights for activism through the means of protests, marches, or judicial action. An example of privileged oppression was on display when the Women's March was organized following the election of Donald Trump, and during the grassroots protests occurring in the Me Too movement. Among communities whose humanity is questioned, life-threatening oppression is at stake. This was the case when the indigenous environmentalist from Honduras, Berta Cáceres, was murdered in 2016. It wasn't the fact that it was exclusively an act of femicide. Instead it was her environmental activism that cost her her life. In 2014, Cáceres motivated a movement that was able to stop the plans of the World Bank and one of the largest companies in China to build a hydropower plant affecting the Rio Gualcarque, which sustains the local indigenous communities such as the Lencas that live in this area. Another example is the disappearance of the 43 Mexican students from the Escuela Normal Rural of Ayotzinapa, which is known for its contestatory politics. Widely agreed-upon evidence suggests these students were kidnapped, murdered, and their bodies burnt by the local police. Up until this point their killers are protected with impunity, even after the many interventions made by human rights international organizations. There are many more examples we could offer that show femicide of prominent activist figures in Latin America. The oppression and assassination of many African American citizens and activists in the United States is linked to the decolonial premise of racism being a matter of the abuse of institutional power that dehumanizes certain communities and not others.

Racism and the Body

A significant theme in this book has been an emphasis on the complexity of identity, and we have noted repeatedly that the modern world makes us up as people with multiple identities. A constructionist analysis takes this into consideration in relation to racism. Yet, at the same time, we are sometimes confronted with circumstances that force us to act on the exact opposite assumption. Take, for example, a young man who commits a crime and is incarcerated in a California state prison. He is White in appearance and has a Spanish last name and a Latinx heritage. On entry to the prison, he is told by inmates, "You have to choose—are you going to be White or Mexican? You can't be both. Your life depends on your joining one group or the other. If you don't choose, you will die in here."

When people are asked to quickly identify how they perceive themselves, White Anglo American students seldom recognize and talk about their Whiteness and instead discuss personal qualities, while people in underrepresented groups and people of color typically identify themselves by their exterior (Neville, Awad, Brooks, Flores, & Bluemel, 2013). Very rarely do we hear a White student in the United States say he is White as the first marker of his identity, but a person of color might claim Asian, African American, Black, Latinx, or Native American status as her first salient identity. Because so many settings are dominated by Whites, color becomes marked as a feature of difference. People of color notice how they are marked as different, and thus color and phenotypic characteristics become internalized as their most salient marker of identity (Holoien & Shelton, 2012). As Jerry Diller (2007) suggests, many Whites see themselves as ordinary members of the human race but not in the first instance as a racial or ethnic group. It continues to surprise many White students when people of color relate to them as a distinct racial group. The experience of surprise, or even shock, does not necessarily identify these individuals as harboring racist intent. It is more likely an effect of the existence of racist assumptions built into the wider social world (Cabrera, Watson, & Franklin, 2016).

This situation may change in future in response to demographic changes. The tide is turning against what was once an unquestioned assumption (among the White majority in the United States) that White European culture was superior in every way. In settings where White people are a minority, Whiteness is becoming a more salient phenomenon. Whiteness is already perceived as salient by people of color, and identity is always partially constituted in relation to how one imagines one is seen by others (DiAngelo, 2011).

The Role of Colonization and Racism

The act of choosing one's salient identity features to present to the world sounds benign enough. In actuality, however, people of color are often denied this choice. Their options are always constrained by the way their skin color and physical features line up with a painful history of racial denigration and abjection produced out of the European colonizing discourses of the last few hundred years (Varga, 2011). (We discussed this history in Chapter 4.) It is still reproduced in the consciousness of a Black child as an experience of inferiority. For example, a Black child is exposed to many beliefs and values of a dominant White culture, while Black culture is represented to the same child in terms of lower academic achievement, association with crime, and lower-paying employment (Banks, 2014; Benner et al., 2018; Bonilla-Silva, 2012; Brown & Segrist, 2016; Piff, Kraus, & Keltner, 2018).

At 10 years old, Monica was already sharply aware of the negative stigma associated with being seen as dark. She says her own aunt was stigmatized by the family and called Blackie. Children at Monica's predominantly White school would say, "Why is your hair like that? Why do you say 'acts' instead of 'asks'? You're not saying it right." She says she felt so much like an outcast at school.

For people in North America and in many other parts of the world, people with Black skin, kinky hair, or stereotypical Asian features and other non-White physical features have been historically assigned inferior status and diminished life opportunity. These markers continue today to be associated with systematic, oppressive experiences of social exclusion, if not outright hatred and loathing. Physical characteristics and linguistic patterns immediately identify people who have been victimized by these colonizing patterns, while Anglo or White populations are associated historically (and sometimes currently) with oppressive and hateful acts. Huge pressures are applied to people of color to avoid the covert and overt acts of racism. Take Sarah, for example.

> I would be scolded for playing outside for fear that my skin complexion would darken. Light skin was emphasized as a symbol of beauty. Time and time again, I was informed that I was very blessed to have such a light complexion. My complexion has been considered a strong trait of beauty and is a sign of status within the Filipino community. My mother and my grandmother ensured that my complexion would remain light by utilizing

Whitening and bleaching creams on a regular basis. Nose shape was also an important physical characteristic in our ethnic group. Each night when I went to bed, my grandmother or mother would pinch the bridge of my nose because they believed that I would have a narrower nose rather than the stereotypical Filipino "pug" nose. At times, they would pinch my nose so hard that I would go to school the following day with a bruise.

Colonizing discourses force people in the margins to try to conform to dominant cultural ideas about beauty and to escape from the effects of racism and racial hatred. Let us pause to note that the origins of racism do not all begin with hatred. While there are gross examples of racial hate, an overemphasis on reducing racism to hatred can lead to the distorted assumption that racism has its origins in hate. It is probably more closely associated with a smug sense of superiority, while anger and hatred are only triggered when this sense of superiority is challenged. The same mistake can be made if we assume that domestic violence always has its origins in the experience of anger. The analysis of violence as an expression of the desire for power and control (often quite coldly expressed) has yielded a more powerful explanation of domestic violence than an explanation based on an excess of anger, and the same might be said for racism. Racial hate often arises when the victims of racism rise up and defy erroneous or arrogant notions of superiority. People captured by racist attitudes of superiority often resent being challenged by those they perceive to be inferior and undeserving. It is this resentment that is the basis of racial hatred (DiAngelo, 2011; DiAngelo & Sensoy, 2014). It is fueled by the same resentment harbored by people who commit acts of domestic violence when they perceive the person in a subjugated position making an effort to resist controlling and oppressive behavior.

Up until the Trump presidency, overt forms of active racism, such as the practices of the Ku Klux Klan and White supremacists, had gone largely underground. It has re-emerged and was on full display as demonstrated in the Charlottesville, Virginia, rally in 2017 (Center for the Study of Hate & Extremism, 2018; Liu, 2017). The legacy of the story of colonization persists (Liu et al., 2019). The European colonizing discourse today generally supports softer versions of what Beverly Tatum (1997) calls passive racism, where people laugh at racist jokes and support or leave unchallenged many forms of exclusionary practice against people of color in education, housing, health, and the workplace (Alvarez, Liang, & Neville, 2016; Douglass, Mirpuri, English, & Yip, 2016). Racism is also expressed in the easy acceptance of social privilege as earned and deserved, along with the assumption that people of other races earn and deserve their exclusion from the same privileges and opportunities (Seaton & Iida, 2019; Sibrava et al., 2019; Wilkins, Wellman, Babbitt, Toosi, & Schad, 2015).

Noticing Ethnic Differences

Racism is founded on the division of people into groups along racial lines, but consciousness of such divisions is not natural. It is learned in the process of being enculturated and supported by institutional social structures. As children progress through school, they learn to notice racial markers (and of course gender, class, and sexual orientation markers, among others) and to accumulate assumptions on the foundation of such noticing. Their own race or ethnicity is also increasingly noticed by others. Ethnic or racial differences are not noticed as much at elementary school, where there is much more mixing in self-contained classrooms. By middle school, recognizable racial groupings are emerging. For example, many White students are tracked into honors programs while many Blacks find themselves in lower tracks. This kind of sorting sends a powerful message to young people (Alamilla, Kim, Walker, & Sisson, 2017; Chavous, Richardson, Webb, Fonseca-Bolorin, & Leath, 2017; Kanter et al., 2017).

As adolescence continues, the mixing between White and Black is lessened. Interracial dating has always been uncommon in the United States (more so than in some other countries) and continues that way today in more conservative states, though there are also many exceptions. Black students are confronted by powerful dominant cultural discourses that suggest that to be Black means you are not smart or will become a mugger, drug dealer, gang member, or some other kind of criminal. The dominant cultural discourses reinforce notions that Whiteness is superior and Blackness inferior. White is the norm and Black or colored is the exception, or the excluded other. There is a growing awareness by adolescence that Black youth are excluded from many aspects of mainstream society in the United States (Benner, 2018; Pittman, Cho Kim, Hunter, & Obasi, 2017). As youth of color become more conscious of inequities, they sometimes develop an oppositional identity (Johnston-Goodstar & VeLure Roholt, 2017; Seroczynski & Jobst, 2016). This identity could be characterized as self-protective but outwardly defiant. It serves to provide some self-protection from the suffering caused by racist practices and also serves to keep the White majority population at a distance.

Barack Obama (2006) speaks about the ongoing effects racism on nonWhite populations:

> None of us—Black, White, Latino, or Asian—is immune to the stereotypes that our culture continues to feed us, especially stereotypes about Black criminality, Black intelligence, or the Black work ethic. In general, members of every minority group continue to be measured largely by the degree of our assimilation—how closely our speech patterns, dress, or demeanor conform to the dominant White culture—and the more that a minority strays from these external markers, the more he or she is subject to negative assumptions. (p. 235)

According to the stereotypes that Obama refers to, if a White person fails to show normal intelligence at school or engages in borderline criminal activity, it is more likely to be considered an instance of individual difference. A person of color in the same situation is more likely to be assumed to be typical of his race.

In middle and high schools across the United States, Black students tend to congregate together, as do Asians and people of other groups. Beverly Tatum's (1997) popular book, titled *Why Are All the Black Kids Sitting Together in the Cafeteria?* speaks to this phenomenon. While there are great within-group differences in all identity groups, the self-selection of social groups formed along ethnic and racial lines continues to dominate many social institutions in North America. It is most notable in schools, prisons, and the residential communities where people live. Part of this gravitation relates to feelings of shared oppression that people of color experience on a day-to-day basis (Kaholokula, 2016; Seaton & Iida, 2019; Smith, Hung, & Franklin, 2011).

Sometimes feelings of oppression shared with others who look similar provide a sense of safety, support, and even protection. Sometimes they also relate to a fear of difference and a desire to keep other groups out. Other factors, such as economic resources, impact where and how people group together. Read the following stories for examples of how racism is made manifest in individual people's lives.

As I grew older, I was undoubtedly exposed to racism and discrimination. I realized I was a Black woman in a White world, and often that was not a good place to be. I repeatedly heard the N word not only being used but being accepted in the workplace. Coworkers would make racist comments to my face and then try to convince me they were not racist. When I was bold enough to tell them I did not appreciate the N word or challenged them to explain what they meant by their "innocent" or "I didn't mean you" racist comments, I was often labeled hostile and confrontational. This is a stereotype that many African American women are subject to.

At the beginning of an interview for a job, the interviewer said, "Oh, you are Black. That is not at all what I was expecting. Your name is not typical for a Black girl."

—Heather Conley-Higgins

"Nigger." Six little letters that when put together in that order have such power over my life. It is more than an insult. It is more than a racial slur. In that one word is a reminder of all that my ancestors went through at the hands of Europeans and Whites in America. In that one word is a reminder of the villages in West Africa that were destroyed and the people who were captured, held in slave castles, and shipped to the "New World." In that one word is the reminder of all who died in the middle passage. In that one word is the reminder of the centuries of backbreaking work from sunup to sundown for no pay. In that one word is the reminder of the women raped, the men beaten, the children separated from their families. In that one word is the reminder of being counted as three-fifths of a person. In that one word is the reminder of the law forbidding Blacks to learn to read. In that one word is the reminder of the years of apartheid in America—also known as Jim Crow. In that one word is a reminder of the water hoses, the dogs, the burning crosses, the lynchings. In that one word is a reminder of the four little girls bombed in a church in Birmingham. In that one word is a reminder of racial profiling, being followed in a store, ladies clutching their purses.

So you see, there is a long history behind those six little letters. When I hear it out of the mouth of a White American, it cuts deep down in my soul. I feel it for all my brothers and sisters in the struggle. I feel it for all that came before me. I feel it for my brothers, my sister, my parents, and my grandmother. I feel all of the unsaid that goes with it. You're nothing. You're worthless. You're nothing more than a chattel. Your opinion doesn't matter. Your thoughts are irrelevant. Your life is unimportant. The hatred behind "nigger" runs too deep.

There is life and death in the power of words. I choose not to let them define me or destroy my spirit. However, I cannot ignore the historical, social, and racial implications of those six little letters.

James Baldwin once said, "You can only be destroyed by believing that you really are what the White world calls a nigger."

I know that I am worth more than gold. I know that my opinion matters. I know that my life is important. I will not be destroyed. But it still hurts. It still cuts deep. Real deep.

—Natasha Crawford

I shouldn't have to work 20 times harder in this world. I shouldn't have to accept your view and ways of life just because you feel you own this land. On the outside I look like I have had an easy life, but on the inside my heart is aching and I long to cry so that I could shed a tear for all the pain my people and I have endured. The anger that I feel inside is boiling from what you have done, so that sometimes I want revenge. But I am better than that. Two wrongs don't make a right. Do you see me now? I don't think you do, because you've heard my story before but you have chosen to ignore it. You have oppressed my race, my family and friends. You are my oppressor. So the hate gets stronger, but so do I, and no matter what you have done or will do to me and my people I will fight for what is rightly ours … Life!

—Deliah

I am writing hoping that maybe, just maybe you'll listen with more than your ears. What you see before you is a typical Asian girl. I've got straight Black hair, dark brown eyes, flat nose, and a short physical stature. That's Asian, right? But sometimes people call me Chinese, Japanese, Vietnamese, or even Oriental! Correction, "Oriental" is for rugs. I am Filipino. And I'd like to tell you that it hurts. It hurts to be described like a rug. But, you know what, most of the time I keep quiet.

What you see before you is an Asian American. I am a citizen of the United States. But sometimes people ask me, "Why don't you just say you are American?" or "Why don't you just be an American?" And I think, why should I have to choose between being Asian and being American? I already feel the pressures to assimilate at the cost of my Filipino culture. And if I don't assimilate, I am going to be labeled as a foreigner in America. Sometimes people see me as a foreigner, a foreign exotic Asian female; like some captive creature you point to in the zoo, or like a mail-order bride who is docile, sexual, and mysterious. I feel dirty, degraded, and dehumanized when treated like a commodity.

Some people tell me that I can achieve the "American dream." From my experience, the American dream is not an equal opportunity for all Americans. There have been institutional barriers, such as laws, that have served as obstacles for those who desire the American dream. Historically, Asian immigrants were prevented from owning land and other property, from attaining citizenship, and from being allowed to immigrate to be with their loved ones. While these laws no longer apply, their legacy and negative effect has influenced the present social, political, and economic struggles of Asian Americans.

—Mary Suzette Tuason

When I started school I could not speak English. When learning English, I could not speak it to my Mandarin-speaking parents. My teachers interpreted my inability to complete work and my lack of participation as a reflection of incompetence. They wrote unsatisfactory comments on my report cards. Because of these reactions, I associated my Chinese heritage with shameful ignorance. I focused on creating an "American identity." I learned to hide my Chinese identity. However, I had limited success. Classmates mocked my Chinese foods, such as rice porridge with dried eel. When I was able to eat hamburgers and fantasize about American pop stars, I began to be accepted by some Anglo American schoolmates.

Despite my very Chinese heritage, Euro-American colonial images were very impactful on my family. As a swimmer, I spent time in the sun and began to develop a strong athletic frame. My mother threatened to pull me out of the swim team because my skin was getting too dark. In my family, dark women were associated with servants or field workers, and pale, thin Chinese women were seen as attractive and of high social status. My mother used to pinch my nose, which was a little flatter than she wanted it to be. She tried to mold it to look like an Anglo American nose. My eyes were not large enough; my lips were too thin.

—Grace Tsai

Discuss

1. Persons of color might be reminded of their own stories of similar experiences and be willing to share them with the class.
2. White students should listen to these stories respectfully and afterward discuss how they are affected by hearing them.
3. What difference does it make to bring these stories into conversation, where they can be heard?
4. How does holding a conversation about racism in class affect relationships in the class?
5. How might holding a conversation about racism in class affect the work you will do as a counselor, social worker, or psychologist?
6. What are some useful strategies that both White counselors and counselors of color can pursue to combat the effects of racism?

Many members of the White majority are quite oblivious to the ongoing effects of racist behavior toward people of color (Bonilla-Silva, 2012; Douglass, Mirpuri, English, & Yip, 2016; Wise, 2005). Some are even convinced that racism is a thing of the past. They focus on the legal changes that have outlawed many of the more egregious overt expressions of racism and ignore the fact that the cultural assumptions and values that live in people's conversation and in their thinking as well as structures of power that impart discrimination are not instantly removed by changes in law. The past continues to cast shadows over the present.

Meanwhile, the media continue to bombard us with stereotypical images of ethnic and racial groupings. Blacks in the United States and other people of color continue to bear the brunt of the harshest forms of racism as they are continually reinforced by media images. These racist discourses are like a fog that penetrates every aspect of people's day-to-day lives (Alvarez, Liang, & Neville, 2016).

Elizabeth Martinez (2007) points out that much of the multicultural literature on racism focuses on White–Black relations and minimizes the Latino/Latina community's experience of racism. Martinez argues that Latino/Latina experiences with racism are ignored because they are invisible. When racism against Latinas and Latinos is recognized, it is often in the form of an insinuation that these people endanger the positions of other ethnic groups.

White Privilege

One cannot understand racism in North America without considering the prominent role that White privilege plays in contemporary society. White privilege is the unearned power that most Whites accrue in the United States society simply because they are White. It has grown out of the last few hundred years of European colonization. The genealogy of many of our struggles today can be traced to the history of racial interactions that we described in Chapters 3 and 4. The identities that we experience in the present are shaped by complex historical patterns of ethnic, racial, gender, religious, sexual orientation, and class relations. For example, dominant cultural discourse in the United States honors the founding fathers' efforts at building the institutions in this country that continue to this day. It is easy to join with this discourse of admiration if you are White. If you are Indian, Black, or Asian, identifying with these historical political figures and honoring their achievements is more complicated. Joining with this discourse may produce conflicting feelings about how your ancestors were treated by these same founding fathers. This is one tiny example of the different positions that history creates for people. And yet White privilege largely rests on the story that racism is solely historical. In this story, slavery ended after the Civil War and civil rights were won in the 1960s, and these structural changes ended the matter.

For many Whites, race and racism are invisible. Joyce King (1991) constructed the term "dysconsciousness" to describe how Whites take for granted their privileged position in society. Many hold to comfortable and unquestioned assumptions of equal individual opportunity. In these assumptions, racism is conceived of only as a set of individual beliefs that get expressed in forms of discrimination and prejudice. Sometimes the word *discrimination* is part of the problem. This word transports the issue of racism into the discourse of individual motivation and intent. For discrimination to be proven in court, such intent needs to be established. The problem is that often the origins of racism and the origins of privilege have little to do with individuals' intended actions. They are instead built into the dominant discourse, into institutional processes, and into taken-for-granted assumptions about how life is. There are, of course, many examples of deliberate discrimination that still take place. But the problem of racism is much larger than anything a word like *discrimination* can encompass. It fails to elucidate situations where there is no personal intent to discriminate and yet inferior status is still ascribed to people of color and privileged status is given to White persons who have not earned it.

Conceiving of racism in terms of individual attitudes blinds people to the more systemic aspects of privilege and disadvantage on racial grounds. As Charles Ridley (2005) says, "Few Whites attribute racial inequality to the structural framework of United States society—a social order where racial victimization is normative" (p. 163). (Notice the structuralist emphasis in this rendering.) White privilege also comes with the option of deciding whether or not to take the initiative in discussing racism.

Another aspect of White privilege is seldom having to think of yourself in terms of race. Not having to identify as a particular race implies choice about the acknowledging or declining of a racial identity. This is a choice Black people do not have. Having the choice, therefore, is itself a privilege. This privilege exists regardless of personal attitude and is therefore not the same as active prejudice. Hence it is often denied on the grounds of lack of personal culpability. Such denials miss the point, and thus the responsibility of Whites to address racism is dismissed. The same lack of primary consciousness exists around other social dividing lines as well. Gender can similarly be less of a defining identity for men than it is for women. Socioeconomic class can be less salient as an identity for the middle class than for those in the lower classes.

Danica Hays and Catherine Chang (2003) define White privilege as the straightforward belief that one's own standards and opinions can be taken for granted as true and accurate (to the exclusion of others'). This taken-for-granted acceptance of one's viewpoint obscures many White persons' perceptions of themselves as located in racial and ethnic relations. A common attitude among the White community is expressed as, "If you work hard, you can succeed in the United States" or "Everybody has the potential to become the president." These ideas illustrate naive assumptions about equality and access to resources. Ronald Jackson (1999) refers to White privilege as a phenomenon that enrolls certain people at birth, without their consent, and brings them up in a favored status. Jerry Diller (2007) suggests that it is easy to deny the existence of White privilege and see oneself as "colorless" so as to avoid noticing ongoing inequalities for people of color.

> If I am White and truly understand what White privilege means socially, economically, and politically, then I cannot help but bear some of the guilt for what has happened historically and what continues to occur. If I were to truly "get it," then I would have no choice but to give up my complacency (Diller, 2007, p. 49)

Many multicultural counseling texts refer to the well-known article "White privilege: Unpacking the invisible knapsack" (McIntosh, 1989), which explains the contemporary systemic advantages of being White in United States society. Peggy McIntosh, a White feminist scholar, identifies a long list of societal privileges that she received simply because she was White. It includes major advantages for middle class Anglo Americans, such as access to a wider range of jobs and housing. She describes the luxury of being confident that the teacher would be unlikely to discriminate against her child on the basis of Whiteness. She lists being able to walk around a department store with little likelihood of being followed by suspicious salespersons. She could be late for meetings and be fairly confident that her lateness wouldn't be attributed to the fact that she was White. She could also express an opinion in a meeting that would not be labeled a White opinion. Many people of color relate easily to McIntosh's list. However, the article is now 15 years old and some people think times have changed.

How much they have not changed may be indicated by a study recently released by the University of California, Los Angeles, which found that 22.7% of freshmen said racial discrimination was no longer a major problem in the United States (Silverstein, 2005). Opinions differed, however, between Whites and minorities on race-related questions. For instance, 23.5% of White freshmen believed that helping to promote racial understanding was essential or very important, while 54.8% of Black freshman and 43.6% of Latino freshmen deemed this essential or very important.

From a social constructionist perspective, privilege is not a static or constant, structurally determined state of being, even though it is recognized as patterned systematically. Rather, it might be considered a property of a relation that is reproduced each time we engage in social practices that assume privileged entitlement. It also shifts in response to contextual events. If a White person enters a Black or Native American context, she may temporarily experience the inverse of White privilege. Neither is privileged entitlement guaranteed for all Whites. Some White people may be excluded from privilege on account of their sexual and gender minority identity, or through being seriously disabled, or elderly, or homeless, or from a White underclass.

These exceptions mean that Whites have to work at maintaining positions of privilege. The need to work at constantly reproducing privilege has two corollaries. It means that privilege is actively reproduced over and over again. And it also means that there are many places where it can be noticed and contested. Many Whites have regular experiences of preferential status. In most business and professional work contexts in North America, White males dominate senior management positions. The mere fact of having White skin still usually protects people from certain degrading, distasteful, and discriminatory experiences (Baruth & Manning, 2007; Liu, 2019). Betsy Lucal (1996) points out that, generally speaking, Whites do not have to expend psychological and monetary resources on recovering from other people's prejudices.

White Fragility and Counseling

According to Leroy Baruth and Lee Manning (2007), White counselors respond to White privilege in different ways. They report that White counselors experience a range of emotional responses—anger, guilt, self-protectiveness, sadness, hopelessness, and confusion. There are variations in how responsible White counselors feel about the role of advocacy in challenging racism and privilege in their communities. The academic Robin D'Angelo, who self-identifies as a White woman, coined the term "White fragility" (2011, p. 54) to address the complex dynamics of White people's relationships with other groups in the United States and how these dynamics benefit them and protect them from any racial confrontations. For her, White fragility is not a weakness but emerges out of racial control born out of superiority, entitlement, and protection of White advantage. D'Angelo observes that many White people demonstrate fragility when engaging in conversations about race. She reports that White fragility can show up with considerable defensiveness and low tolerance for being challenged around racist behavior.

Strong affective responses are sometimes accompanied by an argumentative stand. Instead of seeking to understand how Whites are participating in racist interactions or being empathetic to the negative effects of racism, Whites can shut down, display silence or avoid direct interactions, which D'Angelo reports reinstates a "White racial equilibrium" (2011, p. 54). She reports that it is rare for people in the United States receiving training in cross-cultural work to learn about White privilege and its historical foundations, and this diminishes Whites' abilities to work effectively with non-White groups. This lack of historical study of racism and White privilege contributes to the illusion of the internalized dominance of White people. Racism gets to be understood in terms of problems that ethnically different *others* face and therefore it is not up to Whites to grapple with the problems that racism engenders. For example, it is not uncommon that, in academic training programs in counseling, psychology, or related fields, when there are faculty who are White and people of color, it is the people of color who are considered somehow more qualified to teach courses on race and racism.

D'Angelo (2018) identifies other factors that sustain White fragility due to people living segregated lives within White-dominated societies that reinforce racial entitlement and comfort. Living in segregated communities can promote racial arrogance and positive self-images of the White self in comparison to other groups. She reports that White fragility is undergirded by many Whites experiencing a state of racial belonging in almost all sectors of life and experiencing the psychic freedom to not have to confront the social burden of being othered. Danica Hays, Catherine Chang, and Jennifer Dean (2004) argue that it is good when White counselors experience strong emotions regarding

White privilege, as it may increase their awareness of issues around oppression, advocacy, and counselor awareness. However, our interest is not so much in getting people to feel strong emotions as in getting them to participate in actions toward change. The link between feelings of guilt and motivation to work for change is more often assumed than demonstrated. So it remains questionable.

Reconstructing Whiteness

There is an interesting notion being proposed in the transformational multicultural literature that proposes the possibility of a White identity not characterized as a salient negative identity. It amounts to an attempt to step out of essentialist assumptions of what it means to be White. Instead, it traces a White identity that is oppositional to racism and oppressive practices. Henry Giroux (2002) remarks that, historically,

> whiteness as a marker of identity is confined within a notion of domination and racism that leaves white youth no social imaginary through which they can see themselves as actors in creating an oppositional space to fight for equality and social justice (p. 144).

An alternative discourse of Whiteness can create space for people characterized or identifying as White to become advocates for social justice while diminishing the effects of guilt and shame that the dominant discourse of Whiteness casts on people striving to make a difference in race relations and social and economic equity (Brown & Ostrove, 2013; Obear, 2016; Spanierman & Smith, 2017; Sue et al., 2019). Giroux (2002) sums up his notion of oppositional Whiteness:

> By re-articulating Whiteness as more than a form of domination, White students can construct narratives of "Whiteness" that both challenge, and, hopefully provide a basis for transforming the dominant relationship between racial identity and citizenship, one informed by oppositional politics. (p. 164)

Politicizing Whiteness in this manner opens up new possibilities for Whites to construct new subject positions that strengthen their resolve to support a politics of difference and be partners with people of color in addressing unequal power differentials and unequal distribution of material resources. Alternative discourses of Whiteness will be grounded in a political, historical, cultural, and social reality rather than the previously unmarked and benignly perceived category. Nylund (2006) has experienced this reconstruction of Whiteness as an approach that can help Whites support African American students who wish to express their distress and strong feelings about slavery without their feeling the need to shut down this expression because of the presence of White guilt or fragility. Nylund suggests the reformulation of Whiteness as a discourse of social justice that offers White students an ability to act and not become immobilized by feelings of guilt and shame. Deconstructing Whiteness and positioning it in a discourse of advocacy for justice, equity, and the eradication of racism can be understood as a form of cultural positioning. It provides an opportunity for White students to develop greater cultural respect and is a step toward being culturally responsive to difference.

Discuss

1. When in the United States did *White* become a term used to describe a group of people?
2. How did families identifying as German, Finnish, Irish, or Italian come to identify as White or simply American?
3. Are there any White cultural practices? Is there a White culture? Why do we find it difficult to answer those questions if we are White?
4. How have White people been shaped by the wider culture?
5. How has racism affected their daily lives?
6. How has Whiteness been used politically?
7. What current issues center around Whiteness?
8. What does Whiteness mean to you?
9. How could Whites become antiracist allies?

Source: Adapted from Helfland and Lippin (2001, p. 12).

BOX 7.1 IS SOCIAL JUSTICE A PRINCIPLE OF ACTION OR A MILLENARIAN GOAL?

In his introduction to Jacques Derrida's metaphysical project, Simon Glendinning (2011) argues that Derrida was opposed to the long history in Western thought of millenarian thinking. What is millenarian thinking?

When applied to social justice, it suggests that once all identity groups have achieved freedom, we will reach a heaven on earth or a social nirvana that will last a thousand years. It implies an end to the need for struggle, sometimes referred to as an end of history. Such thinking carries within it the assumption that we can end racism, poverty, sexism, homophobia, and the like. As a clarion call for action, it has appeal. However, we believe we should pause before signing up to "an end to poverty" or its partners.

So what is the problem with millenarian thinking? Well, there are several problems. One lies in the frustration that accrues when history does not end. The result is that those who seek social justice sometimes sound angry that it is not happening. Such frustration, or worse, cynicism, does their cause no good.

Another problem is that sources of injustice do not go away. They are often inventive and figure out new ways to achieve their ends. New injustices are often developing. Social justice advocates need to be prepared and stay constantly alert for new forms of injustice that appear, as much as to win old battles. New analysis constantly has to be done.

Yet another problem is that social justice causes do not uniformly make progress. They often go forwards but sometimes they also go backwards. Progress itself is a grand narrative that does not always apply to a particular social justice cause.

So what is the alternative? It is certainly not to give up on social justice. However, we can treat social justice as an ethical principle rather than as a destination of history. An ethical principle can be like a blowtorch that is used in specific situations to help counselors figure out what to do. It can also be used to help analyze situations that clients find themselves in but are not sure how to proceed justly. In other words, social justice can be used as a principle in counseling as well as in advocacy.

Differing Perspectives on Understanding and Addressing Racism

Racism and its effects can be understood from a variety of perspectives. One's world view and one's understanding of how power and oppression work will influence how one addresses racism and whether its deleterious consequences will diminish. In earlier chapters in this book, we discussed three approaches to power relations—liberal humanist, structuralist, and poststructuralist (and include an analysis of colonial power in Chapter 14)—and how they shape counseling practice. In this chapter we would like to show how these versions of power relations can be applied to give different accounts of racist practices. We shall also explore how racism may be addressed through the lens of these contrasting conceptual tools.

Liberal Humanism and Racism

Liberal humanism, as we explained in Chapter 6, views the individual as the prime mover, responder, and initiator, while the functions of institutional conditions and social structures are downplayed or ignored. Individual free will is favored over any assumption that wider sociocultural influences and colonizing history might shape or determine human volition and action. If individuals are basically free to do as they will, then individual decisions are at the base of discriminatory behavior. Power and the abuse of power is a personal phenomenon and originates from inside the individual and is then acted out against other individuals.

Racism, from this perspective, is commonly understood as an individual attitude of mind or an expression of that mind in behavior. Liberal humanist thinking usually directs us to focus on racism at the individual level. For example, many people consider racial prejudice to be constructed through an individual's making a preconceived judgment or deriving an opinion about a whole group of people on the basis of limited and distorted information. In other words, racial stereotyping is primarily a failure to treat people as individuals. From the liberal humanist perspective, the source of racism might best be understood as located in the corrupted logic of the individual mind. It is an instance of personal failure or is a personal deficit of character. Some have even argued that racism results from the early "hurt" experiences of racist individuals (reported by Ponterotto & Pedersen, 1993). Sometimes people think of it as diseased or irrational thinking that shapes the personal attitudes of individual people. From this perspective, racism has its origins in individual faulty thinking, or personal prejudice, or irrational stereotyping, which is then manifested in discriminatory decisions, practices, laws, and so forth. Thus, racism originates in the individual's psychology, and there will be individual variation in the extent to which racist behavior is expressed.

From a liberal humanist perspective, racism is also understood as a misdirection of a person's personal power. It becomes more damaging when the racist individual has accrued more power than the victims of racism, who may have less personal power and less ability to protect themselves. Racism from this perspective is a by-product of the individual's personality and relational style. Thus, accusing somebody of being racist when he doesn't believe he is racist goes right to the heart. Accused persons experience their essence as being under siege and often go on the attack to protect themselves. The recipient of the racist behavior responds in kind and accepts the protective attack as a personally motivated action that justifies the original accusation. Usually, frustration is the main product of such interactions. Some of the frustration results from conceiving of racism as an intimate act generated and acted out by one individual against another.

From this perspective, the eradication of racism would need to involve a process of individual psychological change in which racist persons are identified, or identify themselves, and then receive corrective training to eliminate their irrational thinking and replace it with more accurate, rational thinking. The role of the counselor or psychotherapist delivering this corrective training might be to help the client "own" her racism and take personal responsibility for her abusive behavior. By helping the client connect with oppression in her own life, the counselor might help her understand and then change her oppressive behaviors.

The liberal humanist perspective on racism is limited, however. Individuals do not usually invent the racist ideas that pepper their utterances and social practices. They more often borrow them from the discourse in which they have been enculturated. They are not in this way the originators of their own thoughts. Most racist social practice comes packaged and ready-made, with little individual thought necessary. It happens because people just accept and go along with how things are done. It is powerful precisely because it seems natural, familiar, and unable to be questioned.

Structuralism and Racism

Another way to understand racism and address its harmful effects is to consider a structural analysis, as discussed in Chapter 6. Racism from this perspective is understood as a systemic process that consistently advantages one group over another based on race (Wellman, 1977). It emphasizes the underlying social structure as the source of racism, rather than racism being a personal property of the individual. Because the structural analysis regards the individual as a product of his position in a social structure, individual people are viewed as having limited abilities to make choices. Since individuals have such little influence within the structure, emphasis is placed on analyzing and changing the structures that shape and influence lives. Those with a structural orientation tend to focus on mobilizing individuals who are the victims of the oppressive structures—that is, those who are victims of racism—and helping them see how the structural constraints are negatively affecting their lives.

A structural analysis is directed at how racism is institutionalized. Institutional racism and discrimination occur when people are excluded or deprived of rights and opportunities as a result of the normal operations of the institution (Gee & Verissimo, 2016). A structuralist analysis can show that even while individuals hold no malicious racist intentions or are unaware of how others are being harmed, there can still be racist outcomes. As Sonia Nieto (2000) notes, racist practices can be produced in schools through inequitable testing practices, rigid ability tracking, low expectations of students based on their identity, and inequitably funded schools. Claude Steele (1992), speaking to the issue of institutional racism, suggested, "Deep in the psyche of American educators is a presumption that Black students need academic remediation, or extra time with elemental curricula to overcome background deficits" (p. 77). Steele spoke of stigma vulnerability, another phrase for racism, and demonstrated how such stigmata are based on the systematic devaluation faced by Blacks and other people of color in schools. Of course, schools are only one location where institutionalized racism occurs. Rewards and punishments are also structurally expressed in the systematic organization of access to housing, employment, and health (Lichter, Parisi & Taquino, 2015; Nagata, Kim, Massey & Tannen, 2015; Santiago-Rivera, Adames, Chavez-Dueñas, & Benson- Flórez, 2016).

As racist behaviors are understood from a structural perspective to be separate from the individual, people are inevitably cast into social groups that represent their structural position in a society. They are considered less as individuals than as members of a group. And that group occupies a structurally determined position that is either oppressing or being oppressed. Individuals may protest their innocence or difference, but they are still seen as part of the group. Beverly Tatum (1997) reserves the term *racist* only for "behaviors committed by Whites in the context of a White-dominated society" (p. 10). While Tatum acknowledges hateful behavior and hate crimes perpetrated by people of color, her overriding concern is to define racism in relation to the structural power differentials afforded Whites in the United States. These power differentials translate into White superiority and White advantage. Individual racism is the downstream effect of this structural superiority. Tatum argues that people of color cannot be racist because they do not automatically benefit from racism and because there is no institutional support for racism by Blacks or other people of color.

Jerry Diller (2007) has a similar perspective when he says that while all people hold prejudices, Whites, because of their access to positions of power, are actually racist, while people of color can only be prejudiced. His formula is that prejudice plus power equals racism. The structuralist perspective shows that racism is a product of systematic privilege for some categories of personhood and systematic penalty for other categories. This structural definition is employed by many people working in the multicultural field. It is a very understandable definition when we consider the history of systematic oppression in the United States. It accounts for racist practice that is anonymous, pervasive, and seemingly not the fault of any individual intent. Many Whites continue to benefit from the cultural privileges that accompany being White and experience considerable distress, anger, and guilt when confronted with this reality.

A therapist using a structural analysis will seek to help individuals identify more closely with their racial group membership. He or she will then teach his or her clients how they are victims of institutional practices and thus help them focus on and identify the oppressive structures rather than blame themselves for the suffering they have experienced. An additional role is to help oppressed groups to rebel and challenge the racial injustices implicit in the institutions that shape day-to-day lives. A counselor focusing on a structural orientation would seek to challenge members of groups that benefit from racist structural conditions to acknowledge their privilege and to use their positions in power structures to help to change the system. This can be very discouraging work, as many individuals question whether they can do anything about institutional racism. They may argue that they are not responsible for an institution's policies. To challenge or question exclusionary practices might seem beyond one's power to change. The typical response is, "I am hardly in a position to change policies I am not responsible for." As Diller (2007) suggests, this is similar logic to that used in the response, "I should not be held responsible for what happened two hundred years ago at the time of the slave trade." People question why they should make sacrifices now to address injustices that happened long ago. Other constraints on action include the sheer effort required to change the status quo, which is often vulnerable to change only at a time of crisis or when the system is completely malfunctioning. For many people, it is difficult to even know where to start.

Closely associated with institutional forms of racism are the phenomena of culturally racist practices in North America. An example is the dominant culture's acknowledging holidays and celebrations such as Christmas and Thanksgiving while ignoring many holidays associated with non-European cultures. Cultural racism can also come in the form of disdain for cultural expressions derived from communal and collective practices and the favoring of individuality and assertiveness. Standard English is

BOX 7.2   RACISM IN PRISON

There is no worse place to see the ugly face of racism than among the over 2,000,000 inmates locked in prison facilities around the United States. It is widely accepted among social scientists that people of color receive harsher sentences than Whites. According to Carson (2018), more than 60% of the people who are incarcerated today are people of color. Black males are six times as likely to be imprisoned as White males, and Hispanic males are nearly three times as likely to end up in prison. In federal prisons, Black males had sentences that were nearly 20% longer than White males between 2011 and 2016.

The prison populations are drawn sharply along racial lines, and in many prisons, when there is trouble, people quickly organize themselves into racial groups. According to Kupers (1999), prisoners of color are more likely than Whites to be sent to solitary confinement rather than receive appropriate psychological treatment. Prison life reminds prisoners of color about all of the systemic injustices in the world. In many prisons the majority of the prison staff are White, including those sitting on hearing and appeals panels. Kupers suggests that prisoners of color are treated in stereotypical ways, resulting in large numbers of complaints against guards on the basis of racial discrimination. He also comments that supervisory positions and training tend to be allocated along racial lines, with higher-status positions going to White inmates. Chung (2016) writes that, because of the dramatic growth of the criminal justice system in the last four decades, felony disenfranchisement has affected the rights of over six million U.S. citizens who are unable to vote because of felony disenfranchisement policies.

expected to be spoken in most institutions in North America, while standard of dress is always measured against European criteria. For example, Afros and braids worn by African Americans can be deemed "ethnic" and not appropriate in many companies and organizations. Cultural icons such as Jesus and Mary are often portrayed as White, while Christ's betrayer Judas is shown as Black. Meanwhile, Band-Aids that are called "skin color" come in shades that approximate only White skin colors.

Some counseling models are constructed so as to empower oppressed groups to challenge the structural inequalities caused by oppressor groups. For example, the Just Therapy Model developed in New Zealand explicitly aims to structure counseling in a way that addresses cultural and racial oppression. One of the interventions aimed at addressing oppression and racism is the forming of caucusing groups among social service agency employees. The dominant group, which could be either White or male, takes responsibility for raising its own consciousness and addressing potential or actual abuses of power and unconscious assumptions of racism. The dominant group takes responsibility for stopping harmful behaviors or discriminatory practices and makes itself accountable to the evaluation and feedback of the nondominant group with regard to its efforts. Group members who are representative of marginalized populations (Maori or Samoan or women) are taught how to identify oppressive practices and to challenge them when they occur (Waldegrave, Tamasese, Tuhaka, & Campbell, 2003). Partnership between the caucuses and accountability of the dominant group to the marginalized are the keys to success. Counseling is provided for families and individuals on the basis of establishing a match between counselor and client with regard to ethnicity and gender.

Another emergent therapeutic model that is in alignment with some of the structural elements described here is the Cultural Context Model (CCM; Hernandez, Almedia, & Dolan-Del Vecchio, 2005). The CCM postcolonial model utilizes culture circles made up of client groups in same-gender or same-race groups. They use a systemic cultural analysis process that involves identifying a variety of forms of domination, including those that relate to racism, and incorporating the analysis and the challenging of oppressive practices into therapeutic work.

Discuss

Have a discussion in small groups on the topic of racism, prejudice, and discrimination.

1. How would you define *racism*, *discrimination*, and *prejudice*?
2. Which definitions included in this chapter do you prefer? Why?
3. How do you think that people learn to behave in racist ways and to show prejudice, and to discriminate against others?
4. What experiences of the various forms of racism described in this chapter have you either experienced or witnessed?
5. What would it mean to you to be described as a racist?
6. Do you know a racist, or is everybody in the world a racist?
7. How do you deal with racism when you encounter it?
8. Can a person change racist behavior? How?
9. Can racism be eliminated? How would you suggest that it could be done?
10. What steps have you taken to help deal with racism?
11. How can counseling practice make a difference to the existence of racism?

Problems with a Purely Structural Analysis of Racism

While Beverly Tatum (1997) eloquently names the insidious, systematic processes of racist behavior and oppression, a challenging part of her analysis occurs when she locates racism as an essential characteristic of White group membership. To call people racist on the basis of their ethnic group membership falls into the same structural logic as racism itself. Like racism, it is an example of essentialist thinking. Structural analyses often create an impression of the inevitability of personal racism that precludes the possibility of personal moral choice about whether or not to resist structural positioning. When people engage with others, they are constructed as falling into alignment with their positions in an organized system of social relations, rather than considered to be speaking out of their personal experience. A structural analysis tends to produce binary groupings made up of oppressors and oppressed. From a structuralist perspective, the oppressor group sets the stage on which the subordinate group operates. The relationship of the oppressor to the oppressed is often one in which the oppressor group assigns itself high status while devaluing the oppressed group in demeaning ways.

While this analysis gets at some important aspects of how discourse operates, to fix people as part of an oppressor or oppressed class limits where you can go in the conversation to address racism and other forms of social injustice. For example, if Whites are part of an oppressor class because they are

White and Blacks are part of an oppressed class because they are Black, there isn't much room for either group to exercise agency. A range of differential responses within each group is obscured from view. It is hard to see how people can make decisions to extricate themselves from these binary positions. A structural analysis also does not easily account for contradictions, reverse racism, White activism against racism, or the subtle nuances of race relations that do not straightforwardly divide into structural binaries.

Shelby Steele (2006), a Black activist of the 1960s whom some describe as a Black conservative, speaks about how Blacks who embrace the status of victims or the oppressed can diminish the extent to which they can act responsibly and powerfully in the world. He states, "Suddenly I could use America's fully acknowledged history of racism just as Whites had always used their race—as a racial authority and privilege that excused me from certain responsibilities, moral constraints, and even the law" (p. 54). He reminisces about authentic Black militancy of the kind shown by Malcolm X, which he termed "hard work militancy," that follows the principles of self-sacrifice, delayed gratification, and the hard-core work ethic. He talks about the troubled analysis of certain social processes that legitimate Blacks' not taking responsibility for their lives and their future. Maintaining an identity as an oppressed victim can undermine people's efforts to take action on their own behalf rather than waiting for the oppressor to stop oppressing them. The assumptions underlying the psychological constructs of internal and external loci of control, first discussed by Julian Rotter (1966), may be of assistance here. An internal locus of control refers to the notion that individuals believe they are in control of their own fate, whereas an external locus of control refers to the notion that individuals are at the mercy of external forces. What is at stake is here is agency, although the internal locus of control idea assumes a liberal humanist version of the ideal individual self.

Many of the multicultural writers, such as Derald Wing Sue and David Sue (2019), have enunciated in depth the influence of the locus of control literature on our understanding of various ethnic groups' responses to change processes. Sue and Sue note how many people of color have developed an external locus of control because of systematic patterns of oppression and believe they are not in charge of their own fate. Charles Ridley (2005) also addresses this issue:

> Shackled by self-doubt, fear, and helplessness, many minorities forgo chances to exploit their potential and opportunities because they are reenacting their past victimization. The secondary gains these individuals realize from such reenactment include avoidance of the consequences of relinquishing the victim role. (p. 115)

He goes on to explain the secondary gains, which include avoiding head-on confrontation with racism, avoiding the discovery of one's true abilities, and avoiding the scorn of other minorities who still hold on to their victim status.

There are further problematic aspects of the dominant/subordinate, oppressor/oppressed binaries. For example, a structural analysis of the abuse of power and the mechanisms of oppression place the following identities in the oppressor category: White, male, able-bodied, cisgendered, Christian, middle class, urban, educated, thin, and attractive. Identities in the oppressed category include colored, female, disabled, sexual minority, non-Christian, poor, rural, uneducated, fat, and unattractive. It is likely that any reader of this text who is placed in some of the categories of the oppressed class will also have membership in oppressor categories. The notion of discrete structural binaries begins to break down when, in any one moment, people are simultaneously part of both oppressor and oppressed polarities. The structural analysis becomes weakened when this kind of diffusion occurs. One of the unfortunate consequences of a structural analysis of racism is that people get seduced into what Elizabeth Martinez (2001) calls the Oppression Olympics—an endless and irresolvable competition among diverse groups seeking a prize for the most victimized and oppressed group. Krishna Guadalupe and Doman Lum (2005) regretfully report that the multicultural movement has been held back because of the conscious or unconscious prioritizing of one set of human diversity attributes over another.

To be called racist is to be labeled with one of the most blameworthy descriptions that can be given a person, especially if the accusation is made by a person of a different ethnicity. *Racist* has become such a loaded word that it often produces a nasty emotional wake, leading to people's withdrawing from one another and erecting barriers to further discussion. We have witnessed many encounters in which an individual or a group of people are told they are racist because of their ethnic membership. Whether the accusation is accurate or not, the quality of the conversation often deteriorates from there. Talking about racism can be intimidating in a roomful of people where some have a family history of active participation in racism while others have a family history of being the recipients of racist acts.

Poststructuralism and Racism

We have emphasized in this book the growing interest in a poststructuralist perspective and its value in our understanding of power and how to intervene to diminish its harm in our communities. As already outlined in Chapter 6, a poststructuralist lens challenges the notion that the world is neatly divided into categories of oppressors and the oppressed. Racism is not assumed to be inherent in the nature of either individuals or groups, or even in social structures.

Instead, we would start from the assumption that racism inheres in social practices, which are performed in discourse. We would argue that these social practices and the discourses that inform assumptions about race are where racism originates. The attitudes of persons, the characteristics of groups, and the structure of social arrangements are all derived from the constant reproduction of these practices. Personal racism is not invented by those individuals who perform racist hate crimes as much as it exists before they are born, and for a complex array of reasons they become recruited into speaking its lines. Structural and institutional racism is not essential to any system, even when it appears to stabilize that system. Neither does structural racism make personal racist assumptions inevitable for members of "oppressor" groups. Nor does it make victimhood and the psychology of abjection essential for members of "oppressed" groups.

The poststructuralist reasoning is instead that social structures are sustained only by pieces of discourse that will shift and change their shape as people remake social discourse. Discourse assigns people positions from which to think, and these are codified and reified into social structures and institutions, but people can and do refuse to act from these positions. They actively contest and modify them on a daily basis.

A poststructuralist analysis of racism needs to take such nuances into account, particularly if we as counselors are intent on helping individuals negotiate their way through life in the midst of a confusing array of positions. From this perspective, the complexity of life makes for a more indeterminate, fluid set of circumstances. People on a moment-to-moment basis make efforts to influence the quality of their own lives and those of others. A poststructuralist analysis pays attention to the microdynamics that both support and undermine racism. To do so means that we don't have to wait for a structural revolution to bring about meaningful change. Nor do we have to rely on changing racism one person at a time. A poststructuralist analysis opens to view a variety of opportunities to challenge the discourse of racism and to diminish its effects.

Discourse, deconstruction, and positioning, as discussed in Chapter 5, are useful conceptual tools that help us name and examine the effects of the cultural discourses that embody racism. The analysis of discourse helps us identify cultural histories that position Blacks as less intelligent than Whites, that suggest that men are superior to women, that see cisgendered as normal and sexual minorities as aberrant. Rather than assigning individuals because of one identity into a dominant group or a subordinate group, and hanging an oppressor or an oppressed label over them, we can explore the effects of these discourses on relations between people. Apart from anything else, labels always run the risk of fixing people in place. A focus on the discourse of racism and its effects provides many avenues to address the problem without resorting to totalizing statements that define people as essentially racists. Such totalizing is no different from defining some people as evil and others as pure. Human beings are always more complex than simplistic descriptions can ever capture.

Addressing racism as a discourse disrupts the tendency to tie the term *racist* in an essential way to a person or to a group. While the emphasis moves on to the discourse and its effects, in no way does this discount the systematic and patterned applications of racist practice that advantage some groups of people over others. Racial privilege can still be deconstructed. Nor does it excuse individuals (of all races and ethnicities) from the challenge of taking moral responsibility for the existence of the social practices of racism. In fact, it opens up the possibility that people who are positioned in places of privilege and people who are positioned in places of marginalization can actually work together against racism. Below is a classroom story that brings out a focus on racism as a discourse that systemically affects groups of people in painful ways and enlists others to perpetuate harm in painful ways.

BOX 7.3 FAMOUS STATEMENTS ABOUT RACE

"Racism ... made me less than I might have been."

—George Jackson, 1971

"The inseparable twin of racial injustice is economic injustice."

—Martin Luther King, Jr., 1963

"Slavery is essential to democracy. For where there are great incongruities in the constitution of society, if the American were to admit the Indian, the Chinese, the Negroes, to the rights to which they are justly jealous of admitting European emigrants, the country would be thrown into disorder, and if not, would be degraded to the level of the barbarous races."

—Lord Acton, 1861

"Blood mixture and the resultant drop in the racial level is the sole cause of the dying out of old cultures."

—Adolf Hitler, 1924

"Never yet could I find that a Black had uttered a thought above the level of plain narration."

—Thomas Jefferson, 1785

"The mental inferiority of the negro to the White or yellow races is a fact."

—Encyclopedia Britannica, 1911

"Now as to the Negroes! I entirely agree with you that as a race and in the main they are altogether inferior to the Whites."

—Theodore Roosevelt, 1906

"I believe in White supremacy until the Blacks are educated to a point of responsibility. I don't believe in giving authority and positions of leadership and judgment to irresponsible people."

—John Wayne, 1971

Racism in the Multicultural Class

In a multicultural counseling class, there was a heated exchange among students wrestling with the issues of racism. Half the group were people of color and the remainder were White. Three women who identified as persons of color expressed serious concerns about a White student who had made a series of racist remarks and told her in direct and strong terms that she was a racist. One of the students had heard the White student relay a comment to another person to the effect that "Black people are homophobic." Now it was being spoken about in the multicultural counseling class.

As the conversation developed, one of the students of color spoke about how much she hated White people. She hated them for what they had done to people of color and how they continued to perpetuate harmful racist behavior as well as support racist cultural practices. The tensions and distress in the room rapidly began to rise. A number of people were feeling under attack for different reasons. The perceived level of safety, which had been very high at an earlier stage, was rapidly being eroded by fear and mistrust.

Some people, both White students and people of color, began linking the racist comment with other remarks that this same White student had made. They began to infer racist undertones in each of these other comments, which further confirmed the opinion of the three students that this White student was indeed racist. Some other group members agreed she was making racist implications, while others disagreed. The accused White student was now shut down and frozen. Many other White students were feeling under attack in the same way that the students identifying as people of color were feeling. The interactions were ready to spiral out of control, and people either wanted to leave the room immediately or began to shut down.

Many educators who have taken on the difficult job of addressing racism have witnessed similar difficult interactions. Exploring the effects of racism is a sensitive and sometimes dangerous task and often runs the risk of unraveling a group. Because many people deny that they are affected by racist attitudes, when they are brought to the surface, it is often very difficult and very painful. That is why many people choose to keep the subject of racism off the table, along with discussions about politics, religion, gender issues, and homophobia. Interactions between group members can so quickly move to attack and defend modes, and then to counterattack and self-protection. Ultimately what is produced is depression, disengagement, and bitterness, rather than significant change toward rooting out racism. Binaries of Us and Them intensify, become more rigid, and thwart efforts to bridge across categories.

There is no doubt that racism was present during these painful interactions. The problem was that individuals were totalized as either racist or as members of a hateful group, and the possibility of challenging racism in a more productive way was shut down. Such conversations also close off opportunities to educate and ultimately address racist behaviors in school, in the workplace, and in the community. We would argue that it is more useful to start from the assumption that racism as discourse is present in all of us. This does not mean that its deleterious effects are felt by all in the same way. Its effects are clearly distributed unfairly. But it does mean that we might share in the process of examining how we are positioned by racist discourse in order to work together to challenge it.

In the next meeting, the facilitator of the class asked permission of the group to talk about the subject of racism in a different way. Instead of attacking the individuals for their various painful remarks, it was suggested that the group identify how they were affected by painful comments rather than going on the attack. Instead of using language like, "I hate White people," "You are a racist," or "You are a perpetrator of injustice," students were asked if they would be prepared to name the discourses of racism that they were personally affected by. Many students used externalizing phrases (White & Epston, 1990) that named the racist behavior without attacking the person. Some students were willing to rephrase their statement "I hate White people" as "I hate what White privilege has done to me."

The group members were able to have some success in referring to the effects of discourse on their lives and to how racism affected them personally. As they continued to practice naming the discourse and its negative effects, the group was able to learn about racism without the conversation turning into personal attack and counterattack. Rather than describing individuals as personally racist, students discovered value in describing as racist the assumption of natural entitlement to privilege on the basis of being White, and the reproduction of the ideology that entrenches these entitlements in patterns of social interaction. Focusing on discourse, we can talk about White privilege and how it can systematically favor Anglo Americans.

This approach is very different from saying that all White people are privileged. We all know of numerous examples of people identified as White who have been exposed to unimaginable suffering from life-threatening disabilities, poverty, and homelessness, or from gay bashing persecution and religious bigotry. While individual people may engage in racist behavior, it is the presence of racist discourses and the social practices they produce that need to be addressed. Individuals participate in the reproduction of these discourses and so become implicated in them, sometimes unconsciously. This perspective is very different from saying that they are the sources of the racist discourse in which they are implicated. Neither does racism originate mysteriously out of the social structures that determine how individuals act. That too would be an essentialist assumption. People are not puppets of institutional or structural racism. They are not programmed to speak and act in racist ways without the possibility of doing otherwise. Asking people to identify systemic patterns of racism in their own families is helpful in addressing and undermining the ongoing effects of racism. Here are two examples of White students who traced racism and gross human injustices in their own family while seeking to play their part to ensure that these histories do not continue.

> *I had a great, great, great uncle who was what my grandpa referred to as a "used slave salesman." This uncle owned more than 150 slaves, whom he sold and rented out to make a profit. It is shameful for me to claim roots in a family system that has played such a blatant role in setting the racist foundation of our country. I have spent the last 10 years of my life living in communities where the dominant groups are people of color. I have had Black boyfriends in the past and my present boyfriend is Black. I really have an affinity with the Black community in my neighborhood and work hard as a school counselor to address racism in the school and community I work in.*
>
> *—Sara*

> *My great-grandfather was a member of the Ku Klux Klan from 1920 to 1932. My great-grandfather preached about "the Klan" all the time. He told my father not to let the Black man or the Mexican take what the White man had earned in America. To my great-grandfather, the KKK was the pride of our family's history. The belief in a superior White race was taught to my grandmother at a young age. Once she came to California, she only saw Whites, so the feeling was not as strong, but I still see evidence of her beliefs today. She still refers to African Americans as "colors" and has even used the word "nigger" in front of me. My father believes that this part of our family's history is gone, but I can still hear negative judgments of other races come from his mouth. While they are not as apparent as "colored" or "nigger," they are still there. I don't believe that this aspect of our family has been passed on to my siblings and me, and I hope it never revisits our cultural world again. It is shameful to admit that my family is associated with a racist past. When racism became socially unacceptable during the Civil Rights Movement of the 1960s, my grandmother hid this aspect of our family. My father hid it from his family as well. I did not learn of our shameful past until recently. At first, I thought that I should keep it hidden, but I realized that this is part of my family's history and I don't need to hide it. Now that I am aware of it, I am making sure that I give back what I believe my family took away from a future integrated society.*
>
> *—Nate*

Internalized Racism

Internalized racism occurs when racist discourses are taken on or adopted by individuals and groups of people targeted by negative stigmatized messages. Racist discourses are all pervasive. The concept of internalized racism is related to the explanation of hegemony that we canvassed in Chapter 6. We believe it can be explained within a poststructuralist analysis of how power operates through discourse. It would make sense that racist discourse as a way of thinking and speaking would be picked up and internalized by people of all races, rather than only by those who benefit from it. Thus, people of color are also easily implicated in the repetition of discourse that disadvantages them. This does not make them racist. Instead it points to the function of discourse as producing racist effects.

Here is an illustration of how internalized racism works. In 2006, a young Black filmmaker (Davis, 2006) replicated the research of Black psychologist Kenneth Clark, who over 67 years ago explored young Black children's responses to White and Black dolls. Black children around six years of age were asked which doll they preferred—the White doll or the Black doll. The Black children overwhelmingly chose the White doll. The children were asked which was the good doll. In large numbers, the children selected the White doll as the good doll and the Black doll as the bad doll. Internalized racism starts at a very early age.

Because discourse is constructed in the exchange of conversation, there is no one who does not participate in it. The contexts where racist discourse is reproduced are the home, the community, and public institutions such as schools, hospitals, and prisons, as well as the most definitive source in the modern world—the mass media. Discourse exchange is the basis of all movies, newspapers, television programs, videos, computer games, Internet sites, and magazines. For generations, racist discourse has penetrated and been reproduced within the very families who have been victims of it. They have often unwittingly handed negative messages on to other family members. Family members who have features most different from Anglo American phenotypic characteristics can be marked as unattractive and can learn within their own family to possess all of the negative traits portrayed by racist discourse, simply because they have darker skin or because their nose is too broad or their hair too kinky. Negative perceptions held by Blacks of other Blacks often arise from individuals not aware of the insidiousness of internalized racism. Embracing negative stereotypes of Blacks and viewing Whites in stereotypical positive terms is an example of internalized racism. It often takes hard work to root out the effects of such internalized discourse.

Many students of color consistently have negative models portrayed for them in the school, the community, and the media. They grow up with a very limited range of models and mentors of their same ethnicity and of whom they can feel proud. So often in schools, most of the historical and contemporary leaders, educators, famous historians, and inventors are Anglo American. The media continue to be full of images such as that of a young Black woman who is a school dropout, a single parent addicted to drugs, and a victim of domestic violence. A young Black male is portrayed with his hands cuffed behind his back, having been arrested for a recent crime.

These images dominate even though they do not represent the majority of young Black men and women. The effect of such discourse as it becomes internalized is sometimes a loss of self-belief and a devaluation of members of one's own ethnic community, including oneself. The result is that many people of color attempt to embrace "Whiteness." Camara Jones (2000) describes this process as one of accepting limitations about one's humanity and the right to determine one's future and constraining or limiting one's self-expression. The use of bleaching creams to lighten the skin, the use of hair straighteners, and the use of cosmetic surgery to reshape the nose and eyes are all examples of internalized racism at work. Other examples include the rejection of one's ancestral or indigenous community, the adoption of racist nicknames, engaging in at-risk behaviors, and failing in school.

Because of the ugliness of racist discourse and the shaming effects it has on victims of this discourse, people of color can minimize or even fail to recognize the implicit and explicit characterizations of racist acts by embracing the apparent safety of being in a state of denial (Henze, Lucas, & Scott, 1998). The oppositional patterns of identity described above also illustrate internalized racism. Beverly Tatum (1997) describes how certain styles of speech, music, dress, and behavior can become characterized as "authentically Black." These behavioral styles may be harmlessly embraced by many Black youths. However, there are also more harmful behaviors that young Black youth can get caught up in that are destructive to themselves, their families, and the community.

Being authentically Black to these youth might come to mean engaging in intimidating and threatening behavior, being disrespectful to any authority figure, and failing to study, leading to low grades and ultimately school failure. Some Black youth are ridiculed by their Black peers for doing their homework, succeeding in school, and respecting their teachers, because this behavior is perceived as "acting White." This is one of the most harmful forms of internalized racism.

When counselors from underrepresented communities are affected by internalized racism, they can feel self-hatred and anger toward their clients of the same ethnicity. Instead of showing empathy with their clients regarding the effects racist practices have had on them, therapists of color can make harsh judgments and be very demanding and blaming. An example might be where a therapist says, "If I can be successful in the United States, so can you."

Internalized racism also helps explain serious racist practices that occur between ethnically underrepresented groups in the United States. Racist treatment of others occurs between Latinxs and Blacks, Asians and Blacks, and within each of these ethnic groupings. Black-on-Black violence is often a consequence of internalized racism, and the same thing can happen among Latinx and Asian communities. When we trace these actions back through a deconstruction of the internalized effects of racism, however, we can often see that such demonstrations of racism within and between people of color are outgrowths of Western colonizing discourse that is more than 400 years old.

Racism and Stereotyping

Another concept that needs to be distinguished in relation to racism is the concept of stereotyping. Many people use the term *stereotyping* to refer to assumptions that fit easily into racist discourse, and many efforts to combat racism aim at disrupting stereotyped thinking. Dictionary definitions of the word *stereotype* commonly refer to conventional but simplistic thinking whereby distorted views of a person or a group become fixed and resistant to being challenged by countervailing information. Kwame Appiah (2005) helps us penetrate farther into the concept of stereotyping by making distinctions among three different types of stereotyping. We shall outline his distinctions here.

Appiah calls the first form of stereotyping *statistical stereotyping*. It occurs when a property is ascribed to an individual on the basis that it is characteristic of a social group to which the individual belongs. If, for example, it is generally thought that women are more "intuitive" than men, then ascribing one woman's responses to her intuitiveness on the basis of this generalization would be an example of stereotyping. Statistical stereotyping, as the name suggests, happens in much social research where statements about a group are made on the basis of probabilities that may not always apply to each individual member of the group. Such stereotyping may not be problematic at the level of generalization but may become problematic if rigidly applied to individuals.

Appiah calls the second form of stereotyping that he identifies *simply false stereotypes.* These are descriptions of a group of people founded on false generalizations or beliefs. As Appiah remarks, many ethnic stereotypes are of this type. They ascribe to a group of people a characteristic that frequently does not pertain to members of that group any more than to any other group. Examples might be that "Scots are stingy," "Americans from the United States are loud," "Women can't think rationally," "Feminists are man-haters," "Mexicans are lazy," and so forth. Such stereotypes frequently create a negative burden for members of the group, which they must work to dispel. They are rationally and empirically false as well as morally wrong in their discriminatory effects.

The third form of stereotyping that Appiah identifies is referred to as *normative stereotyping.* This form of stereotyping occurs when someone does not ascribe a characteristic of a group to an individual but rather judges an individual on whether she is conforming to what a member of a group *should* do. The example Appiah cites is when employers expect women to match gender stereotypes and, for example, wear more "feminine" clothing. Such stereotypes can be thought of as resulting from the normative effects of dominant discourses. They specify how a "proper" or "real" member of a group should behave. They cannot be disproved, as the other two forms of stereotyping can, by challenging their veracity. They cannot be shown to be irrational or incorrect as much as they can be shown to be limiting or restrictive. Indeed, as a result of the work done by dominant discourse, they may often be all too "true" in an empirical sense, because they have the effect of inducing many people to conform to their injunctions. It is Appiah's third category of normative stereotypes that must be examined for its effects on internalized aspects of identity. Such stereotypes are more insidious in getting into our heads than the other two forms. The other two forms of stereotyping can lead to discriminatory acts by others, but this last form conforms to the kinds of internalized technologies of power described by Foucault (see Chapter 6).

With regard to racism, all three forms of stereotyping may be found. They are tools for perpetuating the assumptions of racial superiority and the advantages of racially based privilege. We should be careful, however, of assuming that racism is founded on stereotyping. Racism cannot easily be contested on logical or empirical grounds, as can Appiah's first two forms of stereotyping. Unfortunately, in the history of modernist thinking, racism has not been considered illogical or irrational. It has been all too commonplace. Appiah's third form of stereotyping can be contested not on empirical grounds but on ethical and moral grounds. As a result, it will not be as susceptible to legal challenge on the grounds of discriminatory action or through a rights discourse. It is particularly important because of its insidious insertion into the identity of members of a group. Here is an area of racism that counselors may often find themselves dealing with. Aspects of identity formed by normative processes are of the kind that counselors can be very effective in helping their clients engage with as they encourage them to reconsider their own preferences.

Racism and Counseling Practice

Charles Ridley (2005) judges that the most harmful forms of racism in the mental health professions are associated with the most influential positions in the social services and mental health systems. According to the American Psychological Association, Norine Johnson (2001, cited by Ridley) reported that approximately 5% to 6% of psychologists in the United States are people of color. Because of the small number of ethnically underrepresented therapists, many more inequities may be brought to bear on ethnically underrepresented clients because of the lack of understanding of racism and because of racist behaviors perpetuated by White therapists (American Psychological Association, 2017; Banks, 2014; Comas-Díaz, 2016; Gone et al., 2019; Hartmann, Wendt, Burrage, Pomerville, & Gone, 2019; Houshmand, Spanierman, & De Stefano, 2017; Ibrahim & Heuer, 2016; Nadal, Griffin, Wong, Hamit, & Rasmus, 2014; Neville, Awad, Brooks, Flores, & Bluemel, 2013). There may also be a greater presence of institutional and cultural racism when there are so few people of color to challenge the effects of racist assumptions. Marginalized clients are sometimes struggling to manage their day-to-day affairs and are so negatively affected by racist practices in their communities and in their schools that they often feel hopeless and disoriented (Pérez Huber & Solorzano, 2015; Santiago-Rivera, Adames, Chavez-Dueñas, & Benson- Flórez, 2016; Seaton & Iida, 2019; Sibrava et al., 2019; Skewes & Blume, 2019; Smith, Hung, & Franklin, 2011; Wang, Leu, & Shoda, 2011; Wong-Padoongpatt, Zane, Okazaki, & Saw, 2017; Yip, 2016). Thus, for counselors to ignore the impacts of institutional racism on their clients is for them to unknowingly collude in blaming those who are most victimized by racism.

Counselors can sometimes participate in victim blaming practices by labeling people of color resistant or untreatable and by overdiagnosing underrepresented populations. Diagnostic systems such as the *Diagnostic and Statistical Manual of Mental Disorders* do not attune counselors and psychologists to look for the effects of racist discourse in people's lives. Only when counselors understand the harmful effects of their behavior will they be in a position to address it.

Many people of color who use counseling services will be resistant to trusting "White institutions staffed by White professionals." Charles Gelso and Bruce Fretz (2001) argue that trust is the most important contribution to building a working therapeutic relationship. Marginalized clients often enter a therapy with a significant amount of fear and anxiety. Clients of color are often suspicious of therapy. They are alert to themes of concealment and disguise. To many clients of color, White counselors represent societal oppression. Many scholars continue to find a common theme of mistrust of White counselors among African American, Asian American, Latinx, and Native American clients (Liu et al., 2019; Ridley, 2005; Sue & Sue, 2019; Whaley, 2001). Sometimes clients of color don't trust therapists of color because they feel these professionals have sold out to White establishments and no longer care about the rights of and social justice for marginalized groups. Thus, overcoming a client's mistrust may lead to the greatest success in terms of therapeutic outcome.

It would be a mistake to interpret such resistance in terms of transference originating in family-of-origin dynamics. Since White professionals represent a dominant racist culture to other ethnicities, many people of color may be either guarded or somewhat reactive and ready to act out their frustrations. Charles Ridley (2005) describes this "cultural paranoia" as a healthy reaction to racism by a person of color. It might be disclosed to a Black therapist but not to a White therapist. He also suggests that clients of color may show negative feelings toward White therapists during a counseling session because of what he calls cultural transference. The concept of cultural transference suggests that clients of color can transfer their sufferings caused by racist practices onto a White therapist, who symbolizes and embodies White racist attitudes. Ridley then describes how cultural countertransference can occur when White counselors inappropriately attribute psychological deficiencies to their clients of color because of their own unconscious racist attitudes.

Therefore, there can be significant obstacles to establishing a strong therapeutic alliance between White therapists and people of color. Sensitivity by White therapists to the history of institutional and cultural racist practice is critical in the creation of a strong counselor–client relationship. Ridley (2005) points out that therapists can have good intentions in working with clients of color and yet still engage in racist behavior because of their lack of awareness, knowledge, and understanding of institutional racism. This lack of awareness comes in the form of counselors' assumption that their values, world view, and life experiences are predominantly shared by their clients. Because of colonizing discourse and its systematic privileging of White culture and demeaning of other ethnicities, Black clients and White counselors, for example, have very different experiences of an American (U.S.) way of life. A poststructuralist analysis of racism nevertheless alerts us to the need to study the practices that might build such trust, rather than assuming that it is either possible or not possible on the grounds of the counselor's group membership.

When a White counselor says, for example, "I don't see color; we are all the same underneath," the counselor and client may be immediately talking past each other. The Black client is often immediately in touch with how racism produces systematic oppression and is shocked to hear a White counselor make a comment like this. Meanwhile, the White counselor may be shocked to find that a client is upset, because the intention of the comment was to demonstrate equal treatment of people of all races.

Sarah Knox, Alan Burkard, Adanna Johnson, Lisa Suzuki, and Joseph Ponterotto (2003) found that African American therapists in their sample routinely addressed the subject of race with clients of color and with clients whose race was part of their psychological presentation, but that White psychologists were uncomfortable discussing race and normally avoided mentioning racial issues with their clients. Jairo Fuertes, Lisa Mueller, Rahul Chauhan, Jessica Walker, and Nicholas Ladany (2002) suggest that counselors who are most effective in working across the majority/minority divide show interest in and express appreciation for a client's ethnicity and cultural heritage. There is compelling evidence to suggest that White counselors who directly address race issues with clients of color can establish strong therapeutic relationships with those clients. When this does not occur, clients of color may avoid speaking about race so their therapists won't feel offended or alienated, even when racism is a clear concern.

If counselor values are influenced by racist assumptions, then the potential harm in counseling interactions is all the more alarming. There are many subtle ways in which counselors can act from an unspoken belief that their values are superior to those of their clients. For example, counselors might believe that individualistic decision-making is preferable to, say, a collective, more communal decision-making process. A person being challenged to move from a communal or collective perspective on a decision to deciding for himself and rejecting family or community opinions might be perceived by the counselor as making therapeutic progress. The client, however, may simply be aligning with the counselor's value system and world view. Another example is labeling a client passive when he is behaving in an appropriately deferential position according to his own cultural community.

When clients prematurely cancel their sessions or are subject to psychiatric diagnoses shaped by Eurocentric assumptions, racist discourse can be shown to produce negative outcomes for clients of color. David Smart and Julie Smart (1997) note how the mental health profession generally fails to take into account cultural considerations for diagnosis. They point out that the whole construction of psychiatric and psychological models is based on Eurocentric assumptions with little respect for other cultural practices. For example, several epidemiological studies revealed significant differences between African Americans and Whites with regard to rates of diagnosis of affective disorders. Gordon Johnson, Samuel Gershon, and Leon Hekimian (1968) studied three years' worth of admissions at Bellevue Psychiatric Hospital and did not find a single case of an African American patient diagnosed with a manic depressive disorder. Carl Bell and Harshad Mehta (1980) suggest that misdiagnosis of African American patients is rooted in the notion that manic illness is clustered in higher socioeconomic brackets and is not featured among poor or Black communities. Because lower-class Black patients are denied treatment for affective illnesses, the withholding of appropriate services can be analyzed as a covert form of racism that is institutionalized in psychiatry. When clients are misdiagnosed, they receive inappropriate psychotherapy and medication, fail to receive benefits they would have gained from appropriate treatment, and often are subjected to inappropriate psychopharmacological therapy.

When already misdiagnosed, clients are more likely to be caught in a further cycle of misdiagnosis. Gerald Russell, Diane Fujino, Stanley Sue, Mang-King Cheung, and Lonnie Snowden (1996) sampled 9,000 adults in the Los Angeles County mental health system. They examined the relationship between therapist and client ethnic matching and the therapist's evaluation of overall client functioning based on the Global Assessment Scale. Interestingly, findings indicated that ethnically matched therapists were more likely to judge their clients as having a higher mental health status than therapists and clients working together from different ethnicities. Since most therapists, psychologists, and psychiatrists are White in the United States, it is probable that their clients with non-White identities are more likely to be pathologized.

Other examples of institutional racism in mental health agencies include setting agency fees above the range of what clients of color can afford and thus excluding them from treatment. Standardized psychological tests that do not include data from underrepresented cultural groupings reflect biased test construction and thus perpetuate cultural inequity.

Counselors' unrealistic expectations for therapeutic outcomes for clients of color are other examples of inequitable and possibly racist practice. Therapeutic goals set too low can become self-fulfilling prophecies, while goals set too high can be impossible for clients to achieve. Other forms of unequal treatment can occur when counselors have to spend a long time with their clients to learn about their cultural background when the clients feel that the counselor should already have a basic knowledge of their ethnic community and its cultural history.

Counseling and White Guilt

Writers in the multicultural field have begun to address the role that "White guilt" plays in setting the scene for how Whites and Blacks relate to one another. Essentially, White guilt is the collective and individual shame that Anglo Americans experience as they consider the effects of historical and contemporary oppression thrust upon the Black community by slavery and White institutional racism.

Shelby Steele (2006) has made a powerful argument for how White guilt holds back both White and Black communities from making progress in building meaningful and productive relationships with one another, and stalls positive social and economic initiatives. White guilt can also impact White therapists' behavior with Black clients. For example, Alison Jones and Arthur Seagull (1977) argued that some White professionals are motivated to counsel minorities almost completely out of their guilt about racism. The problem with this motivation is that White counselors are then operating from their own insecurities and trying to work out their own issues rather than being fully present for their clients. In addition, this dynamic of guilt can cause White counselors to seek approval from their clients of color. Charles Ridley (2005) suggests that White therapists may be so focused on their efforts to be nonracist that they set themselves up for counter manipulation by their marginalized clients, who may be keenly aware of their therapists' vulnerability and emotional insecurities. Thus, much time can be wasted on alleviating counselor anxiety, directing the therapy away from meaningful client outcomes.

The Problem of Overidentification with Clients of the Same Ethnicity

According to Charles Ridley (2005), counselors of color can hurt clients of color by assuming that the experiences of clients who look like them are the same as theirs. Even if counselors and clients come from similar backgrounds and have similar upbringings, it does not follow that they share exactly the same challenges. Overidentifying with clients keeps the counselor from being curious about the client's unique circumstances. Counselor interactions become stereotypically based and inflexible. This overidentification produces what Courtland Lee (1996) terms a monolithic perspective. According to Charles Ridley (2005), some counselors gain personal satisfaction from unloading on their clients pent-up feelings from their own experiences of racism. Counseling sessions can then inappropriately become a forum for therapists' own race-related distress.

Counseling Strategies to Circumvent Racist Practices

Because of the complexity and difficulties associated with addressing racism, multiple approaches are necessary to address its causes and effects. Ongoing legal and institutional changes are required. In addition, how to deal with racism should be addressed in counselor training programs and with counseling supervisors and administrators. Racist issues are made all the more difficult when the immediate issues a client struggles with are not directly related to racism but invoke older, painful memories. Shelby Steele (1990) considers the memory of racial victimization to be a particularly powerful wound:

> I think one of the heaviest weights that oppression leaves on the shoulders of its former victims is simply the memory of itself. This memory is a weight because it pulls the oppression forward, out of history and into the present, so the former victim may see his world as much through the memory of his oppression as through his experience in the present. (p. 150)

In this section we look at the important microlevel approaches that counselors might use to address racism in the counseling room. We have discussed at length the value of developing historical and sociocultural awareness of the issues that can negatively affect the work between counselors and clients. An honest examination of one's personal biases, agendas, preferences, and prejudices and how they might impact ethnically different clients is important to undertake. Charles Ridley (2005) says counselors themselves can benefit from seeing a therapist of another race to address their cultural encapsulation and build cultural empathy and understanding.

Charles Ridley (2005) and Larry Lee (2004) have outlined helpful practices in addressing the effects of racism on clients and building trust during counseling, including some of the following:

1. Believe your clients when they describe their experiences of racism.
2. If you are White or are perceived as White by a client of color, don't inadvertently invite your client to behave in a deferential manner.
3. Don't make your client feel she has to diminish her emotional response or reaction to racism. A strong and angry response to an experience of racism may be the client's first step toward rebuilding her dignity and finding her voice. Not accepting and acknowledging the pain caused by racism can lead to an early termination of counseling.
4. When you are conducting psychological assessments, ensure that documentation is made of the effects of racism in a client's profile along with environmental and social factors.
5. Provide information about the counseling time frame. Be careful about how you end the counseling session, especially when a client is preparing to introduce some new information, as he can feel disrespected when the time is up.

When Clients Are Racist

Many multicultural texts focus on helping White counselors grapple with racism and its effects on clients of color. There is currently a growing literature that supports ethnic counselors' of color working with White clients who may exhibit racist behavior. Counselors can sometimes experience troublesome interactions with their clients when clients exhibit blatantly racist behavior. Take this example mentioned by Larry Lee (2004). Lee describes a scenario in which he is counseling a White man and his family. The client has his own tech company and employs many Asians. Lee is Asian American. After the client has engaged in an angry exchange with his wife, Lee makes efforts to interrupt and redirect him. His client spins around and tells him, "Don't interrupt me when I'm speaking. I don't need your help. I can handle this very well without your interference. You know, I really don't know if you are really qualified to help us. I work with a lot of Asians and see that we're different" (p. 95).

These interactions are excruciatingly painful, and counselors can be blindsided by them. Lee gives a wonderful response: "You have a right to express your opinions although I am not comfortable with what you have expressed" (p. 96).

Here are some of the suggestions made by Azmaira Maker (2004) and Larry Lee (2004) to assist counselors of color working with clients from a majority culture:

1. Explore with the client what it is like to work with someone who looks and sounds so different.

2. Ask your client to make an honest response while reassuring her that it is safe to share her feelings and reactions.
3. Adopt an inviting response by asking questions like, "Where do you think I come from?" "Are you wondering about my values and religious beliefs and what I think about you and your family?" and "Do you worry that I might not be able to understand and relate to your experiences?"

Discuss

1. How easy is it to discuss racism in your class? What constraints do you experience? What might make those constraints interfere less?
2. What examples can you recall from your experience of internalized racism?
3. Collect examples of each of Appiah's three forms of stereotyping. Discuss whether these are examples of racism or not.
4. What do you see as the advantages and disadvantages of the poststructuralist analysis of racism?
5. How can counselors work against racism in their practice?

First Response to Chapter 7

KOBUS MAREE,
DED, PHD, DPHIL

Kobus Maree is a professor in the Faculty of Education at the University of Pretoria. His research focuses on career construction (counselling), life design (counselling), emotional-social intelligence, and social responsibility. The author or coauthor of 100+ peerreviewed articles and 60+ books/book chapters since 2009, he supervised 36+ doctoral theses and master's dissertations and read keynote papers at 25+ international and at 25+ national conferences in the same period. He was awarded honorary membership of the Golden Key International Honour Society for exceptional academic achievements, leadership skills, and community involvement in October 2014, the Chancellor's Medal for Teaching and Learning from the University of Pretoria in 2010, and Exceptional Academic Achiever Award on four consecutive occasions. He was awarded a fellowship of the International Association for Applied Psychology in 2017 and the Psychological Society of South Africa's Fellow Award (lifetime award in recognition of a person who has made exceptional contributions to psychology in her/his life) in 2017. Professor Maree is the current editor of the newly established African Journal of Career Development.

The experiences of Alfred, a brilliant fourth-year student from a rural background, illustrate the many one-dimensional notions of cultural groups that are rife in South Africa (SA).

> I really struggled during my first 18 months at the university (particularly with chemistry, physics, and mathematics). The medium of instruction was my biggest problem. Although the lecturers were not unwilling to help, some of them were also experiencing

problems lecturing in their second language. One put it this way: "I don't understand why they bothered to bring Blacks who cannot speak or understand Afrikaans or English properly, to this campus; they have their own universities."

Alfred's quote highlights the fact that Blacks at South African universities are often still assigned inferior status, in typical colonial fashion, and doomed to inferior and diminished opportunities. The embedded suggestion in this remark is the following: "You do not deserve state-of-the-art education." (By and large, Black South African universities have historically been, and still are, greatly disadvantaged). Alfred does not accept being marginalized.

> I have as much right to be here as they do. It is my country, my university, my city too; I visit the same clubs and I belong to the same organizations. Why pick on me?

Alfred intuitively draws attention to the poststructuralist view of racism. He assumes a discursive position in which he refuses to be branded as a helpless, oppressed victim who should merely accept his fate.

> Seemingly even a modern university such as this one is not sufficiently geared toward accommodating people from diverse cultures. When I lost my grandmother (the person who had raised me from birth), I indicated that I, as a member of the extended family, needed to attend her funeral. However, it proved almost impossible to convince many of my lecturers of the need to attend the funeral. One simply retorted, "It seems that all Black people are related to each other. Imagine if every student would apply to attend the funeral of every relative who passed away!"

The lecturer's distorted discourse is a clear example of simply false stereotyping. She shows blatant disrespect for the power and importance of the student's cultural beliefs, and she chooses to discriminate against an already severely traumatized young person.

> I was informed by a lecturer that many persons objected to the fact that Blacks had been "dumped" on "their" university and were "virtually destroying the traditional culture of the place."

This lecturer accepts that her own social privileges have been earned and well deserved, at the same time assuming that the student deserves to be excluded from these privileges.

> We were constantly reminded, directly and indirectly, that Blacks generally achieved poorer results at the end of Grade 12, which "proved" that we did not have the capacity to achieve at the university level.

The lecturers clearly verbalize their support for the stereotypical racist view expressed here, namely that, based on perceived ethnic differences, Blacks are unintelligent (i.e., Whiteness is superior and Blackness inferior).

Acceptance by fellow students was a particularly painful stumbling block. All my fellow Black students consistently complained about racism, being called names, and not being greeted in turn by White students, irrespective of the prevailing circumstances. As one fellow student put it, "Many of us were victims of discrimination this year. It seems as if Whites think that, just because you're Black and poor, you are an animal. I tried to befriend Whites, but they didn't have time to greet me or listen to me."

According to Alfred, Black students continue to suffer rejection and social exclusion at the hands of Whites on account of perceived ethnic (bodily) differences and outmoded colonial practices.

Much as students complained about orientation, we, on the whole, accepted this as a necessary evil. In some instances, though, we perceived the underlying racial motives it created, as well as the lingering bitterness and animosity. In the words of one Black student: "Here we had people who did not respect my culture at all. I felt like a slave, being forced to do things against my will."

Some students whose achievement was not satisfactory at the end of their first, second, or third year were put on a so-called waiting list for residences (*waglys*). This almost inevitably doomed them to a life of roaming the streets of adjacent suburbs (they have no support structures in the region) until (hopefully) one day they were lucky enough to regain access to residences. Conversely, some students turn to squatting as a way of handling an untenable situation with little or no help from administration, which does not seem to understand the frame of reference of changing socioeconomic circumstances and the changing demographic profile of the campus.

Unchallenged, outmoded, and persistent colonizing discourses, which include colonizing patterns of behavior, conspire with unearned White privilege to predestine Black students to untenable situations. I believe Alfred's narrative highlights the need not only to combat racism on all fronts, but, indeed, to strive toward more inclusive perspectives on multicultural counseling, especially an epistemology that would respond satisfactorily to questions about some of the existing theoretical concepts in the field of counseling. In South Africa, in particular, racism impacts the lives of people across diverse cultures. It manifests itself in various forms and in various forums— for example, educational institutions (e.g., schools and universities) and the workplace (where racism and discrimination still abound, despite the best efforts of the powers that be to eradicate this scourge).

Whereas traditional, positivist counseling has failed the needs of the majority of the global population, social constructionism and its emphasis on multiple realities highlights the need for multiple and flexible approaches to data (objective and subjective) collection, for combining approaches, for meaning making and mattering, and offers a window of opportunity—a novel lens that potentially enables psychologists to enter the phenomenological world of clients from across the racial continuum.

Sequel

Reflecting on the situation in South Africa today, almost a decade after my reflections were first published, there is no denying the fact that the South African society is still a work in progress, and that there is still a very long way to go before it can be claimed with any degree of certainty that the dream of "equality" and a nonracial society has been realized; but much has been achieved. Acceptance of an integrative, qualitative–quantitative approach to career counselling and the notion of promoting life design intervention for all is gaining traction. Efforts are afoot to ensure that career counselling is made available to all people in South Africa and not only to a select few. The faculty where Alfred studied is integrated at all levels. The majority of its students are Black and racism has all but disappeared. Free tertiary education for the poorest of the poor has become a reality in South Africa. The discourse on finding ways to address colonialism is alive and well—and it is robust. A sense of mutual trust and respect and a shared sense of destiny are increasingly being experienced. Likewise, realization is dawning that humans and their idiosyncratic behavior must be contextualized and never judged. The importance of enabling all people to draw on and integrate their "stories" and their "scores" to enable them to make meaning, establish a sense of purpose, (re-)kindle their sense of hope, and design successful lives in which they can make social contributions is no longer the domain of a select few. People are increasingly being helped to navigate major career-life transitions; emerge (some would say escape) from their inflicted realities. There is growing evidence of a sincere desire to deal with the scourge of racism.

There is a caveat, though. Not until there is conclusive evidence that the critical mass of our population accepts the inspiring vision embedded in the following quote by the late and great Nelson Mandela will we be able to relax our joint efforts in search of an equal and racism-free society in any way:

> No one is born hating another person because of the color of his skin, or his background, or his religion. People must learn to hate, and if they can learn to hate, they can be taught to love, for love comes more naturally to the human heart than its opposite.

Second Response to Chapter 7

TONIKA DUREN-
GREEN, PHD

Dr. Tonika Duren Green is a Professor at San Diego State University in Department of Counseling and School Psychology. She is a Nationally Certified School Psychologist and received two Presidential Awards of Recognition from NASP for her service as Co-Chair of the Multicultural Affairs Committee and the Chair of the NASP Minority Recruitment and Retention Task Force. She is committed to preparing school psychologists who are multicultural thinkers and actors, who understand how racial, ethnic and sociocultural factors influence student performance. Dr. Green publishes in the areas of social justice within education, recruitment and mentorship, and improving outcomes for youth in foster care. She has been awarded over 3 million dollars in federally-funded grants designed to train school professionals to improve outcomes for marginalized and minoritized youth. Dr. Green's leadership roles include, 18 years of experience as a faculty member, School Psychology Program Director, Grant Director, university and community chairships, and Director and Founder of the African American Mentoring Program (AAMP), which is devoted to recruiting, retaining, and reaching students of African descent. In her newest leadership position, she serves as the Charles Bell Scholar to oversee the Henrietta Goodwin Scholars Program which provides mentorship and academic support for African American freshmen.

My reflection on this chapter is girded up in my lived experiences as an African American woman who is a Christian with a Westernized education, an educator, wife, mother, monolingual, and a native of Richmond, Virginia. While this is not all of who I am, these identities are the most salient in my life as I write this reflection. My response to this chapter is a response that is a result of what I have seen, experienced, and continue to live through. The emotion and critical thought of the chapter will speak from the twisting and coiling of my personal and professional identities. Within the personal, my response will be my heart, mind, and soul reaction to what I have read and how it lines up with what I know to be true in my own life. My professional response will lean on my experience as a university professor and the discussions and discourses that happen in my multicultural counseling classroom. "What would my students feel and think as they read and discuss the chapter?" "How would they respond?" "What would resonate with them and why?" "How would I teach and learn with them?" "How would I sit in my own feelings about racism and effectively move my students through the chapter?" While these questions are of great importance to me as an instructor, my biggest thought was, will this be a chapter that will grip the minds of those that need to hear it and learn from it.

The chapter begins with a powerful quote by Charles Ridley (2005): "Failing to address racism is a form of racism itself. It is like having the ability to rescue a drowning child but failing to do so." Racism attempts to kill the soul of a person with no regard for their life, their experiences, and their purpose on this earth. I appreciate that the chapter defines racism, privilege, and power through a social constructionist lens and from a decolonial perspective. The chapter argues that there is no single kind of racism and that racism is a social power that can be covert or overt. As a person who has experienced both, *the memories of each account of racism are too deep and too wide to share in this reflection*, but reading the chapter provided me with ways to think about each account and the differing perspectives on understanding and addressing it. For example, the chapter explains racism from a liberal humanist perspective. In this context, racism is at the individual level and believed to originate from the inside of an individual. This belief brought my mind back to a time that I was asked by a jeweler for my ID before I was "allowed" to try on a wedding ring in a jewelry store, while my White friend was freely allowed to try on a ring without providing her ID. My friend was more appalled than I was by this act of racism because it was her first time witnessing overt racism and discrimination. My numbness to this encounter was because this was not new, but familiar. In this incident, a liberal humanist perspective would view racism from an individual level. The jeweler made a preconceived judgement about me, which resulted in racial stereotyping.

The chapter also views racism from a structuralist perspective. Racism is considered systemic with underpinnings in the social structure. In this perspective, racist practices are viewed as institutionalized. The chapter provides examples of schools and prisons as the greatest perpetrators of racism. My first experience with institutionalized racism was in the first grade. My White teacher corrected the spelling of my first name (my nickname). My family spelled my name "Nikki," and the teacher told me that the name should be spelled "Nickey." Thirty years later, I shared the experience with my mom, and she thought I wanted to change the spelling of my name, so she never questioned it. How could a teacher erase my identity with a stroke of a pen? Did she not think I could spell? Did she not think my family knew how they wanted my name spelled? Did she not understand the order of the letters of my name were sacred and personal? How could I allow her to change my name? How could my mother allow it? Ironically, this history is repeating itself with my daughter's name, Tori Faith. A name that is very spiritual and sacred to who she is as a person. Her teachers refuse to honor both names and consider it convenient to just call her "Tori," a name she does not identify with. The power differentials are ever present in schools, and the chapter speaks vividly about privilege and power that rests within racism.

Lastly, the chapter discusses postructuralism and racism. In this perspective racism is not an individual or a social structure, but forms from social practices and is lived out in discourse. Rather than seeing a person as racist or tying racism to a person or institution, postructuralism addresses racism as a discourse. For example, I recently wrote an article with colleagues, and we received feedback from the journal reviewers that using the terms African American and Black interchangeably was confusing and inconsistent and to consider choosing one term. After reading this chapter, it solidified for me the microaggressions that continue to exist with those in power. Requesting me to pick one term over another when I identify with both, is similar to asking me to choose one identity over another. I identify with African American as a form of identifying with my ancestors, and I identify with Black as it represents social justice, power, beauty, and pride. A postructuralism perspective would consider the discourse, which in this case is being asked to choose to use one identifying term over another. Addressing this discourse would mean sharing with the reviewers the purpose of using both terms and asking them to reconsider the request. In this, we as authors are educating the reviewers on the purpose and importance of the terms and the reviewers are charged with thinking about the use of the words and how this discourse affects a group of people and potentially evokes feelings of silencing one's identity and choice.

While I wish racism was as easy to codify, identify, and compartmentalize, as the chapter has presented, I am glad that the authors highlighted that there must be a recognition that forms of racism continue to evolve and new injustices surface in our society daily. Additionally, the way people of color and people passionate about addressing racism respond has evolved. With movements like Black Lives Matter, Black Girl Magic, Me Too, and other forms of sociopolitical uprising, the nation has heard the shouts of people who no longer feel powerless, but feel empowered. This empowered formed of action and thought says to oppressors, victimizers, and racism that there are people who are taking a stand against marginalized practices, racist views, discrimination, and oppression. With that comes a love of self and a movement that embraces culture (used broadly). This is beautifully and vividly illustrated in the Black community with Black Girl Magic, Black Girls Rock, and My Melanin is Poppin'. Films like *Black Panther*, with Blacks in leading roles, represent strong sources of pride and beauty. This new sociopolitical platform of self-love to address racism has also been met with discourse in our current political climate, the Make America Great Again movement and its impact on our country's views, position, power, and privilege. This is an important phenomenon that the chapter missed the opportunity to address. Now more than ever we are seeing racism, privilege, and power rise to a devastatingly dangerous height and collide with the empowerment movements. These changes impact what racism is and what it will become, and as a result will bring forth a new form and brand of people who will be entering counseling seeking help on ways to heal and respond to these "new injustices" and new forms of privilege and power. How will we respond? Fortunately, the book offers approaches that can continue to be prevalent in this new era of racism. The counseling approaches that circumvent racism will need to take into account the disappearance and fading of White Guilt and now address the normalization of racism and White Supremacy, White entitlement, and bigotry given our new political climate. Ironically and most unfortunately, this has also crept into communities of color who share views of an Americanized world and who belongs in it. This is a scary reality and one that counselors need to be ready and prepared for.

Chapter 8

Identity Construction

P revious chapters have dealt with macrolevel social processes and power relations that emerge when studying counseling through a cultural lens. We have explored how they play a part in the creation of culture, ethnicity, race, and gender. Considerable emphasis has been placed on the impact of the historical forces of European colonization that have shaped the modern world. This chapter shifts our attention to the microlevel processes of identity construction, but attempts not to lose a sense of the impact of the social dimensions of culture, history, race, ethnicity, and power relations.

The global sociohistorical processes at work around the planet—in particular, the impact of the mass media, technology, and migration, as well as the sustained efforts of many people to generate decolonizing social movements—disrupt the possibility of a stable identity and also the possibility of cultural constancy. The self is saturated (Gergen, 2007) with multiple influences that shape our identities. We have already detailed the complexity of cultural membership in previous chapters and would argue that this complexity is not honored by an approach to intercultural counseling that reduces identity to singular dimensions. We shall now consider the counseling implications of catering to the needs of individuals living with a multiplicity of identities.

In this chapter, we use the notion of identity as a conceptual tool to understand how people make meaning in their personal lives and in their relationships with others. Understanding the process of identity construction as a set of narratives rather than as emerging from a singular core, or personality, can help us understand how psychological problems are produced, and this is at the same time a resource for exploring creative ways to address those problems. We find the construct of identity more useful to us than the notion of personality and would argue that an intercultural perspective in counseling should exercise a preference for identity over personality. In our view, personality is an essentialized, stabilizing construct that does not adequately account for intersecting changes that people make in their lives as they respond to the influences of powerful sociohistorical processes. The notion of ongoing identity construction better represents the dynamic, shifting, and evolving patterns of life that are always responding to the changing cultural contexts that people inhabit.

First, let us specify what we mean by identity construction. The term is used in different ways in accordance with different philosophical traditions.

The Notion of the Singular Self and Personality

Many of us were raised within the influence of a Western cultural tradition to assume without question that we are born with a unique self that expresses itself via a particular personality. From much of the mainstream psychological literature and popular culture, we come to know that we each have different personalities based on certain biological predispositions that we develop when we are young. Most of us accept the fact that these characteristics or dispositions will provide us with a unified, stable sense of who we are throughout our lives. We embrace a prefixed psychological structure that shapes and determines the way we behave. Most of us accept that that personality structure stays with us until the physical breakdown of our bodies. As Vivien Burr (2015) suggests, personality is so taken for granted in Western culture that we could almost imagine that surgeons could open us up to show us our personality. In both academic discourse and in everyday talk, we accept global descriptions of people and their personalities. For example, people are known by their personalities to be extraverted or introverted, generous or mean-spirited.

It would be logical, given our understandings about the self, to expect all cultures to embrace the notion that we have a prefixed personality, but this is clearly not the case. Some cultures don't define certain characteristics as belonging inside people. The Ifaluk, for example, describe people in relationship to community events, rather than as separately locked within their own individual sphere. They talk of justifiable anger not as a privately owned domain but as a moral and public account of some transgression of accepted social practices (Lutz, 1982, 1990). Yet we habitually see qualities such as competitiveness, greed, caring, and love as descriptive of a person rather than of a type of action.

In many ways, the Western or modernist construction of personality could be viewed as pessimistic about possibilities for change. This is due to the widespread notion that deep inside everyone there is just one kind of fundamental truth or essence that really matters and is difficult to change. One could almost say that, in terms of personality, the rest of a person's life journey doesn't really count for much. Mainstream trait-personality theorists suggest that we are born into a particular set of characterological configurations that remain stable over our lives. Other personality theorists suggest that we are shaped by both traits (the biological inclinations we are born with) and states (the situational and environmental influences), from which our personalities are created. This means that heredity and environment play a part in shaping a core identity. People talk about babies having their own personalities and how these personalities will define them as they grow. Certainly we don't dispute the notion that children express certain temperaments and habitual patterns of relating very early in their lives. However, these characterological patterns of relating are a far cry from a fixed set of personality attributes that inherently drive a person's life. The question is whether we think of these patterns as fixed or as contextual, hence constantly changing. Some developmental theorists have proposed that once a person has reached a certain age, her personality is set and not subject to change.

Sigmund Freud's (1938) theories of personality remain a foundation from which many developmental theorists think about personality. The Freudian view of personality is deterministic to the extent that it believes personality is defined by the interplay of irrational forces, unconscious motivations, and instinctual drives regardless of context.

Today, counseling and psychotherapy approaches wrestle with the extent to which people are capable of fundamental and lasting change. In the United States, insurance companies will pay counselors and psychologists to work with clients troubled by psychological problems that are perceived as treatable. They will not pay for counseling and therapy for people whose problems appear to emanate from a personality disorder, since it is believed that a personality disorder is a fixed, stable entity and thus that people with such disorders are not capable of changing their lives. The latest version of the *Diagnostic and Statistical Manual of Mental Disorders* (*DSM-V*; American Psychiatric Association, 2013a), one of the most significant cultural artifacts shaping the fields of psychiatry and psychology, guides mental health professionals in understanding and assessing client problems. It is designed on the basis that we all have a core stable personality and that when that personality is not operating correctly it is disordered in some particular way.

Psychology's Preoccupation with the Self

Psychology and mental health professionals have historically been preoccupied with the notion of the individual and the personality. As we have shown in Chapter 6, liberal humanism has dominated mainstream counseling, psychology, and psychotherapy over the last three decades. Gaining momentum in the 1960s, the liberal humanist tradition, pioneered by psychologists such as Gordon Allport, Abraham Maslow, and Carl Rogers, has traditionally identified the individual as the central agent of all social phenomena and has celebrated the self as independent, stable, and knowable, emphasizing an individual's capacity for choice, freedom, and self-development. The field of counseling and psychotherapy has been dominated by the notion of the unitary self. The central premises of individualism in the helping professions are based on the injunction to "be your own person" and "stand on your own two feet." Clients are supported to be functional human beings who are independent, rational, moral agents responsible for their own welfare and individualistic lifestyle.

Sarah's story clearly illustrates the tensions she experiences with her peer group, who perceive her to be weak and dependent because she is not following the dominant Anglo American pattern of living in a separate dwelling from her parents in her mid 20s.

> *I graduated from UCLA a short while ago. I had a full undergraduate experience, including living in a dormitory and in an apartment separate from my family. Many family members and friends beamed with excitement at the news of my graduation. Then they would ask me, "So what's next in your life?" I'd happily reply that I would be moving back home with my mother and attending graduate school. The mere mention of graduate school brought a sense of pride and joy to their faces, but adding the fact that I would be living at home seemed to make them sneer. I wondered about that, because at first I had no idea what the negativity was all about. In dominant middle-class, Western society, there is the notion that a person over the age of 18 is supposed to be out in the world living on her own. Certainly she should not be living with her mother.*
>
> *In traditional Filipino culture, it is customary that when the children grow up, they take care of their parents. This means that they could all be living under the same roof for as long as they all live. According to my mother, the concept is that they (the parents) took care of you (their child) when you were young, and you should return the favor. The origin of this cultural concept is not known, but it could have to do with the Filipino value of respecting one's elders. Friends and family members who have embraced the Western idea*

that children 18 years of age and older have to move out affects me when I am at family gatherings (usually family parties) or social events with my friends. I mostly feel hurt when they think that it is negative for me to be living at home with my mother, because I truly believe that living at home is a very positive affair. Sometimes I have to stop and self-evaluate for a moment my reasons and objectives for being at home.

My mother and I have a very close relationship, and she has told me time and time again that she loves my being at home. I show, in many ways, that I value the Filipino belief of respecting one's elders through my interactions with my mother. Growing up, I saw how my mother treated my grandmother with utmost respect and kindness, and I have internalized that Filipino value. I plan to take care of her more and more as I get older and have a good career. I use this self-evaluation whenever I feel that people try to impose the stigma of living at home with parents after the age of 18. In other words, I always try to think of my close relationship with my mother and the positive aspects of living at home. At times, however, this dominant cultural attitude of individualism is difficult to weaken.

FIGURE 8.1   Sarah

Interwoven with the liberal humanist perspective of the individual as an independent, autonomous, and unitary being has been the notion that people are fundamentally separate from the social and historical world. With its celebration of individualism, liberal humanism has tended to locate human problems within individuals as distinct and separate from the social, cultural, and political contexts in which they live (McAuliffe, 2019; Neimeyer, 1998; Winslade, Monk, & Drewery, 1997). This dislocation of individuals and their problems from the larger cultural context reflects the humanistic focus on intrapsychic processes. From this viewpoint, the essence of individuality is the feeling self. Feelings are seen as products of nature and bearers of truth about the individual, rather than as products of culture. People's feelings have been revered in counseling as representing a higher level of truth about their nature than their thoughts or words. The dated but nonetheless popular notion of self-actualization, for instance, epitomizes the liberal humanist position that individuals are capable of being in charge of their own lives and grants individuals the freedom to be self-guided, self-governed, and effective in their pursuits of personal growth and development.

The excessive individualism promoted in the liberal humanist movement has tended to ignore the larger sociocultural issues impacting therapists and clients alike. Foreshadowing a contemporary criticism, Allan Buss (1979) observed, "A theory that predisposes one to focus more upon individual freedom and development rather than the larger social reality, works in favor of maintaining that social reality" (p. 47). As a result, the effects of various oppressive practices have frequently been overlooked. For example, the relevance of the humanistic position to the situation of people of color has been challenged (Carter, 1995; Durie, 1989; Jenkins, 2001). Skeptics maintain that because liberal humanist doctrine has portrayed persons as autonomous beings who are primarily responsible for their plight, practitioners within this framework may easily dismiss how racist, sexist, and homophobic discourse impacts them and their clients.

The monolithic conception of the self continues to play a dominant role in modernist schools of thought and continues to be accepted as a fundamental truth on which psychology is founded. This continues despite psychology's best efforts to construct itself as a discipline founded on objective, independent, scientific criteria. The mechanisms by which a society produces fundamental truths were explained by the philosopher Michel Foucault (1969, 1972). In his early writings, he shows how over long periods societies produce certain widely held assumptions about human beings, and how these assumptions come to be accepted as true. Foucault explains how a society then constructs certain protocols and practices based on these "truths." In Chapter 6 we saw how, in the modern world, processes of normalization and surveillance have been constructed to keep these established truths in place. Human behavior is judged in accordance with established norms and found to be appropriate or aberrant. Foucault's argument is that if we examine the work done by the social processes of production of personhood, many of the features of personal identity do not turn out to be straightforward, natural expressions of innate personality. Rather, they are produced into a person's identity as an outcome of the systematic interplay of power relations. We believe that this perspective offers much richer veins to be mined in the development of an intercultural project in the counseling field than those offered by conventional individualistic notions of personality.

Postmodern Psychology and Its Implications

A growing number of social science researchers have rejected the monolithic categories of personality and the notion of the stable self on which the traditions of modern-day psychology are based. They reject the assumption that the individual is both the prime source of all human interaction and the most important unit of social analysis. It is clear from previous chapters that using the individual as the central point of social analysis obstructs our understanding of the profound role that sociocultural processes play in the construction of human expression. The postmodern movement is keenly interested in the link between wider intercultural processes and individual identity construction. Postmodernism has emerged as a powerful challenge to the traditional Euro-American science of modern psychology (Fukuyama & Sevig, 1999; Gergen, 2007; Hare-Mustin & Marecek, 1994; Harvey, 1989; Lax, 1989; Lyotard, 1984). The term postmodernism, however, can be used in a number of ways, and we need to specify the sense in which we are using it here.

Postmodernism is a term applied to a loose collection of intellectual movements in a variety of social fields stretching well beyond the social sciences. Some suggest that its center of gravity lies more in the arts and architecture than in social science (for example, Burr, 2015), but it needs to be considered part of the background against which we can understand the general principles of social constructionist psychology. As the term suggests, postmodernism as an intellectual movement is a reaction to the dominance of modernism, a term referring to the approach to knowledge and truth that grew out of the Enlightenment in Europe in the mid-18th century (Seidman, 1994). Postmodernism casts doubt on the idea that the world can best be understood in terms of the grand narratives or metanarratives (Lyotard, 1984) of modernist science (based on rationality and objective observation), with their promise of ongoing social progress. Steven Seidman (1994) has summarized modernist culture as built on the following set of organizing assumptions or grand narratives: "assumptions regarding the unity of humanity, the individual as the creative force of society and history, the superiority of the west, the idea of science as Truth, and the belief in social progress" (p. 1).

On the basis of these assumptions, Seidman (1994) details a series of institutional edifices that have entrenched the modernist cultural perspective:

> an industrial-based economy; a politics organized around unions, political parties and interest groups; ... the market and state regulation ... role specialization and professionalism ... knowledges divided into disciplines and organized around an ideology of scientific enlightenment and progress; the public celebration of a culture of self-redemption and emancipatory hope. (p. 1)

Charles Taylor (2004) would add to this picture of emancipatory hope a more pessimistic note. He suggests that the modern world has also been characterized by a profound personal sense of alienation.

From a postmodern perspective, modernism is characterized as "in crisis" but far from "abruptly coming to an end" (Seidman, 1994, p. 1). Postmodernism asks uncomfortable questions regarding the adequacy of modernist assumptions about truth, knowledge, the relations between the individual and the social, and the possibility of progress, and argues that many historically and culturally specific assumptions have been masquerading as timeless, universal truths. As Derald Wing Sue and David Sue (2019) have stated, postmodern psychology has fueled interest in understanding alternative realities, spirituality, and indigenous methods of healing. This movement has also raised serious questions about the commonly held assumptions about the nature of the self.

Much of the postmodern literature holds that cultural assumptions of a single definable reality are impositions that dismiss or distort the diversity and indeterminacy of human life. Postmodern writers suggest that understanding anything is a consequence of the coming together of a unique set of circumstances at a particular place and time. Descriptions of human behavior emerging from postmodern literature are generally concerned with local and specific occurrences rather than global descriptions based on context-free laws (Hoshmand & Polkinghorne, 1992).

Many counseling models tend to emphasize the primacy of the rational mind over body and emotion and its capacity to take up one noncontradictory position. Postmodern theorizing, on the other hand, emphasizes the significance of the person as a multipositioned subject, a view quite contrary to unitary notions of the self. Postmodernism has tended to challenge all boundary fixing and the hidden ways in which people subordinate, exclude, and marginalize others (Bernstein, 1983). Advocates of a postmodernist approach, such as Charles Jencks (1992), have suggested that this means an end to a single world view, a resistance to single explanations, a respect for difference, and a celebration of the regional, local, and particular. David Harvey (1989) suggested that the postmodernist position has been characterized as the total acceptance of ephemerality, fragmentation, discontinuity, and the chaotic, while contemporary psychology views chaos and fragmentation as problems to be overcome. The self from this perspective is considered to be in a constant state of change and disequilibrium. The postmodern conception of the self is in stark contrast to the humanist notion of a single, stable, unitary identity.

The nature of the world in the 21st century is characterized by chaos and fragmentation, disorientation and complexity. From a postmodern perspective, the question, "Who are we?" becomes increasingly difficult to answer in the lives that we lead and in the way we describe ourselves in this new century.

BOX 8.1 LINES OF FORCE

The concept of lines of force draws upon descriptions and diagrams in physics of magnetic or electric fields. It was developed by Gilles Deleuze and Felix Guattari (1987) as a way to describe the flows of power in social relations and is a key concept in their social ontology. "Whether we are individuals or groups, we are made of lines" (Deleuze & Parnet, 2007, p. 124.) A line of force exerts a pull on people and events. It establishes norms and creates what we know as normal. It is a device of power that might serve to diminish hope and vitality. We can, therefore, talk about gendered lines of force or racial lines of force in the wider social context, or about lines of force on a smaller scale that regulate the flows of power in a particular family.

Says Luis de Miranda, a line of force is the

> classifying language, the line of prioritisation, of ordering, duty, false oppositions: "family – profession; job – holidays; family – and then school – and then the army – and then the fac-

tory – and then retirement." This is the line of the they: "They tell us: now, you are not a baby anymore." ... This is a line that works collectively, a line of imprisonment in such and such a function or group, a line of training, a line setting in motion the wheels of the social code according to operational models enabling mass containment of the vital flows – necessarily reductive, forced and simplifying. (p. 6)

Lines of force are not originated by any one individual. People ride them like a wave for a while. Thus, for example, a person uttering racist hate speech did not invent racism. He or she merely catches the wave and rides it. This person can be said to mimic what he has heard. Deleuze and Guattari also call lines of force "molar lines," distinguishing them from "molecular lines" or "lines of flight," which are less about colonizing power and more about expressions of vitality.

Multiple Identities and Multiple Selves

To assert that a person has a single identity means to believe that he has a fundamental allegiance, often religious, national, racial, or ethnic, and that having found it he may flaunt it proudly in the face of others. In fact, every person is a meeting ground for many different allegiances. Sometimes these allegiances conflict with one another, and this confronts the person with difficult choices.

The reality is that people's identities change over time. Amin Maalouf (2000) writes of a man who proudly stands up as a Yugoslavian in 1980. Twelve years later, this person denies his identity as a Yugoslavian as the war in Bosnia is waged. Now this same man stands proudly as a Muslim. Today, he may be Bosnian first and Muslim second. What identity will he be in 20 more years?

In the following identity statement, Rosa reflects on the shifts she has made in her religious identity over time.

My great grandparents prayed the rosary every morning and evening and attended Mass every day, and on Sunday they went twice a day. As a child, my mother was told that if she did not attend Mass and pray, she would be committing a mortal sin. These beliefs were taught and believed by many Catholics. In fact, my mom describes my great grandparents as "Catolicos de más" (too Catholic). Today, many among the working class will say, "Si Dios quiere" ("If God wants") or "Si Dios nos da licencia" ("If God permits us"); these sayings are said out loud whenever one is planning on doing something. For example, if a child says that he or she is going to work hard to get better grades in school, the mother will finish off the sentence by saying, "Si Dios te da licencia." Working-class Mexicans believe that if they don't say these phrases, then they are jinxing themselves and will make God mad at them.

Turning to their faith is the only way many working-class Mexicans are able to keep hope despite their unjust living conditions. If one stands outside La Villa, a temple the Virgin Mary asked to be built, one will witness many indigenous and working-class people walking on their knees down the center aisle toward the image of the Virgin Mary. This is done as an act of faith to the patron saint of Mexico. Because of this heritage, I came to believe that religion was imperative for survival. I remember attending Mass every Sunday and praying the rosary every night. This routine carried on until my siblings and I got older and began to work and have other responsibilities. Now that I am older and have had many different experiences in my life and have been exposed to new ways of thinking, I have found myself confused about my own religious and spiritual beliefs. This dissonance originated for me in my first year as an undergraduate. For the first time, I had the opportunity to be exposed to different people, different cultures, and a different environment and did not have my parents deciding what I was to believe. Having these new experiences changed my thought processes. I found out that the religion I practiced does not accept homosexuality; in fact, it is considered a sin to be gay or lesbian. Since many Mexican Americans are Catholics, they are influenced by these teachings and look down on people's sexual and gender identities that are not heterosexual. Among the working class, people not living a heterosexual way of life are ... also perceived as engaging in a shameful way of living. I imagine that these ideas are not influenced just by religious beliefs but also simply by people's being uneducated. My confusion has led me to feel guilty and to feel as if I am a bad Catholic. I am still struggling with this confusion. I know I have faith in God, but I'm not certain I follow all Catholic beliefs. It's a little scary for me to discuss this openly.

My great grandfather told my grandmother that to get married in the Catholic Church meant that "el matrimonio no es para un día ni dos, es para toda la vida. Si tú cruz es libiana o pesada, Dios decidará si va haber una seperación. Si te sale mal el marido, si te golpea, maltrata o lo que sea, tú vas a morir fiel a tú cruz." Meaning, "Marriage is not for a day or two, it's for life. If the weight of your cross is heavy or light, God will be the one to determine if there will be a separation. If your husband turns out bad, if he hits you, mistreats you, or whatever, you will remain loyal to your cross." The advice my great grandfather gave my grandmother exemplifies how marriage was viewed as an extension of Catholic beliefs. During those times, divorce was unheard of, especially among the working-class group. First, there was no money to spend on the process; second, you went down the social class ladder; and third, it was forbidden by the Catholic religion. Witnessing my parents' interactions with each other, I was taught that in a marriage there will be difficult times but that divorce is never an option. Yet, in my American present, I am being taught that divorce is an option. I deal with these two contrasting beliefs by believing that marriage is a sacred union and should not be taken lightly, but not disregarding divorce entirely. I am not saying that I believe in divorce and do not find anything wrong with it; on the contrary, I just don't want to feel trapped, as I think my grandmother once felt.

It is clear that Rosa, like thousands of people, is actively engaged in identity construction. The models of identity laid down for her in her family system about how to be a Christian and a woman do not provide her with all of the cultural knowledge that she needs to negotiate her way into a post-modern world. Migration, the media, and education become powerful contextual elements for Rosa that require her to revise some of her important salient identities.

Mikela is another person in the midst of identity reconstruction, reconciling his Indian-ness with his college education. This is how he describes his identity right now.

> I was the first male from my tribe to graduate from college, and I am the first person from my tribe to go on to graduate school. I am doing things that my people haven't done before, and I fear that this will make me an outsider. Although I do get a lot of praise for what I'm doing, I also get a lot of criticism. My own people think that I'm not Indian anymore because I have a college education. They think that I have "turned White." The process that I have undergone to make it to being a professional has large implications for my culture and me. The more educated I become, the less Indian I am. I fear that when I get everything done, I won't be accepted back into my community. So those that tell me otherwise are usually the ones that solely live on the "rez" but are not connected with their Indian-ness. I sing my songs, and I know in my heart I'm Indian. Another question is, will I not be accepted into the counseling profession because of my Indian-ness? Much racism against my people is still evident, and I fear that being an Indian will create a lot of barriers in my profession. My world view is different, my philosophy is different, and my way of working with kids will be different.
>
> Every individual without exception possesses multiple identities. One only needs to ask a few questions to uncover a person's forgotten divergences and unsuspected allegiances. Sadly, on a large scale, many of us lump the most different people together under the same cultural identity as a "Them" and ascribe to an identity group collective crimes, collective acts, and collective opinions. For example, it is common for people to say, "The Americans destroyed ..." "The English have gone on the offensive ..." or "The Saudis refuse ..." We unthinkingly express sweeping judgments about a whole people in a single breath.
>
> To be born Black is a different matter according to where in the world you come from, whether it be New York, São Paulo, or Addis Ababa. In Nigeria, people are not labeled Black or White but recognized as Yoruba or Hausa (Maalouf, 2000). In his book, The Invention of the White Race, Allen (2011) points out that when the first Africans arrived in Virginia in 1619 there were no "White people." There was certainly a well-developed hierarchy among Europeans on how people were treated, but it occurred around class rather than skin color. During this era it was the Irish who were deemed subhuman and inferior, but it wasn't based upon skin color. The word White didn't appear in any formal category until 1691. African indentured laborers had the same status as European indentured laborers and there were no demarcations around a racial identity. When African laborers were relieved of their indentured status they were free to hire other indentured laborers and did so. There was intermarriage between Africans and Europeans right up until the late-17th century (Haider, 2018). Until the slave trade became fully established in the beginning of the 18th century, Haider stated, "The definitions of Whiteness as freedom and Blackness as slavery did not yet exist" (p. 54).

At the local level of identity construction, identity can take a number of forms, and the context is enormously influential in shaping one's way of understanding oneself and way of relating to the world.

Rosa's identity as a Mexican American woman is significantly affected by the contexts produced by national borders. She discusses the day-to-day conflicts and feelings of identity dislocation that she experiences because of the arbitrary divisions produced between Mexican Americans born in Mexico and those born in the United States.

> *I remember witnessing this division in high school—those born in the United States were perceived as higher class. Often some of the United States–born Mexican Americans did not know the Spanish language as proficiently as the Mexicans, which created a wider division between the two. I was born in the United States, but I had friends from both groups. I remember that one time I wanted to join an organization on campus called MEChA (Movimiento Estudiantil Chicano de Aztlán). I thought that by joining I would learn more about my Mexican roots. At the first meeting I attended, I felt like an outsider. Most of the students were born in Mexico, they were all speaking fluent Spanish, and they had negative images of the "American" lifestyle. I wanted to be a part of them, but at the same time I felt as if I was perceived as the enemy. Needless to say, that was the first and last meeting I attended. Another division among these two groups relies not just on language differences but also on social standing. Those born in Mexico perceive those born in the United States as "fake Mexicans." It's unfortunate that these divisions are a part of growing up as a Mexican American, because they are what make me feel as if I don't belong in the United States or in Mexico. I remember being in Mexico on vacation when I was about 10 and overhearing some ladies refer to me as "the one from the other side." I know that I was born in the United States, but I also know that my roots lie in Mexico. Knowing that my own raza, my own people, do not want me in Mexico or America makes it difficult for me to feel accepted and wanted.*
>
> *Some Mexican Americans consider members of their own group sellouts if they speak English better than Spanish. They believe that those who are not in touch with their Mexican heritage and do not identify with the struggles they may have experienced are not legitimate. I know I have experienced this prejudice.*

Rosa clearly demonstrates the powerful complexities that individuals have to negotiate inside an ethnic category such as Mexican American to feel that they belong. Her identity shifts repeatedly in response to her social context. Rather than seeing her as unfortunately abnormal, we would contend that her experience of multiple reference points is far more normal than dominant discourse usually recognizes. The sad thing is that, rather than feeling valued for her flexible multiplicity, she feels she is required by this discourse to establish singular "roots."

Tristan's story provides some very interesting insights into the nature of identity construction within changing contextual boundaries. Tristan's first public identity was declared in her mostly White elementary school: she was surfer girl. She took after her mother, who wiped "Browns rule" (meaning Latinos) off the blackboard and replaced it with "Surfers rule." She described her parents as a cute beach couple who embraced the surfing lifestyle. When she entered high school, her identity took on a dramatic revision. She transitioned from a predominantly White part of town to a high school that had a large Mexican American population. This was the early 1990s, when rap and hip-hop were becoming popular. This was also a time when gangs and cliques were the thing to be part of. To identify as a gangster was perceived as trendy. Tristan remembers wanting to be part of a gang so badly, but she knew that Mexican students would not allow White people to identify as gangsters. She says her Mexican peers looked down on White people who tried to act like members of another race. However, as time went by, she spent more time with her Mexican peers. She changed her style of clothing and her makeup and started hanging around with students who identified as gangsters. This led to her long-standing White friends turning against her and terminating their friendship. Her mom took notice of her changes and disapproved of this new direction. Tristan began to live an identity that her mother completely despised. Now Tristan was projecting a gangster image that her Mexican friends were beginning to accept. Tristan also became successful in developing an understanding of and adaptation to the expressions of Mexican American culture in her community. She would spend endless amounts of time at her best friend's house, where they would participate in quinceañeras, baptisms, and other important rituals shared by the Mexican American communities. Because of her brown hair and eyes and the people she spent time with more and more, people assumed she was half Mexican and half White. She began to confirm to others that she did have this ethnic heritage. She now began to hide her association with her family. She began to identify so strongly as Mexican American that she no longer felt White. Her dialect, accent, and tone mimicked the tonality of Mexican Americans who speak English as a second language. Her behavioral mannerisms, style of dress, and musical interests were a perfect fit for an Anglo-Mexican American.

Tristan says that since starting college, she has "grown out of that gangster stage." Yet today, as she is in her early 20s, the majority of her friends are still Mexican, as are the men she dates. She keeps her Mexican identity intact. In her workplace, people still consistently speak to her in Spanish or ask, "Aren't you Mexican?" When she replies that she doesn't speak Spanish, Mexican Americans seem to get very upset and ask her why her parents didn't teach her. On the other hand, when White people meet her for the first time and notice her Mexican English accent, they scathingly reject her White identity through their looks and comments.

Tristan's story raises some interesting implications for identity politics. Haider (2018) discusses the case of Rachel Dolezal, an instructor in African American Studies at Eastern Washington University who turns out was a White woman who was passing for Black. This discovery provoked considerable outrage across multiple communities. Despite the scandal this created, she held fast to the notion that she identified Black. Haider suggests passing is a universal condition and suggests that identity is a construction that sometimes brings people together around notions of race and skin color but hides the realities of real class differences in these identity constructions. In his book, *Mistaken Identity*, Haider laments how class is usually marginalized in identity politics, and thus the shared needs of the poor and low-income earners are made invisible in divided racial categorizations. Identity politics formed around race undermine the formation of a collective voice of the underclass to mobilize against the neoliberal and capitalist machine. He points out there are wide variations of privilege occurring within heavily policed racial identity groupings. If people were to check their privilege in racial groupings around their class variation within identity politics, many will be unmasked. He says, "No wonder we are so deeply disturbed by passing—it reveals too much to us about identity; it is the dirty secret of the equation of identity with politics" (p. 81).

Rather than privileging or emphasizing the understanding of people as singular identities, we find it preferable to view the person in terms of complex relational processes manifesting themselves in context and at the site of the individual body. It requires work, however, to shake off some of the individualistic assumptions. We find the term *relational selves* useful in describing the complexity of human identity. We can view the "I" not as a single entity, although it can be portrayed as a singular point from which to view the world, but rather as a product of history that has evolved from institutions and traditions. From this standpoint, the self as a speaking voice is not an individual voice at all but a voice that has been shaped by collective and cultural experiences, carrying the collective stories that people tell one another. These voices carry cultural traditions over hundreds of years. Thus, it becomes critically important to trace relationships within the context of cultural histories to understand how contemporary identities are formed.

Numerous writers have spoken about multiple selves. For instance, Jeffrey Escoffier (1991) referred to overlapping identities. He stressed that the self is often simultaneously connected to a number of different identity discourses and resides within overlapping identities. Kenneth Gergen (2007) described the self as "saturated" with multiple identities. Similarly, John Shotter (1990) stated that "although the postmodern self may be something of a mosaic, no self is completely an island. In postmodern everyday life, as well as in postmodern science, one occupies a multiplicity of standpoints" (p. 19). Maria Root (2003; cited by McGoldrick, Giordano, & Garcia-Preto, 2005, p. 8) proposed a creative challenge to the tendency of people to categorize others in simplistic unitary forms. She was concerned about how many people have a need to categorize others and themselves in uniform boxes, such as one specific ethnicity, religion, or sexual orientation. Root proposed a bill of rights for people who identify themselves as belonging to multiple categories. Her bill of rights seeks to give people permission to not identify as strangers expect them to. She invites people to identify themselves differently in different situations, rather than having to subscribe to a particular category. This approach goes to the heart of building the bridge across the Us and Them divide. People can identify themselves differently from family members, if this better describes their lived identity. She encourages us to recognize loyalties to more than one group and to develop new vocabularies to help communicate about multiple identities; this requires intercultural sensitivities whereby nuanced differences in the articulations of our identities are discovered, acknowledged, sustained, and respected in our everyday interactions.

Border Identities

Any definition of a cultural group establishes a boundary beyond which a person is not considered a member of that group. The more elaborate the definition, the more sharply defined the border will be. At the same time, however, the more we define the border between one identity and another, the more likely we are to find individuals who do not fit our definition, or people who either straddle the border or live very close to it. The term "border identities" (Rosaldo, 1993) was developed to describe these experiences. Tightly defining culture may even define the borders in ways that exclude people from cultural belonging. Their experience of life does not count as the "real" experience of being Black or Native American, if the experience of those deemed to be at the center is used as the sole reference point for what is true. For example, many African Americans struggle with feeling that they are not being "Black enough" or are accused of "acting White" and feel they have to prove to other

African Americans that they truly belong. In these circumstances, particular ideas about culture are functioning in ways that create divisions between people who share common cultural histories. Such divisions are often then policed by those who identify closer to the center of the relevant definition. Sometimes people are pitied or treated as almost abnormal if they owe allegiance to more than one cultural group. In identity terms, they are often invited to make a choice and to adopt one cultural position as their true identity.

If these postmodern critiques have disturbed the comfortable assumptions about culture that have become commonplace, then they are gradually giving way to a new view of culture that is more fluid and less essentializing. Rather than stressing the homogeneity of a people, the postmodern concept of culture has become pluralistic or "polyphonic" (Geertz, 1995, p. 48). Most of us are familiar with how people borrow from different cultural traditions and cannot be defined within one cultural box. We also see that they discard cultural practices when they no longer fit (Narayan, 2000; Yon, 2000).

We would like to emphasize the value of speaking in terms of cultural narratives that run through people's lives, rather than thinking of people as identified in a one-to-one correspondence with a particular cultural identity. Renato Rosaldo (1994) suggests thinking of one's life as an intersection through which cultural narratives are always traveling like vehicles. Kwame Appiah (2005) argues for thinking of identity in terms of a "narrative arc" (p. 23). Seyla Benhabib (2002) suggests that the nature of a culture exists much more in the accounts we give of it, that is, in our interpretations, than in a simple observable reality. Lisa Tsoi Hoshmand (2005) notices how in cultural psychology the concept of narrative has taken on the character of a root metaphor. Critical race theorists, such as Derrick Bell (2000), also argue for the use of narratives to uncover the modern workings of racism. And Edward Said (1978, 1994) suggests that we are always required to take account of the narratives that other people from other cultural backgrounds tell about our People. As a result, the actual lives that people lead are much more fragmented than simplistic uniform accounts of cultural coherence can admit.

Social constructionism enables us at times to ask questions about movements for cultural preservation that would be forbidden by an essentialist perspective. From a constructionist view, such movements appear advantageous to certain people in the power relations among groups within a cultural context. Sometimes it is certain persons' positions of power that are being preserved, rather than the cultural advantages for all cultural members. For example, dominant groups within a culture may seek to preserve selected cultural elements to preserve their own cultural power. Indian feminist Uma Narayan (2000) calls this the process of "selective labeling" of "essential" cultural norms. It ignores, she argues, the ways in which cultural groups have frequently discarded cultural practices in response to changing circumstances.

Essentialist thinking invites people to judge each other's cultural worthiness in relation to established essential norms. You may have heard or even been caught up in arguments about who is a real Native American, who has an authentic right to speak for African Americans and who does not, who is more oppressed than someone else on the basis of cultural membership, who is betraying the essential cause of feminism and who is not. Such arguments can never be resolved. The danger is that they fragment people more than create understanding. Polarization is frequently a direct outcome of such essentialist assumptions. The problem lies in the very idea of seeking to establish a "natural" basis for claims of cultural authenticity, which sets up needless competition for the right to speak and works against a more inclusive and complex approach to the diversity of experience. An important danger of essentialist thinking is that it invites a polarizing stance and tempts people to judge the worthiness of others' experiences, including their experiences of discrimination and oppression. What can result from these kinds of essentialist encounters is that particular voices are not recognized as valid, or as having a right to speak. The conversation then quickly deteriorates and groups retreat without any additional understanding.

A therapeutic process must honor the integrity of the different interconnected cultural contexts within which people's multifaceted ways of being are expressed; this is, in complex, changing, and often contradictory patterns of power relations. As we suggested in Chapter 1, doing otherwise may compromise our humanity. Furthermore, our identities are not fixed or essential, although they are grounded in our lived experience and so are not free floating. Our identities are produced by our physical location, generation, gender, religion, class, status, and numerous other factors. They are products of culturally mediated interpretations arising within dominant, systemic, and continuous social orders woven together in a series of historical, contextual, and dialogic maneuvers within a community (McNamee & Gergen, 1999). From an intercultural perspective, the power differentials that divide humanity in Us and Them categories are problematized so as to find alternatives to connect and work together by recognizing the contextual and fluid nature of our identities. We have laid out in earlier chapters the importance of understanding the contextual and historical influences from which specific cultural identities are formed. Granting significance to the social contexts we inhabit and their impact on the shaping of identity contrasts starkly with individualistic theories and context-independent analyses of the self and relationships.

Language and Identity

Since our ways of understanding the world do not come directly from an objective reality but from cultural, historical, social, political, and relational realities, the role of language becomes pivotal in the production of our concepts and categories. Language is significantly more important in shaping human life and identity than traditional psychology has believed. From a social constructionist perspective, language is more than simply a medium in which we express ourselves. Traditional psychology looks for explanations and understandings inside persons and labels them attitudes, motivations, cognitions, and affective states. When people talk about their personality, they tend to assume that the dimensions of the self exist prior to and separately from the words used to describe them. Language is assumed to serve a representational function to give expression to things that already exist in themselves (Burr, 2003; Davies, 1993; Lather, 1992). Language is regarded as a bundle of labels from which we can choose to describe our internal states. From a constructionist perspective, however, language structures our experience of ourselves in the world and produces the meanings and concepts that make us up.

Rieko, a Japanese school counselor, illustrates this point well as she reflects on her experiences of living in Japan and in the United States.

> When I am speaking in Japanese, I need to speak in a very polite way. I feel very constrained. When I speak English, I feel independent. It reminds me that I have a voice and am allowed to express my opinion and assert myself. In the United States, I feel very confident. I can say what I want to say. I express my ideas and beliefs. I feel that people listen

to me and they don't judge me. They seem to appreciate my contributions. It feels to me that English provides more of a level playing field. The Japanese language is more hierarchical, and as a young woman, in order for me to be respectful in Japan, I must present myself as submissive and quiet. I cannot be as direct, as straight talking. This is particularly the case when I am working in my school and am addressing the principal or senior managers in the school. The language itself directs me into a submissive way of relating. I want to speak in English with my students so I that I can feel independent and self-assured.

Built into the structure of some language forms are social hierarchies that give clear directives to language users about what is allowed to be expressed within the culture. In Japanese cultural communities, it is typical of younger people to convey deference to older people. The language register gives explicit instructions in how to converse across the generations. Rieko was re-confronted with the power of these language hierarchies on returning to Japan. Her experience demonstrates how the Japanese language permits one kind of identity to be lived and expressed. In different social and linguistic contexts, she is permitted different kinds of identity.

Significant shifts of identity occur for most people when they migrate from one country to another and from one language world to another. Members of the family who are not taught the native language of their migrating parents experience profound changes in their identity and in how they make sense of who they are and where they belong.

Nimo is a therapist in a high school working with a very ethnically diverse population. She is also a practicing Muslim, prays five time a day, wears a Hijab, and does not eat pork. Nimo's family fled from civil war in Somalia in the Ogaden region when she was a small child. Her relatives were merchants and camel herders. In the small villages and towns she lived in as a child she could move about without immediate parental oversight. She was living in communal villages where the neighbors all looked out for the children and oversaw their conduct and behavior. By the time she was 8 years old, she spoke four languages of the region, but was not introduced to English until her family flew from Ethiopia to San Diego when she was 10.

Nimo's family had not owned a refrigerator before, so learning in the United States how to refrigerate food and how to not have to buy food from the market everyday was an example of how strange everything was in this big city. Nimo's mother was illiterate but asserted strong authority in the household to support Nimo and her siblings so they would be successful in school. Her dad was yet to migrate from their homeland.

In the United States, Nimo's mother was worried about Nimo losing faith, losing her modesty, and getting caught up with drugs and alcohol and becoming Americanized. Americanized meant talking back to your elders, not being obedient, and pushing for independence. Nimo was having to navigate living two lives. At home she was required to follow the rules of the household. Here she had very little independence and her mother closely monitored the activities Nimo would get involved with because she feared Nimo would lose her way and make terrible choices.

Outside of the home, even by 11 years of age, Nimo was pretty adventurous and wanted to do what her schoolmates were doing—going on field trips, being a spectator at sporting events, swimming at the beach, and going fishing. Her mother's worst fear was Nimo would become rebellious in her teenage years. Now Nimo as a teenager was wanting to do high school, teenage things—see movies, want independence, make new life choices, explore her identity, see "who I am and what fits for me." She entered a teenage, White, adolescent world and was living vicariously through middle-class, White teen adventure novels. In her family she felt like the black sheep as she was exploring realms of life that were foreign to her parents.

She began to watch Oprah on television every week day at 4pm and soaked up all that occurred on Oprah's show. Nimo said, "Oprah raised me." She began to identify with other powerful Black women in the media who had come from nothing, and followed the aspirations these entertainers portrayed in social media. During her adolescence, Nimo was expanding her multiple identities, learning how to live well in her deeply religious home life and be a curious and adventurous young woman experimenting with speaking up and being independent outside of the home.

Today Nimo fully embraces her immigrant identity, Black identity, and Muslim identity, and describes how valuable they are in living her life in the United States as well finding multiple ways to connect with her ethnically and religiously diverse clients. Nimo, in her work context, is part of an outgroup and had the same experience in college as one of a small handful of African Muslim women. At her university her identities were often invisible to other students and her cultures were either unrepresented or vilified within the university as a whole. From that vantage point, Nimo can see clearly the macro- and microlevel aggressions against people of an outgroup, especially during a period like today with growing religious bigotry against Muslims and the demonstration of a new, more emboldened racism in the United States. These experiences of oppression have provided her with strong resources, so as a therapist she is keenly tuned into the needs of her clients, who are navigating culturally different landscapes like she was required to in her teenage years, and is still required to today.

Abbie captures the complexity of identity construction played out by millions of people who, as a result of migration, speak a different language from their parents.

> I do not speak Tagalog, and language is a vital part of Filipino identity. Since I was born, I have been taught to speak English. My father had to endure an American boot camp with no grasp of the English language. He could curse you in English before he could ask where the restrooms were, and once he did learn English, there was nothing he could do to erase the accent he spoke it with. He wanted to spare his children the inferiority he felt when he spoke English. Among my cousins, my sisters and I sound perfectly American, look purely Filipino, and we are the outsiders. I do not speak the language and hence I always feel alienated from other Filipinos.
>
> I do not speak Tagalog, the language of my family, and I have no desire to live outside the United States. I'm slowly gaining independence and learning that, while my family is important, I must also take care of my own needs and wants. In these respects, I am very American. I tried variations of naming what I am to include my American citizenship: Filipino-American with the hyphen, without the hyphen, American citizen who is Filipino. I feel that I am quite simply Filipino American. When I'm with my Tagalog-speaking aunts and uncles, I feel as if I'm an outsider even more keenly than I do in a room full of White people. I become subdued and try to melt into the walls, cloaking myself in invisibility. I wonder why I feel such a profound change in how I feel about myself when I am with my Filipino extended family. Despite incredible feelings of discomfort at times like

this, I still embrace a Filipino identity. In fact, in many ways, how I perceive the world is filtered through that identity. However, things are still not that straightforward. Being in a relationship with an Anglo American has been an interesting experience and impacts how I express myself when I am with him and when I am with my family. That's not to say I change who I am. I just become more overt in certain respects when I am with different people. When I am with my family, we are very vocal, loud, and energetic. I also become much more sensitive to family obligation when I am around them. Some of the main stereotypes that people have about Filipinos are that they are loud and codependent on their families. My friends and my Anglo American husband believe that I am simply an American who happens to have a Filipino background. However, there are certain values and perceptions that I hold that are a result of my being Filipino. A primary example is that I will always be family oriented and I will always emphasize the importance of education.

Because of the changing face of our cultural communities and the elasticity or reconstruction of ethnic membership in the 21st century, there are fewer and fewer familial models and mentors that can help individuals negotiate the kind of person they will be and how they will identify. Historical familial models and ancestral cultural practices are increasingly merging into the background. Abbie comments on the reality of this social process.

Being an American woman is a valued identity for me, which has been problematic for my parents in that I have lived my life according to ideals that are not acceptable in a Filipino Catholic culture. I value the independence that is the cornerstone of American culture and which is denounced in Filipino culture. I value the roles of a female insofar as there should be no traditional roles of a female and that the value of a female is more than just in the preservation of her virginity and in her utility as a housewife and mother. To this day, the fact that I have lived my life a certain way has been a source of conflict between my parents and me. It took a long time before I was able to learn that their approval will not be enough to make me happy if I have to compromise my own self-will, and I would have no one to blame but myself if I did not exert any independence.

My sisters are able to see me and understand that the way my parents live their lives does not necessarily mean that their lives have to be lived in that same manner in order for them to obtain happiness and success. They are slowly becoming able to exert their independence and learning to make moral choices for themselves without having to accept what my parents tell them. I think that they value me as a role model of someone who is able to be independent and still value my family as a Filipino. I think that my independence as a woman is of value to my husband, because I am able to take care of myself and to take care of my needs without being dependent on him for complete support. With the multiplicity of ways that people view themselves and how that changes over time, I feel that it is important to take how they see themselves at the present moment into context. I think that it is difficult for people to really think about how they identify themselves, ethnically, racially, gender wise, and so forth, and to think about what that identity means to them is also a challenge.

As ethnic categories change, individuals look increasingly to the mentors and models from their peer group or from cultural sources portrayed in social media for guidance to help them negotiate how to define themselves. Influencers on YouTube, Tumblr, reality TV shows, soap operas, self-help programs, daytime talks shows, Instagram stories, sports stars, music artists, television and movie stars, and communications via Snapchat or the new modes of communication via the Internet all provide cultural material that young people (sometimes unknowingly) model themselves after. At no other time in recorded history have there been so many choices of identities for people to engage with and perform in their day-to-day lives.

Counseling Implications of Pathologizing and the Challenges for Holding on to Multiple Expressions of Identity

Personality theory suggests that human beings are born with a central, observable core and hold a set of character traits that are set early in life. Therapists influenced by this fixed account of human personality may be constrained in their efforts to support clients because they believe that nothing can be done to change the core. Common notions of a singular and immutable personality can keep counselors from understanding the complexity of human identity and its multiple facets. Many personality-related disorders in the *DSM* are examples of problems assumed to be characterological and thus unresponsive to therapeutic efforts.

Curiosity in therapeutic practice can become a casualty of the notion that people have only single-dimension personality traits. Once a personality is discovered or tested for, the therapist can believe that this is who a person is. Personality diagnosis draws attention away from the complexity, ambiguity, and dynamic nature of human functioning. Nowhere is this kind of understanding of human beings more prevalent than in the mental health field.

Historically, people who have struggled with severe mental illness have been classified by these singular notions of identity. They have a broken core set of character traits. This has been driven by the predominance of modernistic thought in the mental health field that has relied on characterizations of persons along the reductionist lines of mental diagnoses. Following widely embraced scientific principles in the West, one could view the labelling of illness as an invitation to hopefulness and effective treatment. Certainly there is strong evidence that contemporary medical approaches to addressing mental health issues are vastly superior than the dark periods of treatment when people were treated by blood-letting, Trephination (cutting out a piece of the skull), given lobotomies, or provided with exorcisms. There is no doubt that medications in some instances have provided great relief to people who are struggling with some mental health disturbance and that certain categorizations of symptoms have helped mental health professionals target particular troublesome symptoms. There is much to be said for the contributions of science and mental health treatment in improving the mental health and well-being of patients and their families. However, this section of the chapter is not dedicated to the contributions of Western mental health. Rather, what we want to draw attention to is how the proliferation of mental illness categories and the diagnosis and treatments associated with these initiatives have become diminishing of people's identities and disrupting of their ability to live with non-pathologizing facets of their lives.

The culture that has participated in the categorization of mental illness is not purely an effort to diminish people's suffering. The practices associated with the delivery of mental health are in harmony with the economic and ideological commitments of the mental health profession and the associated operations of economic activity in the United States (Ingleby, 2004). Mental illness and diagnosis and treatment are often serving the needs of the dominant cultural groups and have had very real oppressive consequences (Kutchins & Kirk, 1997).

The mental health industry in many ways has, perhaps inadvertently, created what Gergen (1994) termed social hierarchies, community erosion, and self-enfeeblement. The mental health industry in the West has now, for more than a century, wielded an enormous amount power and authority to define what "healthy functioning" looks like, and these constructs have become infused into layperson speak (London, 1986; Margolis, 1966). Implicit in the constructs of what healthy functioning looks like is its binary opposite—those who are mentally sick. Thus, the industry of mental health services has created this demarking of individuals as mentally healthy or mentally sick across cultures. While we may have sympathy for someone battling a difficult anxiety or depression (considered in monocultural terms), it is a very easy next step to feel a sense of superiority and separateness from others who are on the other side of the binary. And for those not displaying "healthy functioning," people are set up to occupy a status of mental health failure. This dynamic sets up a proliferation of harmful hierarchies. "We" are normal, successful, and good and "they" are sick, bad, and a failure.

The creation of categories of mental illness has become a growing menu of global human deficit descriptions that have expanded our vocabulary to pathologize others and their identities, regardless of the particularities of culture, and contributed to what Gergen calls a universal culture of "self-enfeeblement." Gergen (1994) puts it like this:

> Mental deficit [informs] the recipient that "the problem" is not circumscribed or limited in time and space or to a particular domain. [The person] carries the deficit from one situation to another, and like a birthmark or a fingerprint, as the textbooks say, the deficit will inevitably manifest itself. (p. 150–151)

The history of mental deficit language is driven by the mental health profession. The language has been technologized across the globe such that everyday language of one culture that could mean being "really sad" or "really unhappy" is reinterpreted by the monocultural mental health industry as a mental health deficit. Interculturality is therefore at stake by the universalization of articulations of experience by single professional terms. As Gergen (1994), expresses so well,

> The professional now lays claim to knowledge that was once in the common realm. The professional becomes the arbiter of what is rational, irrational, intelligent or ignorant, natural or unnatural. … The layperson is disqualified as a knower. As a consequence, one's normal sense of self as possessing knowledge, insight, and sensitivity is undermined. In effect, those most intimately acquainted with the "problem" must give way to the dispassionate and delimited voices of an alien authority. (p. 152)

The first attempts to categorize mental illness categories in the United States was in 1840. The categories started out as quite crude. Spitzer and Williams (1985) described two categories of mental ill health of this period—idiotic or insane. The history of mental illness categorization is replete with systematic and ongoing bias against White women and women of color as well as minoritized groups. We discussed in Chapter 7 the gender bias contained in mental health categorizations.

Cartwright (1851, cited Kutchins & Kirk, 1997), a supporter of slavery in the deep South, published an article in the prestigious *New Orleans Medical and Surgical Journal* in which he recommended medical advice on how to treat Negros who were mentally ill. He described the outrageous phenomenon of Drapetomania, a disorder peculiar to African slaves in the USA. The mental health disorder manifested itself when a slave exhibited the desire to escape from slavery. His medical advice explained that the cause of wanting to run away was a disease of the mind. The treatment to address the mental health disorder of Drapetomania was for no apparent cause the slave owner should whip "the devil out of them" as a preventive measure until they entered a submissive state (Kutchins & Kirk, 1997, p. 210).

By 1938 there were 40 categories of mental illness. In 1952, the American Psychiatric Association published its first *Diagnostic and Statistical Manual of Mental Disorders* (*DSM*) had listed 128 mental illness categories. Twenty years later the *DSM* had gone through three revisions and now there were 253 recognizable categories. In 2013, with the publication of the *DSM-V*, there are currently 541 categories (Blashfield, Keeley, Flanagan, & Miles, 2014). Once the momentum of deficit language has been expanded, the industry that drives it propels the mental illness field forward. The result is what Gergen (1994) describes as "hierarchies of discrimination, denaturalised patterns of interdependence, and an expanded arena of self-deprecation. The historical process may be viewed as one of progressive infirmity" (p. 155).

Even though the new *Diagnostic and Statistical Manuals* attempt to invite the practitioner conducting the diagnosis to pay attention to social context, the overwhelming thrust of mental categorization disseminated across cultures focuses attention on the individual, dislocated from the sociopolitical and sociocultural factors that negatively affect people's well-being.

Tomm (2014), in his book *Patterns in Interpersonal Interactions: Inviting Relational Understandings for Therapeutic Change*, makes an effort to move away from the pathologizing of individuals and provide tools for mental health professionals to review relational dynamics and build a relationally focused practice that builds bridges for people struggling with mental health challenges, so that difficult disturbances for individuals are located in a wider framework. Relational dynamics are tracked for both identifying problematic patterns of relating as well as identifying relational patterns of resilience. The thrust of the work is to move away from an individualized, deficit-based practice altogether, towards what Gergen (1994) describes as relational intelligibilities.

In the United States, in the last few decades, patients' rights groups invoking civil rights laws in the country energized people who were previously pathologized by the mental health system. Survivors of the mental health system were inspired by the actions of African Americans, White women and women of color, and the gay-lesbian communities to take action to disrupt the traditional model of mental health service delivery and the passive positioning offered to people experiencing what in mainstream psychiatric practice was a severe mental illness (Monk & Hancock, 2015). Psychiatry especially has historically promoted practices where the patient is patronized by expectations of "good behavior," compliance, somebody who follows the rules, takes their meds, and doesn't complain. The compliant patient is usually viewed as permanently disabled, needing to adhere to treatment advice, and to accept their dependency on services. These actions by mental health professionals have promoted disability rather than the prospect of returning to a full life. Zinman (1987) stated, "We are like colonized people, struggling to be free, to reclaim from psychiatry ownership of our lives (p. 7). Survivors started to challenge these attitudes and behaviors, supported a vision of "recovery is possible," and helped build a recovery-oriented system. Shared decision-making between healthcare professionals and the consumer was promoted, and self-directed care was encouraged (Ostrow & Adams, 2012). Never before on such a scale has this recovery movement, led by the survivors of the system, had such a profound influence on the delivery of mental health practice. In effect, survivors of the psychiatric system have been reclaiming their lives back from being "them-ified" to becoming a collective "we." Sarah's story is illustrative of many people being "them-ified" by the deficit-based system of mental healthcare delivery and then winning their lives back through finding community through the peer recovery process.

> *For 12 years I (Sarah) surrounded myself with key mental health practitioners. I followed their guidelines, took the medication necessary as prescribed, dutifully went to all my counseling appointments and group sessions. I worked with many well-intentioned, competent, well-educated and highly skilled mental health practitioners. The missing link between well-intentioned professionals and my life was the absence of hope. It wasn't until I met my first peer support person who had experienced similar challenges to myself that I even knew that living successfully with my mental health challenges was even possible. My doctors and counselors told me real recovery wasn't possible and that my life would continue on the same course for the rest of my life. I resigned myself to their prognosis. In my mind there wasn't really any reason to fight it, it was inevitable, I could see it happening around me. It didn't seem to matter what medication I took, or how*

> *hard I worked at following treatment plans, I just did not feel there was hope. A doctor told me schizophrenia is degenerative, like MS, but with the mind. I was already so bad off, I couldn't imagine it getting worse. When I met my first my peer support person I was so surprised to hear her personal story and her struggles. She taught me what she knew which altered the course of her life. She taught me to run the race as a survivor, not a victim. She taught me to hope. If she could see me now, she'd feel as proud of me. I graduated with my Master's, became a Certified Rehabilitation Counselor, university lecturer, and now share my recovery journey with university students, professionals, and my Emotional Self-Reliance podcast audience.*

FIGURE 8.2   Sarah

Remaining curious about the complexity of individual lives presents counselors with many more therapeutic possibilities with which to respond. Clients who are diagnosed with personality disorders seldom receive resources from health insurance providers, because it is believed that a dysfunctional personality pattern is not susceptible to change. There are still widely held beliefs in the field of psychiatry that people with severe mental illness are destined to live their lives being governed by their diagnosis and prognosis of ongoing ill health. Yet many of us know of individuals, perhaps including ourselves, who have made profound changes in the way they live their lives. Sarah is one inspiring example of someone reclaiming her life and living beyond mental illness categorizations. People who were formally perceived as paranoid may have become more trusting in their relationships. People who were written off as having an antisocial personality can become more respectful and considerate of others. Individuals perceived as avoidant or dependent may in some situations exhibit more confidence and social skill. Descriptions of personality type are usually located within individualistic traditions of psychiatry and psychology, and they are argued to be independent of culture and context. But there are counseling models that are more responsive to complex and multiple identities. Much of psychology, psychiatry, and counseling is focused on the individual as the unit of analysis. This orientation is in alignment with many other modernist practices in the West and follows our attraction to the exploration of human phenomena from deductive and reductionist protocols. What it doesn't allow for is the profound influence that human systems have in shaping human behavior. Historically, the *DSM* invites us to look primarily at what is taking place within the individual rather than between people, regardless of culture. While there have been efforts in the *DSM-V* to include much more context data, the *DSM* is still essentially an instrument that privileges individualistic constructions of life from the lens of a single, Eurocentric culture. As therapists use the *DSM*, they can be drawn away from an appreciation of the relational, systemic, and societal factors in human functioning. In other words, the *DSM* frequently makes intercultural counseling more difficult given that the unique differences whereby suffering is expressed across various communities are ironed out. The journalist Ethan Watters (2010), in his book *Crazy Like Us: The Globalization of the American Psyche*, provides a very good illustration of the intercultural cost of the single adoption of psychiatric terms across cultures to describe locals' experiences of suffering and healing. After traveling through Hong Kong, Zanzibar, Sri Lanka, and Japan, he wrote:

> Over the past thirty years, we Americans [*sic*] have been industriously exporting our ideas about mental illness. Our definitions and treatment have become the international standards. Although this has often been done with the best of intentions, we've failed to foresee the full [intercultural] impact of these efforts. It turns out that how people in a culture think about mental illnesses—how they categorize and prioritize the symptoms, attempt to heal them, and set expectations for their course and outcome—influences the diseases themselves. In teaching the rest of the world to think like us, we have been, for better and worse, homogenizing the way the world goes mad. (p. 2)

Our thrust, by contrast, is to take a serious and careful look at the cultural contexts of our good intentions and professional assumptions by placing greater emphasis on the wider systemic and societal influences that shape identity construction. While we acknowledge that the advances of psychiatry have added significant contributions, we are also careful not to over emphasize such monocultural social constructions as the only alternative by which to understand identity. Other intercultural knowledges must also be considered to counteract homogenous patterns of interaction that put at stake people's rights to relational being. We are conscious that this emphasis renders problematic many counseling theories that center on the individual and treat contextual factors as relevant but peripheral. We don't believe that simply recognizing multiculturalism as a lens through which to understand diverse identities is good enough. Our intercultural theoretical orientation pays close attention to the homogenizing systems of power that compromise our rights of being. In addition, we can be open and curious to explore the interconnectedness across cultures, from where we learn about our identities in contrast to the identities of others. This means that it is not sufficient to understand that a client may have different ways to situate their identity within their own intersecting cultures according to gender, class, body ability, mental health ability, religion, ethnicity, and so on; it is also critically important to inquire and learn about the tangible implications of such differences in their everyday lived experience. For example, as the stories of Nimo, Abbie, and Rosa above illustrated, the identities of Somalis, Filipinxs, and Mexicans are unique to the intercultural complexities of their families and their histories of migration to the United States. An intercultural lens renders visible the contrasting descriptions of people's stories about their identities, and the monocultural conceptualization of personality theory. From this intercultural perspective, identity construction could therefore be characterized in plural terms—as identities—and "outside in" rather than "inside out."

From the stories of people who have described their lives in this chapter, it is clear to us that a person's identity remains always in constant revision. There is no point one can reach in life where one can say, "My identity is set." New contextual factors across cultures will always emerge and invite us to reconfigure ourselves. Our response may be to fall back on old habits or to find the wider contextual factors so compelling that we don't have a choice but to make a new response.

At the same time, we are bombarded with many cultural prescriptions that invite us to figure out who we "really" are. People call for therapy to help them be made whole. Some therapeutic models suggest that it is healthy for people to integrate their lives and eradicate ambiguity. We would suggest that our lives are so complex that integration and wholeness need to be abandoned as therapeutic goals. It is surely impossible to not respond to compelling stimuli in contradictory ways. A more helpful therapeutic response would be to embrace multiplicity and to normalize the experience for those who are troubled by their multiple identities. From our perspective, it is pivotal to recognize that the boundaries surrounding ethnic membership are in a state of flux. There are no static cultural practices that straightforwardly guide people's life paths. All cultural patterns of life are constantly in a state of revision, reconstruction, or even upheaval because of the globalizing and nationalizing trends circulating the planet. Cultural groups cannot be treated as if they were museum pieces frozen in time. People everywhere have to respond to the complex and contradictory intercultural forces that run through their lives, whether they want to or not. Everyone has to choose how to proceed. Awareness of these processes of flux and change, fluidity and complexity, will better equip counselors to work in our multicultural world.

Discuss

1. In what contexts have you experienced challenges to cultural messages you received from your family?
2. In what ways are your own practices different from your parents'? Can you identify the cultural influences that you drew from to make these changes?
3. Can you identify contradictions within your thinking, your experience, your story of who you are?
4. Share stories of situations in which you have been pulled in two (or more) different directions by competing ideas or messages from others. What was that like? Analyze the cultural forces at work in producing these competing ideas.
5. Find examples in the counseling literature of statements that assume the existence of a singular self.
6. Watch a videotape of a counseling session and look for evidence of the counselor's belief in a singular self or in a multiple identity.
7. What are the advantages of thinking about identity as being produced by multiple stories? Are there disadvantages?

Response to Chapter 8

LEAH BREW, PHD

Leah Brew is a licensed professional clinical counselor, a certified clinical mental health counselor, and a nationally certified counselor. She is professor and chair in the Department of Counseling at California State University, Fullerton. Her primary area of research, writing, and teaching is focused on issues of diversity with an emphasis on multiracial identity and intercultural relationships. She co-authored the section on interracial couples for the ACA-endorsed competencies: Competencies for Counseling Multiple Heritage (or Multiracial) Individuals, Multiple Heritage (or Interracial or Multiracial) Families and Couples, and Trans-Racial Adoptive Individuals and Families.

My identity has most definitely been transformed. I remember being without any sense of self or definition; I just was, without self-consciousness. Then, I defined myself according to various cultural affiliations that changed based on my growing knowledge. And I am now returning to an identity-less way of existing, but in a transcended way.

In the third grade, my family moved me to a small town in the South, and other children began to make fun of me because I looked different. They taunted me for being Chinese. I didn't know what this meant, but I was sure it must be bad. I went home and asked my mother if I was Chinese, and to my great relief, she informed me that I was not; I was Japanese. And so I went to school prepared to defend myself. I still didn't know at all what this meant, but I assumed it must be better than Chinese. The kids continued to taunt me. I tirelessly worked to understand what was wrong with being Japanese. Eventually, I recognized through their teasing that my eyes were my downfall; they were small, not large and open like the other kids'. I despised my eyes and would practice making them larger, but to no avail. Thus was the birth of my identity. I defined myself according to this ethnic heritage. That is, until I went to Japan. I quickly recognized that I wasn't Japanese at all. I was much larger, since my father is American (U.S.). I couldn't use chopsticks. I didn't eat fish for breakfast. And, most prominent, I couldn't speak the language. I made many cultural mistakes. I felt lost, without an identity.

In high school, I remember asking my friends if they ever questioned who they were. They looked at me confusedly and had no idea what I was talking about. I felt crazy and weird. I felt certain that something was wrong with me. What I didn't realize then is that they were all part of the dominant culture (White and Christian); I was not. They were fine with their identity.

In college, I met other non-Whites and defined myself as non-White. I also met my ex-husband, who was Thai, and then we defined ourselves as Asian American. I still felt lost, though, because his Thai family was certainly different from the way I was raised. We may both be Asian, but we were no more similar to each other than we were to our White friends. It was only in my culture class as I worked toward my Master's degree in counseling that I began to understand race, ethnicity, and their differences, and began moving through my own identity development.

After completing my degree, I moved to California. I met people from all walks of life: people from various ethnic and religious backgrounds, people with varying gender and sexual identities, even other biracial Japanese Americans. I was so excited! I was in paradise. However, after talking with other Japanese Americans, I realized that we'd had such different experiences that I didn't necessarily belong with them either. I was back to square one. Then something quite fortuitous happened to me. On a trip to Thailand, I attended a presentation on Buddhist psychology. The speaker said something profound. He said that Westerners have a need to create boundaries, boxes, or lines around everything; we are pragmatists. He said that in Thailand, those boundaries don't really exist. I was blown away! Suddenly, I had a solution to my identity problem. I didn't need an identity. That isn't to say that I don't enjoy studying cultural constructs; I do. Instead, I believe that we can transcend our boundaries of self. As a result, I now attempt to respond creatively and consciously (rather than habitually) to each moment in my life, to each person, and to each environment. I recognize how cultural constructions are created, are modified, and affect each of us personally and interpersonally. I am dynamic. I'm a composite of my biology, my interactions with others, my environment, and myriad other things that are constantly changing and impossible to pinpoint. I am like a drop of water in the ocean. How can you define where I begin and end?

Chapter 9

Gender and Sexuality

This chapter explores the impact of the cultures of gender and sexuality on shaping the identities we perform in our individual and relational lives. We consider how gender and sexuality discourses create gendered problems that in turn affect people's mental health. We review too how these cultural influences shape mental health providers' ideas about delivering mental health services when gender issues are in play. We discuss dominant cultural discourses pertaining to gender, gender binaries, intersectionality, gender essentialism, gender entitlement, gender problems, and counseling responses. Finally, we explore different mental health and counseling issues that arise for men and women, because of the way our gendered lives are structured in dominant culture. Counseling approaches are considered for bridging the Us versus Them divide.

Effects of Gender and Sexuality Discourses

Gender and sexuality discourses are among the most powerful shaping influences on people's lives and the most consequential in our engagement with others. These processes are at work as soon as the sex of the child is identified in the womb. There is no problem with the acknowledgment of gender difference, when it involves an appreciation and a valuing of the different biological functions in, for example, childbirth. What is problematic is how biological sex differences have been layered over with differential entitlements in the social world. These discourses produce robust categories that organize the performance of our identities. Counselors generally acknowledge that gender and sexuality are fundamental to the cultural context of living (Brooks & Good, 2001; Gilbert & Scher, 2009; McGoldrick & Hardy, 2019; Murray, Pope, & Willis, 2016). Together with race, ethnicity, and class, gender and sexual identities are institutionalized through the organization of complex cultural and social locations that shape every person's way of being throughout their life. Gender discourses impact human beings' thought patterns, emotions, nonverbal expressions, attractions, life expectations, career aspirations, moral reasoning, value systems, and relationship moves. While some societies are comparatively homogeneous in terms of race or class, no society can ignore gender and sexuality. Every society is founded on assumptions around gender and sexuality differences (Baruth & Manning, 2016; Kimmel & Yi, 2004; Lorber & Farrell, 1991).

Gender and Sexuality

It is helpful to draw distinctions between gender and sex, as they are often used interchangeably. The sex of a person is generally regarded as their biological makeup or chromosomal sex. Gilbert and Scher (2009) state that our sex is whether we are "born biologically female or male" (p. 3). The definition of sex, says Mukherjee (2017), is the anatomical dimensions of female versus male bodies.

This distinction seems unproblematic at first glance, as it is based upon reproductive organs. Yet even the definition of sex is strongly influenced by the binary views society has developed about gender, as some babies, described as intersex, are born with biological characteristics of both sexes (for example, testes and ovaries). In other cases, intersex children can have testes but otherwise be phenotypically female. In the bifurcated world of dominant gendered and sexual discourses, parents and the medical community feel pressure to assign children into an unambiguous sexual category. A few decades ago, many physicians would surgically construct genitalia that would clearly make the child look male or female in the earliest stage of an intersex child's life. More recently this practice has been recognized as harmful (Hird, 2008, cited in Brammer, 2012). Intersex individuals suffer in a world where dominant discourses demand the person fit within the allowable binary options.

Nearly all aspects of Western culture are organized around gender binaries. In most countries categorization of male or female is required for identification on driver's licenses, most official government or organizational documents, and applications for all kinds of purposes. In most literature discussing the differences between gender and sexuality, gender is viewed as constructed within culture and is often understood within a binary framework and as an "expression of his or her sex" (Brammer, 2012). Mukherjee (2017) states that gender is a more complex phenomenon and refers to roles an individual performs in the cultural and psychic senses. "By gender identity I mean an individual's sense of self (as female, versus male, as neither, or as something in between" (p. 356). As Pearson (1996) says, "by using 'gender' as a synonym for 'sex,' we confuse the language and perpetuate the myth that biology is destiny" (p. 329). In the 1990s, postmodern writers and postmodern feminists in particular stated that "women" and "men" are not simple, unproblematic, self-evident gender categories, as the ascriptions "male" and "female" have deep social meanings (Butler, 1992; Davies, 1993; Enns, 1993; Flax, 1990, 1992; Gavey, 1996; Haraway, 1990; Hare-Mustin & Marecek, 1994; Jones & Guy, 1992; Larner, 1995; Mouffe, 1992). Furthermore, there has been insufficient evidence to suggest that either women or men can be categorized into meaningful social groups on the basis of biology alone. As Brammer (2012) argues, explaining gender through a biological lens only captures a small element of who we are. Today, man and woman are inadequate gender descriptions to capture the human lived experience, and the language used to describe sexual and gender expression is constantly changing, often created and disseminated through online forums or blog spaces. As this book goes to press, new gender expression pronouns are being constructed.

Many young people in Western communities around the globe are challenging the gender binaries and choosing different forms of gender expression that do not conform to the typical "she" for woman or "he" for man, and instead adopt alternative, gender-neutral pronouns such as ze/zir/zir or they/them/their. Changing pronouns aligns with a nonbinary expression of gender, affirming these individuals' gender identities. Some people enjoy challenging and disrupting the gender binaries that dominate most societal interactions. Others are exhausted by the judgment and fear of violence from those threatened when individuals cannot be easily categorized as a man or woman.

There is some evidence that a nonbinary identification is being officially recognized. There were at least eight countries in 2018 and four states in the United States (Oregon, California, Washington, and New York) that allowed individuals to adopt a gender neutral option on many legal documents, including birth certificates (Tritt, 2018). More states and countries are likely to follow this trend. There are new developments taking place all the time in growing recognition of nonbinary ways of life. These changes are occurring from dating sites to the growth of nonbinary bathrooms. In the United States and especially in universities and larger towns and cities, unisex toilets have been increasingly put into operation since 2010 (Wikipedia, n.d.).

As addressed further in Chapter 10, it is important for therapists to be up to date with the rapid changes happening within sex- and gender-diverse communities in the United States and other Western countries. The rapid growth of Internet websites dedicated to supporting sex- and gender-diverse people illustrates the transformation occurring within our families, schools, and communities. The changes are so rapid, in fact, that the heteronormative style of textbook writing, such as the language used in this very textbook, can be perceived as becoming redundant and alienating for the IGen population (Mardell, 2016). In part, the dominant culture in the Western world and the wider readership is struggling to catch up to this non–gender binary wave. The research and scholarship cited in this chapter, and in many other chapters of this book, are heavily shaped by a heteronormative lens. Virtually all statistics gathered by major public, private, government, and quasi-government institutions gather data in a binary form of male and female. The remainder of this chapter draws heavily on this binary literature, as that is the only data available to draw on, given the topics tackled in the rest of the chapter. However, where possible, we emphasize the dominant discursive effects of gender and sexuality on persons, rather than reify and essentialize people as belonging to the classical gender and sex binaries.

Gender Discourses and Boys and Men

Gender discourses direct human beings to display what is acceptable and appropriate female and male behavior, and dictate that male and female identity be performed within a narrow bandwidth. Mardell (2016) notes that in Western culture, gender expectations are thrust upon all of us. In the United States, dominant discourses specify how boys dress, play violent video games, or play "rough and tumble." Evans and Davies (2000) found that first-, third-, and fifth-grade literature used in schools reinforces male behavior as competitive, aggressive, and argumentative. For boys, the toys involve action figures, construction objects, science kits, and video games that sometimes portray aggression and violence. Kail and Cavanaugh (2016) reported on a study which found that boys who played with dolls were ridiculed by their same-sex peers.

We know too that many boys have to show a brave face when hurt or scared. Little boys are taught to "man up" and "not be a sissy." Brammer (2012) reports that there are no gender differences in crying in babies and young children. Because it is less acceptable for boys to cry, as children get older, girls cry more than boys. Research by Van Tilburg, Unterberg, and Vingerhoets (2002) shows that older boys cry less than younger boys; and, interestingly, older female children cry more than younger females. Avoiding crying is so critical to manhood that Truijers and Vingerhoets (1999) reported that adolescent boys scored higher than girls on only one item of a shame inventory assessment: "I feel shame when I cry."

BOX 9.1 HETERONORMATIVITY

Heteronormativity is the assumption that heterosexual relations between men and women is the natural order of things. It describes the dominance of heterosexuality over other forms of sexual diversity. It is also about gender performances, not just about sex itself, because it includes domestic and paid work, caring physically and emotionally for family members, and patterns of living across the lifespan. It includes the ideas that govern how a woman or a man should manage adolescent crushes, dating, marriage, family life, and widowhood. It shows how the practices of heterosexual couples are established as normal and how other sexualities are represented as inferior or are regarded as abnormal.

The concept of heteronormativity developed from the early 1990s. It was first used by Michael Warner (1991). The literature on heterosexuality is notably thin, however, as is the literature on being White in the field of racial identity. A notable exception is the (2007) book by Jenny Hockey, Angela Meah, and Victoria Robinson, entitled *Mundane Heterosexualities: From Theory to Practices*. They show that there are a variety of heterosexualities and that heteronormativity is far from monolithic and is widely contested, but it nevertheless represents a powerful force that successfully subjugates other forms of sexual diversity and represents them as abnormal.

Heteronormativity has also shifted over the last few decades. The stigma once attached to cohabitation, divorce, and lone parenthood has weakened considerably. Couples marry later, if they do so at all, and some of them choose to be child-free. Moreover, sex role demarcation in the household is less rigid than it used to be. These are signs that people, especially women, are exercising agency in shaping their lives. However, it is still true that heteronormativity shapes structural arrangements and sets the institutionalized agenda for what individuals must depart from in order to perform a nonconventional identity.

Challenging heteronormativity is not the same as challenging heterosexuality. It is the belief that heterosexuality is the only natural way to be that is the problem. A person can be heterosexual with or without this belief. In its more extreme forms, heteronormativity can lead to homophobia or transphobia.

Like other identities we have discussed in this book, masculinity is embedded in competing discourses. Many dominant discourses direct men in adulthood to avoid behavior that society deems weak or feminine, such as expressing vulnerable emotions of sadness and hurt. Philpot, Brooks, Lusterman, and Nutt (1997) found that men who were regarded as emotionally sensitive were labeled weak. Even apologizing for one's mistakes can be portrayed as weak in mainstream society.

With a focus on self-reliance, control, and invulnerability, dominant discourses invite men to put on a tough guise, or a masculine shield, which can constrain emotional expressions and relational intimacy. "Real men" are invited to show strong competition in almost all areas of life. Even today, male displays of toughness and aggression in politics, the workplace, and in the sporting arena are widely embraced by many men and women. The physical brutality displayed in mixed martial arts (MMA) or even ice hockey matches is highly popular in the media. Verbal abuse and demeaning interactions shown towards others, especially in the political arena, are illustrative of the traditional discourse of male toughness.

Traditional discourses of aggression, even displayed towards those who cannot defend themselves, are sometimes characterized as appropriate and win a certain status as "politically incorrect." The phrasing "politically incorrect" has been used as a rallying cry for a conservative political agenda that criticizes liberals for being excruciatingly sensitive in their mission to address social justice inequities. Being sensitive, attentive, and thoughtful are not the typical attributes of the alpha male identity. The alpha male is viewed within majority culture as emblematic of a "real man" identity conceptualized as "strong, omnicompetent and rational-logical in [his] expression" (Dienhart, 2001, p. 22). Mardell (2016) describes the performance of these characteristics as a display of "toxic masculinity."

The discourse suggests that the only way to be a man is to perform in an aggressive manner, where vulnerable emotions are sealed off from being expressed or even felt. Though there are significant ethnic differences in the way men perform manhood, Fernández, Carrera, Sánchez, Páez and Candia (2000) identified one unifying characteristic. They surveyed 4,784 people who were residing in 21 countries and found that, independent of ethnic identity, men shared the same ability to dismiss negative emotions except for anger. There are different dominant discourses operating on male identity in different ethnic communities. For example, the discourses of African American manhood tend to prize strength and physical and sexual prowess (Parker, Howard-Hamilton, & Parham, 1998). Brammer (2012) reflected a variety of differences in gender performance across a number of mainstream ethnicities in the United States. Many African American couples are more influenced by the discourses that are egalitarian in performing household tasks. Latino manhood emphasizes family leadership, and men protecting and caring for the family. Brammer suggests the dominant discourses of Latino male culture include stoicism, hard work, acting in a dignified manner, and avoiding shame. Brammer (2012) Fernandez, Carrera, Paez and Candia found that many people who identify as Asian have the strongest set of restrictions governing their emotional expressiveness among both men and women. Brammer also suggested that many Asian American men seek to be the figurehead of the family and fulfill the role of taking care of all family members, even though the responsibility for care was picked up by other family members.

Brammer (2012) asserts that a successful male Native American identity arises from a sense of worth born from the immersion with nature, providing for one's tribe/relatives, and gaining wisdom by communing with the spirit world. Vespa (2009) suggests that discourses for Anglo American men directs them to provide less domestic support but to increase the family's income and be successful in their occupations. Lack of egalitarian duties displayed by many men across many ethnic cultures comes back to the interpretation of the "boy code" of acting tough and taking charge. Slovic's (1999) research on men's emotions showed that men lacked fear in many areas. European men were more likely to feel in control of themselves and take calculated risks. Minority men, on the other hand, viewed themselves as more vulnerable and see the world as more risky.

Most of us are familiar with the following discourses that commonly circulate and capture many men:

"Keep your cool."
"Be tough."
"A man doesn't show weakness or emotion."
"A man doesn't need others for emotional support."
"A man should be preoccupied with work, achievement, and success."
"It's a man's duty to financially take care of his family."

"A man's job takes priority over a woman's job even if the salaries are the same."

"A man's sexual desire is natural and compelling."

These discourses reflect what is often considered "common sense" about how men should behave and, because they are "left largely unchallenged and unexamined, they take on an unchangeable and natural nature" (Larsson, 1997, p. 7). Moreover, these discourses exert a powerful influence on the day-to-day interactions of men and women in intimate relationships. As Western society moves into the 2020s, in heterosexual contexts, many women and men will continue to expect heterosexual men to behave in chivalrous ways: buy a woman a drink at a bar, pay for food at a restaurant, open the door for the woman to enter first, protect women and use physical aggression on an adversary, if there is any kind of threat. It is the familiar and taken-for-granted nature of dominant discourses that often constrain heterosexual men's choices. That is, "their influence can most easily remain hidden and difficult to identify and, therefore, to resist" (Gavey & McPhillips, 1999, p. 352).

For adults, the dominant gender discourses continue to dictate what is a proper display of gender identity. In most communities in the United States, dominant culture insists that it is necessary to align biological sex with gender identity. When this does not happen, there is significant social disruption for those individuals who do not want to outwardly perform aligned sex and gender displays. In many Western communities, consider how disruptive it is for a phenotypical male to wear a dress and bra, pluck their eyebrows, and adorn themselves with lipstick and makeup. Even the expression and display of emotion in public settings follows tight gender norms. Men are more permitted to display anger and physical aggression in many settings than are women. Mardell (2016) comments that traditional gender expression limits how people can identify themselves and perpetuates intolerance to any expression outside the norm.

Individuals are not enveloped by discourses in passive ways. The central metaphor used to describe the fluid and dynamic relationship between people and discourse is positioning (Davies & Harré, 1990). People may position themselves in opposition to binary views of gender and sex, and in line with, for example, a discourse that describes gender and sex as existing on spectrums (see, for example, Mardell, 2016). Currently, in more liberal Western contexts people are disrupting gender categorizations, even when there continues to be a strong social stigma associated with having to align biological sex with gender. A biological male may live life conforming to more female-gendered characteristics in ambiguous non–gender defining clothing, getting nails painted, and wearing lipstick and carrying a handbag. A heterosexual man who chooses to go to therapy is also positioning himself in opposition to some dominant discourses about gender roles and in line with other discourses about the possibilities for help from mental health professionals.

Alternative discourses that challenge the more dominant discourses often reflect marginalized cultural ideas circulating within a context or community (Courtenay, 2000). Examples of alternative discourses around masculinity include the following:

"Men express vulnerability and emotions."

"Men are concerned about the relational needs of partnership."

"Men value interdependence in relationships in the home and in the workplace."

"Men are not controlled by their sexual desire."

"Men sustain responsible and loving relationships with children."

Brammer (2012) identifies the impact of the Civil Rights Movement, feminism, and the emerging men's movement, which has created an opportunity for men to perform more diverse occupational and relational roles, such as being primary caregivers for their children and participating in traditionally female occupations. However, at this stage, the numbers are still small. Brammer suggests that men who are enacting traditionally female roles can be subject to new prejudices. For example, men who demonstrate empathetic, caring, and sensitive behaviors in their dealings with others in many workplace contexts, or who are stay-at-home dads parenting young children, are often identified by the hypermasculine discourse as weak, lacking leadership or an authoritative presence, and as unsuccessful in "getting a real job." Many heterosexual women, even in the age of greater gender equality, are not sexually attracted to men who perform a nontraditional masculinity and are often more attracted to the stereotypical "bad boy" who is tough, distant, and emotionally unreachable (Birnbaum & Reis, 2012; Herold & Milhausen, 1999).

Many men have realized the emotional costs of working all the time and are increasingly aware of the constraining view that financial support is the only and best way to provide for a partner and their children. Magnuson (2008) found that more men are deprioritizing work and economic success in favor of attending to one's emotional values and spiritual well-being. According to Lipman (2018), some millennial men between the ages of 18 and 35 are more aware of the value of having an egalitarian relationship. Many younger men are also tuned in to the value of having a work/life balance and playing a greater share in the parenting and the domestic activities in the home. According to the 2016 Deloitte Millennial Survey, men rated a good work/life balance ahead of leadership, promotion, and gaining meaning from work. Lipman finds that younger men ages 18 to 25 strongly disagree with the dominant discourse that men should be the breadwinner and women should be responsible for childcare at home.

Gender Discourses and Girls and Women

Consumer culture is set up along gender lines. Early in the 21st century the color pink is selected by many people to designate girl children from birth. One hundred years ago, pink was not even a feminine color—it was associated with the height of masculinity (Mardell, 2016). There is a huge industry built around girl toys. For example, dolls are to be dressed to show prettiness, and are playthings for domestic activity. Girls are supposed to smell good, stay clean, and look pretty, are discouraged from being too adventurous, and encouraged to "be nice," which often means being compliant and sometimes passive. A KPMG study asked 3,000 professional and college-age women in the United States what lessons they learned in their growing up. In the following order, they listed: "be nice to others"; "be a good student"; "be respectful to authorities/elders"; and "be helpful" (cited by Lipman, 2018, p. 14). At the bottom of the list was: "be a good leader"; "make a difference in society"; "master a skill"; and "share your point of view" (p. 14).

Linguist Deborah Tannen wrote in 1991 about gendered interactions in the United States where little girls learn to get along with other girls by collaborating. In comparison, boys learn to play in a hierarchical fashion, competing and wanting to one-up each other. Girls who do this and try to grab power are shunned by the peer group. Girls get reinforced for being self-effacing, being tentative, and apologizing to others, even when an apology is not deserved. Girls who violate this code are often labelled not nice and instead can be rapidly judged as bossy or mean by both their female and male peers.

Tannen also found out more than 25 years ago that little boys often did not listen to little girls, and less attention is paid to females when male peers are present. Sadly, Lipman (2018) argues with compelling data from the North American workplace that when girls become women in the workforce, they continue with the same stereotypical boy and girl interaction of childhood, with many women being ignored by many men and being punished for bold, strong, and decisive action. While this commentary offered by Lipman (2018) is overlaid by hyperbole, it does have some familiarity to many women in the workplace: "Visit any meeting at any company, anywhere in the world, on any given day, and you will find the same scenario. Men dominate. Women often don't speak at all, or self-censor, or tentatively pose statements as questions. Women who do speak are interrupted or ignored. ... Yet to most men, it is invisible. Meetings, quite simply, are the killing fields of a woman's career" (p. 10).

There are numerous and concerning facts on gender relations in the U.S. workplace today. Kieran Snyder (2014) found that men were likely to interrupt women three times as much as women interrupted men. When women did cut others off, 87% of the time they cut off other women. Startlingly, Jacobi and Schweers (2017), who studied interactions in the U.S. Supreme Court over 12 years, found that female justices were interrupted three times more often than male justices. Lipman (2018) argues that, in many ways, things have gotten worse for women, in part because misogyny and racism against women have become more visible and fanned by the Internet.

Many women are frequently positioned in families as primarily responsible for the socioemotional development of both their husbands and their children, and are more responsible for household duties. While many men are expected to take on assertive, independent, dominant roles, women are invited into roles where they are expected to take up expressive and communal roles and to be relationship-oriented, selfless, emotional, and submissive (Alexander & Fisher, 2003; Cejka & Eagly, 1999). These cultural roles also place women in positions where they are often expected to be primarily responsible for aging parents. Research from the U.S. Bureau of Labor Statistics (2015) shows that women who work outside the home perform household duties on average two hours and fifteen minutes per day, in comparison to men, who work outside the home and perform household duties on average one hour and twenty-five minutes per day. Gender discourses on who is responsible for the care of children in the home drive major inequalities in this area. Yavorsky, Kamp Dush, and Schoppe-Sullivan (2015) found that, in a sample of dual-earner couples, mothers shouldered the majority of childcare and did not decrease their paid work hours after their child was born. Post-birth women completed more than two hours of additional work per day compared to an additional 40 minutes for men. The distressing situation, according to a research poll by Pew Research Center (2016), is that men continue to be largely blind to gender inequity, especially in the workplace, and believe obstacles to women's success are resolved.

Lipman (2018) argues that there is a disturbing trend in Internet search engines such as Google that displays gender biases in images and advertising that are largely the result of hidden prejudices demonstrated in the algorithms that are created by mostly male coders. In fact, Terrell et al. (2017) found that many women are better at writing computer code than many men; but in most tech settings, when the gender of the coder is identified, women's code is rejected at a greater rate than men's. The autofill boxes so commonly used by search engines can reflect male gender bias. A 2013 UN initiative focusing on female inequality ran an ad that showed real-life Google autofills:

Women shouldn't …

> Have rights
> Vote
> Work
> Box

Women need to …

> Be put in their place
> Know their place
> Be controlled
> Be disciplined

Many women adopt a "cool girl" image as a strategy to shrug off the harsh effects of dominant problem discourses and gain entry into the boys' clubs that form inside and outside the workplace.

This behavior is best characterized in Gillian Flynn's (2012) book *Gone Girl*:

Being the cool girl means I am a hot, brilliant, funny woman who adores football, poker, dirty jokes, and burping, who plays video games, drinks cheap beer, loves threesomes and anal sex, and jams hotdogs and hamburgers into her mouth like she is hosting the world's biggest culinary gang bang while somehow managing a size 2. … Cool girls never get angry; they only smile in a chagrined, loving manner and let their men do whatever they want. *(Source:* https://www.goodreads.com/quotes/615369-men-always-say-that-as-the-defining-compliment-don-t-they. First paragraph)

Being a cool girl might be understood as a complex way of navigating multiple choice positions around gender performance as a woman within dominant male culture. A more radical feminist analysis, supported by Lipman (2018), suggests the cost of the cool girl act is putting up with abuse and not challenging sexism and harmful attitudes perpetuated by patriarchal culture.

Wendy Drewery (1986), a passionate feminist using a structuralist analysis, emphasized the value of showing how patriarchy and socially unjust practices contribute to unacceptable conditions in many women's lives. She suggested that the immense burden of individual guilt and self-deprecation from which many women suffer is likely to be only relieved when their experiences are located within the sociocultural practices from which their private experiences have developed. Lipman provides a strong case for how women in the workplace are constantly being passed over and marginalized, and that despite a lot of concern and talk about gender inequity, very little change has been made.

BOX 9.2 ONGOING INEQUITIES IN THE WORKPLACE

A report by the U.S. Bureau of Labor Statistics released in August 2017 stated that in 2016, women had median weekly earnings of 82% of those of men. Almost 40 years ago, women's earnings were 62% of men's. While this reflects progress, in the last 15 years women's-to-men's earnings ratio has been stuck within the low 80% range.

Lipman (2018) reports that the discrepancies are worse for Black women, who are on average earning 63 cents on the dollar, and for Latinx, who earn 54 cents on the dollar in comparison to the male average earnings.

There are many successful businesswomen who report numerous barriers to advancement to senior management (Lyness & Thompson, 2000). For example, when women behave in the workplace in a manner not considered feminine, disadvantages result. Streitfeld (2015) captured the near-impossible balance women are culturally required to perform in the workplace: "Speak up—but don't talk too much. Light up the room—but don't overshadow others. Be confident and critical—but not cocky or negative." When women display a task-oriented style that goes against the dominant discourse of women as, "by nature," relational and demure, they might be rated competent but will receive low likability ratings. When men display the same task-oriented leadership style, they tend to be perceived more favorably (Rudman, 1998, cited by Sue & Sue, 2007). Talented women leaders are often excluded from business domains where male camaraderie exists (for example, on the golf course), which also excludes them from access to good mentoring and to information that might assist them with on-the-job performance. The data on women in leadership positions in large companies is grim. The percentage of women who are CEOs in Standard & Poor's 500 companies is staggeringly low at 5% (Catalyst, 2018) when nearly 50% of the workforce overall is female.

What makes this data more concerning is that 60% of college degrees and more than half of graduate degrees are earned by women. Data from the World Economic Forum (2016) estimates it will be 170 years before women and men have economic parity. Many women know that physical appearance often counts more than a résumé. Lipman (2018) reports on numerous studies that suggest that, among White women, blonds earn 7% more than brunettes, and thin women get better jobs and quicker promotions and earn more than heavier women. Furthermore, men and women deemed attractive by dominant cultural standards have higher incomes than persons deemed less attractive, and women must pay greater attention than men to hair grooming, makeup, and clothing to generate more earnings.

Gender Intersectionality

Gender identity intersects with multiple other identities. We are immediately confronted with the difficulty of understanding gender and sexuality independent of each other, along with ethnicity, class, religion, employment status, age, and a whole host of other identities. Maria Julia (2000) identifies how ethnicity and gender, for example, are "simultaneous, interconnected, inter-determining processes, rather than separate systems" (p. 3). Discussing gender and/or sexuality separately from other identities creates an artificial construction.

The diverse experiences contained within the categories of "men" and "women" make it hard to squeeze women and men into relatively stable or unified subjects relative to consciousness of gender oppressiveness and oppression. Jean Grimshaw (1986) illustrated this by suggesting the following:

> The experience of gender, of being a man or woman inflects on much if not all of people's lives. ... But even if one is always a man or a woman, one is never just a man or a woman. One is young or old, sick or healthy, married or unmarried, a parent or not a parent, employed or unemployed, middle-class or working-class, rich or poor, Black

or White, and so forth. Gender, of course, inflects one's experience of these things, so that experience of any one of them may well be radically different according to whether one is a man or a woman.

But it may also be radically different according to whether one is, say, Black or White, or working-class or middle-class. (pp. 84–85)

Many gender studies have White women as the universal female subject, and this leaves the experiences of women of color marginalized. Sherwin (2008, cited in Brammer, 2012) identified how the fear of racism and associated stresses often affect the health and well-being of ethnic-minority women more than ethnic-minority men and European women. Doman Lum (2000) described women of color as a "double minority" because they are subjected to both racist and patriarchal discourse. Claire Rabin (2005) described the powerful prejudicial imagery and stereotypical forms that impact minority women today. For example, a Black woman can be perceived as the mammy and a submissive, obedient servant, or the aggressive boss of an unruly family and the breeder of countless children, or the dependent welfare mother, or the jezebel, whore, or sexually aggressive woman. Latina women are often portrayed as Madonnas—virtuous, self-effacing, self-sacrificing mothers—or as spitfires, hot blooded and smolderingly erotic. Asian women are depicted as demure china dolls, or as dominating dragons. This discursive imagery is demeaning and implicitly victim-blaming.

White women have been largely exempt from ethnic labeling and stereotyping and have often benefited from White privilege, thus making their day-to-day experiences qualitatively different from those of ethnic-minority women. In some cases, White women have acted as oppressors of women of color, who have been childcare workers for them, while having to abandon the needs of their own children. Because of their ethnicity, White privilege, and/or social class, some women will have more benefits than and influence over some men who are members of an ethnic minority and living within a lower socioeconomic context.

Within sexual, gender, and relationship style minority groups, intersectionality also matters. For example, Elisabeth Sheff points out that the sexual and relational choice afforded by the polyamory community means something different and more empowering for women, who have grown up under patriarchy, than it does for men (Sheff, 2005). Furthermore, people of color who engage in swinging report feeling marginalized within the community (Kimberly & Hans, 2017). While both men and women are assumed to be less sexually appealing and less interested in sex as they age, this assumption is more heavily applied to women than to men. Furthermore, asexual men experience more disparagement than asexual women (Bogaert, 2012).

Gender Essentialism

A number of theories have attempted to explain the etiologic roots of men's and women's behavior, or why men and women are the way they are. There are two dominant explanations in the gender literature. Some scholars maintain an essentialist perspective for male or female behavior, suggesting either a biological (for example, Bancroft, 2002; Guay, 2001; Leiblum, 2002) or psychoevolutionary basis (for example, Archer, 1996; Buss, 1995, 2000). Those advancing a biological perspective propose that essential (genetic and hormonal) differences exist between men and women and that these biological qualities are the source of men's and women's attitudes and behaviors. Others promote a psychoevolutionary account of masculinity and femininity, speculating that men have a completely different evolutionary heritage and face different adaptive challenges than women.

Essentialist views of masculinity remain popular and influential within the psychological literature as well as within popular culture. Essentialist explanations for masculinity are often expressed most plainly in the area of sexuality. For example, it is commonly taken for granted that men's sexual urges are natural and compelling (Hare-Mustin, 1994), while women's naturally have much less intensity (Crawford, Kippax, & Waldby, 1994). Many men and women subscribe to the myths that a man always wants and is always ready for sex, while women need only to be loved, held, and cherished (Bergner, 2013; Braun, Gavey, & McPhillips, 2003; Conley, Moors, Matsick, Ziegler, & Valentine, 2011; Potts, 1998). While men's sex drives are, *on average*, higher than women's, many women have higher sex drives than many men (Laumann, Gagnon, Michael, & Michaels, 2000); and these cultural myths magnify small gender differences and obscure the range of men's and women's desires for sexual and other forms of intimacy.

While essentialist explanations of masculinity offer a certain level of understanding and remind therapists not to ignore biological factors, they fail to capture the nuanced complexities of men's attitudes and behaviors, including their particular professional ambitions, personal aspirations, relational needs, and patterns of relating. Essentialist theories also fail to explain those men who act in ways contrary to their "biological makeup." Moreover, "because of their high regard for the relative immutability of the inherent differences between women and men, essentialist theorists tend to be relatively conservative in their view of possibilities for change" (Brooks & Good, 2001, p. 8).

Essentialist understandings also tell us that as people age, they inevitably become less interested in sex, and dominant discourses further tell us that women become less sexually attractive as they age. Aging women, therefore, are less likely to enact the role of a sexual being, given that cultural messaging tells them that they will be less interested in sex, a less-capable sexual partner, and less sexually attractive. The perception that men's and women's sexual satisfaction is significantly diminished in middle and old age is countered by less culturally validated research indicating that middle-aged adults who no longer have the day-to-day responsibilities of parenthood report increased sexual desire (Bjorklund, 2015), Bjorklund also found that most people over the age of 70 report that they are highly satisfied with their sex lives. Given that diminished sexual satisfaction is more a cultural stereotype than a biological imperative, therapists may be able to help aging clients create preferred local discourses in relation to their sexual identity and activity.

BOX 9.3 THE PATRIARCHAL DIVIDEND

It is common for men to downplay their advantages over women if they have not actively sought to gain or reproduce such advantages. Connell (2005), writing about masculinity, makes a helpful comment on how male hegemony is maintained. She comments that "the number of men rigorously practicing the hegemonic pattern may be quite small" (p. 79). And yet the pattern benefits many more men and gives them social advantages. She uses the term *patriarchal dividend* to explain it. Many men may be complicit with masculine hegemony and tacitly endorse it without running the risks of being what Connell calls "the frontline troops of patriarchy" (p. 79). Such men may show their wives and mothers and daughters considerable respect and never act violently towards them, and yet they draw uncritically on the patriarchal dividend in ways that benefit them in their relations with women. The phrase "patriarchal dividend" is a metaphor drawn from the world of finance and used to explain by analogy the practice of receiving unearned privilege. When people receive a dividend, they are paid but do not have to do any work. It is a use of a theoretical concept that makes redundant any explanation that relies on domination by numbers. What it accounts for is how men can access privilege without having to resort to specific strategies of domination themselves.

Gender Entitlement

Gender discourses have often solidified into dividing lines, and unevenly empowered men with greater agency and choice. More often than not, it has been men who have been privileged by an emphasis on their generally greater physical strength and the development of unified accounts of "superiority" in other domains (intellectual, moral, and so forth). And it has been women who have been assigned second-class social positions on account of their supposed physical, intellectual, and moral "inferiority." Sexism, like racism, has depended on assumptions of superiority and inferiority. And, like racism, gender differences have been developed as elaborate narratives about what is *natural* about these differences. In this way, power relations are shaping many gender differences that have their origins in discourse and have been accorded an authority that is harder to question. If the contours of gender difference and sexual differences and their associated entitlements are based more on discourse and narrative than on nature, then we are necessarily talking about cultural differences.

The history of gender, sexuality, and power has been long, complicated, and contested. It takes different forms in different cultural contexts and is constantly shifting, never static. We should also be careful about applying Eurocentric analyses of gender politics to the cultural positions of women from outside the Western tradition. Even in the West, women have gone through periods of greater and lesser power relative to men. Stephanie Coontz's (2005) writing on the history of heterosexual marriage, for example, shows how many of the particular concerns that have occupied feminists in the last 30 years developed out of the Industrial Revolution, the modern evolution of the love marriage, and the 20th-century breadwinner/homemaker division of labor. Women in earlier centuries might have identified with some but by no means all of the concerns of modern feminists. At the same time, the conservative narrative is that the family is a stable institution from time immemorial that is only now being threatened by such cultural developments as single-parent families, gay marriage, and polyamorous relationships. Coontz shows that the institution of marriage has never been singular or stable, and has, in fact, been through many shifts and changes.

The challenge for counselors is to help men recognize how gender discourse has often placed them in an unearned position of social privilege, which becomes so familiar that an exaggerated sense of entitlement in their relationships with women remains unquestioned. Raquel's story is one woman's account of gendered relationship norms within the family. Notice how she experiences personally the effects of the politics of gender, even though neither she nor her husband is responsible for creating them.

I am an American wife. I wish that meant that I am in an equal partnership where responsibility for income, romance, parenting, entertaining, and so forth are shared. But for me, the word wife frequently means sacrifice, inequality, oppression, powerlessness. This is not just the fault of society, or of my husband, or of myself. Each plays a role in its continuance. Of course, I learned most "rules" from my parents. Popular culture and entertainment also greatly supported what I was learning. The husband is the primary breadwinner. The wife is the homemaker, cook, maid, hostess, relationship counselor, single parent, "arm candy," and entertainment manager. All these titles, but no power. Lesson: husbands are superior and are expected only to make money. Wives are expected to do everything else. The husband is the boss of the home and the decision maker. The wife may speak her opinions, but they do not carry as much weight as the man's in the final decision.

By watching my mother, I learned that sometimes it is easier to hold your tongue in the moment and just do what you want later. Lesson: it's easier to say, "Oops!" or "Sorry" than "May I … ?" and risk hearing "No." But that is not power. While I know he loves and cares for me, my father was not a hands-on parent. In addition to his lack of interest in equal parenting, his career in the military meant he was away from the family a lot, sometimes for months at a time. The emotions he most frequently showed ranged from anger to worry or annoyance.

Because I was a girl, I enjoyed a relationship with my father that was not available to my brothers. Earning his love and approval was very important to me, and I learned which behaviors made him happy and which did not and I adapted. Lesson: if you show your true, imperfect self, you will not be loved.

As with many military families, the ability to adapt to situations and people was necessary and greatly valued. For a long time, it never occurred to me that adapting so much for my father's love might be potentially damaging to my personality. But, through years of playing a role, suppressing my opinions, and learning to ignore my gut and natural tendencies, I lost touch with the real me. In doing so, my own power atrophied from disuse.

I also watched my mother change and suppress her true self in hope of winning my father's love. When my father was away, I observed that my mother was almost a different person. We had fun, certain rules of the house were temporarily lifted, and her dynamic, joyful personality shone more brightly. This shift occurred over and over again each time my father deployed. I learned that it was only safe or appropriate for a wife to be her true self outside the company of her spouse. Lesson: power and freedom are available only when your husband is away. I struggle greatly with this in my own marriage.

Because I was taught to be this way, believing it was "normal," I have made major choices in my life based on that oppressive rule book. I chose a college close to home, because I was sure as a girl that I couldn't make it completely on my own. When I did leave home, I moved directly from my father's house to my husband's house. It never occurred to me, nor was it suggested to me, that my life, my marriage, and my personal worth might benefit from time on my own, from earning things and truly deserving them. In following my husband's career, we moved across country and I had difficulty finding a job relating to my field of study. I was told that any job would do, even part-time at the mall, because he made enough already. He believed he was saying the right thing to relieve my stress and make me feel better. Additionally, he received much fulfillment from his ability to provide for me. But his telling me this did not bring relief. I felt stupid, incapable, held down, and powerless. I equated a job to my own personality, independence, and power, so what I heard was that it didn't matter anyway, because my place in this marriage was subordinate to his. My husband finds traditional gender roles safe and appealing. I'm sure he is quite conscious of the power he holds in our marriage. One reason I think he is scared to give up some of that power is that he fears it will mean losing my love. I find it sad that he views my love as an obligatory response to his power or conditional on his bank account. Who taught him that? It does not escape me that, with every oppressive "rule" I follow, there is a corresponding oppression that bears on him. There is a little voice inside my head saying that I am responsible for my situation; on a logical level I know I am not without power. I know I am a strong, independent, capable person. Yet I remain a victim of this deep-seated belief that as a woman and a wife I cannot make it in this world on my own power, intelligence, and ability. At the end of the day, I am still carrying around with me that same old rule book—and my husband and my culture carry it as well.

Patriarchy and Its Implications for Mental Health Professionals

The mental health field has had a history of supporting patriarchal behaviors during the helping process. Scholars, such as Ivey, D'Andrea, and Ivey (2012), and McDowell, Knudson-Martin, and Bermudez (2018), have explicitly addressed these harmful traditions in their counselor education training, but there is still evidence that these practices continue (Evans, Kincade, & Seem, 2011). Following are some examples that display gendered assumptions held by therapists about family life. Some practitioners had a bias toward assuming that women would benefit from remaining in a marriage. In some instances, there was a bias toward showing more interest in a man's career than a woman's. Often, therapists would hold women more accountable than men for a child's problems and for child-rearing. There was also evidence to suggest that men's needs were prioritized over women's needs.

From a feminist perspective, patriarchal and Eurocentric practices systematically silence women who do not conform to dominant cultural norms. In this way, they require the majority of women to fit their identities into gendered norms and to police those who stray from such norms. These insights inspired many feminist researchers and practitioners to confront mental health professionals for colluding with culturally oppressive practices and failing to attend to the structured inequalities that support sexism (Brown, 2018; Calvert, 1994; Lawson-Te Aho, 1993; Ohlson, 1993; Smith, 1992; Tamesese & Waldegrave, 1993).

A number of researchers in the United States have continued to express concern that gender awareness in therapy has not been adequately addressed (Artkoski & Saarnio, 2013; Rigazio-DiGilio, Anderson, & Kunkler, 1995; Silverstein & Brooks, 2010; Twohey & Volker, 1993). Regarding the supervision of therapists, it has been suggested that supervisors need to be more aware of themselves as gendered beings. Mary Lee Nelson and Elizabeth Holloway's (1990) study illustrated this point when they found that supervisors often failed to encourage female trainees to assume power in supervision. Females tend to defer to more powerful authority figures more quickly than males do. Sandra Rigazio-DiGilio, Stephen Anderson, and Kara Kunkler (1995) suggested that counselor educators must accept the effect that gender differences have on male and female counselors' work. These authors claimed that the socialization of men and women produces different "voices" in clinical practice. Recently, researchers have encouraged supervisors to train therapists to recognize cisgender privilege (Bender-Baird, 2008), and heterosexual privilege (Long & Lindsey, 2004).

Gender entitlement does not only hurt women. For example, Brammer (2012) points out that men can be subject to oppression that is sometimes unrecognized and unaddressed. The oppression comes from the rigid definitions of masculinity. For example, boys' behavior in schools is heavily affected by traditional male discourse. Rodkin, Farmer, Pearl, and Acker (2000) found popular sixth-grade boys who were perceived as cool by their peers were tough, athletic, and antisocial, and were described by their teachers as argumentative, involved in regular fighting, disruptive, and frequently in trouble. Boys are more often diagnosed with ADHD and oppositional defiant disorder (a conduct disorder), or receive diagnoses related to behavioral concerns. These behavioral patterns often result in boys developing lower reading, writing, and speaking abilities throughout their education (Brammer, 2012). Many men in the United States are constrained from showing vulnerability. Even a kiss on the cheek, a typical form of greeting in Italy, is frowned upon by most men in most communities in the United States. The "tough guise" takes a toll on men's mental and physical well-being. Men are often portrayed in the media as creeps, as sexually and physically violent, emotionally incapacitated, incompetent lovers who thwart women's efforts in all arenas in life. Not all men participate in these negative interactions. Those that do suffer themselves from the harm they do to others. Sometimes their suffering is not obvious at first. Many men can use alcohol or other drugs to attempt to alleviate the pressures they may feel in performing the tough guise as they deny their own vulnerable emotions, such as hurt and sadness, that they are not permitted to culturally express. Many men experience stress about their perceived responsibility to be the primary income earner, which is stereotypically viewed as a patriarchal duty. Being laid off at work or experiencing long-term unemployment is a significant psychological threat in addition to the stresses of reduced or no income. When a man's intimate partner demonstrates greater earning power than him, this can sometimes be perceived as threatening his masculinity, making for a conflictual set of interactions in their primary relationship. We will discuss the counseling implications of these gendered limitations, entitlements, and rigidities of male identity on men's emotional and psychological health in a later section.

Selected Counseling Problems that Arise from Dominant Problem Discourse

Violence, Abuse, and Harassment

Feminist therapists and writers have voiced serious criticism, over several decades, of the counseling and therapy field for its failure to adequately address issues of patriarchy (Drewery, 1986; Goldner, 1985; Knudson-Martin et al., 2015; Leslie & Southard, 2009; McKinnon & Miller, 1987; Treadgold, 1983; Waldegrave, 1985; Williams & Knudson-Martin, 2013). The expressions of gendered power relations that are evidenced in male violence and its effects on the psychological experience of women have been a particular focus of this criticism. In the 1990s, feminist structural critiques began to be addressed in therapy with men. In *Becoming Ethical,* Alan Jenkins (2009) built on his 1990 book by outlining ways of taking abusive men from traditional gender patterns through to more ethical and egalitarian relationships with women. Working with men who had used violence or abused women or children, he used the language of male entitlement to explain many men's expectations that women should attend to their physical and social needs. When these men's female partners failed to conform to stereotypical relationship patterns, they felt entitled to resort to abusive behavior.

However, this largely feminist analysis has not adequately acknowledged the frequency of physical and psychological violence enacted upon men by women. In addition, the domestic violence enacted by men on men and women on women is underrecognized. The Intimate Partner Abuse Against Men National Clearinghouse on Family Violence Statistics Canada first collected data on intimate partner abuse of both men and women through its 1999 General Social Survey. The data showed that similar numbers of men (18%) and women (19%) reported emotionally abusive behavior in their intimate relationships; and more men reported being physically abused (slapped, bitten, hit, and/or kicked) than women. Brammer (2012) stated that women initiate physical abuse at least as often, if not more often, than men. Yet, according to Price and Rosenbaum (2007), in the United States, 80% of the arrests for domestic violence are of men. However, this data does need to be viewed in the context of severity.

Caldwell, Swan, and Woodbrown (2012) reported on their research that showed male-on-female intimate partner violence caused significantly more fear and more severe injuries than female-on-male violence. The 1999 General Social Survey reported more severe injuries occur to women in intimate partner violence, typically resulting from being sexually and physically assaulted and choked. Threats from a gun or knife by men towards women also occur at much higher rates. According to the World Health Organization (2017), 38% of murders of women around the globe are committed by a male intimate partner. Petrosky et al. (2017) reported that intimate partner violence (IPV) caused the deaths of nearly half of all 3,519 girls and women murdered in the United States in 2015. Non-Hispanic Black women had the highest rate of IPV death by murder, followed by Native American, Hispanic, non-Hispanic White, and Asian/Pacific Islander women. Fifteen percent of women of reproductive age (18–44 years old) who were murdered by current or previous partners were pregnant or had given birth within the previous six weeks. According to Petrosky et al.'s, research, one in ten victims were exposed to violence in the month before their death. Arguments and expressions of jealousy were common factors leading to IPV-related homicides. In 30% of IPV-related homicides, an argument preceded the victim's death, and this occurred more commonly among Hispanic victims than among non-Hispanic Black and White victims. This data is important for therapists to know to help them be cognizant of the dangers that can be faced when working with families where IPV is present.

Pornography

It is clear from research on men and women's bodies in mainstream Western consumer culture that women's bodies are more sexualized and objectified than men's (Davis, 2018; Vandenbosch & Eggermont, 2016). This objectification has an influence on every aspect of life. The objectification of women's bodies within the porn industry is pervasive and this objectification is increasingly impacting men and male bodies, too. Klaassen and Peter (2015), in their study of objectification and violence portrayed in

BOX 9.4 WORK HARASSMENT AND INTIMATE PARTNER VIOLENCE

Harassment in the Workplace

According to Johnson, Kirk, and Keplinger (2016), 29% of women in the workplace report sexual harassment, and a disturbing 63% of female technologists, engineers, and scientists experienced sexual harassment and 52% quit their positions because of an unsafe work environment.

Fifty-nine percent of women and 27% of men reported unwanted sexual advances or verbal or physical harassment either within or outside of a work context (Graf, 2018).

Fifty-two percent of those who have experienced sexual harassment in the workplace say they made a job change because of the harassment. Only 30% of women and 53% of men strongly agree that their employer handled the incident properly. This discrepancy in the data between the satisfaction that men and women feel when addressing sexual harassment points to more negative experiences that women feel about appropriate and corrective organizational responses (Edison Research, 2018).

Intimate Partner Violence

On average, nearly 20 people per minute are physically abused by an intimate partner in the United States. During one year, this equates to more than 10 million women and men.

> 1 in 3 women and 1 in 4 men have been victims of (some form of) physical violence by an intimate partner within their lifetime.
> 1 in 4 women and 1 in 7 men have been victims of severe physical violence by an intimate partner in their lifetime.
> On a typical day, there are more than 20,000 phone calls placed to domestic violence hotlines nationwide.
> The presence of a gun in a domestic violence situation increases the risk of homicide by 500%.
> Intimate partner violence accounts for 15% of all violent crime.
> Women between the ages of 18 and 24 are most commonly abused by an intimate partner.
> 19% of domestic violence involves a weapon.
> Domestic victimization is positively correlated with depression and suicidal behavior.
> Only 34% of people who are injured by intimate partners receive medical care for their injuries.

Rape

In the United States, 1 in 5 women and 1 in 71 men have been raped in their lifetime. Almost half of female (46.7%) and male (44.9%) victims of rape in the United States were raped by an acquaintance. Of these, 45.4% of female rape victims and 29% of male rape victims were raped by an intimate partner.

Stalking

One in 7 women and 1 in 18 men have been stalked by an intimate partner during their lifetime to the point that they felt very fearful or believed that they or someone close to them would be harmed or killed.

Homicide

A study of intimate partner homicides found that 20% of victims were not the intimate partners themselves, but family members, friends, neighbors, persons who intervened, law enforcement responders, or bystanders.

Seventy-two percent of all murder-suicides involve an intimate partner; 94% of the victims of these murder-suicides are female.

Children and Domestic Violence

1 in 15 children are exposed to intimate partner violence each year, and 90% of these children are eyewitnesses to this violence.

1 in 3 teenage girls has experienced some form of physical violence from a partner.

1 in 3 girls and 16% of boys reported some form of sexual partner violence (Barter et al., 2009).

Economic/Physical/Mental Impact

Victims of intimate partner violence lose a total of 8.0 million days of paid work each year.

Between 21% and 60% of victims of intimate partner violence lose their jobs due to reasons stemming from the abuse.

Women abused by their intimate partners are more vulnerable to contracting HIV or other STIs due to forced intercourse or prolonged exposure to stress.

Studies suggest that there is a relationship between intimate partner violence and depression and suicidal behavior.

Physical, mental, and sexual and reproductive health effects have been linked with intimate partner violence, including adolescent pregnancy, unintended pregnancy in general, neurological disorders, chronic pain, disability, anxiety, and posttraumatic stress disorder, as well as noncommunicable diseases such as hypertension, cancer, and cardiovascular diseases. Victims of domestic violence are also at higher risk for developing addictions to alcohol, tobacco, or drugs (National Coalition Against Domestic Violence, 2018).

Ethnic Differences Among Victims of Violence

Approximately 22% of Black women and 27% of American Indian or Alaska Native women have been raped at some point in their life. Overall, Black and indigenous women were reported to experience rape, stalking, and/or physical violence at rates 30% to 50% higher than those experienced by Hispanic, non-Hispanic White, or Asian or Pacific Islander women. More Black women are killed in America than any other race (Brinlee, 2017).

"amateur porn" on the Internet, found that men were most often the initiators of sex, and women were viewed as less likely to have sex for their own pleasure. These authors found that men were viewed as more dominant and women more sexually submissive in amateur videos, and women appeared to be more manipulated into the sexual encounter. There are also studies that acknowledge that when women create, direct, and watch porn, this can be found to be empowering to many women (Sabo, 2012; Taormino, Penley, Shimizu, & Miller-Young, 2013). The porn industry is far from uniform and unidimensional. In addition, it matters to some people what should be categorized as porn and what should be described as erotica. For example, Kovetz (2006) argues that pornography and erotica are two completely different categories of human experience. She suggests, "The line between erotica and porn isn't thin or fragile. … Erotica is to pornography as a portrait is to a cartoon" (p. 74). She argues that erotica is humanizing and pornography is dehumanizing. However, the distinctions are getting murky. The word pornography has historically been associated with disparaging images (Attwood,

2002). However, Kuhn, Voges, Pope, & Bloxsome (2007) comment that the associations with what is called pornography and erotica today are dependent on the cultural locations of the viewer. Negative images that were defined as pornographic even 20 years ago might now be viewed as erotica. Kuhn et al. claim that the legal definitions of what would be obscene relates how the material is being used. Hartzell (personal communication, December 2, 2018), an experienced sex therapist in San Diego working with men and women who use pornography, suggests it is preferable to use the phrase *sexual images* rather than *pornography* to reduce the charged response that many people have to the word, which has historically invoked reactions of judgment and shame.

Ashton, McDonald, and Kirkman (2018) report that some pornography can be experienced as empowering and educational, and even assists sex partners to enrich and enliven their sex lives. However, there is strong evidence that other forms of pornography can be misogynistic and destructive to both men and women. Lisa Henderson (1991) writes about the "porn wars" among feminists (and others) about the nature and implications of gendered sexual experience involving explicit sexual imagery. She explains that "for anti-porn feminists, female subordination in patriarchy is both cause and effect of female degradation in pornography. Among anti-antiporn feminists on the other hand, suppressing pornography inevitably becomes part and parcel of a long history of female sexual suppression" (p. 173). Enson (2017) argues that pornography is increasingly dominated by themes of aggression and abuse and that it blurs lines for the consumers between what is consensual and pleasurable, and what is coercive and violent. Enson proposes that much of today's pornography conveys messages to men endorsing hypermasculinity and male domination.

One of the most difficult issues for therapists to address with couples is pornography use. The acceptance of the use of pornography for many couples is seldom a "yes or no issue" (Carroll, Busby, Willoughby, & Brown, 2016). Some intimate partners are not troubled by low usage of pornography, but those same partners can be highly distressed by high-frequency use. There tends to be wide agreement among researchers on the negative effects of pornography on intimate partner relationships when one partner is viewing pornography at high frequency and this use is minimized or concealed (Butler & Seedall, 2006; Zitzman & Butler, 2009). Carroll, Busby, Willoughby, and Brown state that concealment and high-frequency use of pornography can harm intimate partner relations, diminish trust, and contribute to isolation, poor self-esteem, depression, and anxiety. Newstrom and Harris (2016) found that many women who discovered their male partner's pornography use viewed this event as traumatic and experienced responses that were similar to those they might feel if their partner cheated. Honesty between partners when using pornography seems to help alleviate mistrust. Olmstead, Negash, Pasley, and Fincham (2013) tellingly found that when one's partner was caught using pornography, rather than engaging in a deliberate discussion about pornography use, this had a very different effect on the couple relationship. The timing of a discussion with one's partner on pornography use also matters, such as whether a frank conversation occurs early in the relationship or much later. Olmstead et al. comment that managing or not managing the dynamics about talking about pornography use with loved ones could be much more influential than the actual pornography use itself. Newstrom & Harris (2016) report that men whose partner knew of their pornography use found it easier to open up about their sexual relationship with their partner. They also found that couples who used pornography together communicated better about their sexual relationship. Kohut, Fisher, and Campbell (2016) found research participants commented that pornography helped improve sexual

BOX 9.5   THE PERVASIVENESS OF PORNOGRAPHY

The growth and size of the pornography industry has brought about significant cultural changes in sexual behavior and sexual expression, and impacts the relational lives of people who consume or are affected by porn. A great deal of pornography is an outgrowth of the influences of dominant gender and sexuality discourses in Western contexts. Lambert, Negash, Stillman, Olmstead, and Fincham (2012, citing Cooper, 1998) comment that the Triple-A Engine driving pornography is accessibility, anonymity, and affordability, and it is being fueled by the rapidly expanding access to the Internet.

Ogas and Gaddam (2012) comment that in 1997, there were approximately 900 pornography sites on the Internet. Writing in 2016, Newstrom and Harris claim that there are well over 2.5 million pornography websites. According to Crouse (2018), 25% of all Internet search requests are for pornography, and every day there are more than 68 million search engine requests for pornography. Consider the sheer number of Internet users who may have access to Internet pornography. Statista (2017) calculated that there are 3.39 billion Internet users in the world, a figure that is double what it was in 2008. In the United States, there are over 272 million Internet users.

Munteanu (2016) cites research by a security technology company (Bitdefender) that found that children are viewing hardcore porn sites at young ages, with 1 in 10 users of graphic porn sites being under ten years of age. Munteanu reported on this same research that shows that under-10-year-olds account for nearly a quarter of online video porn viewing among the under-18 age group. A 2016 NSPCC study cited by Martellozzo et al. (2017) reported that a tenth of 12- to 13-year-olds are concerned about being addicted to pornography.

Carroll, Busby, Willoughby, and Brown (2016) reported that men who were casually dating viewed pornography 42 more times than women who were casually dating, and three to four times as many men viewed pornography alone compared to women. These researchers reported that one-third of women who were married or engaged regarded pornography as a form of "marital infidelity." Over a third of men and women (between 35% and 52%) believed that pornography was objectifying and degrading. Research by Lambert et al. (2012) suggested there was a relationship cost associated with pornography use, and this was specifically related to commitment in romantic relationships. They made a case that pornography consumption was related to infidelity and this association was affected by how committed the partners were to one another.

Ashton et al. (2018), in their research on women's experiences of pornography, described a picture that was complicated, nuanced, and even paradoxical, and showed varying experiences both individually and relationally. De Cadenet, (2015) conducted a, *Marie Claire* survey of 3,000 women studying their pornography use over a two-year period found that 31% of women watched porn every week. Thirty percent said they did so a few times a month and 10% watched porn daily. Sixty percent said they never watch it with a partner. These numbers contradict the belief that most women feel threatened by porn or only watch it to please their partners.

The prominent influence of pornography has to some extent changed cultural norms and people's expectations on sexual behavior and sexual expression. Differences in pornography use and acceptance or rejection of it influence intimate partner relationships. Newstrom and Harris (2016) found that there are both positive and negative effects of pornography when used within committed relationships. For some relational partners the use of pornography is a violation of trust. For others it is viewed as a behavior that enhances the sexual relationship of intimate partners.

communication, experimentation, and sexual comfort, while pornography also produced unrealistic expectations, increased insecurity, and decreased sexual interest. Carroll, Busby, Willoughby, and Brown (2016) suggest it is important for intimate partners to openly discuss pornography use, express their mutual levels of acceptance, and address matters of concealment directly. It is helpful if therapists get comfortable talking about pornography with their clients, who will have a variety of different experiences with this subject, varying from benefiting from its use to being disgusted and harmed by its use. Therapists may be able to help couples establish an agreement about whether, how much, and in what circumstances porn is consumed, and also help intimate partners recognize that most people's bodies and sexual interactions bear little resemblance to what is often depicted in porn, to help counter damaging, unrealistic expectations that porn may engender.

Body Image, Physical Attractiveness, and Physical Well-Being

The effects of gender discourse reach into all areas of people's lives, including how we are directed to relate to the human body, physical attractiveness, and physical well-being. There is abundant research examining the negative experiences women encounter with regard to their physical bodies. There is a much smaller base of research addressing men's concerns with body image and physical attractiveness.

Body Shame in Women

For women, the counseling and psychology literature has the most to say about dieting, eating disorders, body image, body satisfaction, and body esteem (Cash & Smolak, 2011; Grogan, 2016; Maisel, Epstein, & Borden, 2004). Many findings indicate that a large proportion of women are dissatisfied with their bodies and are constantly monitoring their weight and dieting. Most perceive themselves as overweight, regardless of the accuracy of this assessment (for example, Rodin, Silberstein, & Striegel-Moore, 1985; Wooley & Wooley, 1984). In a 1993 national survey, 48% of American (U.S.) women reported experiencing dissatisfaction with their overall appearance as well as a fear of being or becoming overweight (Cash & Henry, 1995). In addition, a recent meta-analysis of 222 body image studies from the past 50 years revealed continual increases in women's body dissatisfaction (Feingold & Mazzella, 1998). Furthermore, females are becoming more concerned about their weight at younger ages (Cavanaugh & Lemberg, 1999). Survey estimates of restrained eating range as high as 45% in third-grade children and as high as 80% among fourth- and fifth-graders (Mellin, Irwin, & Scully, 1992). Finally, studies have demonstrated that females constitute 90% of the eating-disordered population (Striegel-Moore, Silberstein, & Rodin, 1986).

Given the "normative discontent" (Rodin et al., 1985, p. 267), or the widespread nature of women's dissatisfaction with their body and appearance, it is not surprising that a body of literature has been assembled that targets a number of sociocultural factors for their potentially harmful effects on women's status and on their physical and emotional health (Bordo, 1993; Cafri, Yamamiya, Brannick, & Thompson, 2006; Cash, & Smolak,(2011).; Engeln, 2017; Foucault, 1980; Gremillion, 2003; Maisel, Epston, & Borden, 2004; Thompson, Heinberg, Altabe, & Tantleff-Dunn, 1999). Many people are captivated by the appearance culture of many Western societies. Beauty is prominently connected to thinness in the United States. Lemay, Clark & Greenberg (2010) noted that people designated beautiful in the United States are viewed as kinder, more altruistic, more sociable, more enthusiastic, having better sex, and getting better jobs. Women's bodies are inscribed with expectations for attractiveness, including certain clothing and hairstyles, and at this time the most prominent standard for attractiveness for women is thinness. The increasingly thin representation of the feminine body has frequently been referred to as the cultural ideal of thinness or the "tyranny of slenderness" (Chernin, 1981). This normative expectation remains the most frequently implicated sociocultural factor contributing to women's negative body experiences.

Sociocultural constructions of the female body and expectations of physical and sexual appeal lead to a myriad of negative experiences for women, including constant monitoring of one's appearance (the increased prevalence of mirrors contributes), body shame, negative body esteem, restricted eating, and eating problems (McKinley, 1998, 1999; McKinley & Hyde, 1996; Moradi, Dirks, & Matteson, 2005; Tiggemann & Boundy, 2008). Mariette Brouwers (1990) has made a link between negative emotional responses arising from body shame and the eating disorders of anorexia nervosa and bulimia. Therefore, a woman's preoccupation with appearance seems "natural," masking the extent to which external pressures influence women's daily practices, such as makeup application, dieting, and exercise. Because cultural standards for the feminine body are virtually impossible to attain, women often feel shame about their bodies when they internalize these standards (Engeln, 2017; Young, 2003). Negative experiences associated with body shame are widespread and have greater consequences for women and their psychological well-being than they do for men (Gervais, Vescio, & Allen, 2011; Hesse-Biber, Clayton-Matthews, & Downey, 1987; Mintz & Betz, 1986; Silberstein, Striegel-Moore, Timko, & Rodin, 1988).

Ellie gives a personal account of this experience.

> *I internalized the message that a woman's value is proportional to her looks at a very young age, as many girls nowadays probably do, especially those who grow up in places like Southern California. Once, when I was about 13, boarding a chairlift in Vail with my mother, one of the two male attendants gazed at me in a way that made my skin crawl and one commented loudly to the other, "That's a nice shirt. If it was bigger, I'd wear it." I was disgusted and ashamed, as was my horrified mother, but somehow felt that it was my fault. I had attracted his attention, so there must be something wrong with me. Things like that just don't happen to nice girls. In a sick way, I was secretly glad that at some level, I must be desirable. It was horrible to hear comments like that, but in my mind, it would have been infinitely worse to be ugly, or fat. What would people say then? If I continued to be pleasing, I would be safe from criticism that could be devastating to my fragile self-image. The way I looked on the outside became my most salient survival tool, because I was terrified of not being good enough. I was 18, a freshman in college, the first time I threw up my food. I had gone to dinner with one of the guys I'd met. He and most of his teammates at school were from the Midwest. I went to the bathroom at one point, and when I returned to the table I approached him from behind. He was on his cell phone, several drinks deep and talking too loudly, telling his buddy on the other end, "You're going to owe me that eighty bucks, because I'm totally going to fuck her tonight." Too angry and humiliated to call him out, I waited several seconds, then sat down as if nothing was wrong. I was too uncomfortable to address what he had said, and I pretended at the end of the meal that I felt sick. He drunkenly drove me home to my dorm, where I sat and*

cried. I had been at school for only a month and I had never gotten too drunk at a party, danced on a table, taken my clothes off, or done anything that would have somehow justified his (and his teammate's) evaluation of what I apparently was. I cried for a while, then walked to the bathroom and stuck my fingers down my throat. Everything came up so easily and it was like a switch flipped inside of me. That was easy. For the next month I ate nothing, just drank coffee all day and had small salads at night when I ate with my friends. When I got too hungry and ate something "unacceptable" or felt too full, I would throw up. I'd had a perfect body before this, although I didn't think so at the time, but my weight began to fluctuate wildly. I wouldn't eat for months. Then I would get so hungry I would eat everything and throw up. I felt awful all the time. My period stopped and I became extremely depressed. I cut myself with razors and had intrusive thoughts of suicide literally every few moments for several months. I found out that acquaintances of mine at school, my sorority sisters actually, many of whom did cocaine and got blackout drunk every weekend and many weeknights, all talked about how they thought I was a drug addict. Eventually, I dropped out of the house. I could not understand what was wrong with me, why this was happening to me, why I was inherently so horrible and couldn't have a normal functional life like the proverbial "everyone else." My boyfriend became exhausted with me and our relationship deteriorated. I was hurt and newly ashamed of myself and wondered what he must be telling his fraternity friends, who had all probably heard the rumors about me from my sorority "friends." I have never felt so utterly alone.

Somehow I managed to make it through school and overcome the eating problem. It is still a major part of my life, something that will never be completely eradicated, but it is no longer what controls me. I can't say for sure why this happened to me, since there are women who are raped or molested or have encounters far more devastating than my own.

The constant pressure our culture and media bombard women with about how their inherent worth is derived from physical beauty doesn't help. I couldn't help internalizing this and doing the very thing I shouldn't: place all importance on appearance. So how can I blame all the men that hurt me by treating me like an object for doing the same thing? I am working on myself, trying to realize who the person inside is, what she wants and likes. It is still well-nigh impossible for me to approach relationships with the mentality that I have a lot to offer and should do so. I am still terrified of failure of any kind, and I am still learning to accept the simple lesson that mistakes are all right. I hope someday that I will finally be able to do all these things and be happy in my own skin, as a woman.

A few researchers have compared Asian and Hispanic women with White and African American women on measures of body image, body satisfaction, and disordered eating (Ahmad, Waller, & Verduyn, 1997; Akan & Grilo, 1995; Altabe, 1998; Quick & Byrd-Bredbenner, 2013), and one study has compared American Indian women with White and African American women on measures of weight satisfaction (Story, French, Resnick, & Blum, 1995). These findings suggest that body-related concerns are not confined to White females, but that body-related concerns appear less significant among ethnically diverse women relative to White women as a whole (Cash & Henry, 1995; Grabe & Hyde, 2006). The experiences of individual women within each ethnic group, of course, may differ from the normative experience for the group as a whole. What appears to be clearer is that women who identify as a sexual minority tend to report less concern for physical appearance and less drive to be thin than heterosexual women (Beren, Hayden, Wilfley, & Striegel-Moore, 1997; Bergeron & Senn, 1998; Herzog, Newman, Yeh, & Warshaw, 1992; Strong, Williamson, Netemeyer, & Geer, 2000). One explanation for this is that support within the lesbian community buffers lesbians and helps them keep from internalizing the increasingly thin ideal (Heffernan, 1996). This is another example of how alternative discourse positions can provide resources that enable resistance to the norms specified by dominant discourse.

Issues pertaining to body dissatisfaction have led to an enormous increase in plastic surgeries for women. According to a Plastic Surgery Statistics Report (2017), 92% of people undergoing cosmetic plastic surgery are women. Women undergo rhinoplasty to obtain a nose that is small and narrow, liposuction to reduce the size of their thighs and stomach, and breast augmentation. Women of color use bleaching agents to lighten their skin, and some Asian women have surgery on their eyes so they will appear round and Western. As Tracy Robinson-Wood (2017) reported, women will suffer from bunions, corns, and all manner of foot problems to conform to restrictive but socially desirable shoe fashions.

Body Shame in Men

Many men are also increasingly affected by negative body images because of societal notions of attractiveness. A sculpted, triangulated body with washboard abdominal muscles is portrayed in popular culture as an attractive male body. Lillian Emmons (1992) noted that adolescent boys in particular are very prone to a negative self-assessment of their bodies and often engage in unhealthy dieting. Men, like many women, have resorted to fasting, the use of laxatives, and purging. Males are often less concerned with overall weight and much more consumed with muscle definition and the avoidance of fat and flab (Robinson-Wood, 2017). Because men are socialized to believe that manliness is associated with being a protector and provider, being athletic or having superior body strength becomes intimately wrapped up with this identity.

The following story from a young man in his early twenties illustrates how this discourse gets internalized.

> What is difficult about being a male in today's American society is that men are supposed to be the protectors of their friends and family. This means that men need to appear larger than life to create an intimidating persona that others will respect and back down from without any major confrontation. The problem with becoming bigger, faster, and stronger is that men still need to have the defined body that resembles the classical images of ancient Greece, meaning that men need to have the cut washboard abs, tapered V-shaped body, broad shoulders, and well-defined calves. This double standard of "manliness" is an issue that I continually face every day. Being of Asian descent, I am already faced with the fact that most Asians are short. Being short is a genetic shortcoming that cannot be overcome, no matter how much weight training or dieting I do. This puts me at a disadvantage on the "manliness" scale because, when compared to the European American male, whose average height is five inches taller than mine, I cannot appear to be a better protector or a better man. To appear appealing and to be an attractive prospect as a man,

I would need to compensate for the height disadvantage by focusing on what I can control: my weight and body definition.

I grew up as a slim, fit child who was constantly playing sports. I was never too concerned about my body size or image, but I was constantly hearing the mantra "Bigger, faster, stronger!" To do better and dominate the competition, I felt that I had to be those three words. Not knowing much about muscle resistance weight training, I thought that to be bigger I should just eat more. So that's what I did.

Unfortunately, that made me everything that was unattractive and unwanted. While I was not incessantly obese, I was large enough to warrant such comments as "Oh my gosh, you're getting so big," and, "Wow, you need to lose weight!" All that for a kid who was only 13 years old. That was the first time I became overly concerned with my body image, and that insecurity has constantly affected me to this day. Hearing those comments from family members made me wear bigger clothes and eat next to nothing just to keep them from saying these things. I also started attending a gym, where I did weight resistance to bulk up and convert the fat into muscle. While I was seeing improvements in my body, I never got big enough to feel confident or "cut" enough to show off the washboard abs that are so desirable. Wanting to reach these standards, I started developing a disorder known as exercise bulimia. I would constantly work out at the gym. Before meals and after meals, I would go to the gym, because each meal felt like a detriment to my "diet" of achieving a large yet cut body image. I would not have time for any fun or recreation, because the only thought in my head was that I was still fat and needed to bulk up. This mentality actually made problems worse, because it's almost impossible to do both bulking up and cutting fat.

Today I still struggle to feel confident as a man in American society. I don't feel that my body is attractive enough to be perceived as manly, powerful, and respected. I still hear the negative comments of people calling me fat and overweight and still find myself comparing myself to every other male out there, never feeling confident because they have the look I am still striving for. As I see women comment on and fawn over the triangular, defined body shape, I know that that is what is desired and attractive and that that is what a man should be.

Men with physical disabilities often struggle to a great degree with a negative body image, because they are not able to command the same physical strength as able-bodied males. Men sometimes address their negative body image by using and abusing steroids to create a hypermasculine body image (Ham, 1993). Anabolic/androgenic steroid hormones, for example, are used to enhance body size for those seeking to achieve a chiseled body. Steroids are well known to produce adverse effects on the liver, the cardiovascular and reproductive systems, and the psychological health of the steroid user.

Selected Counseling Issues Often Pertaining to Men

There is a strong body of literature that demonstrates that traditional masculine attitudes and adherence to traditional male gender roles are associated with negative outcomes for men (Wester, Vogel, & Archer, 2004), including anxiety (Cournoyer & Mahalik, 1995), depression (Good & Wood, 1995), relationship difficulties (Fischer & Good, 1997), and anger (Blazina & Watkins, 1996). Moreover, the relationship between traditional masculine attitudes and willingness to seek help has been explored and the results support a connection between male socialization and reluctance to seek psychological help (Blazina & Watkins, 1996; Good, Dell, & Mintz, 1989; Robertson, 2001).

Men seek out therapy only half as often as women do (see Box 9.6). There are also differences in how many women and men present themselves to counselors. The counseling literature suggests that men are less aware of their feelings and present more work-related issues (Daniluk, Stein, & Bockus, 1995). Martin Heesacker and his colleagues (1999) found that counselors tend to view men as hypo-emotional or emotionally inexpressive. In a series of six studies, these authors demonstrated that counselors are more likely to blame men for marital difficulties, because of their emotional demeanor.

Increasingly, gender studies are reflecting on the experiences of men through a lens other than that of the oppressor/oppressed binary. Susan Faludi (1999), Michael Gurian (1999), and William Pollack (1998) were integral in provoking considerable debate regarding their assertion that boys, as well as girls, are harmed by a culture that poorly recognizes their needs and stresses (Brooks, 2010; Brooks & Good, 2001). Yet much of the therapeutic literature continues to overlook men as occupants of a unique cultural position that needs to be understood (Brooks, 2010; Brooks & Good, 2001; Dienhart, 2001; Englar-Carlson, Evans, & Duffey, 2014; Rochlen & Rabinowitz, 2014). Anna Dienhart (2001) points out that "there is limited literature in the family therapy field specifically exploring therapeutic techniques aimed at engaging men in the process of therapy" (p. 24). Others agree that there is a particular

---

BOX 9.6 UTILIZATION OF COUNSELING SERVICES BY WOMEN AND MEN

Historically, women have used the mental health system more often than men. About two-thirds of all clients seeking psychological services are women (McCarthy & Holliday, 2004; Vessey & Howard, 1993). This difference occurs even when men experience rates of distress similar to if not higher than those experienced by women (Robertson, 2001). Liddon, Kingerlee, and Barry (2017) found that men find it much more difficult to seek professional mental health support than women. McManus, Bebbington, Jenkins, and Brugha's (2016) research shows that more men than women engage in substance abuse and suggest that men might self-medicate using alcohol and other drugs, rather than use prescription medication.

Liddon et al. (2017) report that men still experience barriers towards help-seeking, because of the stigma associated with having to admit to problems and their difficulty having to be emotionally vulnerable in therapy. These researchers' findings reinforce the discourse that men should be strong and self-reliant, and that seeking help is a sign of weakness. Men find treatment options do not tend to be male-friendly, even though in the higher echelons of the mental health system, men continue to be the largest majority of healthcare professionals. According to John Archer and Barbara Lloyd (2002), approximately three-quarters of psychiatrists and over half of psychologists are male, while only a quarter of those in the social work field are men. Among counselors, women are by far the majority. Seager, Barry, and Sullivan, (2016), believe there is a "male gender blindness" when discussing how the male gender is often unintentionally ignored, which can explain how men's specific therapeutic needs are not fully considered in therapy.

need to investigate the relationship between emotions and men's problems and to design therapeutic interventions to address the restriction of men's emotions (Englar-Carlson, Evans, & Duffey, 2014; Good & Sherrod, 2001; Good, Thomson, & Brathwaite, 2005).

There is a tendency to assume that men are not open to counseling services, which precludes examination of how the mental health system can become more relevant to men (McCarthy & Holliday, 2004; Seidler, Rice, Ogrodniczuk, Oliffe, & Dhillon, 2018). Some therapists may view male clients as impenetrable and "difficult" to work with, or as "resistant," unwilling participants (Dienhart, 2001). Other therapists may unintentionally view men who seek therapy in more negative terms based on traditional notions of masculinity (Dienhart, 2001; Owen, Wong, & Rodolfa, 2009; Robertson & Fitzgerald, 1990). Still others may fail to consider how counselor expectations may align with many men's worst fears; consider this pitch for counseling:

> I'd like you to talk about your emotions in an intimate, vulnerable setting that may leave you feeling a little out of control or helpless. This state is only temporary; it will probably end after you experience a flood of emotions and see yourself in a new way (Brammer, 2012, p. 381).

Pleck (1981) suggested that many men who are beginning to feel emotions will typically rely on women as a surrogate to express vulnerable emotions. For example, a man might wait for his partner to express a vulnerable emotion of hurt, sadness, or fear so that he does not have to. Scher (2001) comments that a male's lack of emotional expression may especially occur in a male-to-male counseling context, because many men have difficulty expressing vulnerable emotions in front of male counselors.

A variety of efforts have been aimed at improving men's access to psychological information and the use of mental health services (Good & Sherrod, 2001; Rochlen & Rabinowitz, 2014; Vogel, Wester, & Larson, 2007; Wexler, 2009). One trend has been reframing or changing the name of mental health services from counseling or psychotherapy to seminar, classes, or coaching in order to attract those men who may hold traditional views of masculinity (Good & Sherrod, 2001; McCarthy & Holliday, 2004; Ogrodniczuk, Oliffe, & Beharry, 2018; Seidler et al., 2018). Some researchers have argued that therapy is too reliant on "feminine" modes of intervention that require verbal expressivity, vulnerability, and emotional awareness, all skills that are difficult for men to acquire in our society (Meth & Pasick, 1990; Seidler, et al, 2018), and that new therapies should be developed that are more congruent with "masculine" styles (Brooks, 2010; Brooks & Good, 2001; Heesacker & Prichard, 1992; Shay, 1996; Wilcox & Forrest, 1992). While these modifications may prove useful, we suggest that therapists pay closer attention to the culture of masculinity as a means of working more effectively with men in families.

Therapists can easily ignore the enormous variation in men's attitudes and behaviors and unwittingly reinforce notions of men as passive participants in their lives. Popular gender-aware (Gilbert & Scher, 2009; Good, Gilbert, & Scher, 1990), gender sensitive (Philpot, 2001), and gender-fair (Nutt, 1991) therapies all reflect the role framework in their attempts to engage men more fully in the context of family therapy. Carol Philpot (2001), describing gender-sensitive family therapy, recommends that the therapist act as a "gender broker" who explains the "male code" to female family members and the "female code" to male family members (p. 628). Philpot cites the case of a couple in conflict over the sharing of childcare and domestic responsibilities to illustrate this approach:

In this common situation, the therapist can help the wife understand that the husband is doing exactly what he believes is expected of him—providing for his family through hard work and dedication to the good provider role. When she understands that his intent is good, she can then approach him from a more compassionate stance. She can correct any misconceptions he may have about her expectations of him and clarify exactly what she wants most. If she chooses, she can ask him to show his love and support in a different way. By reframing the husband's behavior in a positive way, the therapist opens the door for negotiation and change. (p. 629)

The positions assigned to men by dominant gender discourse are not without their liabilities. In studies that address differential diagnoses by gender, men are found to have four or five times higher rates of alcohol abuse and antisocial personality diagnoses. Judith Daniluk, Monika Stein, and Diane Bockus (1995) suggested that when men seek assistance, they frequently present with problems related to career, impulse control, and alcohol or other drug abuse. Kahn (2009) found that men are more likely to smoke, drink, engage in unsafe sexual practice, participate in dangerous occupations and engage in stressful activities than women. Wilson (2001) studied 200 African American teenage boys and found that those who regularly witnessed violence were at higher risk of major health problems like elevated blood pressure, possible heart disease, and stroke. Brooks (2010) found that African American men, who have to cope with high levels of violence in their community, often experienced more mental health issues, unemployment, substance abuse, and health impairment than other ethnic groups.

Hawton and van Heeringen (2000, cited by Archer & Lloyd, 2002) note that suicide rates vary according to age and ethnicity but that men kill themselves in much larger numbers than women. Women, on the other hand, have a higher rate of self-mutilation and self-injurious behavior than men. A number of researchers have suggested that an overdeveloped male gender role sometimes gets expressed by increased risk taking, self-destructive activities, high stress, emotional inexpressiveness, an emphasis on control, and the drive to accumulate money (Green & Jakupcak, 2016; Iwamoto, Cheng, Lee, Takamatsu, & Gordon, 2011; Kimmel & Levine, 1989; Meth, 1990). James O'Neill (1990) stated that men can display "rigid, sexist, or restrictive gender roles learned during socialization, which result in personal restriction, devaluation, or violation of others or the self" (p. 25). While much of this research on presenting problems has focused on the differences between men and women, there appears to be compelling evidence that gender histories shape and influence many of the problems that clients bring to counseling. In addressing these concerns, it is important to note how the relationship between counseling problems and gender-influenced lives is an ongoing sociocultural issue.

For reasons identified earlier in this chapter, many men are affected to such an extent by gender entitlement, gender privilege, and patriarchal histories that their behaviors turn to abuse of women, other men, and children (though, as discussed, the perpetration of violence is not an exclusively male domain). Many men who are perpetrators of physical and sexual violence will struggle to understand the harm and they have caused; be accountable for their actions; and come to terms with the intense societal rejection they can experience because of their violations. The therapist has a responsibility to pay attention to family and public safety as an important goal when individuals have participated in violence and abuse. Providing therapy to these individuals requires specialist training to navigate the safety concerns along with the clinical needs of this population. When individuals engage in violent, coercive, or forced non-consensual sexual acts, mental health professionals must ensure that the victim voices are prominent and present in the therapeutic work, and work closely with the criminal justice and legal systems. The success rates for treatment of IPV are not good. Campbell, Neil, Jaffe, & Kelly (2010) have pointed out the rather grim data that suggests that programs for men addressing their violence have been generally ineffective. Pence and Paymar (1990) suggest that people who perpetrate IPV feel they are losing control of their lives and relationships, and violence sometimes becomes the central method of maintaining control. This classic research suggests that, following an episode of IPV, there is often a honeymoon period that follows the violence, followed by an extended calm. In many cases of IPV the parties wish to stop the violent actions but do not pay attention to solving the underlying relational issues. Brammer (2012) suggests that men may act like a small child, who is sorry for their actions, and then begs for forgiveness, and promises that they will not attack their partner again. The person committing the violence may attempt to convince others that they have changed by purchasing gifts or paying attention to their partners' and families' needs, but often these efforts are temporary fixes. These temporary actions can hook the abused partner to stay in the relationship. If the underlying issues are not addressed, this cycle of events is enacted repeatedly. Martin (1987) noted that conflicts over the management of children and finances are often the issues that can perpetuate the violence by men towards women. In wrestling with these problematic dynamics, it is often difficult to conduct couples counseling when violence is occurring; yet, often couples want to stay together, even when painful violence and abuse has occurred. There is current debate among mental health professionals about whether a therapist should be working on the couple relationship when there is a clear risk of further violence occurring. Some therapists become motivated to help clients exit the relationship when violence is ongoing and want their clients to recognize the likely ongoing effects of the violence. It can be frustrating for therapists who are trying to help clients escape the violence, when the clients themselves are not equipped to exit the relationship, even though the therapist (and sometimes the client) believes it is the logical thing to do.

Braun-Harvey and Vigorito (2015) describe a group of individuals who struggle with out-of-control sexual behaviors (OCSB) that do not involve nonconsensual activity but do cause real harm to self and others. Reid and Woolley (2006) describe OCSB as individuals who have difficulty managing and regulating sexual thoughts, feelings, and behavior. These responses almost always have a negative outcome for the person engaging in OCSB and these actions typically hurt relationships with family members and partners. An example of this would be viewing pornography to such a degree that it is detrimental to other relationships and other important life obligations. Often the behaviors can be completely contradictory to a person's espoused beliefs, values, and goals.

According to Salisbury (2008), OCSB is often driven by unhelpful coping mechanisms to manage emotional distress and reduce anxiety and tension, or is a result of unaddressed trauma earlier in life. Out-of-control sexual behaviors are not exclusively a male domain. Kaplan and Krueger (2010) reported that an extraordinarily wide 8% to 40% of women experience feelings related to OCSB. With a range of that magnitude, it is difficult to know the pervasiveness of OCSB with women. However, Montgomery-Graham (2017) reported that the experiences of women with OCSB are so understudied that it is difficult to reach any conclusions about women's problematic sexual behavior.

Addressing OCSB requires the therapist to comprehend the intense shame that individuals feel as they break societal norms around what is appropriate sexual behavior. Braun-Harvey and Vigorito

(2015) underscore the importance of not conflating the shame-related behavior with the person's identity. Using narrative therapy to separate the person from the problem is especially helpful in providing the context for a client to envision a future in which they can perform a preferred identity that is free from or not dominated by the OCSB. Braun-Harvey and Vigorito express deep concern that many therapists are not open to confronting their own hidden judgments, prejudices, and superficial knowledge about sexuality that they bring to therapeutic interactions with clients struggling with OCSB. They report:

> Offhand remarks, embarrassed silence, stigmatizing comments, or complete uncritical acceptance are not the foundation for the types of conversations that individuals engaging in out-of-control sexual behaviors need. The process of change must begin with an understanding, open, caring, and collaborative conversation with any client considering whether, how, and what to change. (p. xxx)

Braun-Harvey and Vigorito (2015) make a strong case that therapists should receive specialized training to prepare for the explicit and sensitive conversations needed in addressing OCSB.

Selected Counseling Issues Often Pertaining to Women

Women have been found to present with greater affective distress, more anxiety-related disorders, and more relationship-related problems than men (Moore & Leafgren, 1990). Seeing more women present with these problems may lead therapists to construct pathologizing descriptions of the experiences of female clients. There is clear evidence to show consistent biases for certain diagnostic categories that reflect dominant discursive ideas about gender attributes. Women are often identified as having exaggerated emotional expressions, including intense fluctuations in mood. Women are much more frequently diagnosed with personality disorders that relate to stereotypical perceptions of women as being overly emotional or dependent, such as histrionic personality disorder, dependent personality disorder, and borderline personality disorder (Nolen-Hoeksema, 1998).

Royda Crose, Donald Nicholas, David Gobble, and Beth Frank (1992) cite numerous examples of the psychological costs of patriarchal and androcentric culture to women, pointing out that women are more likely than men to receive a diagnosis of mental disorder by their physicians. Women are more often prescribed psychotropic medication and take more prescription and over-the-counter drugs. These authors suggested that women are also more likely to be informally labeled with a hypochondriacal, psychosomatic, hysterical, or dependent personality. Women are also reported to be twice as likely to exhibit depression, anxiety, or phobic disorders. Maye Taylor (1994) reported on surveys revealing that a high percentage of individuals with signs of depression, anxiety, panic, anorexia, and phobia are women, and that they constitute a very large percentage of the client population.

Brammer (2012) suggests the impact of depression on women is more than the sociocultural effects, such as the results of demeaning intimate partner relationships or the female gender training that leads many women to sacrifice their own personal and relational needs for the sake of their partner's and children's needs. This author notes the influence of biomedical factors on depression. For example, many women produce smaller quantities of serotonin than men, a mood-regulating chemical directly connected to depression. Addressing both the biomedical features and harmful sociocultural factors is most likely to yield a positive result.

According to Brammer, normal biological developmental milestones are often embraced and represented as part of the human experience in dominant culture. Male psychosexual development, such as changes in body hair, voice, body mass, and even ejaculation, tend to be welcomed and celebrated by men in their normal development. Perceived physiological delays in these psychosexual milestones can create anxieties with young men, but their onset is widely embraced. However, the dominant discourses around sexual development, including menstruation, often leads young women to feel isolated from one another. Owen (1993) shares a heartfelt story of struggling to understand why she felt different from the women in the tampon commercial who were happily running on the beach wearing White pants. Owen suggested that after the initial pride and excitement about attaining womanhood, these feelings soon turned to shame where she was not allowed to speak openly about menstruation in her family. She described the whole experience of menstruation as a state of being weak and inadequate. While these circumstances may have changed a little in the last 25 years, and some writers, such as Ehrenreich (1999), describe this period as a time for heightened well-being and intellectual clarity, negative attitudes towards menstruation in the wider culture in the West persist. Concerning physical and medical needs may arise from the challenges caused by premenstrual dysphoric disorder (PMDD), which was included in the *DSM-5* (APA, 2013a). These menstrual issues can play havoc with women's bodies, creating serious stress on their general well-being and relational happiness. However, Ussher (2010) makes an important social commentary when she says that, while there are obvious physical and hormonal dynamics, a difficult menstrual cycle should not be categorized as a disorder. She notes that, in some North American contexts, menstruation is situated as a purely negative and debilitating event, whereas in some other contexts menstruation is viewed as natural, and not as a pathological event.

The underlying premise of the multicultural movement in counseling and therapy is the promotion of social justice and cultural democracy among diverse peoples. But therapists can be criticized for promoting and supporting certain ethnic cultural practices on the grounds that they are aligned with cultural traditions that can be harmful to women. Susan Moller Okin (1999), for example, has raised questions about the ethical implications of some forms of multicultural practice for women. She suggests that the defense of certain cultural practices and traditions has the potential to subjugate the rights and the quality of life for women. In many communities, there is very real discrimination against and at times hatred for females, and their freedom and even their right to live are sometimes seriously compromised. The very worst illustrations of these practices, including the ongoing abuse of women through genital circumcision and genital mutilation, female child trafficking, bride burning, infanticide, and the aborting of female fetuses, still occur in many countries of the world.

In North America, there may in some instances be tension between the promotion of multicultural sensitivity and gender and sexual equity. For example, the promotion of gender equity may heighten the possibility of punitive oppressive practices against women. Some cultural traditions urge negative consequences for women who seek outside help. For example, the support by counselors and therapists of women who wish to take a stand against rigid and harmful machismo behavior may not be welcomed in some Latino families. In such instances, therapists who defend traditional ethnic cultural practices ahead of gender equity can produce more negative impacts on women than on men.

Susan Moller Okin (1999) suggested that, because attention to the rights of minority cultural groups must ultimately be aimed at furthering the well-being of these groups, there can be no justification for assuming that the group's self-proclaimed leaders (invariably composed of their older male members) represent the interests of all the family members (p. 24).

Therapists who unquestioningly support particular ethnic traditions without consideration of gender and sexual inequalities can become complicit in the ongoing subjugation of women among immigrant cultures. It is also likely that, in some instances, counselors' promotion of women's rights within a counseling relationship may inadvertently subject those clients to more risk. This retribution effect arises in many situations when women are in abusive relationships and are at risk of being killed, physically hurt, or socially and economically isolated, or when individuals live in contexts that encourage aggression toward homosexual individuals. Therapists must be careful and wise in helping individuals to be removed from potentially lethal situations. Sometimes counselors, following the ethical principle of doing no harm, have to manage the complex tensions between what is best for the family and what is best for the individual. Consultation with supervisors or colleagues can be an essential support to the therapist in this situation.

Physical and sexual violence have devastating psychological effects on women and men. The very common emotional response to these gross forms of violation can be toxic shame and an accompanying numbing silence. Many women subjected to sexual violence can feel sexually, psychologically, and emotionally damaged for the rest of their lives. Rape can leave a person feeling unclean and weak. Rape comes in many guises and therapists have a duty to take the utmost care in addressing the psychological wounds following sexual violence. Brammer (2012) makes it clear that rape is:

> Having sex with a minor.
>
> Forcing someone to have sex or continuing with the sex act after the individual has requested an end to the act.
>
> Having sex with someone who is unable to consent to the act (for example, a person who is drugged or intoxicated, or a person experiencing mental ill health).
>
> Having sex with someone who has not verbally given consent (note: lack of verbal or physical resistance by the victim, resulting from the use of force or threat by the accused, does not constitute consent). (pp. 337–338)

Therapists have a critical role in normalizing a very wide range of emotions that many people might feel following a rape. Sometimes the person enters into a numb, blank state or emotional shock. Often the greatest harm ensues when the person victimized holds themselves responsible, minimizes the sexual violation, or even denies the event. Resnick (2001) reports that following rape many women feel a loss of control and become immensely vulnerable, and experience distressing fear and/or hatred towards men. Normalizing the reactions of the victim to sexual and physical violation require the therapist to not intrude or push in on the client's privacy, or require the traumatized client to share things they are not ready to share. A gentle, careful, and respectful exploration of the concerns of victims of violence is required, allowing the client to set the pace, without rushing them to disclose, enabling the client to experience a sense of control.

When clients are known to be in a dangerous situation where IPV is active, therapists should work with clients to create an escape plan. This may involve inviting the victimized client to monitor signs, nonverbal behaviors, and facial expressions that can occur before violence happens. Strategies can be prepared for escaping from the house, such as having personal items and money ready to go, as well as having preparations made for childcare and/or pet care, a domestic violence shelter number, and trustworthy family and neighbors' contact details at the ready. Escape plans can be rehearsed with the therapist. Survivors of physical violence often engage in placating behavior to stop the violence occurring. Often women hold themselves responsible for the violence and fall prey to being scapegoated. These issues are important areas to address so women can be safe and win back their confidence, self-respect, self-esteem and mental well-being.

Counseling Interactions

When mental health professionals name some of the gendered patterns of identity construction for female and male clients, they are taking the first step toward ensuring that negative patriarchal attitudes do not dominate in the counseling room. Here are some guidelines that therapists can consider when they are addressing gender issues in counseling:

1. There needs to be acknowledgment that in many communities the devaluing of women is a common occurrence. For example, Darcy Haag Granello and Patricia Beamish (1998) identified how women can be pathologized for being codependent when their behavior could be reconceptualized as a nurturing and self-sacrificing demeanor toward family members. At the same time, counselors, especially male counselors, need to guard against chauvinistic behaviors towards women. Male therapists are vulnerable to participating in what McClintock (2016) calls "mansplaining," when a male explains something in a condescending way, especially to a woman. These behaviors conform to dominant discursive actions that reinforce gender inequality.

2. Therapists need to continue to update their knowledge of the biological, psychological, and sociological factors that uniquely impact men and women. For women, counselors can acquire recent knowledge on issues related to menstruation, pregnancy, birth, infertility, miscarriage, and sexuality. For men, therapists can become knowledgeable about prostate issues, vasectomies, steroid use and abuse, the negative effects of patriarchal behaviors, and the like.

3. When cultural traditions emphasize strongly patriarchal assumptions, men and women are ascribed distinct roles in the family and in the community. Communities often place considerable investment in maintaining these elaborate gender narratives, and counselors must, therefore, proceed slowly and respectfully with clients who identify with such cultural traditions, so as not to alienate them. Rhea Almeida, Rosemary Woods, Theresa Messineo, and Roberto Font (1998) have proposed models that include consultants from the client's own cultural communities. Clients are invited to participate in culture circles to grapple with relevant gender, class, and race issues.

4. Whenever gender issues arise in counseling, other identity factors are also likely to be in play. It will be important to take into account other environmental issues that need addressing, such as poverty, racism, sexism, ageism, and other sociocultural and socioeconomic factors. For example, women are subject to pressures to be pretty, feminine, and the loving caregiver, while men are pressured to be the protector, the primary income earner, and the head of the household. When it comes to ageism, older women are often viewed more negatively than older men. Counselors need to be aware of the psychological pressures that accrue for clients as a result of these wider cultural practices.

5. Therapists can use a deconstructive approach toward the impact of gender discourse on clients. Here are some examples of questions that therapists can ask their male and female clients that might open up conversations about the cultural aspects of gender experience:

"Antonio, when you were growing up, what was the significance of work outside the family?" "Where did you get the idea that it was a good idea to work so hard?" "Where do ideas about a man's being financially successful and taking care of the family come from?"

"Xiomara and Andre, to what extent are these ideas about men being the primary bread-winners currently working for you?" "How helpful have ideas about a man's being better suited for money-making activities been to your relationship?"

"Christina, how did you expect that Jaime would show and share his grief after his friend died?" "Jaime, what did you expect to happen when you lost someone close to you?" "Where did you get these expectations about expressing your feelings from?" "Jaime, what does it mean for a man in this society to realize that being strong can be stressful and take a toll on interpersonal relationships?" "What would it mean to you if you didn't have to be strong and feel responsible all the time?"

"Ian, are there any areas of your life where expressing emotion is appropriate?" "Could it be that the constraints on men to be invulnerable and stoic are not as solid as we some-times think?" "Ian, is it possible that you don't have to be so subject to culture's demands?"

Through deconstruction, an astute therapist can support the discovery of alternative discourses, which allow for both personal transformation and also reconstruction of new understandings of how to be in the world.

Discuss

1. Make lists of what standard gender discourse specifies for women and men.
2. Choose one of the stories in this chapter and compare your own experience with that of the student's.
3. Construct a simple questionnaire exploring the effects of gender discourse in couple or family relationships. Answer this questionnaire among the class. Discuss the results.
4. What has the impact of feminism on your own family been?
5. What has the impact of feminism on your career choices been?
6. Collect and share stories of people who defy typical gender specifications in some area of life.

7. Collect a selection of magazines aimed at women and aimed at men. Deconstruct the images presented and speculate on the effects on men and women.

8. Share stories of the impact of gendered norms for body image on your own experience, and comment or speculate about how these impacts may change with age.

9. Watch a counseling videotape and focus specifically on the gender aspects portrayed. How would the counselor responses be different if the client were of a different gender or if the counselor were of a different gender?

Response to Chapter 9

SESEN NEGASH,
PHD, LMFT

Sesen Negash identifies as an Eritrean Black American, 1.5 generation immigrant, heterosexual, middle-class, cisgender woman. She received her master's degree at Purdue University Calumet in Child Development and Family Studies and her doctoral degree in Marriage and Family Therapy from The Florida State University. She is currently an assistant professor at San Diego State University. Her research interests include examining the relational needs of individuals in the correctional reentry population and exploring healthy forms of sexual expression among young adults.

The authors of this chapter present a stimulating discussion of the nuances of gender, sexuality, and intersectionality in ways that challenge the dominant and sometimes destructive cultural discourses that shape clients' experiences. While reading the authors' work, I began to consider how and to what extent the proliferation and viability of the Internet and social media have shaped gender and sexual attitudes, beliefs, and behaviors in recent decades.

The global use of the Internet and social media for information and human interaction challenges the idea that gender expression and sexuality continues to be largely influenced by social location (e.g., geographic location, religion, nationality, and ethnicity). Individuals living in the margins of society, especially those residing in homogenous communities, where harmful and restricting discourses are readily expressed about gender and sexuality, may find the Internet and social media extend their ability to reach ideas, perspectives, and behaviors that are not as accessible within the human interface with loved ones or local community members. For instance, questions like, "Who am I really if I do not identity as cisgender?" "What will my partner think about my use of pornography?" and "Am I the only one who feels ashamed of my body?" can be overwhelming to process and can be met with judgment and intolerance when explored with loved ones. Alternatively, the Internet and social media present a multiplicity of truths around gender and sexuality that some may feel creates a safe and validating space for them to explore their thoughts and ask questions.

The use of the Internet and social media can also be harmful. Thus, individuals are cautioned to set clear boundaries when exploring and expressing their gender and sexuality online. A case example may help crystalize this idea. A former client, who identified as a heterosexual trans woman, presented in therapy with concerns about her body image. The client, who lived in a small community with few residents who identified as transgender, spent years feeling isolated and fearful. The client was, however, resourceful, and over time became very involved with a few online transgender groups. Through those groups she felt supported, accepted, and emotionally fulfilled. Conversely, the client also admitted to spending hours online each day searching for and examining images of individuals who she believed met the beauty standard in the transgender community. Her excessive use of the Internet in this way often left her feeling anxious and distressed, especially on days when she would participate in public engagements. In an effort to defend and advocate for her community, the client also spent considerable time engaging in hostile online conversations with transphobic individuals on social media. It quickly became apparent in therapy that the client both benefited from and psychologically and emotionally suffered from having a presence online. Thus, together the client and I worked to help her set clear boundaries around her use the Internet and social media. Initially the goal was difficult for the client to adopt; however, after a time she learned to maintain a relationship with the Internet and social media that was centered around promoting healthy gender identity.

I implore clinicians reading this chapter to explore their own thoughts and feelings about Internet use and social media, and to assess to what extent their clients use the Internet and social media as a source of information and connection to explore and express their gender and sexuality. Taking these measures may help clinicians adopt a client-centered position about the benefits and risks posed to clients exploring salient aspects of their gender identity and sexuality.

Chapter 10

Affirming Gender, Sexual, and Relational Diversity

Penelope (Nel) Mercer, MA, MS

This chapter builds on the previous chapter by considering the range of gender, sexual, and relational identities, and presents an overview of providing "affirmative" (supportive and validating) therapy to individuals with diverse gender, sexual, and relationship-style identities and practices. Concepts and terminology are sourced primarily in scholarly and academic works and incorporate a diverse range of contributions representing lived experience. This chapter also includes material from comprehensive community-based sources, as there is little research- and theory-based material available on many of the topics; furthermore, community members' voices offer perspectives sometimes missed in the literature.

(a) Overarching Concepts and Themes, (b) Gender Identities and Practices, (c) Sexual Identities and Practices, (d) Relational Identities and Practices, and (e) Therapeutic Considerations.

Overarching Concepts and Themes

Language and Terminology

The language we use has important effects on our own and our clients' ways of thinking. As a relevant example, the word "queer" originally signified strangeness and has been used as a term of homophobic abuse. In the 1980s, it was reclaimed by people in the Lesbian, Gay, Bisexual, and Transgender (LGBT) communities. Today, queer is sometimes used as an umbrella term for anyone who isn't heterosexual and cisgender (identifying with the sex assigned at birth), with the advantages of being more encompassing and tidier than the acronym LGBTQQIP2SAA (for Lesbian, Gay, Bisexual, Transgender, Questioning, Queer, Intersex, Pansexual, Two Spirit, Androgynous, Asexual), often abbreviated as LGBTQ+.

However, use of the word "queer" can also be problematic. Many older people have painful memories of being called queer as a pejorative; and some queer theorists are opposed to "queer" being used as a term denoting fixed identity (Barker & Sheele, 2016) (see Box 10.1 on queer theory). An alternative to the term "queer" or acronym LGBTQ+ is to refer more inclusively to "gender, sexual, and relational diversity" (GSRD).

BOX 10.1 QUEER THEORY

"Queer" used to be an insult that was bandied about with an aim of hurting persons who were not hetero-sexual. It was taken up by people with marginalized sexual and gender identities and embraced in order to emphasize the difference between an essentialized and a non-essentialized account of identity. Part of the aim was to take the heat out of the word "queer" as an insult, but there were other distinctions that were intended. The concept "queer" embraces nondominant versions of sexuality without taking on a fixed iden-tity such as gay or lesbian. Neither though does it completely destroy the identities that have been built up around binary distinctions like straight or gay, male or female.

There is no single theorist who is responsible for queer theory, which originated in the 1980s and 1990s in a variety of critical perspectives, such as feminism, poststructuralism, AIDS activism, and other sources. Queer theory disputes the idea of *normal* sexual preferences. It critiques the dominance of *heteronorma-tivity*: that is, the idea that heterosexuality is normal and natural, and that alternatives, such as same-sex love, are distortions. This idea is shown to be an expression of discursive power that is produced and rein-forced in thousands of big and little ways, including through laws, the media, tax systems, and many other avenues. It works to pressure both gay and straight persons, because it can be found in all sorts of social institutions. Queer theory similarly calls out *homonormativity*, which refers to the replication of heterosex-ist norms and values *within* the queer community, marginalizing some queer individuals, in an attempt to win public approval for "equal" rights. Thus, queer theorists try to break down the power of popular cultur-al narratives by destabilizing them. An alternative to thinking and speaking in terms of dualisms like gay or straight, male or female is to refer to sexual diversity.

Using appropriate terms is the goal; but, despite our best intentions, we will inevitably make mis-takes (for example, by misgendering a client). In these instances, Richards and Barker (2013) suggest correcting the mistake in a matter-of-fact way, apologizing, and moving on. The intention here is to avoid taking up therapy time, or putting responsibility on the client to make the therapist feel better. However, it is important for the therapist to remain in a receptive stance, if the client wants to discuss their thoughts and feelings about the interaction.

This chapter includes and defines many of the terms relevant to GSRD populations that therapists may wish to know; but, as new terms emerge and meanings shift rapidly, the reader might also find online sources useful.

Issues relating to terminology are described in Katie Mercer's statement, below.

> When I realized I was interested in dating women, I struggled with how to present my
> identity to people both within and outside of the LGBTQ+ community. While my first
> relationship with someone of my own gender felt easy and intuitive to me, it took many
> years before coming out to people felt natural. I'm much more comfortable with my queer
> identity now, but the coming out process still doesn't always feel easy, eight years later.
> Even writing this, I wonder whether to identify as pansexual, bisexual, or queer. Pansex-
> ual feels right to me now, but just a few months ago queer resonated more for me. While

FIGURE 10.1   Katie is a 26-year-old graduate student who identifies as White, cisgender, and pansexual.

I was identifying as queer, many people didn't understand the word as I used it, or really understand what it represents. While I identified as bisexual for many years, the label never felt right to me, as it suggests that I experience a 50/50 divide between my attraction to males and females. This is not inclusive of the many beautiful gender identities I'm attracted to, and is inaccurate because my attraction to certain genders changes and fluctuates over time. All of this feels difficult to explain in one simple label for people who are not used to thinking about sexuality and gender on a spectrum.

Katie's comments capture the challenge and importance of finding words to describe her identity. She also refers to conceptualizing sexuality and gender on spectrums, the topic to which we now turn.

From Fixed and Binary to Fluid and Spectrums

Alfred Kinsey, a pioneer in sex research, developed a single-axis model of sexual orientation (the Kinsey Scale; Kinsey, Pomeroy & Martin, 1948), which widely introduced the concept of sexuality as a spectrum, rather than a binary (Barker & Sheele, 2016). To better capture the complexities of sexual orientation, Fritz Klein (2013) later developed the Klein Sexual Orientation Grid (KSOG) to capture changes in sexual orientation over time. While this is viewed by many as an improvement on the Kinsey Scale, it retains the limitation of assuming, and thereby reaffirming, the notion of binary gender categories.

The notion that gender is fixed and binary is challenged both by queer theory and by the lived experience of those whose gender identity is more fluid and/or less dichotomous. Blogger, activist, and writer Ashley Mardell (2016) advocates for gender to be understood not as discrete categories (for example, male/female), but rather as fluid and as spectrums. Mardell offers an inclusive definition of gender identity as the "identifier (or lack of identifier) someone uses to communicate how they understand their personal gender, navigate within or outside our societal gender systems, and/or desire to be perceived by others" (p. 9).

Gender expression, by contrast, is an individual's presentation (for example, physical appearance, clothing, and behaviors) that expresses aspects of gender identity or gender role. Gender identity may or may not correspond with gender expression, primary or secondary sex characteristics, or sex assigned at birth. Therefore, a person's gender identity cannot be assumed from their presentation, and we must rely on their self-identification (American Psychological Association, 2015). This implies that, as Mardell pointedly summarizes, "A man is someone who identifies as a man ... [and] a woman is someone who identifies as a woman" (p. 90, emphasis original). Therapists can invite communication about gender identity by stating their own pronouns during introductions and including their pronouns on email and other written communication. Richards and Barker (2013) further suggest using "ask etiquette": if you are not sure about a client's gender identity, ask.

Generational Differences

Cultural commentator Michael Shulman (2013) writes that the present generation of youth seek "an upending of gender roles beyond the binary of male/female" (paragraph 5), and generally have more fluid and nuanced understandings of sexuality, gender, and relationship styles. Further, coming out in the digital era provides immensely expanded opportunities for exploring nonheteronormative and gender-variant identities (Smith, Arguello, & Dentato, 2016).

This increased ability for young people to self-define gender roles, sexuality, and relationship style, combined with the rapidly changing social mores supported by digital connectivity, contribute to a challenging generational divide. Parents, teachers, and other caregivers may feel alienated, struggle to keep up with terminology and associated conceptual shifts, and, therefore, be less able to support young people with nontraditional gender, sexual, or relational identities (Arguello, 2016). Frank discussions between youth and adults about sexuality, particularly nonheterosexuality, continue to be rare, so young people tend to get most of their information about sexuality online, and often from pornography (Smith, Arguello, & Dentato, 2016). Counselors can support families by identifying these dynamics and facilitating communication. They might also usefully guide clients and family members toward websites with helpful information and supportive online communities for both the client and their families, perhaps co-investigating some web content during session (Zamani, Smith, & Monk, 2013).

The Gender Unicorn infographic (Trans Student Educational Resources, n.d.), is a useful tool for both counselors and clients to conceptualize gender and sexuality on spectrums. The Gender Unicorn also distinguishes among the concepts of gender identity, gender expression, sex assigned at birth, physical/sexual attraction, and romantic/emotional attraction. Try plotting your own identities on the various spectrums of the Gender Unicorn. You might also consider utilizing the Gender Unicorn with clients.

Prejudicial Dominant Discourses

People developing GSRD identities must actively resist and reject many dominant discourses about what is considered "normal" in order to develop a positive identity. Such resistance may involve a struggle against internalized myths that are rampant in the dominant culture, as well as risking legal, social, psychological, economic, and even physical safety in the quest to overcome barriers and express identities.

Prejudicial stereotypes are driven by myths that suggest the following:

> People are homosexual, bisexual, asexual, transgender, or nonmonogamous as a result of a dysfunctional family upbringing.
> People who are gay, bisexual, asexual, transgender, or nonmonogamous are not capable of forming long-lasting partnerships.
> People who are gay, bisexual, transgender, or nonmonogamous should not be engaged in child raising or working with children.
> Publicly living a gay, bisexual, asexual, transgender, or nonmonogamous identity rules out taking up positions of leadership, responsibility, and authority in the community.

People internalize these myths from home and school environments, along with fairy tales, other literature, and Hollywood movies. Some of the myths are overt and easily challenged. Others are subtle, more covert and harder to resist, because they lie hidden as cultural assumptions swallowed up along with stereotypes and assumptions about gender, sexuality, and relationships or theories of "normal" development. Based in part on these and other myths, people in GSRD communities have, historically and presently, been subject to harassment, discrimination, and persecution.

Research confirms that those in GSRD populations are more likely to experience dehumanization and prejudice. MacInnis and Hodson (2012) reported that asexual individuals are viewed as less human and evaluated more negatively than heterosexual individuals; and according to Shucart (2016), a 2012 *Loving More* poll found that 26% of polyamorous individuals had experienced discrimination. Transgender individuals are exposed to especially high levels of discrimination, abuse, and physical violence. According to the 2015 U.S. Transgender Survey, among transgender children in grades K–12 who were "out" or perceived as transgender, 54% reported being verbally harassed, 24% were physically attacked, and 13% were sexually assaulted for being transgender (James et al., 2016).

Therapists should note that these all-too-real aspects of GSRD experience inform clients' choices, attitudes, and expectations, and influence both mental and physical health. Research consistently highlights the stress that gender, sexual, and relational minorities experience, which may lead to higher rates of emotional distress and increased suicide risk (Milton & Coyle, 1999; Butler, 2010; James et al., 2016).

POINTS TO DISCUSS

Catherine Butler (2010) recommends the following group exercise to identify and challenge stereotypes:

1. As a whole group or in small groups, generate stereotypes for each of the following identities or practices and have someone write them on a board: *nonbinary/genderqueer, transgender, cisgender, gay, lesbian, bisexual/pansexual, asexual, BDSM/kink, heterosexual, swinger, polyamorous, people who hook up, monogamous.*
2. Discuss. What commonalities and differences do you notice across the groups? Does it seem that these stereotypes relate to perceived deviance from a "norm"? Do you consider any of the stereotypes particularly damaging or pathologizing? Have you noticed these stereotypes coming up in yourself, or in your clients, and do you see value in identifying/naming them? Do you have alternative knowledges and/or experiences that challenge these stereotypes? What are some ways you might encounter and engage with these stereotypes in your client work?

Identity, Invisibility, and Erasure

Invisibility or erasure of a person's identity occurs when dominant discourses hold that identity to be invalid, immoral, or irrelevant, such that that person's needs go unaddressed and their very existence is called into question. People with GRSD identities experience erasure in countless big and small ways, such as:

not seeing themselves represented in media, except in heavily stereotyped ways;
not finding relevant options for identification on official forms;
having their identity misunderstood, confused, or conflated with other identities;
seeing the lives and accomplishments of people embodying their identity overlooked or obfuscated;
having relevant anti-discrimination laws challenged or dismantled.

The experience of erasure conveys to an individual that their identity does not matter, and, therefore, that they themselves do not matter; and this may lead to anxiety and depression (Ulrich, 2011). Research indicates that those who embody more than one marginalized identity, and those who identify as nonbinary, transgender, asexual, bisexual, and/or intersex, are especially likely to experience erasure of their identity (Barker & Sheele, 2016). Therapists can play an important role in recognizing and validating the many identities that clients embody, as Amanda Mercer's statement, below, conveys. Amanda is a 24-year-old who identifies as White, Jewish, nonbinary, and queer.

> *Our society tries really hard to stomp out any identity that falls outside of the binary norm. One way it tries to do that is by telling nonbinary people that we are confused about our own gender identities. No matter what a person's presentation is or what pronouns they use, if a person says they are nonbinary, they deserve to be seen and believed in their identity. From my perspective, one of the best things a therapist can do when working with a nonbinary client is to wholeheartedly accept the legitimacy of their experience. By validating a nonbinary person's identity, a therapist can help a nonbinary person heal from the trauma of being consistently discounted and disbelieved in their world outside of therapy.*

Discrimination by Medical and Mental Health Professionals

Discrimination by medical and mental health professionals directly and indirectly impacts the physical and mental health of GSRD individuals. Anticipated stigma and/or concern that medical records will not be kept private lead many individuals to not disclose their GSRD status, even when this may be relevant to their care. For example, more than half of individuals who practice kink did not disclose this to their doctor in a study by Waldura, Arora, Randall, Farala, & Sprott (2016); anticipated stigma and concern that the kink activity would be interpreted as interpersonal violence were commonly cited reasons. James et al. (2016) report that 23% of transgender people in a national survey chose not to see a doctor when they needed to because of fear of discrimination or mistreatment, and 33% reported having been refused treatment, verbally harassed, physically or sexually assaulted, or having to educate their provider about transgender issues in order to get appropriate care.

Nichols (2006) writes, "Psychiatry has a rather shameful history of collusion with institutions of political power to marginalize certain subgroups of the population, particularly women and sexual minorities. Most psychological theories are unconsciously biased towards the preservation of prevalent social mores" (p. 282). Therapists can counter these marginalizing effects by helping GSRD clients deconstruct notions of normality, and mental health and illness.

Lillianna, who is polyamorous, describes her experience of biased counseling.

> *Rick and I once saw a couples counselor who interpreted every concern we raised as a product of being poly [polyamorous], even though we asked her to stop and despite the fact that we'd been poly for a decade. She even told me, "Maybe when you work through your issues from the past, you won't need to be poly anymore." Rick and I got some help with communication skills from her, but we didn't continue, because she couldn't stop seeing our choosing polyamory as the cause of any difficulties we faced in our relationship. We knew it wasn't relevant, but she thought that was our denial.*

Conversion or reparative therapy, which attempts to change an individual's sexual orientation or gender identity or expression, is another, stark example of the ways in which GSRD clients have been abused in mental health settings. The practice is widely condemned by the psychiatric, therapeutic, and medical communities as harmful and ineffective; however, only nine states have banned the use of conversion therapy on youth. The Williams Institute estimates that 20,000 youth currently aged 13 to 17 will receive conversion therapy from licensed mental health professionals before turning 18, and another 57,000 youth will receive conversion therapy from religious or spiritual advisers (Mallory, Brown, & Conron, 2018). The continued practice of reparative therapy, rooted in the belief that being gay, bisexual, or transgender is abnormal, bad, and/or wrong, highlights the power of dominant discourses to shape the attitudes of mental health professionals, along with the experiences of individuals and families who seek help.

Pathologization, Medicalization, Objectification, and Activism

Our understanding of psychopathology is strongly influenced by the American Psychiatric Association (APA)'s *Diagnostic and Statistical Manual of Mental Disorders* (*DSM*; APA, 2013a), a dominant taxonomy of mental illness. The *DSM* informs physical and mental health providers, courts, insurance companies, and policy makers, and may be viewed as an important battleground for those whose sexual or gender identities are pathologized as mental illness. Along with the APA's status as a medical body, the notion of scientific objectivity that underpins the *DSM* lends it the credibility of scientific fact, even though the study of mental health and illness is, arguably, not amenable to precise scientific dissection (Rosenau, 1991). The *DSM* also supports what Foucault (1982) termed a "dividing practice" (p. 777), in that people identified as abnormal become subjects of scientific curiosity, and are thus objectified.

Drescher (2015) points out that gay activism was the primary catalyst for changes in the *DSM* regarding homosexuality, which was described as a mental illness in the *DSM*'s first edition (APA, 1952). Based on political pressure and a dearth of empirical evidence that homosexuality is a mental disorder, the *DSM-II* (1973) replaced the diagnosis of "homosexuality" with "ego-dystonic homosexuality," (Federoff, Di Gioacchino & Murphy, 2013). After continued pressure, the APA removed the diagnosis "ego-dystonic homosexuality" from the *DSM-III-R* (1987) supporting a shift from focusing on etiology and blame (that is, "what causes homosexuality?") and medicalization (that is, "how can we treat it or fix it?"), to focusing on the health and mental health needs of gay clients.

More recently, due to concerted efforts by asexual activists (Bogaert, 2012), there was a similar (incomplete) step toward depathologizing asexuality in the *DSM-5* (APA, 2013a), which states that people who show "marked distress" regarding their low levels of sexual attraction should be diagnosed with a mental disorder. Brotto and Yule (2017) argue that this is still unnecessarily pathologizing. It also tends to lead to the medicalization of asexuality (for example, the suggestion of hormone therapy with the goal of increasing sex drive; Bogaert, 2012). Brotto and Yule further argue that the evidence does not support asexuality being a mental illness.

Transsexualism and gender identity disorder, which were identified as mental illnesses in the *DSM-IV-TR* (APA, 2010, have been supplanted in the *DSM-5* (APA, 2013a) with the new diagnosis of "gender dysphoria," to reflect the fact that being transgender, per se, is not a mental illness, a development welcomed by transgender activists, who view this as a positive step in the direction of removing "Gender Dysphoria" from the DSM entirely.

With regard to BDSM (defined below), activism and advocacy by researchers and sex therapists have led to revisions in the *DSM-5* (APA, 2013a). Cross-dressing, fetishes, and BDSM continue to be identified as "paraphilias" (persistent, intense and unusual sexual interests); however, these are newly distinguished from "paraphilic disorders," (involving behaviors that cause mental distress to a person or render that person a serious threat to the well-being of others) (APA, 2013b). In this way, the *DSM-5* has drawn a diagnostic line between consensual, adult BDSM practices and sexual activities that are nonconsensual, intentionally harmful, or involve a minor.

This shift has had an immediate legal impact: the National Coalition for Sexual Freedom (DSM-5, n.d.) states that there was an immediate, sharp rise in the success rate of BDSM-practicing parents seeking custody of children, once the proposed changes in the *DSM-5* (APA, 2013a) depathologizing BDSM were released. The ongoing inclusion of paraphilias in the *DSM-5* continues to be challenged by researchers, clinicians, and activists, such as Charles Moser and Peggy Kleinplatz. Moser & Kleinplatz (2005) criticize the *DSM's* history of "equating particular sexual interests with psychopathology" (p. 91), and argue that the construct of paraphilias is ambiguous and fails to describe a distinct and diagnosable mental disorder (Federoff, Di Gioacchino & Murphy, 2013).

POINTS TO DISCUSS

How do you use the *DSM* (American Psychiatric Association, 2013a) in your practice? Do you see value in identifying a diagnosis? Why or why not?

The Value of GSRD Community

The value of community is a consistent theme in the literature on GSRD (e.g., Alexander, 1999). Community is defined by Mardell (2016) as "a collective group of LGBTQ+ people and organizations, as well as their supporters, who are all united by common identities, cultures, and/or social goals" (p. 8). Community gathering places facilitate recognition, education, and destigmatization among GSRD people, and community involvement may help individuals feel less isolated and allow for political mobilization (Westphal, 2004).

Today, many people find GSRD community online. Arguello (2016) argues that although there are risks associated with online communities and social networking, this aspect of modern Western culture offers "a critical safe space" for GSRD individuals and "facilitates agency and choice" (p. 143). Both real and virtual GSRD communities can offer safe places to challenge dominant discourses and foster identity.

Limitations on the Value of Community

However, not all people have an interest in or have found benefit through community, and people with multiple marginalized identities have more complicated relationships with GSRD communities. For example, bisexual, transgender, and asexual individuals have historically been less supported, overlooked, or even actively discriminated against within GSRD communities (Barker & Scheele, 2016). Richards and Barker (2013) suggest that counselors should, therefore, keep in mind that those embodying multiple GSRD identities, especially across ethnicity and class, may have more trouble finding a community that represents them; and that community involvement that benefits one client may not benefit another client with a similar identity or practice.

Meera, who is a therapist, shares her experience that illustrates some of these points.

> *I am a queer cisgender Indian woman. When I was first exploring attraction and relationships with women I was struck by what it meant to have to choose between cultural identities, and I came to understand and embody intersectionality. A number of years ago, I could not bring my partner to Indian cultural events, but I also did not want to attend them without her. The queer community that was visible and accessible to me was predominantly White. I felt alienated and marginalized in both these community spaces, and I wondered how and where I could find space and community that were more closely aligned with all of the ways that I moved through the world.*
>
> *While my parents slowly became accepting of my partner and my identity, they did not know how to find support from their families, their social circle, or their community; and my being gay, as we called it at that time, became our family secret. Neither my parents nor I were happy with this split, but we struggled to find a resolution for this. I wonder now if a therapist could have helped us bridge this divide and navigate our respective paths while connecting us as a family. At that time it seemed impossible to find someone who could work with us as a family, understanding Indian culture as well as gay identity. If that therapist had been found, they could have helped us through this transition, and have affirmed all of the various connections and community that were so important to us. Perhaps family counseling could have helped us name what was happening, and talk about what we did not have words for.*

Meera's story demonstrates how oppressive dominant discourses can alienate community members, and family members, from one another, and how intersections among identities may make finding supportive community especially difficult. As Meera suggests, a therapist may be able to help family members name these discourses and mitigate their effects.

Intersectionality

Intersectionality refers to the ways in which sexual preference interacts with gender, relationship style, race, ethnicity, and social class, as well as with age, able-bodiedness, religion, immigration/citizenship status, and geographic location, among other aspects of identity. Meera's statement (above) and Mia Little's statement (below), both demonstrate the effects of intersectionality and the ways in which marginalizations can compound.

> *I am a queer genderqueer of color sex worker. Those are key identities that I hold. I was born and raised as a girl. In my 20s with language acquisition and greater understanding about gender I took on genderqueer to accurately describe my gender. I was first aware of my queerness in my youth when I realized that I was attracted to both men and women. Today, in contrast to my gender performance at work, internally my gender is a fluid*

FIGURE 10.2   Mia Little is a graduate of the San Diego
State University Marriage and Family Therapy Program.

blend of masculinity and femininity. Sometimes, not always, I identify as a womxn. My pronouns are they/them/she/her. I am keenly aware of my internal state, but as someone in a body that reads as femme, I am often gendered as female.

As a child I knew that my attraction to women was something that should be hidden because it deviated from the heterosexual dynamics expected in my Filipino upbringing. When I tried to initiate conversations with my parents as a youth to ask about sex, my body, and attraction, I was dismissed and told that I wasn't allowed to date until after college. The assumption was that I would only date men, with the objective of inevitable marriage and then children. Cisgender heterosexuality paired with sex negativity were norms in my culture. In my family, sex was seen as necessary to bring in the next generation; otherwise, it was deeply discouraged, shameful, and dirty. Sexuality was expressed in family members' hidden stashes of pornography and romantic erotic novels, but was never overtly spoken of, except to silence or shame its expression.

When I became a sex worker, I learned how powerful a barrier and marginalizing force stigma can be in the interpersonal, professional, and political arenas. The dominant culture views sex workers as victims to be saved, dirty, objects, subhuman, and unable to make sound decisions over their bodies. I see it in the way people speak about sex workers as criminals or victims. I see it in how casually people make dead hooker jokes that minimize the violent realities sex workers face into something meant to be funny. I see it in how legislation written to combat sex trafficking, but written without the consultation of trafficked people or sex workers, in effect further endangers and marginalizes both trafficked people and sex workers.

A dominant discourse that perpetuates violence against sex workers is that if you sell sex, consent no longer applies to you, and you are open for any and all sexual interactions. This couldn't be further from the truth. Sex workers navigate consent with greater awareness than non-sex workers, because consent informs every aspect of our labor. Sex work has also been an important part of LGBTQIA history and survival of queer individuals.

When it comes to mental health providers, I want them to investigate their own internal sex negativity and discourses on sex, gender, relationships, sexual orientation, desire, sexual shame, body shame, and intimacy. I encourage mental health professionals to divest their internalized sex worker stigma and the layers of sex negativity, slut shaming, and patriarchal bias against sex workers; and to challenge White cisgender heteronormativity as the default. Mental health providers should be mindful of how marginalizations compound and how racism, classism, and other oppressive factors intersect with different identities. Counselors should be prepared with resources to connect clients to professionals and organizations that support those navigating their sexuality and gender—and who are accessible and supportive of Black and Brown people.

An essential way to support a client who is out as a sex worker is to validate their labor, lived experience, and unique positionality. Mental health professionals should see that sex work is a valid form of work and labor; be aware of and willing to learn more about the unique nature of sex work; acknowledge that sexuality is diverse and no one view or social norm can encompass what constitutes healthy sexuality; respect their sex worker client and not try to "save" them or pathologize their work; and recognize that sex workers are entitled to privacy and their own boundaries, just like any other client.

Mia's statement highlights the distinction between gender identity (internal state) and gender performance (external expression), and the oppressive, compounding effects associated with embodying multiple marginalized identities. Mia also identifies the problem of sex negativity (see Box 10.2 on sex positivity) and illuminates how discourses that pathologize and dehumanize sex workers influence our legal system and hurt those individuals.

BOX 10.2 SEX POSITIVITY

This chapter takes a sex-positive stance, understood as a counterpoint to problematic cultural discourses conveying that sex is dirty or sinful (outside of narrowly circumscribed, heteronormative and mononormative contexts). These discourses can promote guilt, fear, and disgust around sexual expression and feelings.

By contrast, sex positivity, as articulated by both sex positive feminism and queer theory (Glick, 2000), promotes acceptance of diverse sexual expression, along with medically accurate sex education and safer sex practices. Beyond consent, sex positivity does not make moral judgments about what form sexuality takes, instead celebrating the diversity of pleasurable, life-affirming, and, for some people, spiritual aspects of sexual and sensual experiences, whether partnered or solo.

Sex positivity, like all discourses, may have different meanings and expressions among people embodying different identities. For example, for those on the asexual spectrum, sex positivity may mean supporting oneself and others in having as little (or as much) sex as they want; and for women of color, who are especially sexualized and fetishized by dominant cultural discourses, sex positivity may involve reclaiming the right to be desexualized (D. Loyoza, personal communication, September 7, 2018). Here, sex positivity refers to celebrating "sexual diversity, differing desires and relationship structures, and individual choices based on consent" (Queen & Comella, 2008, p. 294).

POINTS TO DISCUSS

Are there aspects of Meera's or Mia Little's comments that you particularly relate to, or that make you uncomfortable? How do you think about and make space for the complexity of the intersecting identities that you and your clients embody? What are your thoughts about the concept of sex positivity?

Families of Origin, Families of Choice

Many people embodying gender, sexual, or relational diversity experience rejection and alienation from their families of origin, as parents and siblings are impacted by dominant, disparaging cultural discourses. There is significant research showing that parental attitudes toward GSRD children affect their psychosocial adjustment. Twenty-six percent of transgender individuals report that a family member has rejected or stopped speaking to them (James et al., 2016). Sexual minority youth are 20% more likely to experience parental physical abuse than their nonminority counterparts (Friedman et al., 2011), and D'amico, Julien, Tremblay, and Chartrand (2015) report that parental negative reactions to LGB adolescents' disclosure of sexual orientation are associated with high levels of depression and low self-esteem. Therapists may be able to help family members identify the discursive sources of toxic homophobic and transphobic attitudes that negatively impact everyone in the family system, and develop alternative discourses that foster connection and mutual support.

Many people who have been rejected by families of origin form "families of choice," which provide critical support and an essential social and developmental context (Weston, 1991). Therapists can therefore support clients by recognizing and supporting their relationships with families of choice, which may extend into networks of mutually supportive individuals. The importance of families of choice is particularly evident among aging LGBTQ+ individuals.

LGBTQ+ and Aging

There are unique challenges among aging lesbian, gay, bisexual, and transgender populations. Based on one of the first state-level, population-based studies and a national community-based survey of over 2,500 LGBT older adults, Fredriksen-Goldsen et al. (2011) found that instead of relying on family related by blood or marriage, the majority of LGBT older adults rely heavily on friends and partners, generally of a similar age, for assistance as they age. Fredriksen-Goldsen et al. write that though this reflects the essential, supportive, and caring community created by LGBT individuals, there are limits to the ability of same-age peers to provide care over the long term, and that friends acting as care-givers may be unable to make legal decisions regarding finances or healthcare on behalf of the older adult receiving care.

The older gay male community lost much of their cohort due to HIV/AIDS, which continues to devastate by "interrupting the normal aging process for those who have contracted it and prematurely aging those who care for them" (Brown, Alley, Sarosy, Quarto, & Cook, 2001, p. 41). Fredriksen-Goldsen et al. (2011) report that older LGBTQ+ adults who hold racial and ethnic minoritized identities are at greater risk for aging and health disparities (such as reluctance or inability to access healthcare due to cost or discrimination), as are those with lower incomes and/or less education. Fredriksen-Goldsen et al. report that there is consensus among diverse aging LGBT communities that the most needed services are senior housing, transportation, legal services, social events, support groups, and support-ive, nondiscriminatory long-term care facilities. Therapists may help aging LGBTQ+ clients connect with needed services; they may also consider advocating politically for the needs of this multiply marginalized population.

GSRD and Parenting

Despite the fact that many studies have shown that children raised by people embodying GSRD identities have similar outcomes to children raised in conventional families (Sheff, 2014; Clarke, Ellis, Peel, & Riggs, 2009), due to problematic dominant discourses, many GSRD parents experience social opprobrium, even from mental health professionals (for example, Ruskin, 2013), and GSRD parents may internalize damaging biases. It is also more difficult for people in GSRD communities to adopt children or gain custody of children following a divorce (Sheff, 2014; Ross, Epstein, Goldfinger, & Yager, 2009). Therapists can help clients who are GSRD parents to deconstruct dominant discourses and identify preferred local discourses related to parenting in the context of GSRD; challenge any inter-nalized prejudices regarding child rearing they may hold; describe research on outcomes for children raised by GSRD parents; and maintain lists of medical, legal, and mental health providers who provide affirmative care.

Identities and Practices

Ideally, clients will indicate their own preferred terms for describing their gender, sexual, and rela-tional identities and practices; and will indicate whether the specific sex, gender, or relational topic under discussion represents a practice, an identity, or both. The point here is that practices and identities may or may not overlap. For example, some individuals incorporate kink practices into their sex lives, but do not identify as kinky; and some individuals identify as kinky but are not cur-rently engaging in kink.

The following sections on marginalized gender, sexual, and relational identities and practices constitutes a brief overview, rather than in-depth discussion. Please note that, apart from the lived experience statements, the descriptions are generalizations, and will not be uniformly applicable to individual clients.

Gender Identities and Practices: Transgender, Nonbinary, and Intersex

The transgender, nonbinary, and intersex communities highlight how unforgiving society can be in relation to dominant cultural forces demanding that people live within rigid gendered prescriptions. Intersex, transgender, and nonbinary people are often pathologized and judged as perverted or bad (Brammer, 2012), and experience high rates of medicalization, fetishization, and intrusive questioning about their gender and sexual identities and functioning, in medical, legal, and interpersonal settings. Therapists must pay close attention to helping clients manage their harmful environments, reinforcing the notion that problems are located not inside them, but within the dominant binary discourses that occur in the gender prescriptions.

Transgender (trans)/Gender Nonconforming (GNC)/Gender Diverse (GD)

Trans, GNC, and GD are umbrella terms for gender identities and/or gender roles (social roles and behaviors) that differ, in varying degrees, from sex assigned at birth. This section focuses on people who transition on a full-time basis, rather than on people who "cross-dress," or present in a way that is not societally expected for a person of that birth-assigned gender, on a part-time basis (Richards & Barker, 2013). A trans woman or woman of trans experience is someone who was assigned male at birth (AMAB) and who identifies as, and therefore is, a woman; a trans man or man of trans experience is someone who was assigned female at birth (AFAB) and who identifies as, and therefore is, a man. The descriptors Female to Male (FTM) or Male to Female (MTF) are not often used outside of medical contexts, as the person may never have identified with the gender assigned at birth. The older term *transsexual* is also mainly associated with medical transition and therefore not an umbrella term.

Due to discomfort and distress associated with incongruence among gender identity, sex assigned at birth, primary and secondary sex characteristics, and gender role, trans people who have not transitioned often experience low mood and/or anxiety, termed gender dysphoria (Knudson, DeCuypere, & Bockting, 2010), which is associated with markedly increased risk for suicide and self-harm (James et al., 2016). By contrast, those who transition, socially and/or medically, to a gender expression and role in alignment with their gender identity, tend to have no more psychopathology than the rest of the population (de Vries et al., 2014; Hoshiai et al., 2010).

Richards and Barker (2013) state that some trans people suffer from believing that they are not "real" men or "real" women. Underpinning these troubling feelings of perceived inadequacy are dominant discourses dictating that gender identity is strictly dichotomous and is tied to physiology. Therefore, Richards and Barker encourage therapists to identify alternative discourses highlighting gender spectrums and uncoupling gender identity from physiology (for example, by pointing out that not every female body has a uterus). Richards and Barker argue that medical transition, should it occur, is more successful when clients have already come to think in terms of spectrums of sex and gender, as supported by outcome studies of gender confirmation surgery (e.g., van de Grift et al., 2017).

Transitioning

Transitioning refers to social, psychological, and/or physical changes that an individual makes to better express their gender identity. Social transition involves coming out as trans to family and friends, adjusting gender expression, and changing names and identification documents (Tando, 2016). Medical transition is also undertaken by many, but certainly not all, trans people. A myriad of personal and contextual factors, including the significant cost of surgical interventions, influence trans individuals' decisions about the timing, nature, and extent of transition (Planned Parenthood, n.d.). Therapists working with transgender clients may wish to deconstruct problematic discourses suggesting that a transgender individual who has not transitioned in particular ways (for example, medically) is "less" transgender than one who has.

The first medical intervention is generally hormone therapy, as it is to some extent reversible, while surgeries, which may be undertaken next, are not. Gender affirming surgery (or genital reconstruction surgery/genital reassignment surgery/gender confirmation surgery) include "top surgery" to remove or create breasts, and/or "bottom surgery" to create genitals aligning with the person's gender identity. Richards and Barker (2013) suggest that therapists avoid unnecessarily intrusive questioning about a client's medical transition process. However, supportive aftercare is essential, particularly following bottom surgery, so therapists may assist clients by helping them ensure that they have adequate physical and emotional support post-surgery.

There are many studies finding considerably increased well-being for trans individuals who medically transition (for example, Smith, Van Goozen, & Cohen-Kettenis, 2001; van de Grift et al., 2017). Research has also addressed post-operative regret. Dhejne, Oberg, Arver, and Landen (2014) found that over a 50-year period, just 2.2% of transgender individuals who had received gender confirmation surgery in Sweden were dissatisfied, and that rates of dissatisfaction significantly decreased over the time period of the study. Van de Grift et al. (2017) found that persistent dissatisfaction post-surgery tends to be associated with higher levels of body dissatisfaction entering surgery; loss of physical (including sexual) sensitivity; and surgical complications. Among those who are dissatisfied, some people detransition, or reverse, as much as possible, the effects of hormones and/or surgeries used in the medical transition process.

The World Professional Association for Transgender Health (WPATH, 2011) has issued guidelines regarding healthcare for transsexual, transgender, and GNC people. These suggest that trans people do not need a referral letter from a therapist in order to receive hormone treatment, but should provide referral letters from one mental health professional for top surgery, or from two mental health professionals for bottom surgery. Therefore, therapists continue to act as gatekeepers of the medical transition process, which is one reason trans individuals seek therapy. (Please note that these guidelines are not uniformly applied across medical, legal, and insurance contexts.)

An alternative to this "gatekeeper" model is the "informed consent" model, preferred by many trans advocates (Jacobs, 2019), in which the trans individual and medical care provider explicitly discuss potential risks and benefits, and decision-making power ultimately rests with the trans individual.

Cavanaugh, Hopwood, and Lambert (2016) argue that adoption of this model would allow healthcare providers to deliver better healthcare to trans and GNC patients.

Transgender/Gender Diverse Children and Their Parents

For some young children, expressing a desire to be another gender, or being agender or genderfluid, is temporary; for others, it is not. Not all children who are gender diverse are transgender, but all transgender children are gender diverse (Tando, 2016). A general rule for assessing if a child is transgender, rather than gender diverse, is if the child is consistent, insistent, and persistent about their transgender identity (Rafferty, 2018).

Parents may approach therapists with the request that their child be "fixed" (reparative therapy; Ehrensaft, 2017). With regard to counseling transgender children and adolescents, WPATH considers interventions attempting to align gender identity and expression with sex assigned at birth to be "unethical" (Coleman et al., 2012, p. 175). The American Academy of Pediatrics (Rafferty, 2018) also strongly opposes the "outdated" approach called "watchful waiting" (p. 4), in which a child's gender-diverse assertions are held tentatively until an arbitrary age (generally post-puberty):

> Watchful waiting is based on binary notions of gender in which gender diversity and fluidity is pathologized; in watchful waiting, it is also assumed that notions of gender identity become fixed at a certain age.... More robust and current research suggests that, rather than focusing on who a child will become, valuing them for who they are, even at a young age, fosters secure attachment and resilience, not only for the child but also for the whole family (p. 4).

The position statement also asserts that the evidence "suggests that using an integrated affirmative model results in young people having fewer mental health concerns whether they ultimately identify as transgender" (p. 4).

Tando (2016) advises parents to allow younger children to express a GNC identity and, if desired, socially transition, as this is an affirming but not irreversible step. (Decisions and processes relating to medical transition are, of course, more complex; a team of medical and mental health professionals is likely to be involved.) Tando also writes that some, but not all, parents of trans and GNC children go through their own process of transition, including complex combinations of concern, fear, grief, and loss. Therapists can support parents of GNC children by normalizing parents' feelings and providing a space in which they can safely process any grief or fears related to their child's gender nonconformity and possible transition. Support groups for parents of GNC children (and for the children themselves) may also be helpful, in part by providing a space in which problematic dominant discourses relating to gender may be challenged, and preferred understandings developed and shared. Therapists can also offer practical guidance to parents about the most likely routes to better outcomes for trans and GNC youth, which generally involve acceptance of the child's expressed gender identity and education of social and educational networks (such as schools and clubs; Richards & Barker, 2013).

Many of these concepts are illustrated in Isaac and Monica's stories, below.

Monica is a 52-year-old, cisgender, Mexican woman, and Isaac is her 24-year-old transgender son. Monica talks about her experience of raising Isaac, and Isaac talks about his experience of growing up transgender. Note that Monica goes through a process of profound concern and adjustment, and that she provides affirming support for Isaac. Their stories also highlight the importance of working within social settings, such as a child's school, to facilitate transition.

FIGURE 10.3   Monica and Isaac

Monica writes about her experience of raising a transgender son, below.

> There were so many things I didn't understand when Isaac was growing up. When he was two, he would take his bathing suit top off, and when I asked him why, he'd say, "I'm embarrassed to wear it." I always told him, "You can wear what you want, but you know you're a girl, right?" I found out that sometimes he would use male names when he was introducing himself. He didn't want to take a bath; I didn't realize that it was because he didn't want to see his body.

When we were shopping for preschool, Isaac said, "Mom, can you buy me a penis?" I asked him, "Why do you want one?" He said, "I need one, I don't know why." When he was four, his aunt gave him a dress for his birthday, and when she arrived at his party, he wasn't wearing it. She said, "I bought you that dress to wear for your party." He thought about it and then changed and said, "I'll wear it for you to be happy." That was the last time he wore a dress.

At first I thought Isaac was a lesbian, but when he was eight years old, I realized that my daughter thinks she's a boy—and I googled that. This was sixteen years ago, and there was not much about trans on the Internet. There was a checklist of things to see if your child had gender dysphoria. Almost all the things were true for Isaac. So I knew Isaac had gender dysphoria when he was eight, but I still didn't make all the connections. When he was 10 years old, he kept leaving the mirror door on the bathroom medicine cabinet open. I got mad and said, "Why do you do that?" He said, "Look in the mirror, what do you see?" I did, and I saw myself down to my waist. I realized that he didn't want to see himself, now that he was starting to grow breasts. This was one of the most painful moments of my life, seeing my son, who was assigned female, be in so much pain.

When he started his period, he wouldn't use tampons or pads, he would just bring changes of clothes. Instead of books in his school backpack, he would have extra clothes. About that time, every night for two months, he would cry. I would ask him, "Do you want to be a boy?" He would say, "No. I know how to be a boy, I don't know how to be a girl … but, I'm a girl." One time he lay on the floor and said, "All I want is to die."

I had gotten in touch with the [LGBT] Center and I met Connor, who is a trans man. After Isaac met Connor, he finally said, "Yes, I want to be a boy." One morning I said to him, "Good morning, my boy," and he gave a big smile. So I said to the rest of the family, "Change pronouns today!" He had picked his new name, but he wouldn't tell us what it was. He said, "I don't want to say the name, because I feel like I'm pretending. I'm not going to ask everyone to pretend with me." Finally he said, "My name is Isaac."

I knew he wanted to start hormone blockers and medical transition. There were no services here in San Diego at that time, so we started going to LA Children's Hospital. Dr. Belzer gave Isaac hormone blockers for three months, and then he started testosterone (T). The first day Isaac got T was the most exciting day! We were singing all the way home.

We were lucky, because Isaac was overall a happy kid. His teachers liked him, he made friends easily, and he was a leader. He was a good student and friend, mostly with boys, and they accepted him. The therapist from the hospital had a phone conversation with Isaac once a week. She told us, "I need to have a relationship with Isaac for the future, so that if he has problems he can talk to me. But let's not try to fix what's not broken." She gave him a letter for top surgery. Isaac was only 13. I called so many surgeons and they said, "No," because of his age. I couldn't believe it when we found one who said, "Yes."

There weren't really resources for what we were going through as a family. I finally met some other trans moms through PFLAG (Parents and Friends of Lesbians and Gays). Eventually we created our own chapter of Transforming Family to support others. We have groups for parents, transgender kids, different age groups, and a group for Spanish-speaking parents.

We were so lucky that Isaac's schools were supportive. When he transitioned, the school staff all welcomed him as Isaac, and the principal assured him that he was safe. He was never rejected. He had friends, he started playing soccer as a boy, he went through the lifeguard program, he had a girlfriend. We (his family) participated in Pride. His grandparents, who are very religious, totally understood and were supportive. I feel it is a privilege to be a parent of a transgender kid.

I want counselors to know that when a kid is gender dysphoric, it affects them all the time, every single day, with things that don't even seem related to gender. And of course that makes them anxious, depressed, and self-conscious, and it doesn't allow them to focus on other things in their lives. They can't place themselves in their future lives, so they're scared for the future. A lot of times counselors take the role of "I am the expert and I know when it is best for the child to transition." The counselor Isaac had through Children's Hospital in LA listened to Isaac and to me, and that's what I think they should do. The best way counselors can help families is by working **with** *them: the person who best knows if the kid is trans is the kid. The person who best knows the kid is the Mom.*

Isaac writes about his experience, below. Notice that he suggests that therapists can help by normalizing a client's experience of being trans; and by both acknowledging the broad impact of trans experience on a client's life, and recognizing that a trans client holds other identities as well.

FIGURE 10.4   Isaac at high school graduation

Isaac (L) at age 8, with his sister

I think therapists should know that being trans, it's such a huge part of a kid's life, it can become all-consuming. I had complete discomfort in my body, always being completely uncomfortable. Little experiences, like thinking about my foot position in a toilet stall, or how my pee sounded when it hit the bowl (from close rather than further away), were always on my mind. That's "gender noise."

I think one thing that helped me the most is that my Mom always told me, "Everyone has a challenge. You can deal." So I thought, "This is just my challenge." It's important to remind the kid (and parents) that they're more than a trans kid. There's so much more to a person than their gender. And counselors can normalize young people's experience. Remember not to overgeneralize, everyone's experience of being trans is very particular.

It took me until I was 12 to identify as trans, even though I always felt like a boy. I would see the documentaries and shows about transgender kids that my Mom would show me, but I couldn't identify with them. The people in the shows didn't seem to be sure about their gender, like I was. They weren't my age either. So I didn't really believe I fit the label "trans." In fact, I still haven't fully connected with anyone else's trans feelings. Meeting Connor is what made the difference. I had never met a trans man before. I didn't know you could do that, be a trans man with a normal life. That's why I want to be public about my identity, I want to be there for other kids.

Monica's and Isaac's stories show the tremendous value of supportive family members and highlight the importance of role models and of community, for both a trans person and for their family; they also demonstrate how personal experiences in marginalized communities may translate into community involvement and activism.

Paola, who is a therapist, reflects on her experiences as sister of a sibling with trans experience, and how therapy might have been beneficial for her and her family.

> *It wasn't until middle school that my sister started puberty and we noticed drastic changes in her mood and behavior. She would be very moody, and seemed depressed and withdrawn. This was pre-transition and as a family, we all knew that my sister needed support. From that moment forward, my Mom shared with us everything she had learned and researched about being transgender. It's difficult to see someone you love go through the challenging parts of not having their identity be recognized and affirmed, but you can let them know that their feelings are normal. Even today, I am attuned to monitoring my sister's safety and emotional well-being.*
>
> *Looking back, for me, it would have been beneficial to be in family therapy, or even individual therapy when I was a child and adolescent. As a teen, I always excelled in school and friendships, and seemed to be OK; this might have contributed to others not asking how I was doing. I know that my parents were doing all that they could to support us, but I felt alienated from my mom. A therapist could have helped us to look at the family system and all of our relationships, and helped me find my voice and ask for what I needed. In my Mexican culture, counseling was a taboo and not financially acceptable, but it would have made a difference for me.*
>
> *To me, my sister isn't a trans woman, she's just herself. As a family, we've had to deal with a lot of things, and this is just one aspect of our identity—we're immigrants, we were undocumented. It's a lot harder when you have to deal with intersectionalities in identity. In my family, I learned the power of unconditional love and how to repair and heal in relationship to one another.*

Isaac's, Monica's, and Paola's stories highlight some of the reasons that a trans person might seek therapy. In Isaac's case, he simply needed to see a therapist in order to receive a letter supporting his physical transition. For Paola, family therapy might have provided support for the family system and a safe space in which to recognize and ask for what she needed.

Catherine Butler (2010) writes that trans individuals might also come to therapy if they are dealing with:

stigma, discrimination, and prejudice
rejection by the gender group to which they transitioned
verbal and/or physical aggression
lack of funds due to the cost of treatments and difficulty working due to discrimination
only wanting some kinds of medical intervention, such as hormones, but being pressured to have surgery(ies)
post-operative regret, typically related to poor surgery outcomes and/or unrealistic expectations for the surgery
changing relationships with partners and friends

Therapists may offer family or couple counseling to help partners and family members adjust and maintain a supportive relationship with the person transitioning. If a trans client does not find family and friends to be supportive, online or face-to-face groups or reading material may help the client, family, and friends come to terms with the client's trans identity and transition process.

POINTS TO DISCUSS

If you were working with Isaac and his family, or Paola and her family, what strengths might you identify? What topics would you think it important to address? Are there other things you might you need to know, or resources you might want, to feel comfortable working with them?

If a parent asked you to work with their eight-year-old GNC child to help them become more gender conforming, what conversations would you want to have with the parent and the child?

Nonbinary/Genderqueer

These terms describe a person whose gender identity does not align with a binary understanding of gender. People who identify as genderqueer or nonbinary may redefine gender or decline to define themselves as gendered. They may identify as both male and female (bigender, pangender, androgyne), neither male nor female (agender), moving between genders (genderfluid), or as embodying a third gender.

Amanda (introduced above) writes:

> *I personally identify as a femme and as nonbinary, and for me that means that I feel fluid in my gender from day to day, but being nonbinary can feel and look many different ways. Before I understood or accepted my nonbinary identity, I often experienced discomfort with clothes. On some days, when I would go to school or work in feminine clothes, I felt like I was unwillingly cross-dressing. Not every day—some days I felt and still feel comfortable and like myself in feminine or hyper-feminine clothes. Some days though, in feminine clothes, I feel like a boy being forced to wear a dress when he doesn't want to. It feels awkward and embarrassing, and I don't know what to do with my body in those clothes.*
>
> *These are things I personally would appreciate from a therapist: Encourage me to find big or small ways to affirm my gender every day. Check in with me about safety related to coming out as nonbinary. Encourage me to find more people in my life to share the nonbinary part of my identity. Help me process and release my internalized transphobia that make it hard to love myself in my nonbinary identity. Consistently remind me that I am loved for exactly who I am. Another important thing is for therapists to educate themselves on nonbinary identities and experiences, as well as use resources written by nonbinary people. It is not the job of the client to educate the therapist on definitions and terms related to marginalized identities.*

As Amanda's and Mia Little's (above) statements demonstrate, it is impossible to know a person's gender identity from their voice, mannerisms, primary or secondary sex characteristics, or other aspects of their external presentation, so it is important that therapists not make assumptions about a client's gender identity.

Intersex/Diversity of Sex Development

As discussed in Chapter 9, sex is typically assigned at birth based on the appearance of external genitalia. When the external genitalia are ambiguous, other indicators (for example, internal genitalia, chromosomal and hormonal sex) are considered. Some people's physiology and genetics do not neatly align with the dichotomous male or female categories, referred to as intersex or "disorders of sex development" in the *DSM-5* (APA, 2013a). Richards and Barker (2013) suggest using the alternative term "diversity of sex development." Although estimates vary widely depending on the criteria used, approximately 1 in 50 people has physiology that varies from strictly male or female (Blackless et al., 2000).

People with diversity of sexual development may have any sexual orientation, and may or may not be concerned about their gender identity. For example, many people who have an extra X chromosome (Klinefelter syndrome) consider themselves unambiguously male, despite the fact that their sexual development is not typical. Other people with diversity of sexual development may feel confused about their gender identity, and/or isolated, invalidated, and invisible. As therapists, we can help clients with diversity of sexual development to know that they are not alone, and to deconstruct prescriptive gender and sexual binaries.

Sexual Identities and Practices: Lesbian/Gay, Bisexuality, Asexuality, and BDSM/Kink

Lesbian, Gay, and Bisexual Identities

The experiences of lesbian, gay, and bisexual individuals have many cultural commonalities and also, of course, many differences. This section will seek to highlight some common themes, and also identify some distinct aspects of gay, lesbian, and bisexual individuals' experience.

Terminology

The term "gay" can refer specifically to same-gender attracted men; it is also often used by same-gender attracted women (particularly younger women), and may also be used to refer to anyone who is not cisgender and heterosexual. "Lesbian" refers specifically to any person who feels a connection to womanhood and is attracted to other women, and constitutes an important identity for some. *Bisexuality* may be defined as experiencing emotional, romantic, and/or sexual attraction to more than one gender; *pansexual* and *omnisexual* refer to experiencing attraction to all genders. In this chapter, the term bisexual (bi) will be used, although many young people prefer the terms *fluid* or *pansexual*, or choose not to label themselves (Ulrich, 2011). As discussed above, "queer" is used by many and is inclusive of those who are nonbinary. The term homosexual may be offensive, as it has a long history of association with pathologization. "Sexual preference" implies choice and "alternative lifestyle" is heteronormative; therefore, these may also be offensive; "sexual orientation" and "romantic orientation" are more appropriate. The client's own terms should be used, and employed as adjectives (for example, a bisexual person) rather than nouns (for example, a bisexual), to avoid totalizing a client's identity.

Lesbian/Gay Women

Mallinger (2016) points out that the lives of gay women are intersectional by definition, as they are impacted by both sexism and homophobia; and Swigonski (1995) argues that through their relationships, lesbian women embody a way of living outside of heterosexism, and thereby lay claim to their political power. Mallinger states that lesbian women's confrontation with multiple forms of oppression leads to "learning to function at the synapse of multiple communities" (p. 424) and to the development of valuable skills and knowledge, such as the ability understand personal political power, and to construct preferred meanings.

Richards and Barker (2013) point out that lesbians have historically been less visible to the public eye than gay men and, perhaps for this reason, it has been more important for lesbians to signal their sexual orientation, for example, by cutting their hair short. However, gay women in the 2000s present in a variety of ways, including mainstream feminine presentations, not just in the "butch/femme" dichotomy of the 1950s.

Gay Men

Research indicates that gay and bisexual men identify discrimination and lack of acceptance as the most important issue facing them today. They also name HIV/AIDS, equal rights, and marriage equality (Hamel et al., 2014). With regard to discrimination, Herek (2009) states that 40% of gay men reported person or property crimes based on their sexual orientation in one study—the highest of any sexual minority. Gay men were also more likely to report discrimination in healthcare and public settings than lesbian or bisexual individuals (Bostwick, Boyd, Hughes, West, & McCabe, 2014).

Dentato, Arguello, and Wilson (2016) write that the HIV/AIDS epidemic has had a profound, long-term impact on gay men and gay male culture, with varying effects on different age cohorts. Older gay men lost many of their best friends and partners to AIDS, saw or participated in the rise of gay male activism, found hope with new treatments in the 1990s, and/or began living long term and asymptomatic with HIV. Younger gay men (under 35) are considerably less likely to have lost someone close to them from AIDS or know someone personally who is living with HIV (Hamel, 2014); but few gay men alive today have known a world without HIV/AIDS. Heinous discourses blaming gay men for the AIDS epidemic and viewing the death of gay men as justice meted for sin have negatively impacted gay males' identities, and also contributed to the slow political response in the first years of the epidemic, ultimately giving rise to resistance in the form of activist groups.

Problem dominant discourses equating being gay with weakness and lack of masculinity limit HIV/AIDS prevention and treatment, particularly among gay men of color, those with lower incomes, and those who are younger (Hamel, 2014). A study of men who have sex with men in Tijuana, Mexico, found that internalized homophobia, related to cultural norms of homophobia and machismo, was strongly correlated with not being tested for HIV; by contrast, identifying as gay and being more "out" was associated with HIV testing (Pines et al., 2016). Therefore, one way that therapists can support the mental and physical health of male clients who are having sex with men is by helping them to identify and deconstruct problem dominant discourses and decrease any internalized homophobia.

Halkitis (2000) argues that the lower self-esteem reported by some (particularly urban and aging) gay men may may be due to the high value placed on looks and pressures related to body image prevalent in gay male culture, referred to as the "buff agenda." Halkitis also suggests that the discursive image of the youthful, sculpted gay male body that became highly visible in gay culture of the 1980s reflects the desire to present a healthy and strong gay male body as a counter to images of weakness and frailty associated with HIV/AIDS. Therapists may be able to help counter oppressive discourses dictating that gay men be lean and "buff" by identifying preferred alternative discourses, such as, "There is no one right way to look as a gay man"; and "There is a spectrum of body types, all of which are attractive."

Gay and Lesbian Relationships

Gay, lesbian, and heterosexual romantic relationships are similar in terms of rates of intimacy, conflict resolution, expression of feelings, longevity, and satisfaction (Butler, 2010). However, gay and lesbian partners consistently report more egalitarian relationships than heterosexual peers, with respect to division of household chores and finances, perhaps because they cannot rely on socially constructed gender roles (Esmail, 2010). On the other hand, Kort (2008) argues that there is a heightening of traditional gender roles in same-gender couples, leading to, for example, increased emotional expression in lesbian couples and increased sexual activity in gay male couples. This may help explain research findings that, on average, lesbian couples are more emotionally expressive than gay couples (Garanzini et al., 2017); and gay couples, on average, have more sex at all stages of their relationship than lesbian couples (Baumeister, Catanese, & Vohs, 2001).

Gottman, Levenson, Swanson, Tyson, and Yoshimoto (2003) find that same-sex couples use more affection and humor than heterosexual couples when they bring up a point of conflict, and partners tend to be more positive in how they receive it. Gottman et al. argue that power sharing and fairness are more important and prevalent in gay and lesbian relationships than in heterosexual ones, based on their finding that, on average, same-sex partners demonstrate less belligerence, domineering, and fear in conflict situations than heterosexual couples.

Interpersonal violence (IPV). However, IPV occurs in all relationship forms, and there are extra challenges for lesbian and gay victims of IPV, relating to homophobia. An abusive partner may threaten to "out" the abused partner if they do not comply (McClennen, Summers, & Vaughan, 2002); and lesbians and gay men whose families are unsupportive of their sexuality have fewer sources of support, making it more difficult to leave abusive relationships. Gay and lesbian victims of IPV who are not out are less likely to be comfortable seeking help from the courts, police, or other services due to fears of being outed, embarrassed, or harassed (Merrill, 1998); they may also be concerned that responding police officers would consider the incident to be "mutual combat," possibly resulting in both primary aggressor and victim being arrested (Renzetti, 1998). (However, a 2007 study by Pattavina, Hirschel, Buzzawa, Faggiani, & Bentley indicates that police response to IPV is similar whether the victim is heterosexual, gay, or lesbian.) Furthermore, IPV is typically conceptualized as a male-on-female problem. Therefore, few policies address the specific needs of gay and lesbian IPV victims; domestic violence shelters typically do not admit men (Lyon, Lane, & Menard, 2008); and lesbian women may be less likely to seek refuge, due to concern that they will be misunderstood or stigmatized based on their sexual orientation (Giorgio, 2002). Further, in a number of jurisdictions, legal protections are unavailable to people abused by a partner of the same legal sex (Commission on Domestic & Sexual Violence, 2015).

Bisexuality

Bi invisibility (or bi erasure). Invisibility or erasure is a particularly salient issue for bisexual people. Ulrich (2011) reports that people identifying as bisexual make up a higher proportion of the LGBTQ+ community than people identifying as gay or lesbian; however, "people's assumptions often render bisexuals invisible. Two women holding hands are read as 'lesbian,' two men as 'gay,' and a man and a woman as 'straight.' In reality, any of these people might be bi—perhaps all of them" (p. 1).

Biphobia. Arguello (2016) argues that bisexual individuals are exposed to extremely high levels of stigma, and are often represented in both academic literature and popular media as being:

> confused in their sexual identity, or unable to make a choice
> promiscuous
> unable to commit to long-term relationships
> developmentally stymied or stuck en route to a "true" identity
> in denial of their "true" [homosexual] orientation
> a vector for transmitting diseases, such as HIV, to the heterosexual or lesbian population

Other problematic dominant discourses convey that bisexuals somehow betray lesbian/gay identity; ride on the coattails of lesbian/gay activism; benefit from heterosexual "passing privilege" (the ability to maintain the appearance of being heterosexual); and lead safer, more privileged lives than their gay and lesbian contemporaries. In fact, Kertzner, Meyer, Frost, & Stirratt (2009) find that bisexuality is associated with more social disadvantages than gayness or lesbianism, possibly relating to bi invisibility, and to rejection by both straight and lesbian/gay communities. Bisexual people are, on average, also economically disadvantaged relative to their lesbian/gay peers; for example, bisexual women are more than twice as likely to live in poverty than lesbians (Ulrich, 2011). As a group, bisexual individuals experience higher levels of sexual violence than gay, lesbian, or heterosexual individuals: a study by the National Center for Disease Control (Walters, Chen, & Breiding, 2013) found that the lifetime prevalence of sexual violence is a shocking 75% for bisexual women (compared with 46% for lesbian women and 43% for heterosexual women); and 47% of bisexual men have experienced sexual violence (compared with 40% of gay men and 41% of heterosexual men). Possibly because of these difficulties, bisexual individuals experience higher rates of depression, anxiety, alcohol misuse, negative affect, and suicide plans and attempts (Kertzner, Meyer, Frost, & Stirratt, 2010) than their gay and lesbian peers. Therapists will need to be aware of the social and economic challenges facing bisexual individuals, and help bisexual clients deconstruct biphobic messages they may have internalized.

Katie Mercer, who was introduced above, describes some of these challenges.

> *As someone who identifies as pansexual, the most common negative reaction I've experienced from both the straight community and LGBTQ+ community is being told that my sexual orientation will "sort itself out" at some point, and I'll eventually decide whether I'm gay or straight. My uncle suggested that I keep quiet about my sexual identity until I "saw which way it went." I've had people in the LGBTQ+ community tell me I'll identify*

as gay before long. I've also experienced people telling me how lucky I am to be bi/pansexual, because I'm doubling my dating pool. Beyond this being statistically impossible, given how many women are not actually open to dating other women, and how many people are not open to dating queer people, this comment makes me laugh, because it assumes I'm interested in dating anybody who comes my way! I've explained to straight and gay friends that my dating pool may actually be much smaller than theirs, it just so happens to include people of a range of genders.

Concerns of LGB Clients

Long (1996) researched what lesbian, gay, and bisexual (LGB) clients want therapists to know. Their findings include the sociopolitical history of LGB people, awareness of the impacts of homophobia (including physical violence), and coming out as an ongoing process. Each of these will be addressed below.

The Sociopolitical History of LGB People

LGB people have a long history of oppression at the individual, institutional, and cultural levels. In response, LGB people have demonstrated individual and collective resilience; organized effective activism; coped with oppression, stigma, and stress; and embodied adaptation. Significant milestones in LGB history were summarized by Morris (n.d.):

> In Nazi Germany, gay men were singled out as "sexual deviants" and harassed, arrested, incarcerated, and even castrated. Thousands died in concentration camps.
>
> In the 1950s and earlier, violent and trauma-inducing attempts to "cure" homosexuality were attempted via psychopharmacology, electroshock therapy, lobotomies, and/or medical castration.
>
> The Stonewall riots in New York City, led by LGBTQ+ people in June of 1969, gave rise to the modern LGBTQ+ movement, promoting tolerance, equality, and resistance to oppression. There are, therefore, significant differences in perspective among LGB people who grew up before, during, or after the creation of this civil rights movement (Dentato, Arguello, & Wilson, 2016).
>
> In the 1970s, gay women were frustrated with the underrepresentation of the concerns of women and nonbinary individuals (homonormativity) in most gay liberation groups. Influenced by the feminist movement, they organized politically, forming their own collectives and calling for lesbian rights in mainstream feminist groups.
>
> Gay rights activist Harvey Milk and his ally, San Francisco Mayor George Mascone, were assassinated by Dan White in 1978. White was sentenced for manslaughter but acquitted of murder; in response, a candlelight vigil erupted into civil unrest known as the White Night Riots.
>
> The increasing expansion of a global LGBT rights movement was set back in the 1980s by the AIDS epidemic, which decimated the gay male community. Calls for compassion and demands for medical funding rejuvenated coalitions between gay men and women and channeled anger

at apathetic responses to the health crisis into effective advocacy groups, like Aids Coalition to Unleash Power (ACT UP).

From the time of the Revolutionary War, engaging in homosexual activity constituted grounds for dishonorable discharge from the military (and/or court-martial and imprisonment). Despite these risks, many LGBT individuals served in the armed forces: Fredriksen-Goldsen et al. (2011) report that 41% of older transgender adults, 41% of older bisexual men, 34% of older gay men, and 6% of older lesbian and bisexual women have served in the military. The 1993 "Don't Ask Don't Tell" (DADT) policy theoretically gave protection to LGB service people who were closeted, while barring openly LGB individuals from serving; many LGB service people continued to be expelled under DADT. In 2010, DADT was repealed, allowing LGB individuals to openly serve in the armed forces for the first time.

In 2015, the Supreme Court decision recognizing same-sex marriage marked another legal and cultural turning point; and in spring of 2016, the Supreme Court ruled that a lesbian family adoption in one state had to be recognized in all states.

On June 12, 2016, a shooter killed or injured scores of (primarily) young Latino drag queens and lesbians of color at the Pulse Club in Orlando. This tragedy, along with well-publicized, intense racial profiling confrontations, brought greater attention to intersections of race, class, gender identity, and sexism in the LGBTQ+ community.

Impacts of Homophobia on LGB People's Lives

Stigma and discrimination, rooted in homophobia, have significant effects on the lives of LGB people. According to Dentato, Arguello, & Wilson (2016), *homophobia* is the conscious or unconscious fear of homosexuals, implicitly and/or explicitly expressed, that impacts LGB individuals' willingness to disclose their sexual orientation and ability to seek relationships and intimacy. They argue that the effects of homophobia and stigma on sexual minorities, impacting housing, educational outcomes, employment, healthcare, and the experience of verbal and physical abuse, is often underrecognized.

Mallinger (2016) writes that marginalized youth face higher risks of becoming either victim and/or perpetrator of emotional, physical, and sexual interpersonal violence. She notes that lesbian adolescents are more at risk for bullying than their heterosexual peers, and over 50% of lesbians state that they feel unsafe at school, which is correlated with low self-esteem, depression, anxiety, and school absences—effects that can last well beyond adolescence (Greene, Britton, & Fitts, 2014). Butler (2010) suggests that, possibly due to experiences of discrimination, stigma, and internalized homophobia, LGB individuals have an increased risk of low self-esteem, self-harm, or thoughts of suicide, as well as of problems with relationships, intimacy, risky sexual behavior, and addiction.

Social factors supported by discriminatory dominant discourses contribute to these physical safety risks and mental health challenges. For example, teachers and principals are less likely to intervene in bullying situations when the victim is a sexual minority (Mallinger, 2016); and Hatzenbueller, McLaughlin, Keyes, & Haslin (2010) have shown that the passage of prejudicial institutional policies, such as the constitutional amendments banning gay marriage enacted in various states, are correlated with increased rates of mood, anxiety, and substance-use disorders among LGB individuals.

Coming Out as an Individual Choice and a Multifaceted Process

According to Butler (2010), coming out is a lifelong process of self-acceptance of one's sexual orientation. People initially forge an identity for themselves, and then may reveal it to others; coming out publicly may or may not be part of the process. Common thoughts and emotions associated with coming out include concern about other people's responses, self-doubt, relief at being out/authentic, and perception of new possibilities.

Teeman (2017) writes that "[f]or millennia—with same-sex behavior and trans identity variously legally proscribed or forbidden, or punishable and stigmatized—it suited societies and religions to make LGBT people as invisible as possible. And, to escape detection and persecution, many LGBT people chose to collude with this forced invisibility. Even today, making ourselves visible, coming out, is something every LGBT person considers or does" (paragraphs 1 & 2). Alessi (2008) reminds therapists to avoid imposing normative ideas about coming out on the client, instead supporting the client's level of outness and choices related to disclosure.

Describing their ambivalence about coming out, Amanda (introduced above) writes:

> I feel conflicted: like I have to choose between becoming my office's queer/nonbinary educator or being consistently unseen by my coworkers. The people in my office are open people, and want to be accepting, and at the same time are uninformed about everything queer besides more traditional ideas of being gay or lesbian. When it came up with one of my co-workers that I am queer, she asked me many intrusive questions, such as, "How do lesbians have sex?" and, "Is your sex life like The L Word?" I've never heard her ask anybody else questions like that. People tend to feel free to ask intrusive questions about people in non-hetero relationships.
>
> Since experiencing that, it hasn't felt like an option to disclose that I'm nonbinary. I don't want to field intrusive questions about my body or my gender identity. Further, I don't want to become the gender educator in my office. I don't have the time or mental capacity to take that on right now. It hurts that the co-workers I see every day don't see me the way I see myself, and that they don't know or use my correct pronouns, but I'm making that decision because the alternative isn't better right now. In addition, making that decision feels okay because I am able to be open with and feel seen by my friends and immediate family.

As Amanda's words indicate, coming out (or not) is a multilayered, ongoing, effortful process, rather than a one-time event.

Asexuality Spectrum

There is growing recognition of asexuality as a sexual orientation (Bogaert, 2012). Individuals who identify as asexual or "ace" (approximately 1% of the population; CNN, 2004) experience an unusually limited or absent level of sexual attraction, but other aspects of sexuality, such as romantic attraction, may be present. Asexuality is conceptualized on a spectrum (ace-spec), with gray asexuality (gray-A) referring to the area between asexuality and sexuality; under the gray-A umbrella falls demisexuality.

POINTS TO DISCUSS

Try taking the "Heterosexual Questionnaire" (generally attributed to Martin Rochlin in 1972). Different versions are readily available online (e.g., https://www.uwgb.edu/pride-center/files/pdfs/Heterosexual_Questionnaire.pdf). This tool can also be shared with clients.

Butler (2010) writes that Dominic Davies, founder of the UK organization Pink Therapy, suggests the following exercises:

Buy an LGBT magazine and read it in public.

Go for a drink in an LGBT club or bar.

Wear an LGBT shirt or badge.

Hold hands with a "same-gender" person in public.

Keep your heterosexuality in the closet for a week by ensuring that you don't give it away in conversation. (E.g., don't mention a partner's gender when talking about what you did at the weekend or when talking on the phone with a tradesperson.)

For demisexual individuals, sexual desire is rare and only arises in the context of a deep emotional connection (Asexuality Visibility and Education Network, or AVEN, n.d.).

Asexual people who experience romantic attractions and attachments may have platonic partners; but asexual people also may not experience romantic attraction (aromantic or aro). Note that romantic (affectional/emotional) orientation is also considered to be on a spectrum, and that romantic orientation may or may not align with sexual orientation.

Therapists can help clients on the asexual spectrum to recognize and deconstruct dominant cultural discourses telling them that they are "broken" and need to be "fixed" (AVEN, n.d.). Community gathering places may help facilitate recognition, education, and destigmatization with respect to asexuality, helping to push back against heteronormative cultural narratives dictating that everyone either is, wants to, or should be experiencing sexual attraction (Westphal, 2004).

Sofia, a 24-year-old Latina therapist, writes:

I have identified as an ace-spec lesbian for the past year. For me, this means that I am romantically attracted to women and am interested in dating and loving them but ultimately I don't really experience sexual attraction. About a year ago, I went to a Pride parade, and I recognized that I felt different from the rest of the people celebrating their same-gender attraction, beginning my journey into understanding my asexual identity.

I already knew that there was a spectrum of asexuality in terms of how often or in what context people experienced sexual attraction, and a spectrum for romantic attraction. Recently I went to an ace-spec Meetup, and I learned that there was another spectrum within the community for attitude towards sex. People could be sex favorable, sex indifferent, sex averse, or sex repulsed. I got to talk with someone who identified as a sex-favorable ace. That was an enlightening experience for me, because I feel like a lot of times there's this attitude that if you're asexual you can't have sex. Within the broader LGBT community,

I have encountered people who think that unless you are celibate you're not really asexual. The person I met explained to me that they don't experience sexual attraction, but they still enjoy the act of sex for physical pleasure and building intimacy with their partner. That made me feel like there is more space for my identity, however it may turn out to be. Being at the Meetup also reminded me of how helpful it can be to spend time with other people with similar identities.

BDSM/Kink

BDSM (for Bondage and Discipline; Dominance and Submission; and Sadism and Masochism) is defined by Lin (2014) as "the consensual practice of dominance and submission, and/or the infliction of conventionally perceived unpleasant sensations for erotic purposes" (p. 1). The term BDSM is often used interchangeably with the term kink; however, according to Rehor (2015), kink refers to a broader set of "unconventional sensual, erotic, and sexual behaviors" (p. 825). "Kink" and "kinky" are terms more often used by those in the community and will be employed here. According to Nichols (2006), kink activities generally include one or more of the following: a hierarchical power structure; intense physical or emotional stimulation (for example, spanking or humiliation); sensory deprivation, confusion, or restraint (for example, bondage or blindfolds); role-playing of fantasy scenarios; and use of specific preferred objects and materials (for example, leather, rope) as sexual enhancers ("fetishism").

Barker, Iantaffi, and Gupta (2007) explain that kink activities are not inherently sexual, though they often occur in a sexual context. They also point out that a degree of power or pain exchange is common in many people's sex lives (for example, biting or light spanking, role-playing); however, BDSM "codifies such practices more explicitly and uses terminology such as 'power' or 'pain' exchange in negotiation between partners" (p. 107).

Janus and Janus (1994) estimate that up to 11% of American (U.S.) women and 14% of American (U.S.) men have engaged in BDSM, and BDSM features in fantasies for over 50% of men and women (Joyal, Cossette, & Lapierre, 2015). The kink community is a loose network of individuals connecting at local, national, and/or international levels, by meeting in person (sometimes at "dungeons," which are BDSM play spaces, or "munches," which are casual social gatherings), and/or online. On its homepage, the BDSM social networking site FetLife (fetlife.com) claims more than seven million members.

One of therapists' greatest ethical responsibilities is attention to clients' mental and physical welfare, and therapists unfamiliar with kink may assume that engaging in kink either equates to or stems from abuse, is indicative of mental illness, or is self-destructive. It may, therefore, be helpful for therapists to know that research finds that people who practice kink are generally well-adjusted (Wismeijer & van Assen, 2013), and appear to be psychologically "comparable to both published test norms and to *DSM-IV-TR* estimates for the general population" (Connelly, 2008, p. 72). Furthermore, Moser (2002) finds that the incidence of childhood abuse is no higher in the BDSM community than outside of it.

With regard to potential for sexual and emotional abuse within kink relationships, many writers note that kink relationships, like any relationships, *can* be abusive, but state that they are not *inherently* abusive, as in this post from the National Domestic Violence Hotline blog:

[W]e want to be very clear that BDSM is not inherently or automatically abusive. It's possible to have healthy BDSM relationships, and they require just as much–if not more–of the same things that healthy "vanilla" relationships do: trust, honesty, respect and equality. ... Abuse is about one partner gaining and maintaining power and control over another, whereas healthy BDSM relationships revolve around a consensual power exchange (Melissa, 2018, paragraph 2).

Regarding the notion that engaging in kink is self-destructive, Nichols (2006) writes that there is no evidence that kink is used self-destructively any more often than "vanilla" sex (non-kinky sex; note that the term "vanilla" may be perceived by some as derogatory). The kink community is itself highly focused on issues of safety and personal and collective responsibility, along with negotiating consent and providing logistical and emotional support to its members. The phrase/acronym "Safe, Sane, Consensual" (SSC) is commonly used to describe standards for kink activity. Safe means "being knowledgeable about the techniques and safety concerns involved in what you are doing, and acting in accordance with that knowledge"; sane refers to being sober, of sound mind, and comprehending the difference between fantasy and reality; and consensual means "respecting the limits imposed by each participant at all times" (Best BDSM Practices, n.d., paragraphs 3–5). Another commonly used set of guiding principles is RACK (Risk Aware Consensual Kink), emphasizing practitioners' awareness that engaging in kink entails a degree of risk that may be minimized, but not completely avoided (as does engaging in many sports or other activities).

Some dominant discourses reflecting common misunderstandings about kink practices are described by Nichols (2006) and Barker, Iantaffi, and Gupta (2007):

> *BDSM is mostly about a passive submissive (sub) being exploited by a Dominant (Dom) partner.* In reality, kink scenes (an interaction that includes some kind of kink play) are generally scripted and negotiated ahead of time, with the submissive setting the basic limits. Thus, while the Dominant is putatively in charge, she or he is working within the submissive's guidelines. Furthermore, the submissive is motivated to give consent by pleasure rather than fear.
> *BDSM always relates to pain.* In fact, many kink activities do not include pain; and when they do, it is not pain as it is typically understood (more akin to scratching a lover at the height of passion than bumping one's knee).
> *Once people start engaging in kink they will inevitably try increasingly extreme behaviors and/or become addicted.* While some people may initially be highly focused on kink activities, BDSM activity typically levels off, though the level reached will be different for every individual.
> *People practicing BDSM always take a fixed role of top (the person administering the stimulus, such as a spanking or warm wax) or bottom (the person receiving the stimulus).* On the contrary, some kink practitioners change roles during or in between scenes, referred to as being a Switch.
> *Kinky sex and vanilla sex are incompatible.* Actually, many people enjoy both kinky and vanilla sex, in combination or at different times.

Popular books and movies, such as the *Fifty Shades of Grey* trilogy (James, 2012) and *Secretary* (Shainburg, 2002), have contributed to these myths and misunderstandings about BDSM, while also helping to destigmatize kink practices. Susan Wright, founder of the National Coalition for Sexual Freedom (NCSF), argues that "because of [*Fifty Shades of Grey*], BDSM has burst into the mainstream media, allowing everyone to start talking about kink. Before, the media coverage of BDSM tended to be more negative, but now you can't go on the Internet without finding a new article about exploring your fetish" (Wall, 2015, paragraph 9).

However, the *Fifty Shades of Grey* trilogy (James, 2012) dangerously misrepresents BDSM as a way to coercively push and violate others' limits and boundaries without negotiation (Green, 2015). As previously stated, within the kink community, there is great emphasis placed on informed consent, safety, and respect for emotional and physical limits (while those may be intentionally tested). Power exchange occurs within agreed-upon time limits and negotiated time frames, ranging from a single, brief scene to full-time (termed 24/7); agreements taking both parties' needs and limits into account are developed orally and/or in writing; and bottoms and tops often create understanding about acceptable limits of stimulation by scaling trials. Limits may always be renegotiated, as consent is understood to be an ongoing process, and attending to physical safety, including safer sex practices, as well as emotional safety, including "aftercare" (time and attention given to partners after intense play), are cultural norms.

Kink practitioners who do not conform to community standards in these respects are less likely to be recommended to other potential play partners. Therefore, one of the best ways to play safely is to play within an established community, and therapists can encourage clients to find and join their local and/or online kink communities. It should be noted, however, that many people practice kink without being part of a community.

Therapeutic Considerations

Nichols (2006) writes that the most prominent issue therapists confront when first working with kinky clients is "dealing with their own judgments, feelings, and reactions to this sexual behavior, … [including] … shock, fear, anxiety, disgust, and revulsion" (p. 286). Barker, Iantaffi, and Gupta (2007) comment that it is not necessary for therapists to be comfortable with every BDSM practice that clients might discuss, but that it *is* important that therapists be aware of their comfort level. According to Nichols, when counselors can notice and accept their own discomfort, and recognize that this discomfort may relate to unfamiliarity rather than to inherent problems or dangers associated with kink activity, they are then in a good position both to help clients and to gain insight into internalized shame that clients may have related to their BDSM activities.

Kolmes, Stock, and Moser (2006) found that the attributes kinky clients preferred in therapists were open-minded acceptance, normalizing kinky interests, being willing to ask questions about BDSM, being well-informed on BDSM, and not focusing on kink when it was not relevant. As Barker, Iantaffi, and Gupta (2007) comment, "It is clear that … such a definition of a kink-friendly therapist could be equally applied to any other context, such as bisexuality or race. Therefore, it seems that we could define a kink-friendly mental health practitioner as someone who is willing to engage with the issue of BDSM not as a pathology but as a different cultural context, which may, or may not, be already familiar to them" (p. 19).

Relational Identities and Practices: Polyamory, Swinging, and Hookup Culture

Polyamory, swinging, and hookup culture fall under the umbrella of open relationships and consensual nonmonogamy (CNM). Practitioners of CNM do not view their nonmonogamous activities as cheating, though cultural discourses relating to monogamy and cheating may still influence their thinking and self-perception (Ritchie & Barker, 2006). An estimated 9.8 million American (U.S.) couples

Consider visiting a local BDSM/kink club, Meetup, or organization, to experience the culture of acceptance and community support they often convey (Nichols, 2006). Note your thoughts and feelings as you antici-pate, undertake, and reflect on this experience.

have an agreement to allow outside sexual partners (Shucart, 2016), and a study published in the *Journal of Sex and Marital Therapy* reports that one in five people who are currently single have engaged in some form of open relationship (Haupert, Gesselman, Moors, Fisher, & Garcia, 2017). This study found that men were more likely to report having practiced CNM than women, as were LGB individ-uals, compared with heterosexual individuals. Interestingly, the proportion of participants who had engaged in CNM was the same across age, education level, income, religion, region, political affilia-tion, and race. According to Barker (2011), the most commonly practiced forms of CNM are swinging, gay open relationships, and polyamory, each of which will be addressed below.

CNM brings client and therapist into conflict with one of the most dearly held discourses in West-ern society—that of a romantic, monogamous love union between two individuals, who mate for life. In this discourse, the two members of the couple are understood to be uniquely and fully able to sat-isfy the needs and wants of their partner (Perel, 2015). The practice of CNM subverts this discourse by removing the expectation that each partner will satisfy all sexual, emotional, and logistical needs and wants of the other partner, and calls into question the notion that trust, loyalty, and attachment can only exist in a monogamous framework. As such, practicing CNM is an inherently political act, "call[ing] into question the integrity of monogamy as a stable construct, not rejecting it intact, but pull-ing it apart from the inside out" (Shalandra Phillips, 2009, cited in Perel, 2017, p. 261).

Other dominant discourses that support monogamy, and are challenged by the practice of CNM, were articulated on Tumblr by user nankingdecade (n.d.):

> If you do not experience jealousy, you are not in love.
> Sufficiently intense love overcomes any practical incompatibilities.
> If you are truly in love with your partner, you will not be attracted to anyone else.
> Commitment requires exclusivity.

Therapists can help clients practicing or considering CNM to deconstruct these discourses and develop preferred, local discourses that reflect their choices, values, and experience.

As with any relationship style, the actual practice of CNM will look different for each client. Fur-thermore, the salience of the identity will vary, along with the extent to which clients view their relationship style as an identity, relationship orientation, and/or practice. Some individuals describe CNM as a practice, and may choose to practice monogamy at some junctures and CNM at others; others say that they have never felt comfortable with the concept of monogamy nor been in a monog-amous relationship, and therefore view it as an identity (Sheff, 2016). Ritchie and Barker (2006) suggest that, rather than thinking dichotomously about monogamy/nonmonogamy, it is helpful to think in terms of spectrums. They identify two separate spectrums of monogamy: one for emotional closeness, ranging from entirely monogamous (one close relationship, no other close relationships outside of this) to polyamorous (multiple close relationships); and another for sex and physical contact, ranging from monosex (sexual or physical contact only within a single relationship) to polysex (multiple sexual or physical partners). These spectrums may offer ways for clients to conceptualize and describe their commitments, expectations, and preferences for relationships, whether they identify as monogamous or non-monogamous. Perel (2017) notes that "monogamy was once a subject that was never even discussed in the therapist's office, but today as a matter of course I ask every couple, 'What is your monogamy agreement?'" (p. 278).

POINTS TO DISCUSS

Imagine that you are working with a couple who are approaching their wedding. How might you use the spectrums described above to help the couple clarify their expectations and their understanding of what constitutes "cheating" in their relationship?

Richards and Barker (2013) suggest the following exercise for therapists: Consider where you would put your own (current, past, or ideal) relationship on these spectrums. Where would your (current, past, or ideal) partner put their preference? For example, on the emotional spectrum, what do you think about having a close friendship other than your partner (perhaps with someone of the same gender as them); being friends with an ex-partner; staying up all night talking with someone you just met; or having someone in your life who is as—or even more—important to you than your partner? On the sexual spectrum, how do you feel about fantasizing about a celebrity; watching pornography; flirting with a colleague; having cybersex; or having a one-night stand?

Swinging/The Lifestyle

Swinging is a lifestyle in which sexual activity is viewed as recreational or social. Although single individuals participate in swinging, it more commonly involves couples jointly and consensually having sexual experiences with other individuals or couples (Swing Lifestyle, 2018). In "the lifestyle" (often a preferred term over swinging), the emphasis is on sexual interactions ("playing"), rather than building new romantic relationships, and people in the lifestyle may enact policies to avoid getting romantically close to play partners, such as only engaging with play partners with the consent of their significant other, and/or in the same space, and/or viewing play partners as things or toys. They may also choose to discontinue swinging relationships in which romantic feelings begin to develop (Kimberly & Hans, 2017), though people who meet in the lifestyle do sometimes establish romantic relationships.

The swinging lifestyle both challenges many problematic dominant discourses, such as those that stipulate that "healthy" sex only occurs privately and in a monogamous framework, and reinforces others, such as heteronormativity. For example, bisexual women are prized in swinging communities, as a stereotypical "hot threesome" enacted under a literal or figurative heterosexual male gaze would include two women and a man, with two women to "please" the man and play between the two women taking on a performative nature. By contrast, bisexual men are less celebrated or even welcomed in the lifestyle, and sexual play between men is less accepted, as is kink play (Johnson, 2015).

In the lifestyle, highly stereotyped and bifurcated gender expression tends to be prized and rewarded (such as women wearing sexy lingerie). Yet, some women in the lifestyle report finding it empowering and liberating. Johnson (2015) reports that women do most of the negotiation in swinging encounters: "females drive the lifestyle" (paragraph 4). Thus the gender performance in the lifestyle simultaneously reinforces gender binaries and challenges stereotypical views of women as passive receivers of sexual attention.

Gay Open Relationships

The gay male community has been at the forefront of experimenting with new models of relationship agreements, according to Ester Perel (2017). She comments, "Since the sanctioned heteronormative model was not available to them until recently, they took it upon themselves to be creative and have practiced nonexclusive forms of relating with much success." (p. 261). The late psychologist and gay activist Michael Shernoff described CNM as a "vibrant, normative, and healthy part" of the gay male community that constructively challenges heteronormative assumptions that there is only one correct (heterosexual, monogamous) form for love relationships (Shernoff, nd, cited in Perel, 2017, p. 278).

Polyamory (Poly or Polyam)

Polyamory may be defined as the practice of relating romantically to more than one person, with the knowledge and consent of all involved. Polyamory is distinct from polygamy, in which a man has more than one female partner, and contrasts with swinging by emphasizing romantic relationships over sexual interactions. According to Sheff (2012), polyamory has become more prevalent in the last decade.

Some important subgroups exist within polyamory:

In *hierarchical polyamory*, a *primary* relationship takes priority, and *secondary* relationships are typically only be added with the support of the other primary partner. This hierarchical arrangement may be based on intention (*prescriptive* hierarchy) or circumstances (*descriptive* hierarchy).

In *egalitarian polyamory*, all partners are considered to have equal privilege and power, even if some partners' lives are more intertwined (for example, with shared living space or child-rearing).

Those who practice *solo poly* tend to emphasize individual autonomy in their relationships (for example, forming new partnerships without seeking permission of other partners, and preferring not to combine finances or share a living space with partners).

In *polyfidelity*, three or more primary partners commit to sexual exclusivity within the group. People practicing *relationship anarchy* avoid imposing definitions or labels on relationships (for example, "romantic" or "platonic") and eschew relationship hierarchies (Powers, 2016), thereby subverting multiple social mores.

Therapeutic Considerations

Identifying with and/or practicing a relational style that is outside of the boundaries of social norms is challenging, as it involves confronting and acting in opposition to deeply entrenched values around monogamy and normative sexual practices. Richards and Barker (2013) argue:

> By far the most common problem that people experience around open non-monogamy relates to the difficulties inherent in being non-monogamous in a mononormative world. This may take the form, for example, of family, friends or colleagues not accepting their relationships; of prejudice or discrimination on the basis of their non-monogamy (or the stress of keeping this secret). … Most problems experienced by openly non-monogamous people also relate to wider mononormativity in the sense that they are about not having a 'rulebook.' (p. 208)

As Michaels & Johnson (2015) point out, "designing" one's own relationship(s) provides rich opportunities for growth, and personal and relationship development, as well as requiring navigation of potential minefields of emotionally and physically challenging or even dangerous experiences. Perel (2017) writes that "couples often ask me for help in navigating the new terrain of plural connections. Few social scripts exist as yet. We are all improvising" (p. 261). Therapists can join with clients practicing CNM to help them successfully negotiate the challenges and opportunities of this new terrain.

Communication. Communication is key in CNM; the ongoing negotiation of how and to what extent individuals engage in relational activities, including but not limited to sex, is fundamental. Therapists can help clients practicing CNM to establish and maintain open and direct communication about fears and expectations, sexual health practices, and allocation of resources (particularly time, attention, and money). Capturing expectations and understandings in a written contract or agreement, either during or outside of therapy time, may be a helpful process for clients, and later constitute an important reference point. Veaux and Rikert (2014) urge that any such agreement be viewed as a living document, renegotiated as relationships and circumstances develop and change.

Breakups. The breakup of a nonmonogamous relationship is not inherently less painful than that of a monogamous one; yet, due to mononormativity and fears of stigmatization and discrimination, clients going through breakups of nonmonogamous relationships may have less social support. Richards and Barker (2013) point out that it is critical for therapists to realize that nonmonogamous breakups are no more caused by nonmonogamy than monogamous breakups are caused by monogamy.

Jealousy. As stated above, a dominant discourse supporting monogamy is, "If you don't experience jealousy, you aren't in love." Within the polyamorous community, there is another, problematic discourse suggesting that, instead of jealousy, the successful polyamorist feels only "compersion" (a sense of joy experienced when one's loved one loves another). Dedeker Winston (2017) writes that in reality, whatever their relationship structures, clients may (or may not) experience jealousy, and notes that jealousy can coexist with compersion. In their seminal book, *The Ethical Slut* (2009), Dossi Easton and Janet Hardy suggest that jealousy is a complex emotion, possibly involving feelings of insecurity, loneliness, vulnerability, envy, anger, and/or fear of loss and abandonment. They argue that polyamorous individuals benefit both personally and relationally from learning to manage jealousy, as is described by Greg, below.

Greg, who is a 54-year-old, White, cisgender, polyamorous male, explains:

> *When my primary partner is away with other partners, I feel happy when I think of her being happy. I thought I was weird until I read about compersion, and realized I wasn't alone. But I also feel jealousy sometimes, stemming from a fear of abandonment. The biggest thing is being reassured that she still loves me, isn't planning on leaving me, and doesn't love me any less. Sometimes just a quick text will make all the difference. I also keep myself busy, and I focus on the benefits associated with polyamory. I like feeling strong because I'm able to handle jealous feelings.*

Jane is a cisgender, pansexual, polyamorous woman. She writes:

> *My husband and I see a couples therapist on a regular basis for support in our nontraditional relationship. She has helped us by normalizing our open relationship, pushing us to develop and update a contract, and reminding us to practice safer sex. She prompts and provides space for open and honest communication when uncomfortable feelings—usually jealousies or fears—come up. Perhaps most of all, she consistently conveys that she believes that it is possible for us to have successful polyamorous relationships.*
>
> *I feel a tremendous sense of agency in having more choice about my relational and sexual interactions, and I have become better at countering discourses that tell me that I am foolish to move away from monogamy. On the other hand, shame, fear, and doubt resurface in surprising, irrational ways: Sometimes when I make some kind of innocent mistake, or perhaps have a disagreement with a loved one, I find myself flooded with anxiety and thoughts that I am a "bad" mother, wife, or person, **because I am poly**. This is another way that our therapist helps us: she notices and points out when guilt, shame, and internalized mononormativity show up in unproductive ways. This helps us to make choices that aren't fear based, and align with our beliefs and values.*

Jane's story highlights how a therapist can support a nonmonogamous individual or couple, by highlighting problematic discourses that may underpin anxieties and undermine clients' agency. Therapists also have a role to play in helping CNM clients navigate the decisions and challenges associated with coming out to their children and other family members.

Katie Mercer (introduced above), whose parents opened their marriage, writes about their family's adjustment.

> *Five years after I came out as queer to my family, I found myself on the other side of the conversation when my parents told me they were exploring polyamory together. I felt a huge range of conflicting emotions, partially because of my own sexual identity and the ideas of monogamy I had learned from larger society, and because these were my parents and not just any two individuals in my life. As a member of the LGBTQ+ community, I understood the feeling of not being accepted for your sexual identity and I wanted to*

be supportive. I had polyamorous friends and considered myself to be accepting of poly-
amory and different relationship styles.

When confronted with my parents' opening their marriage, however, I struggled to accept it given the traditional ideas of relationships I didn't even realize I held. Society's ideas about which identities are acceptable and which are not impacted both my own coming out pro-cess and my reaction to that of my parents. I felt our family was threatened by the transition, and was fearful that my parents would have less love for me if they were putting their energy into new romantic partners. I've come to conceptualize love differently now, and understand that my parents can have an infinite amount of love to share with their family, their new partners, and each other. I've read books and talked to people about polyamory, so that my frame of mind allows me to accept and understand polyamory much more easily than I did before. The society I am immersed in promotes monogamy. Movies, stories, songs, reli-gious messages, and what are deemed real relationships, and so much of what we hear, see, and experience promote the idea that humans are meant to be monogamous. I no longer believe this, but I needed to un-learn some of these traditional ideas before I could be fully supportive of and happy about my parents' new relationship structure.

Katie identifies several problematic dominant discourses, such as "the idea that humans are meant to be monogamous," that contributed to her initial sense of threat when her parents revealed their prac-tice of nonmonogamy. A therapist could work with Katie and her family to navigate this transition, by naming these problematic dominant discourses, and providing a safe space in which family members' concerns are acknowledged, and problem solving undertaken, where appropriate.

Hookup Culture

Hookups, which may be defined as uncommitted sexual encounters involving a wide range of behav-iors (for example, kissing, oral, and penetrative sex), are becoming engrained in popular culture (Garcia, Reiber, Massey & Merriwether, 2012). Stinson (2010) reports that hookups, or casual, "no strings attached" sexual encounters, have become the "normative heterosexual relationship on college campuses" (p. 98); and Bogle (2008) states that hookup culture is "a nationwide phenomenon that has largely replaced traditional dating on college campuses" (p. 5). However, Monto and Carey (2014) argue that Bogle's claim is not supported by their analysis of two waves of General Social Survey data, which reveals only a modest increase in reports of casual sex among contemporary college students.

Charlie, who is a sophomore at a small four-year college, offers his perspective:

Hookups are prevalent, but there's still definitely a desire for both [hookups and commit-ted relationships]. I think of hooking up almost like a different category of relationship. Sometimes it's just a destressor. During finals week, I hear way more people saying they're not looking for something long-term.

On our campus, Greek life or apartment parties tend to have a higher number of people purely looking to hook up. Even though some people go to parties to dance, there's more people there with the expectation of hooking up, similar to when you meet on Tinder. Also, in the environment of frat or apartment parties, there's usually alcohol involved, and I've

> *heard many stories of people not using protection, almost to the point of bragging. It's definitely not for everyone…. Some of my friends are interested in hooking up, some aren't at all; it's just not what they're looking for.*

Charlie's description of "a desire for both" hookups and committed relationships is supported by research finding that young people, on average, do not prefer casual sex over committed relationships (Cashman & Walters, 2018). Research also confirms the prevalence of alcohol and sexual risk-taking in hookup culture (Downing-Matibag & Geisinger, 2009).

Friends with Benefits (FWB) Relationships

FWB is another relationship style common among (but not limited to) young adults, according to Knight (2014), in which friends who do not have romantic commitments or expectations enact a sexual relationship. Between 51% and 60% of college students report FWB relationships at one time or another (Bisson & Levine, 2009). Erlandsson, Nordvall, Öhman, and Häggerström-Nordin (2012) report that the FWB relationship is perceived more positively when the partner is a close, comfortable friend; having more than one FWB concurrently is widely accepted; and partners often feel ambivalent about romance within the FWB relationship. As in hookup culture, alcohol use and sexual risk-taking behavior is common in FWB relationships (Erlandsson, et al., 2012).

Gender Differences, Sexual Double Standards and "Slut Discourse"

Cashman and Walters' (2018) survey of college students' FWB relationships finds that while both males and females, on average, report that they are satisfied with their FWB relationship, males are more satisfied than females. Men are also more likely to initiate a FWB relationship, have friends who are supportive of the relationship, and feel comfortable talking to friends about it. Research also indicates that women are more likely than men to report regretting hookups (Uecker & Martinez, 2017).

These gender differences may relate to a sexual double standard; that is, though there is an overall cultural shift toward acceptance of uncommitted sex (Garcia, Reiber, Massey & Merriwether, 2012), male college students have more negative judgments of female college students engaging in casual sex than of males, and women are still likely to be stigmatized ("slut shamed") for their participation in casual sexual encounters (England & Bearak, 2014).

In a more nuanced consideration of "slut discourse," Armstrong, Hamilton, Armstrong, and Seeley (2014) found that high-status female college students label low-status female college students as "slutty" in order to police social boundaries. For example, high-status (generally more affluent) female college students are more likely to be involved in Greek life, and label sexual exploration occurring in this context as "classy," while referring to the sexual activities of lower-status (generally less affluent) female students, typically occurring outside of Greek life, as "slutty."

Heteronormativity and Hookup Culture

As well as being heavily gendered, the college hookup culture is strongly heteronormative, according to Lamont, Roach, and Kahn (2018). They find that LGBTQ+ students are highly critical of dominant hookup culture and attempt to position themselves in relation to preferred local discourses emphasizing consent, communication, and mutual pleasure. According to Pham (2017), research on the college hookup scene privileges the experience of White, middle-class, heterosexual students; less is asked or known about the experience of students who cannot or choose not to participate in hookup culture. Where appropriate, therapists can support clients in deconstructing the heteronormative, classist, and sexist discourses embedded in hookup culture to facilitate clients' sense of agency with regard to sexual activity.

Therapeutic Considerations Relating to Gender, Sexual, and Relationship Diversity

GSRD Affirmative Therapy

The model of "gay affirmative therapy" first developed in the 1980s and 1990s (Malyon, 1982; Davies, 1996) has been widened to include affirmation of all sexual and gender minorities (Butler, 2010), and these principles also apply to therapy with relationship-style minorities. The general assumptions and principles are summarized below.

A Nonpathologizing Stance

Embodying a marginalized gender, sexual, or relational identity reflects human diversity rather than pathology, and, if a mental health issue exists, it is most likely to stem from the experiences of stigma and discrimination, rather than from something intrinsic to the individual.

Self-Awareness

According to Dentato, Arguello, and Wilson (2016), a counselor practicing affirmative therapy must be aware of their own social location and identities. It is critical that counselors, who (like everyone else) are barraged with cultural discourses disparaging GSRD, actively seek to notice and challenge their internalized biases related to gender, sexual, and relational identities and practices. Richards and Barker (2013) encourage therapists to pay attention to feelings of discomfort, threat, or judgment (sometimes referred to as countertransference) that may arise related to a client's GSRD identification or practices, and discuss these with a supervisor or GSRD-friendly colleague.

Education Regarding GSRD Issues/Intercultural Competency

A theme in the literature on working with GSRD clients is the importance of therapists having a foundational knowledge of the population they are working with. Kolmes, Stock, and Moser (2006) found that kinky clients were frustrated by having to educate their therapists about kink; one client explained that she had had to educate her therapist "that it was not abuse, that it was not harmful to me, that I was not self-sabotaging with it, nor acting out past family/spousal abuse. It actually took quite a few sessions to get the therapist over their hang-ups and misconceptions about BDSM. Time that could (have) been better spent on the actual issues I was there for" (p. 315).

Recognizing the Influence of the Client's Social and Cultural Environments

Affirmative therapy emphasizes that clients' relationships, resources, networks, and intersecting identities are of central importance to their well-being, and must therefore be foregrounded throughout the therapeutic process. The therapist should pay attention to the client's experience of their immediate and broader social environment (in terms of homonegativity, and so on), and foster the understanding that social oppression is a societal problem, not the client's problem. Narrative therapy's nonpathologizing stance, and associated assumption that the problems bringing people to therapy are located outside rather than inside of the clients (White & Epston, 1980), make this a particularly helpful therapy modality, according to Dentato, Arguello, and Wilson (2016). They note that narrative therapy may also benefit clients embodying GSRD by highlighting the effects of cultural values and world views on people's lived experience, and the relationships among power, privilege, and individual and collective experience.

Awareness but Not Overemphasis of GSRD-Related Issues

Counselors working in this area should be attuned to potential GSRD-related issues, but also bear in mind that most problems bringing clients to therapy do not relate, or only indirectly relate, to gender, sexual, or relational identities or practices. Richards and Barker (2013) capture this nuance with the following example: "When seeing trans people professionally, not having a metaphorical neon sign saying 'TRANS', but rather a whispered hint behind one's shoulder that there may be a trans theme, is usually the best course of action" (p. 21).

Strengths Perspective

Taking a strengths perspective refers to focusing on the self-determination, well-being, and health of the client, instead of pathologizing the origins of gender, sexuality, or relationship styles, or imposing normative ideas. The therapist conveys that a client's gender, sexual, and relationship styles "are to be valued, accepted, and perceived as positive outcomes" (Butler, 2010, pp. 445–446). Diep and Estrellado (2018) suggest that the therapist might also wish to highlight the client's "positive subjective experiences" and "character strengths." Further, therapists adopting a strengths-based approach recognize the many opportunities for growth associated with embodying one or more marginalized identities. As individuals embodying GSRD develop an awareness that many of the challenges they experience are located not within themselves, but in problematic dominant discourses, they may strengthen personal and collective resilience by resisting these discourses, developing preferred local discourses, and fostering community premised on common values.

David Findlay, 52, who identifies as multiracial, brown-skinned, queer, multiply in love, and as having invisible disabilities, describes how therapy fit into this process for him.

> For me, therapy was a crucial space in which to examine my options and practice new ways of interacting. Friendships, love relationships, work, and other social connections within a diverse urban environment were where I healed. Over time, I learned to navigate a balance among "change self to fit world," "change expectations of world" and "change world to fit all of us" that skewed strongly toward changing the world. I developed an appreciation of the shared perspective arising from the shared experience of occupying many marginalized identity positions. We are never exclusively victim, we are never exclusively occupying bottom-tier positions, we always have some relative social power and with that some responsibility to look out for one another caringly.

David's experience shows how deconstruction of oppressive dominant discourses occurs in social and relational contexts that foster empathy and engagement. He also describes how the process of developing a positive identity may be supported both by affirmative therapy and by interaction with people of diverse gender, sexual, and relational identities.

Other Therapeutic Considerations

Coming out in Session

When therapists practice affirmative therapy, clients are more likely to return to that therapist (and to therapy generally); furthermore, they are more likely to disclose their GSRD identity (Richards & Barker, 2013). When clients come out in session, Nichols (2006) advises therapists to acknowledge that this is an honor, and to provide clients with resources (such as educational and social organizations and networks), as they may particularly benefit from knowing they are not alone at an early stage of coming out.

Sexual Health

When clients are exploring new sexual or relational identities or practices, therapists may want to introduce the topics of sexual health and negotiating sexual boundaries. Therapists can encourage clients to clarify sexual preferences and boundaries, and facilitate planning related to safety precautions, contraception use, and STI testing and prevention.

Condom Use

Richards and Barker (2013) point out that many people regularly use condoms for vaginal or anal sex to reduce STI and/or pregnancy risk; but also, many do not ("barebacking"). Some reasons for this include lack of access to condoms; failure to appreciate risk of STIs (especially common among younger people and among older people becoming sexually active after many years of monogamy or sexual inactivity); impaired judgment associated with drug or alcohol use; and finding it to be more exciting, a demonstration of trust and/or more pleasurable. A therapist may want to discuss these reasons with a client as part of a safer sex conversation.

HIV/AIDS, Health Education, and Stigma

Therapists should also recognize that fear of stigmatization and discrimination is another reason that clients may not use condoms, get tested for HIV, or access potentially lifesaving antiretroviral medications.

A 2014 report by UNAIDS states:

> [R]esearch has shown that stigma and discrimination undermine HIV prevention efforts by making people afraid to seek HIV information, services and modalities to reduce their risk of infection and to adopt safer behaviours lest these actions raise suspicion about their HIV status. Research has also shown that fear of stigma and discrimination, which can also be linked to fear of violence, discourages people living with HIV from disclosing their status even to family members and sexual partners and

undermines their ability and willingness to access and adhere to treatment. Thus, stigma and discrimination weaken the ability of individuals and communities to protect themselves from HIV and to stay healthy if they are living with HIV. (p. 2)

Therapists can help by working with individuals, families, and communities to recognize and reduce stigma and discrimination associated with HIV/AIDS. For clients who are living with HIV, therapists can facilitate involvement in programs emphasizing the rights of people living with HIV, which is a well-documented way to reduce stigma and discrimination and improve access to healthcare (UNAIDS, 2014).

Dentato, Arguello, and Wilson (2016) note that transgender women, and gay and bisexual men who are younger, over the age of 50, and/or of minoritized racial and ethnic backgrounds, continue to bear a disproportional burden in the AIDS epidemic, and suggest that therapists working with these populations be especially prepared to offer advocacy, referrals, and up-to-date information related to STI screenings, window periods (the period between exposure to an STI and when the STI will show up on a test), the use of condoms, and antiretroviral medications that can prevent and/or limit the devastation of HIV/AIDS (both for those who are HIV positive and those at high risk for HIV exposure).

POINTS TO DISCUSS

Imagine you have a 60-year-old male client who has recently begun dating men for the first time. What topics might you want to discuss with your client relating to sexual health and preferences? What emotions and/or concerns do you think might come up for you and/or your client?

Aspects of a GSRD-Friendly Office Environment

An up-to-date list of affirming providers for clients who need referrals to other services (such as legal, medical) or to another therapist

Diversity-affirming magazines and books, posters, brochures, and so on

Personnel who represent diversity and labor policies that support them

Inclusive forms and policies in office and on website:

Parent 1/Parent 2 (rather than Mother/Father)

Multiple options for gender pronouns

Name, and then Legal Name

Relationship configuration (or space to describe romantic relationships that involve more than two people)

Nondiscrimination statements

When the Therapist Is Part of the Community

Therapists who embody GSRD identities have to decide if and/or when it is appropriate to disclose this to clients, and may also need to navigate the issue of dual relationships, if they are active or present in community spaces that clients may share. Barnett (2011) states that factors influencing this decision include the therapist's model of therapy, their professional code of ethics, and the context of therapy (including work culture). However, the primary consideration is clients' best interest, taking into account their treatment needs and personal history, along with the age, ethnicity, gender, and so on, of both the client and the therapist.

Meera's statement below indicates that her work context and therapeutic orientation allow her to comfortably come out to clients, when appropriate, and that this is appreciated by them.

> *I am a queer therapist working within a queer context. As I reflect on my practices and ethical stance with clients and supervisees, there are shared experiences of queer culture and marginalization that inform a spirit of collaboration, social justice, and community. In seeing queerness as present in all parts of someone's life, my therapeutic conversations with clients may inquire about levels of support in various parts of their life, their comfort level with their identity, and what meaning queerness holds for them and the communities they walk in.*
>
> *I am comfortable sharing some of my experiences, as it seems appropriate, in a spirit of transparency and community, which is often greatly appreciated. I participate in rich conversations about how our experience can inform our practice, coming out, and spirituality, fears when connecting to a queer community, and challenges couples may face based on each partner's level of "outness," to name a few. There exists a queer language and culture, based on lived experience, marginalization, and loss, which can be shared between the therapist and client in the counseling process. In the eyes of some of my colleagues, I am privileged in being able to work this way, as their organizations are not as supportive. Now the irony here is that while I am very open professionally and socially where I live, my extended family overseas are still not aware of my queer identity. This is a reality that many of us face, "outness" is very contextual and can be limited to certain spheres of life only.*

Meera's comments remind us of how each of us, therapist and client, engage with issues related to our identities, both in and out of the therapy room, and the importance of reflexive practice. As therapists, whatever our own gender, sexual, and relationship style identities and practices, we are better able to serve our clients' needs when we are comfortable with the range of gender, sexual, and relationship styles our clients may embody, as well as our own.

Conclusion

This chapter has highlighted some problem dominant discourses related to gender, sex, and relationship style, as well as the ways in which those who embody GSRD describe their individual and collective experiences in terms of preferred, local discourses that highlight empowerment and choice. The chapter emphasizes the notion that gender, sexuality, and relationship styles may be usefully conceptualized on spectrums, and suggests that therapists recognize and celebrate the diversity of gender, sexual, and relationship-style identities and practices embodied by clients. We've considered the ways in which intersections among identities offer complex challenges and opportunities for clients and the therapists who work with them (Diep & Estrellado, 2018). Therapists are encouraged to consider their own gender, sexual, and relationship-style identities, and the ways in which they can offer affirmative therapy to GSRD clients.

Response to Chapter 10

ROSE HARTZELL-
CUSHANICK, PHD,
EDS, LMFT

Rose Hartzell works as an AASECT certified sex therapist and licensed marriage and family therapist at San Diego Sexual Medicine, where she works with a world-renowned sexual medicine physician and a number of pelvic floor physical therapists. Dr. Hartzell has written multiple publications and has given over 60 presentations at international and national meetings on sexuality matters. She has published numerous journal articles in professional journals and a number of book chapters discussing sexual health. In 2007, Dr. Hartzell was awarded the Emerging Professional Award from the Society for the Scientific Study of Sexuality. She has conducted sex research with the Kinsey Institute for Research in Sex, Gender, and Reproduction and the Rural Center for AIDS/STD Prevention (RCAP). Dr. Hartzell is an AASECT certified sexuality educator supervisor and has taught numerous classes at San Diego State University, Indiana University–Bloomington, the University of Arkansas–Fayetteville, and National University. She also served as the scientific program co-chair for the Society for the Scientific Study of Sexuality national conferences in 2013 and 2014, and is the current scientific program co-chair for the International Society for the Study of Women's Sexual Health (ISSWSH) meeting. She also serves as a reviewer for the Journal of Sexual Medicine.

This chapter helps provide pertinent information in order to help therapists be more competent when working with individuals and couples. Sexual health conversations are sometimes difficult and awkward for both clients and therapists, yet they often profoundly affect clients' self-identities, mental health, and relationships. When issues related to sexuality are discussed and handled in a sensitive manner, clients are more likely leave therapy feeling empowered, less ashamed, and happier in their lives and relationships.

Due to the stigmatization of various relationship constellations (e.g., consensual nonmonogamy) and sexual practices (e.g., BDSM/kink), the therapist may be the first person outside of sexual partners with whom a client is fully open to regarding their sexuality. It's not uncommon for me to see couples or individuals who have originally gone to other therapists, but have felt like they needed to hide their true sexual identities for fear of judgment by the therapist.

In addition to awareness regarding gender, sexual, and relationship diversity, many people come to therapists with concerns regarding their sexual function (e.g., erectile difficulties, orgasm difficulties, desire discrepancies, arousal disorders, etc.). Behind these concerns is often great shame, conflicting and complicated feelings regarding masculinity/femininity, and a buy-in to societal messages regarding what sex "should" be like.

Through my work as a sex therapist within a sexual medicine practice, I have been exposed to thousands of people from all over the world hoping to improve their sexual function. Although many of the individuals coming to our practice do have some medical issues impacting their sexual function, the issues they are dealing with are often compounded by the societal messages they receive and the narratives they tell themselves regarding their love maps, sexual scripts, and what is "normal."

An example regarding how societal messages and culture can impact sexual health is illustrated by a recent client, who is a cisgender, heterosexual male, originally from India. He came to our practice seeking medical management for his presenting symptoms, which he described as low sexual desire and erectile difficulties. He expressed that when he was engaging in sexual activity with a woman he wasn't interested in or attracted to, he had trouble getting an erection or having sexual desire. He shared that when he is in a relationship with a woman he "likes," however, he does not have trouble with sexual desire, does not have any erectile difficulties, and is able to engage in sexual intercourse two to three times a week. He expressed that his family and friends never talked about sex while he was growing up and that his only exposure to sex education was the sexual imagery that he watched online. When he came to us, he believed that he should have always have sexual desire and be able to get an erection with any woman he came across (regardless of whether he liked her or not). In therapy, I assisted the client in challenging his internalized views of masculinity (that men should ALWAYS have desire and should ALWAYS be able to get an erection on demand). We also discussed the client's desire for "normality" when, in reality, there is such great diversity in sexuality.

Another example of the complexity regarding sexual function and sexual diversity from my practice is a White, cisgender, heterosexual male client who had had his leg amputated in an effort to save him from cancer. During his cancer treatment/amputation he had developed erectile difficulties and was only able to obtain an erection strong enough for intercourse through the help of penile injections. He had recently ended his marriage of over 20 years, since he was interested in BDSM and felt like he could not be his "true self" with his wife. He indicated that he had briefly expressed his interest in BDSM to his wife during couples therapy halfway through their marriage, but that his wife reacted negatively to his disclosure, and the topic of his sexual preferences was never broached again (even by their couples therapist). He expressed that having cancer showed him that his life was too short to waste not being his "true self," and that he could not let the cultural stigma surrounding BDSM keep him from living the life he wanted to live. In therapy, I provided him with support as he navigated dating as a recent amputee, with erectile difficulties, who wanted to find a partner who shared his interest in BDSM.

This chapter is important for all therapists to read in order to be able to meet individuals and couples of diverse genders, sexual function, sexual orientation, and relational constellations where they are, without pathologizing or stigmatizing these individuals or couples in any way. Therapists may be most effective when they can suspend judgment, continue to educate themselves regarding sexual issues, and be curious regarding the sex lives (including gender, orientation, sexual function, and relationship constellation) of the people they work with.

Chapter 11

The Globalization of Identity

The era of globalization has arrived, and with it comes new directions in cultural politics (Eko, 2003). Like it or not, globalization produces common habits, shared cultural norms, and common knowledge systems across diverse cultural populations. These emerging global cultural trends are promulgated by transnational media, mass travel and migration, and technological advances. In order to better understand the intimate and personal issues going on in our clients' lives and to be better equipped as counselors, therapists, and psychologists, it is helpful to grapple with the wider sociocultural dynamics that are currently taking place around the globe.

The Pros and Cons of Globalization

Globalization is a controversial phenomenon. For many, globalization is a contemporary process identified with the accumulation of power in the hands of a limited number of powerful corporations that are now larger than many national economies. In their hands, the globalization of cultural influences can be understood as a subtle new vehicle for political, economic, and cultural domination, a colonizing movement of the 21st century that recapitulates the colonization of previous centuries. There is plenty of evidence for the link between globalization and cultural hegemony. The new global culture certainly seems to privilege Western consumerism, the spread of uncontrolled capitalism and the free market, and deregulated commercialism, and to most benefit those in the most privileged positions in American (U.S.) and European societies.

Nobel Prize-winning economist Joseph Stiglitz (2003) has shown how policies instituted by the International Monetary Fund have served the agendas of the richer industrialized countries at the expense of the developing countries of the world to the extent that globalization (especially the globalization of economic markets) has acquired a bad name around the world and become the target of considerable anger. It is often associated with the continuation of neocolonial policies that ensure that America and Europe maintain an exploitative economic advantage while developing countries are coerced into implementing stringent economic regimens whose negative impact is borne in the end by the poorest people on earth. One such example is corporations' outsourcing of labor to developing countries where labor is cheap and often unregulated. These corporations exploit their workers, profiting from child labor and poor work conditions. Stiglitz nevertheless argues that the problem is not globalization itself as much as unfair and ill-conceived economic policies that ought to and can be corrected.

Koichiro Matsuura, director general of the United Nations Educational, Scientific and Cultural Organization (UNESCO) in the late 1990s, warned that globalization is dangerous, because it floods the third world with cultural artifacts (such as smartphones) from industrialized countries, leading to homogenization and subsequent "global impoverishment" (Caramel & Laronche, 2000). Michael Peters and Tina Besley (2006) argue that the "global interconnected space of communication" (p. 1) is producing new forms of knowledge and new knowledge cultures in which knowledge is exchanged with increasing rapidity. Of course today communication is instantaneous across multiple platforms.

One product of global interconnection is that human societies are tending to become less and less differentiated from one another. When people from different parts of the world form identities around the same musical genres, television shows, and hit movies, there is a strong theme of cultural homogenization at work.

It is of note that while the West may *appear* to dominate the cultural flow across borders, globalizing social processes are not rigid, one-way flows of cultural production. There are numerous examples of reverse flows. Japanese-style management systems have been introduced into Western companies. Musical genres from Brazil, the Caribbean, sub-Saharan Africa, and Asia find audiences in the mainstream of global popular culture. For instance, the Korean hit song and music video "Gangnam Style" went viral in August 2012 and won Best Video at the MTV Europe Music Awards (Billboard, 2012). The Korean music genre known as K-pop is making itself known to people in the West and all over the world. One might argue that what is "Western" and what is "Eastern" is more fluid than it once was. Cultural products emanating from both the West and the East intermingle, resulting in hybrid forms of cultural expression.

Lisa Tsoi Hoshmand (2005) suggests that impactful social processes occurring right now all over the planet are leading to profound changes in human experience and identity. As a result, cultural knowledges are being subjected to processes of assimilation and hybridity. She suggests that we can no longer straightforwardly categorize particular groups of people when the pace of identity formation and identity choices are greater than ever before in the history of the world.

BOX 11.1 ECONOMIC NATIONALISM

Ten years ago, you could be forgiven for believing that the social, economic, and political processes accompanying globalization would continue to march forward, uninterrupted. Sure there were those who argued for globalization and how the market stood to benefit, how everyone would be better off. And sure there were those who detested globalization and took to the streets of Seattle in November 1999 to protest at the World Trade Organization's meeting there. However, for most people the logic of free trade and open economic markets seemed unquestionable. Since World War II, globalization and international organizations had grown steadily in power. There was the United Nations, the European Union, the World Trade Organization, the G7, NATO, and NAFTA, to name a few. Globalization had an inevitability about it and international trade grew exponentially. In fact, international trade had grown 4018% between 1950 and 2017 (World Trade Organization, 2018).

Then the world's economy went into major recession from 2008. The effects were devastating, and enormous sums of money were simply wiped out. Investment companies went to the wall and banks had to be bailed out to survive. It took six years to get back to how things had been before. Nearly everyone, except the wealthy, suffered in some way. Two-thirds of American (U.S.) homeowners owed more in mortgages than their homes were worth. But the poor suffered the most. They bore the brunt of unemployment, their wages stayed stagnant, pension funds were raided, and houses were foreclosed on by banks. They were also blamed by some lenders of dubious subprime mortgages for causing the housing crisis by trying to buy homes they could not afford.

The poor were disaffected by the traditional parties of the left, who they saw as implicated in neoliberal economic policies that had led to economic crisis. In a number of countries, populism grew, along with calls for a return to economic nationalism. In this view, countries were understood as being in economic competition, and protectionist measures like tariffs on international goods prevailed to make local manufacturers more competitive, even if consumers had to pay more.

As voters became more unhappy with globalization, politicians like Donald Trump were happy to throw them a bone. Many believed that too-open immigration policies were leading to immigrants taking their jobs. Others were frustrated with international trade treaties like NAFTA, which they claimed meant corporations were shipping jobs off to China or India. The response was an embrace of Donald Trump, because he was trumpeting economic nationalism at the expense of free market neoliberalism. It mattered little to his supporters that economic nationalism brought with it other uglier forms of nationalism. "Make America Great Again!" his slogan went. The trouble lay in the word "again." "Before what?" was the question begged. Perhaps the answer was before multiculturalism took the privileges the White working class enjoyed. Many thought as much, even if they dared not say so. Steve Bannon had no such compunction. He articulated the deliberate policy for Trump's campaign as a combination of White nationalism and economic nationalism (Kuttner, 2017).

But why did so many vote for Trump? The answer is complex and local twists have to be calculated. However, there was a rejection of globalization. There are multiple possible globalizations, but rejected was the corporate elite version that had previously enjoyed broad support. It was supposed to be "only" way. As Lazzarato (2015) says, "The first watchword of neoliberalism is, 'There is no alternative'" (p. 23).

Jacques Rancière (2010) warns that where there is "consensus," there is elite governance. Only through "dissensus" is the voice of the "demos," of the ordinary person, heard. Well, the demos is being heard through a right-wing rejection of a globalizing consensus, and some right-wing politicians are smart enough to take advantage. The demos is saying no to the consensus of allowing economic elites to profit while ordinary people lose ground. People of color may not vote for Trump like their White, working-class counterparts, but they may vote less enthusiastically, if at all, for the Democrats, who at the moment appear to represent the globalization consensus. Donald Trump offered them someone to blame (immigrants or the elite establishment). For some who feel like they are losing ground daily, such an offer is irresistible. Meanwhile, the Democrats have looked increasingly like the party of immigrants and apologists for the elite establishment (even if they are not) and become something to rebel against.

Horizontal and Vertical Culture

French historian Marc Bloch (1886–1944) once said, "Men [sic] are more the sons [sic] of their time than of their fathers [sic]" (Maalouf, 2000, p. 101). This statement is perhaps more relevant today than it was when Bloch wrote it, as it underscores the point that a citizen today often has greater connection and more shared understandings, values, and meanings with his contemporaries than he does with his own ancestors. This phenomenon is increasingly the case as social change occurs at faster and faster rates. Reflect on the fact that our oldest citizens have to make an effort to recall what their outlook was like in their childhood. In order to understand the self that lived 40 or 50 years ago, we must shed a frame of reference and a lifestyle of habits shaped profoundly by products and tools that a person today cannot do without. Most young people do not have the slightest idea what their grandparents' way of life was like, let alone that of earlier generations. We share some affinities with our contemporaries more than we do with our ancestors. Random passersby on a street in San Diego or Beijing probably have many cultural reference points that are more in common with each other than with their great-grandparents.

Amin Maalouf (2000) suggests that we have two heritages: a vertical one that comes from our ancestors and a horizontal one transmitted by our peers. For example, "I am Mexican American" is a reference to a vertical cultural heritage, whereas "I am into wearing ripped jeans," "I am a Steelers fan," and "I am paleo" are more horizontal cultural allegiances. All may be held by the same person. Nevertheless, the cultural inheritance that most people habitually invoke is the vertical one. Subcultural groups like street gangs demand allegiance to horizontal heritages that construct for their adherents the currency in which identity claims are traded. In the age of globalization, vertical cultural groups often attempt to assert their differences more fiercely in order to ensure that their cultural identities stay distinct. For instance, parents of "ABC" or American-born Chinese children might find it important to teach their offspring traditional ways of the old country in order to preserve their "Chineseness."

Three Major Global Processes

Within the last century, perhaps more than at any other time, life has brimmed with diversity, complexity, discontinuity, and the transitory, chaotic nature of human expression. This is one reason why it is increasingly difficult for us to sustain elaborate descriptions about the specific counseling needs of discrete cultural groups. More than ever before, human beings are simultaneously engaged in both producing new forms of cultural life and carrying forward cultural traditions from their ancestors. As Lisa Tsoi Hoshmand (2005) suggests, we are both culture bearing and culture creating. Cultural life is profoundly shaped and constrained by contemporary social forces.

In this chapter, we have chosen to survey three major social forces at work in the process of globalization that play a profound role in shaping contemporary cultural identity. These are migration, the proliferation and influence of mass media, and the growth of technology. Each of these social phenomena can explain the complexity of the cultural challenges that our clients face us with as we learn about the diverse struggles that they encounter in the process of constructing a life. Since this is not a book about globalization, we have necessarily been selective in our choices, but we would argue that these three themes are usually relevant to the psychological challenges that clients present to counselors.

Migration

Migration across the globe is occurring at levels never before witnessed in human history (Dovidio & Esses, 2001). Such movement of people contrasts starkly with how most human beings lived their lives for many thousands of years prior to the last couple of centuries. While over the centuries there have always been enormous human upheavals caused by war, famine, and widespread disease, numerous communities have lived in relative stability for hundreds of generations. Stability is characterized by generations of individuals and families living in the same place, practicing the same religion, eating the same foods, speaking the same dialect, pursuing the same livelihoods, and following the same child-rearing practices. Cultural practices in many communities around the world have changed very slowly and almost imperceptibly over hundreds of years.

Today, people all over the planet are on the move. In the last few decades, over 150 million people have moved to live outside the country in which they were born. This number increased in 2017 by 258,000, which amounts to approximately 3.4% of the world's population in one year (United Nations, Population Division, 2017). Since 2000, this annual figure has increased by nearly 50%. Today, the largest migration flows are from Latin America and Asia into North America, and from Eastern Europe, the countries of the former Soviet Union, and North Africa into northern and Western Europe. The Middle East receives immigrants from Africa and Asia. The United Nations expects that between 2005 and 2050, at least 98 million people will migrate internationally (United Nations, Population Division, 2004). While there are significant numbers of people on the move between countries, there are an even greater number of people relocating their place of residence within their own country's borders. This trend has been occurring for over 200 years since the industrial revolution, but the acceleration of rural to urban migration in the 20th century was unprecedented and is continuing unabated in the 21st century. For example, in 1800, 3% of the world's population lived in towns and cities. By 1900, the number was 14%. From 1900 to 2000, the urban population increased from 14% to 47% within just 100 years. In 2005, more people around the globe live in an urban setting than a rural one. In China, the 1980s and 1990s witnessed the largest single migration in human history, when approximately 90 million people migrated from rural areas dominated by peasant economies to the new cities of southern China. The Population Reference Bureau, which provides data to the United Nations, has predicted that 60% of the world's population will live in a city by 2030 (United Nations, Population Division, 1999). Today, the cities in countries in Africa and South America, and in India and China, are growing at such an unbelievable rate that in most instances they are stretched beyond capacity to accommodate this human avalanche. According to the OECD, migration of asylum seekers alone into the United States in 2017 reached 329,800 (OECD, 2018).

Moreover, migration is a different phenomenon than it used to be (Rees, 2018). Once, when people migrated to a new part of the world, they had little option but to acculturate to the lifestyle of those around them in their new home. Doing so would require, to some extent, severing connections with their previous cultures and families. However, as renowned scientist Martin Rees points out, nowadays, there is less incentive to acculturate. They can make daily video calls and social media calls at little cost back to their former homes, which enables them, if they choose to do so, to stay in touch with the culture of their homelands much more than immigrants of the past were able to do. Rees talks about a new form of migrant, which he dubs "nomads of the technocratic world" (p. 100).

Movement around the globe is not just about changing residence, however. People from all parts of the globe are traveling for business and vacations in numbers not dreamed of just 20 years ago. Currently, 4.3 billion people per year engage in air travel. China leads the world in rates of new travelers, with a projected annual increase of 12.5% per year. Poland, Hungary, and the Czech Republic are not far behind (Gilden, 2005). It is evident that the world no longer operates as if cultures and communities are isolated from each other, unchanged by contact with other cultures. This volume of people moving around the planet constantly provides opportunities for people to meet face to face with others who follow different cultural practices and lifestyles. As a result, people are continually examining and in some cases modifying their own lifestyles and cultural ideals as they are attracted to and embrace new ways of thinking and new modes of life. In the words of James Clifford (1986), people in different countries now "influence, dominate, parody, translate, and subvert each other ... enmeshed in global movements of difference and power" (p. 22).

These dramatic changes in physical location simultaneously produce profound social, psychological, and cultural changes. Today, there is virtually no place on the planet that is insulated from the powerful cultural forces of urbanization. Life in a city demands dramatic shifts in the way family life is conducted. In the United States, many Anglo American families who have lived here for five or six generations have had many years to adjust to the huge social upheavals brought about by international migration and urbanization. However, for more recent immigrants, these upheavals are still having dramatic effects on their family relationships and personal identities. In many of the indigenous and Black communities, individuals continue to suffer from the circumstances leading to their imposed physical relocation, either within the United States, in the case of Native Americans, or, in the case of African Americans, from the enslavement forced on their ancestors from the continent of Africa.

Huge numbers of citizens have come to the United States in the last few decades to escape atrocious circumstances in their homeland. Large Ethiopian, Somali, Sudanese, Laotian, Cambodian, and Vietnamese communities, among many others, have formed throughout the United States. Many of these people share horrific stories of arriving in North America as refugees fleeing from civil war, violent dictatorships, poverty, and persecution. On their arrival in the United States, they are subjected to new hardships as they attempt to adjust to the cultural life and structural inequalities prominent in the United States. These communities experience profound ruptures of their traditional ethnic identities as younger family members attempt to acculturate to majority norms in a country dominated by European American, middle-class cultural ideals.

Social Impacts on Migrating Families

City life is fast paced and demands that recently arrived urban dwellers quickly develop new cultural strategies just in order to survive. Until a few decades ago, extended families were necessary to plow the fields, plant the crops, harvest the mature produce, and deliver it to the local market for sale. They were also depended on for social security. The struggle for material well-being in cities compels people to compete in ways that rural settings do not. As a result, city life places constraints on how large a family can be. In China, state regulations for decades dictated how many children a family could have, but in October 2015 the Chinese news agency Xinhua announced that the government was planning to abolish the one-child policy. All families are now allowed to have two children. But in many other developed countries, the same restrictions have been achieved without state regulation. In most cities in the world, families have had to become smaller in order to successfully compete for material resources and manage the high material costs of feeding, housing, and educating children. In response, the cultural fabric of kinship systems has necessarily been reconstructed. Many new immigrant mothers and fathers in the United States need to work long hours away from home, leaving their children alone in their homes for long periods. The absence of adults in the family home leaves many children and adolescents to fend for themselves without supervision and to sometimes take on the parental role with younger siblings. These circumstances have a huge influence on family systems and their organization and therefore on the problems that are presented to counselors. Read Mayra's account of the effects of immigration on one family.

I immigrated to the United States from Guatemala with my parents in May 1983. We were the first to come here from both my father's and mother's family. Our immigration was both forced and voluntary. The immigration was forced because my father was trying to escape execution by the Guatemalan government. It was voluntary because my mother decided that she wanted the family to move to the United States.

A new political party had taken over the police force in Guatemala. My father was in the police force and worked as a detective. The new political party wanted to clear the force of corruption, so they fired and executed those whom they believed had corrupted the police force. My father was among those on the list to be executed. Fearing for his life, he fled to the United States in 1981. He left behind his new family: my mother, who was 25, my sister, who was six, and me, three years old at the time.

My father's departure was hard on our family. It was difficult for my mother to take care of two children and work at the same time. My abuelitos (grandparents) were able to provide little support to my mother. My mother struggled for a year on her own to keep my sister and me from going hungry. She rarely heard from my father. On a few occasions he mailed her some American dollars that he had slaved for.

When my father first arrived in the United States, he came to California. He lived in a small city in Los Angeles County named Hawaiian Gardens. He lived there for a few months, then moved to a part of Fresno called Madera. There were many job opportunities for unskilled immigrants in Madera. Jobs were abundant in the fruit fields. My father lived on a ranch. The rancher rented out little shacks to newly arrived immigrants. My father lived in one of those shacks with many other immigrant men. In those days, there were a lot of deportations in Fresno. La Migra *(the immigration authorities) would raid the fruit fields and deport people by the hundreds. My father was deported within a year.*

When he returned to Guatemala, he arrived with absolutely no money. There was a lot of tension that came with my father's arrival. The fact that he was back from "the land of opportunity" with absolutely no money was viewed by the family as very bad. My mother knew that our family would live in poverty if we stayed in Guatemala. So one day in May 1983, she took our family's meager savings out of San Martin de Porres. The money would be used to get my mother, my father, and me to California. Both my parents would leave their families behind in search of a better future in the United States. My sister, who was seven years old at the time, would also be left behind. We had so little money that my mother knew that it would be impossible to bring my sister along with us, so she decided to leave her with my grandmother and come back for her as soon as we had saved enough money. Being left behind devastated my sister.

In May 1983, my mother stuffed a duffle bag with a pair of clothes for each of us, and we set off on our journey to the United States with a duffle bag, 100 dollars, and a heart full of hope. Hope that we would find a better life in the land of liberty and justice for all. Our immigration was very difficult, because we had to cross both the Mexican and United States borders. I do not remember much about crossing the Mexican border, but I do remember crossing the United States border. I remember running in the dark over a dirt field surrounded by bushes with about 20 other people. My little heart was pounding, yet I did not know why I was so scared. I was on my father's shoulders holding on tight to his head, hoping that he would not drop me. I asked him where we were going. He responded, "To Disneyland." We attempted to cross the United States border several times. During our last attempt, my mother and I were separated from my father, who was caught by la Migra. My mother and I were left alone with a Mexican coyote (a person who smuggles undocumented people into the United States), no money, and an address scribbled on a piece of paper. My mother was scared, knowing that this man could harm us if he wanted to. We had no power to stop him, because she was a woman and I a child, and because we were immigrants with no rights in Mexico.

Things got worse for my mother and me as the journey to the United States progressed. After we successfully crossed the border, we waited with the coyote at the San Ysidro train station for a train that would take us to Santa Ana. The coyote would deliver us to the address we had and in return receive money for guiding us across the border and delivering us to our final destination. While we were waiting for the train, the coyote went to the restroom. In the restroom he was caught by la Migra and taken back to Mexico.

Once again, my mother and I were left all alone. Neither of us spoke English, and we had no idea where we were going. When the train arrived, my mother decided that we would not turn back. We would move forward and somehow arrive at the address scribbled on the paper. We boarded the train, hoping that we would not be caught by la Migra. My mother is very light skinned and can pass for a White person. I, on the other hand, am dark skinned. In this situation, my brown skin could get us deported, so my mother wrapped me in her arms to cover my brown skin so that we would not be found out.

During the ride, my mother spotted a Latina, so she moved next to her. My mom began talking to her and told her our story. The lady offered to help us as best she could. She said she would ask her boyfriend, who would be waiting for her at the train stop, to take us to the address we had. The lady knew we had no money, so she offered to buy us some food. My mother thanked her and took up her offer, but only to buy food for me. My mother was too embarrassed and didn't want to take advantage of the lady's kindness by accepting food for both of us. I still remember sitting in that train, eating a sandwich made with wheat bread and drinking milk from a small carton. I was a young child who did not understand the pain and suffering my mom was enduring to get me to this "land of opportunity."

When we got off the train, a tall White man, standing next to a brand new shiny car, was awaiting the arrival of that kind Latina. I remember seeing her walk to him, watching them look at a large paper (which I now know was a map), and then seeing her walk toward us with a sad look on her face. She told my mother that her boyfriend did not know where Hawaiian Gardens was. Even though I was just a little girl, I knew that this was not the truth. In my heart I felt that the Latina's boyfriend wanted nothing to do with us. She handed my mom 20 dollars and wished us luck. So there we were again, alone with nowhere to go.

It was getting dark and my mom began to panic. Where would we sleep, where would we go? We were standing by a liquor store, and my mom saw a Latino man coming out of the liquor store. Desperately she approached him and told him our story. She showed him the address we were trying to get to, and luckily he knew exactly where it was. He told my mother that it was too late to take us to our destination, but that we were welcome to stay the night at his house and that his brother would take us in the morning. He told my mom that he was divorced and lived with his three sons. My mom was scared and hesitant to believe the man. What if he tried to rape her or hurt us? She did not have much choice, so she accepted the man's offer. The man took us to his house and luckily was very respectful and kind to us. He stayed in a room with his sons and offered his room to us. He provided us showers and food from his kitchen.

The next morning, the man was gone. His brother came in the morning, as promised, to drive us to Hawaiian Gardens. We arrived at our final destination and were welcomed with open arms. This was the same house my father had come to when he first came to the United States. Two weeks later, my father arrived. I was in the front of the house, buying an ice cream from the driver of an ice cream truck, when a car pulled up and my dad jumped out of it. I remember feeling so happy that my mother and I were no longer alone.

So far, this is a story of the hardships and stresses of migration. Leave aside the question of immigration legality that may arise in some counselors' minds. Counselors should maintain a position of nonjudgmental responsiveness to the personal and cultural experience that Mayra relates. It is not a counselor's job to engage in the enforcement of legality anyway, but to care for the experiences of their clients no matter what their status with authorities. Read this way, Mayra's story draws on our cultural empathy. Her account of migration does not end, however, with the journey to the new country. It continues through a series of ongoing demands and struggles. Let us take a look at more of Mayra's story from the years that followed.

My parents began to work in the grape fields. I was not old enough to be enrolled in school yet, so my parents would take me to the grape fields with them. One of my first childhood memories is of those grape fields. I was walking up and down the dirt-packed aisles, surrounded by green vines packed with red, plump grapes. I strutted behind my parents, helping them pick the grapes from the vines. My little feet were tired and my hands couldn't reach to pick another grape. I remember looking up at my mom and telling her, "Let's go home now. I think we have enough grapes. Why do you want so many grapes?"

My mother looked at me with a warm, sad look. Now I realize how much meaning that look had behind it. It was an apologetic look that screamed out, "I'm sorry for putting you through this, I'm sorry that you have to work as I did when I was a child. I'm sorry for mistaking this for the land of opportunity." My mother told me that the grapes were not for us and that the reason we picked them was to earn some money.

I was eventually enrolled in school, and that was an experience in itself. I remember walking into the classroom and seeing all the little White, blue-eyed, blond children turning to look at me. I was so different from them. Their language was foreign to me, and my Spanish tongue was foreign to them. I hated being in that classroom. The teacher was a White lady, who was not able to communicate with me. In her frustration to figure out what to do with me and at the same time continue to teach her English-speaking students, she would instruct me to go to the back of the classroom, where I would play all day. I remember yearning to engage in all the activities the other children engaged in. I wanted to read and write as they did. I wanted to learn and was tired of sitting in the back playing by myself. I remember that my first words in English were, "Can I go to the restroom, please?" Often I would raise my hand and ask the teacher, "Can I go to the restroom, please?" Once she excused me, I would sit on the toilet seat, dangle my little feet, and listen to the class speak. I wondered what they said and wished that I could understand. I remember feeling so safe in that little restroom; the four walls protected me from a teacher who did not seem to care and from children who did not accept me.

Working has kept my parents in poverty, from being engaged with their children, and in poor health. They come home so tired from work that they have no energy left to be present with the family, thus creating dysfunction within the family. One of the biggest things my siblings and I have struggled with is the fact that our parents have not been very involved in our lives. We all grew up with little parental supervision and all got into mischief with our freedom. Work shifts have varied for my parents. Sometimes they worked regular hours from 8 a.m. to 5 p.m., but at other times they have worked from 4 p.m. to 1 a.m. and sometimes on weekends, making them unavailable for us. Many people cannot choose working hours that will allow them to be with their families. They just take what is available so they can support their families.

Most jobs available to people who, like my parents, are undocumented and do not speak English, pay a minimum wage or less. The income of two parents working full time at minimum wage is barely enough to pay for rent or mortgage and food. Sometimes there is only one parent in the home, leaving the family to struggle to make ends meet. In both cases, people live in poverty, and sadly stay in poverty because there is little or no room for advancement in jobs open to people like my parents.

I was the first person in my family and one of the few in Hawaiian Gardens to graduate from high school and receive a degree from a university. In my family, I was expected only to graduate from high school, and then to work to help support the family. My family, the community, and my teachers expected this of me. Many youths in Hawaiian Gardens do not graduate from high school for many reasons, the main ones being gangs, drugs and alcohol, poverty, and family dysfunction. Many come from families where there has not been a high level of educational achievement, so parents do not know how to encourage and support their children in school. Many times, education is not a value in the home. Many parents are struggling to make ends meet for their family, so when their children reach working age they are expected to help support the family and not pursue education. Other parents are addicted to drugs or alcohol, and their children struggle to simply survive the pain present in their homes. Many of these homes are very dysfunctional and not the best environment for children to grow up in.

I was kicked out of high school during my freshman year and was not expected to return. At that time I was involved in a gang, doing drugs, and acting out violently in the name of the gang. When I returned to high school, all my teachers and counselors were surprised. I was angry that they expected me to just drop out of high school, angry that at the time when I was expelled they had expected me to never finish my high school education. There are many factors that contribute to a youth's dropping out of high school. Unfortunately, many of those factors are present in low-income neighborhoods.

After I graduated from college, I was able to develop my awareness of all the social injustice around me. I have started to talk to my family about the social injustice present in the community we live in. It amazes me how my desire to help the community has been fostered by my parents and their selflessness in helping the community. My parents are like the social workers of the community. When people first arrive in Hawaiian Gardens from Mexico, or sometimes from Guatemala, they help establish them in the community. They help them find a place to live, and sometimes these immigrants stay with us until my parents find them a place of their own. My dad will teach the men how to work in construction so that they can pick up a job as day laborers. My mom will find jobs for the women in factories. Because my father is one of the older men in Hawaiian Gardens, people look to him for help in getting free of alcohol and drugs. My dad helps out many of the street junkies in the neighborhood. He takes them to rehab homes, or church, and helps them get back on their feet. My mother is like the community counselor for the women. Many of the ladies in the community look to my mom for support when they are having difficulties in their lives. I feel that my parents contribute to the community and try to help the people in it when no one else will. We have a system set up that closes its doors to immigrants. My parents are helping people overcome homelessness, unemployment, drug and alcohol addiction, and poor mental health.

Migration can take a terrible toll on families fleeing from one oppressive culture to another. In Mayra's story, the cycle of oppression continues to keep migrant communities oppressed. In the United States, many poor migrant families are highly vulnerable and are exposed to the ugliest underbelly of life in North America. Many become addicted to street drugs and alcohol. With family cohesion stretched to the breaking point, there is much teenage pregnancy, school truancy, and family violence. Despite the grim struggles Mayra describes, she reports that the family life of U.S. immigrants, even undocumented workers, is possibly easier than the life these people escaped from. Here there is also a story of courage and resilience and of drawing from cultural narratives to create new cultural formations in a new context.

FIGURE 11.1   Mayra Lorenzo and her family endured great suffering and danger when they entered the United States.

The Psychological Effects of Dislocation

Dislocation, or having to leave one's place of origin, can occur for a multitude of reasons, often political, social, religious, or economic in nature. In 2016, 85,000 refugees entered the United States, mainly from the following countries of origin: Democratic Republic of the Congo, Syria, and Myanmar (Connor, 2016). The most frequently reported problems include "separation from family, isolation and socio-economic difficulties ... adaptation difficulties, threat to family, and loss of culture (Carswell, Blackburn, & Barker, 2011, p. 112). Refugees often suffer anxiety around fear of being sent home, delays in processing applications, running into conflict with immigration officials, and not having permission to work (Carswell et al., p. 113). In turn, these challenges often give rise to poverty and all the hardships and psychological stressors that come with lack of resources. Additionally, refugees commonly experience poor access to healthcare and to counselling services at a time when they are most needed (p. 113). Moreover, refugees face adaptation/assimilation difficulties, loss of culture, isolation, and loneliness and boredom (p. 113). These are just a few of the psychological burdens that refugees commonly experience.

Changes in Family Organization

In addition to the growing Asian and African communities in the United States, a sizable proportion of the American (U.S.) population consists of immigrants from Mexico, Central and South America, and the Pacific. Because of dramatic changes in physical location, many extended family systems become stretched, if not ruptured and fragmented. Migration and urbanization push the organization of families toward a nuclear model, rather than extended family structures. Todays grandparents and uncles and aunties who once lived in the same house or were close by are being left behind. The traditional nuclear model has also undergone change. "Despite the rise of childbearing outside of marriage, the majority of ... children under age eighteen live in families with two parents (69 percent)" (United States Census Bureau, 2016). "The second most common family arrangement is children living with a single mother, at 23 percent" (United States Census Bureau). With regard to race, "White householders make up 79 percent of all households in the United States, Black and Hispanic householders each make up 13 percent of households, while Asian householders comprise 5 percent (United States Census Bureau). Concerning marriage, "the median age when adults first marry continues to rise. In 2016, it was age 29.5 for men and 27.4 for women, up from ages 23.7 and 20.5, respectively, in 1947" (United States Census Bureau). Moreover, the number of adults that have never married has increased. "In 2016, almost one third of all adults (32 percent) have never been married, up from about one quarter (23 percent) in 1950)" (United States Census Bureau).

The poverty rate in the United States for 2016 was 12.7% (Poverty USA, 2018).

Of this, almost one in every five children lived in poverty (defined as a family of four making $24,000.00 or less; Poverty USA, 2018). With regard to ethnicity, "the highest poverty rate is found among Native Americans (27.6%), with Blacks (26.2%) having the second highest poverty rate, and Hispanics having the third highest poverty rate (23.4%). Whites had a poverty rate of 12.4%, while Asians had a poverty rate at 12.3%" (Poverty USA).

Given the powerful social and economic forces operating around the globe, people's cultural identities are increasingly being shaped by their access to or exclusion from economic resources. For example, living together in extended families and large groups now often has less to do with ethnic preference for extended family living and much more to do with economic survival. These changes to family organization create increased demands for counseling services.

BOX 11.2 COMPOSITION OF FAMILIES

Geiger and Livingston (2018) reported that more people residing in the United States are living with an unmarried partner, and this figure reached 18 million in 2016, 29% higher than 2007. In 2013, 23% of married people had been married before. In 2015, one in six people were married to someone of a different race or ethnicity. Public support for same-sex marriage has increased in the past decade. In 2017, more people were supportive of (62%) than opposed to (32%) sexual minorities marrying. A 2017 Gallup Poll found that about one in ten LGBT U.S. citizens (10%) were married to a same-sex spouse. In 2018, a majority (61%) of all same-sex couples who live together are married. Significant minorities (40%) of married people have different religious affiliations than their spouse. Most interfaith marriages are between Christians and people who identify as religiously unaffiliated. Interestingly, partnerships and marriages that occur across political party lines are relatively rare in the United States. In 2016, 77% of Democrats and Republicans who were married or living together said their partner was in the same party.

Changes in Religious Belief

The spiritual and religious practices of some people have undergone rapid changes as a result of migration. In an urban environment, people can choose from the wider selection of religious and spiritual practices and not be limited to the faith of their parents and grandparents. With the focus on material survival and material success that so characterizes city life, many young people are replacing deeply held and long-standing family religious values with secular ones, or becoming invested in religious or spiritual expressions very different from those that their parents were brought up with. In August 2005, *Newsweek* and Beliefnet asked 1,004 U.S. citizens how they worshipped and what they believed. Twenty-four percent reported that they had different religious beliefs from those of their parents, and 30% had made some changes in their religious orientation in comparison to their parents (Adler, 2005).

Often younger family members, acculturated to the many social requirements of success in the urban school and workplace, resent the efforts of their parents and grandparents to maintain the social, religious, and linguistic cultural practices brought with them from their rural communities. On the other hand, grandparents and parents become alarmed by the speed with which their children abandon age-old customs, rituals, and ways of life. Family counselors working with immigrant families will encounter the playing out of these themes in people's lives with great frequency.

BOX 11.3   THE HMONG

Migrating indigenous ethnic communities typically face traumatic shifts in their social order and cultural identity upon entering Western-style, consumer-driven societies. The Hmong are a good example of people who have had to survive enormous threats to their social fabric and daily family life.

Many Hmong people, who arrived in the United States as reluctant immigrants in the 1970s and 1980s, explicitly did not want to immerse themselves in the culture and values of middle-class America with its nuclear family patterns. They were not interested in melting pots or salad bowls. Even so, they have gone through profound changes in their family organization and social structure as a result of living in American (U.S.) cities. The Hmong have been historically regarded by many researchers and scholars as one of the most robust and ethnically cohesive social groups in the world. They have deflected many powerful acculturating forces from within Asia over the centuries and within Southeast Asia, specifically, more recently. Now they often find their youth suffering from serious identity crises. Like many American (U.S.) adolescents, some Hmong youths rebel against their parents and elders and reject the cultural practices so carefully protected by their forebears. Instead, they embrace cultural ideals modeled by their adolescent peers (Yang, 1991).

In circumstances of rapid urban migration, elderly members of the family, who were looked to for guidance in addressing life problems in rural settings, find themselves isolated and redundant, because they are not able to provide guidance to younger family members and assist them in dealing with the trials and tribulations of city life. As a result, it is often the young people who become resources for their families, as they acquire the necessary dialects and languages spoken in the cities, in the schools, and in the workplace. Older family members come to rely on younger family members to help them adjust to the changes required to survive in the cities. Customary social roles are thus reversed. Children are cast in the role of primary educators or translators for their families in negotiating with the education system and understanding the economic, healthcare, legal, and political systems. Conflict can result between the older and younger generations.

Anne Fadiman (1998), in *The Spirit Catches You and You Fall Down*, writes about the collision of Hmong culture with middle-class American culture. She describes the phenomenon of role loss that many older migrating family members experience when settling in North America. She describes observing an exercise led by psychologist Evelyn Lee, who asked a group of people at a Southeast Asian mental health conference to role-play a family and line up according to status within Asian culture. She cast each of the individuals in a family, including a grandfather, a father, a mother, an 18-year-old son, and a 12-year-old daughter. They ranked themselves by traditional notions of age and gender, with the grandfather placing himself at the head of the family and the 12-year-old daughter at the bottom of the hierarchy. Lee now told the role players that they had moved to America, where the grandfather has no job, the father is employed performing menial kitchen duties, the son has dropped out of high school, because he cannot learn English, the mother and older daughter work in a factory, and the youngest child has successfully gained entrance to and graduated from the University of California, Berkeley. In the new lineup, there is a reshuffle in the hierarchy, such that it is completely altered. The youngest daughter now earns the most status in the community. This change for the male heads of the household from positions of power and influence to positions of low influence produces "role loss" and all the symptoms of anxiety and depression that accompany this state.

Indigenous Renaissance

Nowhere is this pattern more starkly illustrated than with the demands on families to change their dialect or their language as they enter a new urban environment. Indigenous languages and dialects spoken in small rural communities are often quickly lost in the shift to the large urban environment. In their efforts to help younger family members adjust to the changing demands of life in a new and strange city, parents insist that their children quickly acculturate to the dominant patterns of communication and mode of life in their new place of residence. They encourage their children not to speak their native tongue in order to quickly learn to speak as if they belong with the majority group. José Joachín Brunner (1998) suggests that by the year 2100, based on current projections, fewer than 600 of the world's current 6,200 languages will still be spoken. This trend supports the homogenization argument about globalization. Losing one's mother tongue is a powerful force in disrupting traditional cultural identities and producing dramatic shifts in cultural expression.

There are, however, counter trends that support the localization argument. While families encourage children to move away from their indigenous roots to join mainstream cultural communities, a counter movement often occurs in which families attempt to hold on to or become reacquainted with the language and cultural histories of their ancestors. There are numerous cultural communities on the brink of losing their indigenous languages who take action to reclaim their linguistic traditions. For example, where aboriginal community membership becomes more heterogeneous, a vigorous movement arises to conserve and revitalize traditional languages, teachings, and ceremonial practices (Castellano, 2002). Formal associations and informal networks emerge to support traditional cultural themes, deliberately embracing norms of "sharing and caring" and extending spiritual and practical support to those made vulnerable by family breakdown.

While the dominance of Western cultural ideas is far-reaching, the world is not merely divided between indigenous recipients of cultural messages from the West and cultural transmitters from the West to the developing world. There are societies in every continent that are holding on to their traditions, cultural practices, and, most important, their language. In the United States, the indigenous people have made great efforts to revitalize their cultural traditions. Recreating a new form of education is at the core of this process. Through a dedicated campaign, indigenous communities have transformed the education process to embody indigenous values, for example, developing a "harmonious alignment with the natural world" (Cajete, 2015, p. 76). This new model of indigenous education involves reshaping the collective consciousness around indigenous values, such as

> building knowledge and skills in areas such as personal development, community development, tribal governance, organizational development, native sciences, and sustainable, ecological community planning. (Cajete, 2015, p. 76)

By acknowledging the historical trauma of colonization, and by recreating education in a manner that promotes indigenous values, indigenous people have been making great strides in healing from the harmful long-term effects of colonization and are working to revitalize their cultures (Cajete, 2015, p. 127).

Changing Identities

Amin Maalouf (2000) argues that globalization is owned by only some people. He comments that it is like a huge arena in which there are thousands of jousting matches and complex interactions taking place all at the same time, producing an indescribable and shattering din. The world he suggests has become like "an amphitheatre that anyone is free to enter with his own motto or theme song" (p. 126).

Consumerism and Culture

There is a growing consensus among sociologists and researchers that cultural perspectives conveyed by the mass media supplant among young people many cultural practices previously primarily modeled by families of origin. The increasing availability of mass media outlets threatens the authority of traditional sources of influence, such as the family, school, community, and religion. As a result, many young people brought up in communal and collective cultures are being attracted to individual values, rather than collective or societal values. Lyombe Eko (2003) describes how multinational mass media conglomerates like Disney plunder African cultural motifs, music, landscape, and culture, then de-Africanize them, reduce them to clichés and stereotypes, and repackage them for mass audiences. Robbin Crabtree and Sheena Malhotra (2003) analyzed television programming in India and highlighted an increasing trend toward the promotion of middle-class values, where money is equated with power, authority, and economic advancement. Indian television programmers emulate Western television shows by staging soap operas in lavish settings where the main characters are wealthy and the poor are peripheral. Earlier Indian soaps showed the protagonist as the common person whose goodness was derived from virtue. Indian television portrays prominent characters as breaking away from traditional cultural practices and using Western consumerism as a conduit to do so. Subir Sengupta (1996) compared Indian advertisements with American ones and found that, while the United States still had

BOX 11.4 ASSEMBLAGES

The concept of an *assemblage* is a helpful one for intercultural thinking. Developed first by Gilles Deleuze and Felix Guattari (1987), it refers to the analysis of a force that is a complex ensemble of components "that mesh together well" (DeLanda, 2016, p. 1), some of them social and discursive, some of them technological, physical, and nondiscursive.

For example, take the police actions of violence in the United States against African American youths that has sparked the Black Lives Matter movement. If we are dissatisfied with explanations for the violence that are based in "bad apple" analysis of individual police officers, then a more systematic analysis is needed. The concept of an assemblage fits the bill.

In this case, the assemblage involves as the components a state organization (a police force with authority and legitimacy), weapons (mainly guns), and a discursive set of commands (police procedure) that is suspicious of African American youths and responses that appear to be trained into police officers by an enunciation of fear and an overcoding of police protection. Each component is necessary for the violence to continue. As an assemblage it is characterized by multiplicity that functions together and brings about events. It is often referred to as based in racism because of its selective attention to African American young men, but this is an essentialized generality that defers to what Deleuze and Guattari call "interiority" and deserves to be analyzed in more detail, in particular in the light of its "exteriority" (DeLanda, 2016, p. 2). The advantage of thinking in terms of exteriority is that violent responses might be said to result from what is "coded" or "territorialized" (DeLanda, p. 3), that is, trained into homogenized police procedure. Leaving the explanation as "racism" treats it as a more mysterious internal force (expressing interiority) that originates in the hearts of individuals and is harder to change.

The Black Lives Matter movement started in 2013 from a Facebook post that ended with the expression "Black lives matter," after the death of Trayvon Martin at the hands of George Zimmerman. One of its founders, Patrisse Cullors, has said it aims to "push for Black people's right to live with dignity and respect." It is not just about police actions, nor does it suggest that other people's lives do not matter.

"We are against a system that views people as tools," said Ralikh Hayes of Baltimore. This comment suggests the concept of an assemblage (or a machine with various components) that turns people from individuals into dividuals whose full expression as human beings is not recognized by the functioning of the assemblage. Hence they can easily become objects on which violence is expressed.

more materialistic values, Indian public media were clearly moving in the American (U.S.) direction. Crabtree and Malhotra (2003) give a powerful example of how advertising and consumerism, so intimately interwoven with globalizing trends, are changing family dynamics and cultural values in India:

> What is a kid in a village going to do? Let's take a bar of chocolate. It costs 10 rupees. He is never going to be able to buy a bar of chocolate his whole life. But the commercial is telling him that if his parents love him, they'll buy him that bar of chocolate. (p. 222)

The advertising industry's ability to conflate consumption with love and desire is what consumer culture is built on. These powerful commercial forces have huge shaping influences on identity and family relationships. There is every reason for young people who are not able to attain the monetary goals and wealth promised by the commercial media to be dissatisfied with cultural traditions that have eschewed individualistic agendas. Consumerism is a powerful, disruptive force in societies that construct cultural identities on discourses of collectivism and communality.

Corporate Culture

One of the globalizing forces that has brought serious disruption and sometimes devastation to collective and communal societies is the expansion of international multinational corporations, usually based in Europe or the United States, into many other countries around the world. While sometimes their contributions to their host countries have been helpful through the provision of investment capital and the introduction of goods and services to communities desperately in need, they have also imported corporate culture based on materialistic values, fast-paced competition, and the promise of happiness to be delivered by the quick acquisition of products. Life in the U.S. has been inundated with corporate culture for decades.

In the United States, corporations compete with elected politicians to govern people's lives, and it can be argued that they have achieved the upper hand over the democratic electoral system. Although they often claim to be politically neutral, they also clearly promote particular middle-class norms and practices. Their influence is spreading rapidly as other nations all over the world join the corporate way of life. In Moscow in 2006, an enormous billboard displayed over Red Square advertised an icon of corporate culture: the Rolex watch. Corporate culture sanctions greed by expecting people to devote most of their time and energy to getting richer. Walmart entices thousands of young Chinese to work long hours in its factories, six or seven days a week for three dollars a day, in the hope that they can join in the benefits of the corporate economy.

The expansionist behavior of corporations and the adoption of Western consumerism all around the world are widely admired by those seduced by corporate culture. It compels the wealthy to keep acquiring wealth, even though this behavior could be viewed as compulsive and unhealthy. Ultimately, the corporate promise is usually unsatisfying. When people view themselves through the lens of corporate culture, they become defined culturally through their roles as workers and consumers. The corporate discourse provides them with a personal model of a successful life. It demands that corporate objectives and needs be given the central place of honor in employees' lives. The culture wants all of them. Employees often face demands to work longer hours and struggle to cater to the socioemotional needs of their families. Arlie Russell Hochschild (1997, cited by Kasser & Kanner, 2004) did research on a Fortune 500 company and investigated how parents were able to cater to their children's needs when they were sick.

In one case, the son of a single mother needed surgery, but because she had already used up her sick days and her vacation days, she chose to wait six months to schedule the surgery so she could arrange a day off. In response to her delay, her son's doctor threatened to press charges of child abuse. On another occasion, a supervisor threatened to fire a mother who left work to care for a daughter with a dangerously high fever (Kasser & Kanner, 2004, pp. 169–170).

Such claims on people's lives need to be understood as penetrating not just into work ethics but into the shape of family life. We can see the modern technologies of power (described in Chapter 6) at work through the operation of corporate culture. Corporate culture creates powerful norms that have a structuring effect on the lives of people, who are described as economic units and are required to internalize these descriptions into their cultural perspective on their own lives. The merit of people's lives in corporations is measured by their contribution to a level of production and economic output. Materialistic cultural norms invite people to trivialize any areas of their lives that do not relate to economic substance. As a result of this normalizing judgment, consumer identities are developed and assigned that have intimate effects on all areas of people's lives.

On these grounds, we would argue that we cannot talk about the cultural dimension of life or construct a multicultural perspective in counseling without considering the impact of corporations on people's lives. Corporate culture is a horizontal force that impacts the vertical aspects of cultural identity formation. Its demands are insistent and its control is pervasive. But no one is in control of it. The heads of large corporations may have more decision-making power, but they are just as caught up in the discourse rolling out around them as the consumers at the end of the chain are. And there are examples everywhere of resistance to the power of corporate culture. For instance, local communities in many parts of the United States have joined together to prevent the entry of Walmart into their local cultural context.

Identities Produced in Hollywood

Hollywood movie and television production companies play a significant role in producing contemporary cultural identities. Despite many efforts to develop exceptions, mass media continue to endorse dominant cultural stereotypes. While the world is made up of diverse ethnicities, heterosexual, White, middle-class males still tend to be the main characters in movies and on television. They are especially likely to be portrayed in heroic roles, while other cultural groups are either assigned supporting or villain roles, or remain in the margins. Despite the influence of feminism, mass media frequently continue to encode authoritative gender patterns and reinforce stereotypical gender relations by portraying men as strong and active and women as passive, or as confined to domestic nurturing roles. The way many movies are edited compels the audience to identify with the male character, with the female character often appearing as the "love interest" and frequently being objectified from a male point of view. According to Harry Benshoff and Sean Griffin (2004), there are twice as many men on the movie screen as women, and Hollywood director and producer roles continue to be dominated by men. According to the 21st annual Celluloid Ceiling report, the percentage of women working as directors on the top 250 grossing films declined to 8% in 2018 from 11% in the previous year (Lauzen, 2019). Historically, Hollywood films have been about men, while women have been portrayed in secondary roles drawn from the virgin/whore dichotomy. For example, in Westerns, the guys had the guns and women's roles were reduced to those of either the saloon girl (a euphemism for prostitute) or the virtuous daughter of the mayor of the town or honorable rancher, or perhaps a faithful school teacher. This type of positioning is frequently repeated in music videos.

These gender images are taken up by viewers as powerful cultural prescriptions for the development of their own identities. People mimic the dominant images of the media. As people watch movies, they internalize values and relationship ethics. These images (and the cultural values implicit within them) reach far beyond the borders of America, where the movie narratives are usually constructed. Since young people seek role models from the mass media, the impact of these images on how cultural identities are formed cannot be underestimated.

Early Hollywood films drew from the Victorian era, where women were portrayed as innocent and childlike and in need of protection. Devotion to fathers was transferred to husbands upon marriage. Women were sexually virtuous, cute, and defenseless, and in need of protection by their male suitors from the advances of other men. Many female actors in early Hollywood films were portrayed as childlike. The actor Mary Pickford, featured in films in the 1920s, embodied this innocent character on screen. The set would be constructed with oversize props and chairs to emphasize her innocent, vulnerable, and childlike demeanor (Benshoff & Griffin, 2004). For a short period in the 1920s, some strong female characters, like Greta Garbo, Mae West, and Marlene Dietrich, made it to the movie screen, challenging the dominant images of women at the time. However, when the movie industry in Hollywood became more regulated, these strong female images were eclipsed once more, and challenges to the patriarchal status quo were fleeting. It took World War II to change the popular images of women. Women began to appear as powerful, assertive figures in their own right when women in the United States served in industry and helped run the economy during that period. However, these images never dominated the Hollywood film industry.

After World War II, women continued to be identified as wholesome girls next door aspiring to be stay-at-home mothers and housewives. In the 1950s, 1960s, and 1970s, actors such as Doris Day, Debbie Reynolds, and Sandra Dee epitomized these cultural identities. If it wasn't an innocent, passive female identity being portrayed on television and in the movies, it was an image of women as sexual objects to be lusted for. Movie stars such as Marilyn Monroe, Jayne Mansfield, Mamie Van Doren, Elizabeth Taylor, and Sophia Loren embodied these stereotypical sexualized images.

Today, the media portrayals of the cultural identities of men and women are more diverse and more complex. However, young women continue to be bombarded with heterosexual images that convey a dichotomous view of women as either virtuous and innocent or whorelike and wayward. Men, on the other hand, are subjected to powerful images of rugged individualistic heroes—physically powerful, decisive, independent, and psychologically hardened. The Marlboro Man portrayed in advertising beginning in the mid 1950s is prototypical. Heterosexual images of men as strong protectors and providers dominate, while women are still the nurturers and supporters of their man. It is increasingly common to see gay or lesbian relational images on television and in the movies, but overall they remain in the margins. In the most watched blockbuster movies, Black, Asian, and Latino characters continue to be in secondary roles while their White counterparts continue to have prominence. These dominant mass media images are mapped onto the lives of audiences. They are never the sole cultural influence, but people who come to counseling will be influenced by the messages contained in them. Intercultural counseling should not ignore the influence of these images in the construction of clients' lives.

The Pervasiveness of Western Media

There are virtually no citizens or communities frozen in time and completely isolated from the influences of the mass media. Many have been irrevocably changed by this encroachment. Reality television in its various forms is found in many communities all over the world. Countries such as Kenya, Thailand, Egypt, Japan, and China have experimented with their own reality shows that mimic what has taken place in the West. When traveling around the globe, it is not uncommon to see a variety of versions of the same popular reality shows. For example, Egyptian television has its own homegrown version of *Who Wants to Be a Millionaire*. It has grown in popularity as the media have played a prominent role in shaping a new generation of consumers captured by the materialistic and individualistic goals of many societies in the West (Hammond, 2005). Many themes of these shows illustrate cultural practices that hinge on competition, individualism, and materialism, powerful cultural forces that are shaping cultural identities in all communities throughout the world.

The Times of India has rated *Game of Thrones* the most popular English TV show of 2016 airing in India (The Times of India, 2016). Globally, CBS's *NCIS* has the highest viewership in the world, at over 47 million viewers (Surette, 2017). A Kenyan version of *Shark Tank, Blaze Be Your Own Boss Reality Show*, was reportedly the most watched TV show in Kenya in 2017 (Mboya, 2017). *Blaze* targets young Kenyan entrepreneurs, giving them a platform to pitch their ideas to judges (Mboya). The reality TV craze has made its way to Kenya. The fourth most popular show in Kenya in 2017 was *Nairobi Diaries*, with number five being *Real House-helps of Kawangware* (Mboya). *Nairobi Diaries* "features the lives of young Kenyan socialites, a taste of drama here and there, a love story, and too often, catfights among the girls" while *Real House-helps of Kawangware* "features the day-to-day lives of the house helps in Kenyan households" (Mboya). The popularity of these shows illustrates the influence of Western media on a culture that was at one time insulated from such influence. This is an excellent example of cultural intermingling; the ideas for the shows come from the West, but the content itself is culturally local.

Countries remote and culturally protected from outside influences, such as Myanmar, have changed rapidly and drastically in gaining global accessibility through technological means. After having been under a military dictatorship that had prohibited the use of phones since 1962, Myanmar met 2013

BOX 11.5 MANGAIA

What immediately becomes apparent when one travels from country to country is the extraordinary reach of the mass media and mass communication. During one trip, two of us authors, Gerald Monk and Stacey Sinclair, traveled to a remote Pacific island (Mangaia), where Monk had lived and worked as a secondary school teacher 25 years earlier. Twenty-five years ago, the 1,600 people who lived on this island were virtually cut off from what was going on in the rest of the world. The majority of the population received no newspapers or magazines. There was no electricity other than that produced by seven or eight private generators, no television, and no radio signal strong enough for residents to pick up on an inexpensive radio receiver. Returning to this island 25 years later, we found that most residents had electricity. However, more surprising to us was the view of a large satellite dish dominating the typography, channeling cell phone and television signals to island residents. Today, most Mangaian homes have a television set. At any one time, island citizens are in a position to view a selection of hundreds of television channels broadcast from around the globe. This change in the level of mass media exposure that has occurred on the island of Mangaia over the last quarter of a century is occurring in virtually every corner of the globe.

with rapid development and cultural change after years of global inaccessibility (Leong, 2017, p. 139). By June of 2015 "about 90 percent of the country's 54 million people had access" to a smartphone (Heijmans, 2017).

Devoid of both Internet and cellular phone legacy, the sudden boom of smartphones is (for many) the first experience with wireless communication and with accessing the world wide web (Leong, 2017, p. 140). This means that the Burmese have a somewhat unique outlook and practice when it comes to smartphone use. For instance, the Burmese often use Facebook as a search engine in the same way they use Google (Leong, p. 152). It is of note that, for this population, Facebook is seen and used as a "primary news source" (Leong, p. 153).

Bearing in mind that Myanmar is a country where "most people are farmers, the majority of roads are unpaved, and reliable electricity remains a luxury" there are several advantages as well as disadvantages that come with this new and widespread technology (Heijmans, 2017). From an environmental standpoint, the fact that there are "thousands of cell phone towers sprouting out of forests and remote rice paddies, running off their own solar-powered electricity" is a major downside (Heijmans). Another disadvantage is that people are now getting addicted to online games and other such mindless ways of passing time in non-productive ways (Heijmans).

On the other hand, there are important advantages that come with widespread smartphone use in Myanmar. Some of these advantages are a matter of convenience, such as being able to hail a cab using ride-sharing apps like Uber (Heijmans, 2017). Price is another factor that has undergone major change. Under military dictatorship, a data-enabled card could go for "$2,000 on the black market" (Heijmans). Today, this would go for $1.50 (Heijmans). Communication is an expected implication of smartphone use that has tremendously transformed life for the Burmese. In the past, it was impossible to communicate with family or friends who were working and living in different cities. If someone was working in the city while their family lived in the country, they might go long periods of time without having any contact whatsoever. Another major improvement that came with smartphones is being able to know what is going on in the world in an uncensored and timely manner. In the past, "magazines from the outside world used to arrive weeks late, because censors needed time to comb through them" (Heijmans). In addition to the above advantages, an additional improvement is in the area of finance. Before, Myanmar was "crying out for better financial services." They are now able to "make payments or transfer money, and even withdraw cash at thousands of general stores using nothing besides their smartphones" (Heijmans). As you can see from the above examples, Burmese culture has forever been revolutionized, both for the better and for the worse, given the recent smartphone boom.

Performing New Identities

In a global society increasingly shaped by the role of media and telecommunications, young people are performing identities that arise from multiple cultural sources. Many and varied cultural sources are appropriated by young people in their production of their identity. There are countless examples of people who draw from horizontal as well as vertical cultural influences. For example, Maiko, a Japanese woman in her early twenties, brought up by relatively traditional Japanese parents, traveled to the United States to dedicate her career to hip-hop music. Having been introduced to hip-hop in Japan, she immersed herself in the Black community in central Los Angeles. Many hip-hop lyrics (like other forms of Western music) embody the rhetoric of individualism and the Western cultural formations of the "me" generation. These are not the symbols that one typically associates with a collective Asian culture. And yet they are being invoked by Japanese young people.

The Media and Poverty

Repeatedly, around the globe, the media portray the growing gap between the "haves" and the "have nots," even as the cultivation of consumerism escalates. Consumer behavior must surely be considered as much a part of cultural practice as expressions of family kinship ties. James Petras (1993) graphically describes the effects of consumer culture on the masses everywhere:

> The TV "table of plenty" contrasts with the experience of the empty kitchen; the amorous escapades of media personalities crash against a houseful of crawling, crying, hungry children. … The promise of affluence becomes an affront to those who are perpetually denied. (p. 147)

These are the social forces shaping cultural identity today. As a result, the identity struggles of counseling clients everywhere are made more complex. The influences from traditional vertical cultural traditions are constantly moderated by the immediacy of these horizontal, globalized, cultural influences. How we think about interculturality needs to take these complexities into account. Counselors are always working with clients in their struggles to define an identity. If cultural influences provide the building blocks for such struggles, then counselors need to listen for the echoes of globalized cultural influences as well as the traditional vertical messages from ancestral traditions.

Technology

Access to Technology and Consumer Goods

Consider these events and their potential impact on culture and identity: In Moyabi, Gabon, in the heart of the equatorial rain forest, Africa's most popular commercial FM station broadcasts American (U.S.) and European commercials to societies that are now being bombarded by consumer culture. Timbuktu in Mali was one of the first places in Africa to be wired for the Internet. African television has been overtaken by the regular transmission of American, European, and Asian programming on stations across the continent. From Morocco to Zimbabwe, American popular music, most prominently rap music, blares from radios.

Large sections of humanity are locked into ongoing relationships across the world, because that is how they produce their livelihood. For example, China is producing statuettes of Mexican's patron saint, the Virgin of Guadalupe. The Chinese are also producing traditional Ramadan lanterns to be held by Egyptian children during the fast of Ramadan (Friedman, 2005). These Muslim lanterns play traditional Ramadan tunes and the theme to a television cartoon series in Egypt called *Bakkar*. Who would have guessed the intimate involvement Chinese entrepreneurs have in the religious celebrations of Muslim people thousands of miles away?

Large multinational retail chains like Walmart perpetuate this trend. Walmart has over 8,000 suppliers of goods in China alone, and outlets in 44 countries. It now has 2,276 stores outside the United States. We can travel to the remote reaches of Mexico and find ourselves shopping for groceries alongside the local indigenous Mexican citizens at a Walmart store. There are emerging trends in technology that will continue the march toward an interactive global society.

Technology and the Poor

In most countries around the world, cellular telephone technology has been rapidly introduced. This advancement has made for impressive economic gains in the third world (Pramanik, 2017). It is of note that "in 2000, only 4 percent of people living in low- and middle-income countries had access to mobile phones. By 2015, that number rose to 94 percent," even in places as remote as sub-Saharan Africa (Pramanik, 2017). Phones are getting cheaper and cheaper and soon may be purchased for a few dollars. This technological explosion could connect the entire world with a networked international media in a way that has never been witnessed before. Very different cultural communities are having greater and greater contact because of these profound changes.

Thomas Friedman (2005) argues that we have moved into an era in which human activity around the globe is becoming completely interconnected. He cites examples of how component parts of computers are built in seven or eight countries and constructed and delivered to consumers by companies located in at least three or four other countries. Friedman also describes how Boeing builds its airplanes. Russian engineers based in Moscow help design the planes; contractors at Hindustan Aeronautics in Bangalore, India, digitize the plane designs; and Japanese subcontractors build the wings on some of the aircraft. With computer-designed assembly, they will build the next generation of planes each in three days because the "global supply chain will enable [them] to move parts from one facility to another just in time" (Friedman, 2005, p. 196).

There are vast numbers of citizens around the globe benefiting from this "flattening of the world." The sharing of technology and multinational activity has raised the standard of living for millions of people in numerous countries. Increases in income influence and shape the cultural practices of life in many families. With lowering of the costs of owning satellite-connected television sets, cellular phones, and networked laptop computers, a world has opened to many of those previously excluded from it. These technological shifts create a context in which it is possible for complex cultural identities to form within very short time frames around the globe. On the other hand, while it is clear that cultural landscapes and languages are being transformed, millions experience new forms of alienation and disenfranchisement as it becomes clear that they are not the recipients of the promises of consumerism.

Technology puts culturally different communities into contact with one another faster than they can be prepared for it. This new form of global intimacy leaves vulnerable communities threatened, intimidated, frustrated, and in many cases humiliated by close contact. Thanks to the reach of technology, people see in a graphic way where they stand in relation to everybody else. While this new knowledge may be culturally enhancing, it is equally likely to allow the marginalized and disenfranchised to immediately evaluate their life circumstances and find themselves more disadvantaged and unsatisfied, leading to even stronger experiences of unease and discontentment.

Counseling Implications of Globalization

In this chapter we have underscored the contemporary complexities of seeing cultural groups as neat, stable, and discrete categories. Our primary purpose here is to point to the ramifications, challenges, and nuances of working with cultural diversity in a global context in the 21st century. Human identities are produced through complex social processes, through which the vertical dimensions of race, ethnicity, gender, class, and religion all exert influence. As we have argued in this chapter, the picture is complicated even further by horizontal global forces like migration, the mass media, and technological change. These complex processes make it difficult to identify unambiguous and non-contradictory themes, despite the best efforts of multicultural scholars. As many have commented, within-group differences of an identifiable group often outweigh between-group differences, even when groups of people identify themselves as separate and distinct. Thus, we are very cautious about specifying certain therapeutic practices that might best cater to Whites, Blacks, Asians, Latinos, or others.

While we are concerned about the tendency to overstate the unique needs of one ethnic group in comparison to others (and then extrapolate from there about their specific therapeutic needs), we do not want to lose sight of the real effects of systematic patterns of oppression that have targeted particular ethnic groups. In earlier chapters, we have addressed the disparities that have occurred between many White communities and African Americans, Latinos, and Native Americans as a result of 400 years of European colonization. Such effects are not easily washed away and continue to be reproduced. Significant disparities continue to interact with the horizontal cultural influences outlined in this chapter.

We have described above some of the challenging dynamics confronting individuals and families in the era of globalization. These developments raise serious questions about whether it is adequate for counselors to base their practice on advice about how to counsel an African American, an Asian American, a Latino, or the like. Within a single family, the counseling needs may be very different from one member of the family to another. For example, a Latino family that migrates to the United States will bring with them their traditions, language, and cultural symbols, which are very likely to be different from some of the dominant American (U.S.) cultural practices. The parents have models of childcare, discipline, family rituals, religious practices, and established gender roles that they will likely continue. Their children, however, are growing up in American (U.S.) communities very different from their parents' places of origin. They are subjected to very different gender role models and religious practices. They learn that their friends in the U.S. have very different levels of freedom and rights in the family.

As we have suggested in this chapter, young people today are increasingly exposed to a horizontal heritage, from which they take many of their social cues and much of their cultural guidance. This dynamic produces the occurrence of very different cultural practices within the same household at the same time. Different cultural practices are forever competing and colliding with one another. The result is sometimes serious conflict between parents and children and between siblings, who are all at different places with regard to Western acculturation. This situation is being played out in hundreds of thousands of homes across the United States. Not only are these cultural tensions occurring within families who have recently immigrated from another country, but they are also to be found in families migrating from rural to urban areas and from city to city. Competing cultural practices affect not only migrating families. In fact, in every family whose children are being subjected to significant volumes of horizontal cultural influence, where parents hold to cultural practices that are different from those their children are exposed to, there is great potential for a family culture war. It would not be an exaggeration to suggest that, given the speed of cultural change, many children are brought up in a very different culture from that of their parents. This is the impact of a horizontal heritage at work.

In these circumstances, counselors need to be equipped with more than singular ideas about cultural belonging in order to make sense of what their clients are experiencing. They need a conceptual framework that enables them to identify the complexity of competing background cultural discourses that shape family interactions and produce family conflicts. A counselor helping the family to name the competing and conflicting discourses at work can begin a process in which she assists the family in negotiating, in a more productive and stress-free way, how these cultural forces can be managed. This is very delicate work. It is a big challenge to establish effective and acceptable connections with parents and grandparents as well as to have the skills to connect with and understand children's and young people's perspectives. Democratic problem-solving methods that might be successful with the children may present problems to parents who embrace a more autocratic parenting style. Since every family's needs are different, a way forward can be worked out only on a case-by-case basis. Therapists need to help families gain access to peer resources for information and guidance that fit with the unique family constellations being created in our communities today.

The reliance on horizontal heritage for cultural resources often has a serious negative impact on the role of the elderly. Older people, who once played such a central role in guiding the affairs of a community and family, now have a diminishing presence. In addition, older people who in communal or collective societies could have relied on their children to take care of them through their old age are increasingly having to fend for themselves. The disjuncture between being honored as an integral and guiding cultural resource to the family and taken care of until death, and being isolated and alone, leaves many older people feeling depressed, disoriented, and lonely. Therapists have an important role in supporting the elderly in their quest to make sense of and find positions of integrity in relation to a changed cultural environment. Older people who are not able to keep up with rapid technological change occurring with computers can also be further isolated from what is going on around them. Therapists need to develop specific expertise in working with the elderly, particularly because the numbers of older people are rapidly increasing as the baby boomers age.

With rapid social and cultural change comes rapid change in the cultural practices associated with gender relationships. Historically, men were the primary income earners and family providers. With the growing economic pulling power of many women in families, women's voices have grown in the areas of family life that were traditionally the men's domain. Increasingly, women are less willing to hold down three jobs—one as an income earner for the family; one as a domestic servant who cooks, cleans, and maintains the house; and the third as an emotional and social caregiver for the children and the husband. In many homes, there has been a serious deterioration in couple relationships, because of the changing cultural factors that influence gender roles.

When men and women fail to adjust to these changing cultural trends or women try to sustain all of their previous roles in addition to being a central income earner, the consequence is debilitating stress, conflict, violence, and depression. Therapists have an important role in helping couples and individuals understand the changing gender discourses influencing men's and women's lives. They can help couples renegotiate gender arrangements to fit the new cultural imperatives of gender equity in order to prevent the negative mental health consequences that can otherwise result.

Because of changing cultural trends around income earning, domestic activity, and childcare in families, there are also significant challenges around dating practices and sex. Increasingly, there is confusion about what is the correct cultural behavior. Serious conflicts can occur within families around what is deemed appropriate dating or sexual conduct. Again, the therapist has an important role as a cultural broker to help families negotiate a way forward around what were once intractable cultural positions on these matters.

In many ways, rapidly changing cultural processes taking place around the globe have created serious confusion about how to live in relationships. While there is a sense that particular persons are in charge of these emerging cultural trends, the evidence suggests that nobody is really in control. Religious leaders, politicians, business executives, and educators, while appearing to be leaders in the community, are just as captured and caught up in the cultural changes as everybody else. Nobody is at the helm who can single-handedly influence the discourse. In many ways, we are all participants in creating the direction that our world is heading in.

Additional consequences of these changes include the many emerging subcultures, which are developing their own cultural identity narratives. The Chicano movement is an example of an emergent cultural identity constructed by a disoriented generation among the children of Latino immigrants who felt they belonged to neither a Mexican identity nor an American (U.S.) one. Thousands of young people were simultaneously alienated from White, middle-class America and from their immigrant families. Many Chicanos developed an identity that was not dependent on their speaking Spanish or on their ability to acculturate to the practices of mainstream, middle-class America. But in the face of oppression and prejudice, they did develop a strong political consciousness and a desire for civil rights, together with a deep pride in their Mexican American heritage.

Some of these cultural identities are highly evolved, and the cultural norms underpinning them give clear directives for engaging in day-to-day life. Other subcultural groups are less politically conscious. The most destructive of the new subcultures are the armed gangs in urban and now in rural communities that commit acts of violence against others and against each other. Counselors and therapists who wish to work with the new cultural communities, including gang communities, need to develop a working knowledge of the cultural norms and dominant discourses that prevail in these systems. To build trust and create therapeutic effectiveness, counselors must acquaint themselves with the nuances of these subcultures and their emergent cultural practices.

The increasing focus on material values and the associated Western obsession with body appearance and body shape are powerful cultural themes that many counselors and therapists also need to contend with. Wherever modernist cultural discourses have taken root, there has been serious cultural disciplining of the body. This disciplining produces problems with dieting, starvation, over-exercising, steroid abuse, and overeating. These health problems are lifestyle problems directly related to the dominant cultural messages reinforced every day in the media.

To conclude this chapter, let us reiterate our main theme: counselors and mental health professionals who take seriously the cultural influences on their clients' lives should develop an appreciation of the complexity of cultural narratives that impact the identity development of people's lives. As well as studying the conventional categories of social division formed around ethnicity, sexuality, religion, language, and socioeconomic class, they would do well to attend to the newly emergent elements on the cultural landscape. Cultural influences are not just vertical; they are horizontal as well. Among the horizontal influences, globalization deserves considerable attention. Counselors need to understand especially the profound influence of the media, technology, and mass migration on the shaping of contemporary identities. These cultural strands are becoming pivotal in the task of formulating counseling responses to the bewildering array of complexities that cultural diversity is now composed of.

Discuss

1. Look at the labels of every article of clothing you are wearing right now (including shoes). Make a list of each country that is involved in the manufacturing of your outfit. Look at https://www.dol.gov/ilab/reports/pdf/tvpra_report2014.pdf to find out more about the labor conditions that were likely a part of each garment of clothing according to its country of origin. Take a moment to think about what was involved in the production of each garment. What thoughts and feelings come to mind as you do this?

2. What are some ways in which you have been brought up in a very different cultural background from that of your parents? What horizontal factors are at play? When you were growing up, were there different cultural practices that were competing and colliding with one another? Give examples.

3. Investigate the positive and negative economic effects of globalization for (a) people in Asia and Africa and (b) people in Europe and the United States.

4. How would you prepare yourself as a therapist to engage Mayra Lorenzo and her family?

5. Are there any parts of Mayra Lorenzo's story that stand out to you as being clinically important or relevant? What things do you particularly take note of? What questions would you have for Mayra?

6. What parts of Mayra's story speak to oppression, and what parts speak to resilience? How would your awareness of these themes influence your therapeutic stance or conversations with Mayra?

Response to Chapter 11

SOH-LEONG LIM, PHD, LMFT

Soh-Leong Lim is a licensed marriage and family therapist and emeritus professor at San Diego State University. She is a third-generation Malaysian Chinese and a first-generation immigrant to the United States. She teaches multicultural family therapy, among other courses. She has a passion for bringing global and international awareness to her students in U.S. classrooms. Her research interest is immigrant and transnational families with a focus on acculturation and intergenerational relationships. She lives with her husband in San Diego. They teach internationally and maintain close transnational ties with their family and kin in Asia.

This chapter makes a good case for how vertical and horizontal cultural processes help shape a person's cultural identity. However, I think there needs to be more emphasis on the significance of our vertical cultural processes in addition to the horizontal influences that are going on in our day-to-day lives. My cultural history has been hugely significant in shaping who my family and I have become.

Like weavings of a tapestry, horizontal processes seem more apparent to the observer. The splashes of color catch the eye. Vertical processes, however, are the influences at work that go on silently in one's multigenerational family tapestry. They are passed down from one generation to the next, whether or not the person consciously acknowledges or embraces them at any particular point in his or her life. Though the vertical processes can be masked by globalized forms, they are what constitute the solid framework of one's ethnic identity.

To illustrate this, I would like to share my story. I am a third-generation Malaysian Chinese and a first-generation immigrant to the United States. In my family of five, we have three nuanced identities: my husband and I are OBC (overseas-born Chinese), my first two daughters are ARC (American-raised Chinese), and my youngest daughter is ABC (American-born Chinese). These identities we connect to are a product of horizontal influences, specifically the geographic location of our birth and growing up. However, the common denominator of our identities is that we are Chinese. This is our shared heritage. The vertical influences are very strong for us, although it may appear as if we are losing our Chinese heritage and adopting more American (U.S.) or globalized ways of being through succeeding generations. However, we each tap into these vertical veins and express our Chinese heritage and pride at different junctures of our lives, often in diverse and unexpected ways.

My grandmother migrated to the Malay Peninsula from southern China during the Qing dynasty in the late 19th century. Following her example, my mother carried on the family tradition of ancestor worship blended with elements of Daoist and Buddhist beliefs. We were also deeply influenced by Confucian philosophy, especially the values of education and filial piety. My nine siblings and I grew up in a traditional Chinese home, no different from most Chinese immigrant homes in Malaysia. My father was a magistrate's court interpreter of English, Malay, Mandarin, and seven Chinese dialects; however, with his ten children, he emphasized mastery of the English language. This was the period after British colonial rule in Malaysia when English, used in all official business, was also the medium of instruction in school. My father was a pragmatic man. He saw good education and mastery of the English language as our passport to secure jobs, reflecting the determination of an immigrant set on seeing his young family succeed in the host country. My father did not stress continuity in the Chinese culture, nor did he emphasize mastery of the Chinese language as such. Consequently, while my ethnic heritage is Chinese, I grew up cosmopolitan, imbibing blends of both Eastern (Malay, Chinese, Indian) and Western cultural influences. (I had an English education, grew up with *BBC News*, and enjoyed listening to Johnny Cash.) I spoke English, Malay, and the Chinese Fukien dialect. I also became a Christian at 13 years of age through a deep spiritual experience.

Last year I visited China for the first time in my life. I went to China because I had a teaching assignment. I did not go there with conscious intent to find my roots or to reconnect with my Chinese heritage. Up to that point, I had aligned myself more with my Malaysian Chinese cosmopolitan cultural identity. I was surprised that my time in China stirred in me a pride in being Chinese—a Han Chinese. This was the first time I embraced and celebrated my Chinese identity in such a deep and conscious way. The Chinese in China identified me by the term *hua-chiao*, which means "overseas Chinese." Prior to my trip, I was worried that I could not converse well enough in Mandarin Chinese, and that the fluent Mandarin–speaking Chinese people would look down on me, as those in Malaysia and Singapore often had. This did not happen. Instead, I experienced a sense of homecoming, even though I am not a citizen of China, nor do I have any plans to be one. It had to do with a profound sense of ethnic pride. I am telling this story to illustrate how strong the vertical processes of a Chinese heritage are for me. It seems as if it has been there all the time in the background. It really is the backdrop of my life.

I have three lovely daughters. In all their childhood years, I did not consciously make it a point to instill Chinese culture in my children, but I see these vertical processes at work. For example, three years ago, my American-born daughter, then 16 years old, was at her grandfather's funeral in Malaysia. While surrounded by a throng of relatives, many of whom she had not met before, she took an interest in documenting the family tree of the large extended family network and became known as the Lim family historian. She also took copious pictures of the funeral service, which was a traditional Chinese one, complete with a brass band and Buddhist chants over the five days. She wanted to document this part of her Chinese heritage; all this was of her own accord. She came back to the United States and shared her stories with her two older sisters, who had not been able to leave the country to attend the funeral because of visa restrictions. At that time, my second daughter, a student in visual arts, was struggling with a lack of artistic inspiration. She asked for all the photos, found inspiration from the Chinese rituals and symbols, and incorporated the themes in her metals artwork. Her vertical connections are quietly reflected in her metalsmithing pieces. They are not as loud as the techno music that she dances to with her fun-loving American friends, but they are surely there, treasured as her finely crafted art pieces are. At her senior art show in Texas, I saw her artwork reflecting our heritage, and I was filled with a deep and awesome pride.

To me, this phenomenon is not static. Multigenerationally, I see ebbs and flows. We have our Chinese culture to return to when we so desire or when she stirs in us an awakening. She is like our old faithful friend. We know her strengths and her weaknesses, her prides and her shames. This is what I hope the readers of this volume will understand—that our friend is here to stay; she is strong and she endures the horizontal currents of change. We need to acknowledge her adequately. Counselors should still pay close attention to vertical cultural traditions, as much as they are aware of horizontal forces, in order to be culturally effective.

My therapist friend from China, who grew up under the Cultural Revolution, observed how deeply Confucian and Daoist thought have influenced her and the Chinese people in spite of decades of Maoist rule. "It is in our blood," she reflected. I, as a *hua-chiao*, agree with her. It is indeed in our blood.

Social Class, Poverty, and the American Dream

S ocial class and socioeconomic status are fundamental variables that shape and influence the way life is lived. Class, wealth, and poverty systematically structure our communities, organize where we live, affect our quality of life, constrain or invigorate our aspirations and dreams, impact the quality of our education, channel our access to healthcare, and orchestrate virtually every other aspect of our lives. Social class membership translates into privilege for some and disadvantage for others. It opens or closes the doors of opportunity in life. Since most people agree that social class position is in no way biologically natural, it has to be considered an aspect of the cultural forces that constitute people's lives. It is therefore implicated in the stories that clients tell to counselors, individuals' very access to counseling services, and the resources clients have available for addressing problems.

What Is Social Class?

Defining class is an elusive task. William Ming Liu, Geoffrey Soleck, Joshua Hopps, Kwesi Dunston, and Theodore Pickett (2004) suggest that counselors and healthcare providers speak about class as though everybody knows what it is. According to Liu and his colleagues, counselors too easily assume that they can identify clients' social class membership status. Counselors also often assume that people in a particular class share a homogenous world view, have similar consumer habits, and aspire to similar lifestyle preferences. However, this assumption is unfounded for several reasons. First, it is difficult to separate class from its multiple interactions with other salient social divisions, such as ethnicity, gender, religion, sexuality, geographic location, and mental health status. Class membership makes sense only in relation to other classes and economic privilege or disadvantage and must always be relative to features of a particular social context. The context in which we discuss class shapes our very definition of it. Consider how context might factor into one's perception of social class in the following examples. A dentist could likely be perceived as belonging to a higher class than a manager of a restaurant, even if they earn the same salaries. But, imagine how one's perception might shift if the dentist is an African American woman from the South and the manager is a White male from a WASP-y background. Furthermore, a wealthy Black professional male may have less effective class status than a White professional male in the event that these men get pulled over by the police. In other words, social class status is affected by a variety of contextual dimensions. It is not a fixed or essential category into which people are born and to which they immutably belong.

Another source of confusion is that the very terms in which social class is talked about are not agreed on. The terms *social class* and *socioeconomic status* have very different academic histories, are based on different assumptions, and are used for different purposes. *Socioeconomic status* refers primarily to social groups defined by income level. It is based on a Weberian tradition of sociological research. It informs the collection of data through the census and other databases and is used by social planners to categorize communities on the basis of things like mean income. It lends itself to a liberal humanist account of social relations. (See Chapter 6 for the liberal humanist account of power relations.)

The categories commonly used to define socioeconomic status (SES), such as upper, upper-middle, middle, lower-middle, and lower socioeconomic status, do not always convey the profound differences between wealth and privilege or between poverty and oppression. We live in an era in which the disparities in income between the wealthy and the poor have been widening for several decades. Socioeconomic status can result from both earned and unearned income. Earned income is that produced by employment and occupation. Unearned income includes assets, inheritances, credit lines, employment security, debt load, and how close one can be to being shelterless. All these sources of income are also shaped by ethnicity, gender, and physical and mental well-being.

The term *social class*, on the other hand, has been most strongly influenced by a Marxian analysis of social relations. The Marxian tradition does not so much focus on income level as on positions in economic relations. People are positioned in social classes by their roles as employers or employees, owners of businesses or wage earners, those who have capital to invest and those who sell their labor for wages. Karl Marx (1932) describes classes as being organized in the shape of a pyramid, with the ruling class at the top. The hierarchy is as follows: the ruling class; the nonruling capitalist class; the professional/managerial middle class; the working class, which includes salaried workers of lower social class status; and the lower working class, who live with low wages and no benefits or security. Some writers also discuss an underclass, which consists of the lowest social stratum who are stigmatized and sometimes viewed as the "undeserving poor" (Johnson & Partington, 2017).

Broadly speaking, social class may be defined as a collection of individuals sharing similar economic circumstances. The middle classes and ruling classes have the most decision-making power in the social world and stand to gain the most from economic growth. The working class earns their living by their own labor, and their conditions of work are often characterized, per Marx, by the condition of "alienation." This means that they have no material interest in the economic outcome of their work. If they were to work harder and produce more, they would still earn the same wage. To some extent, the cultural experience of social class is also determined by how free people are in the workplace. Some people are governed as to whether they can have a bathroom break, while others can choose to give themselves bonuses or lay other people off work. In the 19th century, by far the majority of the Western population were working class, and there was a relatively small group in the ruling class and a modest-sized middle class.

One of the problems with a rigid application of the Marxian analysis of class is that the configuration of society has changed considerably since the 19th century. The middle classes have ballooned in size. There have developed a range of occupations that do not fit so easily into the working-class category or the middle-class category. Workers might have some middle-class conditions of work but still be paid working-class wages. The contrast between middle-class workers' interest in and working-class workers' alienation from their work has often become less starkly drawn than it was in the

19th century and has become more complex than previously thought. The range of ways in which people develop relations with economic production and the world of work have become much too diverse to be described by a simple binary opposition between middle-class and working-class interests. Also, the development of an underclass of unemployed and shelterless persons has added to the complexity of the picture of social relations.

There are other problems with the way that social class has been talked about. Essentialist habits of thinking have not been uncommon in relation to social class. For example, many explanations of class are given as distinct and separate from the sociocultural world that people inhabit, including explanations of class culture that refer to individuals' personal and moral attributes, such as dishonesty, reliability, laziness, a strong work ethic, and moral virtue as contributors to their social class position (Johnson & Partington, 2017). Class is thus assumed to be an indication of one's personal worth, and one's social position is merited on the basis of personal talent.

BOX 12.1 THE PRECARIAT

A new concept in the analysis of socioeconomic forces is the term *the precariat*. It owes its popularity to the British sociologist Guy Standing (2011), who claims that we are in the middle of a global socioeconomic transformation and the emergence of the precariat is an aspect of this. The precariat is a class of people whose living conditions and whose participation in the global economy is precarious. It is marked by insecurity.

Says Guy Standing, there is a new class structure emerging from the flexible labor market. At the top is the oligarchy of the increasingly wealthy elites. Underneath them is the shrinking salariat (found in large corporations and government especially). Underneath them is the also shrinking proletariat (what was known as the working class). Underneath them is the rapidly growing precariat (people whose employment and income is insecure because they employed as casual labor with low incomes). Underneath them all lies the unemployed, social misfits, and those on benefits.

Members of the precariat have to accept a life of unstable work. They lack a work narrative that suggests they might be becoming something, such as an occupation. They are faced with uncertainty about whether they should be retraining, or networking, or working an extra job. When they do work, they do not get access to traditional benefits like pensions, paid holidays, medical leave, and so on. Instead, they have to bear economic risks themselves. Therefore, they are always facing debt that they are unable to pay back, especially if they make one mistake, which could lead to them being out on the street.

They are made up of part-time workers, those on short-term contracts, migrants, refugees, and unpaid interns. Guy Standing says that they are becoming increasingly angry. They are the first class of people in human history whose education level is often higher than the work they are able to find. Along with their existence as a social class comes a lack of a work-based career identity, an absence of class solidarity, a sense of alienation, and a susceptibility to populist political movements.

Class Culture

Social research over many years has revealed the complexity of the cultural dimensions of social class identification. People do not just belong to a social class; they construct cultural worlds out of their class membership. These cultural worlds include value systems, habits of thought, relationship patterns, ways of speaking, behaviors, and attitudes toward others. One such pattern has to do with child-rearing practices and the varied patterns that emerge in comparing working-class and middle-class parents. An important example of this is "mastery motivation" defined as "the psychological force that stimulates an individual to attempt independently, in a focused and persistent manner, to solve a problem or master a skill or task which is at least moderately challenging for him or her" (Lavi, Gard, Hagan, Van Horn, & Lieberman, 2015, p. 1). Research findings show that low-income children tend to exhibit lower levels of mastery motivation than their higher SES counterparts. There is speculation as to why this might be the case, but one possibility is that low-income parents' economic stress limits their parenting effectiveness and shapes their child-rearing patterns in a way that doesn't promote mastery motivation (Lavi et al.) Such research has important implications for counseling.

The values that are expressed in counseling theories of self-actualization may often be said to reflect middle-class valuation of self-directed behavior. When counselors look for and reward self-directed behavior in their clients, they may be inadvertently favoring cultural values that are middle class in origin and contradicting the cultural training that working-class children have received in their families.

Discuss

1. How do you locate yourself in terms of social class and socioeconomic status? Discuss factors such as ethnicity, race, or other contextual variables that might affect somebody else's perception of you as belonging to a particular SES.

2. Compare yourself with your parents and grandparents. What have been the generational patterns and trends of social class in your family? What sort of child rearing practices were prevalent in your family of origin?

3. Discuss your experiences with persons who are shelterless, experiencing unemployment, not having health insurance, or holding down two or more jobs. What is the lowest paying job you ever had and what outside support was necessary in improving the situation?

4. What are the conditions of your workplace? Are you able to go to the restroom and take lunch breaks as you please? What sort of impact do these work conditions have on your identity and on your relations with others in the workplace?

5. What does alienation from your labor mean? Have you experienced it? What effect does it have on you?

Being Poor in America

Jesse Jackson gave a speech at the 2000 American Psychological Association annual convention in which he said,

Most poor people work every day. Most poor people in the U.S. are not black, not brown. Most poor people are White, female, young, invisible, and without national leaders.

Most poor people are not on welfare.

They raise other people's children. … They put food in our children's schools. … They clean our offices. … They cut grass. … They pick lettuce. … They work in hospitals, as orderlies. … no job is beneath them. (Jackson, 2000, p. 329)

While the poor contribute so much to our society, they are subject to elevated rates of threatening and uncontrollable life events, noxious life conditions, high infant mortality, violent crime, and homicide. As Bernice Lott (2002) noted, physicians on the whole tend to avoid working in poor areas, even when tempted by generous salary packages. Jonathan Kozol (1992) found that the same is true for the best teachers, who gravitate toward the wealthier school districts, where they are paid more. Mental health workers often feel uncomfortable with low-income clients, finding it difficult to empathize with them. Low-income clients are more likely than middle-income clients to receive therapy that is brief (if they receive any at all) and drug-centered. They are often treated by students and low-status professionals. Lawyers are reluctant to provide services to the poor, and less than a third of low-income people who need an attorney get one. Crime victims who are poor or shelterless receive less attention in the media than those who are more affluent (Viano, 1992). According to a United States Justice Department report ("Deadly Disparities," 2000), 82% of the 682 defendants facing capital charges in federal courts since 1995 were members of a minority and poor. Seventy-four percent of the 183 recommended for the death penalty were also members of a minority and poor.

Poverty is a constant threat to children's well-being. Poor children rarely get access to high-quality childcare facilities. Since poorer parents often work more than one low-paying job and often cannot afford quality childcare at all, there is often very little adult supervision of children in poverty-stricken communities. These same parents usually work in circumstances where there is inadequate sick leave or vacation time. When extended family networks are unavailable, which is increasingly the case, children are frequently left alone. Without adult supervision, children are more likely to spend time engaged in potentially harmful activities, such as watching hours and hours of unmonitored television full of adult sexual and violent content (Garbarino & Bedard, 2001). Children are often free to circulate in a community that is prone to serious unemployment, violence, drugs, deteriorating housing, and declining healthcare services. As a result of violence and gang warfare, children are often isolated and have little access to any form of social support or even physical recreation in the neighborhood (Vera & Shin, 2006). These conditions constitute an ongoing hazardous situation for all members of the community. See Box 12.3 for some statistical summaries of the trends in income levels.

The American Dream

Many people believe that the fate of the poor and marginalized results from their own life choices. The notion that everybody in North America has a chance at the good life if he is willing to work hard and obey the rules continues to be widespread. No one really cares if the boss earns 300 times more than the

BOX 12.2 REDISTRIBUTION OR RECOGNITION?

In recent decades, the emphasis on redistributing material wealth from the well-off to the not-so-well-off that drove the emergence of the welfare state has been replaced in some instances by an emphasis on securing greater recognition of various identity groups. One can think of the contrasting aims of the trade union movement and the gay rights or queer movement. While the former was clearly aimed at redistributing wealth from the elite to the deserving working class, the latter has held out no such aim. It has concentrated on achieving recognition of the right to be heard as different, rather than a claim to be deserving of equal material wealth on account of being the same as everyone else.

Nancy Fraser (1995) has articulated this difference in strategy as well as anyone. She describes many of the identity groups that have emerged recently as more focused on achieving political recognition and celebrating cultural difference, rather than socioeconomic entitlement based on social class. She also complicates the picture by asserting that there are a number of groups of people who make both claims. Specifically, she suggests that injustice in the areas of gender and race are often about the lack of socioeconomic opportunity as well as about cultural identity. However, these strategies do not sit easily together. Socioeconomic claims for redistribution often appear to downplay differences in order to appear similar to others who already receive an economic benefit, while cultural claims for recognition often play up these differences in order to appear distinctive.

Nancy Fraser believes both protests against injustice are justified and deserve to be remedied. She resolves the dilemma between them by distinguishing between affirmative action and transformational action. By the former she means addressing an injustice without disturbing the underlying structure that produced it and by the latter she means changing those same underlying structures. She argues that identity groups that attempt to address these underlying structures need not get caught up in the dilemma of redistribution or recognition.

What is more, she suggests that deconstruction is critical for the transformational purpose. Her advocacy of deconstruction is important for counselors. After all, counselors and educators do not have much that they can redistribute, apart from their own services. However, assisting those who are struggling for recognition, particularly when they have a transformational goal, is very worthwhile.

average worker, as long as the average worker can hope someday to have a shot at the top job. In fact, eight out of ten Americans (U.S.) believe that those who start off poor, if they work hard, can still make pots of money ("Inequality and the American Dream," 2006). This is a central part of the American dream.

The American dream was popularized by the historian James Truslow Adams (1931), who defined the dream of a "land in which life should be better and richer and fuller for every man, with opportunity for each according to his ability or achievement" (p. 404). The dream was based on the idealistic hope that everybody had the right to individual freedom and the chance to succeed. Built into the American dream is the incentive for everyone to strive for upward social class mobility and to become wealthier than she currently is. The dream requires a Protestant work ethic, acceptance of a delay of gratification, individualism, and industriousness. Research on upward mobility suggests that people

BOX 12.3 POVERTY AND WEALTH STATISTICS

According to U.S. Census Bureau, the official poverty rate in 2017 was 12.3%, or 39.7 million people. With regard to formal education, people with at least a bachelor's degree had the lowest poverty rates in 2017. From a gender standpoint, it is of note that in 2017, the median earnings of all male workers increased 3.0% from 2016 to $44,408, while real median earnings for their female counterparts ($31,610) remained unchanged. Women still earn less than men, which implies male privilege over their female counterparts even within the same SES. Moreover, in looking at family households, married couple households had the highest median income in 2017 ($90,386), followed by men with no wife present ($60,843). Family households maintained by women with no husband present had the lowest median income ($41,703), thus indicating greater economic hardship for women living in poverty than their male counterparts.

internalize an expectation to succeed to such an extent that those who are unsuccessful are regarded as deviant (Liu & Pope-Davis, 2003).

The American dream invites us to consider poverty a failure of personal initiative. With this view, the existence of poverty constitutes an irritating reminder of the dark side of the American dream. The American dream is built on individualism. It assumes a valorization of individuals' talents and abilities and a belief in the pervasiveness of personal opportunity. The self envisaged is acontextual to the extent that the constraints on such opportunity put in place by a person's position in relation to social class, race, gender, and disability are at least downplayed, if not trivialized. The spirit of the American dream is firmly rooted in the religious, economic, political, and dominant cultural notions of mainstream US America. These frameworks of belief place most of the burden of accountability for poverty on the poor. They should pull themselves up by their own boot straps. Those who do not achieve such advances are easily deemed worthless as well as poor. This denigration of the poor feeds ongoing political attacks on the United States welfare system and supports plans to dismantle it without providing any alternatives.

bell hooks (2000) claims that "many greedy upper and middle class citizens share with their wealthy counterparts a hatred and disdain for the poor that is so intense, it borders on pathological hysteria" (p. 45). She suggests that US American citizens are socialized to view the poor as "parasites and predators" whose ongoing needs inhibit others' ability to enjoy a good life.

Most social scientists and economists who research patterns of wealth and poverty pretty much agree that the American dream is illusory. Bernice Lott (2002) argued that American (U.S.) psychologists have consistently worked under the assumption that the United States is a classless society, making it seem that socioeconomic status is not an important factor in the treatment of the poor. In the U.S. today, parental income is a better predictor of whether someone will be rich or poor than it is in most other countries, including Canada and most European countries. In the U.S., about half of the income disparity in one generation is generally reflected in the next. By comparison, in Canada and Nordic countries, that proportion is about a fifth. In other words, the American dream is more possible in Canada than it is in the United States. From every measure, it is clear that there has been a continuous trend since 2000 toward a further concentration of income at the very top. No other country has seen such extreme shifts in recent times. The latest research suggests that less than one-half of 1% of children from the bottom fifth of U.S. families attend an elite college; less than half attend any college at all (Chetty, Friedman, Saez, Turner, & Yagan, 2017).

Poor children are often trapped in run-down schools, while wealthier parents are in a position to spend more cash on tutoring their children to ensure they succeed. For many ethnic minorities, new immigrants, and people in the lower socioeconomic strata suffering from institutional discrimination, it is more appropriate to speak of an American nightmare than an American dream (McNamee & Miller, 2004).

In fact, the American dream is systematically denied to numerous social groups by discrimination on the basis of sexual orientation, disability, religion, regional location, and level of physical attractiveness. While gender and ethnicity are generally deemed the most common bases for discrimination, when discrimination happens on other grounds, it is no less real for the victim. Nevertheless, the myth of the American dream holds out hope for many. It can be harmful, however, when it provides an incomplete explanation of an individual's success or failure, or when it continues to mistakenly praise the rich and demonize the poor.

There is a serious disparity between the rich and poor who wish to fulfill the American dream. The wealthy in North America are born near the finish line in terms of maintaining their existing wealth and producing more of it. The poor have a slim chance of accumulating wealth and making the American dream occur in their lives. We hear the success stories in the media of poor individuals who have accrued unimaginable wealth in their short lifetimes. Their numbers, however, are tiny. Success for this population is almost always based on a working-class work ethic and good luck. Table 12.4 shows the immense distance the poor must travel to be financially successful.

BOX 12.4 PRIVILEGE WALK ACTIVITY

1. Have participants form a straight line across the room about an arm's length apart, leaving space in front and behind.
2. Have the facilitators state the following: Listen to the following statements, and follow the instructions given. For example, when I read, "If you are a White male, take one step forward," only White males will move and everyone else will stand still. Each step should be an average length step. No one is going to check up on you, so if you feel you qualify to take a step then do so, if not then you may stay where you are. You are the judge of what you should do.
3. Read the statements one at a time, allowing time for participants to take a step.
4. When all the statements have been read, process the activity using the following questions: What is your "gut reaction" to where you find yourself at the end of this list of privileges? Are you surprised at where you are? How does it feel to be in front? In the middle? In back? Did you come to any new realizations? If so, which one had the most impact?

Here are the statements:

> If you are a White male, take one step forward.
>
> If there have been times in your life when you skipped a meal because there was no food in the house, take one step backward.
>
> If you have visible or invisible disabilities, take one step backward.
>
> If you attended (grade) school with people you felt were like yourself, take one step forward. If you grew up in an urban setting, take one step backward.
>
> If your family had health insurance, take one step forward.
>
> If your work holidays coincide with religious holidays that you celebrate, take one step forward.
>
> If you feel good about how your identified culture is portrayed by the media, take one step forward.
>
> If you have been the victim of physical violence based on your gender, ethnicity, age, or sexual orientation, take one step backward.
>
> If you have ever felt passed over for an employment position based on your gender, ethnicity, age, or sexual orientation, take one step backward.
>
> If you were born in the United States, take one step forward.
>
> If English is your first language, take one step forward.
>
> If you have been divorced or impacted by divorce, take one step backward.
>
> If you came from a supportive family environment, take one step forward.
>
> If you have completed high school, take one step forward.
>
> If you were able to complete college, take one step forward.
>
> If you are a citizen of the United States, take one step forward.
>
> If you took out loans for your education, take one step backward.
>
> If you attended private school, take one step forward.
>
> If you have ever felt unsafe walking alone at night, take one step backward.

Source. State University of New York at Albany School of Social Welfare (n.d.)

The burden of poverty and abuse certainly weighed heavily on me as a child. Poverty is oppressive: cockroaches suck, food stamps and free lunches are embarrassing, and getting the water or electricity shut off, or evicted from your home is, of course, hard stuff for anyone to process. One meal a day was the norm—unless it was a school day and the school would be doing the feeding. Whenever social workers were on their way to do a home inspection, my mom would buy groceries: "Don't you touch any of this food," she would tell us. It was not there for us. It was there so that she could convince the social workers that she did provide for us, though all signs showed this was not the case. We were coached to lie to the social workers and teachers. My absentee father would occasionally stop by when he was in town. He'd ask if he could take us to his apartment for a meal. We knew the answer before my mother said it: "They ate a lot yesterday—they're fine," or "They're plenty fat." Needless to say, on many nights we would comfort each other through hunger pains as we fell asleep.

Hunger was not the only form of physical oppression I experienced. As a child, I couldn't comprehend why we wore (and slept) in the same clothes for a week at a time. In fourth or fifth grade a lifeboat appeared. Two of my sisters and I were allowed to join the local Episcopal church's children's choir. Mainly we rejoiced in the freedom (and food) this afforded us. And bonus upon bonuses, the choir sent us on one all-expenses-paid weekend a year to Camp Stevens in the local mountains. Those two days away from my parents quickly became my favorite two days of the year. We slept in actual beds. We ate three meals a day. We delighted in hikes through the woods and camp activities. It all provided rare childhood joy in my heart. Those were the happiest moments of my childhood, by far.

—Megan

The Growth of Consumer Culture

We are, whether we like it or not, a part of the consumer culture. A belief in capitalism and consumerism tells us that U.S. citizens live in a land of opportunity. Government laws and regulations are designed to protect capitalism, businesses are accorded the right to maximize profit with few restrictions, and our job as consumers is to buy material objects, even if we have to amass debt to do it. Within this culture we are all under tremendous pressure to conform to the tenets of consumerism. Many of us have our world views molded and our identities shaped to live our lives according to goals of consumer practice, such as watching social media, commercial television, shopping in the mall, investing in the stock market, and spending a paycheck. According to Speck and Hasselkuss (2015), "Consumerism has emerged as part of a historical process that has created mass markets, industrialization, and cultural dispositions to ensure that rising incomes are used to purchase an ever-growing output" (p. 23).

As Jeffrey Kottler (1999) suggests, "We are enculturated to want things. We are brainwashed to assess our worth and image according to the products we acquire" (p. 48).

Consumer culture endorses notions of identity that say that we are what we can buy. Everyday consumption practices are heavily driven by social and institutional norms (Speck & Hasselkuss, 2015). Everyone, no matter what his class, is susceptible to the marketing machine of consumer culture, in which a person's value is defined by the acquisition of objects. For the poor, the acquisition of material objects is often used as an antidote to the shame of poverty. Television pumps consumer messages to us through sitcoms, dramas, game shows, and reality television, many of which extol the virtues of acquisition and consumerism. Advertisers have sophisticated techniques to convince us to buy. Tim Kasser, Richard Ryan, Charles Couchman, and Kennon Sheldon (2004) report on the positive correlation between television watching and materialism. Products are being used by famous people or those we find attractive, and we are coached into believing that we might enjoy some of their success if we simply buy that product. Psychological techniques such as classical conditioning and social learning theory (Bandura, 1971) are used to teach us consumptive behavior.

Consumer culture creates cruel illusions as it projects images in the media of human happiness but ultimately does not deliver these things. Consumer culture directs us away from being members of society with an interest in collective issues and focuses us on individual greed and selfishness. It does not promote an interest in the general plight of large portions of the human population who live in poverty, receive limited healthcare, and have inadequate housing and few opportunities. Tim Kasser and Richard Ryan (2001, cited in Kasser & Kanner, 2004) describe a decrease in the likelihood that people oriented toward materialism and consumerism will behave in a prosocial manner. By contrast, when consumerism is reduced, the outcomes usually include improved health, monetary savings, and other interpersonal benefits (Speck & Hasselkuss, 2015). Thus, there is good evidence to suggest that the culture of consumption not only negatively impacts psychological well-being but heightens the dangers of serious environmental and social problems. It also undermines our ability to look for collaborative solutions to our problems.

Discuss

1. What brands or popular products were "all the rage" when you were an adolescent in school?
2. What impact did owning these products have on your personal and social life?
3. What happened to kids who were not able to afford these brand name products?
4. As a child, how did your parents respond when you asked them to buy particular items that were popular at the time?
5. For those who are parents, how does consumer culture work on your children?

The Psychological Effects of Being Poor

Where the consumer culture has taken hold, the social inscriptions of what it means to be poor change. The power of marketing and advertising adds momentum to the myth of a classless society in which wealth is potentially attainable by everyone. bell hooks (2000) suggests that transnational media present consumer culture as a democratic system that is open and free and where anything is possible. The rich are represented as heroic champions of hedonistic consumerism, and the media promote the notion that people already have an equal right to buy anything. hooks makes a case that the poor are demonized in the media and are portrayed as corrupt and dysfunctional, while the rich are depicted as caring and generous. Popular reality television unabashedly celebrates beauty and wealth. The rich and famous dominate our television screens and other forms of media, and many of us vicariously live our lives with them through this medium. We can imagine rising to fame and fortune and think that we too can be part of the fantasy in the popular social media which we consume. hooks gives an example of how consumer culture has undermined the spiritual and moral integrity of young Black leaders:

> While young black gangsta' rappers stand up at award ceremonies and give thanks to God for their fame and fortune, the Christian and Islamic religious beliefs they evoke do not shape their moral values or their actions in the world. They (and their non-black counter parts) mock their gods, and their wanton worship of wealth encourages the young to believe that God is useful only as a tool for taking you to the top. And this top is not Martin Luther King's mountaintop where one embraces a divine vision of social justice and democratic union. (hooks, 2000, p. 87).

The discourse through which poverty is understood inevitably becomes internalized into the psychological experience of the poor. They are susceptible to the invitation to hold themselves personally to blame for their grim and impoverished material circumstances. Many of the lower class and working poor experience feelings of desperation and hopelessness. They are surrounded by middle-class culture and wealth, but none of it seems accessible. As Susan Bray and Marlene Schommer-Aikins (2015) have argued, counselors with a commitment to cultural understandings should be prepared to inquire into and work with the effects of poverty and unemployment. They should understand, for example, the depression that can result from difficult life circumstances as contextually produced rather than just as the result of the action of chemicals in the brain. The production of hedonistic consumerism has created a generation of youth who see little value in hard work but believe that status and power lie only in getting one's material needs met. Success is measured by demonstrating excesses of material consumption. Young African American youth from poverty-stricken communities who become stars in the music industry and in the sporting world often over-exaggerate displays of the conventional status symbols of success to win the respect and approval of their peers. The large diamond-studded necklaces, large rings and jewelry, and even the fashion of wearing diamond-studded teeth is only a different version of materialistic display from that exhibited by movie stars, entrepreneurs, and recipients of inherited wealth who show off jet planes, large yachts, and collections of cars and palaces as status symbols.

Consumer discourse promotes the envy that is exploited by modern advertising. This dynamic has produced a predatory culture in poor urban neighborhoods where young people are slaughtered for their material possessions. Many youth attempt to hide their shame about being poor by masking their background with clothing and material possessions. This is most noticeable in schools, where adolescents often make strong requests to their parents about wearing the current designer labels in order to escape being ridiculed by their peers for wearing out-of-date clothing.

When youth in poor communities are served by poor health and education services, they can look to expedient methods to be free from the shame of being poor and the feelings of worthlessness that can accompany their failure to realize the American dream. In the face of limited possibilities in the inner city, many in the underclass resort to hustling, pimping, prostitution, and drug dealing. In these poor urban communities, families get pulled into the immediate attractions that a prolific drug culture can provide them. Selling drugs buys the necessities and provides the prospect of rapid access to luxuries. The downstream psychological effects of addiction result. Sadly, the infestation of the drug culture in poor communities further undermines the attempts of its citizens to escape the exploitation and violation that accompany drug trafficking. Illicit drugs become attractive pathways to acquiring monetary rewards, allowing an otherwise poor person to drive the same cars and wear the same clothes as the middle and upper classes. Drugs also ease the pain of shame and humiliation and numb the sorrow accompanying entrapment in poverty. Paradoxically, however, it is the same drug culture that frequently destroys the familial bonds that once mitigated the hardships of poverty.

Classism

Classism is the cultural expression of prejudice on the basis of social class membership. It involves the making of a negative judgment about the worth of a person, either oneself or another, on the basis of perceived social class membership. It is similar to racism in that people judge others on the discursive significance of particular attributes and evaluate them on a scale. The scale usually leads to an assumption of superiority or inferiority. Classist discourse is constantly at work informing the perceptions that individuals form about others being above them, below them, or just like them. It becomes a form of rationalization for the assignment of "in" groups and "out" groups.

Classist behavior can show itself in all sections of society. Children engage in this behavior when they tease others because they dress funny or look dorky. Adults warn their children not to get big ideas in life and show them up as inferior. Classist discourse functions as an explanatory system to account for why some people deserve to accumulate resources while others do not.

Colbow and his colleagues (Colbow, Cannella, Vispoel, Morris, Cederberg, Conrad, et al., 2016) expand upon four versions of classism: upward, downward, lateral, and internalized. Upward classism is prejudice and discrimination directed toward individuals who are perceived to be of a higher social class. They are judged to be elitist, snobbish, pretentious, and self-absorbed. Affluent people can be perceived as ruthless, selfish, and uncaring. Downward classism involves prejudicial attitudes and behaviors against people and groups that are perceived by the observer to be "lower" or "below" them. They are assumed on little or no evidence to be lazy, dirty, violent, or a drain on society. Lateral classism is best illustrated by the concept of "keeping up with the Joneses," a phrase that refers to how individuals within a certain economic structure compete with others in that social group to demonstrate that they not only belong to that class grouping, but are a little superior to the others. Those who violate the cultural norms of their class are at risk of being jettisoned from that social group. Lateral classism involves a strong discourse of conformity to the social group, and an individual who moves to the margins of that group may be deemed unworthy to belong. Last, internalized classism functions as a discourse that works on the inside. It occurs when individuals transgress the boundaries of their own internalized cultural norms and expectations. On the basis of deterioration in their financial position or some social or behavioral misdeed, people can judge themselves to be inadequate and to have failed to meet the cultural standards of their class.

There are significant counseling implications for classist behavior, which can be demonstrated by both counselors and clients. For clients experiencing internalized classism, strong feelings of shame, anger, frustration, and depression can dominate their experience (D'Andrea & Daniels, 2001). Men in particular can be deeply troubled when they have not been able to meet their own expectations of wealth accumulation and fail to live up to their own social class world view.

Clark, Moe, and Hays (2017) have suggested that counselors who have not confronted their own classist attitudes may be prone to displaying disrespectful and sometimes abusive behaviors toward their clients that are akin to racism. As therapy is a talking form of healing, the discourse used in the therapy room can be infected with classist language and assumptions. Thus, counselors need to be aware of biases and not judge clients on the basis of, for example, their use of nonstandard English or slang, or their particular accent.

Social Mobility Through Education

Despite the powerful constraining effects of social class, there are many people who are socially mobile. They grow up in working-class families and achieve entry to middle class occupations and lifestyles. Educational achievement is the main pathway to this mobility. Indeed, the opportunity for such educational achievement is sometimes held out to the poor as if it is equally open to all. The impression created is that those who do not achieve social mobility are morally weak and thus less deserving. Many people from a range of non-White ethnic backgrounds and from working-class families nevertheless do achieve educational success. In many cases, these individuals overcome great odds to succeed in school, the university, and the workplace.

Sometimes this success happens because the institutions themselves make efforts to respond to culturally different backgrounds. Affirmative action is an example. More often, however, socially mobile individuals have not only learned the culture of middle-class America, but in many cases also learned to thrive in it. Thriving in the discourse of education is much more straightforward for those groomed in White, middle-class culture from birth (Croninger & Lee, 2001). They are said to have accumulated "cultural capital" (Igarashi, 2014) that gives them profound advantages in the marketplace of education. After they accumulate educational qualifications, they translate this cultural capital back into economic capital through the extra money they can earn in the workplace.

Liu et al. (2004) add to this account by distinguishing between social capital, cultural capital, and human capital. Social capital, for example, is defined by privileged access to specific relationships that enable advancement. It is explained by the well-known phrase, "It's not what you know, but who you know." Human capital is based on personal charisma, interpersonal skills, physical ability, or physical beauty as these things are valued by a particular community. Cultural capital was first defined by Bourdieu (1977) to refer to the particular tastes and aesthetic sensitivities cultivated in one's social class as signals to others that one belongs.

Many middle- and upper-class individuals are groomed to take full advantage of the cultural, social, and human capital they acquire, and to translate it into educational achievement and economic advancement. Others who have not been brought up with cultural capital have to acculturate to the dominant culture of the middle class, sometimes at great cost to themselves and to their indigenous cultural heritage. Sometimes the costs outweigh the advantages, as the stresses of acculturation itself lead to drug addiction, mental illness, family breakup, loneliness, and isolation. There are numerous statistics to support the idea that dynamic and complex shifts in social mobility through education are taking place in North America.

Achieving success in education and in the workplace in the modern world requires the ability to adhere to specific behavioral protocols. Acculturation into these protocols determines to a large extent where one falls in the division between the "haves" and the "have nots." To survive and thrive in educational and corporate institutions, people must negotiate their way through a series of nuanced political requirements and become adept at joining and maintaining a network of positive relationships, especially with those above them in the hierarchy.

Those who are most successful in meeting the cultural expectations of large economic and educational institutions know how to fulfil a complex array of both subtle and not-so-subtle daily tasks. They know the importance of following repetitive routines and managing time. They are able to understand and work within hierarchical structures and are willing to do so. In addition, they learn how to follow the cultural conventions of business and educational etiquette. They can deliver and receive information and acquire particular technological know-how. Less obvious because it is so taken for granted, but most important, is their ability to hold fast to particular standards of dress and hygiene, demonstrate nonverbal attentiveness by engaging in a high degree of eye contact, and demonstrate verbal agility while responding quickly to requests and demands. Successful individuals must also display a particular voice tone, accent, and dialect that mirror the pattern of communication of those who are high in the hierarchy. Those who succeed in contemporary economic systems are generally able to speak fluently in the accents and dialects of the dominant language, which in North America is middle-class English.

There are always a small minority of individuals in diverse cultural communities who "make it" in a capitalist culture even when they do not meet or demonstrate the necessary cultural expectations of the White middle class in school and in business. Many youngsters from underrepresented and marginalized communities aspire to be professional sportsmen and sportswomen, such as professional football, basketball, or baseball stars, or rap or hip-hop artists. In part, these young people know at an early age that their lives do not conform to the cultural expectations prized in school settings. They see physical prowess or musical and dancing talent, rather than the attainment of business acumen or professional mastery in any of the possible career paths that exist, as a way to attain monetary success and social prestige.

The dominant cultural practices in economic institutions may have their origins many hundreds of years ago in Greek, Roman, Chinese, Japanese, and Islamic civilizations. They have been honed and refined by the dominating European civilizations over the last 400 years. In a contemporary American (U.S.) context, the individuals who are most likely to excel in workplace culture are from middle- and upper-class backgrounds and have either a European American or Asian ancestry. In part, they have excelled because their ancestors played a significant role in establishing the cultural practices that accompanied the development of modern-day institutions such as schools, universities, banks, retail stores, factories, hospitals, and construction industries. People without the cultural background that teaches the cultural nuances of contemporary institutions have struggled harder to achieve success in these contexts.

The argument presented here does not deny the history of discrimination that has positively excluded people from success in the workplace on the grounds of skin color or gender. Instead, it explains how privileged access to occupational success is also founded on what happens in our minds and in our daily relational practices. This is the domain of psychology rather than, say, legal rights. It is the psychology of the internalized cultural knowledge that is passed on from generation to generation, much of which we are barely aware of. Its effects are not always immediately obvious, but they are worked out over a lifetime.

Counseling Needs of the Underclass

Members of cultural communities who struggle to participate successfully in the current education system and who drop out and fail to graduate from high school often fall into a large underclass. Included in this group are those who find themselves unemployed or underemployed, or working in menial jobs in dangerous environments at or below the minimum wage. This group typically is caught in a hopeless cycle of poverty from which escape is very difficult. They are also commonly exposed to neighborhood and gang violence and police brutality. They are provided with inadequate social services, and yet they are the most in need of health and counseling services. Current counseling services in North America are mostly underprepared to work with this large and alienated group. While this underclass is made up of many people from African American, Mexican American, Native American, Caribbean, and Pacific Island communities, it also includes many Whites from lower-class backgrounds. People with physical and mental disabilities frequently end up in this underclass, as do seniors who find themselves without adequate financial resources.

In many ways, members of this financially poor, alienated underclass share more day-to-day experiences with each other than they do with more well-off members of the same ethnicity, religion, or sexual orientation. A Community Development Authority report produced by the United States Department of Labor revealed, for example, that the major factors producing child poverty in the United States result from welfare dependence and single parenthood (De Haan & Schreiner, 2018). They state that race per se is not a factor in producing child poverty and does not directly increase or decrease the probability that a child will be poor. When White groups with high levels of single parenthood and welfare dependence (matching those typical in the Black community) are compared to Black groups, the poverty rates for both groups are nearly identical. Yet Black American children are three times more likely to live in poverty than White children are, primarily because Black children are far more likely to live in single parent families and to be on welfare.

Counseling Services and Cultural Acculturation

Counseling and social services need to be tailored for the poor as well as respond to the unique needs of different ethnic groups and gay and lesbian communities. The shared cultural experiences of those who are of the same socioeconomic class are critical resources for the development of culturally respectful and effective counseling approaches for this population.

Those who are schooled in the conventions of middle-class culture are more likely to utilize and benefit from mainstream counseling and psychotherapy services than those who have been rejected, failed, and marginalized by the educational and economic institutions of dominant culture. And yet the frames of reference for most counseling and psychotherapy models are congruent with the cultural assumptions embedded in these same institutions. Many approaches to therapy have been developed by therapists working with middle-class clients. It would therefore not be surprising to find that such approaches do not fit with the cultural values of those who are members of the working class or in poverty. A notable exception to this generalization is Salvador Minuchin's (1974) approach to structural family therapy, which was largely developed among families living in the slums of Philadelphia.

Counseling in Poor Communities

There are some immediate practical issues that need to be taken into account by counselors working in poor communities. Sue, Rasheed, and Rasheed (2015) point many of these out. For example, it is easy to overlook the struggles that many clients with no reliable means of transportation have in attending counseling sessions. Many working-class families also have great difficulty making long-term appointments. People doing shift work or whose working schedule is constantly changing have little control over their working hours and cannot easily schedule services way into the future. They may face greater risk of losing their jobs by taking time off to attend appointments than middle-class clients. Setting 50-minute appointments a week or two in advance may work well for middle-class clients, but not always so well for lower-class clients who are concerned with day-to-day survival (Sue, Rasheed, & Rasheed, 2015). As a result, many families can benefit from mental health services only if counselors are willing to conduct home visits. And yet counselors are often reluctant to make these home visits, particularly in neighborhoods where they feel endangered.

Many people in poor communities have had frequent negative experiences in dealing with public and community agencies, some of which are poorly run and poorly resourced. They also frequently experience such agencies as serving a governing role over their lives, rather than working in solidarity with them in their struggles. As a result, Sue, Sue, Neville and Smith (2019) suggest that many poor people have low regard for punctuality, as they have had numerous experiences of waiting for hours on end in mental health centers, police stations, and various government agencies, just for a few minutes of the professional's time. It is not surprising that clients who have repeatedly had these experiences lack enthusiasm for another appointment and feel indifferent toward counseling professionals. Members of poorer communities have sometimes been described by mental health professionals as more likely to be distrustful and to become frustrated with authority figures. There is perhaps an expectation that mental health professionals won't listen to them and may not value the same things. These self-protective responses may easily be wrongly assessed as poor motivation for counseling.

Living in a harsh environment in a poverty-stricken community does not invite long-range planning and sophisticated, indirect therapeutic strategies. Many people want immediate, concrete advice and tangible support. Salvador Minuchin (1974) describes family relationships in such circumstances as often characterized by a chaotic pattern. He therefore advocates therapeutic interventions that address the building of greater structure in family members' lives. Clients who live in poverty often don't have the resources to pay for mental health treatment and are almost certain not to have health insurance. Instead, they can be completely reliant on public nonprofit health services, which may vary dramatically in quality of services. It is sometimes said that many people who live in poor communities do not necessarily respond to talk therapies.

We want to be very cautious about this conclusion, which can be a quite patronizing and pathologizing assumption made by middle-class counselors who interpret working-class patterns of language use as a lack of intelligence or a lack of ability to communicate. Just because working-class people do not talk in counseling in the ways that a counselor is familiar with, or in ways that match the expectations of a particular therapeutic approach, does not mean that such clients cannot benefit from talking through their struggles with a counselor. The crucial issue is whether the counselor is willing to enter the cultural values implicit in the client's language world, rather than whether talking to a counselor is of no use. In circumstances where such a question arises, the onus is on the counselor to make the effort to join with and respect the client's cultural knowledge and linguistic frames of reference, rather than to write the client off as lacking the skills necessary for participation in counseling. This issue is even more salient when the client's first language is not English. Monolingual English-speaking therapists can easily slip into pathologizing and writing off clients because they do not understand them.

Now we shall turn from the pragmatic issues to the substantive issues that working-class and poor clients raise with counselors. Counselors and therapists can have great difficulty understanding and relating to circumstances and day-to-day challenges that people face in poor communities. It is easy for therapists to interpret failure to overcome powerful systemic and discursive constraints as failures in client awareness or moral courage. In other words, it is easy to individualize the effects of social forces and impute to clients a personal deficit of some kind. Given many of the knowledges that dominate psychology, we can even say that it is understandable that counselors would be pulled in such a direction by their training and professional knowledge base. But what is understandable is not always good enough. It is possible for counselors to understand the processes by which the poor come to internalize feelings of inferiority and failure and become dominated by helplessness (Sue, Rasheed, & Rasheed, 2015), not because of some personal failure, but because these are the interpretations that they are invited to make of themselves by the cultural context in which they live. Jeanne Slattery (2004) comments that sometimes lower-class and working-poor clients feel so hopeless about the quality of their lives and their economic well-being that this hopelessness is transferred to their expectations about therapy. It is also possible for counselors to open opportunities in counseling for clients to contest the negative identity conclusions that they have internalized from the cultural and economic contexts of their lives.

They can also help clients to develop qualities and skill sets that build the resilience, strength, and perseverance necessary to survive in tough and unforgiving communities.

Other times, clients are struggling with basic survival needs, such as having a reliable shelter and finding an adequate source for food. These needs take precedence over some of the agendas important to the counselors assigned to work with folks who are struggling. At the same time, there are internal experiential dimensions and identity stories about obtaining basic survival needs that counseling can help clients process.

Middle-Class Culture and Graduate School

In general, there is very little emphasis on the impact of social class on counseling in counselor training programs. In many programs, counselors are prepared to work with middle-class cultures rather than with the working class and the poor. This emphasis is largely due to the pervasiveness of middle-class culture in many university institutions. As Tracy Robinson-Wood (2017) suggests, graduate culture is steeped in economic privilege. Counselor education programs are shaped and developed within middle-class culture. Graduate students are drilled in cultural practices requiring self-reliance, standard English, and the middle-class work ethic of delayed gratification. Even if members of the student body have not come from well-resourced communities, graduate students have distinguished themselves by succeeding amid the rigors of academia and have acculturated in a middle-class direction, with an emphasis on competing in an individualistic way. Students who have made considerable personal and financial sacrifices to participate in advanced professional training would prefer jobs that show their middle-class standing, and salaries and lifestyle opportunities commensurate with their middle-class grooming. There is compelling evidence to suggest that many counselors are drawn toward working with the young, attractive, verbal, intelligent, and successful client group described by the acronym YAVIS (Schofield, 1964, cited by Robinson-Wood, 2017) rather than working with clients from lower social classes who speak nonstandard English and express themselves in slang and street talk. This tendency is cause for concern in counselor education programs, and counselors who are committed to working in an intercultural way need to address their own assumptions on these issues.

Therapists and Class

For many therapists, it is easy to overlook the constraining social factors pertaining to class and socio-economic status that are impacting their clients. The isolation, self-loathing, and immobilization that occurs for families struggling to survive in poor urban communities can be downplayed. When therapists understand the power of class and socioeconomic factors in shaping people's identities and aspirations, they can help clients feel understood and accepted. Feelings of humiliation, remorse, guilt, and resentment can be alleviated, freeing the individual or family to draw on family and community resources that were not previously available to them.

Counselors and therapists must be prepared to own their socioeconomic privilege, where it exists, and to be watchful about how their class differs from that of their clients and how this gulf may impact the therapeutic relationship. It is not wrong to be economically privileged. The important issue is not *being* privileged as much as how one *uses* one's privilege. If it is used to make a difference in the lives of others who are less privileged, then there should be no criticism. In order to start making such a difference, counselors need to develop consciousness of their own social class influences and be careful of imposing their own class-related assumptions on their clients. Such middle-class markers as speaking standard English can become barriers for therapists whose clients have not learned to look, speak, and act like the middle class. Counselors can, however, work intentionally at minimizing such barriers.

McGoldrick and Hardy (2019) make the point that therapists who are representative of dominant groups, such as the middle class, tend to view their own values as the norm, and therefore must be careful not to judge the meaning of client behaviors or impose their own methods and timetable for when change should occur. They suggest that sometimes even when behavior does not represent a therapist's humanitarian or equitable values, we must understand the cultural context in which a behavior has developed, even as we try to change it. Respectful collaborative conversations about therapists' class dilemmas in therapy can guard against therapists' imposition of social class judgments on individuals of a class different from their own. As we have emphasized repeatedly in this book, it is essential that counseling approaches and theories be examined and redeveloped to address the discourses (historical and current) that underpin present attitudes regarding social class and how it impacts the counseling process.

On the other hand, counselors who have themselves experienced shame and humiliation pertaining to poverty and the prejudices against those who belong to the working class can be immensely positive resources in the lives of poverty-stricken clients. Specifically, therapists can help clients locate the source of their shame and humiliation in the wider cultural practices of the community, rather than inside their character or personal foibles.

But social class differences do not occur only between the middle-class counselor and the working-class client. It can also be challenging for working-class counselors to work with wealthy clients without being intimidated. In this context, counselors may become sensitive to the inadequacies of their physical environment and may evaluate their physical space as not worthy of their client and imagine being negatively judged by their client. Kottler, Montgomery, and Shepard (2004) describe how listening to clients talk about their successes can leave therapists feeling ashamed and inadequate about their own lives. Therapists are just as prone as everybody else to measuring their self-worth according to their financial achievements.

Implications of Poverty and Class for Counseling

Poor or economically disenfranchised clients may perceive the counselor who is middle class (even when she is of similar ethnicity) to have "bought into" Anglo American, middle-class values and cultural practices. Or they may have difficulty disclosing problems to counselors for fear of being judged, out of the middle- and upper-class tendency to vilify the poor. Overtly naming clients' possibly distrustful responses is a helpful way to proceed. For example, a middle-class counselor attempting to build trust with a client from a lower socioeconomic grouping might say, "I notice that you look very uneasy talking to me. We have already established that we are of the same ethnic background, but I am wondering whether you distrust me because my way of talking is very different from yours. It would be really helpful to me if you can be really honest with me and identify any barriers that you think might be getting in the way of our working together."

In many communities where counseling is a foreign practice, there may be significant barriers that keep families from taking advantage of counseling services. The barriers are even greater when these communities are poor and economically disenfranchised. In these communities, people will often take advantage of help from other extended family members, from a family friend, or from somebody deemed to have healing powers, such as a minister or priest. Counselors can play an important role in supporting families' efforts to take advantage of such local resources rather than competing with them.

Linguistic differences and problems with physical accessibility are further barriers between client and counselor. The counselor's knowledge of the language and dialect of the client can be crucial in providing assistance. Counselors who are familiar with nonstandard English can build strong empathy with their clients. There are almost always dialect differences between classes. For example, in some African American communities, a counselor's fluency in ebonics can be a powerful resource for counselors. Understanding and respecting the speech patterns of different cultural communities helps build the kind of counselor–client rapport that is prerequisite to effective counseling.

Counselors who have access to middle-class privilege (perhaps by means of their own social mobility) must be watchful of how they use this privilege with economically disadvantaged clients. Families from lower-class communities can be jealous, cynical, and untrusting of a counselor's economic privileges. Sometimes counselors are tempted to distance themselves from the effects of poverty because of the level of struggle they witness their clients experiencing. Financial hardship may depress client motivation and engagement with the counseling process. Hopelessness caused by the daily struggle to survive does not typically motivate clients to eagerly engage in counseling interactions. Counselors who have been subjected to poverty in their own lives need to remember the experience and empathize.

But to do so, they may have to struggle against an inclination to distance themselves from their own memories of the shame, humiliation, and daily grind they were subjected to in their childhood.

Middle-class clients, on the other hand, may appear to be highly motivated toward the promise of upward economic and social mobility. However, in the desire to "keep up with the Joneses," they may compromise their personal convictions in an effort to "look the part" and achieve material success. Middle-class clients may have suppressed feelings that contradict class-oriented goals of perfection, beauty, and what Jeanne Slattery (2004) calls "interpersonal smoothness." When emphasis is placed on what is expected rather than on what is personally valued, private aspirations for one's life can be compromised. Good counseling can explore the dilemmas that result.

By contrast, some people in lower socioeconomic groups are less concerned about people pleasing—especially when it comes to addressing authority figures. Counselors are often perceived to be authority figures and can be the target of angry and cynical responses by clients who have suffered at the hands of other authority figures. Poor clients may even anticipate adversarial interactions from middle-class professionals and adopt a position of expecting neither to be heard nor to have their strong feelings (including anger) validated. Day-to-day suffering can cause people to develop a tough and invulnerable exterior in which strong, angry emotions serve a protective function.

Whereas middle-class clients may be concerned with attaining beauty and perfection, many lower socioeconomic communities prize resilience, strength, perseverance, and outspokenness. Counselors can provide acknowledgment of these different value systems. Lower-class directness of verbal and physical expression may not conform to middle-class cultural conventions of how to deal with strong emotions. Appreciating these differences as cultural styles can help counselors to not be afraid of such intense emotions.

Response to Chapter 12

PILAR HERNÁNDEZ-
WOLFE, PHD, LMFT

Pilar Hernández-Wolfe is an associate professor in the Marriage, Couple & Family Therapy Program, Lewis & Clark Graduate School of Education and Counseling. She was born and raised in Colombia. She is heterosexual, cisgender, able-bodied, and middle class. In the United States, she is an immigrant and a woman of color. Her areas of interest involve traumatic stress and resilience, the animal-human bond, ecopsychology and Indigenous knowledges relative to healing.

The authors outline three general guidelines to challenge the negative impact of "totalizing" assumptions about class and poverty: (a) understanding the processes by which "the poor" come to internalize feelings of inferiority and failure and exhibit helplessness as the result of cultural interpretations that they are invited to make of themselves in the context in which they live; (b) opening up opportunities in the counseling process to contest the negative identity conclusions these individuals have internalized from the cultural and economic contexts of their lives; and (c) assisting clients in developing qualities, skill sets, hope, and a vision that build the resilience, strength, and perseverance necessary to survive in tough and unforgiving communities.

I would like to call attention to one more way to challenge the negative impact of class-based views on the poor: listening to, tracking, and elaborating on the subjective perception that clients have of their social status. In spite of the real lack of economic resources and quality education and services, and the presence of multiple social ills, it is important to explore how clients perceive their social status in relation to their families and communities. Tapping into people's construction of their social status might prove pivotal in facilitating therapeutic change. The following story illustrates a therapeutic relationship in which many social location factors were salient. However, I would like to emphasize the importance of social status to illustrate my point.

I met Carmen when working at a community mental health center serving low-income clients in New York. She was a client assigned to me after intake with a common description given to female clients—"depressed." Carmen showed symptoms of depression, and at a first glance she fit the profile of many other clients we served: middle-aged, currently unemployed, and living alone, with a high school education, a family history of alcoholism and abuse, a personal history of abusive relationships with men, and two children in their early 20s.

Carmen was soft-spoken and verbal. During our first sessions she candidly shared her personal history and current troubles with me. Carmen was from Puerto Rico and I was from Colombia. Carmen grew up on the island, but her family had migrated to New York in search of better opportunities. However, their economic situation never changed. They struggled to make ends meet. I was an immigrant with a middle-class upbringing and doctoral-level education currently living a middle-class life in the United States.

In spite of these class differences, I realized that we both shared an interest in spirituality. I noticed that she mentioned spirituality a few times here and there in our conversations, and I "knew" that her bracelets and collars had a spiritual meaning based on my knowledge of curanderismo and alternative forms of spirituality. When I engaged her in talking with me about her spiritual beliefs, I tapped in to a treasure full of resources. *Carmen was a spiritual priestess.* Carmen's construction of her social status in relation to her family and community and her actual standing in her social circle played a fundamental role in her perception of who she was as a Puerto Rican woman, mother, and community member. She was a healer, like me. I believe that there were two elements that changed the nature of the therapeutic relationship at this point: (a) she felt treated with the respect that she deserved as a spiritual priestess, and (b) we were able to discuss how healers might not be able to heal themselves. Together we embarked on a process of learning from each other about healing. She helped me understand the meaning of her depressive symptoms in relation to the spiritual test that she had to overcome, but until then had not been successful at mastering. I helped her understand the family legacies around gender, class, sexual orientation, and ethnicity that influenced her experience of abusive relationships with men. I tapped into strengths based on her social status: her power, responsibility, and ability to assert and advocate for herself. We integrated our knowledges to help her overcome the spiritual test that the master spirits had given her. This test involved mourning the loss of a romantic relationship, identifying its abusive aspects, and making the changes necessary to prevent further emotional abuse from happening. We culminated our work with a letting-go ritual at a place near the ocean. At the end of our 18 sessions, Carmen was not taking any medication and the depressive symptoms had disappeared.

I believe that therapeutic change was facilitated by multiple factors, as is the case in any therapeutic relationship. Looking back as I reflect on this therapeutic experience, I think that discovering, acknowledging, and bringing into therapy Carmen's social status as it mattered to her in her community helped us anchor our work to her belief system and strengths. This required that I acknowledged and decentered myself from the middle-class education I was socialized in, and connected through another point of reference relative to change, healing, and relationship. When I was able to use my expert and middle-class knowledge and training as a resource to be considered amongst other knowledges, she and I had truly built a collaborative relationship. From that vantage point of her social position, we were peers.

Discussion Questions

1. What are three ways that your own socioeconomic background might influence or affect the way you work with clients of a different socioeconomic background than yourself?
2. What are some differences in how those from a lower socioeconomic background might view seeing a therapist in comparison to their higher socioeconomic counterparts?
3. Have you ever made assumptions about another's socioeconomic background only to find out that you were mistaken? If so, based on what observations or inferences were you making your assumption? How did you come to realize that you were mistaken in your assumptions?
4. Name some of the privileges that those of a higher socioeconomic status enjoy when it comes to seeing a therapist.

Models of Community

C ommunities, cities, nations, and international bodies must all find a way to respond to cultural diversity. To do so, they must fashion some model of a community in which relations between cultural groups are structured. They must have some image in mind of how cultural relations might look; some sense of ideal community, within which social groups are subsumed. Such an ideal community may not even exist in the present but instead represents a project to work toward. At the very least, communities will develop a social formula as a basis for including immigrant newcomers, recognizing indigenous populations, and providing social inclusion for former slave populations. In this chapter, we shall map out some possible models of community and seek to make sense of them. These are all models that have been recognized, articulated, and sometimes argued over in the last hundred years.

In many counseling texts, even though they focus primarily on working with individuals, we can detect a background imagined community to which a person might aspire to belong. It may be a community that is equitable and just, for example, or warm and sensitive, or respectful of responsible assertiveness. The word *multicultural* in the discourse of multicultural counseling refers more to a community than to an individual, more to social relations than to intrapersonal struggles; and the word *interculturality* also emphasizes knowledge production out of reciprocal encounters among communities. Yet counseling practice is enormously influenced by the theoretical, philosophical, and day-to-day "in-use" ethics, values, and beliefs that guide counselors and therapists in how they work with clients on a one-on-one basis. Counselors might not explain what they do by referencing a model of community, but they will nevertheless be implicitly influenced by larger ideas about what kind of outcome they want to achieve with their clients. Reflecting on and naming the background social processes already at work in our day-to-day lives will give us a language with which to name, challenge, or embrace the models of community advocated in our contemporary modernist society. In addition, by exploring discrete models of community, we can more clearly articulate the political, economic, and social forces bearing down on the fields of counseling, psychology, and psychiatry and shaping of the multicultural field of counseling.

In this chapter, we will explore the genealogy of the melting pot model of community and consider the role it plays in counseling and therapy to support the cultural practices accompanying individualism. We will also give an account of the social forces of segregation in North America and elsewhere as we consider the role of models of segregated service delivery in the helping fields. Dominant multicultural counseling models advocated today have to some extent arisen out of the tensions between culturally specific models of counseling and culturally universal models. Culture-specific models align at least partially with a segregationist model of community. They include, for example, the cultural matching models, where client and counselor are matched by racial membership, by gender, or by religion or sexual orientation. Universal models of counseling align more with integrative models of community. The background histories and contemporary expressions of those segregation and integration models will be examined later in this chapter. In addition, counseling implications of the social movements spurring civil rights, affirmative action, biculturalism, and cultural pluralism will be investigated.

Charles Taylor (2004) refers to this kind of image of a community as a "social imaginary." By this he means something like an implicit sense of how cultural relations might be organized in practice, even if such a sense has not been articulated as a grand idea. He distinguishes carefully between a social imaginary and a theory. The latter is more formal and sometimes may embody a social imaginary. A social imaginary, as Taylor uses the term, is a construction that can be deduced from social practices. His focus is not on academic theorizing so much as on "the way ordinary people 'imagine' their social surroundings" (p. 23). Such images are shared by large groups of people, are often expressed in stories or legends, and give legitimacy to a range of common practices. Taylor's main concern was to articulate some of the major social imaginaries that have evolved in and can serve to characterize the modern era. These are constructs like "the economy," the democratic notion of "popular sovereignty," the "rights" of the individual, and the secular state. Taylor does not extend the concept of the social imaginary to relations between cultures, but we want to use it here for our own purposes to describe implicit models of community that set up cultural relations in particular forms.

There are many different models that can serve this purpose. Which version will apply is usually decided by the group that has political dominance, frequently in the shadow of a history of colonization. Each policy model in effect communicates a message to minority groups, such as, "Come and make sure that you become like us," or "You will never be like us, but we'll tolerate your presence as long as you don't demand too much," or "You can stay for a while, but expect to return home rather than outstay your welcome." Many of the problems that people struggle with on a personal level, and sometimes bring to counselors, are the downstream effects of these messages, and their shaping effects on people's lives can be traced back.

In the modern world, we have developed the concept of populations who can be governed (see Dean, 1999; Foucault, 2000; Rose, 1999). These populations represent categories of belonging for groups of people. In order to be governed, they are first defined in language, often in law. Individuals are assigned membership of these categories through some process of decision-making. Policies are then determined about how populations of people will be counted, treated, legitimated or excluded, manipulated, and, in the worst cases, expelled or eliminated. Counseling is just one of the practices that becomes part of this matrix.

A series of models have been developed for the purpose of developing public policies for the managing and governing of populations of people. Each of these models has been drawn from the discourse of the day and from the available social imaginaries. Each has also been elaborated to some degree in academic knowledge and discussed in public fora of various kinds. The necessity of governing populations of people has led to decisions about how and on what terms people with allegiances to varied cultural traditions will be included in, or excluded from, the mainstream society. Much of this governing function has been administered by the state, by Government with a capital G, through its policing functions, its immigration policies, and its executive spending priorities. Less commonly noticed, however, is the degree to which governing functions have been dispersed throughout a range of bodies. Corporations, health systems, education systems, and the media all exercise part of the function of governing populations of people and of managing how cultural groups will be invited to relate to each other. Each governing body may operate on a slightly different variation of the dominant model of the day for cultural relations. Nevertheless, there is often a rough consensus about the model that everyone knows and tries to operate from. From time to time, however, there may be contests over which model should dominate.

Following Foucault, Nikolas Rose (1990) has proposed that counselors and other mental health practitioners also play a part in the governing of people's lives through their participation in what he calls the "psy complex." The term is an analogical reference to the military-industrial complex (named as such by Dwight Eisenhower) that governs people's lives in other ways. The question that arises is how various counseling practices attempt to govern people's lives. To what sorts of ends do they aspire? What assumptions of cultural relations are, perhaps inadvertently, built in? Our aim is to invite counselors to think carefully about the choices they make. As counselors work with their clients, what kind of world are they seeking to contribute to? What sorts of structural arrangement of cultural relations do particular counseling practices support and reproduce? For that matter, what sorts of structural arrangements do particular practices resist and disrupt? The multicultural agenda requires counselors to distinguish among possible visions of the world and to make informed choices about how they will commit themselves in practice. The intercultural agenda adds to this vision and in our view takes it further. We outline it below.

It is commonplace to suggest that the need to manage life in the midst of diversity is a new demand and that we have never been so diverse. People talk glibly about how "we are becoming more diverse." How accurate is this assumption? It refers, perhaps, to shifts in the demographic trends that shape proportions of identified ethnic groups in the United States, especially the proportion of the population who are identified as White in census data: from 83.5% in 1970 to 69.1% in 2000 (Iceland, 2004). The assumption that we are becoming more diverse, however, deserves further questioning. In the first place, it relies on the existing categories of census data, particularly on the categories of race that are specified by the discourse of the day. These are not fixed categories and have gone through a series of changes historically. The assumption also deserves to be examined in terms of who is saying it and from what background they are drawing in order to say it. It is possible to argue, from the point of view of a minority group, that diversity has always been there and that not much has changed, or perhaps that, as the group's own numbers grow, diversity is actually decreasing. Perhaps, too, there have been shifts in public policy that have made the issue of diversity more visible to those who belong to groups whose traditional privileges have become more visible. The assumption of greater diversity nevertheless persists and often serves to inject a sense of urgency into the conversations about difference, diversity, and cultural relations.

As we study the various models of community that follow, we can notice that none of these models arose out of a social vacuum. Each was a response to particular historical events and trends. Each also gestures toward a future horizon. Each has particular communities of people in mind and rarely encompasses all possible contexts. Some are constructed to address situations of mass immigration.

Others address ongoing relations between settlers and colonizers on the one hand and indigenous populations on the other. Still others are rationalizations of social relations around which the labor market, another social imaginary, is organized. Moreover, in different countries around the world, the models have emerged differently. In highlighting interculturality in this book, we are aware that we are directing your attention towards a social imaginary that has arisen in Latin America and is not as common in the United States as we believe it should be. However, parallels can often be drawn between social imaginaries that are divergently named.

The Melting Pot

In 1908, a play opened for the first time in Washington, DC. It was written by a Jewish playwright named Israel Zangwill, who had immigrated to the United States from England. The play has long since been forgotten, but its title has entered the public lexicon. The play was called *The Melting Pot* (Udelson, 1990). The image was that of a crucible in which various metals are liquefied and then mixed into a new alloy. It was a reference to the vast wave of immigration from Europe that was taking place at the time. Some 18 million people entered the United States as new citizens between 1890 and 1920, first from Ireland and Germany and later from Italy and eastern Europe. A significant proportion of them were Jewish people escaping from various forms of anti-Semitic discrimination, while others were escaping grinding poverty in search of new economic opportunity. The immigrants spoke a variety of languages and brought with them a range of religious and cultural practices.

It is commonly agreed that the melting pot metaphor captured the spirit of what was expected of people by the dominant discourse of the day as the immigrants entered their adopted country. Their cultural identity and traditions would be melted down and they would blend with the dominant Anglo Protestant majority and develop an identity around their newfound position as U.S. citizens. The new alloy that was to be formed was "American." They would feed off the American dream and contribute to the American democratic tradition. The assumption was that immigrants should let go of their cultural past and enthusiastically embrace their new national identity as their preferred cultural identity. The immigrants were expected to assimilate to the cultural customs of the new world, rather than the new world being expected to accommodate itself to include the cultural practices that the immigrants brought with them. It was a one-way accommodation. Theodore Roosevelt made this clear: "There can be no fifty-fifty Americanism in this country. ... There is room only for 100 per cent Americanism, only for those who are American and nothing else" (cited by Rumbaut, 2003, p. 237).

For example, immigrants were expected to learn English and let go of their native languages. Advocates for this model frequently pointed to the immigrants who began in waged jobs and rapidly took up entrepreneurial opportunities and started their own businesses. The image of a society formed in the melting pot was one in which all the contributing "metals" are melted down to form a new U.S. American identity. It was a vision of equality in a sense, since in theory all cultural backgrounds were to be melted down in order to contribute to the new alloy. However, it was also clear that it never quite worked that way. In the first place, there was never any expectation that the existing White, Anglo, Protestant majority should be required to go through the melting process and surrender their culture to help form the new one. It was only the immigrants who were required to assimilate. Secondly, the metaphor was only ever extended to those from Europe who did not disturb the color bar. You could assimilate as long as you were White. Africans and Asians, for example, were not included in this model of community (Birman, 1994). In 1882, for example, the United States Congress passed the Chinese Exclusion Act specifically to ensure that immigrants from China would have minimal impact on the emergent U.S. American culture (Atkinson, Morten, & Sue, 1993). Third, the melting pot metaphor was primarily located in and limited to the experience of New York. It, therefore, was of less significance for areas of the United States as different from New York as the South. Even in New York, it was invoked principally in relation to European migrants and was not so readily applied to African American migrants from the South or to the later waves of Puerto Rican, Dominican, Jamaican, and Asian immigrants. Entrepreneurship has not been as possible a pathway to full admission to the U.S. American dream for the later waves of immigrants.

Moreover, by the 1960s it was clear that the melting pot ideal was not even working. Nathan Glazer and Daniel Patrick Moynihan (later Senator Moynihan) published their classic analysis of this social imaginary entitled *Beyond the Melting Pot* in 1963 (Glazer & Moynihan, 1970). It argued that, while immigrant populations did abandon their native languages and work hard to learn English, they did not on the whole melt their cultural practices down and adopt "U.S. American" lifestyles. Rather, their own cultural expressions evolved in a new context in a wide variety of patterns.

It is interesting to note that the melting pot metaphor was also taken up as an officially sanctioned social imaginary in the new state of Israel. It has since been abandoned, but it was used for a time to organize Israeli thinking about the bringing together of Jewish people from a wide range of countries of origin who brought with them widely divergent cultural practices.

What is now to be made of the melting pot idea? One criticism of it is its tendency to produce cultural blandness, to remove much of the colorful richness of cultural difference from view. If we all melt into one culture, we lose some of the leavening influences that different perspectives can bring. We merge into some kind of drab homogeneity. We might also lose a sense of the difference between modernist cultural expressions and the other streams of Western cultural tradition that have been subsumed under it.

More worrying is the possibility that the melting pot might serve as a ruse to mask something more unpalatable. Behind the scenes of the melting pot crucible, it can be argued, lies a process of cultural domination. As John Berry (2001) comments, when strongly enforced, the melting pot easily "becomes a pressure cooker" (p. 620). The melting pot idea refers really to a process of cultural absorption (Entwhistle, 2000) of all comers into the dominant White, Anglo culture. Those who do not trace themselves back to this tradition should take care to mimic it if they want to get ahead in the "real" world. The process of assimilation it requires means abandoning one's cultural origins and traditions. From the modern point of view, this seems like a tragic loss, but it has to be remembered, as Dina Birman (1994) points out, that in the early-20th century common discourse considered this a better option than the alternative, which was to remain on the margins of the new society.

There are those who argue that the melting pot metaphor still has worth (see Entwhistle, 2000). They claim that some kind of inclusive political vision is needed, because the alternative multicultural vision does not clearly enough specify how to settle intercultural disputes in situations where differences rub against each other. Some worry that multiculturalism wanders off into the marshes of relativism and eventually gets bogged down there. They yearn for a return to the days before postmodern critiques disturbed the settled certainties of modernism.

Our belief is that such a return is not possible. Multiculturalism, interculturalism, and postmodernism are not just academic ideas. They are responses to the material experiences of people who demand more inclusion and more opportunity in life. They are attempts to articulate people's yearnings for something more and their protests against the limits of what is. As attempts to map out a new vision of a social imaginary, they need to be taken seriously, even though there might be flaws in them.

In the counseling field, we might recognize expressions of the melting pot ideal by the tendency to de-emphasize cultural difference and to emphasize the commonalities of culture. The expectation would be that new immigrants should accommodate themselves to the dominant culture, learn English as soon as possible, and seek to get ahead as individuals in the modern world. Hence, this social imaginary would not expect counselors to go out of their way to affirm the cultural knowledges of an immigrant's home country. Bilingual counselors would not be a major priority in schools and mental health settings. This imaginary would have counselors focus on the future and consign the past to history. Each client would be treated first and foremost as an individual human being, rather than as a member of a cultural community, and the focus of counseling would be primarily on individual intrapsychic phenomena. There are, in fact, many approaches to counseling that work in just this way. Their theories are about individuals primarily and not so much about how cultural patterns get inscribed into individual lives. Such theories fit well with a melting pot social imaginary. However, if we are not endeavoring to implement the melting pot agenda, then perhaps we need to look beyond counseling approaches that are focused in this direction.

Segregation

An alternative to the melting pot model of community is the social policy of segregation. It is founded on the assumption that relations between social groups are less troubled when these groups are kept apart. Its ideal community is one in which racial or other groups maintain *separate but equal* communities. Groups of people live parallel lives with minimal interaction. However, in its idealist forms, the segregation or separatism model has usually operated as a smoke screen for practices of domination in which one group maintains control of the separate conditions of the other group and ensures ongoing second-rate levels of opportunity. Such was the case in the long-standing policy of apartheid in South Africa, which finally broke down in the 1990s. It was also the case in the Warsaw ghetto during World War II. There, Jewish people were herded into a separate community as a precursor to being shipped off to the Nazi death camps. These are two of the most well-known examples of segregation used to mask power relations of extreme inequality.

In the United States, the Jim Crow laws in the South also formalized relations between Whites and Blacks in a pattern of segregation. Separate housing, restaurants, shopping facilities, water fountains, bathhouses, schools, and churches were established. Seating on public transport was separate. Intermarriage was prohibited and White children could not be adopted by Black families. White motorists even had right of way over Black motorists at intersections. In order to maintain these separatist laws, voting rights for non-Whites were severely restricted. As in South Africa under apartheid, separate clearly did not mean equal. These laws were challenged and abolished during the Civil Rights Movement of the 1960s.

Around the world, there exist other examples of communities where groups of people are kept separate by legislative or administrative policies of segregation. Sometimes this is the result of inter-communal conflict and segregation is used as a policy to reduce opportunity for contact to produce outbreaks of violence. In Ireland, for example, the "partition" was introduced between the north and the south for this reason. Catholic and Protestant peoples have continued to live alongside each other in Northern Ireland but in segregated communities. In response to ongoing troubles over many decades, the civil rights of the Catholic community especially have been restricted. In Cyprus, since the civil war in 1974, Greek Cypriots and Turkish Cypriots have lived in a totally segregated situation, with a border between them policed by United Nations troops.

In Israel and Palestine, a similar situation exists where Jews and Palestinians are strictly segregated by law and by military force. The Israeli government is currently building a wall around the Palestinian community. It is being built for political reasons, but one of its effects is to further entrench segregation. There are other segregations in Israel, too, which are less entrenched by operations of administrative power and are more voluntary, such as the segregation of the old city of Jerusalem into its Moslem, Jewish, Christian, and Armenian quarters. Israeli Arabs live in their own segregated communities, as do orthodox religious Jews. And the Druze people live in their own segregated community.

Segregation is not always achieved by legislative fiat. This is especially true of residential segregation, which is defined as "the unequal distribution of groups across space" (Iceland, 2004, p. 250). Often such segregation is achieved by individuals' "mobility decisions" (Iceland, 2004), which are in turn influenced by a range of socioeconomic factors and personal preferences. Housing discrimination can play a role, too; for example, in the steering of African American home buyers and renters into certain neighborhoods. There is also a range of social policies that can effectively produce segregated communities, even when they are not required by law. The establishment of expensive gated communities achieves the effect of segregation when there is economic disparity between communities.

Social policy decisions to deliberately build high-rise housing projects right alongside existing African American neighborhoods are also a case in point (Iceland, 2004). Indeed, the most common form of segregation is that established along socioeconomic lines (Iceland, 2004). Wealthier and poorer people do not tend to live beside each other, but withdraw into their own communities (although it is only the wealthy who have the full range of choice). Land values and house prices serve to govern such forms of segregation (as the poor cannot afford a wide range of choice about where to live), and in many instances de facto segregation along racial and ethnic lines tends to piggyback on economic segregation. The growth of ghettos or barrios in the middle of cities or on their outskirts houses the poor and the working class in ethnic enclaves. There is also segregated housing on the basis of age (Iceland, 2004), often fully supported by legislation and public administration. It occurs in the establishment of retirement communities that welcome people only over a certain age.

The development of ethnic homogeneity in what are often referred to as ethnic enclaves is enhanced by the common inner-city phenomenon of "White flight" to the suburbs (Iceland, 2004). No one legislates for White flight. It happens as a result of the personal choices of thousands of individuals and has the effect of producing a pattern of segregation. Research has suggested that Whites have the strongest preferences for living with their own people (Iceland, 2004). As a social trend, segregation is never completely uniform, of course. There are always exceptions, but the exceptions allow those who refuse to see patterns of differential opportunity in life to make the claim that people choose their own lifestyles and that, therefore, there is no issue of injustice involved. As we have shown in Chapter 6, this is a naive view of how power works. In this way, nevertheless, the existence of exceptions works to support the ongoing effects of segregation.

Jonathan Kozol (1992) presented a graphic picture of the results of residential segregation in major U.S. cities. His focus was on educational opportunities in poor and predominantly Black neighborhoods. He showed how a policy of unofficial segregation works just as effectively as any official policy to keep people divided along racial lines with regard to housing, employment, and educational opportunity. Schools in poor neighborhoods in parts of New York and Chicago that are more than 90% African American may not have segregation enforced by law, as schools in the South did before the Civil Rights Movement, but they are effectively segregated all the same. Across town, there are usually suburban schools that are predominantly White. In parts of Los Angeles, there are schools that are predominantly Mexican. Nor is the segregation a case of "separate but equal," as Kozol also shows. Funding for education is sharply differential, and the White kids in the wealthier neighborhoods get usually twice as much spent on their education as the children in the poorer neighborhoods. Kozol presents a series of examples of schools in poorer neighborhoods that do not offer students the same counseling services that children in middle-class neighborhoods are offered. The same is true of quality teachers, because teachers are often paid substantially less in poorer neighborhoods than they would be in wealthier communities. The kind of education offered differs markedly as a result. Often the effects of segregation and differential educational opportunities are then blamed on the poor and minority families themselves. "They are not motivated to learn" and "The parents don't care about their kids' education" are typical comments that circulate in the discourse that justifies the persisting inequalities. Despite the gains made by the Civil Rights Movement in removing official segregation, unofficial de facto segregation is still firmly in place in the cities of the North as much as in the South, and it has the same effects on people's lives as if it were officially sanctioned.

What is happening to residential segregation? Is it diminishing in response to civil rights changes? Or is it increasing in response to recent immigration patterns? John Iceland (2004) has reviewed United States census data on this subject and concludes that the pattern is mixed. Segregation of Blacks in relation to Whites has decreased modestly in recent decades, but segregation is increasing with regard to Hispanics and Asians. He suggests that it is White people who are most sensitive to desegregation and most averse to multiethnic areas. On the other hand, the development of more multiethnic living areas has allowed Hispanics and Asians to serve as "buffers" in the relationship between Whites and Blacks, which has assisted the desegregation of Blacks in the United States to a modest extent.

Not all segregation, however, is imposed. Voluntary segregation, or more accurately a chosen separation, appears in many forms among many social groups. It may arise from the desire of people with shared interests and backgrounds to meet together and support each other. Therefore, there have been forms of separatism that are justified by their supporters in terms of their ability to build strategic power and strengthen the voice of a community. The Black Power movement of the 1970s was an example of this. Many people also choose to live in the ghettos out of preference for being close to family and their own people. Voluntary separation also extends well beyond racial and ethnic groups. Members of the deaf community, for example, have asserted their preference to be together with others who share their language and perspective on life, and to have their own schools and their own university (Gallaudet University in Washington, DC). Feminists have argued for social spaces that can be occupied only by women so that they can listen to themselves and share voices that might be silenced by men if brought into the larger community. Gay bars are an example of separate entertainment venues that aim to be places where people can experience what it is like to be who they are.

Some may object to the term segregation because of its negative connotations. Separation, even temporary separation, has certainly carried a much more positive connotation, as people with similarities have banded together to protect a fragile, often developmental, sense of who they might become when they eventually project this into the world. The theme of becoming introduces a sense of history that is important to appreciate in order to understand the steps that groups of people take in this regard and the variety of political and other objectives they might hold dear. We certainly support such moves as helpful and they should not be misunderstood as situations needing forced integration. For example, in New Zealand, there are now a number of Maori members of parliament. This would quite likely not be the case if the Maori electoral roll had not for over 100 years protected Maori seats in Parliament. We also want to make it clear that voluntary separations are not motivated by the same impulse as when segregation is imposed from above, such as under Jim Crow or apartheid.

In the field of counseling, segregation is largely a question of access to counseling. Where there is residential segregation, then social services will often experience de facto segregation as a downstream effect. More deliberate policies of separatism have been advocated in the counseling field on the basis of social justice agendas. A frequent expression of this principle is the desire to match clients and counselors along the dividing lines by which social groups are defined. Hence, some argue, only women should counsel women, only African Americans should counsel African Americans, only gays and lesbians should counsel gays and lesbians, only deaf people should counsel deaf people, and so forth. Often such decisions are made on the basis of client preferences. When they are made on the basis of agency policy, they are more likely expressions of segregation.

Integration

The first response to the inequalities of forced segregation has often been to call for the opposite social imaginary of integration. Rather than keeping people in separate social institutions, integration throws them together again. Integration stresses the common humanity of people of different cultural backgrounds and invites equality of opportunity through inclusion of difference. It needs to be understood as a response to segregation, and usually to enforced segregation rather than voluntary segregation. Without a previous history of segregation, the social imaginary of integration makes no sense.

Particularly after the overthrow of the Jim Crow laws in the South of the United States in the 1960s, integration was a common catchcry. Rosa Parks's protest about segregated seating on buses led eventually to integrated seating. The *Brown v. Board of Education* decision (1954) led to integrated schooling in the sense that public schools accepted Black and White students into the same schools and classrooms. Integrated housing was harder to achieve, because it was a socioeconomic as well as a racial issue. But some local authorities, particularly in smaller towns, have pursued deliberate policies of granting housing permits and building public housing according to a pepper pot formula that prevents poor areas from developing into large ghettos. Such policies are built on the basis of a social imaginary of integration.

In the United States during the 1970s and 1980s, the cause of integration in education was pursued by means of "busing" students across town to schools outside their immediate neighborhoods in order to ensure racial balance in schools (Pride & Woodard, 1985). The racial composition of each school in a school district was required to reflect the composition of the district as a whole. This was generally achieved by transporting children to a school in a different area of the district. Busing was usually a court-supervised program aimed at combating the lingering effects of segregation in schooling. Without the existence of segregation, it would have made no sense. But it was in the end an unpopular policy that inconvenienced parents and students, and during the early 1990s, in response to a series of court rulings, the policy was tapered off.

One of the aims of the Americans with Disabilities Act (1990) and the Individuals with Disabilities Education Act (1975) was to counter the frequent segregation of persons with disabilities in schools. It gave rise to the mainstreaming movement in special education, which is, in principle, based on the social imaginary of integration in schooling. It envisages equality of educational provision for persons with disabilities through placing them alongside their nondisabled peers, rather than segregating them into special education facilities where they are not expected to achieve educationally to the level of their able-bodied peers.

Integration as a social imaginary has made possible some significant changes in the direction of equality. This has been particularly so with regard to rights of access, whether they be rights of access to education, voting rights, equal employment prospects, or housing. But access is not the full story. Take education, for example. Giving African American children access to the same schools as White persons does not in itself ensure that they will all receive a better education. They may well encounter substantial backlash to integration, a greater likelihood of being tracked into lower classes or special education programs, and a greater likelihood of being expelled or not graduating from high school (Blanchett, Brantlinger, & Shealey, 2005). De facto segregation of housing based on socioeconomic stratification has for many proved just as limiting as blatant segregationist housing laws (Blanchett et al., 2005), which further affects educational achievement, given that living in poverty strongly affects educational achievement (Berliner & Biddle, 1995). Integration is always a policy formed in response to situations of segregation.

Once the rigid structures of segregation have been abolished and have receded further into historical memory, then the need for ongoing assertion of integration also recedes. Integration is in the end a policy that is difference-blind. It works in contrast to discrimination by working for everyone to be treated the same. Where it is limited is in the contexts where equality does not mean equity. Equity sometimes can be obtained only by treating people differently on the basis of their differences. Clients often present to counselors with problems that result from outright discrimination. Good counseling can help a person decide how to respond in such situations. But discrimination is, by definition, intentional and overt, and many of the actions of power, as we saw in Chapter 6, are not personal or intentional but nevertheless have powerful effects. For these effects, the social imaginary of integration does not necessarily help, and therefore counselors need to equip themselves with a more sophisticated vision. Being difference-blind is not enough. We need to be sensitive to the particulars of difference in some way that goes beyond integrating them into the melting pot again.

Civil Rights

A strong social imaginary that galvanized social movements of various kinds in the 20th century is that of civil rights. As we suggested in Chapter 6, the concept of civil rights has developed as a product of the modern era. It grew out of the 18th century idea of "natural rights," as argued by John Locke. Natural rights were those that you were born with just by virtue of being human, rather than some privilege that you earned. Premodern societies would not have been likely to think in this way at all. Gradually the idea of natural rights evolved into what we now call "human rights." They have since been embodied in a variety of landmark legal documents in many countries around the world (the U.S. Constitution was one of the earliest examples of this trend) and into international documents like the United Nations' Universal Declaration of Human Rights, the Geneva Conventions, and so forth. Once the idea of human or civil rights was written into constitutional documents and into laws, it became a lever to be used by social movements seeking to lay legal claims to personal rights in the face of the systematic workings of power to deny these rights to groups of people on the basis of race, gender, class, or disability.

In other words, the concept of civil rights has become not just a philosophical idea; it has become a legal term. Claims for civil rights, as we know them, are in the end legal claims. This means that they are the kinds of claims that can be established through legal means, and the limits of the civil rights social imaginary is likely to be marked by the limits of what can be achieved by the application of law. Laws are by their nature built on universal principles applied across a range of social relations in a way that is supposed to ensure orderly resolution of conflicts. Not all experiences of injustice are illegal. Nor can every expression of power relations be legislated against. Laws cannot reach into the hearts of people and remove hatred or prejudice. Laws cannot exert complete control over discourse either, although they can play a role in determining which discourses will be granted authority and sanction. So there will always be limits to what can be achieved in the way of social change by the application of universal principles through the law.

The social imaginary of civil rights has nevertheless been utilized to powerful effect. The latter half of the 20th century has been notable for a series of assertions of power by cultural groups on the basis of claims of civil rights. The Black Civil Rights Movement of the 1950s and 1960s was the earliest example of this approach. It succeeded in changing the laws in the South of the United States that had institutionalized segregation. It secured legal access for African Americans to voting rights, better educational and employment opportunities, and civic participation. But it also did more than this. It drew attention to the depth of the expressions of racism in U.S. American society. In the words of Martin Luther King, Jr., it inspired people to "dream" of a more just society. Around the world, it inspired other racial and cultural groups to mount their own campaigns of civil rights and indigenous people's rights.

Did it eliminate racism? No, because legal rights and legal processes cannot change people's hearts. Did it shift the dominance of racist discourse in U.S. America or elsewhere? To a limited degree, it did, perhaps, but not completely, because laws cannot completely control discourse. If unjust, racist practices are founded on the discourse of race, then civil rights will only ever go so far to challenge them. Other methods, based on other social imaginaries, will need to take over once the limits of the rights discourse are reached.

The civil rights discourse, based in liberal humanist philosophy, was nevertheless copied by other social groups who saw what it could achieve. The women's movement of the 1970s and 1980s adopted the rhetoric of civil rights in order to advance the cause of women's rights. It challenged a range of laws and practices that rendered women less than full citizens and mounted many successful challenges to male-only exclusionary systems. After the women's movement, the gay rights movement took up the same rhetoric, as did the disability rights movement.

All of these social movements have achieved various degrees of legitimacy for their members by claiming legal rights for individual women, LGBTQ persons, persons with disabilities, and so forth. Civil rights, however, focuses on changes to laws and regulations and on how these are policed. It is a legal focus and does not respond so clearly to situations where there is no law that needs changing, merely practices that serve the purposes of power. Sexual harassment is a case in point. There have been laws passed to outlaw sexual harassment in certain workplaces, but in public and in private it often escapes the radar of the law. Often, counseling clients are experiencing problems in their relations with others that do not cross the threshold into legal rights issues, and in these circumstances the rights discourse does not have so much effectiveness.

Affirmative Action

One method of addressing inequality of opportunity for members of disadvantaged social groups is the introduction of affirmative action policies. In the United States, this has been a topic of huge controversy, because it is seen by many to run counter to the assumption of equal opportunity for individuals by giving "undeserved" preferential treatment to some. Affirmative action policies, however, are not uncommon and have often been accepted as fair without being contested. Official affirmative action policies were first instituted in all United States federal agencies (as well as private contractors with federal agencies) by President Johnson's administration in 1965 (Crosby, Iyer, Clayton, & Downing, 2003; Middleton, Flowers, & Zawaiza, 1996), although the term *affirmative action* has a history in public policy going back to the 1930s (Woodhouse, 2002). The result of Johnson's executive order was that 20% of the U.S. American labor force has since been covered to some degree by affirmative action programs.

Affirmative action can be formally defined as "voluntary and mandatory efforts undertaken by federal, state and local governments; private employers; and schools to combat discrimination and to promote equal opportunity in education and employment for all" (American Psychological Association, 2007). The initial aim of affirmative action policies was to end racial discrimination in employment. Sexual discrimination was added to this agenda by means of the Education Amendments Act of 1972 (Woodhouse, 2002). The goal of affirmative action is not to create unfairness or preferential treatment but to "address the systemic exclusion of individuals of talent, based on their gender or race, from opportunities to develop, perform, achieve and contribute" (Bill Clinton, cited by Middleton et al., 1996, p. 4). It takes aim at the effects of past injustice and seeks to eliminate existing discriminatory policies. The most frequent targets of affirmative action have been women, who are often prevented from gaining access to gender-exclusive careers and to positions of leadership through the existence of the "glass ceiling," and ethnic minorities who have been traditionally excluded from employment or educational opportunity by the existence of systematic prejudicial discourse.

A distinction can be made between active efforts to promote equality of opportunity and more passive assumptions that such equality already exists. Advocates of "equal opportunity" rather than affirmative action argue that the absence of evidence of overt discrimination can be taken to mean that equality of opportunity actually exists. There is a tendency in the United States to assume that constitutional guarantees of individual equality are sufficient to militate against prejudicial stereotyping and the effects of racist or sexist discourse. The intention of affirmative action policies, however, is to redress situations where the existence of systematic discriminatory discourse currently prevents equality of opportunity based on merit in employment or education. At their best, affirmative action policies do not recruit or promote individuals who do not merit the opportunity. They prevent the exclusion of those who do merit it.

Critics of affirmative action primarily object to the institution of quotas for members of minoritized groups, thus granting some individuals unfair, preferential treatment. For example, an affirmative action policy at the medical school at the University of California, Davis, was successfully challenged in court for listing applicants in two lists—one White and one for racial minorities—and reserving 16% of admissions for minority applicants (Crosby et al., 2003). The United States Supreme Court upheld the complaint that setting aside quotas can lead to the granting of access to some on the basis of racial identity, rather than on merit.

On the other hand, Faye Crosby and her colleagues (2003) contend that affirmative action is primarily an effort to strengthen the meritocratic distribution of opportunity. They argue that the primary effort of affirmative action is to set in place systems for monitoring the proportions of under-represented groups in workforce statistics. When such monitoring reveals unmerited preferential treatment, affirmative action policies should affirm the right of minority groups to equal treatment based on merit, and corrective action should be taken. In fact, in the realm of government employment, the institution of quotas and consequent preferential treatment for minorities has never been part of public policy in the United States. And yet the perception persists for many opponents that this is exactly what affirmative action is about.

Let us now consider the model of community envisaged in the affirmative action idea. It is clearly a policy intended for the governing of relations between social groups. It embodies the hope of creating greater social justice by ensuring a more equitable distribution of opportunity to individuals. It is based, however, on the assumption that individual merit exists and that it can be measured and estimated accurately. It relies to a large extent on a liberal humanist analysis of power relations. In this model, power is conceived of as being in the possession of individuals, and it is fairly shared if individuals from various cultural backgrounds are given proportionate opportunity. It leaves the categories of distinction along ethnic, racial, and gender lines in place and even strengthens them through turning them into facts that can be counted and measured in the workplace.

On the other hand, it involves a small shift away from the exclusively individual model of community relations. Crosby and her colleagues (2003) argue that affirmative action policies place the primary responsibility for creating social justice on the institution or company, rather than on the individual. The company or the government department has to take responsibility for actively monitoring its own practices. The onus is taken off the individual, who must otherwise register a complaint against unjust treatment and risk being accused of being a troublemaker. Crosby and her colleagues summarize evidence from psychological studies to support the existence of stereotyping and of (usually unconscious) systematic injustice in testing processes and selection criteria. They also cite evidence that opponents of affirmative action are more likely to support racist or sexist discourse. Such evidence suggests that the need for affirmative action is based on the power of racist and sexist discourse to have effects on the life chances of persons and that passive assumptions of equal opportunity do not undermine these effects.

What are the implications of this discussion about affirmative action policies for counseling? Counselors, especially career counselors, are likely to meet individuals who are in the midst of constructing educational or employment directions in their lives. As they do so, they will be experiencing the effects of employment or education practices of one kind or another, whether or not such practices are shaped by affirmative action policies. One of our counseling tasks needs to be to help individuals to make sense of the employment or education environments they live in. We believe that counselors are better equipped for this task if they have developed a strong understanding of discursive and systematic forces at work in the construction of such social contexts. This can position them to respond to clients in ways that do not encourage them to take personal responsibility for unjust situations and that also do not encourage an unrealistic sense of entitlement when they are the recipients of privilege. Another possibility is that individual clients may overestimate the influence of discriminatory discourse in situations where affirmative action policies do exist. Crosby and her colleagues refer to the phenomenon of perceived "stereotype threat" and its inhibitory effects on performance in, for example, job interviews or tests.

Counselors need to have their eyes open to the workings of injustice. They may at times need to be advocates on behalf of those on the receiving end of racist or sexist discourse. This may mean advocating the introduction of affirmative action policies where they do not exist. But counselors also need to help their clients make assessments of the world in which they live and to chart their own pathways in life. Sometimes this will mean helping them find expression for resistance to injustice. Sometimes it will mean helping them develop greater consciousness of how injustice works. Sometimes it will mean helping them name injustices that they were scarcely aware of, and sometimes it will mean helping them reconsider internalized conclusions of self-blame when they are rejected as a result of unjust practices.

Multiculturalism

A social imaginary of a new form of community that has developed in recent decades as an alternative to earlier proposals for a melting pot or for either segregation or integration is the vision of a multicultural society. The multicultural society has its historical roots in the concept of a society that grants religious toleration to people of different faiths. The ideal of religious toleration (which is by no means universal) grew out of the stalemates that emerged in Europe after centuries of religious wars. It was expressed in the Constitution of the United States as the separation of church and state. Charles Taylor (2004) traces the shift from the premodern to the modern world as being founded on the social imaginary of a more secular state. In the last few decades, the model of religious toleration has been extended beyond religious differences to cultural differences. However, as Jacques Derrida (Borradori, 2003) points out, the idea of "toleration" is a flawed one. It is in the end based on the position of the dominant group, who are entitled to exercise their magnanimity and grant a place of toleration to those who are "different." Thus, it leaves the dominant group's dominance in place, it relies on the continuance of generosity by this group, and it positions minoritized groups in the expectation that they should be vigilant for opportunities to show gratitude and accept without complaint what they have been offered. Toleration is extended like charity.

Nevertheless, despite a history of many setbacks, there have been a series of significant openings created for people who are different as a result of policies of religious toleration. For example, despite his ruthless colonization of the Irish in the 17th century, Oliver Cromwell introduced religious toleration for the Jews into England during his reign. In France, Abbé Grégoire persuaded the revolutionary council in the aftermath of the French Revolution to grant religious toleration to Jews. And it is well known that Queen Elizabeth I told Parliament as it established the Church of England that she would not "make windows into men's souls."

In the multicultural social imaginary, people are not required to relinquish their cultural distinctiveness. They are instead urged to retain it and value it and to wear it proudly for all to appreciate. Cultural difference should be given greater visibility, rather than remain hidden in the background (Entwhistle, 2000). From this perspective, those who have been cut off from their cultural history have been encouraged to find their cultural "roots" (Haley, 1976) and develop their cultural identity. Multiculturalism is about embracing cultural particularity rather than merging into the generality of the dominant culture. Searching for roots, immersing oneself in one's cultural history and traditions, centering oneself in the heart of a cultural identity—all this has been encouraged, usually at the expense of acknowledging the complexity of competing pulls.

Nowhere has the vision of a multicultural society been articulated more fully and given more formal public substance than in Canada. Multiculturalism was granted official status as Canadian government policy in 1971 and has since been written into a series of laws (Mock, 1997). The 1982 Charter of Rights and Freedoms entrenched multiculturalism in Canada as a constitutional principle, and in 1988 the Canadian Multiculturalism Act specified further the responsibilities of government departments to implement multicultural policies. This act clearly states that it "recognizes the diversity of Canadians as regards to race, national or ethnic origin, colour and religion as a fundamental characteristic of Canadian society" (Mock, 1997, p. 127).

It is instructive to look at how the meaning of multiculturalism has evolved in Canada over the last three decades. It began with the recognition of English and French as two official languages and was expanded to include the perspectives of "other" communities. In contrast to the melting pot impulse, multiculturalism was at first declared to be about programs to encourage "cultural retention and cultural sharing" (Mock, 1997, p. 123). Rather than allowing their cultural background to be melted down, new immigrants were encouraged to retain their cultural practices in a society that would celebrate differences among groups. Laws against hate crimes were introduced or strengthened. Immigration policy was liberalized.

Later, in response to ongoing dissatisfaction among cultural groups (especially aboriginal Canadians) and in the face of some racial incidents, it was realized that celebrating difference was not enough. Attention began to turn to more active policies of promoting equality. Systemic inequality required more than freedom from discrimination if it was to change significantly. It also could not be addressed by policies that focused mainly on individual freedoms. The emphasis in Canada has therefore shifted to programs that actively promote equality across a range of social institutions.

A variety of metaphors have been suggested as shorthand references to the social imaginary of a multicultural society. Rather than the melting pot, multiculturalism has envisaged the "cultural mosaic" (Benhabib, 2002; Entwhistle, 2000; Sue et al., 1998). In this image, each cultural group contributes a distinctive color to the overall picture of a society. Others have imagined a multicultural society as a "salad bowl," in which each cultural group contributes a flavor to the meal (Anderson, 2000). Another frequently used metaphor is the "tapestry," in which each different colored thread is woven into the overall effect (Entwhistle, 2000). More critically, the shallowness of multiculturalism has been questioned in that it merely celebrates differences without performing any analysis of power in cultural relations, and likening it to putting "parsley on the plate" (Wise, 2005). It adds color but little nutritional value.

The social imaginary of multiculturalism has often been invoked in the field of education. The vision of multicultural schooling is not just about access to public schools for people of all cultures. It is also about what happens at school. For example, it is about curriculum designed to be inclusive of the experiences of all students. Multiculturalism, as a social imaginary, works well for this purpose. It supports moves toward the study of a history that does not portray just White men as heroes and leave out the experience of other people (Lawrence, 1997). It urges a study of art and literature that goes outside the established canon of European art and includes artists and writers who speak to the life experience of many cultural groups. Inclusion of the stories of many peoples provides students with role models, validates their cultural identities, and gives people the experience of recognition.

Charles Taylor (1994) argues that "recognition" is one of the chief goals of multiculturalism. If policies that promote integration are difference-blind, then multiculturalism is the opposite. It pays attention when people demand to be treated differently on the basis of their cultural identity. Multiculturalism is not about equal treatment for individuals as much as it is about equal recognition of different cultural groups and equal respect for cultural practices (Taylor, 1994). One problem that critics of multiculturalism have brought up is the question of how to decide on the merits of pieces of art, music, and literature once you have disestablished the traditional canon. Multiculturalism itself does not establish grounds for decisions on this issue. Taylor (1994) suggests that such decisions will become possible only if we work toward a future horizon where diverse cultural values meet and fuse in a way that allows for cultural respect that goes beyond condescension.

However, other problems have been emerging with the multicultural vision in recent years. For example, an issue has arisen in France during the last decade over Muslim girls wearing the *hijab* headscarf to public schools (Benhabib, 2002). This was taken as a symbol of religious expression, which contradicted the modernist tradition of secularism in school. So the French government in 2004 banned the wearing of the hijab, arguing that it contradicted school dress codes. At the same time, the wearing of Christian crosses, Jewish yarmulkes, and other religious symbols was also banned. An uproar arose among the large Muslim community in France as a result. The issue is not an easy one to resolve. On the one hand, the hijab is a piece of clothing closely associated with personal modesty as it is understood from a Muslim cultural perspective. On the other hand, it is read as a religious statement and criticized from a Western feminist perspective as restrictive for women.

Moreover, as Seyla Benhabib points out, some of the students claiming the right to wear the hijab did so explicitly as a political statement, not just as a religious expression. From the perspective of government, some kind of decision that promotes equality for all is needed. One of the aims of democratic secularism in education is just such difference-blind equality. From the perspective of a minority community, however, this decision is interpreted as an instance of the cultural hegemony of the majority. They claim the right to differential recognition as a minoritized group, and special protection of their cultural practices, not just same-as-everyone equality. Official policies of multiculturalism here ran afoul of administrative decision-making. A decision was made that could not please everyone and attracted accusations of cultural hegemony.

Similar issues are raised in courts of law. Seyla Benhabib (2002) cites several examples of criminal court cases in which a defendant has successfully mounted a defense on the grounds that "my culture made me do it." Here is one example:

> In California, a young Laotian American woman is abducted from her work at Fresno State University and is forced to have intercourse against her will. Her assailant, a Hmong immigrant (one of the boat people who fled Cambodia and Laos in the final stages of the Vietnam War) explains that among his tribe this behavior is accepted as the customary way to choose a bride. He is sentenced to 120 days in jail, and his victim receives $900 in reparations. (p. 87)

Benhabib shows how, in this instance and in other instances, the law courts are helpless when it comes to establishing principles to accept cultural differences and at the same time provide equality of protection for individuals, especially women and children. Protection from the effects of power relations is widely affirmed but not really clarified by multiculturalism.

A question often asked regarding a multiculturalist vision that seeks inclusion for all is, inclusion in what? Clearly, inclusion in a singular nationalistic vision dominated by the majority culture is just a path back to assimilation. Opponents of multiculturalism, therefore, frequently fall back on the melting pot at this point (for example, Entwhistle, 2000; Schlesinger, 1991). Proponents of multiculturalism have to work hard at constructing an alternative vision of a social world that might contain different rights within it and resolving disputes between cultural groups over competing demands.

Counseling Implications of Multiculturalism

Counseling that takes a multicultural vision into account has evolved through a series of cycles. At first, it focused on White counselors and invited them to break out of the place of being "culturally encapsulated" (Wrenn, 1962). The development of cultural sensitivity through the gathering of knowledge about other main cultural groups was advanced as a goal of multiculturalism (Patterson, 1996; Sue & Sue, 1981). Training a more diverse generation of counselors was another goal of the multicultural counseling movement (Patterson, 1996). Culture-specific counseling methods have been advocated and advanced (Pedersen, 1976; Waldegrave, Tamasese, Tuhaka, & Campbell, 2003) and also critiqued (Patterson, 1996). More recently, multiculturalism in counseling in the United States has settled on an agenda of competencies that counselors should master (see Chapter 14). These involve a strong emphasis on developing awareness of one's own and others' cultural assumptions and processes of cultural identity development. In this book, we introduce interculturality as a critique of the notion of cultural competency, adding to the great advances of multicultural counseling.

The multicultural social imaginary is strong on inviting counselors to become aware of diversity and value it. What has been less evident in most of the mainstream approaches to multicultural counseling is what is generally missing from multiculturalism in general, which interculturality emphasizes (see Chapter 14). The mosaic metaphor does not specify an analysis of power relations among the various races and cultures. How the pieces of the mosaic should relate to each other is always a little vague. The conception of a social world in which differences among cultures might not just be appreciated and valued in our awareness but actually debated and negotiated with some give and some take is seldom articulated. Such a conversation is probably limited by the available social imaginaries of a multicultural world. These social imaginaries rarely embody any elaboration of the assumption that culture is dynamic and always evolving, rather than static and fixed. We believe that this is the challenge for the future of multiculturalism.

Multiculturalism is also a social imaginary that portrays an overarching vision of a social world in which different cultures can live. As an overarching vision, its weakness lies in its hegemonic stance toward relations between particular cultures. It asks these cultures to put their faith in the overarching vision and has little to say about relations between cultures. That accounts for its shallow account of power relations. Now let us turn to some social imaginaries that do more to account for such power relations.

Biculturalism

The social imaginary of biculturalism differs in its history from multiculturalism. It has been developed in circumstances where the community has been founded on the basis of an indigenous culture and a colonizing culture. This idea has had the greatest currency in New Zealand, but it is known in other parts of the world as well. The ideal community imagined from a bicultural perspective is founded on a partnership between the indigenous people and the former colonists.

BOX 13.1 INTERSECTIONALITY

Intersectionality is a basis for social analysis that addresses how a person's experiences are affected by multiple forms of subordination. It has its origins in feminist activism, where women of color argued that they were oppressed on the grounds of their race as well as their gender. The concept has grown from there to include the various ways in which women have also been subjected to power relations and domination on the basis of social class, disability, sexual orientation, and so on.

The term was founded on the division of society into sections made up of a majoritized section and a minoritized section. It was first used by Kimberlé Crenshaw (1989) in a paper written for the University of Chicago Legal Forum, in which she argued that one could not understand Black women's experience of things like domestic violence and rape without taking race into consideration. Their experience was markedly different from White women's experience of similar things. While the concept might have been a relatively recent invention, the experience has a much longer history. Many women of color, from Sojourner Truth through to Patricia Hill Collins, bell hooks, Audre Lourde, and Gloria Anzaldua, have addressed the same theme.

The claim by many activists is that feminist concerns are too White, middle class, cisgendered and able-bodied. Therefore, they claim that the intersectional experience is more than the sum of its parts. Something new is created when two or more intersectionalities are acknowledged.

In New Zealand, this partnership was founded on an actual treaty, known as the Treaty of Waitangi, which was signed in 1840 by representatives of the British Crown and about 150 Maori leaders (Orange, 1987). Similar treaties were signed in other parts of the world—for example, in Canada and the United States—between European colonizing powers and indigenous cultures. However, the New Zealand treaty happened some decades after the colonization of North and South America and Australia, at a time when the British Home Office was influenced by a liberal group in London called the Aboriginal Protection Society (Orange, 1987). This group's influence led the British government to send an emissary to sign a treaty that would afford the Maori people some protection from the worst ravages of colonial rule that had taken place in other parts of the world, such as wholesale theft of land and genocidal slaughter. Maori leaders, for their part, were fully cognizant of what could happen to them and were eager to negotiate a partnership that would advantage their people in the future. The result was the founding document of New Zealand as a nation. However, because the British settlers who came to New Zealand in the wake of the treaty did not always have the high ideals of the Aboriginal Protection Society at heart, they hated its provisions and sought to set it aside at every opportunity. It was not until over a hundred years later that the treaty was actually honored by the New Zealand government and gradually written into constitutional law as a founding document. (Maori had campaigned in a series of mostly nonviolent movements for this to happen for over one hundred years.) The result has been the rise of a movement arguing for New Zealand to embrace biculturalism as a national social imaginary.

Biculturalism entails the official recognition that two cultures have equal roles to play in a social world. It is echoed in countries that have officially instituted bilingualism. Belgium comes to mind in its embrace of Flemish and French as official languages. The imaginary of biculturalism has evolved into a call for the recognition of the roles and obligations of two different peoples to each other in a relationship. These roles are not necessarily exactly the same. Hosts and guests have different roles in a situation of hospitality. Biculturalism does not require each group to melt down and form a new alloy. It rests on the remembering of a partnership agreement that represents the best moments of a shared history, rather than looking at the history and shuddering at the sight of the ugliness of the colonizing process.

This is not to imply that there were not ugly aspects of the colonizing process in New Zealand. There certainly were many abuses of power by the colonists, but the Treaty of Waitangi rendered many of these illegal, and since the latter part of the 20th century many Maori have been pursuing legal means of exacting compensation for the worst excesses of illegality (especially illegal land confiscation).

It is worth taking note here that there is another usage of the term bicultural that we are not referring to here. Sometimes in the literature on race and culture, the term *bicultural* is used to refer to an individual born of parents from two different racial or cultural groups. This usage is not uncommon in the United States. The parents may be referred to as a bicultural couple and the child as a bicultural child. However, the focus in this usage is on the individual and not on the social imaginary. Therefore, the two meanings are quite different. In this chapter, we are focusing on the social imaginary rather than the individual. It is the meaning that is common in New Zealand that we are employing.

The advantage of a bicultural social imaginary is that it specifies, in a way that multiculturalism often does not, the official recognition of the places of two different cultural groups in legitimate partnership. It has strength because of its location in history, rather than seeking to be the expression of an abstract ideal. It recognizes the colonial past out of which current debates and conflicts have arisen. It even acknowledges the power relations that have shaped that history and specifies a model for shared power. Even when that model is not honored by one of the partners, it creates a ground from which critique can be mounted. It assumes that there will be an ongoing dialogue between the bicultural partners and that neither partner's position will be completely negated in that dialogue. It avoids the call for a singular base for a social world, such as that expected in a social imaginary of integration or a melting pot. In so doing, biculturalism recognizes a dual perspective on reality and rejects the singular definition of truth that science has often sought.

However, there are some downsides to the social imaginary of biculturalism. One question that quickly arises is, what about other cultures that come to settle in the arrangement set up by two initial partners? The bicultural partnership can appear to them like a comfortable binary that leaves them out. An answer sometimes given in New Zealand is that there needs to be a special place of privilege for the indigenous people in a partnership, since there is nowhere else that their culture will be protected. But this answer does not always satisfy people of Asian or Pacific Island descent who have immigrated to New Zealand in the wake of the British colonists. Neither does it address the situation of succeeding generations of the settlers' descendants, who have nowhere else to call home.

A better argument perhaps is that the two partners who signed the original treaty have set up the form of a relation. Other immigrants have been slotted into this relation in different ways. It is a power relation in which a contest of different interests is worked out. Subsequent immigrants are typically slotted into this power relation in the position of either of the two original partners. The bicultural social imaginary allows for an analysis of the privileges and disadvantages of both of these positions.

Still, in the long run, this social imaginary has limits. It may have historical value and serve particular purposes in particular contexts, but it should not be regarded as applicable to every aspect of relationships between all cultures. It leaves out too many people. What it does offer to other countries is the vision of a different ideal, that of deliberate partnership. This is a vision of a power relation that has been set up not to favor one side over the other. Even if this ideal is not lived out, it can serve as a model for what might be. There is no such equivalent in multiculturalism, which does not usually have a highly developed analysis of power relations or such a potent vision of an ideal.

Cultural Pluralism

Another social imaginary that is sometimes invoked is that of cultural pluralism. It is often used interchangeably with multiculturalism, and many writers make no distinction between the two. We think there are possibly some subtle differences and shall try to articulate them here. Nowhere that we know of does there exist any kind of formalized consensus on the kind of cultural pluralism we imagine. Rather, we see signs of an emergent perspective that is arriving in the discourse and that may eventually lead us a step beyond multiculturalism and biculturalism. Some writers, such as Iris Marion Young, Seyla Benhabib, and Jürgen Habermas, have been endeavoring to articulate this vision in theoretical terms. And there are some emergent social trends and social practices that we can point to that suggest that in many places people are extending feelers toward an as yet unknown social imaginary. Cultural pluralism is simply the best name we can think of for this chimerical image.

Cultural pluralism refers to an image of a social world in which there is pluralism of cultural difference not just in a positive sense, but also in a normative one. In other words, it is not just that different groups of people exist, but that they are granted differential rights to exist. They are recognized as members of a group as well as individuals, and perhaps there are rights granted to groups of people as well as to individual human beings.

Given that the Enlightenment-sponsored democratic vision has extended rights only to individuals, such an idea amounts to new forms of democracy that recognize cultural forces more directly than democracy does at present. It is a vision of a democratic system that gives overt legitimate status to differences. It is more than just tolerant of differences; it welcomes them. Imagining such a world is difficult, because there is as yet no consensus on this emergent social imaginary, just a sense of movement toward some new cultural forms that have not yet been born.

One of the problems that cultural pluralism needs to solve is how to address the needs of minoritized cultural groups and protect them from the tyranny of the majority. In other words, it needs to address the problems that limit the melting pot and integrationist visions. Another problem is how to settle differences when cultural groups come into conflict without falling back into segregationist solutions. Currently, these issues are dealt with in most democratic traditions on the level of individual rights. But there may be other alternatives. Let's list some examples that come to mind.

In New Zealand and in Canada at the moment, some experiments are being undertaken with regard to the handling of criminal offenses. In New Zealand, the Maori people have lobbied for, and in some cases been granted, the right to try their own people using protocols drawn from pre-European traditions. "Marae justice" experiments have been cautiously explored and have achieved some success—so much so that "family group conferences," as they have become known in the youth justice arena, have been made normative for all youth offenders, regardless of cultural background. What is distinctive here is that a cultural minoritized group succeeded in establishing a differential practice for its own people, and then had this extended to the whole community. In Canada, "sentencing circles" for dealing with crimes in native communities have been introduced by a similar process (Stuart, 1997). These practices are linked together under the banner of restorative justice.

New Zealand is also an example of a nation that has moved politically (during the 1990s) toward a proportional representation model of parliamentary elections. Seyla Benhabib acknowledges that this political model allows a greater opportunity for minority interests to be represented in government decision-making. Two-party, first-past-the-post electoral systems such as those that prevail in Britain and the United States do not include the range of political and cultural voices that proportional representation does, and minority cultural interests are forced to remain represented by lobby groups on the outside of the official decision-making process. Exceptions to this include the granting of limited sovereignty to cultural minorities, such as that given on Indian reservations. In the cultural pluralism social imaginary, this kind of sovereignty would increase but would also be matched by greater opportunity for the negotiation of differences among cultural groups along the lines envisaged under bicultural partnership models.

In Boston, the Public Conversations Project (Chasin et al., 1996) has developed a method of facilitating conversations between groups of people who are polarized on cultural issues. Their approach draws from the experience in family therapy of most of the key members of the project. It is not a method of mediation aimed at producing an agreement as much as it is a method of building within each group an understanding of and greater familiarization with the other group's experience and commitment to a different viewpoint. Public conversations began with the abortion debate, bringing "pro-choice" and "pro-life" people together to talk. Other topics that the public conversations model has been used with have included environmental land use, gay priests in churches, and the terrorist attacks of September 11, 2001. The authors of this book also used the public conversations model to generate conversations between Greek Cypriots and Turkish Cypriots, who are divided by the Cyprus problem. This is an example of how it is possible for conversations across differences to occur without there being a need to reach a synthesis that produces unity.

These examples suggest some principles that the cultural pluralism of the future might embody. First of all, they are not just about equality before the law in the sense of everyone's being treated the same. A pluralistic social imaginary has room for people to be treated differentially according to their cultural preferences. But it also does so within an overall system that does not end up in separatism or segregation, but engages people in dialogue. It is a dialogic vision, in the sense that Mikhail Bakhtin (1981) envisioned, of a never-ending exchange in which mutual learning continues to take place. This does not have to be dialogue in which a unified outcome is produced. This is its key difference from an integration model. Neither does it conclude that "never the twain shall meet" and surrender to a spirit of segregation. Instead, it regards cultural groups as capable of a degree of sovereignty within their own jurisdiction, on the condition that they will also play a part in the creation of an overall society. It deliberately creates situations of mutual accountability among the different cultural groups within a polity, rather than a winner-takes-all form of democracy. It is built on a trust born of mutual accountability rather than on treating everyone exactly the same.

Those who try to articulate a vision of what a culturally pluralist social world might look like speak of the need for a unifying vision as well as a recognition of difference. This vision is sometimes referred to as one of "deliberative democracy" (Benhabib, 2002). Along with the vision of pluralistic cultural values that a person can borrow from, as from a lending library, comes a vision of serious efforts to communicate across differences rather than regard them as incommensurable. It involves the formation of a basis for commitment from places of difference to create a sense of belonging without insisting on a comprehensive national culture or uniform values or ways of doing things. This needs to be a more robust vision of citizenship than the current U.S. American liberal emphasis on tolerating difference (in culture and religion) in the private sphere while requiring uniformity in the public sphere. Its precise forms are still to be elaborated and the social imaginary is nowhere near as clearly captured in metaphor as the melting pot or the cultural mosaic.

Interculturalism

Interculturality is a new social imaginary arising from an Andean experience. This new social imaginary takes into account the more pluralistic, less essentialist versions of culture that we have been tracing through this book. The emergent perspective takes us a step beyond the challenges we find in multiculturalism and biculturalism. The project of interculturality belongs first to geocultural locations other than the United States. We discuss below the Latin American, Andean experience from which we can also learn.

The Andean experience of interculturality invokes the construction of other imaginaries that are mobilized in response to the challenges presented by a history of colonial oppression. Governmental entities have a history of "officially" determining what are to be regarded within a multicultural social imaginary as legitimate rights, justice, or equality. They also specify how morality and ethics are to be enforced and who monitors them. New imaginaries expose continuing colonial activity that present in the form of Eurocentric definitions of well-being reinforced through narrow academic fields of inquiry and professional activity. For example, in the mental health field, what are deemed appropriate mental health services are highly regulated by professional associations. Furthermore, Eurocentric, monocultural approaches, as well as bicultural partnerships, are problematized from an intercultural perspective, because diverse ethnic communities are often left out or ignored. In the Andean case, many African and Campesinas/Peasant communities have been completely marginalized (Walsh, 2009). Within the Andean colonial imaginary, the aspirations and needs of African communities have been systematically left out, silenced, and rendered invisible within many Latin American countries like Colombia, Bolivia, and Ecuador. Often indigenous communities' aspirations have been privileged over African communities' in these countries. As a response to the colonial legacy, interculturality can only occur insofar as an analysis of power and its effects on the development of intercultural alliances is in place. Decolonial activists focus such analysis of power on coloniality (see Chapter 14), which multiculturalism misses, as we highlighted above.

The project of interculturality is a "bottom up" ideological and political activity most clearly illustrated within the African, Indigenous, and Campesinxs social movements (Walsh, 2012). Interculturality is a social imaginary grounded on what Mignolo and Walsh (2018) describe as an experiential base of local lived experience rather than being research-driven. Yet, Walsh (2012) emphasizes that interculturality is not a self-serving, ethnic, or more widely defined cultural project that only considers the rights of Indigenous or African communities. Neither is it a project solely about the promotion of difference pertaining to individuals in these communities. Rather, interculturality is a relational global project with concern for all human and non-human sectors of society. As Albán (2008) argues, interculturality aims at existence and life itself, supported by *another* imaginary of living *with*. But it is a living with in a particular relation that is sensitive to colonizing power. It envisions forms of living in community with relational aspirations other than neoliberal ones of a "better life" but instead of *el buen vivir* or good living. These relational aspirations include living with integrity and justice for the reclamation of subaltern subjectivities and political, epistemological, and ontological existence from modern hierarchical, racializing, and individualizing essentialisms.

This means that the project of interculturality has a clear agenda of action, transformation, and construction beyond being an intellectual consideration of embracing cultural differences or engaging in dialogue. Interculturality is, therefore, considered a praxis, which requires action and critical reflection for the purposes of social transformation (see Chapter 14).

As interculturality emerges from existence-based social movements, it has escaped (although not entirely) its institutionalization when adopted as a model of a nation, a profession, a vision for education, and so on, as has been the case with multiculturalism. For example, in some Latin American countries, such as Colombia and Bolivia, multiculturalism has become interwoven in their nations' constitutions. Colombia's constitution of 1991 for the first time recognized Afro-Colombian and Indigenous communities' rights to have political, cultural, and legal participation. Decolonial activists critiqued initiatives like this from an intercultural stance. They judged them to be colonizing practices of inclusion (that is, minoritized communities were included into the neocolonial organized governance of a state or nation). The result was the silencing of minoritized communities.

Interculturality does not limit itself to the construction of political, social, and cultural spaces, but considers culturally negotiated understandings of knowledge, being, living, and the very consideration of life itself (Walsh, 2012). It holds concern for ontological, epistemological, and theoretical exclusion and subalternization when privileging only Eurocentrism, as we have highlighted throughout this book. Most likely, differences are being listened to by the counselor from the epistemological and ontological foundations that inform the listening skills shaped by the Eurocentric counseling frameworks. When considering interculturality in counseling, conversations across differences, such as those, for example, pertaining to gender, sexual orientation, social class, and religion, mean that counselors address differences by not only locating them in their cultural contexts, but also implementing interventions that belong to world view of the client.

Discuss

1. What is your understanding of the concept of the "psy complex"? How are counselors involved in the governing of people's lives?
2. What are the arguments for and against affirmative action?
3. Debate the pros and cons of each of the social imaginaries with regard to relations among cultures.
4. Investigate the word *rhizome*, suggested by Gilles Deleuze and Felix Guattari (1983) and below by Jung Min Choi. What might be its implications for multicultural counseling?

Response to Chapter 13

JUNG MIN CHOI, PHD

Jung Min Choi is an associate professor of sociology at San Diego State University. His areas of interest are race relations, globalization, democracy, and postmodern theory. He has published numerous articles and book chapters and has coauthored several books on issues related to social justice and democracy. His recent work revolves around the issue of democratic education and narrative health. His latest book is Narrative Medicine and Community-Based Health Care and Planning.

In this chapter, the authors do an excellent job of providing a historical sketch of the various perspectives on communities and communal identities that have emerged in sociopolitical writings throughout the 20th century. Beginning with the melting pot theory and progressing to integration, multiculturalism, and pluralism, the authors point out how each has attempted to explain, and at times justify, the existing social order. Of all the perspectives mentioned throughout this chapter, multiculturalism and "cultural pluralism" seem to be most viable within the tenets of democracy. Indeed, both perspectives seem to be grounded on the notion of "inclusion" as a basis for maintaining society. The problem, however, is that neither perspective (along with all the other perspectives mentioned in the chapter) truly embraces the ontology of difference that is necessary to sustain an egalitarian society. Albeit in different degrees, all the perspectives mentioned in this chapter maintain a form of essentialism that restricts interaction among individuals as equals.

Beyond the various perspectives of society described in this chapter, what other imaginaries are viable in maintaining society? Martin Buber (1978) believes that in a democratic society, all social relationships should reside in the "in-between," or *dazwischen* (pp. 202–205). For Michel Foucault (1983), communities are "discursive formations" where communal boundaries are (re)interpreted and (re)understood continually without a particular telos. A "patchwork" of locally determined frameworks is the most appropriate way to describe society (Lyotard, 1993). This understanding of linguistic communities defies predetermination, essentialism, genetic superiority, and structured hierarchies based on fallacious concepts of integration, a melting pot, assimilation, and pluralism. Having said this, there is no question that, in our society, the impact of assimilation and pluralism has been enormous.

For example, as a nine-year-old Asian American boy growing up in the outskirts of East Los Angeles in the 1970s, I wanted to be integrated into the "norm" that I was surrounded by. Even at an early age, it was evident that fitting in was important. There were no other Koreans in my neighborhood and I was constantly looked at by the other kids as weird in many ways; the language I spoke, the food I ate, and the culture that I practiced were all ridiculed. I got picked on just about every day in school. At times, I got into physical altercations, which usually ended in my being jumped by two or three other students. Rather than having fun and playing games during recess, I either stayed inside the classroom or just sat in a corner out in the quad. Going to school became a recurring nightmare.

So I did everything I could to assimilate as fast as possible. I learned to speak English, ordered my mom to cook burgers and fries, and shunned many of my cultural practices and beliefs. Slowly but surely, this worked! I had friends who would stand up for me and protect me from bullies, and I was able to play tag during recess and lunch. Unwittingly, I was pursuing assimilation and integration at the expense of my cultural identity.

This pursuit of assimilation continued throughout my adolescence into the early part of my college years. In fact, as a high school kid living in Riverside, California, in the early 1980s, I was ashamed to be an Asian American. I didn't want to be associated with the newly arriving "boat people" (as they called many of the Vietnamese refugees), nor did I want to be associated with the "model minority" status given to many Asians. It seemed to me that being an Asian American meant that I had a truncated existence. I was either a war refugee who had no rights or privileges or a bookworm who lacked any other human desires—such as dating, playing sports, being mischievous, or simply being lazy. The model minority status really bothered me. It seemed as though they were saying that I was the "best of the worst." How flattering! I so desperately wanted to have blue eyes and blond hair so that people could see me as a person and not an abstraction.

Once in college, the pursuit of assimilation turned into an obsession with pluralism. This idea seemed really liberating. I heard someone say that rather than a melting pot, we should have a society that resembles a salad bowl. This, I thought, was so progressive. I could hold on to my cultural and ethnic identity and still be an integral part of the larger society. However, many argued that the problem with pluralism is that there is too much difference and diversity, which will eventually destroy the basic fabric of American (U.S.) life.

Nevertheless, as I write this piece 20 some years later—having neither been melted in a pot nor chopped up like a salad—I muse about the power of certain social imaginaries, like assimilation and pluralism, that place individuals into discrete categories.

If we are to have a truly open society where diversity is protected and celebrated rather than feared and repressed, we need an ethical social order where all views reside on a single horizontal plane. A *rhizome*, according to Gilles Deleuze and Felix Guattari (1983), provides an excellent social imaginary of this kind. Rhizomes have no apparent beginning or end, and these plants do not have centralized roots to sustain their growth. At the same time, rhizomes do not sprout haphazardly. In fact, the dispersion of these plants is orderly, yet decentered. By adopting the image of the rhizome, Deleuze and Guattari attempt to illustrate the applicability of difference in constructing social order.

Without a firm anchor to sustain society, isn't chaos inevitable? Absolutely not, claims Alfred Schutz (1976). Chaos can be averted with people's "growing old" together, where each person is tuned in to the experiential realm of the Other. A "multiplicity of worlds of names, the insurmountable diversity of cultures" does not require a grand narrative to provide a fixed formula for sustaining social order (Lyotard, 1993, p. 31). The point is that social order can emerge from individuals' asserting and accepting each other's opinions in the absence of an imposing structure. According to Deleuze and Guattari (1983), so called-universal structures that are uncompromising may only serve to alienate citizens. Instead of relying on static constructs for guidance, persons are able to use interpretations to lead them down the "path of the dancer's soul" (p. 71). By employing the image of a dancer, Deleuze and Guattari emphasize creativity. Unlike a programmed robot, a dancer's next step can change without a moment's notice and yet not disrupt the harmonious movement. This is why Deleuze and Guattari view social order as a process of "becoming" (p. 49). Clearly stated, order is not the product of a pre-established reality, but rather order and reality "become," or emerge, out of direct interaction between persons. Living at the boundary of one's interpretive reality allows the Other to approach and be approached. Instead of the traditional asymmetrical version of social reality, society can be based on "a series of exclusively lateral relations" (Foucault, 1983). According to Michel Foucault, an ethical social order is one where all views reside on a single horizontal plane. In a society modeled after the rhizome, persons living in different interpretive communities are able to construct reality in the absence of a metaphysical presence such as the "melting pot" or "integration," "multiculturalism" or even "interculturality."

Chapter 14

Bridging the Divide—Towards Interculturality

I n response to the changes in the demographic landscape of United States' society, given its history
of immigration, multicultural writers have dedicated over three decades to developing multicultural
counseling practices in attempts to help counseling practitioners achieve "competency" in working
with diverse client groups. The advances they have made in promoting what is known in the field
as "cultural competence" have benefited therapists and clients alike. Today, most major professional
organizations offering mental healthcare expect practitioners to be culturally competent (Middleton, Stadler, & Simpson, 2005). Clinical multicultural competence has been formalized in program
accreditation standards such as those of the American Psychological Association (2002), Council for
Accreditation of Counseling and Related Education Programs (2016), Association of Multicultural
Counseling and Development (1996), Association for Counselor Education and Supervision (1993),
and National Career Development Association (1997). Efforts have been made to help counseling
organizations as a whole become more responsive to cultural difference, more knowledgeable about
contextual factors, and ultimately more competent in their work.

   In this chapter we would like to take a critical look at the development of the cultural competence
movement. We may become a little more provocative than we have been in previous chapters. We suspect that you will not always agree with us. We are, after all, attempting to scan hidden possibilities,
and we can easily misread what is there. Some readers will see different options from whatever vista
their particular vantage point affords. We address key concepts underpinning cultural competence
and also problematize the challenges of ascribing to the notion of achieving cultural competency. We
also outline the possibilities that the project of cultural humility and interculturality offer. Finally, we
lay out a decolonial perspective, and what it may suggest for advancing culturally responsive therapeutic practices, particularly as they relate to addressing social injustices relating to race, ethnicity, class,
religion, ableism, gender, and sexuality.

Defining Cultural Competence

There are many perspectives that might define cultural competence, yet the multicultural counseling literature has been dominated in the last two decades by the three-pronged developmental model
composed of awareness, knowledge, and skills (Fowers & Davidov, 2006). These three dimensions
have become widely accepted, and addressing multicultural awareness, multicultural knowledge, and

multicultural skills has created a prolific literature base (for example, Arredondo, Gallardo-Cooper, Delgado-Romero, & Zapata, 2014; Lum, 2007; Santiago-Rivera, Arredondo, & Gallardo-Cooper, 2002; Sue & Sue, 2016). In their book on cultural competence, Sue & Sue (2019) named a much broader summary that emphasizes understanding and valuing cultural diversity, pluralism, equity, social justice, and cultural democracy, and advocates the "study" of multiple cultures and multiple perspectives. We find Sue and Sue's idea of studying "others" as a means to become culturally competent problematic. We believe that traditional multicultural textbooks that produce research depictions of cultures may result in essentializing and racializing cultures. Communities are at risk of being depicted as uniform and there is the possibility that counseling services will then be delivered in homogeneous ways—a practice we have critiqued in this book. The traditional multicultural work has reinforced a hierarchical relationship between those who study and those who are being studied, and gives the illusion that research can encompass the characteristics of a culture.

Despite the large body of literature exploring multicultural competence, there is still no clear definition of it (Cornish, Schreier, Nadkarni, Metzger, & Rodolfa, 2010; Sue, Gallardo, & Neville, 2014; Sue & Sue, 2016). While there are some common themes in the definition of cultural competence, there is often a failure to name the epistemological foundations of this construct. Sue & Sue (2019) suggest that it is not possible to have a unified definition of cultural competence, as it is still evolving. However, that does not constrain them from articulating a working definition of cultural competence:

> Multicultural counseling competence is defined as the counselor's acquisition of awareness, knowledge, and skills needed to function effectively in a pluralistic democratic society (ability to communicate, interact, negotiate, and intervene on behalf of clients from diverse backgrounds), and on an organizational/societal level, advocating effectively to develop new theories, practices, policies, and organizational structures that are more responsive to all groups. (p. 58)

Many have taken this statement as a working definition. For us, it raises many questions. Of the range of possible awarenesses, or cultural knowledges, or practice skills, which ones are important to acquire? Once we have decided that, how much of this learning represents competence? Indeed, from what cultural basis might we decide that competence has been achieved? Doman Lum (2011) contends that cultural competence should go beyond racial and ethnic groups to include gender, social class, and sexual orientation groups. He suggests that where there are advocates for women, gays, lesbians, immigrants and refugees, and "spiritual" persons, there will be a broad application of cultural competence with diverse populations. These debates are not conclusive and will no doubt continue, but they seem to militate against the establishment of any consensus on what kind of cultural competence should be aimed at. While the competence movement emphasizes the development of awareness, knowledge, and skills, there is an assumption that the attainment of competence involves a profound personal journey of self-exploration. Derald Wing Sue and David Sue (2019) point out that competence is gained by facing the painful realities about oneself, about one's cultural group, and about society as prejudiced and racist. Such an assertion targets cultural competence especially in those who identify with dominant cultural groups. Thus, cultural competence really involves addressing one's personal cultural constraints and blindnesses and doing so through extensive personal transformation.

Among the challenges for those seeking to define cultural competence is that it requires therapists to determine which groups they will learn to be competent in working with. In our view, this further replicates racism and discrimination between targeted cultures that are deemed more or less relevant to "learn" about. This is deeply problematic, as the pursuit of competence inadvertently diminishes fulfilling the promises the developers of the construct of cultural competence were hoping for in the first place. There are taken-for-granted assumptions built into the entire profession that are problematic. There are mandates in the statutes for each profession's licensing boards, which are culturally produced, yet rarely scrutinized. They shape larger systemic processes at institutional levels. Currently, as mental health professionals, we are required to engage in long periods of graduate study, complete rigorous licensing requirements, and continually engage in lifelong education to remain up to date with the changing needs of the discipline. Hence, we are required to convey to our clients, to our employers, and to those who supply resources for our research, training, and service activities that we are competent to perform. These are the multiple and complex tasks required of a mental health professional seeking to attain the elusive construct of cultural competence. We are instructed to abide by standard definitions of multicultural competence as an important indicator of our professional attainment. We feel obliged to demonstrate cultural competence that implies that as counselors or therapists we will be *successful* at developing the necessary awareness, knowledge, and skills to work with a culturally different Other. Yet, in actual fact we can knowingly or unknowingly participate in othering people by believing we can study them as a category, and further establish a divide between them and us.

Cultural Competence as Academic Racism

It is wonderful for mental health professionals to learn to be more responsive, respectful, compassionate, and effective with all clients when considering culture as a context marker for their historically, politically, and socially forged experiences. We appreciate the efforts of those who have gone before us in introducing the cultural competence movement into the counseling and helping professions, and who have helped counselors grapple with the important ongoing changes in United States society. Like our colleagues, we are mindful of the enormous complexity involved in demonstrating socially just and antiracist engagement with all clients, understanding that we may inhabit very different cultural worlds. In fact, authors attuned to the complexities of cultural contexts recognize the profound nature of the transformation that must take place, if we are to practice in culturally responsive ways (McDowell, Knudson-Martin, & Bermudez, 2018). We would like to problematize the concept of cultural competency because we think it requires considerably more attention. We suggest practitioners should be exposed to a broader literature, which can offer alternative perspectives that could also be helpful for counselors.

Competence is generally defined as being well qualified to perform a particular role, and this role includes being knowledgeable about intersecting, culturally different communities. We find affinity with some of the literature published in the field of medicine and nursing from authors who have been reviewing and critiquing the concept of cultural competency to train practitioners. Tervalon & Murray-García (1998) consider the idea of competency as deceptive and unattainable. Crigger, Brannigan, and Baird (2006) also challenge the notion that it is possible to competently care for all cultural communities, while noting that the helping disciplines neglect to recognize that learning about diverse cultures and addressing their needs is an ever-changing, constant, and ongoing process. Isaacson (2014) highlights the challenges of engaging in a practice that assumes there exists a priori knowledge of the client's culture that can be learned from research or textbooks, which in actual fact, may not be generalizable. Isaacson warns us of the naive practitioner who has participated in "cultural training" who overestimates their knowledge and skill in working with communities whose cultures have been "studied." For example, practitioners might study how to conduct therapy with Latinx's communities. They could learn about values of *familismo*, in a heterosexual family with a *machista* father and a *marianista* mother who is self-sacrificing. They might study too how families have grandparents who are wise and godparents who are resourceful (Sue & Sue, 2019). Some of this literature can inadvertently produce stereotypes and a simplistic caricature of a cultural community that has, like every other cultural community, complex, dynamic, and ever-changing dimensions. If a counselor is considered to be competent to work with Latinx families by engaging with these stereotypical assumptions, families are being listened to from racializing referentials. We agree with Gordon Pon (2009), who writes about the field of social work in Canada, describing cultural competency as a "new racism" and proposing jettisoning the entire construct of cultural competency. We would argue that cultural competency could be understood as an activity of academic racism. Pon suggests that the practices of cultural competence often turn into othering others "without using racialist language ... (while) deploying modernist and absolutist views of culture" (p. 60). Similar to the definitions of cultural competency we discussed above, and the views of multiculturalism we addressed in previous chapters, Pon suggests that the quest for cultural competency completely fails to theorize and critique systems of power and oppression that underpin the social structures of racism. Sakamoto (2007) states that cultural competency tends to assume a depoliticized as well as dehistoricized view of culture, as if it was neutral and not implicated in social structures of power relations, as we have emphasized throughout this book.

The construct *cultural competence* has a strong association with the epistemology of modernism—the very same modernism that gave rise to racism and justified it "scientifically." As we have already established in previous chapters, the agendas of modernism are an outgrowth of the European colonization from the 16th century on. There is a surprising irony in that multiculturalists committed to advancing the cause of social justice, equity, and respect in counseling practices toward all cultural groups use the tools of modernist epistemology to facilitate change. The ability to measure competence and to validate it is an example of this modernist dream.

The construct of cultural competence is easily weaponised and becomes a punitive cultural product by which people are scrutinized and analyzed in tests and exams. The right answers on these tests may or may not be close to what people actually do in confidential counseling and psychotherapy interactions. The cultural competence movement risks becoming a mechanism of institutional scrutiny that subjects individuals to particular forms of evaluation based on the latest iteration of Western psychological theory. Doman Lum (2011) indicates a concern about the evaluation of the cultural competence of students through measurement instruments. Numerous studies have been conducted to explore the attainment of cultural competence (for example, Constantine & Sue, 2005; Green, 2005; Teasley, 2005). Many of the instruments are self-report surveys in which people tend to overinflate their evaluation of their cultural competence, because it has become socially desirable to be culturally competent. We believe that these tendencies lead counselors to detach themselves from the very same purpose of adopting culturally responsive practices that matters most: social change through the means of social justice and antiracism.

Social Constructionism and Cultural Competence

In an extensive exploration of culturally competent practice, Doman Lum (2011) identifies social constructionism as a robust theoretical underpinning to the rather elusive construct of cultural competence. We have used this theoretical lens to view the whole multicultural movement in general. Let us consider now the value of social constructionism as a way of grappling more fully with the cultural competence construct and the challenges of attaining meaningful and effective therapeutic outcomes across cultures.

Social constructionism does not embrace the notion of the therapist as the content expert. Rather than aspiring to cultural competence, the constructionist aspires to what we call a persistent curiosity (Monk, Winslade, Crocket, & Epston, 1997). Clients are considered experts on their own lives and assumed to possess detailed local knowledge (Geertz, 1983) of cultural significance that can serve as the wellspring of resourcefulness for change. Therapists cannot hope to learn enough about the details of a client's cultural contexts to know what will make a difference. Rather, they can use their expertise to help clients deconstruct the complexity of the cultural issues that are in different ways both constraining and strengthening their responses to the challenges they face (De Jong & Berg, 2002).

Gerald Corey (2008) suggests that constructionism in fact disavows the role of the therapist as expert and places greater emphasis on client consultation and collaboration.

In the second chapter, we referred to sample quotations from the work of Sigmund Freud, Carl Jung, B. F. Skinner, and Carl Rogers, all of whom played leading roles in shaping psychological practice. In different ways they drove the modernist agenda in its search for understanding the "essence" of what it meant to be a human being (they define humanity in phenomenological terms as an essence that makes up a human being). Today, that quest is being displaced by a desire to understand the wider sociocultural world and how it constructs persons as cultural beings. Gerald Corey (2008) describes the changes in epistemology like this: "The modernist search for human essence and truth, is being replaced with the concept of socially storied lives" (p. 386). Corey suggests that constructionists are distrustful of "knowing" because the dominant culture becomes the lens by which families and society are understood. A constructionist approach emphasizes a curious posture where there is a mutual search for understanding and exploring of ways to solve problems.

Harlene Anderson and Harold Goolishian (1992) described this quality as a "talking with" rather than a "talking to" one another. They articulated a "not knowing" position in therapy as a useful stance from which to come to understand the culturally different Other. This stance requires an active curiosity unbound by a strong therapist agenda about what should be explored. Taking a not knowing position is about entering the world of another with a fierce curiosity and a persistent interest in codiscovery between therapist and client. The expectation here is not that one can become a cultural expert in the way that some literature on cultural competence appears to suggest. Instead, therapy from this position involves an open and inquiring stance of wanting to come to understand what the client is conveying and actively eschewing any certainty that one has fully understood.

Solution-focused therapy (Corey, 2008), for example, is in alignment with this philosophy and emphasizes clients' capacity to engage effectively with challenging circumstances, but assumes that they are temporarily blocked, contextually, from accessing their cultural and linguistic resources. Clients are perceived from this perspective as having the capacity to change and adapt and as doing the best they can while confronted with difficult problems. John Walter and Jane Peller (2000) suggest that therapists should work alongside their clients and trust clients' intentions to solve their problems.

Social constructionist approaches emphasize the value of seeking to understand the dominant narratives or life stories in the counseling process. From this perspective, problem situations are communicated indirectly through narratives. These narratives speak not only to the past but to what is currently taking place and what is possible in the future. Even when they amount to reports of what has already happened, they are also constructions that have effects on the decisions that shape this future. Some traditional psychotherapy models define health and illness through a dominant cultural lens. A constructionist orientation operates on the central premise that problems and solutions lie in the social, political, and historical discourse rather than within the nature of individuals. Narrative therapists, for example, concentrate on the cultural narratives that are dominating and subjugating at both the personal level and at the wider sociocultural level.

At the heart of this work are sociopolitical assumptions about how problems are constructed. A social constructionist embarks upon therapeutic work in a deconstructive spirit to more clearly expose the cultural assumptions that are part of the client's difficulties. When people become aware of how social practices can oppress them, they can then notice opportunities for new perspectives to emerge. Out of the plot elements of problem stories can emerge the coproduction of preferred, uplifting, and resourceful narratives.

Cultural Humility

Critics of cultural competence among health professions have proposed *cultural humility* instead, a literature which has made its way into some of the counseling, family therapy, and psychology professions, and aligns with social constructionism. For Tervalon and Murray-García (1998), cultural humility situates culture from the particular vantage point of members of that culture, hence it is not knowledge the practitioner could have a priori. Most importantly, it involves a position by the counselor, in this case, to be aware and humble enough to "say that they do not know when they do not know" (p. 119) and to recognize that, agreeing with Levi (2009) "it is impossible to be adequately knowledgeable about cultures" (p. 97). Assuming a not knowing position then means that the counselor ought to be equipped with other sets of skills of situated learning, or preparedness to learn, in the very same encounter with the client. This is where we believe interculturality could provide us with some possibilities, which we discuss more thoroughly below.

The proponents of cultural humility emphasize a shift in the therapist's listening skills, as listening from a knowledgeable position is quite different than from a not knowing position. At the same time, like proponents of cultural competency, they highlight the importance of therapists' ongoing processes of self-reflection, self-critique and self-awareness. The suggestion is that therapists be attuned to their own responses to what they are learning about the cultures of clients, at the same time that they are listening carefully to the client's accounts. The American physician DasGupta (2008) introduces the term "narrative humility" (p. 980) to depict a listening stance of practitioners who are witnesses to the stories of sufferings of patients. She recognizes that the culturally negotiated stories of suffering come into being in the patient's act of telling them and they belong entirely to them (not to the researchers' findings or to textbooks' authors). Clients' stories of experience cannot always be translated into forms that are understandable to therapists (Cushman, 1990; Lutz, 1988; Monk, 1998). In contradiction to liberal humanist claims of universality, there are discourses that position clients in places that may not be shared in the experience of counselors. For example, it would be a challenge for a therapist who has spent much of her/hir/his life positioned in discourses that are predominantly racist to assume understanding of clients who have been directly targeted by those very discourses. Listening from a cultural humility position, considers DasGupta, is "like the act of the careful reader, who enters into the metaphor of the poem while allowing the metaphor of the poem to enter him [her, hir], granting yet undiscovered meaning to his [her, hir] life's events" (p. 980). Hence, it is not possible for the practitioner to predict exactly how the stories of suffering of clients will start or end within their respective cultural contexts. She adds, "We cannot ever claim to comprehend the totality of another's story, which is only ever an approximation of the totality of another's self" (p. 980). This does not mean, she clarifies, that scientific or professional knowledge about the contextual social, historical, and political aspects of suffering ought to be abandoned, but that we ought to adopt a position of receptivity to understand how these important markers are impacting and shaping the person's suffering.

Some have critiqued the concept of humility by arguing that it places the burden on the client to inform the therapist about their culture. Learning about the cultural contextual markers of the person's experience does not necessarily mean being an ethnographic or anthropological expert in learning about the client in order for the therapy to begin. Showing cultural humility is part of intercultural engagement in the therapeutic process, by which the cultural differences between therapist and clients are discovered as possibilities from where change can happen, drawing from the client's meanings and responses to their social, political, and economic circumstances.

Unlike the idea of competency, which is subject to be assessed in terms of measurable outcomes, as we mentioned above, to determine one's proficiency or expertise, cultural humility is proposed as an ongoing commitment. Taking a culturally humble approach, the practitioner understands culture as culturally negotiated and fluid, as we have discussed in previous chapters.

For Tervalon and Murray-García (1998), adopting a humble position means that the practitioner "relinquishes the role of *expert* to the patient, becoming the students of the patient with a conviction … of the patient's potential to be a … full partner in the therapeutic alliance" (p. 121). Therefore, practitioners are reflexive, ongoing learners who become knowledgeable about communities' lives that are conveyed through the sufferings of clients. Tervalon and Murray-García consider that learning about the cultural circumstances of clients opens possibilities for community-oriented work and advocacy, drawing from the resources and assets learned from the communities themselves, to build alliances and culturally responsive initiatives.

Institutional Humility and Psycho-Politics

Unfortunately, the selection of the three main areas of cultural competence (awareness, knowledge, and skills) leaves out what Tervalon and Murray-García (1998) highlight in terms of humility at the

BOX 14.1 ADVOCACY

Counselors have often felt uneasy about working one on one with clients and then sending them back into the same world that produced their problems in the first place. Hence, multicultural and social justice counseling have for a long time urged counselors to be involved more widely as clients' advocates in clients' communities.

Courtland Lee, a past president of the American Counseling Association, suggests that, "the basic principles of advocacy — helping people to be their best — have always been a part of the profession in some ways." He continued, "As it evolved, advocacy became part of the multicultural and social justice movements" (Meyers, 2014, para 4).

A well-known spokesperson for advocacy and social justice is Rita Chi-Ying Chung, a professor at George Mason University in Virginia. Here, she reflects on a time early in her career:

> "I felt that we were creating kind of a revolving door where we would see clients, they would feel better, and then leave and go back in their world and get exposed to whatever issues or injustices that were happening to them, and their pain and difficulties would just come back." (Meyers, 2014, para 7)

A set of Advocacy Competencies were endorsed by the ACA Governing Council in 2003. They were created to define advocacy and give counselors strategies for working with clients and their communities to identify appropriate actions. They include six domains of action:

1. client/student empowerment
2. client/student advocacy
3. community collaboration
4. systems advocacy
5. public information
6. social/political advocacy

These advocacy competencies are outlined further at the following URL: https://www.counseling.org/docs/default-source/competencies/aca-2018-advocacy-competencies.pdf?sfvrsn=1dca552c_6

Counselors can become advocates by addressing the context that led to the problem. It might mean making a phone call, contacting a social service agency, speaking to politicians or policy makers, or recommending a course or a program. Advocacy tends to be direct and practical and does not leave it up to the client to flounder.

institutional level, involving self-reflection and self-critique. A psycho-politics perspective adds to the examination of institutional systems of power that support the profession and its practices. Psycho-politics is the practice of explicitly naming and exposing the taken-for-granted epistemologies, practices, concepts, models, and theories reviewed against the background of the particular historical, cultural, and political conditions of the time. Madsen (2014) suggests that counseling is informed by a "global psychological mentality and discourse about individuality" (p. 2). For example, counseling in its day-to-day application tends to pathologize, and categorize human behavior in simplistic, narrowly defining ways from a priori text books that outline treatment plans according to Eurocentric conceptualizations of suffering, such as "depression," "anxiety," "deficits of attention," and so on. The practice of psycho-politics makes visible how totalizing these descriptions of suffering are; it invites us to deconstruct the dominant cultural practices that replicate Eurocentric diagnostic practices across cultures within the disciplines of psychiatry and psychology. Such deconstruction opens space for the culturally negotiated language of clients to be more fully expressed in therapy. Responding to client need might include psychopharmacological alternatives or professional interventions but might also include prayers, herbal remedies, consultation with loved ones or priests, and so on.

De Sousa Santos (2008) calls the limiting labelling and monochromatic defining of human action epistemicide. For de Sousa Santos, unequal exchanges of knowledges among cultures implies "the death of the knowledge of the subordinated culture, hence the death of the social groups that possessed it" (p. 15). In this process, so much of what can be seen and known outside of these myopic Eurocentric categorizations of human action remains unacknowledged, unseen, or undervalued. It exposes the overreach of the psychological and psychiatric categorizing of human behavior. The application of psycho-politics exposes the insidious practice of imposing narrow descriptions of mental health and counseling. China Mills (2014) traced the global mental health institutional trends to make psychiatric interventions a reality for "all." She commented that implementing a universal standardized treatment across all cultures promotes a world view where every cultural community is forced to adopt the language of "globalizing tropes of 'brain disease' and 'biochemical imbalances'" (p. 14). Such implementation is often made in the name of human rights and equality. While it is certainly well intended, the negative effects are far-reaching. Eurocentric institutions with the economic power and authority to promote an ethnocentric, universal, deficit-based agenda of mental health (mostly psychiatrically defined) is not respectful or socially just to indigenous and culturally diverse communities' local knowledge. This deficit-based system is often sustained by educational, governmental, and nonprofit organizations, among others. Consequently, an entire world is represented as "all," regardless of cultural difference, and interventions are delivered globally and uniformly to all. This is what the fine-sounding language of "all" translates into.

Hence, the creation of a global mental health system ultimately becomes a colonizing force even though it is developed in the name of equality and human rights. It appears, at first glance, to promote the inclusivity of treatments, but actually delivers exclusionary practices in spite of democratic intentions. Global tropes of how to promote mental health as the only legitimate alternative or response to suffering consequently results in the exclusion of other local, culturally negotiated possible alternatives. The downstream effects of these global tropes actually end up as anti-democratic activity instead of democratic practice. The critique of the current Eurocentric view of democracy is important to understand when providing mental healthcare for many communities. The decolonial Andean activists, such as Mignolo (2014) and Quijano (2014), ask us to take a closer look at Western versions of democracy that were originally developed to contest aristocratic rule in Europe. This democratic model was never intended, no matter how it is dressed up, to protect an individual's ordinary human rights and to defend citizens against exploitation, domination, and oppression. This current democratic model has now been appropriated by neoliberal forces to satisfy the needs of a select group of individuals and their interests. One group of elite aristocrats has been replaced by another elite. This calls for what de Sousa Santos (2014) describes as the need to democratize democracy. For us, engaging in a project of interculturality could be a contribution to the counseling field where both European and non-European articulations of human problems, interventions, and solutions are equally prized as legitimate counseling knowledge and practice. Learning through intentionally discovering, acknowledging, and engaging cultural difference as a requirement to articulate responses to suffering presents a democratic pathway forward. It creates new possibilities for how our lives could be transformed. The flowering of difference is in itself evidence of democratic vitality. It should be sought out and brought forward. The heroes of democracy are not the exalted, but the ordinary folk.

However, we cannot only rely on our professional bodies to achieve this. It is important to disrupt the hold and power of academia and the professional institutions that drive particular notions of truth and allow for local voices to be heard. Such ruptures are the pathway to genuine social change and contributions to a renewed commitment to a true representational democracy. Improving democracy is about giving all people a fair chance to participate in the world, to have social justice, human rights, and access to the humanity of humanness. This is not just about democracy as electoral politics. It is about giving more people more of a say in the construction of their own lives. This democracy needs to be more respectful of different ways of knowing, where new knowledges can be brought forth and create new opportunities for well-being and happiness for those who currently are typically marginalized by Eurocentric universalisms. These exist in *DSM* diagnoses, in counseling as it is taught, in textbooks, in counseling tests, and in counseling ethics.

The practice of psycho-politics can help counselors understand more explicitly that all therapeutic practice is, of course, a polycultural system in itself that is not apolitical. Psycho-politics views the culture of therapy as sets of belief systems, assumptions, and theories about the nature of the self, the family, and the community embedded in structures of power that have tangible effects in people's lives and their relationships; as well as the preferred cultural pathways of response. The epistemological, theoretical, historical, and political assumptions embedded within these descriptions often go unexamined. The knowledge usually focused on is knowledge of the cultural world views of clients, rather than the knowledge that informs counseling itself. Lisa Tsoi Hoshmand (2005) makes the comment that counseling systems not only mirror their cultures of origin, but continue to replicate what is portrayed in popular culture. She adds that dominant cultural viewpoints lie at the cornerstone of the psychology professions and are seldom considered problematic, because they are products of our age and support the basic assumptions and beliefs of the dominant Western culture. This has not changed markedly since when Lisa Tsoi Hoshmand wrote it.

China Mills (2014) examines the psycho-political effects of the globalization of mental health and how they shape the local understandings of communities' experiences. She illuminates the global exportation of hegemonic, psychological, and psychiatric terminology. She discusses how the application of a psychiatric diagnosis puts at risk the possibility for communities from different cultures to learn from one another about their own articulations and practices of response to suffering within their own traditions. Mills argues that the globalization of mental health alienates how people come to understand themselves within their own cultural contexts. They get to learn about their suffering through the Eurocentric mental health lenses or language, which displaces their local, cultural representations of experience. Similar patterns can occur in therapy conversations. For example, if the exchange of cultural knowledges between therapists' professional interventions and clients' local cultural knowledges do not take place, what is at stake is the integrity of their narratives, world views, and practices. In turn, clients would not be listened to within their own social, economic, historical, political contexts. They are heard instead within a confined Eurocentric context of a priori counseling of a textbook version of suffering. In turn, this can displace culturally responsive therapeutic engagement that respects the integrity of the client's narrative.

Derald Wing Sue and David Sue (2019) argue that much of what counts as professional knowledge is supposedly constructed on a sound empirical base. However, it actually emerges from folk wisdom and from the cultural assumptions and traditions of the dominant cultures in the West. They suggest that most ethnocentric psychotherapies share common therapeutic characteristics that make it difficult to attend to the unique cultural requirements of some client groups. For example, therapy most often occurs in a one-to-one relationship, and the responsibility for change in client behavior belongs with the client. The therapeutic medium is usually verbal, and clients are expected to self-disclose their most intimate thoughts and feelings. These are all cultural assumptions that no amount of empirical testing can validate, although we do not mean to suggest that they have not brought about change in therapy. They are parallel to more collaborative and intercultural practices where there is shared responsibility for therapeutic change and where the unique cultural requirements are learned through the therapeutic process

Multiculturalists acknowledge that therapy is inherently a cultural product and shaped by sociocultural, historical, and sociopolitical forces. Arredondo et al. (2014) suggest that counseling practices and ethics are infused with values informed by cultural elements. Clearly, the cultural, economic, and institutional context of mental health practice shapes the definition of clients' problems and influences what might be deemed appropriate therapeutic responses. For example, the primary mental health frameworks and their corresponding interventions originated in the United States, in English, by Euro-American scholars within a cultural context where individualism and independence is highly valued. These frameworks are then disseminated mostly through journals in the United States and European contexts.

Just as specific cultural identities influence and shape world views, cultural values influence and shape the theoretical orientations of mental health professionals. So much of therapeutic practice taught in graduate school has evolved from therapeutic outcomes with the White middle class. Sue and Sue (2019) quite rightly identify that many of the cultural conventions of therapy contravene the cultural practices of some indigenous communities that do not embrace the therapeutic taboos. For example, the particular formulations of confidentiality that are taught in counseling often run counter to indigenous practices. If these biases are part and parcel of the discourse practices (theoretical orientations) of counseling itself, then it is not surprising that counselors struggle not to impose their personal cultural biases and assumptions on their clients.

In addition, many counseling practices suggest that clients should not receive advice, because it can encourage dependency, and that the giving of advice defies the therapeutic imperatives of helping clients connect with their own resources and strengths. Some clients expect that they will be given advice when they see a therapist, and there is thus a significant cultural disconnect that can occur. Most counselors and psychologists are trained not to disclose their thoughts and feelings, because to do so is perceived as unprofessional. Yet many clients resent the fact that they are expected to be trusting, highly disclosing, and vulnerable, while the therapist wears a professional mask and hides a compassionate and caring human response. We are taught that bartering with clients is inappropriate, because it negatively affects the therapeutic relationship, yet gift giving in some communities is essential to developing respect and a bond of mutuality. These ethical practices may contravene the dominant modes of respectful human interaction among some client groups, and yet the counselor or therapist is somehow still required to exhibit cultural competence in what is for the client a foreign medium.

Sue and Sue (2019) link Western psychology with the philosophical traditions of the Greek scholars, such as Socrates, Hippocrates, Plato, and Aristotle. They find the link between contemporary psychology and these ancient philosophers' writings in the idea that individualistic, autonomous, independent behavior is illustrative of good mental health. They contrast these theories with those of the ancient Chinese scholars, such as Lao Tzu, Confucius, and Mo Tzu, whose theories about healthy living stressed collectivism and interpersonal connectedness, values very much marginalized by a Western world view. China Mills (2018) describes this individualistic view as "psychocentrism" (p. 305), which she considers leads to internalized, pathologizing, depoliticized, dehistoricized, and decontextualized understandings of clients' suffering. Suffering is therefore approached as a problem of the client's mind and not linked to a structural social problem embedded within the dynamics of power. This psychocentrism has strongly informed the conceptualization and institutionalization of treatments in counseling and related areas. The World Health Organization and global mental health initiatives have institutionalized mental health treatment. A priori, monocultural, standardized understandings of suffering and its treatments adopted in psychocentrism compromise intercultural opportunities for change.

Unearthing the genealogy of the institutional structures of power of Eurocentric, psychological ideas and Euro-American practices shows how embedded Western cultural assumptions are in contemporary psychological theory. This tracing of the Eurocentric cultural genealogies of therapy demonstrates how much political and historical forces are on display. It is not surprising, however, that therapists and psychologists, rather than considering an epistemological foundation that could support a more collective or communal approach to working with families, are pulled into an individualistic mindset when they approach their clients, and a lack of self-critique of the practices we adopt remains. For example, Eurocentric therapy frameworks, such as cognitive behavioral therapy, solution-focused therapy, psychoanalysis, emotionally focused therapy, and so on, are taught internationally without careful consideration of the geographies, cultures, genders, and social class of where they originated, by whom they are being adopted, and for whom they are being implemented. Counseling can be advanced by explaining human problems not just through the lens of cognitive distortions, emotional processing, and the study of mechanisms of behavior change, but also through the realities that accompany people's cultural relationships. These relationships need to be carefully examined, however, and the colonial systems within which they take place to be more directly addressed.

Another example lies in the family therapy concept of enmeshment. This form of family engagement is negatively regarded in favor of the Eurocentric stance of a family in which persons are more separate, individualized, and potentially more distant from each other. There are many cultures in which this Western idea of the family might come under suspicion and yet it is taught as a norm to be aspired to.

The emphasis on monocultural individualism, psychological mindedness, pathologization, and so-called "rational" approaches to problem solving is so pervasive in therapeutic practice that many practitioners would be challenged to exhibit skills to engage interculturality in their practice. Consequently, interdependence, instead of being perceived as healthy, might be pathologized as codependency and enmeshment.

BOX 14.2 NEPANTLA

Nepantla is a concept that has developed to describe an aspect of Latinx experience. It derives from the Nahuatl word that means "in the middle." It is used to describe the experience of living in between two cultural worlds. In this liminal space, life may be experienced as painful, because a familiar sense of self has been crushed. But it can also be a transformational space, as Gloria Anzaldúa points out, even though it is precarious and unstable. It can become not just a place of threat but also of connection with others who share the in-between experience.

The term dates back to the Aztecs, who were encountering colonization in the 16th century, but has recently been made more popular, particularly through the writings of Gloria Anzaldúa (2012). She writes about how the borderlands offers both restraints that produce pain and possibilities for creation. Liminal spaces can also be thresholds to something new. They allow us to draw from two different cultural worlds and allow, therefore, a doubling of experience. In the borderlands, people become multiple selves in response to the forces they encounter but they also retain a sense of "I," the autobiographical self that maintains continuity. Especially in her later writings, Anzaldúa rejected an oppositional form of identity politics that was based on binary distinctions rooted in institutional norms.

Given that our counseling theories and research are dominated by Eurocentric cultural systems and assumptions about culturally responsive practice, when working interculturally, practitioners must pay special attention to how underlying world views direct and influence therapeutic moves in the counseling room. These underlying world views are embedded in structural systems of power, as we have discussed in previous chapters.

Modern and Colonial Systems of Power

We have articulated throughout this book our critique of the multicultural lack of analysis of power in counseling, and how this absence also features in understanding cultural competence. In Chapter 6 we have engaged in a thorough discussion of different accounts of power and privilege. Going forward in understanding the project of interculturality and contemporary practices of counseling in the United States and other Western locations, it is critically important to examine the intricately intertwined histories of modern and colonial power and the harm they have perpetuated in the name of providing mental health services and well-being across cultures.

Interculturality, as we have adopted it here, as we mentioned earlier, is a project proposed from decolonial activism in the Andean region. It emerged as an Indigenous and African bottom-up act of response to colonial patterns of power embedded in Eurocentric, universal, monocultural, and modern conceptions of thinking, sensing, being, believing, and doing (Walsh, 2012). It is a project that emerged from the very same experiences of response to the effects of systems of power (colonial power in this case). Therefore, its conceptualization and adoption cannot be detached from it. It is at the heart of the intercultural project to understand the pervasive effects that systems of power have in the development and establishment of intercultural initiatives and practices.

Above, we discussed the institutional systems of power whereby counseling practices are centered on European epistemologies, displacing *other* representations of suffering and responses to suffering from *other* cultural vantage points, resulting in epistemological racisms (between the superiority of certain theories and inferiority or inexistence of others, as we discussed in Chapter 12) or in epistemicide. Furthermore, such counseling practices have prevented intercultural collaborations whereby new paradigms, forms of relating, social orders, and political, cultural, and social transformations can take place in counseling (Walsh, 2012).

While poststructuralism/postmodernism offers a helpful understanding of power as something that is at work in the day-to-day interactions between people, and not always visible, this understanding of power at its very foundation is linked to a modern Eurocentric vision and the accompanying injustices that have occurred within the modernist framework. Understanding power from a decolonial, intercultural lens locates the analysis of power in colonial action and the particular history of colonialism in Latin America. Decolonial and postcolonial scholars critique a poststructuralist analysis of modern systems of modern power. These scholars consider that their descriptions of societal processes is an intra-analysis, given that poststructuralism is also Eurocentric, and poststructuralist scholars do not take into account the history of colonization in their analysis. Andean decolonial scholars reference in their writing the Spanish colonization experience in their region, while postcolonial writers tend to reference the history of the British colonization of India. In the United States, writers describing the colonization experience of Black communities depict unique historical, political, and social conditions and their ongoing replication, which have limited generalizability to other contexts. There is not one homogenous colonial pattern.

Decolonial activists describe coloniality as the "darker" side of modernity and intricately connected to it. Walter Mignolo (2011) considers them as two sides of the same coin. Therefore, there is no modernity without coloniality (and vice versa). Modernist ideas (deemed superior) have predominated through centuries, because colonial patterns of organization have been put in place to sustain European epistemologies, theories, and practices, which continue to remain at the center of the organization of the world. The Peruvian sociologist Anibal Quijano (2000) called this structural system between a superior center and an inferior periphery the *colonial matrix of power*, which has its origins in the 16th century. For decolonial and postcolonial scholars, colonizing actions are kept in place and embedded within the preeminent bifurcation of categories of humanity, defined as superior and inferior, and reinforced and sustained by the universal promotion of Eurocentric knowledge. This structure, the colonial matrix of power, has remained throughout history in various ways determined by the geolocation and history of different regions around the world. Anibal Quijano (2000) discusses how the existence and sustainability of the matrix is maintained throughout the centuries. As discussed in previous chapters, the world and its institutional structures are organized by various racial and social markers that not only reference color but also include markers such as social class, religiosity, sexual orientation, gender, body abilities, nationality, language, and mental illness. For Quijano, racism is constitutive of the matrix of colonial power (not a cause or a result of it). The end of coloniality would mean an end to the construct of race as a determinant of our humanity. In a decolonial world we would no longer view ourselves as Black, White, Latinx, Asian, and so on. A decolonized world would dismiss essentializing descriptions of people but also geographical spaces as we know them, such as Europe, Latin

America, Asia, and North America. This is a division sustained by the idea of modern nation states, and a European colonial legacy.

Attaining the end of coloniality would require a serious shift of epistemology and ontology by recognizing that other paradigms have existed outside of European ones. The vision of interculturality is a world in which humans are not categorized, let alone by tiers of racial superiority and inferiority. We argue it is time to shift away from racialized practices in the counseling field and support moving away from the categorizations of humanity as a means to frame how counseling services should be delivered. We have become suspicious of the development of specialized services tailored to categories of persons such as Latinxs, Asians, or LGBTQIA, as this essentializing of identities pulls us back to simplistic, artificially created, homogenized communities. Quijano argues that continuing to support the creation of a homogenous European perspective (that dismisses as well the wide diversity of European cultures and histories) constructs forms of knowledge that sustain and are sustained by the colonial matrix of power, discussed previously.

Eurocentrism has been used to naturalize and essentialize culture and identity. Academics and others employing Eurocentric counseling practices have unfortunately utilized multiculturalism as a movement to further compartmentalize groups of people and attempt to confine them to narrow categories, from which tailored psychological services are manufactured. Decolonial scholars and activists consider the multicultural movement to be a long-lasting epistemic phenomenon (Mignolo & Walsh, 2018) that continues to universalize knowledge, and define subjectivity and identity from a purely modernistic, rational perspective.

The project of multiculturalism in counseling that appeared at first blush to provide more access to services for those in need actually has become a force to keep the inequalities and the provision of care frozen in time. From the decolonial position, the multicultural movement at its heart falls within the colonial matrix of power, ensuring that the fundamental verities of Eurocentric universalism remain completely intact. In many ways, the inequalities experienced by so many peoples from various cultural contexts across the world are maintained within the status quo of current societal power relations. Many people feel their concerns are not legitimized by the present power structures and in many ways experience isolation, invisibility, and a sense of being replaceable. The application of the colonial matrix of power exposes the racializing of psychological needs across all cultures, along with the universalization of European knowledge, which further alienates those stuck at the inferior/nonexistence end of the superior/inferior binary. This oppressive disparity is often dressed up in academia as some form of evidence-based research and serves the multicultural agenda.

Being skilled to be culturally responsive requires therapists to continually revise the threads of power that sustain the cultural assumptions embedded in Eurocentric counseling practice. We need to critique patterns of racism and Eurocentrism and their influence on helping and healing practices, and guard against replicating colonial patterns. We do not mean that European practices should disappear or we should ignore their contributions. Instead, we need to challenge the systems that centered them as the only alternative for providing health services, thus displacing other representations of knowledge and casting indigenous, Black, or local practices at the periphery. This is easy to say and hard to do. Becoming skilled and practiced using an intercultural process is quite demanding. It involves learning about cultural difference while at the same time deconstructing patterns of power that might negatively affect what counselors do to their clients. Using an intercultural process may require critiquing the institutions that may inadvertently support racism and unjust practices.

Dangers of Centering European Counseling Practices

The historical legacy of European colonial patterns of power has had deleterious effects on many cultural communities, and the negative impacts have been uneven. Out of desperation, or because of externally imposed mandates, people who have experienced difficulties have sometimes had to attend counseling and therapy sessions, and the results have been destructive to themselves and others. People already caught up in institutionalized social systems such as criminal justice or social welfare, or those who have suffered within a schooling context or more informal systems, such as marriage, have often experienced embarrassment, humiliation, shame, and guilt (Cooper Stein, Wright, Gil, Miness, & Ginanto, 2018; Wright, Whitaker, Khalifa, & Briscoe, 2018; Wright, 2018). Some of these individuals who are experiencing great vulnerability in their lives, when entering a counseling context, have sometimes suffered even more negative consequences. After counseling, the process has left them feeling even less equipped to deal with difficult personal and family problems.

It was this series of multiple negative consequences experienced by underrepresented populations that galvanized researchers and practitioners to develop and promote a multicultural counseling competency movement in the first place. These consequences have been well documented in the multicultural counseling literature. According to the President's Commission on Mental Health (*Report to the President*, 1978), counseling clients reported that they often felt harassed, intimidated, and abused by nonminority personnel delivering mental health services. Derald Wing Sue and David Sue (2019) reported that many people of color complained that mental health professionals could not relate to their life circumstances and were insensitive to their needs. Many described how they did not feel respected and were treated with arrogance and contempt when they received services.

At the heart of the move toward cultural competence has been the recognition that counseling practices have often been enormously harmful to specific racial and ethnic populations. Non-White populations in particular have had their cultural belief systems and cultural practices labeled as at worst deviant and pathological and at best unhelpful and outdated across disciplines. Such invalidation of people's life experiences and treasured cultural beliefs has denied many communities access to culturally appropriate resources that could have assisted them with serious mental health concerns and threats to their physical, psychological, and socioemotional well-being (White et al., 2016). Many dominant Eurocentric therapy practices are often unhelpful and irrelevant to marginalized populations. Services have often been imposed on communities in such a manner as to alienate those most in need of assistance.

As a consequence, the multicultural counseling literature has documented that people of color are almost twice as likely as Whites to terminate counseling services early (Sue & Sue, 2016). The aim of the cultural competence movement, understood through a Eurocentric lens, has been to address these serious negative consequences for minority populations. In this context, it is ironic that the "minority" populations are steadily heading toward becoming the "majority" (in terms of numbers) in the United States. We can, of course, still talk about them as "minoritized" communities even if they are numerically in the majority.

What we find concerning about the multicultural movement's attempts at developing practices that are more inclusive of minoritized communities is that they sustain a hierarchy between a professional community and a "clinical" community. Eurocentric ideas of suffering and response to suffering are often understood through an expert-driven, highly individualistic framework where categories of pathology are employed. Such a dynamic is clearly demonstrated in the way clients' experiences are diagnosed and psychiatrized while only adopting diagnostic criteria to interpret clients' problems. These initiatives go against the project of interculturality, since they further replicate the patterns of the colonial matrix of power, of racializing and minoritizing communities and displacing their culturally negotiated knowledges, epistemologies, and theories about their suffering by the imposition of Eurocentric mental health language to address their circumstances.

Non-Utilization of Counseling Services

A relatively small proportion of people in the United States utilize counseling and psychological services. Few people view therapy as a realistic and helpful response to their suffering. However, when viewing popular media, one would think that everyone goes to counseling and therapy. Many movies and television shows write into their scripts the central characters consulting therapists. Newspapers reporting on traumatic events customarily mention that survivors are receiving counseling. In the first decade of the 21st century, talk shows have grown in popularity and they frequently display a parade of experts dispensing advice about how to deal with life's problems. The Moroccan sociologist Eva Illouz's (2008) research on therapy as a worldwide cultural phenomenon argues that therapy has been spread on such a scale that it could be comparable to other popular cultural movements originating in the United States. Illouz suggests that the popularization of therapy in social media has made it a site for accessing cultural legitimacy, "within which we invent ourselves as individuals, with wants, needs, and desires to be known, categorized, and controlled for the sake of freedom" (p. 3). She believes that it is a site within which our choices about addressing suffering have been managed and controlled and often manipulated at an institutional level. Michel Foucault claims that this emphasis has built a "confessional society."

Yet, despite the global popularity of therapy, seeing a counselor, therapist, or psychologist is still an alien notion to many people. In the public sphere, we continue to hear people speak about avoiding seeking therapists for fear of being labeled crazy by others who have judgments about the value and role of mental health professionals. In Chapter 9, we discussed how alien an idea seeking psychological or counseling assistance is for many men.

The most likely reason that people troubled by the notion of going to therapy end up seeing a counselor is that they are forced to by somebody else. Popular culture portrays attending therapy as a voluntary process. However, the reality for many is that people's personal troubles have become so distressing that conventional healthcare professionals or federal or state agencies have become involved and have ended up mandating psychological treatment. Alien as the experience of seeing a counselor or therapist is to many people in the White middle classes and in the dominant Western cultural groupings, it is an even greater source of alienation, estrangement, and mystery for minoritized and marginalized populations (Sue & Sue, 2016). There are many explanations for this, and we will identify some specific issues below.

Many individuals do not perceive counseling as an activity with which they have a positive relationship, or view psychotherapy as culturally relevant to the ways in which their communities view suffering and how it should be responded to. It is foreign to many people, in many cultures, to sit down with a perfect stranger and, within a brief time, disclose deeply personal material in a supposedly private forum, and thus become immensely vulnerable to this stranger's efforts to be helpful. How much greater might the risk appear when the client and counselor inhabit very different cultural worlds and when the counselor is straining to make meaning of the client's experience, which only remotely matches the counselor's. For example, Derald Wing Sue and David Sue (2019) suggest that among some Asian American communities, discussing family problems with a stranger is a source of embarrassment and an indication of failure. In fact, for many cultural groups, seeing a counselor is deeply embarrassing and perhaps even humiliating. From an intercultural perspective, the non-utilization of services by certain communities should not trigger the exact same Eurocentric efforts to enhance access to mental health services for cultural groups who have not found these services helpful in the past. Eurocentric efforts to bring communities of all cultural representations to therapy has not succeeded in the past. What we would advocate instead is a need to expand the conceptualization and practice of counseling outside of Eurocentrism, to discover alternative means to become more responsive and supportive of the cultural nuances of suffering and responses to suffering experienced by diverse communities. An intercultural approach is an effort from a humble position to engage people experiencing difficulties in a reciprocal or mutual exchange of knowledges, and address as much as possible the power differentials between client and counselor. Taking this position makes it more possible to learn how to articulate new alternatives to providing services, which ought to take place both at the institutional level and the therapy level. For example, counselors could find themselves working closely with communities and community leaders to create alliances by which both could learn from each other to ensure there is an appropriate approach to therapy in harmony with local responses to suffering. The purpose of advancing support to communities and their key members is to articulate and structure such responses into services that may, or may not, include European interventions. Therefore, communities are not just passive recipients of counseling services, but active contributors to the development of appropriate mental health interventions.

Morality and Privilege

The influence of moral decision-making and the effects that power and privilege have on the counseling relationship and how this impacts cultural competence, we argue, cannot be ignored. If we were to thoroughly deconstruct all of the main notions that underpin Western psychology, we would find the discipline embedded within a complex social and political nexus. Its influence goes well beyond the reach of simple descriptive techniques that are supposed to work with people from different cultural communities. As Lisa Tsoi Hoshmand (2005) suggests, value issues are seldom part of the therapy discourse. Inherently, the scientific method that has so dominated the field of psychology hides the very epistemological foundations on which it is built. It is the scientific assumption of neutrality or objectivity in psychology that leaves psychotherapists and counseling practitioners unconscious of the extent to which they are actually facilitators of moral reflection. This assumption explains why counselors and therapists avoid facing the very real moral and political challenges in working across diverse communities.

As Hoshmand (2005) contends,

> The old approach of attempting to maintain neutrality has to be replaced by a conscious attempt to acknowledge the moral spaces in which psychotherapists and clients are located as well as the role we play in enabling, questioning, or diminishing the client's moral responsibilities. (p. 16)

If counseling is a place for moral reflection on clients' intentions and purposes in their lives, then surely it is important for therapists to be more consciously aware of how they are engaging clients in inevitable moral consequences and dilemmas on the basis of their interventions. This requires much more than knowing some general outline of how to counsel a particular group of people. When counselors consider the basis of their moral, social, and political acts in their exchanges with clients, they are going beyond the mere application of "how-to" techniques with different cultural and ethnic groups. These actions could contribute to demonstrating a committed agenda to social justice as well as countering racism in its many expressions.

It is encouraging to note that multiculturalists are increasingly speaking of multicultural competence that acknowledges the power differentials that exist within a counseling relationship. As Hervé Varenne (2003) notes, the authority granted to therapists by the wider community places them within political structures of social control. Because of the differential access to power, influence, and privilege that therapists have, it is important for therapists from all cultural positions to understand and address how power and privilege work in the lives of counselors and clients. It is helpful as well to pay attention to how our professional institutions regulate therapists' professional and therapeutic activities and how these influences can affect the lives of diverse cultural groups.

Moving from Multicultural Competency Towards Interculturalism

While the intercultural project that we have been discussing throughout this book emerged outside of the realities of the communities in the United States and within the particularities of the experiences of communities of the Andean region of Abya Yala (Kuna name of Latin America), we believe that the translation of their proposals into North American contexts can contribute to disciplines of counseling, psychology, family therapy, and related fields. We have added this material to introduce a decolonial paradigm, making overt its particular geocultural location as one foreign to the various communities of the United States but also relevant. Our intention has been to bridge the knowledge division between North and South America to invite you, the reader, to think about your counseling practice more critically; and to recognize that, much like a decolonial intercultural project, there are many other sources of knowledge from within and outside of the United States from which counselors can learn. We think it is important to keep clear the sources of these distinct epistemological perspectives and not mash North and South perspectives together into some eclectic soup. Introducing these fresh decolonial perspectives alongside Eurocentric practices can open up new possibilities, and help us rethink our responses to human suffering and how these fresh perspectives can contribute to social transformation. Similar to the proposals of social constructionism and cultural humility discussed above, interculturality is a new option to be considered in a North American context and should be disseminated widely. The practice of interculturality invites the counselor to learn mental health knowledges and their application outside the realm of exclusively Eurocentric evidence-based knowledge. In doing so, the practitioner can discover what is inherent in the intercultural encounter, where both client and practitioner are legitimate contributors in grappling with the aftermath of social, historical, political, and relational suffering. We envision interculturality being applied at the microlevel in a therapeutic conversation by which the practitioner is working in a genuine partnership with clients.

We refer to interculturality throughout the book as a "project." We have done so since it is a decolonial praxis (simultaneous reflection and action in the Freirean sense, for purposes of social transformation) that operates in everyday life. This means that adopting interculturality as an ongoing process in counseling does not mean adopting yet another concept to learn from a textbook or multicultural training in order to secure our culturally responsive stance. It is intricately linked to an ideology that necessarily translates into a way of being and doing in the world that goes beyond the act of engaging in dialogues among cultural differences. Mignolo and Walsh (2018) propose that interculturality "points toward the building of radically different societies, of an 'other' social ordering, and of structural economic, social, political, and cultural transformations" (p. 57). For Walsh, interculturality assumes a permanent and active process of interrelation that sustains difference in order to affirm it and consider it as the fundamental element of the cocreation of new understandings, collaborations, coexistences, solidarities, and relationalities. Difference provides added value and new contributions. Mignolo and Walsh affirm that difference should be embraced, not discounted, renegotiated, eradicated, ignored, or discriminated against. They write,

> Interculturality is a process and project in continuous insurgence, movement and construction, a conscious action, radical activity, and praxis-based tool of affirmation, correlation, and transformation. As such, it can be best be understood not as a noun but, more critically … as what Ronaldo Vásquez calls a verbality that advances from modernity's margins and outside. (p. 59)

The intercultural project goes beyond a multicultural premise that continues to sustain a colonialist syndrome of cultural superiority. For example, the term "diverse groups" is usually defining diversity and difference in relation to Whites as the "zero point of reference" (Castro Gomez, 2010, p. 23). While notions of self-reflection and self-critique are present within the literature on competency and cultural humility as required elements in culturally responsive practices, this terminology does not show up in the decolonial literature of interculturality. Notions of self-reflection and self-critique are embedded in the individualistic, European conceptualization of personhood as a self with the ability to reflect upon one's essences. In contrast, within interculturality, reflection instead seems to be a process that occurs at the borders where differences meet. In other words, interculturality is a reflective, relational process.

A project of interculturality requires that counselors keep working at developing a vision of a social world that not only prizes the virtues of difference but also cocreates alternatives for change. We need to bring forth new sets of social imaginaries that remind us that differences ought to coexist. These social imaginaries have to some extent been driven by White feminists and women of color feminist movements, the Chicano movement, the Zapatista movement, the Gay Rights movement, the Black Lives Matter movement, and the Me Too movement. These movements must be recognized as drivers that contribute to the democratization of humanity. Interculturalism is about efforts to facilitate contexts where new terms of negotiated relations are generated. This effort is about valuing the construction of pluricultural worlds and identities to resist and problematize neoliberal systems of power at play. This includes paying astute attention to how much we have all been implicated in the replication of unjust systems of power, even in the name of democracy. It is time for an intercultural project in counseling that articulates what this profession might offer the world in an effort to promote democracy. For example, at the microlevel, in a therapy session, as we mentioned above, these ideas would invite practitioners to renew their listening skills so as to not merely listen for evidence in clients' stories that confirm a previously made professional, individualistic knowledge. Instead, therapists can listen openly to discover and learn from their clients' culturally informed world views. In so doing, the therapist can pay close attention to how their own culturally informed world views are shaping their counseling interactions and how those interactions might be affecting their client. This approach will provide the opportunity for the therapist to attune their responses to the vantage points taken by their clients. In so doing, the therapist is in a better position to attend to how the systems of power are at play in their counseling interactions. This also requires practitioners to engage in inquiry and discovery, rather than dispensing previously defined interventions across cultures. Inquiries would include human and nonhuman relationships alike, and their importance to clients. Narrative therapy, for example, draws heavily from a practice of inquiry. Additionally, to further the construction of pluriversal worlds, intercultural practitioners would include in their inquiries practical options for social change that include how both practitioners and clients envision their further participation in or exclusion from the current systems of power at play. This could take them beyond the therapy goals limited to the achievement of individual emotional, cognitive, or behavioral change. For example, in my (marcela) work, I have learned about the ways in which women have taken action to intervene in responses to patriarchy by developing support groups in their homes for immigrant women responding to domestic violence; young children who resist animal cruelty by feeding animals who reside in the streets; and men who oppose the marginalization of people of advanced age by helping the elderly and their families in their neighborhood maintain the upkeep of their homes. We hope for the arrival of new forms of counseling that are yet to be articulated that might emerge by taking up the ideas shared here. We should also be open to new possibilities offered by other disciplines working at addressing mental health and well-being.

Interculturality and Improving Democracy

In the end, the goal of adding an Andean, decolonial intercultural project building upon the multicultural, cultural humility and social constructionist approaches to improving the field of counseling must be to advance social justice. The goal is a democratic one. We are not referring here just to the process of electing governments through majority voting. There are many instances where "democratic" elections occur and yet where democratic conditions of life are not upheld. The democratic vision is much more than mere electoral politics. It is a vision that goes beyond the Eurocentric idea of democracy and humanity. According to Mignolo (2008, 2014), democracy was reappropriated by Europeans during the early stages of modernity to think about the future of their nations founded on their Western ideals, including the protection of human rights. For Mignolo and Walsh (2018), human rights advanced an imperial European invention of the model human being based on a model of justice and rights that has been sustained by the colonial matrix of power. This matrix was supported by an institutional control of authority through the creation of sovereign nation states. This structure is emblematic of a political expression of modernity (Quijano, 2014; Mignolo & Walsh, 2018; Walsh, 2008). The modernist democratic system, in turn, has been implicitly motivated by the economic market and military power (Quijano, 2005). Boaventura de Sousa Santos (2014) proposes then to democratize democracy via intercultural translations in contrast to how democracy is currently situated. He states,

> More and more frequently we witness the massive violation of human rights in the name of human rights, the destruction of democracy in the name of democracy, the killing of innocent civilians in the name of supposedly protecting them, the devastation of livelihoods in the name of development, and the massive deployment of surveillance techniques and restrictions of basic freedom in the name of preserving freedom and security. The ideological investments used to conceal such discrepancy are as massive as the brutality of such practices. (p. 22)

The pursuit and realization of a democratization of democracy and human rights opens a path to agency in vital sectors of social existence that are identified in the local experiences clients bring to therapy conversations. Counselors would need to open their psychiatric or psychological repertoire to become educated about clients' cultural perspectives about their sufferings. This requires counselors to understand that their problems and solutions are embedded in European values and are only one possible approach to interpreting client experience. What is critically important is understanding clients' own interpretations of issues offered on their own terms, which can help clients to regain a sense of agency in creating change. These actions will support the reclamation of subjectivities and knowledges from within the cultural contexts to which they belong, rather than only from professional and institutional contexts. Such initiatives provide the staging for constructing new knowledge (versus applying a priori Eurocentric knowledge) to work *with* clients to intervene in the circumstances and structures of power that bring therapists and clients together in the first place. We could argue that, in the end, the goal of counseling from a multicultural or intercultural perspective is to improve democracy and to make it more just for more people. Culturally responsive counseling practices are about working to ensure participation in and promotion of these new initiatives. As we see it, the intercultural agenda is first and foremost about creating social change.

The philosopher Jacques Derrida speaks about "democracy to come." In French, there is an added strand of meaning to this phrase. *Democratie á l'avenir* has a double meaning because the word *avenir* refers to what is arriving or coming and also to the future. So Derrida is speaking about the democracy of the future, and he is at the same time speaking about democracy as always in the process of arriving, as always promising a future, better world. Derrida was serious about the hope that his own work would bring out this process of improving democracy, of excavating the hidden possibilities in the idea of democracy and exposing them to light. He saw his idea of deconstruction as endeavoring to give birth to new meanings and new possibilities. We like this idea, and we see it as critically relevant to intercultural counseling. There is much in the social world and in the practice of counseling that can benefit from the kind of deconstruction that opens up new possibilities. At its best, we think counseling is not about adjusting people to accept the "reality" of the imperfect world in which they live, but about generating and unleashing forces of change that would create new realities, albeit primarily in the limited and local domains of personal living.

There are two corollaries that go with this assertion. One is that a project of interculturality in counseling recognizes the idea that there is much in current reality that needs changing. We do not live in a world that readily embraces, respects, honors, or engages cultural difference. Rather, we live in a world that values and rewards practices of unification, domination, and exclusion on racial, cultural, and other grounds. This is in some instances as true in the so-called developed countries that trumpet democracy around the world as it is in those that would not presume to call themselves democracies. However, the old practices and institutions of the modern world and the discourses that have supported them have given birth to some noble and useful democratic traditions in our political systems that need not so much to be jettisoned as further developed.

The other corollary is that a project of interculturality in counseling must embrace an analysis of power in order to understand the personal effects of cultural relations in people's lives and to be effective in offering movement toward change. Using social change to harness multiple sites of difference needs to be taken much more seriously in the counseling field. We are aware that to do so might be uncomfortable and challenging, since we need to do more than just assert it. We need to keep working with the concept of cultural difference to decolonize it in ways that render it central to what democratizing democracy in counseling is about. For this, counseling theories and practices would have to go through some significant changes. Counseling itself needs to be more rigorously examined from an intercultural perspective to change the ongoing divide between the "them" and "us." The fundamental assumptions of Eurocentrism that are built into counseling and psychological knowledge, and that masquerade as solid and universal scientific truth, need to be opened up to make room for a more cultural analysis. The truths of psychology and counseling often need to be understood as more local than universal, which does not have to rob them of all their value. This shift is indeed happening in some quarters, but there is much more room for this trend to develop.

Conclusion

In applying deconstructive knowledge and expertise, therapists are going to have varying degrees of success. Confronting one's cultural encapsulation and cultural limitations can be deeply distressing and can engender a genuine sense of dislocation. Rethinking cultural competence requires an extraordinary degree of openness and sensitivity, serious institutional revision, and painful cultural and relational discovery. The goal, however, is still worth striving for. The journey may be unsettling but also hopeful. We argue that profound changes can come from intercultural projects that sustain difference among the lives and communities across cultures.

This requires a continual effort to overcome those deeply entrenched life experiences that produce knee-jerk reactions to events that are culturally new and different. Transformation comes after a serious engagement in thoroughly questioning lifelong loyalties to the presumed rightness and universality of a cultural world view. As part of a profession that is regulated by structural Eurocentric academic and professional institutions that hold control over the production of knowledge that pertains to the personal praxis of living, we consider it imperative for counselors to assume ethical responsibilities in our work to ensure that counseling practices are integrated into a serious commitment to create social change.

Discuss

1. Find some books that have chapters on how to counsel particular ethnic groups. Locate yourself in relation to one of these groups. Consider the advice given. How would this advice be helpful to you as a client? How would it not be helpful?
2. Discuss another chapter with someone of a different ethnicity from yours. Interview this person about what he or she would find helpful or not helpful.
3. Discuss aspects of who we are that escape descriptive accounts of ethnic groups.
4. Research the list of multicultural competencies promoted by one professional organization. What are the strengths and weaknesses of this list?

Response to Chapter 14

WONYOUNG L. CHO,
PHD LMFT

Wonyoung Cho is an assistant professor in Marriage, Couple, and Family Therapy (MCFT) program at Lewis and Clark Graduate School of Education and Counseling. Her clinical experiences include working in a multidisciplinary treatment team at a children's hospital outpatient psychiatry department and supervising students as an AAMFT-approved clinical supervisor at a community clinic serving culturally diverse clientele. Her research interests include culturally-relevant practices and pedagogy, multilingual mental health services, and narrative identity construction.

Culture is such an elusive *thing* to capture and discuss. It is such a pervasive and integral *thing* that impacts and shapes every corner of human experience that it is of critical importance to know how to identify, conceptualize, and interact with culture(s) as culturally responsive professionals. And yet we are limited by what we can identify. We grow awareness of our own cultural contexts by contrasting it to something that is *other*. In other words, it is difficult to become aware of who we are and what we do unless we see or experience something different. I think this is why those who are and live consistently as the "norm" of a certain cultural context are at a disadvantage in becoming culturally self-aware, because they are surrounded by so much that is taken for granted and expected. Those who live in diasporas and live in communities that experience different cultural contexts all at the same time are at a particular advantage in becoming culturally self-aware. Let me explain what I mean.

As a Korean American woman living in the United States, I've spent the majority of my life trying to articulate and participate in this *thing* called culture. It was crucial to my social survival that I learn the rules of this *thing*, especially when the *thing* shifted and changed depending on whether I was home, at school, in my neighborhood, or in particular social communities. It depended on who I wanted to connect with and who I wanted to please, whether I had the social power to control my context or if I needed to have someone as my ally for my social survival. As I began to navigate successfully in a variety of these spaces, I was then invited and expected to translate and bridge between them.

I don't think I'm alone in these experiences. Everyone, whether they identify as the majority or not, has to perform within different social locations that involve nuanced cultural shifting and bridging. The difference is that throughout my journey I was also met with a steady stream of questions with sometimes benign, sometimes hostile intentions: Who am I? Where am I from? What am I eating? Why do my parents do that? Why do I do that? Why do I think that? Why do I say that? These questions had me constantly reflecting and aware of the choices I was making, the ways I was relating, and groups I was identifying with. Furthermore, these questions always seemed to have a same question at their core: *Are you one of us or one of them?* And this particular question of cultural belonging is a question that many people who identify as non-majority experience quite early and consistently throughout their life.

I've worked hard to answer this question. It required me to learn who is "us" and "them." I tried to figure out whether I had features of the particular "us" group, and whether I wanted to join and belong to the particular "them" group. These questions were asked by people who I might consider as "ingroup" as well as those I might consider as "outgroup." I found that the differences between "us" and "them" often blur and shift; and the question becomes challenging to answer because it depends on who, when, and the context in which these questions are asked. Through having this arduous journey of answering questions, I've grown an acute level of cultural self-awareness that I may not otherwise have developed. And these questions always emerged when I was in contexts where I was different than the norm and/or deviated from the expectations of my context.

For example, when I got invited to a friend's house for a birthday party for the first time following my family's move to the United States, I prepared for that social event the best I knew how. My parents helped me buy a birthday present and I wrote a card to go along with it. I dressed in jean overalls which was popular in those days, and my parents dropped me off at my friend's house. But I could not have prepared for a series of strange experiences that left me feeling very displaced. When I was invited in, I was first surprised that everyone wore their shoes inside, tracking in all the dirt and dust from the ground outside into the living space. Then I was surprised that my friend called her parents by their names, which seemed pretty rude and disrespectful, but her parents did not betray any sign of annoyance or concern. Finally, as I was leaving their house, no one came out to follow me to my car to say goodbye—an experience which left me feeling dismissed and insulted.

If I was not under the premise that I was on someone else's cultural turf with someone else's rules, I might not have questioned my initial reactions of feeling offended. I might have attributed these "rude behaviors" to my friend and her family's character. But I knew I was the foreigner here and my social expectations were under question. Why did I assume that everyone took off their shoes in their homes? Why did I assume that adults should not be referred to by their names? Why did I expect the host of the party follow me to my car and bid me farewell? From these differences, I was able to identify some social (or cultural) customs that I took for granted, which were unique to the contexts of my upbringing: the distinct and clear separation of private inside and public outside, as indicated by taking off shoes when entering a home; the sacredness of names and respect for elders, which resulted in referring to adults by my relation to them rather than their names (i.e., my friend's mother, my dad's co-worker, or my homeroom teacher); and the social protocol of seeing guests out the door when they leave. At first, I attributed these differences to "American" culture: Americans do not care about the cleanliness of their homes; Americans do not respect their elders; Americans do not see their guests to the door and say goodbye. And these differences solidified in my young eight-year-old heart that I was not American, but Korean.

But as an "American" audience living in the United States today, you might raise some objections. Perhaps you also take off your shoes when you enter your home and ask your visitors to do the same. Perhaps you also adhere to some sort of social hierarchy based on age and experience, and perhaps you do not refer to your parents by their names either. Perhaps you also express respect for elders, just in a different way, and you always see your guests to the door.

These customs are not essentially Korean or American, and my original distinction of *us* and *them* start to blur. The us–them defined here is not necessarily American and Korean anymore, it is whether we wear our shoes inside the house, whether we adhere to a certain value and respect for elders expressed in a particular way, and whether we follow our guests to the door. With continued experiences of "American" culture that diversified my understanding of who and what the United States of America is, I know now that there are diverse cultures represented within the United States and that "American" culture is more complex and diverse than the caricatures of the Anglo middle-class represented in Norman Rockwell paintings.

I also found out I have become American to a certain degree when I traveled back to Korea and visited my extended family years later. I found out that I was a foreigner in my homeland by the way I wrote my numbers fours and sixes, by the length of my hair, and the way I was able to pronounce R and L in a Korean English class—I was not Korean anymore, not in the way I thought I was. And Korean people in Korea were different than the way I had remembered them. My definition of what it means to be Korean was that of the late 1980s and early 1990s—the memories of Korea when I was last there. Korean culture and social customs continued to morph and change, as all cultures do. My distinction of us–them shifted again.

In the years following, I explored Korean American identity and found out I did not quite fit in initially because my Korean was too good, or my English was too good, or because I didn't bleach strips of my hair (which was a thing back then). The point I am trying to make here is not that I am Korean, or American, or Korean American. Ultimately, it isn't the answer but it was the process of answering questions that helped me articulate my unique cultural makeup. And by being able to articulate my unique cultural makeup that is not quite Korean, not quite American, and not even quite Korean American, I am also able to recognize the *other* in ways that are more nuanced and complex.

I'm not suggesting that I am self-aware in all aspects of my life and that I am completely knowledgeable in all things cultural. Nor am I suggesting that I am unique in my experiences. My experiences, along with others who straddle multiple worlds as non–majority identified people, are a little more defined and articulated because we have lived our lives under the premise that we are in multiple cultural contexts where norms and expectations continue to shift. This premise has us self-reflecting and examining our own taken-for-granted assumptions. My experiences make me more acutely aware of certain aspects of my identity, and the diverse cultural contexts I've lived in.

Perhaps this next movement in culturally relevant practices is not about knowing more about the other cultures. Rather than becoming preoccupied about who, what, and how others are, it is about knowing more about ourselves as counselors and therapists. To effectively bridge between us and them and develop culturally relevant practices, the questions we ask ourselves are crucial. We need to know who and what we mean when we say "us," and we need to learn about who and what we mean when we say "them." I don't mean just the racial and/or ethnic other, the sexual orientation and/or gender identity other, or the spiritually and/or secular other. Sometimes "us" means those who speak the Western psychology language, use "therapy-speak," or use the language of psychiatric diagnoses. Sometimes "us" means those who are comfortable sharing feelings, thoughts, and relationships with strangers who have professional licenses. Sometimes "us" means those who have had the privilege and ability to take graduate-level courses, write academic papers, and pass licensure exams to become professional counselors and therapists.

Being knowledgeable about others is just the tip of the iceberg, and the practitioners who are culturally sensitive and ethical often embody cultural self-awareness that is not bound in professional contexts. They often have an acute awareness of their sociocultural, political, educational, and historical location in their personal as well as their professional lives. Thus, as professionals striving for culturally relevant practices, we need to constantly be asking the questions that cultural minorities face: Who am I? Where am I from? What am I eating? Why do I do that? Why do I think that? Why do I say that? And ultimately, we have to ask ourselves: *Am I one of "us" or one of "them"?*

We have to ask these questions consistently in our shifting contexts and throughout our personal and professional growth, because the answer always depends.

Appendix

Meeting CACREP Standards for Intercultural Counseling

M aterial in this book, as indicated by the chapter numbers below, supports students' mastery of the following CACREP standards:

Section 2: Professional Counseling Identity

1. **PROFESSIONAL COUNSELING ORIENTATION AND ETHICAL PRACTICE**

   a. history and philosophy of the counseling profession and its specialty areas

   Chapter 2

   b. the multiple professional roles and functions of counselors across specialty areas, and their relationships with human service and integrated behavioral healthcare systems, including interagency and interorganizational collaboration and consultation

   Chapter 14

   c. counselors' roles and responsibilities as members of interdisciplinary community outreach and emergency management response teams

   Chapter 14

   d. the role and process of the professional counselor advocating on behalf of the profession

   Chapters 8, 14

   e. advocacy processes needed to address institutional and social barriers that impede access, equity, and success for clients

   Chapters 8, 14

   i. ethical standards of professional counseling organizations and credentialing bodies, and applications of ethical and legal considerations in professional counseling

   Chapter 14

k. strategies for personal and professional self-evaluation and implications for practice

Chapters 1, 2, 3, 4, 5, 6, 7, 8, 9, 10, 11, 14

2. **SOCIAL AND CULTURAL DIVERSITY**

a. multicultural and pluralistic characteristics within and among diverse groups nationally and internationally

Chapters 1, 2, 3, 4, 5, 6, 7, 8, 9, 10, 11, 12, 13, 14

b. theories and models of multicultural counseling, cultural identity development, and social justice and advocacy

Chapters 2, 8, 14

c. multicultural counseling competencies

Chapter 14

d. the impact of heritage, attitudes, beliefs, understandings, and acculturative experiences on an individual's views of others

Chapters 1, 2, 3, 4, 5, 6, 7, 8, 9, 10, 11, 12, 13, 14

e. the effects of power and privilege for counselors and clients

Chapters 3, 5, 6, 9, 10, 14

f. help-seeking behaviors of diverse clients

Chapter 14

g. the impact of spiritual beliefs on clients' and counselors' world views

Chapters 11, 14

h. strategies for identifying and eliminating barriers, prejudices, and processes of intentional and unintentional oppression and discrimination

Chapters 1, 2, 3, 4, 5, 6, 7, 8, 9, 10, 11, 12, 13, 14

3. **HUMAN GROWTH AND DEVELOPMENT**

c. theories of normal and abnormal personality development

Chapter 8

e. biological, neurological, and physiological factors that affect human development, functioning, and behavior

Chapter 1

f. systemic and environmental factors that affect human development, functioning, and behavior

Chapters 1, 2, 3, 4, 5, 6, 7, 8, 9, 10, 11, 12, 13, 14

g. effects of crisis, disasters, and trauma on diverse individuals across the lifespan

Chapter 3

i. ethical and culturally relevant strategies for promoting resilience and optimum development and wellness across the lifespan

Chapter 14

5. **COUNSELING AND HELPING RELATIONSHIPS**

a. theories and models of counseling

Chapters 2, 14

b. a systems approach to conceptualizing clients

Chapters 1, 2, 3, 4, 5, 6, 7, 8, 9, 10, 11, 12, 13, 14

e. the impact of technology on the counseling process

Chapters 1, 11

f. counselor characteristics and behaviors that influence the counseling process

Chapters 1, 2, 3, 4, 5, 6, 7, 8, 9, 10, 11, 12, 13, 14

g. essential interviewing, counseling, and case conceptualization skills

Chapters 5, 8

k. strategies to promote client understanding of and access to a variety of community-based resources

Chapter 14

n. processes for aiding students in developing a personal model of counseling

Chapters 1, 2, 3, 4, 5, 6, 7, 8, 9, 10, 11, 12, 13, 14

Section 5: Entry-Level Specialty Areas

A. **CLINICAL MENTAL HEALTH COUNSELING**

1. FOUNDATIONS

a. history and development of clinical mental health counseling

Chapters 2, 6, 14

b. theories and models related to clinical mental health counseling

Chapters 2, 14

2. **CONTEXTUAL DIMENSIONS**

b. etiology, nomenclature, treatment, referral, and prevention of mental and emotional disorders

Chapters 1, 2, 3, 4, 5, 6, 7, 8, 9, 10, 13, 14

i. legislation and government policy relevant to clinical mental health counseling

Chapter 14

j. cultural factors relevant to clinical mental health counseling

Chapters 1, 2, 3, 4, 5, 6, 7, 8, 9, 10, 11, 12, 13, 14

l. legal and ethical considerations specific to clinical mental health counseling

Chapter 14

3. PRACTICE

b. techniques and interventions for prevention and treatment of a broad range of mental health issues

Chapter 14

e. strategies to advocate for persons with mental health issues

Chapters 8, 14

B. **MARRIAGE, COUPLE, AND FAMILY COUNSELING**

1. FOUNDATIONS

a. history and development of marriage, couple, and family counseling

Chapters 2, 6, 14

b. theories and models of family systems and dynamics

Chapters 1, 11

d. sociology of the family, family phenomenology, and family of origin theories

Chapters 3, 4, 9, 10, 11

2. **CONTEXTUAL DIMENSIONS**

   b.   structures of marriages, couples, and families

      Chapter 10

   e.   human sexuality and its effect on couple and family functioning

      Chapters 9, 10

   f.   aging and intergenerational influences and related family concerns

      Chapter 11

   g.   impact of crisis and trauma on marriages, couples, and families

      Chapters 3, 7, 13

   h.   impact of addiction on marriages, couples, and families

      Chapter 3

   i.   impact of interpersonal violence on marriages, couples, and families

      Chapters 3, 4, 6

   j.   impact of unemployment, under-employment, and changes in socioeconomic standing on marriages, couples, and families

      Chapters 1, 9, 13

   k.   interactions of career, life, and gender roles on marriages, couples, and families

      Chapter 9

   m.   cultural factors relevant to marriage, couple, and family functioning, including the impact of immigration

      Chapters 1, 2, 3, 4, 5, 6, 7, 8, 9, 10, 11, 12, 13, 14

3. PRACTICE

   c.   techniques and interventions of marriage, couple, and family counseling

      Chapters 5, 6, 8, 9, 10, 13, 14

References

Abramian, A. (2018, 25 July). Harnessing the positive effects of social media for your teen. *Forcefield*. Retrieved from https://forcefield.me/positive-social-media/

Adames, H. Y., Chavez-Dueñas, N., Sharma, S., & La Roche, M. (2018). Intersectionality in Psychotherapy: The experiences of an AfroLatinx queer immigrant. *Psychotherapy, 55*, 73–79. doi: 10.1037/pst0000152

Adams, J. T. (1931). *The epic of America.* Boston, MA: Little, Brown.

Adler, J. (2005, August 29). In search of the spiritual. *Newsweek* (U.S. ed.), p. 46.

Adorno, T., Aron, B., Levinson, M., & Morrow, W. (1950). *The authoritarian personality.* Chicago, IL: Wiley.

Ahmad, S., Waller, G., & Verduyn, C. (1997). Eating attitudes and body satisfaction among Asian and Caucasian adolescents. *Journal of Adolescence, 17*(5), 461–470.

Akan, G. E., & Grilo, C. M. (1995). Sociocultural influences on eating attitudes and behaviors, body image, and psychological functioning: A comparison of African-American, Asian American, and Caucasian college women. *International Journal of Eating Disorders, 18*(2), 181–187.

Alamilla, S. G., Kim, B. S. K., Walker, T., & Sisson, F. R. (2017). Acculturation, enculturation, perceived racism, and psychological symptoms among Asian American college students. *Journal of Multicultural Counseling and Development, 45*, 37–65. http://dx.doi.org/10.1002/ jmcd.12062

Albán, A. (2008). ¿Interculturalidad sin decolonialidad? Colonialidades circulantes y prácticas de re-existencia. Interculturality without decoloniality? Circulating colonialities and practices of re-existence] In W. Villa & A. Grueso (Eds.), *Diversidad, interculturalidad y construcción de ciudad* (pp. 64–96). Bogotá, Colombia: Universidad Pedagógica Nacional.

Alzendi, D., Zamani, N. & Ashoor, A. (2017). I have a dream! A study on mental health and Gender Based Violence (GBV). Iraqi youth and Syrian families of newcomers to San Diego, California. San Diego, CA: Bridge Collaborative Communities

Alessi, E. J. (2008). Staying put in the closet: Examining countertransference and clinical issues in work with gay men married to heterosexual women. *Clinical Social Work Journal, 36*, 195–201.

Alexander, J. (1999). Beyond identity: Queer values and community. *International Journal of Sexuality and Gender Studies, 4*(4), 293–314.

Alexander, M. G., & Fisher, T. D. (2003). Truth and consequences: Using the bogus pipeline to examine sex differences in self-reported sexuality. *Journal of Sex Research, 40*(1), 27–35.

Alinsky, S. D. (1969). *Reveille for radicals.* New York, NY: Vintage Books.

Allen, T. W. (2011). *The invention of the white race: Volume 2: The origin of racial oppression in Anglo-America.* London, UK: Verso Books.

Almeida, R., Woods, R., Messineo, T., & Font, R. (1998). The cultural context model: An overview. In M. McGoldrick (Ed.), *Revisioning family therapy.* New York, NY: Guilford Press.

Altabe, M. (1998). Ethnicity and body image: Quantitative and qualitative analysis. *International Journal of Eating Disorders, 23*(2), 153–159.

Alvarez, A. N., Liang, C. T. H., & Neville, H. A. (Eds.). (2016). *The cost of racism for people of color: Contextualizing experiences of discrimination.* Washington, DC: American Psychological Association.

American Psychiatric Association. (1952). *Diagnostic and statistical manual of mental disorders.* Washington, DC: Author.

American Psychiatric Association. (2008). *Diagnostic and statistical manual of mental disorders* (4th ed.). Washington, DC: Author.

American Psychiatric Association. (2013a). *Diagnostic and statistical manual of mental disorders* (5th ed.). Washington, DC: Author.

American Psychiatric Association. (2013b). Paraphilic disorders. *Diagnostic and statistical manual of mental disorders* (5th ed.). Washington, DC: Author.

American Psychological Association. (2002). *American Psychological Association guidelines on multicultural education training, research, practice, and organizational change for psychology.* Retrieved from www.apa.org

American Psychological Association. (2007). *Affirmative action: Who benefits?* Retrieved from http://www.apa.org/pubinfo/affirmaction.html

American Psychological Association. (2015). Guidelines for psychological practice with transgender and gender nonconforming people. *American Psychologist, 70*(9), 832–864. doi.org/10.1037/a0039906

American Psychological Association. (2017). *Multicultural guidelines: An ecological approach to context, identity, and intersectionality, 2017*. Retrieved from http://www.apa.org/about/policy/multiculturalguidelines.pdf

Americans with Disabilities Act of 1990, Pub. L. No. 101–336, 104 Stat. 328 (1990).

Anderson, B. (2000). *America's salad bowl: An agricultural history of the Salinas Valley*. Monterey, CA: Monterey County Historical Society.

Anderson, H., & Goolishian, H. (1992). The client is the expert: A not-knowing approach to therapy. In S. McNamee & K. J. Gergen (Eds.), *Therapy as social construction* (pp. 25–39). Thousand Oaks, CA: SAGE.

Antone, R., Hill, D., & Myers, B. (1985). *Power within people: A community organizing perspective*. San Francisco, CA: Diane L. Hill Publisher.

Anzaldúa, G. (2012). *Borderlands/La frontera: The new mestiza* (4th ed.). San Francisco, CA: Aunt Lute Books.

Appiah, K. A. (2005). *The ethics of identity*. Princeton, NJ: Princeton University Press.

Archer, J. (1996). Sex differences in social behavior: Are the social role and evolutionary explanations compatible? *American Psychologist, 51*, 909–917.

Archer, J., & Lloyd, B. (2002). *Sex and gender* (2nd ed.). Cambridge, UK: Cambridge University Press.

Arguello, T. M. (2016). Identity development. In M. P. Dentato (ed.), *Social work practice with the LGBT community* (pp. 115–155). New York, NY: Oxford University Press.

Armstrong, E. A., Hamilton, L. T., Armstrong, E. M., & Seeley, J. L. (2014). "Good girls": Gender, social class, and slut discourse on campus. *Social Psychology Quarterly, 77*(2), 100–122. doi.org/10.1177/0190272514521220

Arnold, M. (1865). *Essays in criticism*. New York, NY: Macmillan.

Arredondo, P., Gallardo-Cooper, M., Delgado-Romero, E. A., & Zapata, A. L. (2014). *Culturally responsive counseling with Latinas/os*. Alexandria, VA: American Counseling Association.

Artkoski, T., & Saarnio, P. (2013). Therapist's gender and gender roles: Impact on attitudes toward clients in substance abuse treatment. *Journal of Addiction, 2013*.

Asexuality Visibility and Education Network. (n.d.). Retrieved from http://www.asexuality.org/

Ashton, S., McDonald, K., & Kirkman, M. (2018). Women's experiences of pornography: A systematic review of research using qualitative methods. *The Journal of Sex Research, 55*(3), 334–347.

Association for Counselor Education and Supervision. (1993). *Ethical guidelines for counseling supervisors*. Retrieved from http://www.acesonline.net/ethical_guidelines.asp

Association of Multicultural Counseling and Development. (1996). *Standards for multicultural assessment. Association for Assessment in Counseling*. Retrieved from http://www.aac.ncat.edu/Resources/documents/

Atkinson, D. R., Morten, G., & Sue, D. W. (Eds.). (1993). *Counseling American minorities* (4th ed.). Dubuque, IA: Brown.

Attwood, F. (2002). Reading porn: The paradigm shift in pornography research. *Sexualities, 5*(1), 91–105.

Augusta-Scott, T., & Dankwort, J. (2002). Partner abuse group intervention: Lessons from education and narrative therapy approaches. *Journal of Interpersonal Violence, 17*(7), 783–805.

Augusta-Scott, T. (2001). Dichotomies in the power and control story: Exploring multiple stories about men who choose violence in intimate relationships. *Gecko: A Journal of Deconstructive and Narrative Ideas in Therapeutic Practice, 2*, 31–68.

Avenanti, A., Sirigu, A., & Aglioti, S. M. (2010). Racial bias reduces empathic sensorimotor resonance with other-race pain. *Current Biology, 20*(11), 1018–1022.

Bakhtin, M. (1986). *Speech genres and other late essays* (C. Emerson & M. Holquist, Eds.; V. W. McGee, Trans.). Austin, TX: University of Texas Press.

Bakhtin, M. M. (1981). *The dialogic imagination* (C. Emerson & M. Holquist, Trans.). Austin, TX: University of Texas Press.

Baldwin, E., Longhurst, B., McCracken, S., Ogborn, M., & Smith, G. (2000). *Introducing cultural studies*. Athens, GA: University of Georgia Press.

Bancroft, J. (2002). Biological factors in human sexuality. *Journal of Sex Research, 39*(1), 15–21.

Bandura, A. (1971). *Psychological modeling: Conflicting theories*. Chicago, IL: Aldine-Atherton.

Banaji, M. R., & Greenwald, A. G. (2013). *Blindspot: Hidden biases of good people*. New York, NY: Delacorte Press.

Banks, K. H. (2014). "Perceived" discrimination as an example of color blind racial ideology's influence on psychology. *American Psychologist, 69*, 311–313. http://dx.doi.org/10.1037/a0035734

Barker (2011). Monogamies and non-monogamies: A response to "The challenge of monogamy: Bringing it out of the closet and into the treatment room". Sexual and Relationship Therapy 26(3), 281–287. Doi/abs/10.1080/14681994.2011.595 401

Barker, M., Iantaffi, A., & Gupta, C. (2007). Kinky clients, kinky counselling? The challenges and potentials of BDSM. In L. Moon (Ed.), *Feeling queer or queer feelings: Radical approaches to counselling sex, sexualities and genders* (pp. 106–124). London, UK: Routledge.

Barker, M., & Landridge, D. (2009). *Understanding non-monogamies.* New York, NY: Routledge.

Barker, M.-J., & Scheele, J. (2016). *Queer: A graphic history.* London, UK: Icon Books Ltd.

Barnett, J. E. (2011). Psychotherapist self-disclosure: Ethical and clinical considerations. *Psychotherapy, 48*(4), 315–321. doi: 10.1037/a0026056

Barter, C., McCarry, M., Berridge, D. & Evans, K. (2009). Partner exploitation and violence in teenage intimate relationships. London: NSPCC.

Baruth, L. G., & Manning, M. L. (2007). *Multicultural counseling and psychotherapy: A lifespan perspective* (4th ed.). Upper Saddle River, NJ: Pearson Merrill Prentice Hall.

Baruth, L., & Manning, M. (2016). *Multicultural counseling and psychotherapy: A lifespan approach.* New York, NY: Routledge.

Battiste, M. (Ed.). (2000). *Reclaiming indigenous voice and vision.* Vancouver, British Columbia, Canada: UBC Press.

Baumeister, R. F., Catanese, K. R., & Vohs, K. D. (2001). Is there a gender difference in strength of sex drive? Theoretical views, conceptual distinctions, and a review of relevant evidence. *Personality and Social Psychology Review, 5*(3), 242–273.

Beaudoin, M. N., & Zimmerman, J. (2011). Narrative therapy and interpersonal neurobiology: Revisiting classic practices, developing new emphases. *Journal of Systemic Therapies, 30*(1), 1–13.

Bell, C. C., & Mehta, H. (1980). The misdiagnosis of black patients with manic depressive illness. *Journal of the National Medical Association, 72,* 141–145.

Bell, D. A. (2000). After we're gone: Prudent speculations on America in a post-racial epoch. In R. Delgado & J. Stefancic (Eds.), *Critical race theory: The cutting edge* (2nd ed., pp. 2–8). Philadelphia, PA: Temple University Press.

Bender-Baird, K. (2008, June 22). Examining cisgender privilege while conducting transgender research. Presentation at National Women's Studies Association Conference, Cincinnati, OH.

Benedict, R. (1945). *Race and racism.* London, UK: Routledge and Kegan Paul.

Benhabib, S. (2002). *The claims of culture: Equality and diversity in the global era.* Princeton, NJ: Princeton University Press.

Benner, A. D., Wang, Y., Shen, Y., Boyle, A. E., Polk, R., & Cheng, Y. P. (2018). Racial/ethnic discrimination and well-being during adolescence: A meta-analytic review. *American Psychologist.* Advance online publication. http://dx.doi.org/10.1037/amp0000204

Benshoff, H. M., & Griffin, S. (2004). *America on film: Representing race, class, gender, and sexuality at the movies.* Malden, MA: Blackwell.

Beren, S. E., Hayden, H. A., Wilfley, D. E., & Striegel-Moore, R. H. (1997). Body dissatisfaction among lesbian college students: The conflict of straddling mainstream and lesbian cultures. *Psychology of Women Quarterly, 21*(3), 431–445.

Bergeron, S. M., & Senn, C. Y. (1998). Body image and sociocultural norms: A comparison of heterosexual and lesbian women. *Psychology of Women Quarterly, 22*(3), 385–401.

Bergner, D. (2013). *What do women want?: Adventures in the science of female desire.* New York, NY: Harper Collins.

Berliner, D. C., & Biddle, B. J. (1995). *The manufactured crisis: Myths, fraud, and the attack on America's public schools.* Reading, MA: Addison-Wesley.

Bernstein, R. (1983). *Beyond objectivism and relativism: Science, hermeneutics, and praxis.* Philadelphia, PA: University of Pennsylvania Press.

Berreby, D. (2005). *Us and them: Understanding your tribal mind.* Boston, MA: Little, Brown and Company.

Berry, J. W. (2001). A psychology of immigration. *Journal of Social Issues, 57*(3), 615–631.

Berscheid, E., & Reis, H. T. (1998). Attraction and close relationships. In D. T. Gilbert, S. T. Fiske, & G. Lindsay (Eds.), *Handbook of Social Psychology* (4th ed., vol. 2, pp. 193–281). Boston, MA: McGraw-Hill.

Best BDSM practices (n.d.). Retrieved from https://www.ncsfreedom.org/component/k2/item/579-best-practices

Billboard. (2012). Rap Songs 2012-10-20. Retrieved from https://www.billboard.com/charts/rap-song/2012-10-20

Bilton, N. (2014, September 10). Steve Jobs was a low-tech parent. *New York Times.*

Birman, D. (1994). Acculturation and human diversity in a multicultural society. In E. Trickett, R. Watts, & D. Birman (Eds.), *Human diversity: Perspectives on people in context* (pp. 261–284). San Francisco, CA: Jossey-Bass.

Birnbaum, G. E., & Reis, H. T. (2012). When does responsiveness pique sexual interest? Attachment and sexual desire in initial acquaintanceships. *Personality and Social Psychology Bulletin, 38*(7), 946–958.

Bisson, M. A. & Levine, T. R. (2009). Negotiating a friend's with benefits relationship. *Archives of Sexual Behavior, 38*(1), 66–73.

Bjorklund, B. R. (2015). *The journey of adulthood* (8th ed.). Boston, MA: Pearson.

Blackless, M., Charuvastra, A., Derryck, A., Fausto-Sterling, A., Lauzanne, K., & Lee, E. (2000). How sexually dimorphic are we? Review and synthesis. *American Journal of Human Biology, 12,* 151–166.

Blanchett, W., Brantlinger, E., & Shealey, M. (2005). Brown 50 years later—exclusion, segregation, and inclusion. *Remedial and Special Education*, *26*(2), 66–69.

Blashfield, R. K., Keeley, J. W., Flanagan, E. H., & Miles, S. R. (2014). The cycle of classification: *DSM-I* through *DSM-5*. *Annual Review of Clinical Psychology*, *10*(1), 25–51. doi: 10.1146/annurev-clinpsy-032813-153639

Blazina, C., & Watkins, C. E., Jr. (1996). Masculine gender role conflict: Effects on college men's psychological well-being, chemical substance usage, and attitudes toward help-seeking. *Journal of Counseling Psychology*, *43*, 461–465.

Bogaert, A. F. (2012). *Understanding asexuality* [Kindle version]. Lanham, MD: Rowman & Littlefield. Retrieved from https://www.amazon.com/Understanding-Asexuality-Anthony-F-Bogaert-ebook/dp/B008UTMYMU

Bogle, K. A. (2008). *Hooking up: Sex, dating, and relationships on campus*. New York, NY : New York University Press.

Bonilla-Silva, E. (2012). The invisible weight of Whiteness: The racial grammar of everyday life in contemporary America. *Ethnic and Racial Studies*, *35*, 173–194.

Bordo, S. (1993). *Unbearable weight: Feminism, Western culture, and the body*. Berkeley, CA: University of California Press.

Borradori, G. (2003). *Philosophy in a time of terror: Dialogues with Jürgen Habermas and Jacques Derrida*. Chicago, IL: University of Chicago Press.

Bostwick, W. B., Boyd, C. J., Hughes, T. L., West, B. T., & McCabe, S. E. (2014). Discrimination and mental health among lesbian, gay, and bisexual adults in the United States. *American Journal of Orthopsychiatry*, *84*(1), 35–45. doi: 10.1037/h0098851

Bourdieu, P. (1977). *Outline of a theory of practice*. New York, NY: Cambridge University Press.

Bourdieu, P. (1980). *The logic of practice*. Redwood City, CA: Stanford University Press.

Bouteldja, H., & Valinsky, R. (2017). *Whites, Jews, and us: Toward a politics of revolutionary love*. Los Angeles, CA: Semiotext.

Brammer, R. (2012). *Diversity in counseling* (2nd ed.). Boston, MA: Cengage.

Braun, V., Gavey, N., & McPhillips, K. (2003). The "fair deal"? Unpacking accounts of reciprocity in heterosex. *Sexualities*, *6*(2), 237–261.

Braun-Harvey, D., & Vigorito, M. A. (2015). *Treating out of control sexual behavior rethinking sex addiction*. New York, NY: Springer Publishing Company.

Bray, S. S., & Schommer-Aikins, M. (2015). School counselors' ways of knowing and social orientation in relationship to poverty beliefs. *Journal of Counseling & Development*, *93*(3), 312–320.

Brinlee, M. (2017). More Black women are killed in America than any other race. *Bustle*. Retrieved from https://www.bustle.com/p/more-black-women-are-killed-in-america-than-any-other-race-a-new-cdc-report-says-71955

Brooks, G. (2010). *Beyond the crisis of masculinity: A transtheoretical model for male-friendly therapy*. Washington, DC: American Psychological Association.

Brooks, G. R., & Good, G. E. (2001). Introduction. In G. R. Brooks & G. E. Good (Eds.), *The new handbook of psychotherapy and counseling with men* (vol. 1, pp. 3–21). San Francisco. CA: Jossey-Bass.

Brotto, L. A., & Yule, M. (2017). Asexuality: Sexual orientation, paraphilia, sexual dysfunction, or none of the above? *Archives of Sexual Behavior*, *46*(3), 619–627. https://doi.org/10.1007/s10508-016-0802-7

Brouwers, M. (1990). Treatment of body image dissatisfaction among women with bulimia nervosa. *Journal of Counseling & Development*, *69*(2), 144–147.

Brown v. Board of Education, 347 U.S. 483 (1954).

Brown, B. (2017). *Braving the wilderness: The quest for true belonging and the courage to stand alone*. New York, NY: Random House.

Brown, D. L., & Segrist, D. (2016). African American career aspirations: Examining the relative influence of internalized racism. *Journal of Career Development*, *43*, 177–189. http://dx.doi.org/10.1177/0894845315586256

Brown, K. T., & Ostrove, J. M. (2013). What does it mean to be an ally? The perception of allies from the perspective of people of color. *Journal of Applied Social Psychology*, *43*, 2211–2222. http://dx.doi.org/10.1111/jasp.12172

Brown, L. (2018). *Feminist Therapy*. Washington, DC: American Psychological Association.

Brown, L. B., Alley, G. R., Sarosy, S., Quarto, G. Q., & Cook, T. (2001). Gay men: Aging well. *Journal of Gay and Lesbian Social Services*, *13*(4), 41–54. Retrieved from https://www.tandfonline.com/doi/abs/10.1300/J041v13n04_06

Brueck, H. (2018, September 10). The US suicide rate has increased 30% since 2000 and tripled for young girls. Here's what we can do about it. *Business Insider*. Retrieved from https://www.businessinsider.com/us-suicide-rate-increased-since-2000-2018-6

Brunner, J. J. (1998). *Globalización cultural y postmodernidad* [Cultural and postmodern globalization]. Santiago, Chile: Fondo de Cultural Economica.

Buber, M. (1978). *Between man and man*. New York, NY: Macmillan.

Burman, E. (1994). *Deconstructing developmental psychology*. London, UK: Routledge.

Burr, V. (2003). *Social constructionism* (2nd ed.). London, UK: Psychology Press.

Burr, V. (2015). *Social constructionism* (3rd ed.) Hove, UK: Routledge.

Buss, A. R. (1979). *A dialectical psychology*. New York, NY: Irvington.

Buss, D. M. (1995). Psychological sex differences: Origins through sexual selection. *American Psychologist, 50*, 164–168.

Buss, D. M. (2000). The evolution of happiness. *American Psychologist, 55*, 15–23.

Butler, C. (2010). Sexual and gender minorities: Considerations for therapy and training. In C. Butler, A. O'Donovan, & E. Shaw (Eds.), *Sex, sexuality, and therapeutic practice: A manual for therapists and trainers* [Kindle version] (pp. 143–206). Retrieved from https://www.amazon.com/Sex-Sexuality-Therapeutic-Practice-Therapists-ebook-dp-B003PJ7AX8/dp/B003PJ7AX8/ref=mt_kindle?_encoding=UTF8&me=&qid=

Butler, J. (1992). Contingent foundations: Feminism and the question of postmodernism. In J. Butler & J. W. Scott (Eds.), *Feminists theorise the political* (pp. 3–21). London, UK: Routledge.

Butler, J. (2011). *Bodies that matter: On the discursive limits of sex*. New York, NY: Routledge.

Butler, M. H., & Seedall, R. B. (2006). The attachment relationship in recovery from addiction. Part 1: Relationship mediation. *Sexual Addiction & Compulsivity, 13*(2–3), 289–315.

Cabrera, N. L., Watson, J. S., & Franklin, J. D. (2016). Racial arrested development: A critical Whiteness analysis of the campus ecology. *Journal of College Student Development, 57*, 119–134. http://dx.doi.org/10.1353/csd.2016.0014

Cafri, G., Yamamiya, Y., Brannick, M., & Thompson, J. (2006). The influence of sociocultural factors on body image: A meta-analysis. *Clinical Psychology: Science and Practice, 12*, 421–433.

Cajete, G. (2015). *Indigenous community: Rekindling the teachings of the seventh fire*. St. Paul, MN: Living Justice Press.

Caldwell, J. E., Swan, S. C., & Woodbrown, V. D. (2012). Gender differences in intimate partner violence outcomes. *Psychology of Violence, 2*(1), 42–57. doi: 10.1037/a0026296

Calvert, S. (1994, March). Psychology and a feminist practice: Opponents or complements? *Bulletin of the New Zealand Psychological Society, 80*, 21–23.

Campbell, M., Neil, J., Jaffe, P., & Kelly, T. (2010). Engaging abusive men in seeking community intervention: A critical research & practice priority. *Journal of Family Violence, 25*(4), 413–422.

Caramel, L., & Laronche, M. (2000). We must fight for cultural diversity. *Le Monde*.

Carpenter, S. (2008). Buried prejudice [PDF file]. *Scientific American Mind, 35*. Retrieved from http://siricarpenter.com/wp-content/uploads/2010/02/Buried-Prejudice1.pdf

Carroll, J. S., Busby, D. M., Willoughby, B. J., & Brown, C. C. (2016). The porn gap: Differences in men's and women's pornography patterns in couple relationships. *Journal of Couple & Relationship Therapy, 16*(2), 146–163.

Carson, E. A. (2018). *Prisoners in 2016*. Washington, DC: Bureau of Justice Statistics.

Carswell, K., Blackburn, P., & Barker, C. (2011). The relationship between trauma, post-migration problems and the psychological well-being of refugees and asylum seekers. *International Journal of Social Psychiatry, 57*(2), 107.

Carter, J. (2014, November 21). Patriarchy and violence against women and girls. *The Lancet, 385*, 40–41.

Carter, R. T. (1995). *The influence of race and racial identity in psychotherapy: Toward a racially inclusive model*. New York, NY: Wiley.

Case, A., & Deaton, A. (2015). Rising morbidity and mortality in midlife among white non-Hispanic Americans in the 21st century. *Proceedings of the National Academy of Sciences, 112*(49), 15078–15083.

Cash, T. F., & Henry, P. E. (1995). Women's body images: The results of a national survey in the U.S.A. *Sex Roles, 33*(1–2), 19–28.

Cash, T. F., & Smolak, L. (2011). *Body image: A handbook of science, practice, and prevention*. New York, NY: Guilford Press.

Cashman, E. G. & Walters, A. S. (2018). *"I made my Facebook page Benefits so when you add me it says, you're friends with benefits": Young adults' attitudes about FWB Relationships*. Poster Presentation at American Association of Sexuality Educators, Counselors, and Therapists 50th Annual Conference, Denver, CO.

Castellano, M. B. (2002). *Aboriginal family trends: Extended families, nuclear families, families of the heart*. Retrieved from http://www.vifamily.ca/library/cft/aboriginal.html

Castro Gomez, S. (2010). *La hybris del punto cero: Ciencia, raza e ilustración en la Nueva Granada (1750–1816)*. [Zero point hubris: Science, race, and enlightenment in New Granada] Bogotá, Colombia: Editorial Pontificia Universidad Javeriana.

Catalyst. (2018). *Women CEOs of the S&P 500* [Data file]. Retrieved from https://www.catalyst.org/knowledge/women-ceos-sp-500

Cavalli-Sforza, L. L., & Feldman, M. W. (2003). The application of molecular genetic approaches to the study of human evolution. *Nature Genetics, 33*(3s), 266–275. doi: 10.1038/ng1113

Cavanaugh, C. J., & Lemberg, R. (1999). What we know about eating disorders: Facts and statistics. In R. Lemberg (with L. Cohn, Eds.), *Eating disorders: A reference sourcebook* (pp. 7–12). Phoenix, AZ: Oryx.

Cavanaugh, T., Hopwood, R., & Lambert, C. (2016). Informed consent in the medical care of transgender and gender-nonconforming patients. *AMA Journal of Ethics, 18*(11), 1147–1155. doi: 10.1001/journalofethics.2016.18.11.sect1-1611

Cejka, M. A., & Eagly, A. H. (1999). Gender-stereotypic images of occupations correspond to sex segregation of employment. *Personality and Social Psychology Bulletin, 25,* 413–423.

Centers for Disease Control and Prevention (2018). Suicide rates rising across the U.S. https://www.cdc.gov/media/releases/2018/p0607-suicide-prevention.html.

Center for the Study of Hate & Extremism. (2018). *Report to the nation: Hate crimes rise in the U.S. cities and counties in time of division & foreign interference.* Retrieved from https://csbs.csusb.edu/sites/csusb_csbs/files/2018%20Hate%20Report%205-141PM.pdf

Chasin, R., Herzig, M., Roth, S., Chasin, L., Becker, C., & Stains, R. (1996). From diatribe to dialogue on divisive public issues: Approaches drawn from family therapy. *Mediation Quarterly, 13*(4), 323–344.

Chavez-Dueñas, N. Y., Adames, H. Y., Perez-Chavez, J. G., & Salas, S. P. (2019). Healing ethno-racial trauma in Latinx immigrant communities: Cultivating hope, resistance, and action. *American Psychologist, 74,* 49–62. http://dx.doi.org/10.1037/amp0000289

Chavous, T. M., Richardson, B. L., Webb, F. R., Fonseca-Bolorin, G., & Leath, S. (2017). Shifting contexts and shifting identities: Campus race-related experiences, ethnic/racial identity, and academic motivation among Black students during the transition to college. *Race and Social Problems, 10,* 1–18. http://dx.doi.org/10.1007/s12552-017-9218-9

Chernin, K. (1981). *The obsession: Reflections on the tyranny of slenderness.* New York, NY: Harper & Row.

Chetty, R., Friedman, J. N., Saez, E., Turner, N., & Yagan, D. (2017). *Mobility report cards: The role of colleges in intergenerational mobility* (No. w23618). National Bureau of Economic Research.

Chomsky, N. (2003). *Hegemony or survival: America's quest for global dominance.* New York, NY: Henry Holt.

Choudhury, S. (2015). *Deep diversity: Overcoming us vs. them.* Toronto, Ontario, Canada: Between the lines.

Chung, J. (2016). *Felony disenfranchisement: A primer.* Washington, DC: The Sentencing Project.

Clark, M., Moe, J., & Hays, D. G. (2017). The relationship between counselors' multicultural counseling competence and poverty beliefs. *Counselor Education and Supervision, 56*(4), 259–273.

Clarke, V., Ellis, S. E., Peel, E., & Riggs, D. W. (2009). *Lesbian, gay, bisexual, trans and queer psychology: An introduction.* Cambridge, UK: Cambridge University Press.

Cleary, L. M., & Peacock, T. D. (1998). *Collected wisdom: American Indian education.* Boston, MA: Allyn & Bacon.

Clifford, J. (1986). Introduction: Partial truths. In J. Clifford & G. E. Marcus (Eds.), *Writing cultures: The poetics and politics of writing ethnography.* Berkeley, CA: University of California Press.

CNN.com. (2004). Study: One in 100 adults asexual. Retrieved from www.cnn.com/2004/TECH/science/10/14/asexual.study/index.html?iref=allsearch

Coe, M. D. (1996). *Mexico: From the Olmecs to the Aztecs.* New York, NY: Thames & Hudson.

Colbow, A. J., Cannella, E., Vispoel, W., Morris, C. A., Cederberg, C., Conrad, M., et al. (2016). Development of the Classism Attitudinal Profile (CAP). *Journal of Counseling Psychology, 63*(5), 571.

Coleman, E., Bockting, W., Botzer, M., Cohen-Kettenis, P., DeCuypere, G., Feldman, J., Zucker, K. (2012). Standards of care for the health of transsexual, transgender, and gender nonconforming people (7th ver.). *International Journal of Transgenderism, 13,* 165–232. http://dx.doi.org/10.1080/15532739.2011.700873

Collins, P. H., & Bilge, S. (2016). *Intersectionality.* Malden, MA: Polity Press.

Comas-Díaz, L. (2016). Racial trauma recovery: A race-informed therapeutic approach to racial wounds. In A. N. Alvarez, C. T. H. Liang, & H. A. Neville (Eds.), *The cost of racism for people of color: Contextualizing experiences of discrimination* (pp. 249–272). Washington, DC, US: American Psychological Association. http://dx.doi.org/10.1037/14852-012

Commission on Domestic & Sexual Violence. (2015). *American Bar Association report to the House of Delegates* [Resolution 109B]. Retrieved from https://www.americanbar.org/content/dam/aba/administrative/domestic_violence1/LGBT/109B.authcheckdam.pdf

Conley, T. D., Moors, A. C., Matsick, J. L., Ziegler, A., & Valentine, B. A. (2011). Women, men, and the bedroom: Methodological and conceptual insights that narrow, reframe, and eliminate gender differences in sexuality. *Current Directions in Psychological Science, 20*(5), 296–300.

Connell, R. W. (2005). *Masculinities* (2nd ed.). Berkeley & Los Angeles, CA: University of California Press.

Connelly, P. H. (2008). Psychological functioning of bondage/domination/sado-masochism (BDSM) practitioners. *Journal of Psychology and Human Sexuality, 18*(1), 79–120. doi.org/10.1300/J056v18n01_05

Connor, P. (2016). *U.S. admits record number of Muslim refugees in 2016.* Retrieved from http://www.pewresearch.org/fact-tank/2016/10/05/u-s-admits-record-number-of-muslim-refugees-in-2016/

Constantine, M. G., & Sue, D. W. (Eds.). (2005). *Strategies for building multicultural competence in mental health and educational settings.* Hoboken, NJ: Wiley.

Cook, N. D. (1981). *Demographic collapse, Indian Peru, 1520–1620.* New York, NY: Cambridge University Press.

Coontz, S. (2005). *Marriage, a history: From obedience to intimacy, or how love conquered marriage*. New York, NY: Viking Press.

Cooper, A. (1998). Sexuality and the Internet: Surfing into the new millennium. *CyberPsychology & Behavior*, *1*, 187–193.

Cooper Stein, K., Wright, J., Gil, E., Miness, A., & Ginanto, D. (2018) Examining Latina/o students' experiences of injustice: LatCrit insights from a Texas high school. *Journal of Latinos and Education*, *17*(2), 103–120. doi: 10.1080/15348431.2017.1282367

Cordell, L. S., Lightfoot, K., McManamon, F., & Milner, G. (Eds.). (2008). *Archaeology in America: An encyclopedia* [4 volumes]. Santa Barbara, CA: ABC-CLIO.

Corey, G. (2008). *Theory and practice of counseling and psychotherapy* (8th ed.). Belmont, CA: Thomson Learning.

Cornell, S., & Hartmann, D. (1998). *Ethnicity and race: Making identities in a changing world*. Thousand Oaks, CA: Pine Forge Press.

Cornish, J. A. E., Schreier, B. A., Nadkarni, L. I., Metzger, L. H., & Rodolfa, E. R. (Eds.). (2010). *Handbook of multicultural counseling competencies*. Hoboken, NJ: John Wiley & Sons.

Council for Accreditation of Counseling and Related Education Programs. (2016). *2016 CACREP standards*. Retrieved from https://www.cacrep.org/for-programs/2016-cacrep-standards/

Cournoyer, R. J., & Mahalik, J. R. (1995). Cross-sectional study of gender role conflict examining college-aged and middle-aged men. *Journal of Counseling Psychology*, *42*(1), 11–19.

Courtenay, W. H. (2000). Constructions of masculinity and their influence on men's well-being: A theory of gender and health. *Social Science & Medicine*, *50*, 1385–1401.

Crabtree, R. D., & Malhotra, S. (2003). Media hegemony and the commercialization of television in India: Implications to social class and development communication. In L. Artz & Y. R. Kamalipour (Eds.), *The globalization of corporate media hegemony* (pp. 213–228). New York, NY: State University of New York Press.

Crawford, J., Kippax, S., & Waldby, C. (1994). Women's sex talk and men's sex talk: Different worlds. *Feminism & Psychology*, *4*, 571–587.

Creek, S. J., & Dunn, J. L. (2011). Rethinking gender and violence: Agency, heterogeneity, and intersectionality. *Sociology Compass*, *5*(5), 311–322.

Crenshaw, K. (1989). Demarginalizing the intersection of race and sex: A Black feminist critique of antidiscrimination doctrine, feminist theory and antiracist politics. *University of Chicago Legal Forum*, *1989*(1), Article 8.

Crenshaw, K. (1991). Mapping the margins: Intersectionality, identity politics, and violence against women of color. *Stanford Law Review*, *43*(6), 1241–1299.

Crigger, N. J., Brannigan, M., & Baird, M. (2006). Compassionate nursing professionals as good citizens of the world. *Advances in Nursing Science*, *29*, 15–26.

Croninger, R. G., & Lee, V. E. (2001). Social capital and dropping out of high school: Benefits to at-risk students of teachers' support and guidance. *Teachers College Record*, *103*(4), 548–581.

Crosby, F., Iyer, A., Clayton, S., & Downing, R. (2003). Affirmative action: Psychological data and the policy debates. *American Psychologist*, *58*(2), 93–115.

Crose, R., Nicholas, D. R., Gobble, D. C., & Frank, B. (1992). Gender and wellness: A multidimensional systems model for counselling. *Journal of Counseling & Development*, *71*, 149–156.

Crosslin, A. (2010). Leader lunch 30. *Pearls of wisdom*. Retrieved from https://www.youtube.com/watch?v=SruVfefMlSs

Crouse, J. S. (2018, February 7). Five ways porn affects us all. *The Washington Times*. Retrieved from https://www.washingtontimes.com/news/2018/feb/7/metoo-culture-product-porn-industry/

Curiel, O. (2007). Crítica poscolonial desde las prácticas políticas del feminismo antirracista. [Postcolonial critique from antiracist feminist politics practices]. *Nómadas*, *9*, 92–101.

Curtin, P. D. (Ed.). (1971). *Imperialism*. New York, NY: Walker.

Curtis, S. (2016, September 19). One in 10 visitors to porn sites are under 10 years old. *Mirror*. Retrieved from https://www.mirror.co.uk/tech/one-10-visitors-porn-sites-8868796

Cushman, P. (1990). Why the self is empty: Toward a historically situated psychology. *American Psychologist*, *45*(5), 599–611.

Cusicanqui, S. (2018). *Un mundo ch'ixi es posible: Ensayos desde un presente en crisis*. Cusicanqui, S. (2018). *Un mundo ch'ixi es posible: Ensayos desde un presente en crisis* [A ch'ixi world is possible: Essays from the present in crisis]. Buenos Aires, Argentina: Tinta Limón Buenos Aires, Argentina: Tinta Limón.

D'amico, E., Julien, D., Tremblay, N., & Chartrand, E. (2015). Gay, lesbian, and bisexual youths coming out to their parents: Parental reactions and youths' outcomes. *Journal of GLBT Family Studies*, *11*(5), 411–437.

D'Andrea, M., & Daniels, J. (2001). RESPECTFUL counseling. In D. Pope-Davis & H. Coleman (Eds.), *The intersection of race, class, and gender in multicultural counseling* (pp. 417–466). Thousand Oaks, CA: SAGE.

D'Angelo, R. (2011). White fragility. *International Journal of Critical Pedagogy*, *3*(3), 54–70.

D'Angelo, R. (2018). White fragility. Why it is so hard for White people to talk about racism? Boston, MA: Beacon Press.

Daniluk, J. C., Stein, M., & Bockus, D. (1995). The ethics of inclusion: Gender as a critical component of counselor training. *Counselor Education and Supervision, 34*(4), 294–307.

DasGupta, S. (2008). The art of medicine: Narrative humility. *The Lancet, 371*, 980–981.

Davies, B. (1993). *Shards of glass: Children reading and writing beyond gendered identities.* St. Leonards, New South Wales, Australia: Allen & Unwin.

Davies, B., & Harré, R. (1990). Positioning: The discursive production of selves. *Journal for the Theory of Social Behavior, 20*(1), 43–63.

Davies, D. (1996). Towards a model of gay affirmative therapy. In D. Davies & C. Neal (Eds.), *Pink therapy: A guide for counsellors and therapists working with lesbian, gay and bisexual clients* (pp. 24–40). Maidenhead, BRK, England: Open University Press.

Davies, N. (1995). *The Incas.* Niwot, CO: University Press of Colorado.

Davis, A. J. (Ed.). (2017). *Policing the Black man.* New York, NY: Pantheon Books.

Davis, F. J. (1991). *Who is black? One nation's definition.* University Park, PA: Pennsylvania State University Press.

Davis, K. (2006). *A girl like me* [Motion picture]. Retrieved from http://www.uthtv.com/umedia/ show/2052/

Davis, S. E. (2018). Objectification, sexualization, and misrepresentation: Social media and the college experience. *Social Media + Society, 4*(3). https://doi.org/10.1177/2056305118786727

De Cadenet, A. (2015, October 19). More Women Watch (and Enjoy) Porn Than You Ever Realized: A Marie Claire Study. Here, 3,000+ women get real. https://www.marieclaire.com/sex-love/a16474/women-porn-habits-study/

De Haan, M., & Schreiner, R. C. (2018). *The intergenerational transmission of welfare dependency* (No. 7140). CESifo Working Paper.

De Jong, P., & Berg, I. K. (2002). *Interview for solutions* (2nd ed.). Pacific Grove, CA: Thomson Brooks/Cole.

De Miranda, L. (2013). Is new life possible? Deleuze and the lines (trans. M-C. Courilleault). *Deleuze studies., 7* (1), 106-152. DOI: 10.3366/dls.2013.0096

de Sousa Santos, B. (2008). *Another knowledge is possible: Beyond Northern epistemologies.* New York, NY: Verso.

de Sousa Santos, B. (2014). *Epistemologies of the south: Justice against epistemicide.* New York, NY: Routledge.

de Vries A., McGuire J., Steensma, T., Wagenaar, E.C., Doreleijers, T.A., Cohen-Kettenis, P.T. (2014). Young adult psychological outcome after puberty suppression and gender reassignment. *Pediatrics, 134*, 696–704.

Deadly disparities. (2000, September 17). *New York Times,* p. 18.

Dean, M. (1999). *Governmentality: Power and rule in modern society.* London, UK: SAGE.

DeLanda, M. (2016). *Assemblage theory.* Edinburgh, UK: Edinburgh University Press.

Deleuze, G. (2004). *Difference and repetition.* London: Continuum.

Deleuze, G., & Guattari, F. (1983). *On the line.* New York, NY: Semiotext(e).

Deleuze, G., & Guattari, F. (1987). *A thousand plateaus.* Minneapolis, MN: University of Minnesota Press.

Deleuze, G., & Guattari, F. (1994). *What is philosophy?* (H. Tomlinson & G. Burchell, Trans.) New York, NY: Columbia University Press.

Deleuze G., & Parnet, C. (2007). *Dialogues.* New York, NY: Columbia University Press.

Deloitte Touche Tohmatsu Limited (2016). The 2016 Deloitte Millennial Survey Winning over the next generation of leaders. Retrieved from https://www2.deloitte.com/content/dam/Deloitte/global/Documents/About-Deloitte/gx-millenial-survey-2016-exec-summary.pdf

Deng, F. M. (1997). Ethnicity: An African predicament. *Brookings Review, 15*(3), 28–31.

Dentato, M. P., Arguello, T. M., & Wilson, C. (2016). Practice with the gay male community. In M. P. Dentato (Ed.), *Social work practice with the LGBT community* (pp. 423–459). New York, NY: Oxford University Press.

Derrida, J. (1976). *Of grammatology* (G. C. Spivak, Trans.). Baltimore, MD: Johns Hopkins University Press.

Derrida, J. (1978). *Writing and difference.* Chicago, IL: University of Chicago Press.

Derrida, J. (1994). The deconstruction of actuality: An interview with Jacques Derrida. *Radical Philosophy, 68*, 28–41.

Dhejne, C., Oberg, K., Arver, S., & Landen, M. (2014). An analysis of all applications for sex reassignment surgery in Sweden, 1960-2010: Prevalence, incidence, and regrets. *Archives of Sexual Behavior, 43*(3), 1535–1545. doi: 1007/s10508-014-0300-8

Diamond, J. (1999). *Guns, germs and steel: The fates of human societies.* New York, NY: Norton.

DiAngelo, R. (2011). White fragility. *International Journal of Critical Pedagogy, 3*, 54–70.

DiAngelo, R., & Sensoy, Ö. (2014). Getting slammed: White depictions of race discussions as arenas of violence. *Race, Ethnicity and Education, 17*, 103–128. http://dx.doi.org/10.1080/13613324.2012.674023

Dienhart, A. (2001). Engaging men in family therapy: Does the gender of the therapist make a difference? *Journal of Family Therapy, 23*, 21–45.

Diep, H., & Estrellado, J. (2018, August 4). At the intersection of language, gender, and identity. Workshop sponsored by the San Diego Psychological Association.

Diller, J. V. (2007). *Cultural diversity: A primer for the human services* (3rd ed.). Belmont, CA: Thomson Brooks/Cole.

Dominguez, V. R. (1986). *White by definition: Social classification in Creole Louisiana.* New Brunswick, NJ: Rutgers University Press.

Douglass, S., Mirpuri, S., English, D., & Yip, T. (2016). "They were just making jokes": Ethnic/racial teasing and discrimination among adolescents. *Cultural Diversity & Ethnic Minority Psychology, 22,* 69–82. http://dx.doi.org/10.1037/cdp0000041

Dovidio, J., & Esses, V. (2001). Immigrants and immigration: Advancing the psychological perspective. *Journal of Social Issues, 57*(3), 375–387.

Downing-Matibag, T. M. & Geisinger, B. (2009). Hooking up and sexual risk taking among college students: A health belief model perspective. *Qualitative Health Research, 19*(9), 1196–1209. doi.org/10.1177/1049732309344206

Drescher, J. (2015). Out of DSM: Depathologizing homosexuality. *Behavioral Science, 5*(4),565–575. doi: 10.3390/bs5040565

Drewery, W. (1986). The challenge of feminism and the practice of counselling. *New Zealand Counselling and Guidance Association Journal, 8*(1), 18–28.

Drewery, W. (2005). Why we should watch what we say: Position calls, everyday speech and the production of relational subjectivity. *Theory & Psychology, 15*(3), 305–324.

Drewery, W., & Monk, G. (1994). Some reflections on the therapeutic power of poststructuralism. *International Journal for the Advancement of Counselling, 17*(4), 303–313.

Drewery, W., Winslade, J., & Monk, G. (2000). Resisting the dominating story: Toward a deeper understanding of narrative therapy. In R. Neimeyer & J. Raskin (Eds.), *Constructions of disorder: Meaning-making frameworks for psychotherapy* (pp. 243–264). Washington, DC: American Psychological Association.

Du Bois, W. E. B. (1903). *The Souls of Black Folk.* Chicago, IL: A.C. McClurg & Co.

Duhigg, C. (2019, January/February). Why are we so angry? *The Atlantic,* pp. 64–75.

Dukes, K. N., & Gaither, S. E. (2017). Black racial stereotypes and victim blaming: Implications for media coverage and criminal proceedings in cases of police violence against racial and ethnic minorities. *Journal of Social Issues, 73,* 789–807. http://dx.doi.org/10.1111/josi.12248

Duran, E. (2006). *Healing the soul wound: Counseling with American Indians and other native peoples.* New York, NY: Teachers College Press.

Durie, M. H. (1989). A move that's well overdue: Shaping counselling to meet the needs of Maori people. *New Zealand Counselling and Guidance Association Journal, 11*(1), 13–23.

Dutton, D. G., & Corvo, K. (2006). Transforming a flawed policy: A call to revive psychology and science in domestic violence research and practice. *Aggression and Violent Behavior, 11*(5), 457–483.

Easton, D., & Hardy, J. H. (2009). *The ethical slut: A practical guide to polyamory, open relationships & other adventures.* Berkeley, CA: Celestial Arts.

Edison Research. (2018, June 21). *Sexual Harassment in the Workplace.* Retrieved from http://www.edisonresearch.com/sexualharassmentworkplace/

Ehrenreich, B. (1999, March 8). The real truth about the female body. *Time, 153*(9). Retrieved from http://www.time.com/time/magazine/article/0,9171,20616,00.html

Ehrensaft, D. (2017). Gender nonconforming youth: Current perspectives. *Adolescent Health, Medicine and Therapeutics, 8,* 57–67. doi: 10.2147/AHMT.S110859

Eko, L. (2003). Globalization and the mass media in Africa. In L. Artz & Y. R. Kamalipour (Eds.), *The globalization of corporate media hegemony* (pp. 195–212). Albany, NY: State University of New York Press.

Ellis, A. (1985). *The case against religion: A psychotherapist's view and the case against religiosity.* Austin, TX: American Atheist Press.

Emmons, L. (1992). Dieting and purging behavior in black and white high school students. *Journal of the American Dietetic Association, 92*(3), 306–312.

Engeln, R. (2017). *Beauty sick: How the cultural obsession with appearance hurts girls and women.* New York, NY: Harper Collins.

England, P., & Bearak, J. (2014). The sexual double standard and gender differences in attitudes toward casual sex among U.S. university students. *Demographic Research, 30*(1), 1327–1338. doi: 10.4054/DemRes.2014.30.46

Englar-Carlson, M., Evans, M., & Duffey, T. (2014). *A counselor's guide to working with men.* Alexandria, VA: American Counseling Association.

Enns, C. Z. (1993). Twenty years of feminist counseling and therapy: From naming biases to implementing multifaceted practice. *Counseling Psychologist, 21*(1), 3–87.

Enson, S. (2017). Evaluating the impact of pornography on the lives of children and young people. *British Journal of School Nursing, 12*(7), 326–330.

Entwhistle, H. (2000). Educating multicultural citizens: Melting pot or mosaic. *International Journal of Social Education, 14*(2), 1–15.

Erlandsson, K., Nordvall, C. J., Öhman, A., Häggström-Nordin, E. (2012). Qualitative interviews with adolescents about "friends-with-benefits" relationships. *Public Health Nursing Populations at Risk Across the Lifespan: Case Studies.* https://doi.org/10.1111/j.1525-1446.2012.01040.x

Escoffier, J. (1991). The limits of multiculturalism. *Socialist Review, 21*(3–4), 61–73.

Esmail, A. (2010). "Negotiating fairness": A study on how lesbian family members evaluate, construct, and maintain "fairness" with the division of household labor. *Journal of Homosexuality, 57*(5), 591–609. doi.org/10.1080/00918361003711881

Espinosa Miñoso, Y. (2009). Etnocentrismo y colonialidad en los feminismos latinoamericanos: complicidades y consolidación de las hegemonías feministas en el espacio transnacional. [Ethnocentrism and coloniality in Latin American feminisms: Complicities and consolidation of feminist hegemonies in the transnational space]. *Revista Venezolana de Estudios de la Mujer, 14*(33), 37–54.

Evans, K., Kincade, E., & Seem, S. (2011). *Introduction to feminist therapy: Strategies for social and individual change.* Thousand Oaks, CA: SAGE.

Evans, L., & Davies, K. (2000). No sissy boys here: A content analysis of the representation of masculinity in elementary school reading textbooks. *Sex Roles, 42*, 255–270.

Ewing, J., Estes, R., & Like, B. (2017). Narrative neurotherapy (NNT). In M-N. Beaudoin & J. Duvall (Eds.), *Collaborative Therapy and Neurobiology: Evolving Practices in Action* (pp. 87–100). London, UK: Routledge.

Fadiman, A. (1998). *The spirit catches you and you fall down: A Hmong child, her American doctors, and the collision of two cultures.* New York, NY: Noonday Press.

Fairclough, N. (1992). *Discourse and social change.* Cambridge, UK: Polity Press.

Faludi, S. (1999). *Stiffed: The betrayal of American men.* New York, NY: Morrow.

Fanon, F. (1952). *Black skin, White masks.* New York, NY: Grove Press.

Fanon, F. (1963). *The wretched of the earth.* New York, NY: Grove Press.

Farley, M. (2018). Risks of Prostitution: When the Person Is the Product. *Journal of the Association for Consumer Research, 3*(1), 97–108. doi:10.1086/695670

Fay, B. (1987). *Critical social science: Liberation and its limits.* Cambridge, UK: Polity Press.

Federoff, J.P, Di Gioaccino, L., Murphy, L. (2013). Problems with paraphilias in the DSM-5. Current Psychiatry Reports 15, 363. Doi: 10.1007/s11920-013-0363-6

Federici, S. (2018). *Witches, witch-hunting, and women.* Oakland, CA: PM Press.

Feingold, A., & Mazzella, R. (1998). Gender differences in body image are increasing. *Psychological Science, 9*(3), 190–195.

Feldman, S., & Zaller, J. (1992). The political culture of ambivalence: Ideological responses to the welfare state. *American Journal of Political Science, 36*(1), 268–307.

Felitti, V. J., Anda, R. F., Nordenberg, D., Williamson, D. F., Spitz, A. M., Edwards, V., et al. (1998). Relationship of childhood abuse and household dysfunction to many of the leading causes of death in adults. *American Journal of Preventive Medicine, 14*(4), 245–258.

Fernández, I., Carrera, P., Sánchez, F., Páez, D., & Candia, L. (2000). Differences between cultures in emotional verbal and non-verbal reactions. *Psicothema, 12*, 83–92.

Ferrante, J., & Brown, P., Jr. (2001). *The social construction of race and ethnicity in the United States.* Upper Saddle River, NJ: Prentice Hall.

Ferraro, K. J. (1996). The dance of dependency: A genealogy of domestic violence discourse. *Hypatia, 11*(4), 77–91.

Fischer, A. R., & Good, G. E. (1997). Masculine gender roles, recognition of emotions, and interpersonal intimacy. *Psychotherapy, 34*, 160–170.

Fisher, P., & Maloney, T. (1994). Beliefs, assumptions and practices of two feminist therapists. *Bulletin of the New Zealand Psychological Society, 80*, 17–20.

Flax, J. (1990). Postmodernism and gender relations in feminist theory. In L. J. Nicholson (Ed.), *Feminism/postmodernism* (pp. 39–62). New York, NY: Routledge.

Flax, J. (1992). The end of innocence. In J. Butler & J. W. Scott (Eds.), *Feminists theorise the political* (pp. 445–463). London, UK: Routledge.

Flynn, G. (2012). *Gone girl: A novel.* New York, NY: Broadway Books.

Foucault, M. (1969). *The archaeology of knowledge* (A. M. S. Smith, Trans.). London, UK: Tavistock.

Foucault, M. (1972). *The order of things: An archaeology of the human sciences* (A. M. S. Smith, Trans.). New York, NY: Pantheon.

Foucault, M. (1978). *The history of sexuality: An introduction* (vol. 1; R. Hurley, Trans.). New York: Vintage Books.

Foucault, M. (1980). *Power/knowledge: Selected interviews and other writings*. New York, NY: Pantheon Books.

Foucault, M. (1982). The subject and power. *Critical Inquiry, 8*(4), 777–795. Retrieved from http://www.jstor.org/stable/1343197

Foucault, M. (1983). *This is not a pipe* (J. Harkness, Trans.). Berkeley, CA: University of California Press.

Foucault, M. (2000). *Power: Essential works of Foucault, 1954–1984* (vol. 3; J. Faubion, Ed.; R. Hurley, Trans.). New York, NY: New Press.

Foucault, M. (2005). *The hermeneutics of the subject: Lectures at the College de France* (F. Gros, F. Ewald, & A. Fontana, Eds.; G. Burchell, Trans.). New York, NY: Palgrave Macmillan.

Fowers, B. J., & Davidov, B. J. (2006). The virtue of multiculturalism: Personal transformation, character, and openness to the other. *American Psychologist, 61*(6), 581–594.

Frankenberg, R. (1993). *White women, race matters: The social construction of whiteness*. Minneapolis, MN: University of Minnesota Press.

Fraser, N. (1995). From redistribution to recognition? Dilemmas of justice in a 'post-socialist' age. *New Left Review, 212*, 68–94.

Fredriksen-Goldsen, K. I., Kim, H.-J., Emlet, C. A., Muraco, A., Erosheva, E. A., Hoy-Ellis, C. P., et al. (2011). The aging and health report: disparities and resilience among lesbian, gay, bisexual, and transgender older adults [executive summary]. Retrieved from http://age-pride.org/wordpress/wp-content/uploads/2012/10/Executive_Summary10-25-12.pdf

Freire, P. (1976). *Pedagogy of the oppressed*. Harmondsworth, UK: Penguin Books.

Freud, S. (1938). *The basic writings of Sigmund Freud* (A. Brill, Ed. & Trans.). New York, NY: Modern Library.

Friedman, M. S., Marshal, M. P., Guadamuz, T. E., Wei, C., Wong, C. F., Saewyc, E., et al. (2011). A meta-analysis of disparities in childhood sexual abuse, parental physical abuse, and peer victimization among sexual minority and sexual nonminority individuals. *American Journal of Public Health, 101*(8), 1481–1494. doi: 10.2105/AJPH.2009.190009

Friedman, T. L. (2005). *The world is flat: A brief history of the twenty-first century*. New York, NY: Farrar, Straus and Giroux.

Fuertes, J. N., Mueller, L. N., Chauhan, R. V., Walker, J. A., & Ladany, N. (2002). An investigation of European American therapists' approach to counseling African American clients. *Counseling Psychologist, 30*, 763–788.

Fukuyama, F. (2018) *Identity: The demand for dignity and the politics of resentment*. New York, NY: Farrar, Straus & Giroux.

Fukuyama, M. A., & Sevig, T. D. (1999). *Integrating spirituality into multicultural counseling*. Thousand Oaks, CA: SAGE.

Garanzini, S., Yee, A., Gottman, J., Gottman, J. Cole, C., Preciado, M., et al. (2017). Results of Gottman Method couples therapy with gay and lesbian couples. *Journal of Marriage and Family Therapy, 43*(4), 674–684. doi.org/10.1111/jmft.12276

Garbarino, J., & Bedard, C. (2001). *Parents under siege*. New York, NY: Free Press.

Garcia, J. R., Reiber, C., Massey, S. G., & Merriwether, A. M. (2012). Sexual hookup culture: A review. *Review of General Psychology, 16*(2), 161–176. http://dx.doi.org/10.1037/a0027911

Gavey, N. (1996). Women's desire and sexual violence discourse. In S. Wilkinson (Ed.), *Feminist social psychologies: International perspectives* (pp. 51–65). Philadelphia, PA: Open University Press.

Gavey, N., & McPhillips, K. (1999). Subject to romance: Heterosexual passivity as an obstacle to women initiating condom use. *Psychology of Women Quarterly, 23*, 349–367.

Gee, C. G., & Verissimo D. O. (2016). Racism and behavioral outcomes over the life course. In A. N. Alvarez, C. T. H. Liang, & H. A. Neville (Eds.), *The cost of racism for people of color: Contextualizing experiences of discrimination* (pp. 133–162). Washington, DC: American Psychological Association.

Geertz, C. (1983). *Local knowledge: Further essays in interpretive anthropology*. New York, NY: Basic Books.

Geertz, C. (1995). *After the fact*. Cambridge, MA: Harvard University Press.

Geiger, A., & Livingston, G. (2018). *8 facts about love and marriage in America*. Retrieved from http://www.pewresearch.org/fact-tank/2018/02/13/8-facts-about-love-and-marriage/

Gelfand, M. J. (2018). *Rule makers, rule breakers: How culture wires our minds, shapes our nations, and drives our differences*. London, UK: Hachette UK.

Gelso, C., & Fretz, B. (2001). Counseling psychology (2nd ed.). Fort Worth, TX: Harcourt.

Gerber, D. A. (2011). *American immigration: A very short introduction*. New York, NY: Oxford University Press.

Gergen, K. (2015). From mirroring to world-making: Research as future-forming. *Journal for the Theory of Social Behaviour, 45*(3), 287–310.

Gergen, K. J. (1994). *Reality and relationships: Soundings in social construction*. Cambridge, MA: Harvard University Press.

Gergen, K. J. (1999). *An invitation to social construction*. London, UK: SAGE.

Gergen, K. J. (2007). *The saturated self.* .New York, NY: Basic Books.

Gergen, K. J. (2009). *The relational being: Beyond self and community*. New York, NY: Oxford University Press.

Gergen, K. J., & Davis, K. (Eds.). (1985). *The social construction of the person*. New York, NY: Springer.

Gervais, S., Vescio, T., & Allen, J. (2011). When what you see is what you get: The consequences of the objectifying gaze for women and men. *Psychology of Women Quarterly, 35*(1), 5–17.

Gilbert, L. A. (1980). Feminist therapy. In N. A. Brodsky & R. T. Hare-Mustin (Eds.), *Women in psychotherapy* (pp. 245–265). New York, NY: Guilford Press.

Gilbert, L., & Scher, M. (2009). *Gender and sex in counseling and psychotherapy*. Eugene, OR: Resource Publications.

Gilden, J. (2005). As the number of fliers soars, expansion efforts are underway. *Los Angeles Times*. Retrieved from http://www.latimes.com/news/local/valley/la-tr-airports23jan23,1, 29058.story

Giorgio, G. (2002). Speaking silence: Definitional dialogues in abusive lesbian relationships. *Violence Against Women, 8*(10), 1233-1259. Doi/abs/10.1177/107780120200801005

Giroux, H. A. (2002). *Breaking into the movies: Film and the culture of politics*. Malden: MA: Blackwell.

Gladwell. M. (2007). *Blink: The power of thinking without thinking*. New York, NY: Little, Brown and Company.

Glazer, N., & Moynihan, D. P. (1970). *Beyond the melting pot* (2nd ed.). Cambridge, MA: MIT Press.

Glendinning, S. (2011). *Derrida: A very short introduction*. Oxford, UK: Oxford University Press.

Glick, E. (2000). Sex positive: Feminism, queer theory, and the politics of transgression. *Feminist Review 64*(1), 19–45.

Goffman, E. (1986). *Stigma: Notes on the management of spoiled identity*. New York, NY: Touchstone.

Goldberg, D. T. (1993). *Racist culture: Philosophy and the politics of meaning*. Cambridge, MA: Blackwell.

Goldner, V. (1985). Feminism and family therapy. *Family Process, 24*, 31–47.

Gone, J. P., Hartmann, W. E., Pomerville, A., Wendt, D. C., Klem, S. H., & Burrage, R. L. (2019). The impact of historical trauma on health outcomes for indigenous populations in the USA and Canada: A systematic review. *American Psychologist, 74*, 20–35. http://dx.doi.org/10.1037/amp0000338

Good, G. E., Dell, D. M., & Mintz, L. B. (1989). Male role and gender role conflict: Relations to help seeking in men. *Journal of Counseling Psychology, 36*, 295–300.

Good, G. E., Gilbert, L. A., & Scher, M. (1990). Gender aware therapy: A synthesis of feminist therapy and knowledge about gender. *Journal of Counseling & Development, 68*, 376–380.

Good, G. E., & Sherrod, N. B. (2001). Men's problems and effective treatments: Theory and empirical support. In G. R. Brooks & G. E. Good (Eds.), *The new handbook of psychotherapy and counseling with men* (vol. 1, pp. 22–40). San Francisco, CA: Jossey-Bass.

Good, G. E., Thomson, D., & Brathwaite, A. (2005). Men and therapy: Critical concepts, theoretical frameworks, and research recommendations. *Journal of Clinical Psychology, 61*(6), 699–711.

Good, G. E., & Wood, P. K. (1995). Male gender role conflict, depression, and help seeking: Do college men face double jeopardy? *Journal of Counseling & Development, 74*, 70–75.

Goodman, N. (1978). *Ways of worldmaking*. Indianapolis, IN: Hackett.

Goodwin, G. C. (1977). *Cherokees in transition: A study of changing culture and environment prior to 1775*. Chicago, IL: University of Chicago, Department of Geography.

Gore, J. (1992). What we can do for you! What can "we" do for "you"? Struggling over empowerment in critical and feminist pedagogy. In C. Luke & J. Gore (Eds.), *Feminisms and critical pedagogy* (pp. 54–73). New York, NY: Routledge.

Gorospe, J. (2007, March). *Deadly silent: Filipino American adolescents and emotional disturbance*. Paper presented at the annual conference of the National Association of School Psychologists, New York.

Gossett, T. F. (1963). *The history of an idea in America*. Dallas, TX: Southern Methodist University Press.

Gottman, J. M., Levenson, R. W., Swanson, C., Tyson, R., & Yoshimoto, D. (2003). Observing gay, lesbian and heterosexual couples' relationships: Mathematical modeling of conflict interaction. *Journal of Homosexuality, 45*(1), 65–91.

Grabe, S., & Hyde, J. (2006). Ethnicity and body dissatisfaction among women in the United States: A meta-analysis. *Psychological Bulletin, 132*, 622–640.

Graf, N. (2018, September 27). *Sexual harassment at work in the era of #MeToo*. Retrieved from http://www.pewsocialtrends.org/2018/04/04/sexual-harassment-at-work-in-the-era-of-metoo/

Graham, D. A. (2012, September 27.). Really, would you let your daughter marry a Democrat? *The Atlantic*. Retrieved from https://www.theatlantic.com/politics/archive/2012/09/really-would-you-let-your-daughter-marry-a-democrat/262959/

Gramsci, A. (1971). *Selections from the prison notebooks*. New York, NY: International.

Granello, D. H., & Beamish, P. M. (1998). Reconceptualizing codependency in women: A sense of connectedness, not pathology. *Journal of Mental Health Counseling, 20*(4), 344–358.

Green, A. R., Carney, D. R., Pallin, D. J., Ngo, L. H., Raymond, K. L., Iezzoni, L. I., et al. (2007). Implicit bias among physicians and its prediction of thrombolysis decisions for black and white patients. *Journal of General Internal Medicine, 22*(9), 1231-1238.

Green, E. (2015, February 10). Consent isn't enough: The troubling sex of fifty shades. *The Atlantic*. Retrieved from https://www.theatlantic.com/entertainment/archive/2015/02/consent-isnt-enough-in-fifty-shades-of-grey/385267/

Green, J., & Jakupcak, M. (2016). Masculinity and men's self-harm behaviors: Implications for non-suicidal self-injury disorder. *Psychology of Men & Masculinity*, *17*(2), 147–155.

Green, T. (2005). Multicultural counseling lecture series. Unpublished PowerPoint presentation, Department of Counseling and School Psychology, San Diego State University, San Diego, CA.

Greene, D. C., Britton, P. J. & Fitts, B. (2014). Long-term outcomes of lesbian, gay, bisexual, and transgender recalled school victimization. *Journal of Counseling & Development*, *92*(4), 406–417. doi.org/10.1002/j.1556-6676.2014.00167.x

Greenwald, A. G., & Banaji, M. R. (2017). The implicit revolution: Reconceiving the relation between conscious and unconscious. *American Psychologist*, *72*(9), 861.

Gremillion, H. (2003). *Feeding anorexia*. Durham, NC: Duke University Press.

Griffith, D. M., & Cornish, E. K. (2018). "What defines a man?": Perspectives of African American men on the components and consequences of manhood. *Psychology of Men & Masculinity*, *19*, 78–88. http://dx.doi.org/10.1037/men0000083

Griffith, J. L., & Griffith, M. E. (1994). *The body speaks: Therapeutic dialogues for mind-body problems*. New York, NY: Basic Books.

Grimshaw, J. (1986). *Philosophy and feminist thinking*. Minneapolis, MN: University of Minnesota Press.

Grogan, S. (2016). *Body image: Understanding body dissatisfaction in men, women and children*. London, UK: Routledge.

Grosfoguel, R. (2000). Developmentalism, modernity, and dependency theory in Latin America. *Neplanta: Views from South*, *1*(2), 347–374.

Grosfoguel, R. (2012). The dilemmas of ethnic studies in the United States: Between liberal multiculturalism, identity politics, disciplinary colonization, and decolonial epistemologies. *Human Architecture: Journal of the Sociology of Self-Knowledge*, *10*(1), 80–88.

Grossberg, L., Nelson, C., & Treichler, P. (1992). *Cultural studies*. New York, NY: Routledge.

Grzanka, P. R., Santos, C. E., & Moradi, B. (2017). Intersectionality research in counseling psychology. *Journal of Counseling Psychology*, *64*(5), 453–457. http://dx.doi.org/10.1037/cou0000237

Guadalupe, K. L., & Lum, D. (2005). *Multidimensional contextual practice: Diversity and transcendence*. Belmont, CA: Thomson Brooks/Cole.

Guay, A. T. (2001). Advances in the management of androgen deficiency in women. *Medical Aspects of Human Sexuality*, *1*, 32–38.

Guess, A., Nyhan, B., & Reifler, J. (2018). Selective exposure to misinformation: Evidence from the consumption of fake news during the 2016 US presidential campaign [PDF file]. *European Research Council*. Retrieved from http://www.ask-force.org/web/Fundamentalists/Guess-Selective-Exposure-to-Misinformation-Evidence-Presidential-Campaign-2018.pdf

Guilfoyle, M. (2005). From therapeutic power to resistance? Therapy and cultural hegemony. *Theory & Psychology*, *15*(1), 101–124.

Gurian, M. (1999). *A fine young man: What parents and educators can do to shape adolescent boys into exceptional men*. New York, NY: Tarcher.

Hacking, I. (1995). The looping effects of human kinds. In D. Sperber & A. J. Premack (Eds.), *Causal cognition* (pp. 351–383). Oxford, UK: Oxford University Press.

Hagan, W. T. (1993). *American Indians* (3rd ed.). Chicago, IL: University of Chicago Press.

Haider, A. (2018). Mistaken identity: Race and class in the age of Trump. London, UK: Verso Press.

Haley, A. (1976). *Roots: The saga of an American family*. New York, NY: Doubleday.

Halkitis, P. (2000). Masculinity in the age of AIDS: HIV-seropositive gay men and the "buff agenda". In P. Nardi (Ed.), *Gay masculinities* (pp. 130–151). Thousand Oaks, CA: Sage Publications.

Hall, S., Evans, J. & Nixon, S. (2013*). Representation: Cultural representations and signifying practices*. Thousand Oaks, CA: Sage.

Ham, M. D. (1993). Empathy. In J. L. Ching, J. H. Liem, M. D. Ham, & G. K. Hong (Eds.), *Transference and empathy in Asian-American psychotherapy: Cultural values and treatment needs* (pp. 35–62). Westport, CT: Praeger.

Hamel, L., Firth, J., Hoff, T., Kates, J., Levine, S., & Dawson, L. (2014). HIV/AIDS in the lives of gay and bisexual men in the United States [report]. Retrieved from Kaiser Family Foundation website: http://files.kff.org/attachment/survey-hivaids-in-the-lives-of-gay-and-bisexual-men-in-the-united-states

Hammond, A. (2005). *Pop culture Arab world! Media, arts, and lifestyle*. Santa Barbara, CA: ABC-CLIO.

Hanson, R. (2009). *Buddha's brain: The practical neuroscience of happiness, love, and wisdom*. Oakland, CA: New Harbinger Publications.

Haraway, D. (1990). A manifesto in cyborgs: Science, technology and socialist feminism in the 1980s. In L. Nicholson (Ed.), *Feminism/postmodernism* (pp. 190–233). London, UK: Routledge.

Hare-Mustin, R. T. (1994). Discourses in the mirrored room: A postmodern analysis of therapy. *Family Process*, *33*, 19–34.

Hare-Mustin, R. T., & Marecek, J. (1994). Feminism & postmodernism: Dilemmas and points of resistance. *Dulwich Centre Newsletter*, *4*, 13–19.

Hart, R. (1971). *Witchcraft*. London, UK: Wayland.

Hartmann, W. E., Wendt, D. C., Burrage, R. L., Pomerville, A., & Gone, J. P. (2019). American Indian historical trauma: Anticolonial prescriptions for healing, resilience, and survivance. *American Psychologist*, *74*, 6–19. http://dx.doi.org/10.1037/amp0000326

Harvey, D. (1989). *The condition of postmodernity*. Oxford, UK: Blackwell.

Haslam, N., & Whelan, J. (2008). Human natures: Psychological essentialism in thinking about differences between people. *Social and Personality Psychology Compass*, *2*(3), 1297–1312. doi: 10.1111/j.1751-9004.2008.00112.x

Hatzenbuehler, M. L., McLaughlin, K. A., Keyes, K. M., & Hasin, D. S. (2010). The impact of institutional discrimination on psychiatric disorders in lesbian, gay, and bisexual populations: A prospective study. *American Journal of Public Health*, *100*(3), 452–459. doi: 10.2105/AJPH.2009.168815

Haupert, M. L., Gesselman, A. N., Moors, A. C., Fisher, H. E. & Garcia, J. R. (2017). Prevalence of experiences with consensual nonmonogamous relationships: Findings from two national samples of single Americans. *Journal of Sexuality and Marital Therapy*, *43*(5), 424–440. doi: 10.1080/0092623X.2016.1178675

Hawton, K., & van Heeringen, K. (2000). *The international handbook of suicide and attempted suicide*. Hoboken, NJ: John Wiley & Sons.

Hays, D. G., & Chang, C. Y. (2003). White privilege, oppression, and racial identity development: Implications for supervision. *Counselor Education and Supervision*, *43*(2), 134–145.

Hays, D. G., Chang, C. Y., & Dean, J. K. (2004). White counselors' conceptualization of privilege and oppression: Implications for counselor training. *Counselor Education and Supervision*, *43*, 242–257.

Hechter, M. (1975*). Internal colonialism: The Celtic fringe in British national development, 1536–1966*. London, UK: Routledge and Kegan Paul.

Heesacker, M., & Prichard, S. (1992). In a different voice, revisited: Men, women, and emotion. *Journal of Mental Health Counseling*, *14*, 274–290.

Heesacker, M., Wester, S. R., Vogel, D. L., Wentzel, J. T., Mejia-Millan, C. M., & Goodholm, C. R., Jr. (1999). Gender-based emotional stereotyping. *Journal of Counseling Psychology*, *46*(4), 483–495.

Heffernan, K. (1996). Eating disorders and weight concern among lesbians. *International Journal of Eating Disorders*, *19*(2), 127–138.

Heid, M. (2017, August 2). You asked: Is social media making me miserable? *Time*. Retrieved from http://time.com/4882372/social-media-facebook-instagram-unhappy/

Heijmans, P. (2017, July 10). The unprecedented explosion of smartphones in Myanmar. *Bloomberg Businessweek*. Retrieved from https://www.bloomberg.com/news/features/2017-07-10/the-unprecedented-explosion-of-smartphones-in-myanmar

Helfland, J., & Lippin, L. (2001). *Understanding whiteness/unraveling racism: Tools for the journey*. Cincinnati, OH: Thomson Learning Custom Publishing.

Helms, J. E. (1994). *The conceptualization of racial identity and other "racial" constructs*. In E. Trickett, R. Watts, & D. Birman (Eds.), *Human diversity: Perspectives on people in context* (pp. 261–284). San Francisco, CA: Jossey-Bass.

Helms, J., & Cook, D. (2007). *Using race and culture in counseling and psychotherapy*. Upper Saddle River, NJ : Prentice Hall.

Hemming, J. (1970). *The conquest of the Incas* (1st American ed.). New York. NY: Harcourt, Brace, Jovanovich.

Henderson, L. (1991). Lesbian pornography: Cultural transgression and sexual demystification. Reprinted in S. Munt (Ed.), *New lesbian criticism: Literary and cultural perspectives* (pp. 173–191). London, UK: Harvester Wheatsheaf.

Henn, B. M., Cavalli-Sforza, L. L., & Feldman, M. W. (2012). The great human expansion. *Proceedings of the National Academy of Sciences*, *109*(44), 17758–17764. doi: 10.1073/pnas.1212380109

Henriques, J., Hollway, W., Urwin, C., Venn, C., & Walkerdine, V. (1984*). Changing the subject: Psychology, social regulation, and subjectivity*. London, UK: Methuen.

Henze, R., Lucas, T., & Scott, B. (1998). Dancing with the monster: Teachers discuss racism, power, and white privilege. *Urban Review*, *30*(3), 187–210.

Herek, G. M. (2009). Hate crimes and stigma-related experiences among sexual minority adults in the United States: Prevalence estimates from a national probability sample. *Journal of Interpersonal Violence*, *24*(1), 54–74. doi.org/10.1177/0886260508316477

Hernandez, P., Almedia, R., & Dolan–Del Vecchio, K. (2005). Critical consciousness, accountability, and empowerment: Key processes for helping families heal. *Family Process*, *44*(1), 105–119.

Herold, E. S., & Milhausen, R. R. (1999). Dating preferences of university women: An analysis of the nice guy stereotype. *Journal of Sex & Marital Therapy, 25*(4), 333–343.

Herzog, D. B., Newman, K. L., Yeh, C. J., & Warshaw, M. (1992). Body image satisfaction in homosexual and heterosexual women. *International Journal of Eating Disorders, 11*(4), 391–396.

Hesse-Biber, S., Clayton-Matthews, A., & Downey, J. A. (1987). The differential importance of weight and body image among college men and women. *Genetic, Social, and General Psychology Monographs, 113*(4), 509–528.

Hetherington, M., & Weiler, J. (2018). *Prius or pickup? How the answer to four simple questions explain America's great divide.* New York, NY: Houghton Mifflin Harcourt.

Hill, D.L., Antone, R. A. & Myers, B.A. (1986). Power Within People: A Community Organizing Perspective. Multiple Nations: Diane Hill.

Hindmarsh, J. H. (1987). Letting gender secrets out of the bag. *Australia and New Zealand Journal of Family Therapy, 8*(4), 205–211.

Hindmarsh, J. H. (1993). Alternative family therapy discourses: It is time to reflect (critically). *Journal of Feminist Family Therapy, 5*(2), 5–28.

Hird, M. (2008). *Queering the non/human.* Aldershot, UK: Ashgate Publishing Limited.

Hochschild, A. R. (1983). Attending to, codifying, and managing feelings: Sex differences in love. In L. Richardson & V. Taylor (Eds.) *Feminist frontiers: Rethinking sex, gender, and society*, (pp. 250–262). Boston, MA: Addison-Wesley.

Hochschild, A. R. (1997). *The time bind: When work becomes home and home becomes work.* New York, NY: Metropolitan Books.

Hockey, J., Meah, A., & Robinson, V. (2007). *Mundane heterosexualities: From theory to practices.* Basingstoke, UK: Palgrave MacMillan.

Hollinger, D. (1995). *Postethnic America: Beyond multiculturalism.* New York, NY: Basic Books.

Holoien, D. S., & Shelton, J. N. (2012). You deplete me: The cognitive costs of colorblindness on ethnic minorities. *Journal of Experimental Social Psychology, 48*, 562–565. http://dx.doi.org/10.1016/j.jesp.2011.09.010

hooks, b. (2000). *Where we stand: Class matters.* New York, NY: Routledge.

Hopkins, M. (1647). *The discovery of witches.* Witch finder, The benefit of the whole kingdome, M.DC. XLVII.

Horsman, R. (1981). *Race and manifest destiny: The origins of American racial AngloSaxonism.* Cambridge, MA: Harvard University Press.

Hoshiai, M., Matsumoto, Y., Sato, T., Ohnishi, M., Okabe, N., Kisimoto, Y., et al. (2010). Psychiatric comorbidity among patients with gender identity disorder. *Psychiatry and Clinical Neurosciences, 64*(5), 514–519. doi: 10.1111/j.1440-1819.2010.02118.x

Hoshmand, L. T. (Ed.). (2005). *Culture, psychotherapy, and counseling: Critical and integrative perspectives.* Thousand Oaks, CA: SAGE.

Hoshmand, L. T., & Polkinghorne, D. E. (1992). Redefining the science-practice relationship in professional training. *American Psychologist, 47*(1), 55–66.

Houshmand, S., Spanierman, L. B., & De Stefano, J. (2017). Racial microaggressions: A primer with implications for counseling practice. *International Journal for the Advancement of Counseling, 39*, 206–216. http://dx.doi.org/10.1007/s10447-017-9292-0

Hsu, J. (2009, June 7). People choose news that fits their views. *Live Science.* Retrieved from https://www.livescience.com/3640-people-choose-news-fits-views.html

Huntington, S. P. (2004). *Who are we? The challenges to America's national identity.* New York, NY: Simon & Schuster.

Ibrahim, F., & Heuer, J. (2016). Understanding acculturation and its use in counseling and psychotherapy. In A. Marsella (Ed.), *Cultural and social justice counseling* (pp. 77–98), Geneva, SW: Springer. http://dx.doi.org/10.1007/978-3-319-18057-1_4

Iceland, J. (2004). Beyond black and white metropolitan residential segregation in multiethnic America. *Social Science Research, 33*, 248–271.

Igarashi, H. (2014). Cosmopolitanism as cultural capital: Exploring the intersection of globalization, education and stratification. *Cultural Sociology, 8*(3), 222.

Individuals with Disabilities Education Act (Education for All Handicapped Children Act of 1975), Pub. L. No. 94–142, 89 Stat. 773.

Inequality and the American dream. (2006, June 15). *Economist*, p. 28.

Illouz, E. (2008). *Saving the modern soul: Therapy, emotions, and the cultures of self-help.* Berkeley, CA: University of California Press.

Ingleby, D. (2004). Critical psychiatry: The politics of mental health. London?: Free Association.

Inglehart, R. (2018). *Cultural evolution: Peoples motivations are changing and reshaping the world.* Cambridge, UK: Cambridge University Press.

Intimate Partner Abuse Against Men National Clearinghouse. (1999). *Family violence statistics Canada* [PDF file]. Retrieved from http://www.phac-aspc.gc.ca/ncfv-cnivf/familyviolence/pdfs/Intimate_Partner.pdf

Isaacson, M. (2014). Clarifying concepts: Cultural humility or competency. *Journal of Professional Nursing, 30*(3), 251–258.

Ivey, A. E. (1993). On the need for reconstruction of our present practice of counseling and psychotherapy. *Counseling Psychologist, 21*(2), 225–228.

Ivey, A. E., D'Andrea, M. J., & Ivey, M. B. (2012). *Theories of counseling and psychotherapy: A multicultural perspective.* Thousand Oaks, CA: SAGE.

Iwamoto, D. K., Cheng, A., Lee, C. S., Takamatsu, S., & Gordon, D. (2011). "Man-ing" up and getting drunk: The role of masculine norms, alcohol intoxication and alcohol-related problems among college men. *Addictive Behaviors, 36,* 906–911.

Iyengar, S., & Westwood, S. J. (2014). Fear and loathing across party lines: New evidence on group polarization. *American Journal of Political Science, 59*(3), 690–707. doi: 10.1111/ajps.12152

Izard, M. (1975). Slavery and social death. Cited in D. Berreby (2005), *Us and them: Understanding your tribal mind.* Boston, MA: Little, Brown and Company.

Jackson, R. L. (1999). White space, white privilege: Mapping discursive inquiry onto the self. *Quarterly Journal of Speech, 85*(1), 38–54.

Jackson, J. (2000). What *ought* psychology to do? *American Psychologist, 55*(3), 328–330. DOI 10.1037//0003.066x.55.3.328

Jacobi, T., & Schweers, D. (2017). Justice, interrupted: The effect of gender, ideology and seniority at Supreme Court oral arguments (October 24, 2017). 103 Virginia Law Review 1379 (2017); Northwestern Law & Econ Research Paper No. 17–03.

Jacobs, L.A. (2019, June). *Transgender care and informed consent: The person is radical.* PowerPoint presentation at American Association of Sexuality Educators, Counselors, and Therapists 51st Annual Conference, Philadelphia, PA.

James, E. L. (2012). *Fifty Shades Trilogy.* New York, NY: Vintage.

James, S. E., Herman, J. L., Rankin, S., Keisling, M., Mottet, L., & Anafi, M. (2016). The report on the 2015 Transgender Survey. Retrieved from https://www.transequality.org/sites/default/files/docs/USTS-Full-Report-FINAL.PDF

James, W. (1981). *The principles of psychology.* Cambridge, MA: Harvard University Press. (Originally published 1890.)

Janus, S. S., & Janus, C. L. (1994). *The Janus report on sexual behavior.* Hoboken, NJ: John Wiley and Sons.

Jencks, C. (1992). *The postmodern reader.* London, UK: Academy Editors.

Jenkins, A. (2009). *Becoming ethical: A parallel, political journey with men who have abused.* Lyme Regis, UK: Russell House Publishing.

Jenkins, A. H. (2001). Humanistic psychology and multiculturalism: A review and reflection. In K. J. Schneider, J. F. T. Bugental, & J. F. Pierson (Eds.), *The handbook of humanistic psychology: Leading edges in theory, research, and practice* (pp. 37–45). Thousand Oaks, CA: SAGE.

Jenkins, R. (2003). Rethinking ethnicity: Identity categorization and power. In J. Stone & R. Dennis (Eds.), *Race and ethnicity: Comparative and theoretical approaches* (pp. 59–71). Oxford, UK: Blackwell.

Johnson, G., Gershon, S., & Hekimian, L. J. (1968). Controlled evaluation of lithium and chlorpromazine in the treatment of manic states: An interim report. *Comprehensive Psychiatry, 9*(6), 563–573.

Johnson, J. H., & Partington, A. (2017). Corpus assisted discourse study of representations of the "Underclass" in the English-language press. In E. Friginal (Ed.) *Studies in corpus-based sociolinguistics* (293–318). New York, NY: Routledge.

Johnson, J. L. (2015, April 2). "TJ's Lasting Impressions" lifestyle club [Blog post in Queer Culture Collection]. Retrieved from https://sites.psu.edu/245spring2015/author/jlf5352/

Johnson, N. G. (2001). Women helping men: Strengths of and barriers to women working with men clients. In G. R. Brooks & G. E. Good (Eds.), *The new handbook of psychotherapy and counseling with men* (vol. 1, pp. 696–718). San Francisco, CA: Jossey-Bass.

Johnson, S., Kirk, J., & Keplinger, K. (2016, Oct 4). Why we fail to report sexual harassment. *Harvard Business Review.* Retrieved from https://hbr.org/2016/10/why-we-fail-to-report-sexual-harassment?autocomplete=true

Johnston-Goodstar, K., & VeLure Roholt, R. (2017). "Our kids aren't dropping out; they're being pushed out": Native American students and racial microaggressions in schools. *Journal of Ethnic & Cultural Diversity in Social Work, 26*(1–2), 30–47. http://dx.doi.org/10.1080/15313204.2016.1263818

Jones, A., & Guy, C. (1992). Radical feminism in New Zealand: From Piha to Newtown. In R. Duplessis, P. Bunkle, K. Irwin, A. Laurie, & S. Middleton (Eds.), *Feminist voices: Women's studies texts for Aotearoa/New Zealand* (pp. 300–316). Auckland, New Zealand: Oxford University Press.

Jones, A., & Seagull, A. A. (1977). Dimensions of the relationship between the black client and the white therapist. *American Psychologist, 32*(10), 850–855.

Jones, C. P. (2000). Levels of racism: The theoretical framework and a gardener's tale. *American Journal of Public health*, *90*(8), 1212–1215.

Joyal, C. C., Cossette, A., & Lapierre, V. (2015). What exactly is an unusual sexual fantasy? *Journal of Sexual Medicine*, *12*, 328–340.

Judis, J. B., & Teixeira, R. (2004). *The emerging Democratic majority*. New York, NY: Simon and Schuster.

Julia, M. (Ed.). (2000). *Constructing gender: Multicultural perspectives in working with women*. Belmont, CA: Thomson Brooks/Cole.

Jung, C. (1983). *Jung: Selected writings* (A. Storr, Ed.). London: Fontana.

Kahn, J. S. (2009). *An introduction to masculinities*. Chichester, UK: Wiley-Blackwell.

Kaholokula, J. K. A. (2016). Racism and physical health disparities. In A. N. Alvarez, C. T. H. Liang, & H. A. Neville (Eds.), *The cost of racism for people of color: Contextualizing experiences of discrimination* (pp. 163–188). Washington, DC: American Psychological Association.

Kail, R. V., & Cavanaugh, J. C. (2016). *Human development: A life span view*. Singapore: Cengage Learning Asia Pte.

Kanter, J. W., Williams, M. T., Kuczynski, A. M., Manbeck, K. E., Debreaux, M., & Rosen, D. C. (2017). A preliminary report on the relationship between microaggressions against Black people and racism among White college students. *Race and Social Problems*, *9*, 291–299. http://dx.doi.org/10.1007/s12552-017-9214-0

Kaplan, M. S., & Krueger, R. B. (2010). Diagnosis, assessment, and treatment of hypersexuality. *Journal of Sex Research*, *47*(2–3), 181–198.

Kasser, T., & Kanner, A. D. (Eds.). (2004). *Psychology and consumer culture: The struggle for a good life in a materialistic world*. Washington, DC: American Psychological Association.

Kasser, T., & Ryan, R. M. (2001). Be careful what you wish for: Optimal functioning and the relative attainment of intrinsic and extrinsic goals. In P. Schmuck & K. Sheldon (Eds.), *Life goals and well-being: Towards a positive psychology of human striving* (pp. 116–131). Gottingen: Hogrefe.

Kasser, T., Ryan, R. M., Couchman, C. E., & Sheldon, K. M. (2004). Materialistic values: Their causes and consequences. In T. Kasser & A. D. Kanner (Eds.), *Psychology and consumer culture: The struggle for a good life in a materialistic world* (pp. 11–28). Washington, DC: American Psychological Association.

Kawagley, A. O. (1995). *A Yupiaq world view: A pathway to ecology and spirit*. Prospect Heights, IL: Waveland Press.

Kertzner, R. M., Meyer, I. H., Frost, D. M., & Stirratt, M. J. (2009). Social and psychological well-being in lesbians, gay men, and bisexuals: The effects of race, gender, age, and sexual identity. *American Journal of Orthopsychiatry*, *79*(4), 500–510. http://dx.doi.org/10.1037/a0016848

Khalifa, M. A., Gooden, M. A., & Davis, J. E. (2016). Culturally responsive school leadership: A synthesis of the literature. *Review of Educational Research*, *86*(4), 1272–1311. doi: 10.3102/0034654316630383

Kimberly, C., & Hans, J. D. (2017). From fantasy to reality: A grounded theory of experiences in the swinging lifestyle. *Archives Sexual Behavior*, *46*, 789–799. doi: 10.1007/s10508-015-0621-2

Kimmel, D., & Yi, H. (2004). Characteristics of gay, lesbian, and bisexual Asians, Asian Americans, and immigrants from Asia to the USA. *Journal of Homosexuality*, *47*(2), 143–171.

Kimmel, M., & Levine, M. (1989). Men and AIDS. In M. Kimmel & M. Messner (Eds.), *Men's lives* (pp. 344–354). New York, NY: Macmillan.

King, J. C. (1981). *The biology of race*. Berkeley, CA: University of California Press.

King, J. E. (1991). Dysconscious racism: Ideology, identity, and the miseducation of teachers. *Journal of Negro Education*, *60*(2), 133–146.

King, M. (2003). *The Penguin history of New Zealand*. Auckland, New Zealand: Penguin Books.

Kinsey, A. C., Pomeroy, W. B., & Martin, C. E. (1948). *Sexual behavior in the human male*. Philadelphia, PA: Saunders.

Klaassen, M. J., & Peter, J. (2015). Gender (in) equality in Internet pornography: A content analysis of popular pornographic Internet videos. *The Journal of Sex Research*, *52*(7), 721–735.

Klein, F. (2013). *The bisexual option*. London, UK: Routledge.

Klein, M. A. (1998). *Slavery and colonial rule in French West Africa*. New York, NY: Cambridge University Press.

Knight, K. (2014). Communicative dilemmas in emerging adults' friends with benefits relationships: Challenges to relational talk. *Emerging Adulthood*, *2*(4), 270–279. https://doi.org/10.1177/2167696814549598

Knox, S., Burkard, A. W., Johnson, A. J., Suzuki, L. A., & Ponterotto, J. G. (2003). African American and European American therapists' experiences of addressing race in crossracial psychotherapy dyads. *Journal of Counseling Psychology*, *50*(4), 466–481.

Knudsen, G., DeCuypere, D. G., & Bockting, W. (2010). Response of the World Professional Association for Transgender Health to the proposed DSM 5 criteria for gender incongruence. *International Journal of Transgenderism*, *12*(2):119–123. doi: 10.1080/15532739.2010.509214

Knudson-Martin, C., Huenergardt, D., Lafontant, K., Bishop, L., Schaepper, J., & Wells, M. (2015). Competencies for addressing gender and power in couple therapy: A socio emotional approach. *Journal of Marital and Family Therapy*, *41*(2), 205–220.

Kohut, T., Fisher, W. A., & Campbell, L. (2016). Perceived effects of pornography on the couple relationship: Initial findings of open-ended, participant-informed, "bottom-up" research. *Archives of Sexual Behavior*, *46*(2), 585–602.

Kolmes, K., Stock, W., & Moser, C. (2006). Investigating bias in psychotherapy with BDSM clients. In P. Kleinplatz & C. Moser (Eds.), *SM: Powerful pleasures* (pp. 301–324). Binghamton, NY: Haworth Press.

Kort, J. (2008). *Gay affirmative therapy for the straight clinician: The essential guide*. New York, NY: Norton & Co, Inc.

Kottler, J. A. (1999). *Exploring and treating acquisitive desire*. Thousand Oaks, CA: SAGE.

Kottler, J., Montgomery, M., & Shepard, D. (2004), Acquisitive desire: Assessment and treatment. In T. Kasser & A. D. Kanner (Eds.), *Psychology and consumer culture: The struggle for a good life in a materialistic world* (pp. 149–168). Washington, DC: American Psychological Association.

Kovetz, L. B. (2006). Sisters are doin' it for themselves. *Publishers Weekly*, *253*(35), 74. Brisbane, Australia: Griffith University.

Kozol, J. (1992). *Savage inequalities: Children in America's schools*. New York, NY: Harper.

Kroeber, A. L., & Kluckhohn, C. (1952). *Culture: A critical review of concepts and definitions*. Cambridge, MA: Peabody Museum of Harvard University.

Krook, J. (2014). *Us vs Them: A case for social empathy*. Self-published.

Kuhn, K., Voges, K., Pope, N., & Bloxsome, E. (2007, September 28). *Pornography and erotica: Definitions and prevalence*. Presentation at 2007 International Nonprofit and Social Marketing Conference Social Entrepreneurship, Social Change and Sustainability.

Kupers, T. A. (1999). *Prison madness: The mental health crisis behind bars and what we must do about it*. San Francisco, CA: Jossey-Bass.

Kurdi, B., Seitchik, A. E., Axt, J. R., Carroll, T. J., Karapetyan, A., Kaushik, N., et al. (2018). Relationship between the Implicit Association Test and intergroup behavior: A meta-analysis. *American psychologist*. Advance online publication. http://dx.doi.org/10.1037/amp0000364

Kutchins, H., & Kirk, S. A. (1997). *Making us crazy: DSM; the psychiatric bible and the creation of mental disorders*. London, UK: Constable.

Kuttner, R. (2017). White nationalism and economic nationalism. *American Prospect*, *28*(4), 30–33.

Lacan, J. (1977). *Ecrits: A selection* (A. Sheridan, Trans.). New York, NY: Norton.

Ladd, J. M. (2011). *Why Americans hate the media and how it matters*. Princeton, NJ: Princeton University Press.

Lakoff, G. (1987). *Women, fire, and dangerous things: What categories reveal about the mind*. Chicago, IL: University of Chicago.

Lambert, N. M., Negash, S., Stillman, T.F., Olmstead, S.B., & Fincham, F.D. (2012). A love that doesn't last: Pornography consumption and weakened commitment to one's romantic partner. *Journal of Social and Clinical Psychology*,31 (4),410–438.

Lamont, E., Roach, T., & Kahn, S. (2018). Navigating campus hookup culture: LGBTQ students and college hookups. *Sociological Forum*, *33*(4), 1000–1022. https://doi.org/10.1111/socf.12458

Lankford, A. (2009). Promoting aggression and violence at Abu Ghraib: The U.S. military's transformation of ordinary people into torturers. *Aggression and Violent Behavior*, *14*(5), 388–395. doi: 10.1016/j.avb.2009.06.007

Larner, W. (1995). Theorising "difference" in Aotearoa/New Zealand. *Gender, Place and Culture, 2*(2), 77–191.

Larsson, C. B. (1997). Masculinities: A social constructionist perspective (Doctoral dissertation, Massachusetts School of Professional Psychology, Boston). *Dissertation Abstracts International, 58*, 5B.

Lather, P. (1992). Post-critical pedagogues: A feminist reading. In J. Gore & C. Luke (Eds.), *Feminisms and critical pedagogy* (pp. 120–137). New York, NY: Routledge.

Laumann, E. O., Gagnon, J. H., Michael, R. T., & Michaels, S. (2000). *The social organization of sexuality: Sexual practices in the United States*. Chicago, IL: University of Chicago.

Lauzen, M. M. (2019). The celluloid ceiling: Behind the scenes employment of women in the top 100, 250 and 500 films of 2018. Retrieved from https://womenintvfilm.sdsu.edu/wp-content/uploads/2019/01/2018_Celluloid_Ceiling_Report. pdf

Lavi, I., Gard, A. M., Hagan, M., Van Horn, P., & Lieberman, A. F. (2015). Child-parent psychotherapy examined in a perinatal sample: Depression, posttraumatic stress symptoms and child-rearing attitudes. *Journal of Social and Clinical Psychology, 34*(1), 64–82.

Lawrence, V. J. (1997). Multiculturalism, diversity, cultural pluralism... "Tell the truth, the whole truth and nothing but the truth." *Journal of Black Studies, 27*(3), 318–333.

Lawson–Te Aho, K. (1993). The socially constructed nature of psychology and the abnormalisation of Maori. *New Zealand Psychological Society Bulletin, 76*, 25–26.

Lax, W. D. (1989). Postmodern thinking in a clinical practice. In J. Shotter & K. J. Gergen (Eds.), *Texts of identity* (pp. 69–85). London, UK: SAGE.

Lazzarato, M. (2015). *Governing by debt* (J.D. Jordan, Trans.). Pasadena, CA: Semiotext.

Leach, C. W., Spears, R., Branscombe, N. R., & Doosje, B. (2003). Malicious pleasure: Schadenfreude at the suffering of another group. *Journal of Personality and Social Psychology, 84*(5), 932–943. doi: 10.1037/0022-3514.84.5.932

Lears, T. J. (1985). The concept of cultural hegemony: Problems and possibilities. *American Historical Review, 90*(3), 567–593.

LeDoux, J. (1996). *The emotional brain: The mysterious underpinnings of emotional life*. New York, NY: Simon and Schuster.

Lee, C. C. (1996). MCT theory and implications for indigenous healing. In D. W. Sue, A. Ivey, & P. Pedersen, *A theory of multicultural counseling and therapy* (pp. 86–98). Pacific Grove, CA: Thomson Brooks/Cole.

Lee, L. J. (2004). Taking off the mask: Breaking the silence—the art of naming racism in the therapy room. In M. Rastogi & E. Wieling (Eds.), *Voices of color: First-person accounts of ethnic minority therapists* (pp. 91–115). Thousand Oaks, CA: SAGE.

Leiblum, S. R. (2002). Reconsidering gender differences in sexual desire: An update. *Sexual and Relationship Therapy, 17*, 57–68.

Lemay, E., Clark, M., & Greenberg, A. (2010). What is beautiful is desired: Physical attractiveness stereotyping as projection of interpersonal goals. *Personality and Social Psychology Bulletin, 36*(3), 339–353.

Leong, L. (2017). Mobile Myanmar: The development of a mobile app culture in Yangon. *Mobile Media & Communication, 5*(2), 139–160.

Leslie, L. A., & Southard, A. (2009). Thirty years of feminist family therapy: Moving into the mainstream. In Lloyd, S., Allen, K. & Few, A. (Eds.), *Handbook of Feminist Family Studies* (328–339). Thousand Oaks, CA: Sage

Levi, A. (2009). The ethics of nursing student international clinical experiences. *Journal of Obstetric, Gynecologic & Neonatal Nursing, 38*, 94–99.

Lévi-Strauss, C. (2001). Race, history and culture. *UNESCO Courier, 54*(12), 6–9.

Lewis, T., Amini, F., & Lannon, R . (2000). *A general theory of love*. New York, NY: Random.

Lichter, D. T., Parisi, D., & Taquino, M. C. (2015). Toward a new macro segregation? Decomposing segregation within and between metropolitan cities and suburbs. *American Sociological Review*, 80, 843–873. http://dx.doi.org/10.1177/0003122415588558

Liddon, L., Kingerlee, R., & Barry, J. A. (2017). Gender differences in preferences for psychological treatment, coping strategies, and triggers to help-seeking. *British Journal of Clinical Psychology, 57*(1), 42–58.

Lieberman, M. D. (2013). *Social: Why our brains are wired to connect*. Oxford, UK: Oxford University Press.

Lin, K. (2014). The medicalization and demedicalization of kink: Shifting contexts of sexual politics (MA Thesis, University of Delaware). Retrieved from http://udspace.udel.edu/bitstream/handle/19716/16960/2014_LinKai_MA.pdf?sequence=1&isAllowed=y

Linehan, C., & McCarthy, J. (2001). Reviewing the "community of practice" metaphor: An analysis of control relations in a primary school classroom. *Mind, Culture, and Activity, 8*(2), 129–147.

Lipman, J. (2018). *That's what she said*. New York, NY: Harper Collins.

Liu, W. M. (2017). White male power and privilege: The relationship between White supremacy and social class. *Journal of Counseling Psychology, 64*, 349–358. http://dx.doi.org/10.1037/cou0000227

Liu, W. M., Liu, R. Z., Garrison, Y. L., Kim, J. Y. C., Chan, L., Ho, Y. C. S., et al. (2019). Racial trauma, microaggressions, and becoming racially innocuous: The role of acculturation and White supremacist ideology. *American Psychologist, 74*, 143–155. http://dx.doi.org/10.1037/amp0000368

Liu, W. M., & Pope-Davis, D. B. (2003). Moving from diversity to multiculturalism: Exploring power and its implications for multicultural competence. In D. B. Pope-Davis, H. L. K. Coleman, W. M. Liu, & R. L. Toporek (Eds.), *Handbook of multicultural competencies in counseling and psychology* (pp. 90–102). Thousand Oaks, CA: SAGE.

Liu, W. M., Soleck, G., Hopps, J., Dunston, K., & Pickett, T., Jr. (2004). A new framework to understand social class in counseling: The social class worldview model and modern classism theory. *Journal of Multicultural Counseling, 32*(2), 95–122.

London, P. (1986). *The modes and morals of psychotherapy*. New York, NY: Hemisphere Publishing Corporation.

Long, J., & Lindsey, E. (2004). The sexual orientation matrix for supervision: A tool for training therapists to work with same-sex couples. In J. J. Bigner & J. L. Wetchler (Eds.), *Relationship therapy with same-sex couples* (pp. 123–135). New York, NY: Haworth Press.

Long, J. K. (1996). Working with gays, lesbians, and heterosexuals: Addressing heterosexism in supervision. *Family Process*, *35*, 377–388.

Lopez, G. (2018). There are huge racial disparities in how US police use force. *Vox*. Retrieved from https://www.vox.com/identities/2016/8/13/17938186/police-shootings-killings-racism-racial-disparities

Lopez, I. F. H. (2000). Institutional racism: Judicial conduct and a new theory of racial discrimination. *Yale Law Journal*, *109*(8), 1717–1884.

Lorber, J., & Farrell, S. A. (1991). *The social construction of gender*. Newbury Park, CA: SAGE.

Lott, B. (2002). Cognitive and behavioral distancing from the poor. *American Psychologist*, *57*(2), 100–110.

Lucal, B. (1996). Oppression and privilege: Toward a relational conceptualization of race. *Teaching Sociology*, *24*, 245–255.

Lum, D. (2000). *Social work practice and people of color: A process-stage approach*. Belmont, CA: Wadsworth.

Lum, D. (Ed.). (2007). *Culturally competent practice: A framework for understanding diverse groups and justice issues* (3rd ed.). Belmont, CA: Thomson Brooks/Cole.

Lum, D. (2011). *Culturally competent practice: A framework for understanding diverse groups and justice issues*. Princeton, NJ: Recording for the Blind & Dyslexic.

Lutz, C. A. (1982). The domain of emotion words on Ifaluk. *American Ethnologist*, *9*(1), 113–128.

Lutz, C. A. (1988). *Unnatural emotions: Everyday sentiments on a Micronesian atoll & their challenge to Western theory*. Chicago, IL: University of Chicago press.

Lutz, C. A. (1990). Morality, domination and understandings of "justifiable anger" among the Ifaluk. In G. R. Semin & K. J. Gergen (Eds.), *Everyday understanding: Social and scientific implications* (pp. 204–226). Thousand Oaks, CA: SAGE.

Lyness, K. S., & Thompson, D. E. (2000). Climbing the corporate ladder: Do female and male executives follow the same route? *Journal of Applied Psychology*, *85*(1), 86–101.

Lyon, E., Lane, S., & Menard, A. (2008, October). *Meeting survivor's needs: A multi-state study of domestic violence shelter experiences*. Washington, DC: National Institute of Justice.

Lyotard, J. F. (1993). *The postmodern condition: A report on knowledge* (G. Bennington & B. Massumi, Trans.). Minneapolis, MN: University of Minnesota Press.

Maalouf, A. (2000). *On identity*. London, UK: Routledge.

MacInnis, C. C., & Hodson, G. (2012). Intergroup bias toward "Group X": Evidence of prejudice, dehumanization, avoidance, and discrimination against asexuals. *Group Processes and Intergroup Relations*, *15*(6), 725–743.

Madsen, O. J. (2014). *The therapeutic turn: How psychology altered Western culture*. London, UK: Routledge.

Maerz, L., & Augusta-Scott, T. (2017). Complex trauma and dominant masculinity: A trauma-informed, narrative therapy approach with men who abuse their female partners. In *Innovations in Interventions to Address Intimate Partner Violence* (pp. 75–92). New York, NY: Routledge.

Magnuson, E. (2008). Rejecting the American Dream. *Journal of Contemporary Ethnography*, *37*(3), 255–290.

Maisel, R., Epston, D., & Borden, A. (2004). *Biting the hand that starves you: Inspiring resistance to anorexia/bulimia*. New York, NY: W.W. Norton.

Maker, A. H. (2004). Post 9/11: Combating racism in the sanctity of healing. In M. Rastogi & E. Wieling (Eds.), *Voices of color: First-person accounts of ethnic minority therapists* (pp. 155–168). Thousand Oaks, CA: SAGE.

Mallinger, G. (2016). Practice with the lesbian community: A roadmap to effective micro, mezzo, and macro interventions. In M. P. Dentato (Ed.), *Social work practice with the LGBT community* (pp. 423–459). New York, NY: Oxford University Press.

Mallory, C., Brown, T. N. T., & Conron, K. J. (2018). *Conversion therapy and LGBT youth* (executive summary). The Williams Institute. Retrieved from https://williamsinstitute.law.ucla.edu/wp-content/uploads/Conversion-Therapy-LGBT-Youth-Jan-2018.pdf

Malyon, A.K. (1982). Psychotherapeutic implications of internalized homophobia in gay men. *Journal of Homosexuality* *7*(2–3) 59–69. Doi: 10.1300/J082v07n02_08

Mamdani, M. (2001). *When victims become killers*. Princeton, NJ: Princeton University Press.

Mardell, A. (2016). The ABC's of LGBT+. Coral Gables, FL: Mango Media.

Margolis, J. (1966). *Psychotherapy and Morality: A Study of Two Concepts*. New York, N.Y.: Random House

Marshall, J. D. (2007). Michel Foucault: Educational research as problematisation. In M. A. Peters & A. C. Besley (Eds.), Why Foucault? New directions in educational research (pp. 15–28). New York, NY: Peter Lang.

Martellozzo, E., Monaghan, A., Adler, J. R., Davidson, J., Leyva, R., & Horvath, M. A. H. (2017). "I wasn't sure it was normal to watch it". Retrieved from https://learning.nspcc.org.uk/research-resources/2016/i-wasn-t-sure-it-was-normal-to-watch-it/

Martin, G. L. (1987). *Counseling for family violence and abuse*. Waco, TX: World Books.

Martin, L., Gutman, H., & Hutton, P. H. (1988). *Technologies of the self: A seminar with Michel Foucault*. Boston, MA: University of Massachusetts Press.

Martinez, E. (2001). *Latino politics: Seeing more than black & white*. Retrieved from https://www.indigenouspeople.net/blackwht.htm

Martinez, E. (2007). Seeing more than Black and White: Latinos, racism, and the cultural divides. In M. L. Andersen & P. H. Collins (Eds.), *Race, class, and gender: An anthology* (6th edn) (pp. 105–111). Belmont, CA: Wadsworth/Thomson Learning.

Marx, K. (1932). *Capital, the communist manifesto and other writings by Karl Marx* (M. Eastman, Ed.). New York, NY: Modern Library.

Maslow, A. H. (1956). Self-actualizing people: A study of psychological health. In C. E. Moustakas (Ed.), *The self* (pp. 160–194). New York, NY: Harper Colophon.

Mason, L. (2018). *Uncivil agreement: How politics became our identity*. Chicago, IL: University of Chicago Press.

Masson, J. M. (1984). *The assault on truth: Freud's suppression of the seduction theory*. New York, NY: Farrar, Straus and Giroux.

Mboya, L. (2017). Most watched TV shows In Kenya 2018. Retrieved from https://trending.co.ke/watched-tv-shows-kenya-2017/

McAuliffe, G. (2019). *Culturally alert counseling: A comprehensive introduction* (3rd ed.). Thousand Oaks, CA: SAGE.

McCarthy, J., & Holliday, E. L. (2004). Help-seeking and counseling within a traditional male gender role: An examination from a multicultural perspective. *Journal of Counseling & Development*, 82, 25–30.

McClennen, J. C., Summers, A. B., & Vaughan, C. (2002). Gay men's domestic violence: Dynamics, help-seeking behaviors and correlates. *Journal of Gay and Lesbian Social Services*, 14(1), 23–49.

McClintock, E. A., (2016, March 31). The psychology of mansplaining. *Psychology Today*. Retrieved from https://www.psychologytoday.com/us/blog/it-s-man-s-and-woman-s-world/201603/the-psychology-mansplaining

McDaniel, R., & Twist, M. L. C. (2016). Designer relationships: A guide to happy monogamy, positive polyamory, and optimistic open relationships, edited by Mark A. Michaels and Patricia Johnson, Sexual and Relationship Therapy. doi: 10.1080/14681994.2016.1192596.

McDowell, T., Knudson-Martin, C., & Bermudez, J. M. (2018). *Socioculturally attuned family therapy: Guidelines for equitable theory and practice*. New York, NY: Routledge/Taylor & Francis Group.

McGoldrick, M., Giordano, J., & Garcia-Preto, N. (2005). *Ethnicity and family therapy* (3rd ed.). New York, NY: Guilford Press.

McGoldrick, M., & Hardy, K. V. (2019). *Re-visioning family therapy: Race, culture, and gender in clinical practice*. New York, NY: Guilford Press.

McIntosh, P. (1990). White privilege: Unpacking the invisible knapsack. *Independent School*, 49, 2, 31–36.

McKinley, N. M. (1998). Gender differences in undergraduates' body esteem: The mediating effect of objectified consciousness and actual/ideal weight discrepancy. *Sex Roles*, 39(1–2), 113–123.

McKinley, N. M. (1999). Women and objectified body consciousness: Mothers' and daughters' body experience in cultural, developmental, and familial context. *Developmental Psychology*, 35(3), 760–769.

McKinley, N. M., & Hyde, J. S. (1996). The objectified body consciousness scale: Development and validation. *Psychology of Women Quarterly*, 20(2), 181–215.

McKinnon, L., & Miller, D. (1987). The epistemology and the Milan approach: Feminist and socio-political considerations. *Journal of Marital and Family Therapy*, 13(2), 139–155.

McManus, S., Bebbington, P., Jenkins, R., & Brugha, T. (Eds.). (2016). *Mental health and wellbeing in England: Adult Psychiatric Morbidity Survey 2014*. Leeds: NHS Digital.

McNamee, S., & Gergen, K. J. (1992). *Therapy as social construction*. London, UK: SAGE.

McNamee, S., & Gergen, K. J. (1999). *Resources for sustainable dialogue*. Thousand Oaks, CA: SAGE.

McNamee, S. J., & Miller, R. K., Jr. (2004). *The meritocracy myth*. Lanham, MD: Rowman & Littlefield.

Meares, R. (1999). The "adualistic" representation of trauma: On malignant internalization. *American Journal of Psychotherapy*, 53(3), 392–402.

Medina, D. A. (2016, September 23). Dakota Pipeline Company Buys Ranch Near Sioux Protest Site, Records Show. *NBC News*. Retrieved from https://www.nbcnews.com/storyline/dakota-pipeline-protests/dakota-pipeline-company-buys-ranch-near-sioux-protest-site-records-n653051

Melissa. (2018, April 6). Can BDSM be healthy? [Blog post]. Retrieved from http://www.thehotline.org/2017/04/06/healthy-bdsm-relationships

Mellin, L. M., Irwin, C. E., & Scully, S. (1992). Prevalence of disordered eating in girls: A survey of middle class children. *Journal of the American Dietetic Association*, 92, 851–853.

Memmi, A. (1967). *The colonizer and the colonized*. Boston, MA: Beacon Press.

Merrill, G. S. (1998). Understanding domestic violence among gay and bisexual men. In R. K. Bergen (Ed.), *Issues in intimate violence* (pp. 129–142). Thousand Oaks, CA: SAGE.

Meth, R. L. (1990). The road to masculinity. In R. L. Meth & R. S. Pasick (Eds.), *Men and therapy: The challenge of change* (pp. 3–34). New York, NY: Guilford Press.

Meth, R. L., & Pasick, R. S. (1990). *Men in therapy: The challenge of change.* New York, NY: The Guilford Press.

Meyers, L. (2014, April 23). Advocacy in action. *Counseling Today* (Cover story). Retrieved from https://ct.counseling.org/2014/04/advocacy-in-action/

Michaels, M.A. & Johnson, P. (2015). Designer relationships: A guide to happy monogamy, positive polyamory, and optimistic open relationships. Jersey City, N.J.: Cleis Press.

Middleton, R. A., Flowers, C., & Zawaiza, T. (1996). Multiculturalism, affirmative action, and Section 21 of the 1992 Rehabilitation Act Amendments: Fact or fiction? *Rehabilitation Counseling Bulletin*, *40*(1), 11–31.

Middleton, R. A., Stadler, H. A., & Simpson, C. (2005). Mental health practitioners: The relationship between white racial identity attitudes and self-reported multicultural counseling competencies. *Journal of Counseling & Development*, *83*(4), 444–456.

Mignolo, W. (2007). Coloniality of power and de-colonial thinking. *Cultural Studies*, *21*(2–3), 155–167.

Mignolo, W. (2008). Hermenéutica de la democracia: el pensamiento de los límites y la diferencia colonial. Hermeneutics of democracy: The thinking of limits and the colonial difference] *Tabula Rasa*, *9*, 39–60.

Mignolo, W. (2011). *The darker side of Western modernity: Global futures, decolonial options.* London, UK: Duke University Press.

Mignolo, W. (2014). Democracia liberal, camino de la autoridad humana y transición al vivir bien. Liberal democracy, human authority's path and transition into good living] *Sociedade e Estado*, *29*(1), 21–44. doi: 10.1590/S0102-69922014000100003

Mignolo, W., & Walsh, C. (2018). *On decoloniality: Concepts, analytics, praxis.* Durham, NC: Duke University Press.

Millennial Survey 2016—Deloitte Library. (n.d.). Retrieved from https://deloittelibrary.com.cy/hotnews/millennial-survey-2016

Miller, R. (2016, July 11). Black Lives Matter: A primer on what it is and what it stands for. *USA Today*. Retrieved from https://www.usatoday.com/story/news/nation/2016/07/11/black-lives-matter-what-what-stands/86963292/

Mills, C. (2014). *Decolonizing global mental health: The psychiatrization of the majority world.* London, UK: Routledge.

Mills, C. (2018). 'Dead people don't claim': A psychopolitical autopsy of UK austerity suicides. *Critical Social Policy*, *38*(2), 302–322.

Mills, C. W. (2014). White time: The chronic injustice of ideal theory. *DuBois Review: Social Science Research on Race*, 11, 27–42. http://dx.doi.org/10.1017/S1742058X14000022

Milton, M., & Coyle, A. (1999). Lesbian and gay affirmative psychotherapy: Issues in theory and practice. *Sex and Marital Therapy: The Journal of the British Association for Sexual and Relationship Therapy*, *14*(1) 43–60.

Mintz, L. B., & Betz, N. E. (1986). Sex differences in the nature, realism, and correlates of body image. *Sex Roles*, *15*(3–4), 185–195.

Minuchin, S. (1974). *Families and family therapy.* Cambridge, MA: Harvard University Press.

Mock, K. (1997). 25 years of multiculturalism—past, present, and future, part 1. *Canadian Social Studies*, *31*, 123–127.

Monk, G. (1998). *Developing a social justice agenda for counselor education in New Zealand: A social constructionist perspective* (Unpublished doctoral dissertation). University of Waikato, Hamilton, New Zealand.

Monk, G., & Hancock, S. (2015). Recovering a life with severe mental illness. Psychologists and peer support specialists working together. *Psychology Aotearoa*, *7*(2) 112–118.

Monk, G., Winslade, J., Crocket, K., & Epston, D. (Eds.). (1997). *Narrative therapy in practice: The archaeology of hope.* San Francisco, CA: Jossey-Bass.

Montagu, A. (1962). The concept of race. *American Anthropologist*, *65*(5), 919–928.

Montgomery-Graham, S. (2017). Conceptualization and assessment of hypersexual disorder: A systematic review of the literature. *Sexual Medicine Reviews*, *5*(2), 146–162.

Monto, M. A., & Carey, A. G. (2014). A new standard of sexual behavior? Are claims associated with the "hookup culture" supported by General Social Survey data? *The Journal of Sex Research*, *51*(6), 1–11. doi: 10.1080/00224499.2014.906031

Moore, D., & Leafgren, F. (Eds.). (1990). *Problem-solving strategies and interventions for men in conflict.* Alexandria, VA: American Association for Counseling and Development.

Moradi, B., Dirks, D., & Matteson, A. V. (2005). Roles of sexual objectification experiences and internalization of standards of beauty in eating disorder symptomatology: A test and extension of objectification theory. *Journal of Counseling Psychology*, *52*, 420–428.

Moradi, B., & Grzanka, P. R. (2017). Using intersectionality responsibly: Toward critical epistemology, structural analysis, and social justice activism. *Journal of Counseling Psychology*, *64*, 500–513. doi: 10.1037/cou0000203

Morris, B. J. (n.d.). A brief history of lesbian, gay, bisexual and transgender social movements. *American Psychological Association*. Retrieved from https://www.apa.org/pi/lgbt/resources/history.aspx

Moser, C. & Kleinplatz, P.J. (2006). DSM-IV-TR and the paraphilias. *Journal of Psychology & Human Sexuality, 17*(3–4), 91-109, DOI: 10.1300/ J056v17n03_05

Moser, C. (2002, May). *What do we really know about S/M: Myths and realities.* Paper presented at the 34th conference of the American Association of Sex Educators, Counselors, and Therapists, Miami, Florida.

Mouffe, C. (1992). Feminism, citizenship and radical democratic politics. In. J. Butler & J. W. Scott (Eds.), *Feminists theorise the political* (pp. 369–384). London, UK: Routledge.

Moy, S. (1992). A culturally sensitive, psychoeducational model for understanding and treating Asian-American clients. *Journal of Psychology and Christianity, 11*(4), 358–367.

Mukherjee, S. (2017). *The gene: An intimate history.* London, UK: Vintage.

Murray, C., Pope, A., & Willis, B. (2016). *Sexuality counseling: Theory, research, and practice.* Thousand Oaks, CA: SAGE.

Mutz, D. C. (2018). Status threat, not economic hardship, explains the 2016 presidential vote. *Proceedings of the National Academy of Sciences of the United States of America.* Advance online publication. http://dx.doi.org/10.1073/pnas.1718155115

Myers, D. G. (2007). The powers and perils of intuition. *Scientific American Mind, 18*(3), 24–31.

Nadal, K. L., Griffin, K. E., Wong, Y., Hamit, S., & Rasmus, M. (2014). The impact of racial microaggressions on mental health: Counseling implications for clients of color. *Journal of Counseling and Development, 92*, 57–66. http://dx.doi.org/10.1002/j.1556-6676.2014.00130.x

Nagata, D. K., Kim, J. H. J., Massey, D. S., & Tannen, J. (2015). A research note on trends in Black hypersegregation. *Demography, 52*, 1025–1034. http://dx.doi.org/10.1007/s13524-015-0381-6

Nagata, D. K., Kim, J. H. J., & Wu, K. (2019). The Japanese American wartime incarceration: Examining the scope of racial trauma. *American Psychologist, 74*, 36–48. http://dx.doi.org/10.1037/amp0000303

nankingdecade (n.d.). What I mean when I say "toxic monogamy culture" (Tumblr post). Retrieved from http://kateordie.tumblr.com/post/164844109602/what-i-mean-when-i-say-toxic-monogamy-culture

Narayan, U. (2000). Essence of culture and a sense of history: A feminist critique of cultural essentialism. In U. Narayan & S. Harding (Eds.), *Decentering the center: Philosophy for a multicultural, postcolonial & feminist world* (pp. 80–100). Bloomington, IN: Indiana University Press.

National Career Development Association. (1997). *Career counseling competencies* (rev. ed.). Columbia, OH: National Career Development Association.

National Coalition Against Domestic Violence. (2018). *Statistics* [Data set]. Retrieved from https://ncadv.org/statistics

Neimeyer, R. A. (1998). Social constructionism in the counseling context. *Psychology Quarterly, 11*(2), 135–149.

Nelson, M. L., & Holloway, E. L. (1990). Relation of gender to power and involvement in supervision. *Journal of Counseling Psychology, 37*, 473–481.

Neville, H. A., Awad, G. H., Brooks, J. E., Flores, M. P., & Bluemel, J. (2013). Color-blind racial ideology: Theory, training, and measurement implications in psychology. *American Psychologist, 68*, 455–466. http://dx.doi.org/10.1037/a0033282

Newstrom, N. P., & Harris, S. M. (2016). Pornography and couples: What does the research tell us? *Contemporary Family Therapy, 38*(4), 412–423.

Nichols, M. (2006). Psychotherapeutic issues with "kinky" clients: Clinical problems, yours and theirs. *Journal of Homosexuality 50*(2–3), 281–300. Retrieved from https://www.ncbi.nlm.nih.gov/pubmed/16803768

Nieto, S. (2000). *Affirming diversity: The sociopolitical context of multicultural education* (3rd ed.). New York, NY: Longman.

Nolen-Hoeksema, S. (1998). *Abnormal psychology.* Boston, MA: McGraw-Hill.

Northcott, C. (2016, September 2). Life in the Native American oil protest camps. *BBC News.* Retrieved from https://www.bbc.com/news/world-us-canada-37249617

Nosek, B. A., Banaji, M. R., & Greenwald, A. G. (2002). Harvesting implicit group attitudes and beliefs from a demonstration website. http:// dx.doi.org/10.1037/1089-2699.6.1.101

Nutt, R. (1991). Ethical principles for gender-fair family therapy. *Family Psychologist, 7*(3), 32–33.

Nylund, D. (2006). Critical multiculturalism, whiteness, and social work: Towards a more radical view of cultural competence. *Journal of Progressive Human Services, 17*(2), 27–42.

Obama, B. (2006). *The audacity of hope: Thoughts on reclaiming the American dream.* New York, NY: Crown.

Obear, K. (2016). *But I'm not racist! Tools for well-meaning Whites.* McClean, VA: The Difference Press.

OECD. (2018). *International Migration Outlook 2018.* Paris, FR: OECD Publishing. Retrieved from https://doi.org/10.1787/migr_outlook-2018-en

Ogas, O., & Gaddam, S. (2012). *A billion wicked thoughts: What the Internet tells us about sexual relationships.* New York, NY: Plume.

Ogrodniczuk, J. S., Oliffe, J. L., & Beharry, J. (2018). HeadsUpGuys: Canadian online resource for men with depression. *Canadian Family Physician, 64*, 93–94.

Ohlson, T. H. (1993). The Treaty of Waitangi and bicultural issues for psychologists. *New Zealand Psychological Society Bulletin, 76*, 8–9.

Okin, S. M. (1999). *Is multiculturalism bad for women?* In J. Cohen, M. Howard, & M. Nussbaum (Eds.), *Is multiculturalism bad for women?* (pp. 9–24). Princeton, NJ: Princeton University Press.

Olds, J., & Schwartz, R. S. (2009). *The lonely American: Drifting apart in the 21st century.* Boston, MA: Beacon.

Olmstead, S. B., Negash, S., Pasley, K., & Fincham, F. D. (2013). Emerging adults' expectations for pornography use in the context of future committed romantic relationships: A qualitative study. *Archives of Sexual Behavior, 42*(4), 625–635.

Olssen, M. (1991). Producing the truth about people. In J. Morss & T. Linzey (Eds.), *Growing up: The politics of human learning* (pp. 188–209). Auckland, New Zealand: Longman Paul.

O'Neill, J. M. (1990). Assessing men's gender role conflict. In D. Moore & F. Leafgren (Eds.), *Problem-solving strategies and interventions for men in conflict* (pp. 23–38). Alexandria, VA: American Counseling Association.

Ong-Van-Cung, K. S. (2011). Critique and subjectivation: Foucault and Butler on the subject. *Actuel Marx, 49*, 148–161. doi: 10.3917/amx.049.0148

Orange, C. (1987). *The Treaty of Waitangi.* Wellington, New Zealand: Allen & Unwin.

Ostrow, L., & Adams, N. (2012). Recovery in the USA: From politics to peer support. *International Review of Psychiatry, 24*(1), 70–78. doi:10.3109/09540261.2012.659659

Owen, J., Wong, Y. J., & Rodolfa, E. (2009). Empirical search for psychotherapist' gender competence in psychotherapy. *Psychotherapy Theory, Research, Practice, Training, 46*(4), 448–458.

Owen, L. (1993). *Her blood is gold: Celebrating the power of menstruation.* San Francisco, CA: Harper & Row Publishers.

Parker, I. (1992). *Discourse dynamics: Critical analyses for social and individual psychology.* London, UK: Routledge.

Parker, W. M., Howard-Hamilton, M., & Parham, G. (1998). Counseling interventions with African American males. In W. M. Parker (Ed.), *Consciousness-raising: A primer for multicultural counseling* (pp. 147–175). Springfield, IL: Charles C. Thomas Publishing.

Parker-Guilbert, K. S., Leifker, F. R., Sippel, L. M., & Marshall, A. D. (2014). The differential diagnostic accuracy of the PTSD Checklist among men versus women in a community sample. *Psychiatry Research, 220*(1/2), 679–686.

Pattavina, A., Hirschel, D., Buzzawa, E., Faggiani, D., & Bentley, H. (2007). A comparison of the police responses to heterosexual versus same-sex intimate partner violence. *Violence Against Women, 13*(4), 374–394.

Patterson, C. H. (1996). Multicultural counseling: From diversity to universality. *Journal of Counseling & Development, 74*, 227–231.

Pauketat, T. R. (2015). *The Oxford Handbook of North American Archaeology.* Oxford, UK: Oxford University Press.

Payne, B.K. (2006). Weapon Bias Split-Second Decisions and Unintended Stereotyping. *Association for Psychological Science,*15(6), 287–291.

Pearson, G. A. (1996). Of sex and gender. *Science, 274*(5286), 324–329.

Pedersen, P. B. (1976). The field of intercultural counseling. In P. B. Pedersen, W. J. Lonner, & J. G. Draguns (Eds.), *Counseling across cultures* (pp. 17–41). Honolulu, HI: University of Hawaii Press.

Pence, E. (1993). *Education groups for men who batter: The Duluth model.* New York, NY: Springer.

Pence, E., & Paymar, M. (1990). *Power and control, tactics of men who batter: An educational curriculum.* Duluth, MN: Minnesota Program Development.

Perel, E. (2015). Sex, stability, and self-fulfillment (TED talk). Retrieved from https://www.youtube.com/watch?v=CK0geTiYyds

Perel, E. (2017). *The state of affairs: Rethinking infidelity.* New York, NY: Harper-Collins.

Pérez Huber, L., & Solorzano, D. G. (2015). Visualizing everyday racism: Critical race theory, visual microaggressions, and the historical image of Mexican banditry. *Qualitative Inquiry, 21*, 223–238. http://dx.doi.org/10.1177/1077800414562899

Perkins, J. (2004). *Confessions of an economic hit man.* San Francisco, CA: Berrett-Koehler.

Perrin, A., Jingjing, J. (2018, March). About a quarter of U.S. adults say they are 'almost constantly' online. *Pew Research Center.* Retrieved from https://www.pewresearch.org/fact-tank/2018/03/14/about-a-quarter-of-americans-report-going-online-almost-constantly/

Peters, M. A., & Besley, A. C. T. (2006). *Building knowledge cultures.* Lanham, MD: Rowman & Littlefield.

Petras, J. (1993). Cultural imperialism in the late 20th century. *Journal of Contemporary Asia, 23*, 139–148.

Petrosky, E., Blair, J., Betz, C., Fowler, K., Jack, S., & Lyons, B. (2017). Racial and ethnic differences in homicides of adult women and the role of intimate partner violence — United States, 2003-2014. *Morbidity and Mortality Weekly Report, 66*, 741–746.

Pham, J. M. (2017). Beyond hookup culture: Current trends in the study of college student sex and where to next. *Sociology Compass*, *11*(8). doi.org/10.1111/soc4.12499

Phillips, U. B. (1968). The slave economy of the old south. In E. D. Genovese (Ed.), *Selected essays in economic and social history* (pp. 269–276). Baton Rouge, LA: Louisiana State University Press.

Philpot, C. L. (2001). Family therapy for men. In G. R. Brooks & G. E. Good (Eds.), *The new handbook of psychotherapy and counseling with men* (vol. 1, pp. 622–638). San Francisco, CA: Jossey-Bass.

Philpot, C., Brooks, G., Lusterman, D., & Nutt, R. (1997). *Bridging separate gender worlds: Why men and women clash and how therapists can bring them together.* Washington, DC: American Psychological Association.

Piff, P. K., Kraus, M. W., & Keltner, D. (2018). Chapter two—Unpacking the inequality paradox: The psychological roots of inequality and social class. *Advances in Experimental Psychology*, *57*, 53–124. http://dx.doi .org/10.1016/bs.aesp.2017.10.002

Pines, H. A., Goodman-Meza, D., Pitpitan, E. V., Torres, K., Semple, S. J., & Patterson, T. L. (2016). HIV testing among men who have sex with men in Tijuana, Mexico: A cross-sectional study. *BMJ Open.* doi: 10.1136/bmjopen-2015-010388

Pinker, S. (2015). *The village effect: Why face-to-face contact matters.* London, UK: Atlantic Books.

Pittman, D. M., Cho Kim, S., Hunter, C. D., & Obasi, E. M. (2017). The role of minority stress in second-generation Black emerging adult college students' high-risk drinking behaviors. *Cultural Diversity & Ethnic Minority Psychology*, *23*, 445– 455. http://dx.doi.org/10.1037/cdp0000135

Planned Parenthood (n.d.). *What do I need to know about transitioning?* Retrieved from https://www.plannedparenthood.org/learn/sexual-orientation-gender/trans-and-gender-nonconforming-identities/what-do-i-need-know-about-transitioning

Plastic Surgery Statistics Report [PDF file]. (2017). Retrieved from https://www.plasticsurgery.org/documents/News/Statistics/2017/plastic-surgery-statistics-full-report-2017.pdf

Pleck, J. H. (1981). *The myth of masculinity.* Cambridge, MA: MIT Press.

Pollack, W. S. (1998). *Real boys: Rescuing our sons from the myths of boyhood.* New York, NY: Basic Books.

Pon, G. (2009). Cultural competency as new racism: An ontology of forgetting. *Journal of Progressive Human Services*, *20*(1), 59–71. doi: 10.1080/10428230902871173

Ponterotto, J. G., & Pedersen, P. B. (1993). *Preventing prejudice: A guide for counselors and educators.* Newbury Park, CA: SAGE.

Poster, M. (1989). *Critical theory and poststructuralism: In search of a context.* Ithaca, NY: Cornell University Press.

Potts, A. (1998). The science/fiction of sex: John Gray's Mars and Venus in the bedroom. *Sexualities*, *1*(2), 153–173.

Poverty USA. (2018). The Population of Poverty USA. Retrieved from https://povertyusa.org/facts

Powers, A. (2016). The coffee break primer on polyamory (blog). Retrieved from https://medium.com/@adampowers/the-coffee-break-polyamory-primer-6c64b4dc53de

Pramanik, A. (2017). The technology that's making a difference in the developing world. U.S. Global Leadership Coalition. Retrieved from https://www.usglc.org/blog/the-technology-thats-making-a-difference-in-the-developing-world/

President's Commission on Mental Health (1978). *Report to the President* (4 vols.). Washington, DC: U.S. Government Printing Office.

Price, B., & Rosenbaum, A. (2007). *National survey of batterer intervention programs.* Paper presented at the International Family Violence and Child Victimization Research Conference, Portsmouth, NH.

Pride, R. A., & Woodard, J. D. (1985). *The burden of busing: The politics of desegregation in Nashville, Tennessee.* Knoxville, TN: University of Tennessee Press.

Prinz, J. J. (2014). *Beyond human nature: How culture and experience shape the human mind.* New York, NY: WW Norton & Company.

Putnam, R. D. (2000). Bowling alone: America's declining social capital. In In L. Crothers & Ch. Lockhart (Eds.), *Culture and politics* (pp. 223–234). New York, NY: Palgrave Macmillan.

Queen, C., & Comella, L. (2008). The necessary revolution: Sex-positive feminism in the post-Barnard era. *The Communication Review*, *11*(3), 274–291. doi: 10.1080/10714420802306783

Quick, V. M., & Byrd-Bredbenner, C. (2013). Disordered eating, socio-cultural media influencers, body image, and psychological factors among a racially/ethnically diverse population of college women. *Eating behaviors*, *15*(1), 37–41.

Quijano, A. (2000). Colonialidad del poder, eurocentrismo y América Latina. [Coloniality of power, Eurocentrism and Latin America]. In E. Lander (Ed.), *La colonialidad del saber: Eurocentrismo y ciencias sociales. Perspectivas Latinoamericanas* (pp. 246–275). Buenos Aires, Argentina: CLACSO, Consejo Latinoamericano de Ciencias Sociales.

Quijano, A. (2005). El "movimiento indígena," la democracia y las cuestiones pendientes en América Latina. [The "indigenous movement," democracy and pending issues in Latin America] *Polis*, 10.

Quijano, A. (2010). Coloniality and modernity/rationality. In W. D. Mignolo & A. Escobar (Eds.), *Globalization and the Decolonial Option* (pp. 22–32). Oxford, UK: Routledge.

Quijano, A. (2014). *Estado-nación, ciudadanía y democracia: cuestiones abiertas*. [State-nation, citizenship and democracy: Open issues]. Buenos Aires, Argentina: CLACSO, Consejo Latinoamericano de Ciencias Sociales.

Rabin, C. L. (2005). *Understanding gender and culture in the helping process: Practitioners' narratives from global perspectives*. Belmont, CA: Thomson Wadsworth.

Rader, J. E. (2003). *The egalitarian relationship in feminist therapy* (Doctoral dissertation, The University of Texas at Austin). Retrieved from https://repositories.lib.utexas.edu/bitstream/handle/2152/866/raderje039.pdf

Rafferty, J. (2018). Committee on Psychosocial Aspects of Child and Family Health, Committee on Adolescence, Section on Lesbian, Gay, Bisexual, and Transgender Health and Wellness. Ensuring comprehensive care for transgender and gender-diverse children and adolescents (American Association of Pediatrics Policy Statement). *Pediatrics*, *142*(4), 1–16.

Rancière, J. (2010). *Dissensus: On politics and aesthetics* (S. Corcoran, Trans.) London, UK: Continuum.

Ratts, M., & Pedersen, P. (2014). *Counseling for multiculturalism and social justice*. Alexandria, VA: American Counseling Association.

Rauch, J. (2019, January/February). Don't call me LGBTQ. *The Atlantic*, pp. 16–18.

Rawlings, E. I., & Carter, D. K. (1977). Feminist and non-sexist psychotherapy. In E. I. Rawlings & D. K. Carter (Eds.), *Psychotherapy for women* (pp. 49–76). Springfield, IL: Charles C Thomas.

Reed, I. (1989). America's "black only" ethnicity. In W. Sollors (Ed.), *The invention of ethnicity* (pp. 226–229). New York, NY: Oxford University Press.

Rees, M. (2018). *On the future: Prospects for humanity*. Princeton, NJ: Princeton University Press.

Rehor, J. (2015). Sensual, erotic, and sexual behaviors of women from the "kink" community. *Archives of Sexual Behavior*, *4*(44), 825–836. Retrieved from https://link.springer.com/article/10.1007%2Fs10508-015-0524-2#citeas

Reid, R., & Woolley, S. R. (2006). Using emotionally focused therapy for couples to resolve attachment ruptures created by hypersexual behavior. *Sexual Addiction & Compulsivity*, *13*, 219–239.

Reinke, T. (2017). *12 ways your phone is changing you*. Wheaton, IL: Crossway.

Renzetti, C. M. (1998). Violence and abuse in lesbian relationships. In R. K. Bergen (Ed.), *Issues in intimate violence* (pp. 117–128). Thousand Oaks, CA: SAGE.

Resnick, J. (2001). From hate to healing: Sexual assault recovery. *Journal of College Student Psychotherapy*, *16*(1–2), 43–63.

Bouteldja, H., Valinsky, R. & West, C (2017). *Revolutionary love*. South Pasadena, CA: Semiotext(e).

Richards, C., & Barker, M. (2013). *Sexuality and gender for mental health professionals, a practical guide*. London, UK: SAGE.

Ridley, C. R. (2005). *Overcoming unintentional racism in counseling and therapy: A practitioner's guide to intentional intervention* (2nd ed.). Thousand Oaks, CA: SAGE.

Ridley, C. R., Mendoza, D. W., & Kanitz, B. E. (1994). Multicultural training: Reexamination, operationalization, and integration. *Counseling Psychologist*, *22*(2), 227–289.

Rigazio-DiGilio, S. A., Anderson, S. A., & Kunkler, K. P. (1995). Gender-aware supervision in marriage and family counseling and therapy: How far have we actually come? *Counselor Education and Supervision*, *34*(4), 344–355.

Ritchie, A., & Barker, M. (2006). 'There aren't words for what we do or how we feel so we have to make them up': Constructing polyamorous languages in a culture of compulsory monogamy. *Sexualities*, *9*(5), 584–601. doi.org/10.1177/1363460706069987

Robertson, J. M. (2001). Counseling men in college settings. In G. R. Brooks & G. E. Good (Eds.), *The new handbook of psychotherapy and counseling with men* (vol. 1, pp. 146–169). San Francisco, CA: Jossey-Bass.

Robertson, J. M., & Fitzgerald, L. F. (1990). The (mis)treatment of men: Effects of client gender role and life-style on diagnosis and attribution of pathology. *Journal of Counseling Psychology*, *37*, 3–9.

Robinson-Wood, T. L. (2017). *The convergence of race, ethnicity, and gender: Multiple identities in counseling*. (5th Ed) Thousand Oaks, CA: SAGE.

Roccas, S., & Brewer, M. B. (2002). Social identity complexity. *Personality and Social Psychology Review*, *6*(2), 88–106.

Rochlen, A. B., Rabinowitz, F. E. (Eds.). (2014). *Breaking barriers in counseling men: Insights and innovations*. New York, NY: Routledge/Taylor & Francis Group.

Rodin, J., Silberstein, L., & Striegel-Moore, R. (1985). Women and weight: A normative discontent. In T. B. Sonderegger (Ed.), *Psychology and gender: Nebraska Symposium on Motivation* (pp. 267–307). Lincoln, NE: University of Nebraska Press.

Rodkin, P. C., Farmer, T. W., Pearl, R., & Acker, R. V. (2000). Heterogeneity of popular boys: Antisocial and prosocial configurations. *Developmental Psychology*, *36*(1), 14–24.

Rodriguez, C. E. (1999). *Changing race: Latinos, the census, and the history of ethnicity in the United States.* New York, NY: New York University Press.

Rogers, C. R. (1973). *Carl Rogers on encounter groups.* New York, NY: Harper & Row.

Root, M. P. P. (2003). Bill of rights for racially mixed people. In M. P. P. Root & M. Kelly (Eds.), *The multiracial child resource book: Living complex identities.* Seattle, WA: Mavin Foundation.

Rosaldo, R. (1993). *Culture and truth: The remaking of social analysis.* Boston, MA: Beacon Press.

Rosaldo, R. (1994). Cultural citizenship and educational democracy. *Cultural Anthropology, 9*(3), 402–411.

Rose, N. (1985). *The psychological complex: Psychology, politics and society in England, 1869–1939.* London, UK: Routledge and Kegan Paul.

Rose, N. (1990). *Governing the soul: The shaping of the private self.* London, UK: Routledge.

Rose, N. (1999). *Powers of freedom: Reframing political thought.* New York, NY: Cambridge University Press.

Rosenau, P. M. (1991). *Post-modernism and the social sciences: Insights, inroads, and intrusions.* Princeton, NJ: Princeton University Press.

Ross, H. (2008). Exploring Unconscious Bias. Retrieved from https://culturalawareness.com/wp-content/uploads/2017/03/Unconscious-Bias-White-Paper.pdf

Ross, L. D. (1977). The intuitive psychologist and his shortcomings: Distortions in the attribution process. In L. Berkowitz (Ed.), *Advances in experimental social psychology* (vol. 10, pp. 173–220). Cambridge, MA: Academic Press.

Ross, L. E., Epstein, R., Goldfinger, C., & Yager, C. (2009). Policy and practice regarding adoption by sexual and gender minority people in Ontario. *Canadian Public Policy / Analyse de Politiques, 35*(4), 451–467.

Rotter, J. B. (1966). Generalized expectancies for internal versus external control of reinforcement. *Psychological Monographs, 80*(1), 1–28.

Roy, A. (2004). *An ordinary person's guide to empire.* Cambridge, MA: South End Press.

Rumbaut, R. (2003). Assimilation and its discontents. In J. Stone & R. Dennis (Eds.), *Race and ethnicity: Comparative and theoretical approaches* (pp. 237–259). Oxford, UK: Blackwell.

Ruskin, K. (2013). Polyamory – not healthy for children. Retrieved from https://www.drkarenruskin.com/polyamory-not-healthy-for-children/

Russell, G. L., Fujino, D. C., Sue, S., Cheung, M.-K., & Snowden, L. R. (1996). The effects of therapist-client ethnic match in the assessment of mental health functioning. *Journal of Cross-Cultural Psychology, 27*(5), 598–615.

Sabo, A. (2012). *After pornified: How women are transforming pornography and why it really matters.* Blue Ridge Summit, PA: John Hunt Publishing.

Said, E. (1978). *Orientalism.* New York, NY: Pantheon Books.

Said, E. W. (1993). *Culture and imperialism.* New York, NY: Vintage Books.

Said, E. W. (1994). *Orientalism.* New York, NY: Vintage Books.

Sakamoto, I. (2007). An anti-oppressive approach to cultural competence. *Canadian Social Work Review, 24*(1), 105–114.

Salisbury, R. M. (2008). Out-of-control sexual behaviours: A developing practice model. *Journal of Sexual & Relationship Therapy, 23,* 131–139.

Sampasivam, S., Collins, K. A., Bielajew, C., & Clément, R. (2016). The effects of outgroup threat and opportunity to derogate on salivary cortisol levels. *International journal of Environmental Research and Public Health, 13*(6), 616.

Sampson, E. (1989). The deconstruction of the self. In J. Shotter & K. J. Gergen (Eds.), *Texts of identity* (pp. 1–19). London, UK: SAGE.

Santiago-Rivera, A. L., Adames, H. Y., Chavez-Dueñas, N. Y., & Benson- Flórez, G. (2016). The impact of racism on communities of color: Historical contexts and contemporary issues. In A. Alvarez, C. Liang, & H. A. Neville (Eds.), *Contextualizing the cost of racism for People of Color* (pp. 229–245). http://dx.doi.org/10.1037/14852-011

Santiago-Rivera, A. L., Arredondo, P., & Gallardo-Cooper, M. (2002). *Multicultural aspects of counseling series, Vol. 17. Counseling Latinos and la familia: A practical guide.* Thousand Oaks, CA: SAGE.

Sapolsky, R. M. (2018). *Behave: The biology of humans at our best and worst.* New York, NY: Penguin Books.

Sasse, B. (2018). *Them: Why we hate each other and how to heal.* New York, NY: St. Martin's Press.

Schechter, S. (1982). *Women and male violence: The visions and struggles of the battered women's movement.* Boston, MA: South End Press.

Scheepers, D., & Derks, B. (2016). Revisiting social identity theory from a neuroscience perspective. *Current Opinion in Psychology, 11,* 74–78.

Scher, M. (2001). Male therapist/male client: Reflections on critical dynamics. In G. Brooks & G. E. Good (Eds.), *A new handbook of counseling and psychotherapy for men.* San Francisco, CA: Jossey-Bass.

Schlesinger, A. M. (1991). *The disuniting of America: Reflections on a multicultural society.* New York, NY: Norton.

Schofield, W. (1964). *Psychotherapy: The purchase of friendship.* Englewood Cliffs, NJ: Prentice Hall.

Schutz, A. (1976). *Collected papers II: Studies in social theory*. The Hague, Netherlands: Martinus Nijhoff.

Seager, M., Barry, J., & Sullivan, L. (2016). Challenging male gender blindness: Why psychologists should be leading the way. *Clinical Psychology Forum, 285*, 35–40.

Seaton, E. K., & Iida, M. (2019). Racial discrimination and racial identity: Daily moderation among Black youth. *American Psychologist, 74*, 117–127. http://dx.doi.org/10.1037/amp0000367

Seidler, Z. E., Rice, S. M., Ogrodniczuk, J. S., Oliffe, J. L., & Dhillon, H. M. (2018). Engaging men in psychological treatment: A scoping review. *American Journal of Men's Health, 12*(6), 1882–1900.

Seidman, S. (1994). *The postmodern turn: New perspectives on social theory*. Cambridge, UK: Cambridge University Press.

Selden, S. (1999). *Inheriting shame: The story of eugenics and racism in America*. New York, NY: Teachers College Press.

Sengupta, S. (1996). Understanding consumption related values from advertising: A content analysis of television commercials from India and the United States. *Gazette: The International Journal of Communication Studies, 57*, 81–96.

Seroczynski, A. D., & Jobst, A. D. (2016). Latino youth and the school-to-prison pipeline: Addressing issues and achieving solutions. *Hispanic Journal of Behavioral Sciences, 38*, 423–445. http://dx.doi.org/10.1177/0739986316663926

Shainburg, S. (Director), & Beardsley, J., Fierberg, A., Hobby, A., Posner, J., Posner, P. J., Roban, M., et al. (Producer). (2002). Secretary (Motion picture). USA: Lionsgate.

Shay, J. J. (1996). "Okay, I'm here, but I'm not talking!" Psychotherapy with the reluctant male. *Psychotherapy, 33*, 503–513.

Sheff, E. (2005). Polyamorous women, sexual subjectivity and power. *Journal of Contemporary Ethnography, 34*(3), 251–283.

Sheff, E. (2012). Three waves of non-monogamy (Blog). Retrieved from https://elisabethsheff.com/2012/09/09/three-waves-of-polyamory-a-select-history-of-non-monogamy/

Sheff, E. (2014). *The polyamorists next door*. Lowman, MA: Rowman & Littlefield.

Sheff, E. (2016). *When someone you love is polyamorous: Understanding poly people and relationships*. Portland, OR: Thorntree Press.

Sherif, M. (1954). *Experimental study of positive and negative intergroup attitudes between experimentally produced groups: Robbers cave study*. Norman, OK: University of Oklahoma Press.

Shernoff, M. (n.d.). Resisting conservative social and sexual trends: Sexual nonexclusivity and male couples in the United States. Unpublished paper shared by author.

Sherwin, B. (2008). Hormones, the brain, and me. *Canadian Psychology, 49*(1), pp. 42–48.

Shotter, J. (1990). Getting in touch: The metamethodology of a postmodern science of mental life. *Humanistic Psychologist, 18*, 7–22.

Shotter, J., & Gergen, K. J. (1989). *Texts of identity*. London: SAGE.

Shriver, L. (2016, September 13). Lionel Shriver's full speech: 'I hope the concept of cultural appropriation is a passing fad.' *The Guardian*. Retrieved from https://www.theguardian.com/commentisfree/2016/sep/13/lionel-shrivers-full-speech-i-hope-the-concept-of-cultural-appropriation-is-a-passing-fad

Shucart. (2016). Polyamory by the numbers. Retrieved from https://www.advocate.com/current-issue/2016/1/08/polyamory-numbers

Shulman, M. (2013). Generation LGBTQIA. Retrieved from http://www.nytimes.com/2013/01/10/fashion/generation-lgbtqia.html

Sibrava, N. J., Bjornsson, A. S., Perez Benitez, A. C. I., Moitra, E., Weisberg, R. B., & Keller, M. B. (2019). Posttraumatic stress disorder in African American and Latinx adults: Clinical course and the role of racial and ethnic discrimination. *American Psychologist, 74*, 101–116. http://dx.doi.org/10.1037/amp0000339

Siegel, D. (2007). *The mindful brain*. New York, NY: W.W. Norton & Company Inc.

Siegel, D. (2009). *Mindsight*. New York, NY: Random House.

Siegel, D. (2010). *The mindful therapist*. New York, NY: W.W. Norton & Company Inc.

Silberstein, L. R., Striegel-Moore, R. H., Timko, C., & Rodin, J. (1988). Behavioral and psychological implications of body dissatisfaction: Do men and women differ? *Sex Roles, 19*(3–4), 219–232.

Silverstein, L. B., & Brooks, G. R. (2010). Gender issues in family therapy and couples counseling. In J. Chrisler & D. McCreary (Ed.), *Handbook of gender research in psychology*. New York, NY: Springer.

Silverstein, S. (2005, January 31). Racial issues lose urgency, study finds. *Los Angeles Times*, p. B.

Sinclair, S. L. (2007). Back in the mirrored room: The enduring relevance of discursive practice. *Journal of Family Therapy, 29*(2), 147–168.

Sinclair, S. L., & Monk, G. (2004). Moving beyond the blame game: Toward a discursive approach to negotiating conflict within couple relationships. *Journal of Marital and Family Therapy, 30*(3), 335–347.

Skewes, M. C., & Blume, A. W. (2019). Understanding the link between racial trauma and substance use among American Indians. *American Psychologist, 74*, 88–100. http://dx.doi.org/10.1037/amp0000331

Skinner, B. F. (1968). *The technology of teaching.* Englewood Cliffs, NJ: Prentice Hall.

Slattery, J. M. (2004). *Counseling diverse clients: Bringing context into therapy.* Belmont, CA: Thomson Brooks/Cole.

Slovic, P. (1999). Trust, emotion, sex, politics, and science: Surveying the risk-assessment battlefield. *Risk Analysis, 19*(4), 689–701.

Smart, D. W., & Smart, J. F. (1997). DSM-IV and culturally sensitive diagnosis: Some observations for counselors. *Journal of Counseling & Development, 75*(5), 392–398.

Smedley, A., & Smedley, B. D. (2005). Race as biology is fiction, racism as a social problem is real: Anthropological and historical perspectives on the social construction of race. *American Psychologist, 60*(1), 16–28.

Smith, D. L. (2012). *Less than human: Why we demean, enslave, and exterminate others.* New York, NY: St. Martin's Press.

Smith, G. H. (1992, November). *Tane-nui-a-Rangi's legacy, propping up the sky: Kaupapa Maori as resistance and intervention.* Paper presented at the joint conference of the New Zealand Association of Research in Education and the Australian Association of Research in Education, Geelong, Australia.

Smith, M., Arguello, T. M., & Dentato, M. P. (2016). The coming out process. In M. P. Dentato (Ed.), *Social work practice with the LGBT community* (pp. 156–189). New York, NY: Oxford University Press.

Smith, W. A., Hung, M., & Franklin, J. D. (2011). Racial battle fatigue and the miseducation of Black men: Microaggressions, societal problems and environmental stress. *The Journal of Negro Education, 80*, 63–82.

Smith, Y. L. S., Van Goozen, S. H. M., & Cohen-Kettenis, P. T. (2001). Adolescents with gender identity disorder who were accepted or rejected for sex reassignment surgery: A prospective follow-up study. *Journal of the American Academy of Child and Adolescent Psychiatry, 40*(4), 472–488.

Snyder, K. (2014, July 23). How to get ahead as a woman in tech: Interrupt men. *Slate.* Retrieved from https://slate.com/human-interest/2014/07/study-men-interrupt-women-more-in-tech-workplaces-but-high-ranking-women-learn-to-interrupt.html

Somerville, S. (1994). Scientific racism and the emergence of the homosexual body. *Journal of the History of Sexuality, 5*(2), 243–266.

Sowell, T. (1998). *Conquests and cultures: An international history.* New York, NY: Basic Books.

Spanierman, L. B., & Smith, L. (2017). Roles and responsibilities of White allies: Implications for research, training, and practice. *Counseling Psychologist, 45*, 606–617. http://dx.doi.org/10.1177/0011000017717712

Speck, M., & Hasselkuss, M. (2015). Sufficiency in social practice: Searching potentials for sufficient behavior in a consumerist culture. *Sustainability: Science, Practice, & Policy, 11*(2), 14–32.

Spickard, P. R. (1992). The illogic of American racial categories. In M. P. P. Root (Ed.), *Racially mixed people in America* (pp. 12–23). Thousand Oaks, CA: SAGE.

Spickard, P. R., & Fong, R. (1995). Pacific Islander Americans and multiethnicity: A vision of America's future? *Social Forces, 73*(4), 1365–1383.

Spitzack, C. (1990). *Confessing excess: Women and the politics of body reduction.* New York, NY: State University of New York Press.

Spitzer, R. L., & Williams, J. B. (1985). Classification of mental disorders. In H. L. Kaplan and B. J. Sadock (Eds.), *Comprehensive textbook of psychiatry* (pp. 580–602). Baltimore, MD: Williams and Wilkins.

Stam, H. J. (Ed.). (1998). *The body and psychology.* Thousand Oaks, CA: SAGE.

Standing, G. (2011). *The precariat: The new dangerous class.* London: Bloomsbury Academic.

State University of New York at Albany School of Social Welfare. (n.d.). Module 5: Privilege Walk Activity [PDF file]. Retrieved from https://www.albany.edu/ssw/efc/pdf/Module%205_1_Privilege%20Walk%20Activity.pdf

Statista. (2017). Number of internet users worldwide 2005-2018. Retrieved from https://www.statista.com/statistics/273018/number-of-internet-users-worldwide/

Steele, C. M. (1992, April). Race and the schooling of black Americans. *Atlantic Monthly*, pp. 68–78.

Steele, I. K. (1994). *Warpaths: Invasions of North America.* New York, NY: Oxford University Press.

Steele, S. (2006). *White guilt: How blacks and whites together destroyed the promise of the civil rights era.* New York, NY: HarperCollins.

Stiglitz, J. (2003). *Globalization and its discontents.* New York, NY: Norton.

Stinson, R. D. (2010). Hooking up in young adulthood: A review of factors influencing the sexual behavior of college students. *Journal of Psychotherapy for College Students, 24*(2), 98–115.

Stone, J. (2003). Max Weber on race, ethnicity and nationalism. In J. Stone & R. Dennis (Eds.), Race and ethnicity: Comparative and theoretical approaches (pp. 28–42). Oxford, UK: Blackwell.

Story, M., French, S. A., Resnick, M. D., & Blum, R. W. (1995). Ethnic/racial and socioeconomic differences in dieting behaviors and body image perceptions in adolescents. *International Journal of Eating Disorders, 18*(2), 173–179.

Streitfeld, D. (2015, March 5). In Ellen Pao's suit vs. Kleiner Perkins, world of venture capital is under microscope. *The New York Times*. Retrieved from https://www.nytimes.com/2015/03/06/technology/in-ellen-paos-suit-vs-kleiner-perkins-world-of-venture-capital-is-under-microscope.html

Striegel-Moore, R. H., Silberstein, L. R., & Rodin, J. (1986). Toward an understanding of risk factors for bulimia. *American Psychologist, 41*(3), 246–263.

Strong, S. M., Williamson, D. A., Netemeyer, R. G., & Geer, J. H. (2000). Eating disorder symptoms and concerns about body differ as a function of gender and sexual orientation. *Journal of Social and Clinical Psychology, 19*(2), 240–255.

Strong, T., & Paré, D. A. (2004). Striving for perspicuity. In T. Strong & D. A. Paré (Eds.), *Furthering talk: Innovations in the discursive therapies* (pp. 1–14). New York, NY: Kluwer Academic/Plenum.

Stuart, B. (1997). Sentencing circles: Making "real differences." In J. Macfarlane (Ed.), *Rethinking disputes: The mediation alternative* (pp. 201–232). London, UK: Cavendish.

Sue, D. W. (2018). Microaggressions and student activism: Harmless impact and victimhood controversies. In G. C. Torino, D. P. Rivera, C. M. Capodilupo, K. L. Nadal, & D. W. Sue (Eds.), *Microaggression theory: Influence and implications* (pp. 229–243). Hoboken, NJ: Wiley.

Sue, D. W., Alsaidi, S., Awad, M. N., Glaeser, E., Calle, C. Z., & Mendez, N. (2019). Disarming racial microaggressions: Microintervention strategies for targets, White allies, and bystanders. *American Psychologist, 74*, 128–142. http://dx.doi.org/10.1037/amp0000296

Sue, D. W., Carter, R., Casas, J. M., Fouad, N., Ivey, A., Jensen, M., et al. (1998). *Multicultural counseling competencies: Individual and organizational development.* Thousand Oaks, CA: SAGE.

Sue, D. W., Gallardo, M., & Neville, H. (2014). *Case studies in multicultural counseling and therapy.* Hoboken, NJ: Wiley.

Sue, D. W., Rasheed, M. N., & Rasheed, J. M. (2015). *Multicultural social work practice: A competency-based approach to diversity and social justice.* Hoboken, NJ: John Wiley & Sons.

Sue, D. W., & Sue, D. (1981). *Counseling the culturally different: Theory and practice.* New York, NY: Wiley.

Sue, D. W., & Sue, D. (1990). *Counseling the culturally different: Theory and practice* (2nd ed.). New York, NY: Wiley.

Sue, D. W., & Sue, D. (2007). *Counseling the culturally diverse: Theory and practice* (5th ed.). New York, NY: Wiley.

Sue, D. W., Sue, D., Neville, H. & Smith, L. (2019). *Counseling the culturally diverse: Theory and practice* (8th ed.). New York, NY: Wiley

Surette, T. (2017). Guess which show is the biggest in the entire world? *TV Guide*. Retrieved from https://www.tvguide.com/news/most-watched-show-in-world-ncis/

Swigonski, M. E. (1995). Claiming a lesbian identity as an act of empowerment. *Affilia, 10*(4), 413–425. doi.org/10.1177/088610999501000405

Swing Lifestyle. Retrieved from https://www.kinkly.com/definition/723/swing-lifestyle

Tamesese, K., & Waldegrave, C. (1993). Cultural and gender accountability in the "just therapy" approach. *Journal of Feminist Family Therapy, 5*(2), 29–45.

Tando, D. (2016). *The conscious parent's guide to gender identity: A mindful approach to embracing your child's authentic self.* Avon, MA: Adams Media.

Tannen, D. (1991). *You just don't understand: Women and men in conversation.* New York, NY: Ballantine.

Taormino, T., Penley, C., Shimizu, C., & Miller-Young, M. (2013). *The feminist porn book: The politics of producing pleasure.* New York, NY: The Feminist Press at the City University of New York.

Tatum, B. V. (1997). *"Why are all the black kids sitting together in the cafeteria?" And other conversations about race.* New York, NY: Basic Books.

Taylor, C. (1994). *Multiculturalism: Examining the politics of recognition.* Princeton, NJ: Princeton University Press.

Taylor, C. (2004). *Modern social imaginaries.* Durham, NC: Duke University Press.

Taylor, M. (1994). Gender and power in counselling and supervision. *British Journal of Guidance & Counselling, 22*(3), 319–326.

Teasley, M. L. (2005). Perceived levels of cultural competence through social work education and professional development for urban school social workers. *Journal of Social Work Education, 41*, 85–98.

Teeman, T. (2017). This is why the erasing of LGBT Americans on the 2020 Census matters. *The Daily Beast*. Retrieved from https://www.thedailybeast.com/this-is-why-the-erasing-of-lgbt-americans-on-the-2020-census-matters

Teixeira, R., & Rogers, J. (2000). *America's forgotten majority: Why the white working class still matters.* New York, NY: Basic Books.

Terrell, J., Kofink, A., Middleton, J., Rainear, C., Murphy-Hill, E., Parnin, C., et al. (2017). Gender differences and bias in open source: Pull request acceptance of women versus men. *PeerJ Computer Science* 3:e111 https://doi.org/10.7717/peerj-cs.111

Tervalon, M., & Murray-García, J. (1998). Cultural humility versus cultural competence: A critical distinction in defining physician training outcomes in multicultural education. *Journal of Health Care for the Poor and Underserved, 9*(2), 117–125.

The Kinsey Scale. (n.d.). The Kinsey Institute. Retrieved from https://www.kinseyinstitute.org/research/publications/kinsey-scale.php.

The Times of India (2016). Top 10 English TV shows of 2016. *The Times of India.* Author. Retrieved from https://timesofindia.indiatimes.com/tv/news/english/top-10-english-tv-shows-of-2016/photostory/56164934.cms

Thomason, T. C. (1991). Counseling Native Americans: An introduction for non–Native American counselors. *Journal of Counseling & Development, 69*(4), 321–327.

Thompson, J. K., Heinberg, L. J., Altabe, M., & Tantleff-Dunn, S. (1999). *Exacting beauty: Theory, assessment, and treatment of body image disturbance.* Washington, DC: American Psychological Association.

Tiggemann, M., & Boundy, M. (2008). Effect of environment and appearance compliment on college women's self-objectification, mood, body shame, and cognitive performance. *Psychology of Women Quarterly, 32,* 399–405.

Tomm, K. (2014). *Patterns in interpersonal interactions: Inviting relational understandings for therapeutic change.* New York, NY: Routledge.

Trans Student Educational Resources. (n.d.). The gender unicorn. Retrieved from http://www.transstudent.org/gender

Treadgold, R. (1983). Two issues in the counselling of women. *New Zealand Counselling and Guidance Association Journal, 5,* 23–29.

Treyvaud, R. (2017). The positive effects of social media on teenagers. *Wangle Family Insights.* Retrieved from familyinsights.net/advice/positive-effects-of-social-media-on-teenagers/

Tritt, A. (2018, April 2). States are starting to recognize a third gender: Here's what that means for nonbinary youth. *Vox.* Retrieved from https://www.vox.com/identities/2018/3/28/17100252/trans-nonbinary-third-gender-youth-legal-recognition

Truijers, A., & Vingerhoets, A. (1999). Shame, embarrassment, personality, and well-being. Second International Conference on the (non) Expressions of Emotions in Health and Disease, Tilburg, The Netherlands.

Tucker, R. C. (1978). *The Marx-Engels readers* (2nd ed.). New York, NY: Norton.

Tuhiwai-Smith, L. (2012). *Decolonizing methodologies: Research and indigenous peoples.* Dunedin, New Zealand: Otago University Press.

Turkle, S. (2010). *Alone together: Why we expect more from technology and less from each other.* New York, NY: Basic Books.

Turkle, S. (2015, September 26). Stop googling. Let's talk. *New York Times,* 27.

Turner, T. (1993). Anthropology and multiculturalism: What is anthropology that multiculturalists should be mindful of it? *Cultural Anthropology, 8*(4), 411–429.

Twenge, J. (2001). Changes in women's assertiveness in response to status and roles: A crosstemporal meta-analysis, 1931–1993. *Journal of Personality and Social Psychology, 81*(1), 133–145.

Twenge, J. M. (2017). *iGen.* New York, NY: Atria Books.

Twohey, D., & Volker, J. (1993). Listening to the voices of care and justice in counselor supervision. *Counselor Education and Supervision, 32,* 189–197.

Tylor, E. (1871). *Primitive culture.* New York, NY: Harper.

Udelson, J. H. (1990). *Dreamer of the ghetto: The life and works of Israel Zangwill.* Tuscaloosa, AL: University of Alabama Press.

Uecker, J. E., & Martinez, B. C. (2017). When and why women regret sex in hookups more than men do: An analysis of the online college social life survey. *The Sociological Quarterly, 58*(3), 470–494. doi.org/10.1080/00380253.2017.1331716

Ulrich, L. (2011). *Bisexual invisibility: Impacts and recommendations.* San Francisco Human Rights Commission LGBT Advisory Committee. doi.org/10.1177%2F1464700109343258

UNAIDS. (2014). *Reduction of HIV-related stigma and discrimination* (guidance note). Retrieved from http://www.unaids.org/sites/default/files/media_asset/2014unaidsguidancenote_stigma_en.pdf

United Nations Declaration on the Rights of Indigenous Peoples for Indigenous Peoples. (n.d.). Retrieved from https://www.un.org/development/desa/indigenouspeoples/declaration-on-the-rights-of-indigenous-peoples.html

United Nations, Population Division. (1999). *World urbanization prospects: The 1999 revision.* Retrieved from http://www.un.org/esa/population/pubsarchive /urbanization/ urbanization.pdf

United Nations, Population Division. (2004). *World population prospects: The 2004 revision.* Retrieved from http://www.un.org/esa/population/publications/WPP2004/ wpp2004.htm

United Nations, Population Division. (2017). *World population prospects: The 2017 revision | multimedia library—United Nations Department of Economic and Social Affairs.* Retrieved from https://www.un.org/development/desa/publications/world-population-prospects-the-2017-revision.html

U.S. Bureau of Labor Statistics (2015). American Time Use Survey. *Retrieved from* https://www.bls.gov/tus/charts/household.htm

U.S. Bureau of Labor Statistics. (2017, August). Highlight of women's earnings in 2016. *BLS Reports, 1069*. Retrieved from https://www.bls.gov/opub/reports/womens-earnings/2016/home.htm

U.S. Census Bureau. (2016). Census Bureau Reports. Retrieved from https://www.census.gov/newsroom/press-releases/2016/cb16-192.html

Ussher, J. (2010). Are we medicalizing women's misery? A critical review of women's higher rates of reported depression. *Feminism & Psychology, 20*(1), 9–35.

Van de Grift, T. C., Elaut, E., Cerwenka, S. C., Cohen-Kettenis, P. T., De Cuypere, G., Richter-Appelt, H., et al. (2017). Effects of medical interventions on gender dysphoria and body image: A follow-up study. *Psychosomatic Medicine, 79*(7), 815–823 doi: 10.1097/PSY.0000000000000465

Vandenbosch, L., & Eggermont, S. (2016). The interrelated roles of mass media and social media in adolescents' development of an objectified self-concept. *Communication Research, 43*, 1116–1140.

Van der Kolk, B. (2015). *The body keeps the score: Mind, brain and body in the transformation of trauma*. London, UK: Penguin Books.

Van der Kolk, B. A. (1998). Trauma and memory. In *Psychiatry and Clinical Neurosciences 52*(S1), S52–S64.

Van der Kolk, B. A. (2006). Clinical implications of neuroscience research in PTSD. *Annals of the New York Academy of Sciences, 1071*(1), 277–293.

Vannucci, A., Flannery, K. M., & Ohannessian, C. M. (2017). Social media use and anxiety in emerging adults. *Journal of Affective Disorders, 207*, 163-166 doi:10.1016/j.jad.2016.08.040

Van Tilburg, M. A., Unterberg, M. L., & Vingerhoets, A. J. (2002). Crying during adolescence: The role of gender, menarche, and empathy. *British Journal of Developmental Psychology, 20*(1), 77–87.

Varenne, H. (2003). On internationalizing counseling psychology: A view from cultural anthropology. *Counseling Psychologist, 31*(4), 404–411.

Varga, D. (2011). Look-normal: The colonized child of developmental science. *History of Psychology, 14*, 137–157. http://dx.doi.org/10.1037/a0021775

Veaux, F., & Rickert, E. (2014) *More than two: A practical guide to ethical polyamory*. Portland, OR: Thorntree Press.

Vera, E. M., & Shin, R. Q. (2006). Promoting strengths in a socially toxic world: Supporting resiliency with systemic interventions. *Counseling Psychologist, 34*(1), 80–89.

Verdant Labs. (2015). *Democratic vs Republican occupations* (data file). Retrieved from http://verdantlabs.com/politics_of_professions/

Vespa, J. (2009). Gender ideology construction. *Gender & Society, 23*(3), 363–387.

Vessey, J. T., & Howard, K. I. (1993). Who seeks psychotherapy? *Psychotherapy: Theory, Research, Practice, Training, 30*, 546–553.

Viano, E. C. (1992). The news media and crime victims: The right to know versus the right to privacy. In E. C. Viano (Ed.), *Critical issues in victimology: International perspectives* (pp. 24–34). New York, NY: Springer.

Wagner, R. (1981). *The invention of culture*. Chicago, IL: University of Chicago Press.

Waldegrave, C. (2003). *Just Therapy—a journey: A collection of papers from the Just Therapy team, New Zealand*. Adelaide, Australia: Dulwich Centre Publications.

Waldegrave, C. T. (1985). Mono-cultural, mono-class, and so called non-political family therapy. *Australia and New Zealand Journal of Family Therapy, 6*(4), 197–200.

Waldegrave, C., Tamasese, K., Tuhaka, F., & Campbell, W. (2003). *Just Therapy: A journey*. Adelaide, South Australia: Dulwich Centre.

Waldura, W. F., Arora, I. A., Randall, A. M., Farala, J. P., & Sprott, R. A. (2016). Fifty shades of stigma: Exploring the health care experiences of kink-oriented patients. *The Journal of Sexual Medicine, 13*(12), 1918–1929. doi.org/10.1016/j.jsxm.2016.09.019

Wall, K. (2015, February 10). Fetish lovers begging for freedom: '*Fifty Shades of Grey* is our Stonewall moment'. The Guardian. Retrieved from https://www.theguardian.com/lifeandstyle/2015/feb/10/fetish-lovers-fifty-shades-of-grey-stonewall-moment

Walsh, C. (2009). Critical interculturality and decolonial pedagogy: In-surgir, re-existing and re-living. In. V. M. Candau (Ed.), *Intercultural education in Latin America: Between conceptions, tensions and proposals* (pp. 12–43). Rio de Janeiro, Brazil: 7 Letras.

Walsh, C. (2008). Interculturalidad, plurinacionalidad y decolonialidad: Las insurgencies político-epistémicas de refundar el Estado [Interculturality, plurinationality and decoloniality: Political-epistemological insurgencies to refound the State]. *Tabula Rasa, 9*, 131–152

Walsh, C. (2012). *Interculturalidad crítica y (de)colonialidad: ensayos desde Abya Yala* [Critical interculturality and (de) coloniality: essays from Abya Yala]. Quito, Ecuador: Ediciones Abya Yala.

Walter, J. L., & Peller, J. E. (2000). *Recreating brief therapy: Preferences and possibilities.* New York, NY: Norton.

Walters, M. L., Chen, J., & Breiding, M. J. (2013). *The National Intimate Partner and Sexual Violence Survey (NISVS): 2010 findings on victimization by sexual orientation.* Atlanta, GA: National Center for Injury Prevention and Control, Centers for Disease Control and Prevention.

Wang, J., Leu, J., & Shoda, Y. (2011). When the seemingly innocuous "stings": Racial microaggressions and their emotional consequences. *Personality and Social Psychology Bulletin, 37,* 1666–1678. http://dx.doi.org/10.1177/0146167211416130

Warner, M. (1991). Introduction: Fear of a queer planet. *Social Text, 29,* 3–17.

Watters, E. (2010). *Crazy like us: The globalization of the American psyche.* New York, NY: Free Press.

Weinrach, S. G., & Thomas, K. R. (1998). Diversity-sensitive counseling today: A postmodern clash of values. *Journal of Counseling & Development, 76*(2), 115–122.

Wellman, D. (1977). *Portraits of white racism.* Cambridge, UK: Cambridge University Press.

Wester, S. R., Vogel, D. L., & Archer, J., Jr. (2004). Male restricted emotionality and counseling supervision. *Journal of Counseling & Development, 82,* 91–98.

Weston, K. (1991). *Families we choose: Lesbians, gays, kinship.* New York, NY: Columbia University Press.

Westphal, S. P. (2004). Feature: Glad to be asexual. *New Scientist.* Retrieved from https://www.newscientist.com/article/dn6533-feature-glad-to-be-asexual/

Wetherell, M., & Potter, J. (1992). *Mapping the language of racism: Discourse and the legitimation of exploitation.* New York, NY: Harvester Wheatsheaf.

Whaley, A. L. (2001). Cultural mistrust of white mental health clinicians among African Americans with severe mental illness. *American Journal of Orthopsychiatry, 71*(2), 252–256.

Whelehan, I. (1995). *Modern feminist thought: From the second wave to "post-feminism."* New York, NY: New York University Press.

White, J., Marsh, I., Kral, M. J., & Morris, J. (2016). *Critical suicidology: Transforming research and prevention for the 21st century.* Vancouver, British Columbia, Canada: UBC Press.

White, M. (1989). The externalisation of the problem and the re-authoring of relationships. In M. White, *Selected papers* (pp. 5–28). Adelaide, AU: Dulwich Centre Publications.

White, M. (1992). Deconstruction and therapy. In D. Epston & M. White (Eds.), *Experience, contradiction, narrative, and imagination* (pp. 109–152). Adelaide, South Australia: Dulwich Centre.

White, M. (2002). Addressing personal failure. *International Journal of Narrative Therapy and Community Work, 2002*(3), 33–76.

White, M. (2006). Working with people who are suffering the consequences of multiple trauma: A narrative perspective. In D. Denborough (Ed.), *Trauma: Narrative responses to traumatic experience* (pp. 25–85.) Adelaide, Australia: Dulwich Centre

White, M. (2009). Narrative practice and conflict dissolution in couples therapy. *Clinical Social Work Journal, 37*(3), 200–213.

White, M., & Epston, D. (1980). *Narrative means to therapeutic ends.* New York, NY: W.W. Norton & Co.

White, M., & Epston, D. (1990). *Narrative means to therapeutic ends.* New York, NY: Norton.

Wijeyesinghe, C., Griffin, P., & Love, B. (1997). Racism curriculum design. In A. Bell & P. Griffin. (Eds.). *Teaching for diversity and social justice: A sourcebook* (pp. 82–109). New York, NY: Routledge.

Wikipedia. (n.d.). Unisex public toilet. Retrieved from https://en.wikipedia.org/wiki/Unisex_public_toilet

Wilcox, D. W., & Forrest, L. (1992). The problems of men and counseling: Gender bias or gender truth? *Journal of Mental Health Counseling, 14,* 291–304.

Wilkins, C. L., Wellman, J. D., Babbitt, L. G., Toosi, N. R., & Schad, K. D. (2015). You can win but I can't lose: Bias against high-status groups increases their zero-sum beliefs about discrimination. *Journal of Experimental Social Psychology, 57,* 1–14. http://dx.doi.org/10.1016/j.jesp.2014.10.008

Wilkinson, R. G. (2001). Mind the gap: Hierarchies, health and human evolution. New Haven, CT: Yale University Press.

Williams, J. C. (2017). *White working class: Overcoming class cluelessness in America.* Boston, MA: Harvard Business Press.

Williams, J. C., & Boushey, H. (2010). The three faces of work-family conflict: The poor, the professionals, and the missing middle. *SSRN Electronic Journal.* doi: 10.2139/ssrn.2126314Williams, K., & Knudson-Martin, C. (2013). Do therapists address gender and power in infidelity? A feminist analysis of the treatment literature. *Journal of Marital and Family Therapy, 39*(3), 271–284.

Willig, C. (2001). *Introducing qualitative research in psychology: Adventures in theory and method.* Buckingham, UK: Open University Press.

Wilson, D. K. (2001). *Violence may affect blood pressure in Black boys.* Presented at the 16th scientific meeting and exposition of the American Society of Hypertension, San Francisco, California.

Wilson, T. D. (2004). *Strangers to ourselves.* Cambridge, MA: Harvard University Press.

Winslade, J. (2005). Utilising discursive positioning in counseling. *British Journal of Guidance & Counselling, 33*(3), 351–364.

Winslade, J., & Monk, G. (2007). *Narrative counseling in schools: Powerful and brief* (2nd ed.). Thousand Oaks, CA: SAGE.

Winslade, J., Monk, G., & Drewery, W. (1997). Sharpening the critical edge: A social constructionist approach in counselor education. In T. L. Sexton & B. L. Griffin (Eds.), *Constructivist thinking in counseling practice, research, and training* (pp. 228–248). New York, NY: Teachers College Press.

Winston, D. (2017). *The smart girl's guide to polyamory: Everything you need to know about open relationships., non-monogamy, and alternative love.* New York, NY: Skyhorse Publishing.

Wise, T. (2005). *White like me: Reflections on race from a privileged son.* New York, NY: Soft Skull Press.

Wismeijer, A. A. J., & van Assen, M. A. L. M. (2013). Psychological characteristics of BDSM practitioners. *Journal of Sexual Medicine, 10*(8), 1943–1952. doi: 10.1111/jsm.12192

Wong-Padoongpatt, G., Zane, N., Okazaki, S., & Saw, A. (2017). Decreases in implicit self-esteem explain the racial impact of microaggressions among Asian Americans. *Journal of Counseling Psychology, 64,* 574–583. http://dx.doi.org/10.1037/cou0000217

Woodhouse, S. (2002). The historical development of affirmative action: An aggregated analysis. *Western Journal of Black Studies, 26*(3), 155–158.

Wooley, S. C., & Wooley, O. W. (1984, February). Feeling fat in a thin society. *Glamour,* pp. 198–252.

World Economic Forum Annual Meeting 2016. (n.d.). Retrieved from https://www.weforum.org/events/world-economic-forum-annual-meeting-2016

World Health Organization. (2017). *Violence against women.* Retrieved from https://www.who.int/news-room/fact-sheets/detail/violence-against-women

World Professional Association for Transgender Health. (2011). Standards of care for the health of transsexual, transgender, and gender nonconforming people (7th version). Retrieved from https://www.wpath.org/publications/soc

World Trade Organization. (2018). *World Trade Report.* Geneva, Switzerland: Author. Retrieved from https://www.wto.org/english/res_e/publications_e/world_trade_report18_e_under_embargo.pdf

Wrenn, C. G. (1962). The culturally encapsulated counselor. *Harvard Educational Review, 32,* 444–449.

Wright, J. (2018). Diversifying approaches to educational leadership: The impact of tradition in a changing educational landscape. *Journal of School Leadership, 28*(6), 815–833.

Wright, J., Whitaker, R. W., Khalifa, M., & Briscoe, F. (2018). The color of neoliberal reform: A critical race policy analysis of school district takeovers in Michigan. *Urban Education.* Advance online publication. doi: 10.1177/0042085918806943

Yang, D. (1991). Generational conflict among the Hmong in the United States. *Hmong Forum, 2,* 35–38.

Yang, E., Zald, D. H., & Blake, R. (2007). Fearful expressions gain preferential access to awareness during continuous flash suppression. *Emotion, 7*(4), 882.

Yavorsky, J. E., Kamp Dush, C. M., & Schoppe-Sullivan, S. J. (2015). The production of inequality: The gender division of labor across the transition to parenthood. *Journal of Marriage and Family, 77*(3), 662–679.

Yip, T. (2016). To be or not to be: How ethnic/racial stereotypes influence ethnic/racial disidentification and psychological mood. *Cultural Diversity & Ethnic Minority Psychology, 22,* 38–46. http://dx.doi.org/10.1037/cdp0000046

Yon, D. A. (2000). *Elusive culture: Schooling, race, and identity in global times.* Albany, NY: State University of New York Press.

Young, I. M. (2003). Breasted experience: The look and the feeling. In R. Weitz (Ed.), *The politics of women's bodies* (pp. 152–163). New York, NY: Oxford University Press.

Zamani, N. J., Smith, G., & Monk, G. (2013). Online forums as definitional ceremonies. *Journal of Systemic Therapies, 32*(4), 1–18. doi.org/10.1521/jsyt.2013.32.4.1

Zinman, S. (1987). Definition of self-help groups. In S. Zinman, H. Harp, & S. Budd (Eds.), *Reaching across: Mental health clients helping each other* (pp. 7–15). Riverside, CA: California Network of Mental Health Clients.

Zinn, H. (2003). *A people's history of the United States: 1492–present.* New York, NY: HarperCollins.

Zitzman, S. T., & Butler, M. H. (2009). Wives' experience of husbands' pornography use and concomitant deception as an attachment threat in the adult pair-bond relationship. *Sexual Addiction & Compulsivity, 16*(3), 210–240.

Index

N

NAFTA, 326–327
Nairobi Diaries, 345
Narayan, Uma, 59
Narrative humility, 411
National Center for Disease Control, 303
Nationality, equating geo-culture and, 54
Native Americans, 330, 337, 349, 370
  and border identities, 225
  and dominant discourses, 243
  and IPV death, 255
  counseling, 370
  enslavement, 330
  poverty rate among, 337
Nazis, 16, 384
Negash, Sesen, 274–275
Nepantla, 416
Neville, H., 371
New Orleans Medical and Surgical Journal, 233
Newsweek, 338
New York Times, 27, 30, 32
New Zealand, multicultural policies, 396–399
Nicholas, David, 151
Nieto, Sonia, 189
Nonbinary/genderqueer, 299–300
Normative stereotyping, 201
North America, 72
Northern Ireland, 385

O

Obama, Barack, 179
Objectification, and GSRD communities, 284–286
Online identities and aloneness, 33–36
Oppression, against immigrants, 335
"Orientalism", 70
Out-of-control sexual behaviors (OCSB), 268–269

P

Paraphilias, 284
Paraphilic disorders, 284
Paré, David, 138
Parenting, and GSRD community, 290
Passive racism, 178
Pathologization
  and counseling, 231–236
  and GSRD individuals, 285–287
Patriarchal dividend, 250–251
Patriarchy, and mental health professionals, 253–254
Patterns in Interpersonal Interactions: Inviting Relational Understandings for Therapeutic Change (Tomm), 233

Patterson, Cecil, 54, 395
Pedersen, Paul, 63
Pence, Ellen, 147
Perkins, John, 86
Personality, 214–215
  and postmodern psychology, 218–220
Peters, Michael, 326
Petras, James, 347
Phillips, Ulrich Bonnell, 67
Physical attractiveness, 260–264
Physical violence, and women, 271
Physical well-being, 260–264
Pickett, Theodore, 355
Pickford, Mary, 344
Plastic Surgery Statistics Report, 263
Political tribal identities, 27–28
Polyamory, 313
  egalitarian, 313
  hierarchical, 313
Polyfidelity, 313
Pon, Gordon, 408
Ponterotto, Joseph, 203
Popular culture, 250
  and counseling, 421
Population Reference Bureau, 329
Pornography, 255–260
  pervasiveness of, 258
Positioning, 128–129
  defined, 128
  examples of, 130–131
Postmodernism, 218–219, 384, 418
  culture and, 55–57
Postmodern psychology, and personality, 218–220
Poststructuralism, and racism, 194–196
Poststructuralist account of power relations, 153–164
  confessional society, 160–161
  dividing practices, 161–163
  power/knowledge, 159–160
  resistance, 163–164
  sovereign power and disciplinary power, 156–159
Potter, Jonathan, 53
Poverty, 330–331, 336–337
  and media, 347
  and technology, 348
  and wealth statistics, 361
  counseling needs relating to, 371–372
  implications of, 374–375
  in the United States, 358–359, 382, 388
  psychological effects of, 365–366
Power, 159–160
  advantages for counselors of post-structuralist analysis of, 164–168
  and dominant meanings, 139–140

colonial system of, 417–420
concept of hegemony, 149
confessional society, 160–161
disciplinary, 156–159
dividing practices, 161–163
European colonial patterns of, 420–421
gender, race, and class, 149–153
liberal humanist view of, 143–146
modern system of, 417–420
poststructuralist account of power relations, 153–164
resistance, 163–164
sovereign, 156–159
structural view of, 146–153
three approaches to, 142–164
Power relations, 395–396, 398, 408, 419
Pre-European societies, colonization in, 75–76
Prejudice, 351, 366–367, 373, 389, 406
Prejudicial dominant discourses, 281–282
Prejudicial stereotypes, 281
Premenstrual dysphoric disorder (PMDD), 270
Primacy of fear, 8–10
Prison, racism in, 190
Privilege, 153
  and counseling, 421–422
Production of Us and Them, 8–18
Psychological effects of colonization, 76–78
psychological effects, of dislocation, 336
Psychology professionals, and self, 215–217
Psycho-politics, 411–417
Psy complex, 381
Public Conversations Project, 399

Q

Queer, 277, 300
  as insult, 278
  concept of, 278
  theory, 278
Quijano, Anibal, 418

R

Rabin, Claire, 249
Race, 389–390, 393, 395–397, 405, 418
  and ethnicity, 105–107
  as a defining domain, 92
  biological differences among different, 95–97
  counseling implications of, 111–115
  effects of the construction of, 102–103
  genealogy of the term, 92–94
  matching in therapy, 379

About the Authors

Gerald Monk, PhD, identifies as Pakeha from Aotearoa (New Zealand). He is a professor in the Department of Counseling and School Psychology at San Diego State University and is the director of the Marriage and Family Therapy Program. He teaches cross-cultural counseling classes at the graduate level. Gerald is a practicing marriage and family therapist in California and a mediator and trainer in couples counseling and collaborative divorce. Gerald worked as a psychologist and counselor educator in New Zealand for 15 years before moving to the United States in 2000. He has a long-standing commitment to working with the bicultural issues that have arisen from the abuses of Maori by the history of European colonizing practices in Aotearoa over the last 260 years. He has participated in extensive bicultural programs in New Zealand and introduced many students to working with indigenous healing practices on marae, the sacred ground of the Maori. Gerald has a strong interest in promoting constructionist

theories in counseling and family systems work. He is well known for his contributions to developing and expanding the applications of narrative therapy and narrative mediation internationally. Gerald has published numerous articles and co-authored seven books on the subject of culture and therapy, narrative therapy, and narrative mediation.

John Winslade, PhD, is an emeritus professor at California State University, San Bernardino. He is a New Zealander of Pakeha ancestry, and he conceives of Pakeha culture not just as an expression of White, British, or European heritage, but also as being about living in relation to Maori and Pacific cultural narratives in Aotearoa. Two of his grandchildren belong to Ngati Awa (a Maori tribe). His academic work has focused mainly on the application of social constructionist and narrative ideas to the fields of counseling and conflict resolution. His interest in these ideas lies not just in their novel modes of practice but also in their potential for helping people articulate responses to new developments in our conditions of life in the 21st century. He believes that counseling and psychology need to adapt to current cultural shifts, rather than continuing to repeat older solutions. In addition to numerous articles, John has written and co-authored 12 books on narrative counseling, mediation, narrative grief counseling, and

teaching. John has a strong interest in conflict resolution, restorative justice, and peace building in personal, organizational, and community contexts. He has taught workshops on narrative counseling and mediation in the United States, Canada, Britain, Ireland, Denmark, Sweden, Norway, the Netherlands, Italy, Romania, Australia, New Zealand, Cyprus, Hong Kong, Singapore, China, Japan, and Israel.

Stacey L. Sinclair, PhD, is director of the Weber Honors College at San Diego State University. Her research, publications, and teaching focus on cultural studies, discourse and therapy, and conflict resolution. She has published numerous journal articles and book chapters on these topics and presents her work at the national and international level.

Her primary teaching focus lies in the area of cultural studies and grounding culture in political, economic, and social contexts. This curriculum starts from the premise that popular culture, far from being a frivolous or debased alternative to "high" or "real" culture, is in fact an important site of popular expression, social instruction, and cultural conflict and thus deserves critical attention. Stacey's teaching pays special attention to the ways popular culture affects individuals' daily lives, producing a range of physical, social, and emotional consequences. Stacey also has a strong background in developing a range of interdisciplinary international education programs for students from diverse academic backgrounds, including leading programs in Costa Rica, China, Cyprus, Estonia, Finland, and New Zealand.

marcela polanco, PhD, is an African, Muisca, and European Colombian immigrant in the United States. She is part of the faculty team of the Master of Science in Counseling at San Diego State University. As a family therapist, marcela positions her research, teaching, supervision, and practice geopolitically. In her immigrant English, she is strongly influenced by the social justice politics and literary framework of narrative family therapy. In her Colombian Spanish, she has been immersing herself into the politics, epistemologies, and ontologies of the work of Andean decolonial academic and social activists. Additionally, she borrows from the work of Latin American literary writers of magical realism. marcela's work is driven by academic activism searching for intercultural and interlanguage encounters of knowledge fair trades between Eurocentrism and decoloniality. She is interested in the development of alter-narratives that would support the integrity of the construction of new pluriversal and deracialized responses to social suffering and the systems of power that support it.

Penelope (Nel) Mercer, MS, MA, is the author of Chapter 10. She identifies as White, cisgender, pansexual, and polyamorous. Nel is a longtime student and educator, having studied and worked in different parts of the United States, United Kingdom, and Israel, earning an MA in Socio-Legal Studies, an MA in Psychology, and, most recently, an MS in Counseling. She has taught Lifespan Development and other psychology classes at community colleges, given presentations on polyamory to MFT students with her husband, George Mercer, and currently works as an Associate Marriage and Family Therapist in a private practice, where she learns from and with clients embodying gender, sexual, and relational diversity. Nel is grateful to have had the opportunity to contribute to this book, and to those whose lived experience informed the writing.

CPSIA information can be obtained
at www.ICGtesting.com
Printed in the USA
LVHW061354200820
663736LV00003B/485

9 781516 533503